ARISTOPHANES

WASPS

ARISTOPHANES
WASPS

EDITED WITH

INTRODUCTION AND COMMENTARY

BY

DOUGLAS M. MacDOWELL

PROFESSOR OF GREEK IN
THE UNIVERSITY OF GLASGOW

CLARENDON PRESS · OXFORD

Oxford University Press, Great Clarendon Street, Oxford OX2 6DP

Oxford New York
Athens Auckland Bangkok Bogota Bombay
Buenos Aires Calcutta Cape Town Dar es Salaam
Delhi Florence Hong Kong Istanbul Karachi
Kuala Lumpur Madras Madrid Melbourne
Mexico City Nairobi Paris Singapore
Taipei Tokyo Toronto
and associated companies in
Berlin Ibadan

Oxford is a trade mark of Oxford University Press

Published in the United States by
Oxford University Press Inc., New York

© *Oxford University Press 1971*

First issued as a Clarendon Paperback 1988

British Library Cataloguing in Publication Data
Data available

Library of Congress Cataloging in Publication Data
Wasps/Aristophanes; edited with introduction and
commentary by Douglas M. MacDowell.
Greek text; English introduction and commentary.
Includes bibliographical references and indexes.
I. MacDowell, Douglas M. (Douglas Maurice) II. Title.
PA3875.V5 1988 882'.01—dc19 88-3780
ISBN 0-19-814465-2

3 5 7 9 10 8 6 4 2

Printed in Great Britain on acid-free paper by
J. W. Arrowsmith Ltd., Bristol

PREFACE

BECAUSE it is many years since the last annotated edition of *Wasps* appeared and it may be some years before there is another, I have tried to make this edition useful to every sort of reader. For the advanced scholar I provide more information than previous editors about the readings of the manuscripts, and I offer some discussion of textual, historical, and dramaturgical problems. For the sixth-former or undergraduate who has read no play of Aristophanes before, I provide a good deal of help with translation; and textual criticism and a few other specialized matters are segregated in square brackets, for easy skipping.

The presentation of the text closely follows that of Professor K. J. Dover's *Clouds*, to assist readers who turn from one play to the other. I follow his practice in the indentation of lines (even though it differs somewhat from the arrangement which I should otherwise have preferred), and in the *apparatus criticus* I use his symbols and abbreviations.

In the introduction and commentary one of my main aims is to approach the play not as a work of literature but as the script of a performance. Aristophanes's purpose was not to produce a book for readers, but to entertain and impress Athenian spectators in 422 B.C. So I try to reconstruct the performance as far as is possible from the text, and to consider what effect the various parts of the play are likely to have had on the original audience.

I do not confine myself to providing information and discussing questions of fact; I venture also to assess. In discussing metre, for example, instead of just describing arrangements of long and short syllables, I make an attempt to judge their artistic effectiveness. This will probably displease some metrical purists, who prefer an austerely descriptive approach. Certainly my approach involves some loss of objectivity;

nevertheless I believe it to be right for a commentator to help his readers not just to understand but to appreciate. I happen to think that *Wasps* is one of the world's best comedies, and it is proper that I should give my grounds for this opinion by explaining what I believe to be the play's qualities.

For advice and suggestions on various points I am grateful to several colleagues and friends. Mr. D. Mervyn Jones was particularly generous: he lent me his own extensive notes on the play, and also his photographs of one of the manuscripts. Above all, I owe a great deal to Professor Dover's acute and thorough criticism.

D. M. M.

Manchester
January 1969

CONTENTS

ABBREVIATIONS

Most of my abbreviations are like those of LSJ (= Liddell and Scott
A Greek-English Lexicon, revised by H. S. Jones), except that I do not
usually Latinize Greek names. I list below only a few which might
cause doubt.

Ancient Authors and Works

Ais.	Aiskhines
Akh.	*Akharnians*
Ant.	Antiphon the orator
Ek.	*Ekklesiazousai*
Lex. Rhet.	*Lexeis Rhetorikai*, cited by page and line of Bekker's *Anecdota Graeca*
Lys.	Lysias
Lys.	*Lysistrate*
Plu. *Eth.*	Plutarch *Ethika*
Pol.	Polydeukes (Pollux) *Onomastikon*
Th.	Thucydides
Th.	*Thesmophoriazousai*
X. *Apom.*	Xenophon *Apomnemoneumata*
Σ	scholia or scholiast

Modern Books and Periodicals

ATL	B. D. MERITT, H. T. WADE-GERY, and M. F. McGREGOR *The Athenian Tribute Lists* (1939–53).
Beer	C. BEER *Ueber die Zahl der Schauspieler bei Aristophanes* (1844).
Dale²	A. M. DALE *The Lyric Metres of Greek Drama* 2nd edition (1968).
Denniston	J. D. DENNISTON *The Greek Particles* 2nd edition (1954).
*Dith. Trag. Com.*²	A. W. PICKARD-CAMBRIDGE *Dithyramb, Tragedy and Comedy* 2nd edition, revised by T. B. L. WEBSTER (1962).
*Dram. Fest.*²	A. W. PICKARD-CAMBRIDGE *The Dramatic Festivals of Athens* 2nd edition, revised by JOHN GOULD and D. M. LEWIS (1968).
Flor. Chrest.	FLORENT CHRESTIEN's notes on *Wasps*, printed in the editions of Portus (1607) and Kuster (1710).

HSCP	*Harvard Studies in Classical Philology.*
Holzinger	KARL HOLZINGER 'Erklärungen umstrittener Stellen des Aristophanes' (*Akademie der Wissenschaften in Wien, Philosophisch-historische Klasse: Sitzungsberichte* ccviii [1928].)
Mn. I, II, etc.	*Mnemosyne* series I, II, etc.
Taillardat	JEAN TAILLARDAT *Les Images d'Aristophane* (1962, corrected reprint 1965).
Thompson *Birds, Fishes*	D'ARCY W. THOMPSON *A Glossary of Greek Birds* 2nd edition (1936), *A Glossary of Greek Fishes* (1947).
Tyrwhitt	T. TYRWHITT *Conjecturae in Aeschylum, Euripidem et Aristophanem* 2nd edition (1822).
Wilamowitz	U. VON WILAMOWITZ-MOELLENDORFF 'Über die Wespen des Aristophanes' (*Sitzungsberichte der königlich Preussischen Akademie der Wissenschaften* [1911] 460–91, 504–35), reprinted in his *Kleine Schriften* (1935) i 284–346. References are to the original page numbers, given in the margins of the reprint.
Willems	ALPHONSE WILLEMS *Aristophane: traduction avec notes et commentaires critiques* i (1919).

All three-figure dates are B.C. Figures with a diagonal stroke, such as '423/2', denote an Athenian official year, from midsummer to midsummer. A figure followed by 'n.' refers to my commentary; thus '38 n.' means 'see my note on line 38'.

INTRODUCTION

I. ARISTOPHANES, KLEON, AND THE LAW-COURTS

Wasps was performed at the festival of the Lenaia early in 422
B.C. Aristophanes was by then well established as a comic
dramatist; six or seven of his comedies had been performed,
and at least three of them had won the first prize in their
respective contests. Among the most successful had been
Akharnians (performed in 425) and *Knights* (424). Both of
these dealt mainly with political themes and contained
satirical attacks on war-mongers, especially Kleon. In 423
Clouds, with a more intellectual theme, was a comparative
failure, and no doubt it was partly in order to recover his
popularity that in 422 he returned to a political subject.

Kleon was now at the height of his fame, the most popular
politician in Athens. This loud-voiced man first came to
prominence by criticizing Perikles's timid conduct of the war
against Sparta in 431 and 430 (Plu. *Per.* 33. 8, 35. 5). After
the death of Perikles in 429 he developed the policy of
aggression towards Sparta and severity towards the allied
cities which formed the Athenian empire. His great military
triumph came in 425, when he managed (with Demosthenes)
to capture the Spartans besieged on the island of Sphakteria.
However, in the spring of 423 the Athenians made a truce
with the Spartans for one year, so that in the following winter
war was not in progress, and it is not for his aggressive foreign
policy that Aristophanes attacks Kleon in *Wasps*.

In recent years Kleon had been making increasing use of
the law-courts for political and personal ends. He represented
himself as being the watch-dog of Athens (cf. *Wasps* 970), who
brought to justice anyone guilty of harming Athens, and
especially officials who made money at the state's expense. In
Athens an official at the end of his term of office was required

to submit to an examination of his actions with special reference to his handling of public money, and if he was thought to be guilty of peculation or other misconduct he was prosecuted in a law-court. The examination was called εὔθυνα and a man subject to it ὑπεύθυνος. Kleon and some of his friends and supporters made a habit of prosecuting ὑπεύθυνοι. It may seem praiseworthy in a politician to be zealous in bringing offenders to justice, but Aristophanes evidently thought that the zeal went much too far, and that many of the prosecutions were due not to a wish to see justice done but to personal vindictiveness, to vote-catching, and even to the hope of making money out of the accused men by blackmail. He had already alluded to Kleon's legal witch-hunting in *Knights* (774–6), and in a play performed in 423 he had satirized prosecutions made from ulterior motives (*Wasps* 1037–42). Now in 422 he returned to the theme.

But *Wasps* is not just about Kleon. Whereas in *Knights* Kleon is a constant object of attention throughout the play, in *Wasps* there are long passages in which he is not mentioned at all, and in the prologue we are told 'We aren't going to make mincemeat of the same man a second time' (63). The main object of attack is rather the legal system which facili-tated unfair prosecutions and convictions.

The most important feature of the Athenian legal system was the large volunteer juries. Any Athenian citizen over thirty years of age could be a juror. Volunteers were called for at the beginning of each year, and a list of six thousand jurors for the year was made out. The jury for each case was drawn from this list. The jury varied in size according to the type of case. It was often five hundred, sometimes more; in one case it is said to have been six thousand (And. 1. 17), but that was exceptional.[1] Each juror was paid three obols for each day on which he sat to try cases.

A jury was regarded as representing the whole Athenian people, and any attack on the jurors was treated as an attack

---

[1] In the fourth century odd numbers were used to avoid a tie in the voting, but there is no evidence for odd numbers in the fifth century.

on the Athenian democracy. There was no appeal against a jury's verdict, because in Athens the people were supreme. Through the law-courts the people controlled not only all Athenians but also the allied cities of the Athenian empire (many of whose legal cases were tried in Athens); and the jurors could regard themselves as rulers, while the allies were their 'slaves' (cf. [X.] *Ath. Pol.* 1. 18), who supported them by paying tribute.

It is undoubtedly true that this system was democratic, and that the large juries were more representative of the Athenian people than small juries or individual judges would have been. Another advantage was that a large jury was hard to bribe. But there were some serious disadvantages too.

One was that a jury was a crowd rather than a number of individuals. It was easily influenced by a skilful orator (like Kleon), but it could not easily give rigorous scrutiny to the details of a case or appreciate the merits of a case which was badly presented. This defect was the more serious because in an Athenian court there was no judge to give the jury impartial advice; a magistrate presided, but he did not explain the law or sum up the evidence. In *Wasps* Aristophanes satirizes and parodies various devices which speakers used to pull wool over jurors' eyes and to distract their attention from the weaknesses of a case.

A second disadvantage was that jurors tended to regard jury service as a permanent paid occupation. Because the pay was low, an able-bodied man would not usually volunteer to spend a year as a juror when he could earn more money in other ways; but a man too old for ordinary work would volunteer year after year, and his pay as a juror would practically serve the purpose of an old-age pension. Such men relied for their livelihood on the politicians (like Kleon) who provided them with cases to try by bringing politically motivated prosecutions, and who persuaded the assembly to keep up their pay. It was probably Kleon who got the daily rate of jurors' pay raised to three obols a few years before (Σ^{R} *Wasps* 88). Certainly Kleon claimed the credit for keeping up the

Athenian revenues (especially by seeing that peculators were severely fined, and that the allies paid large amounts of tribute) so that the jurors' pay would be secure: 'I shall feed him and take care of him, finding fair means and foul for him to have his three obols' (*Knights* 799–800). The natural result was that the jurors did their best to please Kleon by condemning men he said were guilty.

Thus the defects of the jury system were giving rise to a very dangerous state of affairs, in which a leading politician could control the verdicts of the courts. Kleon and his associates pretended to be servants and protectors of the democracy, but really they were manipulating the people's decisions for their own personal advantage—or so Aristophanes would have us believe. If the situation was really as serious as he makes out, he did a great public service in showing it up. One must remember, though, that the Athenians were people of an independent turn of mind; they were not sheep (despite *Wasps* 31–6). Probably the picture was not as black as he paints it.[1] What he does is not so much to present to his audience precisely what is happening in 422, but to show them what will happen if present tendencies are allowed to develop unchecked. The play consists of satirical exaggeration; and it is strikingly successful because it manages to make its serious points and be highly entertaining at the same time.

II. THE STRUCTURE OF THE PLAY

Wasps tells the story of an old man named Philokleon ('Love-Kleon') who has a strange disease: he is passionately addicted to being a juror, and believes that the life of a juror is happy and powerful. His son Bdelykleon ('Loathe-Kleon'), who knows better, tries to cure him, first by keeping him away from the law-courts by force and later by reasoned argument. By gradual stages the old man is brought round, and is per-

[1] T. A. Dorey (*Greece & Rome* iii [1956] 132–9) argues that Kleon, though a violent and oppressive politician, was not venal and corrupt.

suaded to take up a different and gayer way of life. At one stage of his cure he is allowed to have a private law-court at home, and the trial of a dog for stealing some cheese is a hilarious parody of proceedings in the real law-courts. Later the courts are largely forgotten, and the centre of amusement is the old man's grotesque attempts to adopt new standards of behaviour and enter high society.

The play is well constructed, in a manner which exemplifies Old Comedy at its best. Although our evidence is meagre, since we have no complete comedy by any author earlier than Aristophanes, it seems possible that by his time there existed a traditional pattern of comedy including the following features:[1] a prologue, introducing the theme of the play; the entrance-song of the chorus (πάροδος); one or more symmetrical scenes (sometimes called 'epirrhematic syzygies', in which the second half approximately corresponds to the first in form and metre), including a contest or debate (ἀγών);[2] a passage of set metrical form in which the chorus address the audience (παράβασις), followed later in the play by a passage similar in form to the second half of it ('second parabasis'); further episodes with dialogue, alternating with short songs; and a concluding scene (ἔξοδος) of revelry or festivity. In many of Aristophanes's plays some of these features either contribute little to the main theme or even are omitted altogether: *Peace* has no agon, *Clouds* has no concluding festivity, *Frogs* has no full parabasis but only a 'second parabasis', and so on. Not so in *Wasps*; here all the traditional features are used, and all are made to contribute to the purpose of the play. The prologue introduces the character of Philokleon, and the parodos reveals the hardship of the jurors' life. Two symmetrical scenes show the conflict of views about Philokleon's life as a juror, and a third (the agon)

[1] On the form of Old Comedy see *Dith. Trag. Com.*[2] 194–229. Some problems connected with it are discussed by Paul Händel *Formen und Darstellungsweisen in der aristophanischen Komödie* (1963).

[2] For a detailed study of this form of scene, see T. Gelzer *Der epirrhematische Agon bei Aristophanes* (1960).

shows the reasons on which each of the opinions is based. The parabasis justifies the author's approach to comedy, and further describes the character of the jurors; the second parabasis defines further the author's attitude to Kleon. A series of episodes shows the successive stages of Philokleon's conversion, and the drinking and dancing in the final scenes demonstrate the pleasures of his new way of life. This is the sequence:

1–229	Prologue.
230–316	Parodos.
317–333	Song by Philokleon.
334–364 365–402	Symmetrical scene.
403–460 461–525	Symmetrical scene.
526–630 631–724	Symmetrical scene (agon).
725–759	Song (conclusion to agon).
760–862	Episode.
863–890	Song.
891–1008	Episode.
1009–1121	Parabasis.
1122–1264	Episode.
1265–1291	Second parabasis.
1292–1449	Episode.
1450–1473	Song.
1474–1537	Exodos.

All this is not just one incident after another; the arrangement has a satisfying unity. The critique of the jury system is placed in the central portion of the play (526–1008), which consists of a verbal discussion of the system (the agon) followed by a satirical example of its working in practice (the trial of the dog). But the play is not just an attack on the jury system; it is the story of Philokleon. The first third of the play shows his old way of life, and the last third his conversion to a new one. The gay social life at the end is in exact contrast to the austerity presented in the prologue and the parodos, and his new mania for the joyful activity of dancing is the reverse of his old passion for the severe activity of judging. He reaches a point precisely opposite to the one from which he started, and this makes one feel that the story is complete. Some other plays of Aristophanes create an effect of anticlimax: in *Peace*, for instance, Peace is rescued at line 520 and the rest of the play (three-fifths of the whole) contains little but celebration of that event. In *Wasps* this kind of anticlimax is avoided, because Philokleon is not fully converted at the end of the agon; his conversion continues step by step through the following episodes, and is not finished until the final scenes.[1] The last scene (the exodos) makes a climax, both because it completes the transformation of his character and also because the display of dancing is an exciting spectacle, making a fine visual end to the play.

III. THE CHARACTERS AND THE CHORUS

Philokleon has rightly been called 'a triumph of characterization, one of the best comic figures in literature'.[2] He is supposed to be an old man, and from time to time allusions are made to weaknesses due to age (165, 357, 809–10, 1343, 1380–1), but his behaviour is exceedingly lively; in nearly every scene there is slapstick to give plenty of scope to an actor who is an expert clown. His mind is as lively as his body. Like other Aristophanic heroes[3] he is quick-witted and crafty. In the prologue he is so full of ideas for escaping from the

---

[1] The superficial view that the last third of the play has too little connection with the rest is refuted by C. F. Russo *Aristofane, autore di teatro* (1962) 198–201, and W. Kassies *Aristophanes' Traditionalisme* (1963) 79–80. The incidents of the later scenes are foreshadowed from the prologue onwards (e.g. 116, 341, 504–6, 736–40), and themselves contain references to the themes of earlier scenes (e.g. 1335–40, 1367).

[2] A. W. Gomme *More Essays in Greek History and Literature* (1962) 79. For another discussion of the character see C. H. Whitman *Aristophanes and the Comic Hero* (1964) 143–66.

[3] Cf. Whitman *Aristophanes and the Comic Hero* 21–41.

house that Bdelykleon and Xanthias can hardly keep up with him. Even when they think they have seen through his plan to escape with the donkey, it turns out to be a more ingenious one than they realized (174–89). He continues to show equal comic resourcefulness in later scenes, for instance when he tries to pass off a flute-girl as a torch (1361–77). His normal mood is one of complete confidence in himself and scorn for all opponents: 'I'm excellent in this line' (635) and 'He'll be gulped down' (1502) are typical of his boastful talk. He has no sense of morality (1262–3). Above all, he is thoroughly hard-hearted (δύσκολος) towards the accused men whom he tries. To him condemning is not only a duty but a pleasure too.

He is, in short, an old scallywag. And yet one cannot help liking him. One point in his favour (in Aristophanes's eyes at least) is his preference for what is old-fashioned, in music and dancing for instance (269 and the exodos). His ignorance of modern fashions is amusing, and yet one feels it to be forgivable; why *should* he have to discard his dear old cloak (1122–67)? Although he behaves badly when he gets drunk, the raucous woman and the two pompous men who threaten to summon him are unattractive because of their litigiousness, and one is glad when he outfaces them. Besides, he is not as hard-hearted as he pretends to be: at the end of the trial scene he actually sheds tears of pity for the accused, though he hastily pretends that they were caused by his hot soup (982–4). But the most important thing is that we are made to feel that he is not really responsible for the harm which he does in the law-courts. He is the dupe of Kleon and Kleon's friends. They are the villains. Philokleon is an ordinary man who has been led astray by them. When his eyes are opened, the truth comes to him as a surprise and a shock (696–7, 713–14). And it is because he evokes our sympathy as well as our laughter that he is a great comic character, perhaps the greatest in ancient comedy.

Bdelykleon is comparatively colourless. He is a good son, and sincerely desires his father's welfare. He is also a firm and efficient controller of his slaves, who stand in some awe of him

(134–7). But those are not characteristics which contribute much to the humour of a comedy. His main function is to present the sensible view of any question, and especially to point out the truth (as Aristophanes sees it) about Kleon and the law-courts. He serves as a foil to Philokleon, a standard of normality by which the old man's absurdities may be measured. His lines are almost always serious. But occasionally he shows some dry humour or sarcasm (146, 150–1, 173, 186, 209–10, 1387), and it is these passages which make him something more than just a necessary part of the mechanism of the play.

The slaves are a couple of good-natured fellows who warm up the audience by their chatter at the beginning of the play, and are a useful dramatic device for introducing the character of Philokleon (54–135), the character of the chorus (211–29, where Bdelykleon needs a questioner), and fresh turns in the plot at several points later in the play (835–43, 1292–1325, 1474–81). Like most slaves in ancient comedy they show signs of laziness, cowardice, stupidity, and lack of imagination (compare 225–9 with 426–7), but this does not mean that they are bad or unlikeable; it is natural (in the Greek view) for slaves to be inferior to free men in these ways. There is no perceptible difference in character between the two of them, and indeed in some parts of the play one cannot be certain which of them is speaking. Some editors attribute the lines to 'Slave A' or 'Slave B' or merely 'Slave', but since the names Xanthias and Sosias are given in the text (1, 136, 456) I have thought it more helpful to the reader to use them. Xanthias is addressed in line 456, and so I assume that it is Sosias who leaves the stage at 141 and that all subsequent lines spoken by a slave belong to Xanthias. But the correctness of this assumption cannot be proved.

Other characters perform useful dramatic functions in single scenes. The dog of Kydathenaion provides a satirical picture of Kleon and his methods of oratorical attack. The three accusers of Philokleon are stooges for comic behaviour on his part; but they also satirize Athenian litigiousness, and in particular the Bread-seller, a loud-mouthed defender of her own rights and dignity, is a character very vividly drawn in only a few lines. The boy who converses with the chorus-leader in the parodos adds much to the pathos of this passage by drawing attention to the poverty and decrepitude of the old jurors. Although it is unrealistic for old men to have such young children, the departure from realism is justified here because the contrast between youth and age is dramatically very effective; and the boy's mischievous threats (254–7, 299) and wheedling (291–8) make him the most lifelike child in any surviving Greek play.

The jurors who form the chorus are also well character-ized; in this play 'the poet has created the most vividly drawn chorus in his entire work'.[1] In their youth they fought in the Persian wars (1060–1101), which makes them, if the audience cares to calculate (as most would probably not), about eighty years old or more.[2] Of course most Athenian jurors will not have been as old as this; but some no doubt were. So, in making his jurors remember the Persian wars, Aristophanes is not making an arithmetical mistake or an absurd exaggeration; he is just showing that some jurors belong to the oldest living age-group.

Although the members of the chorus are old and poor like Philokleon, they differ from him in two respects. First, Philo-kleon is so perverse as to be poor by choice. He has a rich son who would be glad to keep him in luxury, but he obstinately prefers his old cloak and chilblains (1167), until in the later scenes he is gradually led to see the advantages of a different way of life. But the chorus do not enjoy their poverty at all. This illustrates an important fact about Aristophanes's method of satirizing the jurors: it is the chorus who show what Athenian jurors are really like (in his view), whereas the main character is not a typical juror but an absurd comic exaggeration.

[1] W. Kassies *Aristophanes' Traditionalisme* (1963) 81.
[2] If 1081 refers to Marathon, that makes them even older. But that line is not explicit, and the other reminiscences could all refer to the years 480–479 or later.

The second difference between Philokleon and the chorus is that they are much less lively than he is. In this respect too they are more realistic. He is a clown whose antics amuse the audience. They are afflicted by the weaknesses of genuine old age. Walking along an Athenian street is hard work for them (230–2). Mud and stones are obstacles (246–8). Many of their contemporaries are dead, and they look back nostalgically to the days of their youth and vigour (233–9, 354–5, 1060–1101). In conversation they tend to ramble into irrelevance (237–9, 259–65). They are just feeble old men—except when angered; then their waspish nature is revealed.

Their animal character must not be exaggerated.[1] The chorus of *Birds* are birds. The first chorus of *Frogs* are frogs. But the chorus of *Wasps* are not wasps; they are men who sometimes behave like wasps. The chief point of resemblance is that Athenian jurors, when roused, punish their victims with a seemingly irrational fury; but other similarities are also wittily suggested (1102–21). Their costume is adapted to make them look like wasps: they have visible stings[2] and narrow waists (420, 1071–5), and possibly other features not mentioned in the dialogue, such as tunics with black and yellow stripes.[3] All this is concealed under long cloaks when they first appear. In the parodos they are simply old men. But when Bdelykleon provokes them they become waspish; they throw off their cloaks (408) and their stings become visible (420). It is in this scene that they play their most active part. Once the fight is over they become spectators for

---

[1] Cf. H.-J. Newiger *Metapher und Allegorie* (1957) 74–80.

[2] Some scholars have thought that the sting was the phallos which was a normal part of the costume of performers in a comedy, but that is a mistake. Such lines as 225 and 420 prove that the sting is something which ordinary men like Bdelykleon and Xanthias do not have, and 1075 proves that the sting is attached to the rump.

[3] This costume is not worn by Philokleon. In fact he is never called a wasp at all. In 366 he is called 'little bee', but that is just an affectionate mode of address like the American 'honey'. In 107 he is compared to a bee, but that does not mean that he is a bee; only two lines earlier he is compared to a limpet.

the rest of the play; they sing their songs, but they take no further part in the action.

IV. HUMOUR AND ARTISTRY

The chief purpose of a comedy is to amuse, and Aristophanes shows considerable versatility in his use of different sorts of humour and fun. The most important sort is that in which something is said or done which is not quite appropriate to the circumstances. When Philokleon exclaims 'How thoroughly convicted he'll be!' (893), it is funny because he says it before knowing who is being accused. This sort of humour often consists of combining two things which separately would be unremarkable but seem incongruous when put together. It is natural for a juror to enter a law-court, and it is natural for a man celebrating the rites of the Korybantes to have a drum, but to take the drum into the law-court (119–20) is incongruous and therefore funny.

This humour of inappropriateness may take more purely verbal forms. It is funny when addiction to being a juror is called a disease (87–8), because 'disease' is a word which is not generally applied to such conditions. It is funny when Philokleon uses the language of tragedy to express his longing to be in a law-court (750–9), because exclusion from a jury is not a sufficiently serious affliction to justify this kind of melodramatic utterance. Anticlimax or bathos is funny, when a word or speech is inappropriate because it is somehow on a lower level than what has just been said: 'Give me a sword —or else a penalty tablet' (166–7).

A different but related sort of humour is that in which a situation or action is developed logically to an absurd conclusion, the sort of humour which is often employed by Lewis Carroll and in the more recent 'Theatre of the Absurd'.[1] Something which in real life would be an insuperable practical obstacle is disregarded, and, almost before the audience

[1] I am thinking of such dramatists as Eugène Ionesco and N. F. Simpson.

can realize what is happening, the action moves from realism to fantasy. There is less fantasy in *Wasps* than in some of Aristophanes's other plays, but even this play has some fantastic features. One is the trial of the dog in the domestic law-court. Since Philokleon wants to try cases and his son wants him to stay at home, the obvious conclusion is that he should try cases at home; cases tried at home must be for offences committed in the household; the sort of offence committed in a household is the theft of food by a dog; therefore a dog must be tried; naturally his accuser must be another dog; so the speech for the prosecution is made by a dog. Each stage of the development seems logical, and yet the conclusion is absurd, because Aristophanes has disregarded what would normally be an insuperable practical obstacle: dogs can't talk.

Another sort of fun is produced by being disrespectful to persons or things that are usually treated respectfully and seriously. People laugh when an important man is treated rudely, and they laugh more if they think that he deserves it; and so it is funny, especially to their opponents, when Aristophanes says rude things about Kleon and other prominent politicians. It is even funnier if the rude remark is made inadvertently by the victim himself or by a person who means to praise him, if Kleon calls himself a thief (928) or Philokleon calls him 'the shout-conqueror' (596). The spectators laugh because they feel released from the inhibitions which normally prevent them from being rude to an important man. The obscenity which appears from time to time in Aristophanes has a similar explanation. A line like 739 is funny because it says openly something which people usually feel inhibited from saying.

Then there is the humour which arises from play on words, or from words which are funny in themselves. Sometimes Aristophanes invents a funny word, like 'pomposnortical' (135) or 'to waggle-bottom' (1173). A kind of verbal humour which he particularly likes is the pun. In the twentieth century puns have become unfashionable, but many people still find them funny. In fifth-century Athens, to judge from Aristophanes, they were as popular as in Victorian England. Sometimes a pun is a good one, in the sense that the two words involved are identical in form, for example ἀσπίς meaning 'asp' and ἀσπίς meaning 'shield' (15–19). But Aristophanes is equally happy to use two words which are only similar, like ὀπή meaning 'chink' and ὀπία meaning 'cheese' (350–3). Some puns seem to have been old favourites which had become traditional: the mere utterance of the word σύκινος was apparently enough to raise a laugh without any need to mention συκοφάντης at all (145, 897).

These are only some of the sorts of humour which Aristophanes uses most often; it is hardly possible to make a complete list, or to categorize every joke. Different sorts of humour are not mutually exclusive, and one line may be amusing in two or three ways. A comic compound name may be used to express rudeness to a prominent politician (e.g. 459, 592). A comically melodramatic utterance may prepare the way for bathos (e.g. 312–13). One sense in a pun may be a laughable obscenity (e.g. 808). A pun and a comic invented name may be involved in a parody of a myth which is itself based on a logical absurdity (184–6).

And one must remember that the script is not the whole performance. An Aristophanic comedy includes some slapstick farce. In many places we can get from the text some idea of the accompanying actions, for instance when Bdelykleon claps down the chimney-cover on Philokleon's head (148); putting a lid on someone always makes a satisfying piece of clowning. But the original performance of *Wasps* will certainly have contained a good deal of comic business which does not appear in the text at all. The reader must resign himself to the loss of most of the visual humour—unless he likes to invent some of his own.

Other elements of the play which are completely lost are the music and the choreography. The plays which the Athenians had at their festivals were not only their drama but also their opera and their ballet, and many of them probably thought the singing and dancing the most important and entertaining parts of the performance. The dancing must have been particularly spectacular at two points in *Wasps*. One is the scene in which the chorus of jurors show their waspish character and attack Bdelykleon and Xanthias; here there is great scope for picturesque or exciting charges, withdrawals, and flank movements. The other is the exodos, where the three sons of Karkinos give a display, Philokleon makes some comic contribution, and the chorus join in at the end.

The songs, one may feel, are not as completely lost as the dances, since at least we have the words. True, a song without its music is only a shadow of itself; who would care about the words of *The Marriage of Figaro* or *Tosca* if they had no music? But still the words of a song may have some value, either as poetry or as comic verse. The lines about Amynias (1265–74), for instance, are a good little comic lyric, with their tripping trochaic rhythm and their neatly arranged sentences, working up step by step to the concluding pun.

There is little or no great poetry in *Wasps*. But there is some excellent verse. Aristophanes has a superb control of the various metres which he uses,[1] especially the smooth-flowing iambics, the hurrying trochees, and the pounding anapaests.[2] They invigorate the whole play, because the insistent rhythms give the words an impetus such as prose can never have.

---

[1] For an account of the metrical rules see pages 21–9. Some examples which are only briefly mentioned in the introduction are more fully explained in the commentary.

[2] Some readers may object to my interpretation of various metres as fast, slow, smooth-flowing, and so on. I freely admit that all such interpretations are to some extent uncertain, because it is always *possible* for any passage in any metre to be delivered either fast or slowly, smoothly or jerkily, lightly or ponderously. Nevertheless it does seem to me that some metres lend themselves more easily than others to certain modes of delivery, and that we may fairly assume that for each passage Aristophanes selected a metre which lent itself easily to the tempo and manner of delivery he intended for that passage rather than a metre which did not. His purpose in using different metres was to produce artistic effects; therefore we ought to make some attempt to understand and appreciate those effects, despite the difficulties and uncertainties.

Nearly always the lines seem to run on effortlessly. Each character says just what the author wishes him to say, and hardly ever does one feel that the metre has obstructed the author's wish by compelling a different choice of words or a distortion of the usual word-order. On the contrary, Aristophanes can manipulate the metre to suit the sense. When he wants to talk about slowness, the metre slows down (e.g. 230). When he wants to move faster, the metre speeds up (e.g. 246, 248). When the mood changes, the metre changes with it (e.g. 323–4, 1291). When the audience gasps in amazement, the metre misses a beat (1526–7).

Sometimes, especially in the iambic trimeters of ordinary dialogue, the lines seem to run on continuously, and one is hardly conscious of a verse as a separate entity, so closely does the end of one verse adhere to the beginning of the next (e.g. 1193–4). Yet even an iambic trimeter can have an artistic unity. A single complete verse may be answered or balanced by another single complete verse (e.g. 1–2); the two may even rhyme (e.g. 65–6). Within a verse, the words before the caesura may be rephrased and reinforced by the words after it (e.g. 992). Or a verse may be divided in the proportions 3:4:5, giving a triplet of increasing length and dignity (e.g. 978, 1005). Other effective rhythms are also evolved in this same metre. Line 979 is an amazing example of Aristophanes's control of the iambic trimeter; without breaking the rules of comic iambics it assumes the insistent rhythm of anapaests, and the last word makes a climax and a conclusion, both in sound and in sense.

Language is used no less effectively than metre. Sometimes the characters seem to chat in the most ordinary language, and even become grammatically slipshod: verbs are colloquially omitted (e.g. 142), and a subordinate clause may have no apparent grammatical connection with its main clause (e.g. 517–18). But what is important is not the observance of grammatical conventions but the effective expression of meaning, and Aristophanes's sentences hardly ever fail to make their points clearly and forcefully. He has a wide range of rhetorical devices for vigorous expression, such as balanced antithesis (e.g. 65–6), repetition of a word (e.g. τυραννίς in 488–507), and short staccato sentences in asyndeton (e.g. 1214–17). He knows how to arrange a sentence in such a way that the final word comes as a comic climax (e.g. 15–19, 717–18).

But the most important feature of his language is the imagery.[1] He makes lavish use of similes, metaphors, and other sorts of comparative and pictorial expression. It is these more than anything else which distinguish his language from the language of ordinary prose writing and from the language of real-life conversation, by making it more attractive and more vivid. Comparisons with animals are especially common: Philokleon is like a limpet (105), a bee (107), a jackdaw (129), a sparrow (207), or a thieving cat (363), while Kleon is a horrific mythological monster (1031–5). Actions are often seen in military or naval terms, or else in the terms of agriculture or other labour in the countryside: to struggle against difficulties is to fight a sea-battle (479); to resist sleep or a cold wind is like withstanding a Persian invasion (11–12, 1123–4); to do something new is to open up a mine (876); corrupt orators are like a pair of sawyers (694); and Aristophanes himself is an unreliable vine-stake (1291). A tough man is a dog-leash (231), an accuser is a fever (1038), and boasters are smoke (324–5, 459). A look may be mustard (455), a smell may be clever (1059); to be cheated is to be encircled (699).[2] If Aristophanes is, as he claims, a charioteer

---

[1] For detailed studies of his imagery, see Jean Taillardat *Les Images d'Aristophane* (1962), and Anna M. Komornicka *Métaphores, Personnifications et Comparaisons dans l'œuvre d'Aristophane* (1964). Taillardat's book is the more thorough and useful of the two.

[2] There are several references to encirclement in *Wasps* (132, 395, 432, 699, 924), and circular dancing is mentioned several times in the exodos (1517, 1523, 1528–31). Whitman (*Aristophanes and the Comic Hero* 161) argues that these references have a symbolic significance for the play as a whole, conveying 'the underlying idea of the vicious circle where all things return upon themselves'. But encirclement in a trap is really quite different from rotation in a pirouette, and I doubt whether this symbolism was intended by Aristophanes.

who drives past his rivals (1050), his use of vivid imagery is not the least of the means which enable him to do so.

V. THE PERFORMANCE

The festival of the Lenaia was held each year in Gamelion (the month corresponding approximately to January).[1] In early times the plays at this festival were performed at the precinct of the Lenaion.[2] Later the performances were transferred to the theatre of Dionysos, beside the Akropolis. It is not known at what date this transfer took place. Some scholars believe that it was before the career of Aristophanes began, but there is no clear evidence for this, and the question remains open.[3]

Fortunately it hardly matters as far as *Wasps* is concerned, because this play needs no unusual scenic arrangements and could be performed in any sort of theatre, whether permanent or temporary. The only scenery needed is a building to serve as the house, with one door, one window at a higher level, and a roof on which Bdelykleon can lie and stand in the prologue. If the building has any other doors and windows, they are kept shut and ignored throughout the play.[4] In front of the house there is some kind of raised stage or rostrum or steps (1341); there is also an altar (used in 820, 860-90).

At the beginning of the play the scene is the front of the house of Bdelykleon and Philokleon, but it would be pedantic to insist that the whole play is supposed to take place there, even though changes of locale are not explicitly indicated in

---

[1] For an account of the festival see *Dram. Fest.*[2] 25-42.

[2] Its location is doubtful; see R. E. Wycherley in *Hesperia* xxxiv (1965) 72-6, *Dram. Fest.*[2] 37-9.

[3] For recent discussions see W. B. Stanford in *Hermathena* lxxxix (1957) 65, C. F. Russo *Aristofane, autore di teatro* (1962) 1-21, *Dram. Fest.*[2] 39-40.

[4] A. M. Dale (*JHS* lxxvii [1957] 205-11) argues that there are two windows but only one door, K. J. Dover (*Proc. Cambridge Philol. Soc.* cxcii [1966] 2-17) that the number of doors is not necessarily limited to one.

the text. During the trial of the dog, and again in the scene
following the parabasis, we may, if we wish, imagine that we
are inside the house.[1] When Philokleon is on his way home
from the party the scene may be in the Agora (1372), though
we are back in front of the house by the end of it (1444).
Some passages have no particular location. And even if
a location is clearly stated, the characters are at the same time
actors performing in the theatre and can converse with the
audience (54–135, 1497–1500).

Time is as vague as place; it is indicated when it is important, and otherwise we need not think about it at all. It is
night when the play begins, and dawn at line 366. It must be
afternoon or evening when Philokleon and Bdelykleon go out
to dinner (1264), and dark when Philokleon returns with
a torch (1326). But other passages are not at any particular
time. It is pointless to ask, for instance, whether the final
dance takes place in the middle of the night. This is one of the
advantages of an open-air theatre: imaginary darkness is
easily forgotten.

It is not known for certain how many speaking actors
Aristophanes could use in a comedy, but the number was certainly not less than four. In *Wasps* four speaking actors are
needed at 1412–15, where there is no time for one actor to
change from the part of the Bread-seller to that of the Accuser,
while Philokleon and Bdelykleon are both present. If one
actor played Philokleon and one Bdelykleon, it would be
possible for two actors to play all the other speaking parts
between them. More actors would be needed for the various
silent parts.

The chorus of a comedy in Aristophanes's time had twenty-
four members. In this play the chorus are accompanied in the
parodos by some boys (not necessarily as many as twenty-
four), who depart at line 414. The boy performers who took
these roles may also have played the puppies and witnesses in
the trial scene.

[1] But there is, as A. Müller showed (*Philologus* lxxii [1913] 442–4), no
reason to suppose that the *ekkyklema* was used in this play.

Some details of the contest for which *Wasps* was entered are given at the end of the first hypothesis (ancient introduction to the play), but unluckily that passage is confused. The statement that the play was produced by Philonides instead of by Aristophanes himself seems to be clearly wrong.[1] Philonides apparently produced one of the other plays in the competition, *Proagon*, which possibly, though not certainly, was written by Aristophanes. According to the received text of the hypothesis *Proagon* won the first prize and *Wasps* came second, but some scholars have proposed to emend the text in such a way as to reverse the order. There is general agreement that Leukon's *Ambassadors* came third.

Modern performances of *Wasps* have been few. There was a famous production at Cambridge in 1909, for which Vaughan Williams composed some charming but very un-Aristophanic music; but in recent years the play has been performed less often than it deserves.

[1] See note on hyp. i line 32.

THE METRES

SINCE rhythmical effects form an important part of the artistry of Aristophanes, and a reader who does not understand them fails to attain a full appreciation of the play, I offer here a general introduction to the commoner metres in *Wasps*. It is intended especially for those who have not read an Aristophanes play before, but I assume that readers are already familiar with the use of iambic trimeters in tragedy.

Metres used in only one or two passages in the play and special metrical difficulties in individual lines are not explained here, but in the commentary.[1]

Prosody

The scansion of individual syllables in Aristophanes is generally the same as in tragedy. But the following features may deserve special mention.

1. *A short vowel before a mute and a liquid consonant.*

(*a*) Before β or γ or δ followed by λ or μ or ν, as in tragedy, a short vowel is normally scanned long. But it is short in 570 ἄμᾰ βληχᾶται (570 n.).

(*b*) Before other combinations of a mute and a liquid (κλ, πν, τρ, χμ, etc.) a short vowel is usually scanned short (except in the preposition ἐκ). In iambic trimeters it is nearly always short, unless tragedy is being parodied; but it is long in 837 ἱπνὸν (837 n.).

2. *ε combined with a following vowel.* When ε is immediately followed by another vowel in the same word, the two are occasionally scanned together as one long syllable; e.g. 1067 νεᾱνικὴν.

[1] For fuller discussion and statistics see J. W. White *The Verse of Greek Comedy* (1912). For analyses of the lyric passages see Otto Schroeder *Aristophanis Cantica* (1909), Carlo Prato *I canti di Aristofane* (1962); but the analyses in my commentary sometimes differ from theirs.

3. *Correption.*

(a) αι is sometimes scanned short in adjectives in -αιος; e.g. 40 δείλαιος.

(b) οι is sometimes scanned short in οἶος, ποῖος, and τοιοῦτος, and also in ποιῶ[1] and ποιήτης; e.g. 25, 261, 318, 1016, 1369.

(c) In the demonstrative οὑτοσί a long vowel or diphthong immediately before the -ί is scanned short; e.g. 256 τουτουί, 262 οὑτοιί, 807 αὑτηί.

(d) Any long vowel or diphthong ending a word is scanned short (except in cases covered by 4, 5, and 6 below) if the next word begins with a vowel; e.g. 291 μοῖ οὖν, 699 ὅπῃ ἐγκεκύκλησαι. (But this is avoided in iambic trimeters.)

4. *Synizesis.* The long vowel concluding ἐγώ, ἦ, μή, τῇ, τῷ, and occasionally other words, if immediately followed by another vowel, is scanned with it as one long syllable; e.g. 827 τῇ οἰκίᾳ is − ∪ −, 1224 ἐγὼ εἴσομαι is ∪ − ∪ −.

5. *Elision of a diphthong.*

(a) αι at the end of a verb (in -μαι, -σαι, -ται, -σθαι, or -ναι) may be elided; e.g. 273 φαίνετ᾽, 1426 δέομ᾽.

(b) οι at the end of οἴμοι may be elided; e.g. 1449.

6. *Hiatus* is allowed after εὖ, περί, τί or τι, ὅτι, and exclamations, e.g. ὦ, ἰή. (Aristophanes also has οὐδὲ εἷς and οὐδὲ ἕν in other plays, but there is no instance in *Wasps*.)

7. *Brevis in longo.* As in tragedy and other Greek verse, at the end of a metrical group (at the end of each line in 'stichic' metres like the iambic trimeter and the iambic, trochaic, and anapaestic tetrameter; at the end of each period in a lyric) a syllable which otherwise would be short is counted as long, because a pause follows it. I mark such syllables ⌢.

Iambic trimeters

The iambic trimeter is the usual metre for dialogue. It is used for almost half the lines in *Wasps*. Although for some pur-

---

[1] For the alternative spelling without ι, 261 n.

poses it is preferable to treat the line as three metra (one metron being ×–∪–),[1] I shall here follow the usual and convenient practice of treating it as six feet:

$$× – ∪ – \quad × – ∪ – \quad × – ∪ –$$

Aristophanes departs from tragic practice in these ways:

1. He admits trisyllabic feet more freely. Any of the first five feet may be ∪∪∪ or ∪∪– (979 is an exceptionally striking example). The first, third, and fifth feet may be –∪∪ There is possibly one case in *Wasps* of ∪∪∪∪ in the second foot (967).

2. Porson's law, restricting the use of a long syllable at the beginning of the fifth foot, is not observed.

3. Word-break[2] within an anapaestic foot is sometimes allowed, even between the two short syllables; e.g. 25, 155, 1369. Similarly word-break is allowed in a tribrach or dactyl even between the second and third syllables; e.g. 3, 172, 767.

4. Caesura is sometimes neglected.

Although this metre was evidently considered suitable for conversation in a play, that does not mean that it resembles the rhythm of prose conversation in real life, and Aristophanes's audiences must always have been conscious that they were listening to verse, not prose. The reason for the metre's popularity is perhaps its versatility: a word of almost any metrical shape can, if necessary, be fitted in without seriously obscuring the rhythmical beat (e.g. the awkward name Ἀλκιβιάδης in 44–6). And Aristophanes shows great skill in producing different kinds of effect with it (cf. page 16).

---

[1] × marks a position which may be occupied by either a short or a long syllable (anceps).

[2] The space in our printed texts between a prepositive (the definite article, most prepositions, καί, ἀλλά, ἤ, εἰ, etc.) and the following word, or between a postpositive (most enclitic words, μέν, δέ, γάρ, οὖν, etc.) and the preceding word, does not, to Greek ears, constitute a break between words. For a fuller list of prepositives and postpositives see K. J. Dover *Greek Word Order* (1960) 12–19.

Iambic tetrameters

An iambic metron is $\times - \cup -$, and iambic tetrameters are catalectic (that is, the last metron is a syllable short, so that there is a slight pause at the end of each line). So the line is:

$$\times - \cup - \quad \times - \cup - \quad \times - \cup - \quad \cup - -$$

The fourth metron never begins with a long syllable. The second or fourth syllable of each metron (except the last) may be resolved from $-$ to $\cup\cup$, though such resolution is not frequent; e.g. 246:

χωρῶμεν, ἅμα τε τῷ λύχνῳ πάντῃ διασκοπῶμεν.
$$- - \cup\cup\cup \ \cup - \cup - \ | \ - - \cup - \ \cup - -$$

Diaeresis (word-break at the end of a metron) is usual at the end of the second metron (marked | in the example above), but sometimes does not occur there; e.g. 235, 634.

The regularity of the beat (caused by the rarity of resolved syllables) and the pause at the end of each line (caused by the catalectic metron) make this a suitable metre for the plodding entry of the chorus of old men (230–47).

Trochaic tetrameters

A trochaic metron is $- \cup - \times$. Otherwise a trochaic tetrameter is just like an iambic one, with a catalectic metron at the end:

$$- \cup - \times \ - \cup - \times \ - \cup - \times \ - \cup -$$

As in an iambic tetrameter, diaeresis at the end of the second metron is usual but not invariable. The first or third syllable of each metron (but not the last syllable of the line) may be resolved from $-$ to $\cup\cup$; e.g. 462:

εἴπερ ἔτυχον τῶν μελῶν τῶν Φιλοκλέους βεβρωκότες.
$$- \cup\cup\cup - \ - \cup - - \ \cup\cup\cup - \cup \ - \cup -$$

But such resolution is not used a great deal, so that usually the trochaic beat, long and short syllables alternating, is very pronounced. Besides, the first metrical beat of the line falls on the first syllable (whereas in iambics it is on the second). So the effect is one of strong drive and urgency, and this metre is suitable for scenes of excitement. It is used, for instance, for the wasps' attack on Bdelykleon (403–525).

Anapaestic tetrameters

An anapaestic metron is ∪ ∪ − ∪ ∪ −, and anapaestic tetra-meters, like trochaic and iambic, are catalectic (which in this case means that the last ∪ ∪ is omitted), giving the line:

∪ ∪ − ∪ ∪ − ∪ ∪ − ∪ ∪ − ∪ ∪ − ∪ ∪ − ∪ ∪ − −

The end of the line is always − ∪ ∪ − −, but elsewhere ∪ ∪ − is often changed to − − or − ∪ ∪. But Aristophanes pre-fers to avoid any such substitution which produces four consecutive short syllables; so − ∪ ∪ is not followed im-mediately by ∪ ∪ − (for exceptions, 397 n.). It is rare for the second metron to end with − ∪ ∪ (but it does so in 350, 397).

There is usually (but not quite always: 568 n.) diaeresis at the end of the second metron, often at the end of the first, and sometimes at the end of the third too; e.g. 352:

πάντα πέφρακται κοὐκ ἔστιν ὀπῆς οὐδ' εἰ σέρφῳ διαδῦναι.

− ∪ ∪ − − | − − ∪ ∪ − | − − − − | ∪ ∪ − −

Because the substitution of − − for ∪ ∪ − is very common, there is sometimes a considerable number of long syllables in succession (e.g. 387 has twelve, the maximum possible); trochaic and iambic tetrameters never have more than three consecutive long syllables. This fact, together with the fact that each metron is longer than a trochaic or iambic one, makes the anapaestic tetrameter a slower and more dignified line, but not less forceful: one has the impression of a rhythm pounding relentlessly on and on until the whole of the long line is completed. It is one of Aristophanes's favourite metres, and in *Wasps* it is the next commonest after the iambic trimeter. It is used, as usual, for the main part of the parabasis (1015–50) and in the agon (546–619, 648–718).

Iambic, trochaic, and anapaestic runs ('dimeters')

Sometimes iambic, trochaic, or anapaestic metra, instead of being grouped in fours (three full metra with one catalectic) to make tetrameters, follow one after another in a longer continuous run before being brought to a conclusion or a pause by a catalectic metron. This occurs both in songs and in dialogue; it is often hard to guess how far music was used in the performance of a particular passage, and no hard and fast distinction can be drawn between spoken and lyric passages.

For example, 1482–95 is a passage of dialogue consisting of 26 anapaestic metra, of which only the last is catalectic. 324–33 is part of a song; there is a short run of anapaests ending with a catalectic metron in 326, and then a longer run ending with a catalectic metron in 333. 1265–74 is a song in trochaics, divided into four 'stanzas' or 'periods' by the catalectic metra which make pauses at the ends of 1266, 1267, 1270, and 1274. A run of this sort is often used to round off a passage of tetrameters: thus 346–57 are anapaestic tetrameters, and 358–64 are a run of 14 anapaestic metra (13 full and the last catalectic).

In these runs the same kinds of substitution are allowed as in tetrameters: in anapaests − − or − ∪ ∪ is often substituted for ∪ ∪ −, and in trochaics and iambics ∪ ∪ is occasionally substituted for −. In anapaests a diaeresis at the end of the metron (except when the next metron is catalectic) is common but not invariable, but in trochaics and iambics there is no regular diaeresis or caesura. Such runs have been given the name πνῖγος ('choker') on the assumption (probably false) that they were delivered by the actor in a single breath.

In manuscripts and editions the metra are generally written in pairs, as though they formed a series of dimeters.[1] This

---

[1] The first editor to arrange such passages in dimeters was probably the Alexandrian scholar Aristophanes of Byzantion. For the view, with which I do not agree, that the dimeter is a genuine unit in anapaestic passages see Dale[2] 49.

is misleading, because in fact there is not a pause after each alternate metron (as is clear from the way in which words run on from one metron to the next; e.g. 629–30, 754, 1268–70), and sometimes there is an odd number of metra, not exactly divisible into pairs. A passage like 719–24 should not be regarded as five and a half dimeters but (if a name is needed) as one big hendecameter.

To get an impression of the effect of a passage of anapaestic tetrameters concluding with a run of anapaests, it may be helpful to listen to (or, failing that, read) the Lord Chancellor's nightmare song in Act II of Gilbert and Sullivan's *Iolanthe*. Gilbert was strongly influenced by Aristophanes, and that song, though it differs from Aristophanes's metrical practice in certain respects (it is based on stress rather than quantity; and spondees are never substituted for anapaests, so that the rhythm seems much faster), clearly shows the effectiveness of comic anapaestic tetrameters leading up to a πνῖγος.

Reduced trochaics

In several trochaic passages in *Wasps* some of the metra, instead of having the full form $- \cup - \times$ (or with resolution $\cup \cup \cup - \times$ or $- \cup \cup \cup \times$), are reduced[1] in one of the following ways.

The last syllable may be omitted, leaving $- \cup -$. (Metricians dispute whether this should be called 'syncopated trochaic' or 'cretic'.) This is the same as the catalectic metron regularly found at the end of a trochaic tetrameter or run, or at a pause; but in the passages now under discussion it is found in other places, where there is no pause. For example, 418–19 are two tetrameters in which every metron is $- \cup -$, and in 413–14 the last three metra of a run are all $- \cup -$.

[1] I avoid here the term 'syncopated' because it implies the entire suppression of a syllable. When $\cup \cup - \cup$ is used for a trochaic metron no syllable has been entirely suppressed. On the other hand 'syllable-counting' (Dale[2] 89) will not cover the use of $- \cup -$ in place of $- \cup - \times$. I use 'reduced' to cover both phenomena.

Alternatively the first or third syllable of a metron may be short instead of long. $- \cup \cup \cup$ is fairly common; e.g. 370 ἀλλ' ἔπαγε, 1062 τοῦτο μόνον. (Some metricians prefer to regard this not as $- \cup - \cup$ with the third syllable short instead of long, but as $- \cup -$ with the third syllable resolved.) $\cup \cup - \cup$ is rarer, but occurs in 342 -τι λέγεις τι, 343 περὶ τῶν νε-. In one catalectic line (where one might expect $- \cup - \times \quad - \cup -$) no fewer than three long syllables have shorts substituted for them: 339 τίνα πρόφασιν ἔχων scans $\cup \cup \cup \cup \quad \cup \cup -$.

Where a strophe and antistrophe occur, responding to each other metrically, such reduced metra are often found in the same places in both. But not always; 1062 τοῦτο μόνον responds to 1093 -ους, πλέων ἐ-, and there is similar inexact responsion in 339 ∼ 370, 342*b* ∼ 374, 343 ∼ 375.

410–14 will serve as an example of the combination of full and reduced trochaic metra:

καὶ κελεύετ᾽ αὐτὸν ἥκειν	$- \cup - \cup$	$- \cup - -$
ὡς ἐπ᾽ ἄνδρα μισόπολιν	$- \cup - \cup$	$- \cup \cup \cup$
ὄντα κἀπολούμενον, ὅτι	$- \cup - \cup$	$- \cup \cup \cup \cup$
τόνδε λόγον εἰσφέρει,	$- \cup \cup \cup$	$- \cup -$
μὴ δικάζειν δίκας.	$- \cup -$	$- \cup -$

What is the purpose of reducing metra in this way? No certain answer can be given, because of our ignorance of the manner in which the lines were delivered. But my guess is that the purpose is to give an effect of slowness within a more rapid trochaic rhythm. Within any one passage the rhythmi-cal beat is, presumably, regular; that is, each metron occupies the same length of time in delivery. If an individual metron has fewer syllables, or a short syllable in place of a long one, the syllables have to be delivered more slowly (or with a pause at some point) to fill up the time. The actor lingers over his words, or he pauses for breath in the middle of them.

This guess is supported by consideration of some of the passages in which the reduced metra are used. The chorus have a good many before and after their fight with Bdely-kleon (403–29, 463–87). They are excited and active, but they are old men and they get out of breath. The trochaic rhythm easily lends itself to rapid delivery, to give an effect of excited activity; the reduction of some of the metra conveys the impression that they are too breathless to keep up the pace. It is significant that in the longer speeches (403–14, 463–70) the proportion of reduced metra increases towards the end. It is also significant that there are none in the speeches of Bdelykleon and Xanthias; they are young, and able to keep up the pace of the fight without getting out of breath.

In 1060–5 a different effect is obtained by the reduced metra. There the chorus are singing nostalgically of days long past, and they linger affectionately over their memories. At 1066 they turn to the present; the pace becomes brisker, and the reduction of metra ceases.

Metrical symbols

—	long syllable
◡	short syllable
×	position occupied by either – or ◡ (anceps)
○○	position occupied by – – or – ◡ or ◡ –
⌒	syllable which would be short if no pause followed but is counted as long because a pause does follow (brevis in longo)
‖	pause whose presence is proved by hiatus or by ⌒
|	word-end (caesura or diaeresis)

Where a symbol appears above another in the analysis of a responding passage (▽, ⌣, etc.), the upper symbol refers to the strophe and the lower to the antistrophe.

THE MANUSCRIPTS

The principal manuscripts[1]

THE oldest manuscript of *Wasps* is Π, a fragmentary papyrus of the fifth century A.D. It contains only bits of about 150 lines from the middle of the play.

The oldest manuscript containing the whole play is R, the renowned Ravenna manuscript of about A.D. 1000, in the Biblioteca Classense in Ravenna. It is the only manuscript containing all the eleven extant plays of Aristophanes.

The next oldest is V, which is in the Biblioteca Nazionale di S. Marco in Venice.[2] It contains seven plays (*Wealth, Clouds, Frogs, Knights, Birds, Peace, Wasps*).

Γ is a fourteenth-century manuscript in the Biblioteca Mediceo-Laurenziana in Florence. It must have been copied from a defective exemplar, which had lost a number of pages. It contains (besides various other plays of Aristophanes and Euripides) about three-fifths of *Wasps*, lines 421–1396. In addition the closing lines of the play (1494–1537) appear between 705 and 706; presumably a loose page of the exemplar had been put back in the wrong place.

J is one of the Palatine manuscripts in the Vatican library.[3] It contains only three plays (*Knights, Akharnians, Wasps*). It belongs to the fifteenth century, and previous editors of *Wasps* have classed it with other late manuscripts and paid

---

[1] For a complete list of the manuscripts containing *Wasps*, giving their full names, see page 41.

[2] Its date is uncertain, but it has usually been attributed to the eleventh century. W. J. W. Koster (*Rev. Ét. Gr.* lxvi [1953] 25, *Mn.* IV xvi [1963] 141) has maintained that it cannot be earlier than the late twelfth century, but this view is rebutted by A. Colonna (*Riv. Fil.* xxxii [1954] 318–20); cf. K. J. Dover *Aristophanes: Clouds* (1968) page cv n. 3.

[3] J is my symbol for the manuscript which J. W. White (*Class. Phil.* i [1906] 17) called Vp3.

little or no attention to it. But its merit is that it is free from the Byzantine conjectures which are found in the other fifteenth-century manuscripts (described below), and it has preserved a number of good readings which are not in *ΠRVΓ*. It is particularly useful in those parts of the play which *Γ* does not contain (see, for example, lines 7, 21, 53, 58, 59, 90, 152, 419, 1428, 1461). So this edition, unlike earlier editions of the play, contains a full report of its readings.

It is, in my opinion, a mistake to try to construct a stemma showing the relationships between *ΠRVΓ*J, because it is an 'open recension'. That is, these manuscripts and their lost ancestors were not simply copied each from a single exemplar, but after (or even while) being copied one manuscript was often compared with others, and they were corrected (or corrupted) by reference to one another, so that any one manuscript may contain readings drawn from several different sources. Between them our surviving manuscripts show what variant readings were current in medieval times, but no one of them consistently preserves a separate tradition from the rest. This is shown by passages in which the same error is found in two or more manuscripts although others avoid it: no manuscript consistently has the same partners in error. A short list of examples will illustrate the fact that almost every possible division and combination occurs. This is a list (not exhaustive, but only a selection) of false readings shared by two or more manuscripts but not by all: 7 *ὕπνου* RV, 175 *ἵνα θᾶττον* VJ, 263 *ὁ ζεὺς* RV, 508 *οὐδὲν* ΠΓ, 570 *-τ' ἀπο-* ΠV, 602 *οὖσαν* om. VΓ, 668 *περιπεμφθεὶς* RVΓ, 675 *δωρο-δοκοῦσιν* RΓJ, 693 *τι* om. VΓJ, 802 *ἀνοικο-* RΓ, 950 *-μένους* RVJ, 1009 *ταχέως* ΓJ, 1211 *κατακλιθῆναι* RJ.

Furthermore it cannot be assumed that RVΓJ are all descended from a single text which alone survived the dark ages.[1] Sometimes an error found in only some of them is

[1] The view of Wilamowitz and others that only one manuscript of Aristophanes survived into the ninth century to be transliterated from uncial into minuscule script has been rejected by Max Pohlenz (*Nachrichten*

shared by Π. For example, in 570 ΠV have -τ' ἀπο-, where
the correct -θ' ἅμα is preserved in ΓJ (and virtually in R).
This shows that -τ' ἀπο- was already current in the fifth
century, and both readings have been passed on from that
time into the Middle Ages, either in different manuscripts or
in a manuscript which included variant readings and not
just a single text.

So in these manuscripts age is not a criterion of superiority,
and a reading found in R or V should not automatically be
preferred to one found in Γ or J. Each reading must be judged
on its merits.

Later manuscripts

P, H, L, Vv17, and B are manuscripts affected by the
conjectures of late Byzantine editors.[1] P and Vv17 are in the
Vatican library, H is in the Kongelige Bibliotek in Copen-
hagen, and B is in the Bibliothèque Nationale in Paris. L is
a manuscript from the Earl of Leicester's library at Holkham,
now in the Bodleian Library in Oxford. The significance of
L and Vv17 has only recently been noticed.[2] This is the first
edition of *Wasps* to make use of H, L, and Vv17.

These five manuscripts contain a number of emendations,
most of which were evidently attempts to restore the metre in
passages which were thought not to scan. Some of these cor-
rections are certainly or probably right (e.g. 28 ἔστιν, 200
ἔμβαλλε). But in some places an editor has been led astray by
a little learning. For example, in 747 these five manuscripts
all have νῦν οὖν ἴσως τοῖς σοῖς λόγοισι πείθεται : some editor has
carefully adapted the text to make an iambic trimeter—but

---

der Akademie der Wissenschaften in Göttingen, Phil.-hist. Klasse [1952] 95–103)
and W. J. W. Koster (*Rev. Ét. Gr.* lxxvi [1963] 381–4).

[1] I do not mean to imply that RVΓJ contain no conjectural emendations. But the readings in RVΓJ which look like conjectures are few, and
most of them appear to have been made not in order to correct the
metre (like most of those in PHL̈Vv17B) but to explain or clarify the
sense; e.g. 7 ὕπνου, 263 ὁ ζεύς.

[2] L has been fully described by N. G. Wilson (*CQ* xii [1962] 32–47)
and Vv17 by Seth Benardete (*HSCP* lxvi [1962] 241–8).

unluckily for him this passage is not written in iambic trimeters. Another series of examples occurs in 248–72; someone thought that these lines should be in the same metre as 230–47, and so B has an extra syllable (usually an otiose γε or δή or νῦν) inserted in the middle of every line in the passage.

Three stages of this conjectural activity can be detected: conjectures which appear in all the five manuscripts, conjectures which are in LVv17B but not in PH, and conjectures in B only. One may thus speak of three 'editions' of *Wasps* made in the late medieval period.

The first was the one which I call *q*. The editor of *q* seems to have taken as his basis a manuscript resembling J (though not J itself) and made emendations in it, possibly also comparing it with other manuscripts. P and H are derived from *q* and do not contain the emendations attributable to later editions. A number of obvious mistakes appear in both P and H, and some in P only, and some in H only; these show that P and H are independent copies of a manuscript which itself was a copy of *q*. So a reading may be attributed to *q* if it appears in P or H or both and also in LVv17B; but a reading which is in PH but not in LVv17B cannot safely be attributed to *q*, since it may be only a mistake made in the exemplar of PH.

The next edition was the one called *t*. The editor took *q* as his basis and made further emendations in it. L and Vv17 are derived from *t* and do not include any subsequent emendations. L is evidently a very accurate copy of *t*, in which fresh mistakes are rare and trivial. In Vv17 obvious mistakes are far more numerous, and some of these mistakes are shared by B (e.g. 348 ποιήμην, 418 θεοεχθρία, 1076 εὐμενεῖς), but not all. This shows that Vv17 and B are both derived independently from a manuscript which itself was a copy of *t*. So a reading may be attributed to *t* if it appears in L and also in Vv17 or B or both; but a reading which is in Vv17B but not in L cannot safely be attributed to *t*, since it may be only a mistake made in the exemplar of Vv17B.

The third edition was based on a copy of *t*, with more conjectures added. Since B is the only surviving representative of this edition, we may call the edition B, though really it is more likely that B is not the original text but only a copy of it.

The interrelation of these manuscripts in *Wasps* is shown in the following diagram. Asterisks represent lost manuscripts whose existence must be assumed, but there may have been more of these intermediate manuscripts than the diagram shows.

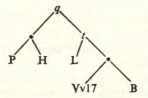

Who were the editors of *q*, *t*, and B? Since many of the conjectures are metrical, one of them was almost certainly the early-fourteenth-century scholar Demetrios Triklinios, who made a special study of metre. Indeed it is possible that all three editions were the work of Triklinios, who may well have gone over the play several times.[1] But perhaps the likeliest guess is that, though *q* and *t* may have been the work of Triklinios, the editor whose work is preserved in B was a scholar of a later date.[2]

After these editions (or perhaps before B) came the first printed edition, the Aldine (abbreviated as Ald). It was edited by the Cretan scholar Mousouros and published by Aldus Manutius at Venice in 1498. Mousouros seems to have used several manuscripts closely related to PHLVv17B, though probably not any of these actual five. He also made some conjectures of his own. In individual cases, therefore,

[1] As he did with other plays; see for example G. Zuntz *An Inquiry into the Transmission of the Plays of Euripides* (1965), especially Chapter II.

[2] Cf. N. G. Wilson 'The Triclinian Edition of Aristophanes' (*CQ* xii [1962] 32–47).

the source of a reading in Ald is often doubtful. Yet, although
the editors of *q*, *t*, B, and Ald must all have been able to use
one or more manuscripts which are not extant now, it does
not appear that those manuscripts contained anything of
value which is not preserved also in at least one of our older
surviving manuscripts. So any reading of the later manuscripts or Ald which does not appear in RVΓJ should generally
be regarded as either a conjecture or a mistake.

But there is one notable exception to this principle. B has
here and there an alternative reading written above the line
by a different scribe (B₂), often coinciding with the reading
of Γ. For example, in 901 B (like all other manuscripts
except Γ) has ἐξαπατήσειν, but above the middle of the word
the letters αναστή have been written by B₂; the reading of Γ
is ἐξαναστήσειν. Clearly B₂ did not conjecture these readings
himself, but found them in another manuscript. Now, some
of his readings are in parts of the play which Γ does not contain; this shows that they come not from Γ itself but from an
ancestor (or from a copy of an ancestor) of Γ. Thus the
readings of B₂ deserve serious consideration alongside those of
RVΓJ, where they occur; there are however not many of
them.

There are three other manuscripts which are merely copies
of older surviving manuscripts. G is a copy of V; Δ is a copy
of B; and C (written by a very careless scribe) contains
Knights, *Akharnians*, *Wasps* copied from J (or possibly from
a copy of J),[1] followed by other plays copied from some

[1] E. Cary (*HSCP* xviii [1907] 171–3), followed by D. Mervyn Jones
(*CQ* v [1955] 39), maintains that C is not a copy but a twin of J, but this
view seems to me less likely. Whereas C contains dozens of errors not
found in J, there are hardly any places in *Wasps* where J has an error and
C the right reading, perhaps only four: 413 εἰσφέρῃ J: εἰσφέρει C
464 τυραννίς J: τυραννίς C   674 λαγαρυζόμενον J: λαγαριζόμενον C
756 τελευσταῖος J: τελευταῖος C. (There is not a fifth in 1237, since Cary's
statement in *HSCP* xxx [1919] 30 that J there has δοξιᾶς is incorrect; it
results from a misreading of the ligature for εξ.) The omission of a letter
and the confusion of η and ει, υ and ν, and υ and ι are such common
errors that these four readings of C may easily be due to accident. Cary
says that the writing of J is too clear and distinct to justify the frequent

manuscript similar to P. These manuscripts therefore have no independent authority, and may generally be ignored. But there are two places where the scribe of one of them has made a copying mistake which by coincidence has counteracted the mistake of a predecessor so as to produce a correct reading not preserved in other manuscripts (C in 674, G in 1193).

Facsimiles and collations

A photographic facsimile of V was published in 1902, and one of R in 1904. Collations of RVΓJCPHB for *Wasps* have been published by E. Cary (*HSCP* xxx [1919] 1–35). I have made my own collations of RVΓJPHLVv17BAld (L in the original, RV from the published facsimiles, and the other manuscripts from photographs or microfilms). I have found some errors in Cary's, but only small ones; nowhere would the discrepancies affect anyone's view of Aristophanes's text, but in a few places it will be found that Cary's collations are contradicted by my *apparatus criticus* (e.g. 325, 692). For Π I have relied on the text given by B. P. Grenfell and A. S. Hunt in *The Oxyrhynchus Papyri* xi (1915) no. 1374.

Scholia

Some of the manuscripts contain notes (scholia, for which the symbol *Σ* is used) written in the margins: there are some in R and a much bigger number (to a great extent identical) in VΓLAld. Some of these notes are merely comments by Byzantine scholars, sometimes intelligent and sometimes stupid. Others are much older, and may be attributed to Hellenistic scholars who had sources of information (including other plays by Aristophanes and his contemporaries) not now available to us. It is often hard to assess the value of a particular note. Occasionally it is clear that the author of

errors of C, but in fact a careless scribe can copy even a clear exemplar badly; and another possible explanation is that C was copied not directly from J but from a less clearly written copy of J.

a note had a different reading in his text of the play from the one which now appears in our manuscripts, and this may enable us to correct a corrupt reading (e.g. 1050).

An edition of the scholia found in R was published by W. G. Rutherford (1896). The scholia on *Wasps* in VΓAld have no edition more recent than the one by F. Dübner (1842), and those in L have not yet been printed at all (except for a few in *CQ* xii [1962] 41).

Testimonia

Another source of information is the quotations from *Wasps* in other books (testimonia). Many lines from the play are quoted in the tenth-century lexicon entitled *Souda* (sometimes called 'Suidas'; I use the symbol S for it), and a smaller number in other authors, two of them (Plutarch and Athenaios) as early as the second or third century A.D. In some cases the quotations are obviously inaccurate and must have been made from memory, but in other cases they must have been copied from manuscripts earlier than any now available to us, and sometimes they give us correct readings not preserved in our manuscripts (e.g. 699, 1348). In this edition testimonia are listed at the foot of the text, above the *apparatus criticus*.

The apparatus criticus

In general the *apparatus criticus* in this edition gives a full report of ΠRVΓJ and of the testimonia which are listed above it; that is, it reports every instance in which any of these authorities gives a reading different from the one printed in the text. But the following exceptions should be noticed.[1]

1. Variations of accents, breathings, punctuation, and ι subscript (which in the manuscripts is sometimes subscript,

---

[1] Readers interested in the kinds of variation which I have omitted may consult Cary's collations (*HSCP* xxx [1919] 1–35).

sometimes adscript, and sometimes omitted) are generally neglected. In particular the *apparatus* does not record that the manuscripts generally have ἀνύσας, ἀνήρ, ἄνθρωπος, ἄρχων, and ἡλιαστής where my text has ἀνύσας, ἀνήρ, ἄνθρωπος, ἄρχων, and ἡλιαστής.[1]

2. Where the manuscripts are divided between -μεθα and -μεσθα, or ἐς and εἰς, or σύν and ξύν, or the dative forms -οις (-αις) and -οισι (-αισι), or between the inclusion and the omission of ν *ephelkystikon*, or between elided (or prodelided) and unelided forms of a word, and the metre shows beyond doubt which form is right,[2] the fact that some manuscripts are wrong is not reported. But if the metre leaves the correct form in doubt, or if the correct form is not preserved in any of the manuscripts ΠRVΓJ but is restored from a later manuscript or by editorial conjecture, the readings of ΠRVΓJ are reported.

3. Variations in the attribution of words to speakers are recorded in the *apparatus*.[3] But no distinction is made between different abbreviations of the same name; thus, for example, attribution of a line to Xanthias may be indicated in different manuscripts by ξ or ξα or ξαν or ξανθ or ξανθίας or even οἰκέτης ξανθίας, but all these are shown in the *apparatus* as Ξα. Similarly οἰκέτης and θεράπων are both shown as Οἰ. Abbreviations for ἡμιχόριον are shown as Ἡμ. Sometimes (especially in R and V) instead of a speaker's name there is

---

[1] For ἡλιαστής, 195 n.

[2] I assume that ν *ephelkystikon* should be written at the end of a verse, whether the next verse begins with a vowel or not. Cf. K. Zacher in *Philologus* Supp. vii (1899) 465–8.

[3] It may well be thought that manuscripts' attributions are not worth recording, since they are probably not inherited from Aristophanes's original manuscript, but are due to the conjectures of Hellenistic and Byzantine editors and scribes; cf. J. C. B. Lowe in *Bull. Inst. Class. Studies* ix (1962) 27–42. However, one cannot be sure that none of them at all is inherited from Aristophanes himself; and so I have, after some hesitation, included them in the *apparatus*.

In testimonia words are not generally attributed to speakers; so the omission of a speaker's name in a testimonium is not significant, and is not recorded in the *apparatus*.

simply the sign— (paragraphus) at the start of a line, or the sign : (dicolon) or a space in the middle of a line, to indicate a change of speaker; but the use of any of these signs instead of a speaker's name is not reported unless there is doubt which speaker the sign is meant to indicate. Where the *apparatus* reports a name or sign of a change of speaker and nothing either in the *apparatus* or in the text indicates the point in the line at which it occurs, that means that it is at the beginning of the line.[1]

The symbol **a** signifies agreement of RVΓJ or (in passages not preserved in Γ) of RVJ. Readings of the later manuscripts and Ald are reported only when they seem to be of some importance or interest. The symbol *q* signifies agreement of P or H or both with LVv17B or L or Vv17B; *t* signifies agreement of L with Vv17 or B or both.

[1] In R, when a change of speaker is marked in the middle of a line, there is sometimes (not always) also a paragraphus at the beginning of the next line, meaning only that the new line is the first complete line attributed to the new speaker and not that there is a further change of speaker at this point; e.g. 38, 41, 49. But since this sign is ambiguous (because sometimes there is indeed a further change of speaker at the beginning of the new line), it is reported in the *apparatus* each time it occurs in such a situation.

In V a change of speaker at the beginning of a line is occasionally marked by a dicolon at the end of the previous line. In the *apparatus* this sign, where it needs to be reported, is reported as if it stood at the beginning of the new line; e.g. '852 dic. V' means that V has : at the end of 851.

SIGLA

Π   *POxy* 1374 (V p.C.) ; vv. 443–67, 486–513, 558–77, 607–25, 746–
         60, 790–808, 814–19, 825–30, 863–9, 875–8

R   Ravennas 429 (X vel XI)
V   Venetus Marcianus 474 (XI vel XII)
Γ   Laurentianus 31. 15 (XIV) ; vv. 421–1396, 1494–1537
J   Vaticanus Palatinus 128 (XV)

a   consensus codicum RVΓJ vel (ubi deficit Γ) RVJ

P   Vaticanus Palatinus 67 (XV)
H   Havniensis 1980 (XV)
L   Holkhamensis 88 (XV)
Vv17   Vaticanus Graecus 2181 (XIV)
B   Parisinus Regius 2715 (XVI)

q   consensus codicum PH (vel P vel H) et LVv17B (vel L vel
         Vv17B)
t   consensus codicum LVv17B (vel LVv17 vel LB)

Ald   editio Aldina (1498 p.C.)
G   Venetus Marcianus 475 (XV)
C   Parisinus Regius 2717 (XVI)
Δ   Laurentianus 31. 16 (XVI)

Σ   scholium
⊂   colligi potest e glossemate vel scholio
*   littera erasa
+   spatium quod uni litterae sufficit
[ ]   periit vel non legi potest
dic.   dicolon
par.   paragraphus

Notae adscriptae (e.g. R^{ac}, V^{gp}, $^{\lambda}\Sigma\Gamma$, B$_2$)

ac   ante correctionem, dummodo correxerit ipse scriba vel non
         distingui possit corrector
gl   glossema suprascriptum
i   in linea
mg   in margine

pc	post correctionem (cf. ad 'ac')
s	supra lineam vel sub linea
γρ	varia lectio quam memorat scriba vel scholiastes vocabulis usus τινες δέ, γρ(άφεται), vel sim.
λ	in lemmate scholii
1	ipsius scribae manus
2	una et altera e manibus recentioribus

Sigla quae ad testimonia tantum pertinent

S	Suda
Sch.	scholium apud testem
v.l.	varia lectio
§	fabulam non nominat testis
§§	nec fabulam nec poetam nominat testis
†	verba fabulae adeo transposuit omisit corrupit testis ut nullius pretii sit omnia memorare
‡	verba quae in Vespis legimus alii fabulae tribuit testis

ΥΠΟΘΕΣΕΙΣ

I

*Φιλοκλέων Ἀθηναῖος φιλοδικαστὴς ὢν τὴν φύσιν ἐφοίτα περὶ
τὰ δικαστήρια συνεχῶς. Βδελυκλέων δὲ ὁ τούτου παῖς, ἀχθόμενος
ταύτῃ τῇ νόσῳ καὶ πειρώμενος τὸν πατέρα παύσειν, ἐγκαθείρξας
τοῖς οἴκοις καὶ δίκτυα περιβαλὼν ἐφύλαττε νύκτωρ καὶ μεθ'
ἡμέραν. ὁ δέ, ἐξόδου αὐτῷ μὴ περικειμένης, ἔκραζεν. οἱ δὲ* 5
*συνδικασταὶ αὐτοῦ σφηξὶν ἑαυτοὺς ἀφομοιώσαντες παρεγένοντο,
βουλόμενοι διὰ ταύτης τῆς τέχνης ὑποκλέπτειν τὸν συνδικαστήν·
ἐξ ὧν καὶ ὁ χορὸς συνέστηκε καὶ τὸ δρᾶμα ἐπιγέγραπται. ἀλλ'
οὐδὲν ἥννον οὐδὲ οὗτοι. πέρας δὲ τοῦ νεανίσκου θαυμάζοντος
τίνος ἕνεκα ὁ πατὴρ οὕτως ἥττηται τοῦ πράγματος, ἔφη ὁ* 10
*πρεσβύτης τὸ πρᾶγμα εἶναι σπουδαῖον καὶ σχεδὸν ἀρχὴν τὸ
δικάζειν. ὁ δὲ παῖς ἐπειρᾶτο τὰς ὑποψίας ἐξαίρειν τοῦ πράγματος
νουθετῶν τὸν γέροντα. ὁ δὲ πρεσβύτης μηδαμῶς νουθετούμενος
οὐ μεθίει τοῦ πάθους, ἀλλ' ἀναγκάζεται ὁ νέος ἐπιτρέπειν αὐτῷ
φιλοδικεῖν. καὶ ἐπὶ τῆς οἰκίας τοῦτο ποιεῖ, καὶ τοῖς κατὰ τὴν* 15
*οἰκίαν δικάζει. καὶ δύο κύνες ἐπεισάγονται πολιτικῶς παρ' αὐτῷ
κρινόμενοι· καὶ κατὰ τοῦ φεύγοντος ἐκφέρειν συνεχῶς τὴν ψῆφον
μέλλων, ἀπατηθεὶς ἄκων τὴν ἀποκαταδικάζουσαν φέρει ψῆφον.*

*περιέχει δὲ καὶ δικαιολογίαν τινὰ τοῦ ποιητοῦ ἐκ τοῦ ποιητικοῦ
προσώπου, ὡς σφηξὶν ἐμφερεῖς εἰσιν οἱ τοῦ χοροῦ, ἐξ ὧν καὶ τὸ* 20
*δρᾶμα· οἵ, ὅτε μὲν ἦσαν νέοι, πικρῶς τοῖς Πέρσαις ἐφήδρευον,
ἐπεὶ δὲ γέροντες γεγόνασι, κεντοῦσι τοῖς κέντροις. ἐπὶ τέλει δὲ
τοῦ δράματος ὁ γέρων ἐπὶ δεῖπνον καλεῖται, καὶ ἐπὶ ὕβριν
τρέπεται, καὶ κρίνει αὐτὸν ὕβρεως ἀρτόπωλις· ὁ δὲ γέρων πρὸς
αὐλὸν καὶ ὄρχησιν τρέπεται, καὶ γελωτοποιεῖ τὸ δρᾶμα.* 25
*τοῦτο τὸ δρᾶμα πεποίηται αὐτῷ οὐκ ἐξ ὑποκειμένης ὑποθέ-
σεως, ἀλλ' ὡσανεὶ γενομένης· πέπλασται γὰρ τὸ ὅλον. διαβάλλει*

δὲ Ἀθηναίους ὡς φιλοδικοῦντας, καὶ σωφρονίζει τὸν δῆμον ἀποστῆναι τῶν δικῶν. διά τοι τοῦτο καὶ τοὺς δικαστὰς σφηξὶν
30 ἀπεικάζει κέντρα ἔχουσι καὶ πλήττουσι. πεποίηται δ᾽ αὐτῷ
χαριέντως.

ἐδιδάχθη ἐπὶ ἄρχοντος Ἀμεινίου διὰ Φιλωνίδου ἐν τῇ πθ'
Ὀλυμπιάδι. β' ἦν εἰς Λήναια. καὶ ἐνίκα πρῶτος Φιλωνίδης
Προάγωνι· Λεύκων Πρέσβεσι γ'.

1–25 Greg. Cor., Rh. vii. 1333–4

In codicibus hypothesis prior secundam sequitur. 1 φιλόδικος R
περὶ] εἰς J: πρὸς Greg. 2 τὰ om. J 3 τῇ τοιαύτῃ νόσῳ Greg.
παύειν V Greg.: παῦσαι J 4 ἐφύλακτε R: ἐφύλαττεν V νύκτωρ
τε Greg. 5 ἐξόδους Greg. ἑαυτῷ R Greg. μὴ περικείμενον
ἔκραζεν R: ἐζήτει Greg. 6 αὐτοῦ om. J σφηγξὶν R αὐτοὺς J
ἀφωμοι- R: ὁμοι- Greg. 8 -στηκεν R 10 τοῦ πράγματος om.
Greg. 11 εἶναι om. R Greg. σπουδῆς Greg. σχεδὸν] καὶ R: om.
Greg. ἀρχῆς VJ Greg. 12 δικάζεν R 13 πρέσβυς Greg.
14 τοῦ πάθους] τὸ πρᾶγμα J ἀλλ᾽ ἀναγκάζεται] ἀναγκάζεται οὖν Greg.
15 τοῦ οἴκου Greg. ποιεῖν Greg.: ποιεῖν μόνον J 15–16 καὶ τοῖς . . .
δικάζει om. Greg. τοῖς om. J 16 δικάζειν J παρεισάγονται J:
εἰσέρχονται Greg. παρ αυτῶ πολιτευτικῶς J 17 κρινόμενοι]
δικαζόμενοι Greg. 17–18 κατὰ τοὺς φεύγοντας ἐκφέρειν . . .
φέρει ψῆφον J: κατὰ τοῦ φεύγοντος ἐκφέρει τὴν ψῆφον RV: τὴν ψῆφον
ἐκφέρει κατὰ τοῦ φεύγοντος Greg. 18 ἀποδικάζουσαν Brunck
19–22 περιέχει . . . κέντροις om. Greg. 19 ποιητοῦ] χοροῦ J
ποιητικοῦ] ποιητοῦ J 20 ὡς] διὰ τὸ J εἰσιν οἵ] εἶναι τὰ J 21 τοῖς
Πέρσαις van Leeuwen: ταῖς δίκαις a 22 δὲ (secundum) om. J
23–4 ἐπὶ δεῖπνον τρέπεται καὶ εἰς ὕβριν χωρεῖ Greg. 24 καὶ om. J
αὐτῶ J ὕβρεως ἀρτοπώλης VJ: ἀρτόπωλις ὕβρεως Greg. 25 τρέπεται, ἀφεὶς δικάζειν ὡς μισητόν τι χρῆμα καὶ ἀποτρόπαιον Greg., et hic
desinit 27 γὰρ] δὲ J 29 διά τοι] καὶ διὰ J σφηγξὶν R
30 εἰκάζει V: εἱμάζει J πεποίηται om. J 32 Ἀμεινίου Brunck:
ἀμυνίου a διὰ Φιλωνίδου del. Petersen πθ' Kanngiesser: πόλει a
33 ὀλυμπίων J ἦν β' J: ἔτει β' Kanngiesser 33–4 πρῶτος· Φιλωνίδης
Προάγωνι δεύτερος· Petersen 34 προάγων γλευκεῖς J πρέσβεις VJ
τρεῖς J

II

ΑΡΙΣΤΟΦΑΝΟΥΣ ΓΡΑΜΜΑΤΙΚΟΥ

Φιλοῦντα δικάζειν πατέρα παῖς εἴρξας ἄφνω
αὐτός τ' ἐφύλαττεν ἔνδον οἰκέται θ', ὅπως
μὴ λανθάνῃ μηδ' ἐξίῃ διὰ τὴν νόσον.
ὁ δ' ἀντιμάχεται παντὶ τρόπῳ καὶ μηχανῇ.
εἶθ' οἱ συνήθεις καὶ γέροντες, λεγόμενοι   5
σφῆκες, παραγίνονται βοηθοῦντες σφόδρα
ἐπὶ τῷ δύνασθαι κέντρον ἐνιέναι τισὶν
φρονοῦντες ἱκανόν. ὁ δὲ γέρων τηρούμενος
ξυμπείθετ' ἔνδον διαδικάζειν καὶ βιοῦν,
ἐπεὶ τὸ δικάζειν κέκρικεν ἐκ παντὸς τρόπου.   10

ΑΡΙΣΤΟΦΑΝΟΥΣ om. J   *ΓΡΑΜΜΑΤΙΚΟΥ* om. VJ   2 τ' om.
VJ   οἰκουντα V : οἰκοῦνθ' J   θ' om. RJ   4 ὁ δ'] ὁκ' J   καὶ] τι J
5 συνέθεις J   6 om. R   βοηθοῦντι J   7 ἰέναι VJ   post 7 σφῆκες
παρόντες ἐκ ταυτοῦ κακοῦ add. R   9 συμπείθεται R : ξυμπόθετ' J
δικάζειν RJ   10 ἐπεί] ἐπὶ VJ

ΤΑ ΤΟΥ ΔΡΑΜΑΤΟΣ ΠΡΟΣΩΠΑ

οἰκέται β'
Βδελυκλέων
Φιλοκλέων
χορὸς ἐκ γερόντων σφηκῶν
παῖδες   5
ἀρτόπωλις
συμπότης
Κυδαθηναιεὺς κύων

1–8 φιλοκλέων· οἰκέται δύο· παῖδες· βδελυκλέων· συμπότης· χορὸς ἐκ
γερόντων σφηκῶν· κηδαθηνευς· κύων· κῆρυξ J   8 Κυδαθηναιεὺς
Portus : κυδαθηνεὺς RV

ΤΑ ΤΟΥ ΔΡΑΜΑΤΟΣ ΠΡΟΣΩΠΑ

ΣΩΣΙΑΣ οἰκέτης Βδελυκλέωνος
ΞΑΝΘΙΑΣ οἰκέτης Βδελυκλέωνος
ΒΔΕΛΥΚΛΕΩΝ
ΦΙΛΟΚΛΕΩΝ
ΠΑΙΣ υἰὸς τοῦ κορυφαίου
ΚΥΩΝ Κυδαθηναιεύς
ΑΝΗΡ ὑπὸ Φιλοκλέωνος ὑβριζόμενος
ΑΡΤΟΠΩΛΙΣ
ΚΑΤΗΓΟΡΟΣ

ΧΟΡΟΣ δικαστῶν

κωφὰ πρόσωπα

ΟΝΟΣ Βδελυκλέωνος
ΠΑΙΔΕΣ υἱοὶ τοῦ χοροῦ
ΟΙΚΕΤΑΙ Βδελυκλέωνος
ΛΑΒΗΣ κύων
ΤΥΡΟΚΝΗΣΤΙΣ
ΣΚΕΥΗ ἐκ τοῦ ἱπνοῦ ἄλλα
ΚΥΝΙΔΙΑ παιδία Λάβητος
ΔΑΡΔΑΝΙΣ αὐλητρίς
ΑΝΔΡΕΣ ὑπὸ Φιλοκλέωνος ὑβριζόμενοι
ΧΑΙΡΕΦΩΝ κλητὴρ τῆς ἀρτοπώλιδος
ΚΛΗΤΗΡ τοῦ κατηγόρου
ΥΙΟΙ ΚΑΡΚΙΝΟΥ τρεῖς
ΚΑΡΚΙΝΟΣ

ΣΦΗΚΕΣ

ΣΩΣΙΑΣ

  Οὗτος, τί πάσχεις, ὦ κακόδαιμον Ξανθία;

ΞΑΝΘΙΑΣ

  φυλακὴν καταλύειν νυκτερινὴν διδάσκομαι.

Σω. κακὸν ἄρα ταῖς πλευραῖς τι προυφείλεις μέγα.
  ἆρ᾽ οἶσθά γ᾽ οἷον κνώδαλον φυλάττομεν;

Ξα. οἶδ᾽, ἀλλ᾽ ἐπιθυμῶ σμικρὸν ἀπομερμηρίσαι.   5

Σω. σὺ δ᾽ οὖν παρακινδύνευ᾽, ἐπεὶ καὐτοῦ γ᾽ ἐμοῦ
  κατὰ τοῖν κόραιν ἤδη τι καταχεῖται γλυκύ.

Ξα. ἀλλ᾽ ἦ παραφρονεῖς ἐτεὸν ἢ κορυβαντιᾷς;

Σω. οὔκ, ἀλλ᾽ ὕπνος μ᾽ ἔχει τις ἐκ Σαβαζίου.

Ξα. τὸν αὐτὸν ἄρ᾽ ἐμοὶ βουκολεῖς Σαβάζιον.   10
  κἀμοὶ γὰρ ἀρτίως ἐπεστρατεύσατο
  Μῆδός τις ἐπὶ τὰ βλέφαρα νυστακτὴς ὕπνος.
  καὶ δῆτ᾽ ὄναρ θαυμαστὸν εἶδον ἀρτίως.

Σω. κἄγωγ᾽ ἀληθῶς οἷον οὐδεπώποτε.
  ἀτὰρ σὺ λέξον πρότερος.

Ξα.   ἐδόκουν αἰετὸν   15
  καταπτάμενον εἰς τὴν ἀγορὰν μέγαν πάνυ

---

1 Ap. Dys. 1. 21. 15   13–51 Greg. Cor., Rh. vii. 1334–6

---

2 διδάσκομαι om. V 3 Σω. BAld: Ξα. J: par. R: om. V
προυφείλεις Elmsley: προύφειλες a 4 Σω. J οἶσθας οἷον J 5 Ξα.
om. V: par. R μικρὸν J 6 οὖν] αὖ R 7 τοῖν Hirschig: ταῖν a
ἤδη] ὕπνου RV 8 Ξα. om. V 9 Σω. om. V ἀλλ᾽ om. V
10 Ξα. om. V 11 ἀρτίως τίς J 14 Σω. om. V κἀγὼ δ᾽ Greg.
15 πρότερον Greg. Ξα. om. V: + + J ἀετὸν Greg. 16 τὴν
ἀγορὰν] τὸν ἀέρα Greg.

ἀναρπάσαντα τοῖς ὄνυξιν ἀσπίδα
φέρειν ἐπίχαλκον ἀνεκὰς εἰς τὸν οὐρανόν,
κἄπειτα ταύτην ἀποβαλεῖν Κλεώνυμον.

Σω.   οὐδὲν ἄρα γρίφου διαφέρει Κλεώνυμος.   20

Ξα.   πῶς δή;

Σω.   προερεῖ τις τοῖσι συμπόταις, λέγων
ὅτι "ταὐτὸν ἐν γῇ τ᾽ ἀπέβαλεν κἀν οὐρανῷ
κἀν τῇ θαλάττῃ θηρίον τὴν ἀσπίδα."

Ξα.   οἴμοι, τί δῆτά μοι κακὸν γενήσεται
ἰδόντι τοιοῦτον ἐνύπνιον;

Σω.   μὴ φροντίσῃς·   25
οὐδὲν γὰρ ἔσται δεινόν, οὐ μὰ τοὺς θεούς.

Ξα.   δεινόν γέ πού 'στ᾽ ἄνθρωπος ἀποβαλὼν ὅπλα.
ἀτὰρ σὺ τὸ σὸν αὖ λέξον.

Σω.   ἀλλ᾽ ἔστιν μέγα.
περὶ τῆς πόλεως γάρ ἐστι τοῦ σκάφους ὅλου.

Ξα.   λέγε νυν ἀνύσας τι τὴν τρόπιν τοῦ πράγματος.   30

Σω.   ἔδοξέ μοι περὶ πρῶτον ὕπνον ἐν τῇ Πυκνὶ
ἐκκλησιάζειν πρόβατα συγκαθήμενα,
βακτηρίας ἔχοντα καὶ τριβώνια.
κἄπειτα τούτοις τοῖσι προβάτοις μοὐδόκει
δημηγορεῖν φάλλαινα πανδοκεύτρια,   35
ἔχουσα φωνὴν ἐμπεπρημένης ὑός.

31 § Hdn. *Philet.* [Dain] 13   36 Sch. Luc. *Tim.* 30

17 ταῖς Greg.   20 Σω. q: Ξα. J: par. RV   ὀδὲν R   γρύφου
διαφέρει J: διαφέρει γρίφου Greg.   21 Ξα. et Σω. Bentley: om. a
Greg.   προσερεῖ VJ   dic. ante λέγω RV   22 ταυτὸν θηρίου ἐν
γῇ κἂν οὐρανῶ J   23 par. R   κἂν ἐν θαλάσσῃ Greg.   θηρίον] τ᾽
ἀπέβαλε J   24 Ξα. q: Σω. J: par. RV   25 Σω. J: dic. RV
26 ἔσεται Greg.   28 αὖ om. Greg.   ἔστιν t Greg.: ἔστι a   30 Ξα.
om. V   τι om. J   31 Σω. om. V   πυκὶ J Greg.: νυκτὶ
Hdn.   34 τοῖς προβάτοισί J   35 δημηγορεῖν R   φάλαινα V Greg.
36 ἐμπεπρησμ- VJ Greg.   -ένην RV Sch. Luc.   υίος V: συός J

Ξα.   αἰβοῖ.

Σω.   τί ἐστι;

Ξα.   παῦε παῦε, μὴ λέγε·
       ὄζει κάκιστον τοὐνύπνιον βύρσης σαπρᾶς.

Σω.   εἶθ' ἡ μιαρὰ φάλλαιν' ἔχουσα τρυτάνην
       ἵστη βόειον δημόν.

Ξα.   οἴμοι δείλαιος·   40
       τὸν δῆμον ἡμῶν βούλεται διιστάναι.

Σω.   ἐδόκει δέ μοι Θέωρος αὐτῆς πλησίον
       χαμαὶ καθῆσθαι τὴν κεφαλὴν κόρακος ἔχων.
       εἶτ' Ἀλκιβιάδης εἶπε πρός με τραυλίσας·
       "ὁλᾷς; Θέωλος τὴν κεφαλὴν κόλακος ἔχει."   45

Ξα.   ὀρθῶς γε τοῦτ' Ἀλκιβιάδης ἐτραύλισεν.

Σω.   οὔκουν ἐκεῖν' ἀλλόκοτον, ὁ Θέωρος κόραξ
       γιγνόμενος;

Ξα.   ἥκιστ', ἀλλ' ἄριστον.

Σω.   πῶς;

Ξα.   ὅπως;
       ἄνθρωπος ὢν εἶτ' ἐγένετ' ἐξαίφνης κόραξ·
       οὔκουν ἐναργὲς τοῦτο συμβαλεῖν, ὅτι   50
       ἀρθεὶς ἀφ' ἡμῶν ἐς κόρακας οἰχήσεται;

---

41 St. Byz. 228. 10   44–6 § Plu. *Alc.* 1. 7   45 §§ Hermog.
451. 16; §§ Eust. 1764. 41

---

37 Ξα. (prius) om. V   παῦε παῦε, μὴ λέγε om. Greg.   38 par. R
39 φάλαιννα V: φάλαιν' Greg.   40 ἔστη J   41 par. R   διιστά-
νειν J Greg. St. Byz.   42 Σω. om. V   αὑτοῦ Greg.   πλησίον J
45 ὁλᾷς Θέωλον; Plu.   θέωρος J   κόρακος J   ἔχων Greg.   47 Σω.
om. RV   οὔκουν om. Greg.   ἐκεῖνο δ' Greg.   ἀλλώκοτον V   48 γινό-
μενος Greg.   Ξα. (prius) om. V   ἥκιστά γ' J   49 par. R:
+ + + J   ἦν J Greg.   ἐγίνετ' V   50 om. et γιγνόμενος ἥκιστ' ex 48
iterat V   ἐναργῶς Greg.   συμβάλλειν R: ξυμβαλῇ Greg.

Σω.   εἶτ᾽ οὐκ ἐγὼ δοὺς δύ᾽ ὀβολὼ μισθώσομαι
      οὕτως ὑποκρινόμενον σαφῶς ὀνείρατα;

Ξα.   φέρε νυν, κατείπω τοῖς θεαταῖς τὸν λόγον,
      ὀλίγ᾽ ἄτθ᾽ ὑπειπὼν πρῶτον αὐτοῖσιν ταδί,   55
      μηδὲν παρ᾽ ἡμῶν προσδοκᾶν λίαν μέγα,
      μηδ᾽ αὖ γέλωτα Μεγαρόθεν κεκλεμμένον.
      ἡμῖν γὰρ οὐκ ἔστ᾽ οὔτε κάρυ᾽ ἐκ φορμίδος
      δούλω διαρριπτοῦντε τοῖς θεωμένοις,
      οὔθ᾽ Ἡρακλῆς τὸ δεῖπνον ἐξαπατώμενος,   60
      οὐδ᾽ αὖθις ἀνασελγαινόμενος Εὐριπίδης·
      οὐδ᾽ εἰ Κλέων γ᾽ ἔλαμψε τῆς τύχης χάριν,
      αὖθις τὸν αὐτὸν ἄνδρα μυττωτεύσομεν.
      ἀλλ᾽ ἔστιν ἡμῖν λογίδιον γνώμην ἔχον,
      ὑμῶν μὲν αὐτῶν οὐχὶ δεξιώτερον,   65
      κωμῳδίας δὲ φορτικῆς σοφώτερον.
      ἔστιν γὰρ ἡμῖν δεσπότης ἐκεινοσὶ
      ἄνω καθεύδων, ὁ μέγας, οὑπὶ τοῦ τέγους.
      οὗτος φυλάττειν τὸν πατέρ᾽ ἐπέταξε νῷν,
      ἔνδον καθείρξας, ἵνα θύραζε μὴ ᾽ξίῃ.   70
      νόσον γὰρ ὁ πατὴρ ἀλλόκοτον αὐτοῦ νοσεῖ,
      ἣν οὐδ᾽ ἂν εἷς γνοίη ποτ᾽ οὐδὲ ξυμβάλοι,
      εἰ μὴ πύθοιθ᾽ ἡμῶν· ἐπεὶ τοπάζετε.

Σω.   Ἀμυνίας μὲν ὁ Προνάπους φήσ᾽ οὑτοσὶ
      εἶναι φιλόκυβον αὐτόν.

Ξα.   ἀλλ᾽ οὐδὲν λέγει,   75
      μὰ Δί᾽, ἀλλ᾽ ἀφ᾽ αὑτοῦ τὴν νόσον τεκμαίρεται.

Σω.   .   .   .   .

      52 Σω. om. V   53 σοφῶς RV   οὐ εἴρατα J   55 ἄτθ᾽ Portus:
ἄττα RV: om. J   πρότερον J   57 κεκλαμμένον Σ^Ald Ald   58 οὐδὲ
RV   καρυί V   59 διαριπ- V   -τοῦντες RV   66 δὲ om. J
69 ἐπειταξε J   70 καθεύδειν JB₂   71 ἀλόκοτον V   72 οὐδὲ]
οὐδ᾽ ἂν RV   -βάλῃ R   73 τοπάζεται J   74 Σω. B: om. a
ἀμυννοίας V   75 Ξα. Meineke: dic. RV: om. J: Σω. q   post 76
Σω. et lacunam Bergk: om. a

Ξα.   οὔκ, ἀλλὰ "φιλο-" μέν ἐστιν ἀρχὴ τοῦ κακοῦ.

Σω.   ὁδὶ δέ φησι Σωσίας πρὸς Δερκύλον
        εἶναι φιλοπότην αὐτόν.

Ξα.   οὐδαμῶς γ', ἐπεὶ
        αὕτη γε χρηστῶν ἐστιν ἀνδρῶν ἡ νόσος.   80

Σω.   Νικόστρατος δ' αὖ φησιν ὁ Σκαμβωνίδης
        εἶναι φιλοθύτην αὐτὸν ἢ φιλόξενον.

Ξα.   μὰ τὸν κύν', ὦ Νικόστρατ', οὐ φιλόξενος,
        ἐπεὶ καταπύγων ἐστὶν ὅ γε Φιλόξενος.
        ἄλλως φλυαρεῖτ'· οὐ γὰρ ἐξευρήσετε.   85
        εἰ δὴ 'πιθυμεῖτ' εἰδέναι, σιγᾶτέ νυν·
        φράσω γὰρ ἤδη τὴν νόσον τοῦ δεσπότου.
        φιληλιαστής ἐστιν ὡς οὐδεὶς ἀνήρ·
        ἐρᾷ τε τούτου τοῦ δικάζειν, καὶ στένει
        ἢν μὴ 'πὶ τοῦ πρώτου καθίζηται ξύλου.   90
        ὕπνου δ' ὁρᾷ τῆς νυκτὸς οὐδὲ πασπάλην·
        ἢν δ' οὖν καταμύσῃ κἂν ἄχνην, ὅμως ἐκεῖ
        ὁ νοῦς πέτεται τὴν νύκτα περὶ τὴν κλεψύδραν.
        ὑπὸ τοῦ δὲ τὴν ψῆφόν γ' ἔχειν εἰωθέναι
        τοὺς τρεῖς ξυνέχων τῶν δακτύλων ἀνίσταται,   95
        ὥσπερ λιβανωτὸν ἐπιτιθεὶς νουμηνίᾳ.
        καὶ νὴ Δί' ἢν ἴδῃ γέ που γεγραμμένον
        υἱὸν Πυριλάμπους ἐν θύρᾳ Δῆμον καλόν,
        ἰὼν παρέγραψε πλησίον "κημὸς καλός".
        τὸν ἀλεκτρυόνα δ', ὃς ᾖδ' ἀφ' ἑσπέρας, ἔφη   100

80 §§ S a 4470   88 S § (1) η 215; § (2) φ 326

___

77 Ξα. om. V: par. R   φιλόδικος R   78 Σω. B: om. a   79 Ξα.
Bothe: dic. RV: Σω. J   80 ἀνδρῶν ἐστιν J   81 Σω. Bothe: par. R:
Ξα. J: om. V   αὖ J   σηαμβ- J   83 Ξα. Bothe: Σω. J: om. RV
84 τε J   85 Ξα. J: par. R   87 νόσου J   90 'πὶ om. RV
91 ἐρᾷ R   92 οὖν] αὖ B   καταμηνύσῃ R   93 πέταται J
94 ἔχειν γ' VJ   97 ἢν] ἂν J   98 υἱὸν] τὸν J   δῆμον J   99 ἰδὼν B
παρέγραψεν R   πλησίου κημὶς J   100 τήν B₂   ἀλεκτυόνα R   ᾖδεν ἐφ'

ὄψ' ἐξεγείρειν αὐτὸν ἀναπεπεισμένον,
παρὰ τῶν ὑπευθύνων ἔχοντα χρήματα·
εὐθὺς δ' ἀπὸ δορπηστοῦ κέκραγεν ἐμβάδας,
κἄπειτ' ἐκεῖσ' ἐλθὼν προκαθεύδει πρῷ πάνυ,
ὥσπερ λεπὰς προσεχόμενος τῷ κίονι.   105
ὑπὸ δυσκολίας δ' ἅπασι τιμῶν τὴν μακρὰν
ὥσπερ μέλιττ' ἢ βομβυλιὸς εἰσέρχεται
ὑπὸ τοῖς ὄνυξι κηρὸν ἀναπεπλασμένος.
ψήφων δὲ δείσας μὴ δεηθείη ποτέ,
ἵν' ἔχοι δικάζειν, αἰγιαλὸν ἔνδον τρέφει.   110
τοιαῦτ' ἀλύει· νουθετούμενος δ' ἀεὶ
μᾶλλον δικάζει. τοῦτον οὖν φυλάττομεν
μοχλοῖσιν ἐνδήσαντες, ὡς ἂν μὴ 'ξίῃ.
ὁ γὰρ υἱὸς αὐτοῦ τὴν νόσον βαρέως φέρει.
καὶ πρῶτα μὲν λόγοισι παραμυθούμενος   115
ἀνέπειθεν αὐτὸν μὴ φορεῖν τριβώνιον
μηδ' ἐξιέναι θύραζ'· ὁ δ' οὐκ ἐπείθετο.
εἶτ' αὐτὸν ἀπέλου κἀκάθαιρ'· ὁ δ' οὐ μάλα.
μετὰ τοῦτ' ἐκορυβάντιζ'· ὁ δ' αὐτῷ τυμπάνῳ
ᾄξας ἐδίκαζεν εἰς τὸ Καινὸν ἐμπεσών.   120
ὅτε δῆτα ταύταις ταῖς τελεταῖς οὐκ ὠφέλει,
διέπλευσεν εἰς Αἴγιναν· εἶτα ξυλλαβὼν
νύκτωρ κατέκλινεν αὐτὸν εἰς Ἀσκληπιοῦ·
ὁ δ' ἀνεφάνη κνεφαῖος ἐπὶ τῇ κιγκλίδι.
ἐντεῦθεν οὐκέτ' αὐτὸν ἐξεφρίομεν·   125
ὁ δ' ἐξεδίδρασκε διά τε τῶν ὑδρορροῶν

123 Priscian. *Inst.* (1) 18. 184; (2) 18. 198

---

101 ἐγείρειν J   102 παραυτῶν V   103 εὐθυσ' ἀπὸ J   δορπι-
στου V   ἐμβδας V   108 ὑποπε- J   109 δήσας R   110 ἔχῃ J
113 ἐγκλείσαντες J   118 κἀκαθαιρ' Bentley: καὶ κάθαιρε J: κακκάθαιρ'
RV   ὁ δ' οὐ μάλα] καὶ μαλκ J   119 τοῦδ' R: ταῦτ' J   -τίαζ' J
120 ἐς τὸ κενὸν J   121 δῆτα] δὲ ταῖς J   ταῖς om. J   τελευταῖς V
122 συλ- J   124 γιγγλιδ V   125 ἐξεφρείομεν J   126 -σκεν V
ὑδρορόων R

καὶ τῶν ὀπῶν· ἡμεῖς δ' ὅσ' ἦν τετρημένα
ἐνεβύσαμεν ῥακίοισι κἀπακτώσαμεν·
ὁ δ' ὡσπερεὶ κολοιὸς αὑτῷ παττάλους
ἐνέκρουεν εἰς τὸν τοῖχον, εἶτ' ἐξήλλετο·   130
ἡμεῖς δὲ τὴν αὐλὴν ἅπασαν δικτύοις
καταπετάσαντες ἐν κύκλῳ φυλάττομεν.
ἔστιν δ' ὄνομα τῷ μὲν γέροντι Φιλοκλέων,
ναὶ μὰ Δία, τῷ δ' υἱεῖ γε τῳδὶ Βδελυκλέων,
ἔχων τρόπους φρυαγμοσεμνάκους τινάς.   135

ΒΔΕΛΥΚΛΕΩΝ

  ὦ Ξανθία καὶ Σωσία, καθεύδετε;

Ξα. οἴμοι.

Σω. τί ἐστι;

Ξα.   Βδελυκλέων ἀνίσταται.

Βδ. οὐ περιδραμεῖται σφῷν ταχέως δεῦρ' ἅτερος;
ὁ γὰρ πατὴρ εἰς τὸν ἰπνὸν ἐξελήλυθεν,
καὶ μυσπολεῖ τι καταδεδυκώς. ἀλλ' ἄθρει   140
κατὰ τῆς πυέλου τὸ τρῆμ' ὅπως μὴ 'κδύσεται.
σὺ δὲ τῇ θύρᾳ πρόσκεισο.

Ξα.   ταῦτ', ὦ δέσποτα.

Βδ. ἄναξ Πόσειδον, τί ποτ' ἄρ' ἡ κάπνη ψοφεῖ;
οὗτος, τίς εἶ σύ;

ΦΙΛΟΚΛΕΩΝ

  καπνὸς ἔγωγ' ἐξέρχομαι.

135 § S φ 747 143 (τί . . .) § S κ 343

---

128 ἐνεβρύ- J 130 ἐξήλετο V 134 τῳδὶ] τῶδε J
135 -σεμνακ- J -ους τινάς S: -ουστίνας V: -ουστίνους RJ
137 Ξα.] Οι. RV Σω.] dic. R: ἔτε. V Ξα.] dic. V: om. R
138 -μεῖσθον J ἕτερος J 139 εἰσελή- RJ 140 τὶς RJ -δεδοι-
κώς R 141 ὅπως om. V 142 Ξα. Beer: Οι. a 143 Βδ.
om. R: ὁ δε. V σοφεῖ S 144 Φι. οὗτος J Βδ. καπνὸς J

Βδ.   καπνός; φέρ' ἴδω, ξύλου τίνος σύ;

Φι.   συκίνου.   145

Βδ.   νὴ τὸν Δί', ὅσπερ γ' ἐστὶ δριμύτατος καπνῶν.
       ἀτὰρ οὐκ ἐσερρήσεις γε; ποῦ 'σθ' ἡ τηλία;
       δύου πάλιν. φέρ', ἐπαναθῶ σοι καὶ ξύλον.
       ἐνταῦθά νυν ζήτει τιν' ἄλλην μηχανήν.
       ἀτὰρ ἄθλιός γ' εἴμ' ὡς ἕτερος οὐδεὶς ἀνήρ,   150
       ὅστις πατρὸς νυνὶ Καπνίου κεκλήσομαι.

Φι.   παῖ.

Ξα.   τὴν θύραν ὠθεῖ.

Βδ.   πίεζέ νυν σφόδρα,
       εὖ κἀνδρικῶς· κἀγὼ γὰρ ἐνταῦθ' ἔρχομαι.
       καὶ τῆς κατάκλειδος ἐπιμελοῦ καὶ τοῦ μοχλοῦ,
       φύλαττέ θ' ὅπως μὴ τὴν βάλανον ἐκτρώξεται.   155

Φι.   τί δράσετ'; οὐκ ἐκφρήσετ', ὦ μιαρώτατοι,
       δικάσοντά μ', ἀλλ' ἐκφεύξεται Δρακοντίδης;

Ξα.   σὺ δὲ τοῦτο βαρέως ἂν φέροις;

Φι.   ὁ γὰρ θεὸς
       μαντευομένῳ μοὔχρησεν ἐν Δελφοῖς ποτε,
       ὅταν τις ἐκφύγῃ μ', ἀποσκλῆναι τότε.   160

Ξα.   Ἄπολλον ἀποτρόπαιε, τοῦ μαντεύματος.

Φι.   ἴθ', ἀντιβολῶ σ', ἔκφρες με, μὴ διαρραγῶ.

Ξα.   μὰ τὸν Ποσειδῶ, Φιλοκλέων, οὐδέποτέ γε.

Φι.   διατρώξομαι τοίνυν ὀδὰξ τὸ δίκτυον.

145 Βδ. om. V   τίνος ξύλου J   146 ὥσπερ R   147 εἰσερρήσεις
J: ερρήσεις R   150 ἕτερός γ' RV   151 νῦν RV   152 Φι.
MacDowell: Οι. a   παῖ om. RV   Ξα. MacDowell: om. a   Βδ.
Rogers: om. a   156 μιαρώτατε J   157 ἀλλ'] οὐκ J   158 Ξα.
Beer: Βδ. a   Φι. Bentley: dic. R: om. VJ   160 μή μ' J   ποτὲ J
161 Ξα. Beer: par. RV: Φι. J   162 Φι. Bentley: om. a   ἔκφρες
Buttmann: ἐκφερέ a   163 Ξα. Beer: par. R: Βδ. J: om. V
164 Φι. om. V: par. R

Ξα. ἀλλ' οὐκ ἔχεις ὀδόντας.

Φι.   οἴμοι δείλαιος.   165
πῶς ἄν σ' ἀποκτείναιμι; πῶς; δότε μοι ξίφος
ὅπως τάχιστ', ἢ πινάκιον τιμητικόν.

Βδ. ἄνθρωπος οὗτος μέγα τι δρασείει κακόν.

Φι. μὰ τὸν Δί' οὐ δῆτ', ἀλλ' ἀποδόσθαι βούλομαι
τὸν ὄνον ἄγων αὐτοῖσι τοῖς κανθηλίοις·   170
νουμηνία γάρ ἐστιν.

Βδ.   οὔκουν κἂν ἐγὼ
αὐτὸν ἀποδοίμην δῆτ' ἄν;

Φι.   οὐχ ὥσπερ γ' ἐγώ.

Βδ. μὰ Δί', ἀλλ' ἄμεινον.

Φι.   ἀλλὰ τὸν ὄνον ἔξαγε.

Ξα. οἵαν πρόφασιν καθῆκεν, ὡς εἰρωνικῶς,
ἵν' αὐτὸν ἐκπέμψειας.

Βδ.   ἀλλ' οὐκ ἔσπασεν   175
ταύτῃ γ'· ἐγὼ γὰρ ᾐσθόμην τεχνωμένου.
ἀλλ' εἰσιών μοι τὸν ὄνον ἐξάγειν δοκῶ,
ὅπως ἂν ὁ γέρων μηδὲ παρακύψῃ πάλιν.
κάνθων, τί κλάεις; ὅτι πεπράσει τήμερον;
βάδιζε θᾶττον. τί στένεις, εἰ μὴ φέρεις   180
'Οδυσσέα τιν';

Ξα.   ἀλλὰ ναὶ μὰ Δία φέρει
κάτω γε τουτονί τιν' ὑποδεδυκότα.

Βδ. ποῖον; φέρ' ἴδωμαι.

165 Ξα. Beer: par. RV: Βδ. J   166 ἐποκτείναιμι J   μοι om. J
168 δρασείει Rᵖᶜ: ει δρασει Rᵃᶜ: δράσει VJ   169 τὸν om. J   172 γ'
q: om. a   173 Βδ. om. R   Φι. Beer: om. a   174 Ξα. Brunck:
Οι. a   175 ἵνα θᾶττον VJ   Βδ. om. R   176 par. R   ταύτην V:
ταῦτα J   179 σήμερον V   181 ὁδασέα J   τιν' Elmsley:
τινά a: τινά γ' q   Ξα. Brunck: Οι. a   183 Βδ. (prius) om. V
ἴδωμεν J

Ξα.   τουτονί.

Βδ.   τουτὶ τί ἦν;
τίς εἶ ποτ', ὦ 'νθρωπ', ἐτεόν;

Φι.   Οὖτις, νὴ Δία.

Βδ.   Οὖτις σύ; ποδαπός;

Φι.   Ἴθακος Ἀποδρασιππίδου.   185

Βδ.   Οὖτις μὰ τὸν Δί' οὔτι χαιρήσων γε σύ.
ὕφελκε θᾶττον αὐτόν. ὦ μιαρώτατος,
ἵν' ὑποδέδυκεν· ὥστ' ἔμοιγ' ἰνδάλλεται
ὁμοιότατος κλητῆρος εἶναι πωλίῳ.

Φι.   εἰ μή μ' ἐάσεθ' ἥσυχον, μαχούμεθα.   190

Βδ.   περὶ τοῦ μαχεῖ νῷν δῆτα;

Φι.   περὶ ὄνου σκιᾶς.

Βδ.   πονηρὸς εἶ πόρρω τέχνης καὶ παράβολος.

Φι.   ἐγὼ πονηρός; οὐ μὰ Δί', ἀλλ' οὐκ οἶσθα σὺ
νῦν μ' ὄντ' ἄριστον; ἀλλ' ἴσως, ὅταν φάγῃς
ὑπογάστριον γέροντος ἡλιαστικοῦ.   195

Βδ.   ὤθει τὸν ὄνον καὶ σαυτὸν εἰς τὴν οἰκίαν.

Φι.   ὦ ξυνδικασταὶ καὶ Κλέων, ἀμύνατε.

Βδ.   ἔνδον κέκραχθι τῆς θύρας κεκλεισμένης.
ὤθει σὺ πολλοὺς τῶν λίθων πρὸς τὴν θύραν,
καὶ τὴν βάλανον ἔμβαλλε πάλιν εἰς· τὸν μοχλόν,   200

192 S π 296

---

183 Ξα. Brunck: dic. RV: Οι. J   184 ὦ 'νθρωπ'] ἄνθρωπ' J
185 οὗτος J   Φι. om. V   186 οὗτις γε μὰ J   σύ R^{pc}: σὺ ἔσει R^{ac}
V: σὺ ἔσῃ J   189 κρατῆρος J   190 ἐάσετ' R: ἐασεσθ' V   ἡσύχως
RV   191 Βδ. om. V: par. R   Φι.] dic. RV   192 Βδ. om. R:
par. V   193 par. RV   οἶαθα J   194 dic. ante ἀλλ' R
196 Βδ. om. V: par. R   197 om. J   Φι. q: par. R: om. V
198 Βδ. q: par. R: Φι. J: om. V   κέκραθι V   κεκλησ- J   200 ἔμβαλλε
BAld: ἔμβαλε a

καὶ τῇ δοκῷ προσθεὶς τὸν ὅλμον τὸν μέγαν
ἀνύσας τι προσκύλισον.

Ξα.   οἴμοι δείλαιος·
πόθεν ποτ' ἐμπέπτωκέ μοι τὸ βωλίον;

Βδ.   ἴσως ἄνωθεν μῦς ἐνέβαλέ σοί ποθεν.

Ξα.   μῦς; οὐ μὰ Δί', ἀλλ' ὑποδυόμενός τις οὑτοσὶ   205
ὑπὸ τῶν κεραμίδων ἡλιαστὴς ὀροφίας.

Βδ.   οἴμοι κακοδαίμων· στροῦθος ἀνὴρ γίγνεται·
ἐκπτήσεται. ποῦ ποῦ 'στί μοι τὸ δίκτυον;
σοῦ, σοῦ, πάλιν, σοῦ. νὴ Δί' ἦ μοι κρεῖττον ἦν
τηρεῖν Σκιώνην ἀντὶ τούτου τοῦ πατρός.   210

Ξα.   ἄγε νυν, ἐπειδὴ τουτονὶ σεσοβήκαμεν,
κοὐκ ἔσθ' ὅπως διαδὺς ἂν ἡμᾶς ἔτι λάθοι,
τί οὐκ ἀπεκοιμήθημεν ὅσον ὅσον στίλην;

Βδ.   ἀλλ', ὦ πόνηρ', ἥξουσιν ὀλίγον ὕστερον
οἱ ξυνδικασταὶ παρακαλοῦντες τουτονὶ   215
τὸν πατέρα.

Ξα.   τί λέγεις; ἀλλὰ νῦν γ' ὄρθρος βαθύς.

Βδ.   νὴ τὸν Δί', ὀψὲ γοῦν ἀνεστήκασι νῦν.
ὡς ἀπὸ μέσων νυκτῶν γε παρακαλοῦσ' ἀεί,
λύχνους ἔχοντες καὶ μινυρίζοντες μέλη

205 (ὑπο- . . .)–206 Poll. 10. 183   208 (ποῦ ποῦ . . .)–209 (. . .
πάλιν, σοῦ) S §§ (1) ε 2807; (2) σ 792   209 (νὴ . . .)–210 §§ S σ 614
213 Phot. s.v. στίλην; §§ S σ 1112   219 (μιν- . . .)–220 S §§ (1) α
4075; § (2) μ 1103

202 -κύλισον Cobet: -κύλιε a   Ξα. Beer: Οι. a   ὤιμοι R: ὦμοι J
204 Βδ. Beer: par. R: Οι. J: ετερος οικέτ. V   σοί] συ V   205 Ξα.
Beer: par. RV: Οι. J   206 κεραμίων Poll.ᵛ·ˡ·   207 Βδ. Bentley:
par. R: Οι. J: om. V   γίγν- q: γίν- a   208 μου RVS   210 par. R
τούτου] τοῦδε J   211 Ξα. Beer: par. RV: Οι. J   νυν] δὴ V
212 ἔτι λάθοι] ἐπιλάθοι R   213 οὐ κατεκοι- Phot.   215 συν- J
-καλοῦν J   216 Ξα. B: dic. RV: Οι. J   γ' om. RJ   ὄρθροι βα J
217 γοῦν q: γὰρ a: γ' ἀρ' Porson   218 γε om. J

ἀρχαιομελισιδωνοφρυνιχήρατα,   220
οἷς ἐκκαλοῦνται τοῦτον.

Σα.   οὐκοῦν, ἢν δέῃ,
ἤδη ποτ' αὐτοὺς τοῖς λίθοις βαλλήσομεν.

Βδ. ἀλλ', ὦ πόνηρε, τὸ γένος ἤν τις ὀργίσῃ
τὸ τῶν γερόντων, ἔσθ' ὅμοιον σφηκιᾷ.
ἔχουσι γὰρ καὶ κέντρον ἐκ τῆς ὀσφύος   225
ὀξύτατον, ᾧ κεντοῦσι, καὶ κεκραγότες
πηδῶσι καὶ βάλλουσιν ὥσπερ φέψαλοι.

Σα. μὴ φροντίσῃς· ἐὰν ἐγὼ λίθους ἔχω,
πολλῶν δικαστῶν σφηκιὰν διασκεδῶ.

ΧΟΡΟΣ

χώρει, πρόβαιν' ἐρρωμένως. ὦ Κωμία, βραδύνεις.   230
μὰ τὸν Δί' οὐ μέντοι πρὸ τοῦ γ', ἀλλ' ἦσθ' ἱμὰς κύνειος·
νυνὶ δὲ κρείττων ἐστί σου Χαρινάδης βαδίζειν.
ὦ Στρυμόδωρε Κονθυλεῦ, βέλτιστε συνδικαστῶν,
Εὐεργίδης ἆρ' ἐστί που 'νταῦθ', ἢ Χάβης ὁ Φλυεύς;
πάρεσθ' ὃ δὴ λοιπόν γ' ἔτ' ἐστίν, ἀππαπαῖ παπαιάξ,   235
ἥβης ἐκείνης, ἡνίκ' ἐν Βυζαντίῳ ξυνῆμεν
φρουροῦντ' ἐγώ τε καὶ σύ· κᾆτα περιπατοῦντε νύκτωρ
τῆς ἀρτοπώλιδος λαθόντ' ἐκλέψαμεν τὸν ὅλμον·
κᾆθ' ἥψομεν τοῦ κορκόρου κατασχίσαντες αὐτόν.
ἀλλ' ἐγκονῶμεν, ὦ 'νδρες, ὡς ἔσται Λάχητι νυνί·   240

---

232 (κρεί- . . .) §§ S χ 115   235 (ἀπ- . . .) §§ S ε 2807

---

220 ἀρχαῖα R   -μελι- ⊂ΣᵛS(1)(2) : -μελη- a   -χάρατα J   221 ἐκβαλ-
J   Σα. Beer : dic. R : Οι. J : om. V   222 par. R   223 Βδ.
om. V   225 ὀσφύος V   226 ᾧ] ὃ R   καὶ om. R   227 βάλ-
λωσιν V   228 Οι. J : par. V   230 ΧΟΡΟΣ om. V   ὦ ἀκμία J
231 par. R   ἡμᾶς J   232 κρεῖττον VSᵛ·ˡ·   234 χάρης J
235 γ' om. R   ἔτ' om. J   παππαιάξ J   237 φρουρῶν V
περιπατοῦνται V   239 ἤψαμεν VJ   240 ἀγκονῶμεν ἄνδρες J
εστιν V

σίμβλον δέ φασι χρημάτων ἔχειν ἅπαντες αὐτόν.
χθὲς οὖν Κλέων ὁ κηδεμὼν ἡμῖν ἐφεῖτ᾽ ἐν ὥρᾳ
ἥκειν ἔχοντας ἡμερῶν ὀργὴν τριῶν πονηρὰν
ἐπ᾽ αὐτόν, ὡς κολωμένους ὧν ἠδίκησεν. ἀλλὰ
σπεύσωμεν, ὦ 'νδρες ἥλικες, πρὶν ἡμέραν γενέσθαι.   245
χωρῶμεν, ἅμα τε τῷ λύχνῳ πάντῃ διασκοπῶμεν,
μή που λίθος τις ἐμποδὼν ἡμᾶς κακόν τι δράσῃ.

ΠΑΙΣ

ὤ.
τὸν πηλόν, ὦ πάτερ πάτερ, τουτονὶ φύλαξαι.

Χο.   κάρφος χαμᾶθέν νυν λαβὼν τὸν λύχνον πρόβυσον.

Πα.   οὔκ, ἀλλὰ τῳδί μοι δοκῶ τὸν λύχνον προβύσειν.   250

Χο.   τί δὴ μαθὼν τῷ δακτύλῳ τὴν θρυαλλίδ᾽ ὠθεῖς,
καὶ ταῦτα τοῦ 'λαίου σπανίζοντος, ὦ 'νόητε;
οὐ γὰρ δάκνει σ᾽, ὅταν δέῃ τίμιον πρίασθαι.

Πα.   εἰ νὴ Δί᾽ αὖθις κονδύλοις νουθετήσεθ᾽ ἡμᾶς,
ἀποσβέσαντες τοὺς λύχνους ἄπιμεν οἴκαδ᾽ αὐτοί.   255
κἄπειτ᾽ ἴσως ἐν τῷ σκότῳ τουτουὶ στερηθεὶς
τὸν πηλὸν ὥσπερ ἀτταγᾶς τυρβάσεις βαδίζων.

Χο.   ἦ μὴν ἐγώ σου χἀτέρους μείζονας κολάζω.
ἀλλ᾽ οὑτοσί μοι βόρβορος φαίνεται πατοῦντι.
κοὐκ ἔσθ᾽ ὅπως οὐχ ἡμερῶν τεττάρων τὸ πλεῖστον   260

241 § S ε 947   242–3 (. . . ἥκειν) § S ε 3887   257 §§ S a 4307;
An. Bachm. 162. 1

---

241 σίμβολον V: σίμβουλον J: ἔμβολον S: ἔμβολα S^{v.l.}   φησι R
ἅπαντες om. S   242 par. R   ὁ κηδεμὼν om. S   244 κολω- V₂:
χολού- V₁: κολου- J: καλου- R   -μενος V   ἀλλὰ γὰρ RJ   245 σπεύδωμεν J   247 λαθών RJ   ἡμᾶς ἐμποδὼν J   248 ΠΑΙΣ om. V
σὺ τουτονὶ a: σὺ del. Flor. Chrest.   249 Χο. om. V゙   χαμόθεν V
σὺ τὸν RJ   250 μοι γε R: μοι γε νῦν J   251 Χο. om. V   θρυαλίδ᾽
V   252 'νόητε σύ RJ   254 -δύλοις q: -δύλοισι a   νουθετήσετ᾽ RV
255 ἄπειμεν V   256 τουτοὶ V   257 ἀτταγῆς J   258 Χο. om. RV
259 μοι] μὴ R   βάρβαρος V   πατοῦντα V   260 πλεῖστον om. J

ὕδωρ ἀναγκαίως ἔχει τὸν θεὸν ποιῆσαι.
ἔπεισι γοῦν τοῖσιν λύχνοις οὑτοιὶ μύκητες·
φιλεῖ δ᾽, ὅταν τοῦτ᾽ ᾖ, ποιεῖν ὑετὸν μάλιστα.
δεῖται δὲ καὶ τῶν καρπίμων ἄττα μή 'στι πρῷα
ὕδωρ γενέσθαι κἀπιπνεῦσαι βόρειον αὐτοῖς.   265
τί χρῆμ᾽ ἄρ᾽ οὐκ τῆς οἰκίας τῆσδε συνδικαστὴς
πέπονθεν, ὡς οὐ φαίνεται δεῦρο πρὸς τὸ πλῆθος;
οὐ μὴν πρὸ τοῦ γ᾽ ἐφολκὸς ἦν, ἀλλὰ πρῶτος ἡμῶν
ἡγεῖτ᾽ ἂν ᾄδων Φρυνίχου· καὶ γάρ ἐστιν ἀνὴρ
φιλῳδός. ἀλλά μοι δοκεῖ στάντας ἐνθάδ᾽, ὦ 'νδρες,   270
ᾄδοντας αὐτὸν ἐκκαλεῖν, ἤν τί πως ἀκούσας
τοῦ 'μοῦ μέλους ὑφ᾽ ἡδονῆς ἑρπύσῃ θύραζε.

τί ποτ᾽ οὐ πρὸ θυρῶν φαίνετ᾽ ἄρ᾽ ἡμῖν   στρ.
    ὁ γέρων οὐδ᾽ ὑπακούει;
    μῶν ἀπολώλεκε τὰς ἐμβάδας; ἢ προσέκοψ᾽ ἐν   275a
    τῷ σκότῳ τὸν δάκτυλόν που,   275b
εἶτ᾽ ἐφλέγμηνεν αὐτοῦ   276a
τὸ σφυρὸν γέροντος ὄντος;   276b
καὶ τάχ᾽ ἂν βουβωνιῴη.   277a
ἢ μὴν πολὺ δριμύτατός γ᾽ ἦν τῶν παρ᾽ ἡμῖν,   277b
καὶ μόνος οὐκ ἀνεπείθετ᾽,
    ἀλλ᾽ ὁπότ᾽ ἀντιβολοίη   279a
    τις, κάτω κύπτων ἂν οὕτω   279b
"λίθον ἕψεις" ἔλεγεν.   280

264 (πρῷα) § Poll. 7. 152   268–9 (. ̇ . . -χου) S ε 3944
276 § Zonar. 936

---

261 ποῆσαι R   262 λίχνοις V   μυοῦντες J   263 τοῦτ᾽ ᾖ
Flor. Chrest.: ᾖ τουτὶ a   ποεῖν R   ὁ ζεὺς ὑετόν R: ὁ ζεὺς υἱετόν V
264 πρώιμα J   266–89 post 316 transtulit Srebrny   266 par. R
269 ἔστι γ᾽ J   271 ἐκβαλεῖν RJ   272 ἐξερπύσῃ RJ   273 Χο. R
275 -κοψ᾽ ἐν Bentley: -κοψεν RV: -κοψε J   276 -μηνες J   τὸν V
277 δρυμύ- R   278 ἂν ἐπείθετ᾽ RJ   279 κτω J   280 ἐψεῖ σε
λέγων R

τάχα δ' ἂν διὰ τὸν χθεσινὸν ἄνθρω-   ἀντ. 281 a
  πον, ὃς ἡμᾶς διεδύετ'   281 b
  ἐξαπατῶν καὶ λέγων ὡς φιλαθήναιος ἦν καὶ
  τἀν Σάμῳ πρῶτος κατείποι,   283 a
  διὰ τοῦτ' ὀδυνηθεὶς   283 b
  εἶτ' ἴσως κεῖται πυρέττων.
  ἔστι γὰρ τοιοῦτος ἀνήρ.   285
  ἀλλ', ὦ 'γάθ', ἀνίστασο, μηδ' οὕτω σεαυτὸν
  ἔσθιε, μηδ' ἀγανάκτει.
    καὶ γὰρ ἀνὴρ παχὺς ἥκει   288 a
    τῶν προδόντων τἀπὶ Θρᾴκης·   288 b
  ὃν ὅπως ἐγχυτριεῖς.

ὕπαγ', ὦ παῖ, ὕπαγε.   290

Πα. ἐθελήσεις τί μοι οὖν, ὦ   στρ.
     πάτερ, ἤν σού τι δεηθῶ;

Χο. πάνυ γ', ὦ παιδίον. ἀλλ' εἰ-
     πέ, τί βούλει με πρίασθαι
     καλόν; οἶμαι δέ σ' ἐρεῖν ἀσ-   295
     τραγάλους δήπουθεν, ὦ παῖ.

Πα. μὰ Δί', ἀλλ' ἰσχάδας, ὦ παπία· ἥδιον γάρ—

Χο.   οὐκ ἂν
     μὰ Δί', εἰ κρέμαισθέ γ' ὑμεῖς.

Πα. μὰ Δί' οὔ τἄρα προπέμψω σε τὸ λοιπόν.

Χο. ἀπὸ γὰρ τοῦδέ με τοῦ μισθαρίου   300
     τρίτον αὐτὸν ἔχειν ἄλφιτα δεῖ καὶ ξύλα κῶψον·
     σὺ δὲ σῦκά μ' αἰτεῖς.

281 χθιζινὸν Hermann   286 οὔπω V   288 ταχὺς R
289 αἰσχυνεῖς ἐγχυτριεῖς J   290 par. R: ἐκ τῶν γερόντων J
297 Χο. om. V   298 κρέμαισθέ Dobree: κρέμεσθε V: κρέμοισθέ RJ
299 Πα. om. V   300 Χο. om. V

Πα. ἄγε νυν, ὦ πάτερ, ἢν μὴ   ἀντ.
     τὸ δικαστήριον ἄρχων
     καθίσῃ νῦν, πόθεν ὠνη-   305
     σόμεθ᾽ ἄριστον; ἔχεις ἐλ-
     πίδα χρηστήν τινα νῷν ἢ
     πόρον Ἕλλας ἱερόν;

Χο. ἀπαπαῖ φεῦ. μὰ Δί᾽ οὐκ ἔγωγε νῷν οἶδ᾽   309/10
     ὁπόθεν γε δεῖπνον ἔσται.

Πα. τί με δῆτ᾽, ὦ μελέα μῆτερ, ἔτικτες;

Χο. ἵν᾽ ἐμοὶ πράγματα βόσκειν παρέχῃς.

Πα. ἀνόνητον ἄρα σ᾽, ὦ θυλάκιον, γ᾽ εἶχον ἄγαλμα.
     ἐέ.   315
     πάρα νῷν στενάζειν.

Φι. φίλοι, τήκομαι μὲν   317a
     πάλαι διὰ τῆς ὀπῆς   317b
     ὑμῶν ὑπακούων.   318a
     ἀλλὰ γὰρ οὐχ οἷός τ᾽ εἴμ᾽   318b
     ᾄδειν, τί ποιήσω;   319a
     τηροῦμαι δ᾽ ὑπὸ τῶνδ᾽, ἐπεὶ   319b
     βούλομαί γε πάλαι μεθ᾽ ὑ-   320
     μῶν ἐλθὼν ἐπὶ τοὺς καδίσ-
     κους κακόν τι ποιῆσαι.
     ἀλλ᾽, ὦ Ζεῦ μεγαβρόντα,

     ἤ με ποίησον καπνὸν ἐξαίφνης
     ἢ Προξενίδην ἢ τὸν Σέλλου   325
     τοῦτον τὸν ψευδαμάμαξυν.

303 Πα. om. V   304 ὤρχων V   305 καθεσηι R   307 νῶιιν R
308 ἐλὰς R   ἱρὸν J   309 Χο. om. V   ἀπαπαῖ J   311 ὀπόθε V
313 Χο. Cobet: om. a   314 Πα. Meineke: par. R: Χο. J: om. V
ἀνώνητον R   315 par. V: Πα. J   316 νῶιιν R   318 ἀλλ᾽
ἀτὰρ V   319 ποήσω V   320 πάλαι q: πάλαι πάνυ a   322 ποή-
σαι RV   324 ποήσον RV   ἐξαίφης V   325 προξενιάδην J: πρὸς
ξενιάδην R   326 ψευδαμ- BAld: ψευδομ- a

τόλμησον, ἄναξ, χαρίσασθαί μοι,
πάθος οἰκτίρας· ἤ με κεραυνῷ
διατινθαλέῳ σπόδισον ταχέως,
κἄπειτ' ἀνελών μ' ἀπυφυσήσας   330
εἰς ὀξάλμην ἔμβαλε θερμήν·
ἢ δῆτα λίθον με ποίησον, ἐφ' οὗ
τὰς χοιρίνας ἀριθμοῦσιν.

Χο. τίς γάρ ἐσθ' ὁ ταυτά σ' εἴργων κἀποκλείων   στρ.
     τῇ θύρᾳ; λέξον· πρὸς εὔνους γὰρ φράσεις.   335

Φι. οὑμὸς υἱός. ἀλλὰ μὴ βοᾶτε· καὶ γὰρ τυγχάνει
     οὑτοσὶ πρόσθεν καθεύδων. ἀλλ' ὕφεσθε τοῦ τόνου.

Χο. τοῦ δ' ἔφεξιν, ὦ μάταιε, ταῦτα δρᾶν σε βούλεται;
     τίνα πρόφασιν ἔχων;

Φι. οὐκ ἐᾷ μ', ὦ 'νδρες, δικάζειν οὐδὲ δρᾶν οὐδὲν κακόν· 340
     ἀλλά μ' εὐωχεῖν ἕτοιμός ἐστ', ἐγὼ δ' οὐ βούλομαι.

Χο. τοῦτ' ἐτόλμησ' ὁ μιαρὸς χα-   342a
     νεῖν, ὁ Δημολογοκλέων, ὅτι λέγεις τι   342b
     περὶ τῶν νεῶν ἀληθές;
     οὐ γὰρ ἄν ποθ' οὗτος ἀνὴρ   344a
     τοῦτ' ἐτόλμησεν λέγειν, εἰ   344b
     μὴ ξυνωμότης τις ἦν.   345

     ἀλλ' ἐκ τούτων ὥρα τινά σοι ζητεῖν καινὴν ἐπίνοιαν,
     ἥτις σε λάθρᾳ τἀνδρὸς τουδὶ καταβῆναι δεῦρο ποιήσει.

330–1 S a 3646; *An. Bachm.* 137. 3–4   330 (ἀπο- . . .)–331 Ath.
385 d

---

327 τίμησον J   328 οἰκτίρας van Herwerden: οἰκτείρας a   ἤ με]
ἦλθε J   329 σπόνδισον V: πόνεσον J   331 ἅλμην *An. Bachm.*
ἔνβαλε R   θερμόν Ath.^v.l.   332 πόησον RV   334 ἔστ' R   κατα-
κλείων V   335 τὰς θύρας RJ   337 πρόσθες V   338 ἐφέξειν
VJ   340 Φι. om. RV   341 ἐσθ' R : ἐστιν J   344 ἄν om. RJ
ἐτόλμησε VJ   346 τούτων] πάντων R   347 τουδὶ Flor.
Chrest.: τοῦδε a   δεῦρο] χειρο J   πόησει RV

Φι.   τίς ἂν οὖν εἴη; ζητεῖθ᾽ ὑμεῖς, ὡς πᾶν ἂν ἔγωγε ποιοίην·
οὕτω κιττῶ διὰ τῶν σανίδων μετὰ χοιρίνης περιελθεῖν.

Χο.   ἔστιν ὀπὴ δῆθ᾽ ἥντιν᾽ ἂν ἔνδοθεν οἷός τ᾽ εἴης διορύξαι,   350
εἶτ᾽ ἐκδῦναι ῥάκεσιν κρυφθεὶς ὥσπερ πολύμητις Ὀδυσ-
σεύς;

Φι.   πάντα πέφρακται κοὐκ ἔστιν ὀπῆς οὐδ᾽ εἰ σέρφῳ διαδῦναι.
ἀλλ᾽ ἄλλο τι δεῖ ζητεῖν ὑμᾶς· ὀπίαν δ᾽ οὐκ ἔστι γενέσθαι.

Χο.   μέμνησαι δῆθ᾽ ὅτ᾽ ἐπὶ στρατιᾶς κλέψας ποτὲ τοὺς ὀβελίσκους
ἵεις σαυτὸν κατὰ τοῦ τείχους ταχέως, ὅτε Νάξος ἑάλω;   355

Φι.   οἶδ᾽· ἀλλὰ τί τοῦτ᾽; οὐδὲν γὰρ τοῦτ᾽ ἔστιν ἐκείνῳ προσ-
όμοιον.
ἥβων γάρ, κἀδυνάμην κλέπτειν, ἴσχυόν τ᾽ αὐτὸς ἐμαυτοῦ,
κοὐδείς μ᾽ ἐφύλαττ᾽, ἀλλ᾽ ἐξῆν μοι
φεύγειν ἀδεῶς. νῦν δὲ ξὺν ὅπλοις
ἄνδρες ὁπλῖται διαταξάμενοι   360
κατὰ τὰς διόδους σκοπιωροῦνται,
τὼ δὲ δύ᾽ αὐτῶν ἐπὶ ταῖσι θύραις
ὥσπερ με γαλῆν κρέα κλέψασαν
τηροῦσιν ἔχοντ᾽ ὀβελίσκους.

Χο.   ἀλλὰ καὶ νῦν ἐκπόριζε μηχανὴν ὅ-   ἀντ. 365
πως τάχισθ᾽· ἕως γάρ, ὦ μελίττιον.

Φι.   διατραγεῖν τοίνυν κράτιστόν ἐστί μοι τὸ δίκτυον.
ἡ δέ μοι Δίκτυννα συγγνώμην ἔχοι τοῦ δικτύου.

349 §§ S χ 596

---

348 ζητεῖσθ᾽ V   ἂν (secundum) Bentley: om. a   ποοί- RV   -μην J
349 κιττῶι R : κιττῶμαι S   χοιρίνης] χρόνον J   350 Χο. om. R
ὄπηι R   τ᾽ Ald : τε a   εἴης] ἧς VJB₂   351 ῥάκεσσιν Rᵃᶜ : ῥάκεσι
VJ   κρυφθὸς J   353 ἡμᾶς J   354 Χο. om. R   355 κατ αὐτοῦ V
ταχέως om. J   356 Φι. om. R   ἔστιν q: ἔστ᾽ a   ἐκεῖνο R
358 ἐφύλατ᾽ R   359 ξυνόπλους V   365 Χο. om. V   366 τάχιστ᾽
R   μελίττιον q: μελίτιον a   367 Φι. om. V   368 δίκτυννα RJ
συγγνώμην R

Χο. ταῦτα μὲν πρὸς ἀνδρός ἐστ' ἄνοντος ἐς σωτηρίαν.
ἀλλ' ἔπαγε τὴν γνάθον.   370

Φι. διατέτρωκται τοῦτό γ'. ἀλλὰ μὴ βοᾶτε μηδαμῶς,
ἀλλὰ τηρώμεσθ' ὅπως μὴ Βδελυκλέων αἰσθήσεται.

Χο. μηδέν, ὦ τᾶν, δέδιθι, μηδέν·
ὡς ἐγὼ τοῦτόν γ', ἐὰν γρύξῃ τι, ποιή-
σω δακεῖν τὴν καρδίαν καὶ   375
τὸν περὶ ψυχῆς δρόμον δρα-
μεῖν, ἵν' εἰδῇ μὴ πατεῖν τὰ
τῶν θεῶν ψηφίσματα.

ἀλλ' ἐξάψας διὰ τῆς θυρίδος τὸ καλῴδιον εἶτα καθίμα 379
δήσας σαυτὸν καὶ τὴν ψυχὴν ἐμπλησάμενος Διοπείθους.

Φι. ἄγε νυν, ἢν αἰσθομένω τούτω ζητητόν μ' ἐσκαλαμᾶσθαι
κἀνασπαστὸν ποιεῖν εἴσω, τί ποιήσετε; φράζετε νυνί.

Χο. ἀμυνοῦμέν σοι τὸν πρινώδη θυμὸν ἅπαντες καλέσαντες
ὥστ' οὐ δυνατόν σ' εἴργειν ἔσται· τοιαῦτα ποιήσομεν ἡμεῖς.

Φι. δράσω τοίνυν ὑμῖν πίσυνος. καὶ μανθάνετ', ἤν τι πάθω
'γώ,   385
ἀνελόντες καὶ κατακλαύσαντες θεῖναί μ' ὑπὸ τοῖσι δρυφάκτοις.

Χο. οὐδὲν πείσει· μηδὲν δείσῃς. ἀλλ', ὦ βέλτιστε, καθίει
σαυτὸν θαρρῶν κἀπευξάμενος τοῖσι πατρῴοισι θεοῖσιν.

Φι. ὦ Λύκε δέσποτα, γείτων ἥρως (σὺ γὰρ οἷσπερ ἐγὼ
κεχάρησαι,

369 Χο. om. R: par. V   ἐστιν J   εἰς J   371 Φι. om. V: par. R
διατέτρωται τοῦ γ' J   372 ὅπω R   373 Χο. om. V: par. R
δειδιθι V   374 τοῦτόν] τὸ J   ποήσω RV   377 πατῆ J
378 ταῖν θεαῖν VJ   379 καθίμω V   381 αἰσθομένωι R   ἐγκαλ-
R : ἐκκαλ- J   382 ποεῖν R   ἔσω V   ποήσετε V   383 Χο. om. V
384 ἔσται] τὰ RJ   ποήσομεν RV   385 Φι. om. V   386 κλαύ-
σαντες RJ   387 Χο. om. V   πείσῃ VJ   388 θαρῶν RJ
389 Φι. om. V   ἐγὼ] ἐκ J   κεχάρηται R : κεχαρης V

τοῖς δακρύοισιν τῶν φευγόντων ἀεὶ καὶ τοῖς ὀλοφυρμοῖς·
ᾤκησας γοῦν ἐπίτηδες ἰὼν ἐνταῦθ' ἵνα ταῦτ' ἀκροῶμαι,   391
κἀβουλήθης μόνος ἡρώων παρὰ τὸν κλάοντα καθῆσθαι),
ἐλέησον καὶ σῶσον νυνὶ τὸν σαυτοῦ πλησιόχωρον,
κοὐ μή ποτέ σου παρὰ τὰς κάννας οὐρήσω μηδ' ἀπο-
        πάρδω.

Βδ.   οὗτος, ἐγείρου.

Ξα.   τί τὸ πρᾶγμ';

Βδ.   ὥσπερ φωνή μέ τις ἐγκεκύκλωται.   395
μῶν ὁ γέρων πῃ διαδύεται αὖ;

Ξα.   μὰ Δί' οὐ δῆτ', ἀλλὰ καθιμᾷ
αὑτὸν δήσας.

Βδ.   ὦ μιαρώτατε, τί ποιεῖς; οὐ μὴ καταβήσει.
ἀνάβαιν' ἀνύσας κατὰ τὴν ἑτέραν καὶ ταῖσιν φυλλάσι παῖε,
ἤν πως πρύμναν ἀνακρούσηται πληγεὶς ταῖς εἰρεσιώναις.

Φι.   οὐ ξυλλήψεσθ', ὁπόσοισι δίκαι τῆτες μέλλουσιν ἔσεσθαι,
ὦ Σμικυθίων καὶ Τεισιάδη καὶ Χρήμων καὶ Φερέδειπνε;
πότε δ', εἰ μὴ νῦν, ἐπαρήξετέ μοι, πρίν μ' εἴσω μᾶλλον
        ἄγεσθαι;   402

Χο.   εἰπέ μοι, τί μέλλομεν κινεῖν ἐκείνην τὴν χολήν,
ἤνπερ ἡνίκ' ἄν τις ἡμῶν ὀργίσῃ τὴν σφηκιάν;
νῦν ἐκεῖνο νῦν ἐκεῖνο   405

394 (οὐ . . . οὐρήσω) Poll. (1) 7. 176; (2) 10. 183

390 δακρύοισιν B : δακρύοισι a   394 περὶ Poll. (1)(2)ᵛ·ˡ·   395 par.
R   Ξα. Hermann : Οι. VJ : om. R   Βδ. (secundum) om. R : dic. V
ἐγκέκλωται J   396 par. R : Οι. J   αὖ Dindorf : om. a   Ξα.
MacDowell (Οι. β' Coulon) : dic. V : Βδ. J : om. R   dic. et par. ante ἀλλὰ R
397 δείσας J   Βδ. van Leeuwen : dic. RV : Οι. J   ποεῖς RV
καταβήσῃ R   398 par. R : Βδ. J   ταῖσιν Bentley : ταῖσι a   399 ἤν]
εἴ V   ἀνακρούρηται V : ἀνακούσηται J   400 Φι. om. VJ   ὁπόσοι RJ
401 Φι. VJ : par. R : om. PHB   Τεισιάδη van Herwerden : τισιάδη a
402 δ'] τ' R   403 μοι om. J   μέλομεν V   ἐκείνη R   σχολὴν J

τοὐξύθυμον, ᾧ κολαζό-
μεσθα, κέντρον ἐντέτατ' ὀξύ.
ἀλλὰ θαἰμάτια λαβόντες ὡς τάχιστα, παιδία,
θεῖτε καὶ βοᾶτε, καὶ Κλέωνι ταῦτ' ἀγγέλλετε,
καὶ κελεύετ' αὐτὸν ἥκειν   410
    ὡς ἐπ' ἄνδρα μισόπολιν
    ὄντα κἀπολούμενον, ὅτι
    τόνδε λόγον εἰσφέρει,
    μὴ δικάζειν δίκας.

Βδ.   ὦ 'γαθοί, τὸ πρᾶγμ' ἀκούσατ', ἀλλὰ μὴ κεκράγατε.   415

Χο.   νὴ Δί', εἰς τὸν οὐρανόν γ'.

Βδ.   ὡς τόνδ' ἐγὼ οὐ μεθήσομαι.

Χο.   ταῦτα δῆτ' οὐ δεινὰ καὶ τυραννίς ἐστιν ἐμφανής;
    ὦ πόλις καὶ Θεώρου θεοισεχθρία,
    κεἴ τις ἄλλος προέστηκεν ἡμῶν κόλαξ.

Ξα.   Ἡράκλεις, καὶ κέντρ' ἔχουσιν. οὐχ ὁρᾷς, ὦ δέσποτα;   420

Βδ.   οἷς γ' ἀπώλεσαν Φίλιππον ἐν δίκῃ τὸν Γοργίου.

Χο.   καὶ σέ γ' αὐτοῖς ἐξολοῦμεν. ἀλλ' ἅπας ἐπίστρεφε
    δεῦρο κἀξείρας τὸ κέντρον εἶτ' ἐπ' αὐτὸν ἵεσο,
    ξυσταλείς, εὔτακτος, ὀργῆς καὶ μένους ἐμπλήμενος,
    ὡς ἂν εὖ εἰδῇ τὸ λοιπὸν σμῆνος οἷον ὤργισεν.   425

Ξα.   τοῦτο μέντοι δεινὸν ἤδη, νὴ Δί', εἰ μαχούμεθα.
    ὡς ἔγωγ' αὐτῶν ὁρῶν δέδοικα τὰς ἐγκεντρίδας.

---

408 βαλόντες B₂   τὰ παιδία RV   409 θεῶτε J   ἐλέωνι V
ἀγγέλετε V   412 καὶ πολούμενον V   413 εἰσφέρῃ J   414 μὴ
Dindorf: ὡς χρὴ μὴ a   415 κεκράγετε q   416 δία R: δία γ' V
Βδ. Dobree: om. a   τὸν δε γ' ἐγὼ V   417 Χο. B: par. R: Βδ. J:
om. V   δη γ' V   418 Ἡμ. RJ   πόλις q: πόλι a   θεοισεχθρία
Bentley: θεὸς ἐχθρία a   419 ὑμῶν RV   421 incipit Γ   Βδ. om.
R: dic.V   φίλιπον R   422 Χο. om. J   σέ γ'] σ' J   αὐτοῖς Hirschig:
αὗτις RΓJ: αὐτῆς V   423 καὶ ξείρας Γ   424 ἐμπλησμένος J
425 ὤργησεν R: ὤργια Γ   426 Ξα.] οικετ βδε V   427 κεντρίδας R

Χο.   ἀλλ' ἀφίει τὸν ἄνδρ'· εἰ δὲ μή, φήμ' ἐγὼ
      τὰς χελώνας μακαριεῖν σε τοῦ δέρματος.

Φι.   εἶά νυν, ὦ ξυνδικασταί, σφῆκες ὀξυκάρδιοι,   430
      οἱ μὲν εἰς τὸν πρωκτὸν αὐτῶν εἰσπέτεσθ' ὠργισμένοι,
      οἱ δὲ τὠφθαλμὼ κύκλῳ κεντεῖτε καὶ τοὺς δακτύλους.

Βδ.   ὦ Μίδα καὶ Φρὺξ, βοήθει δεῦρο, καὶ Μασυντία,
      καὶ λάβεσθε τουτουὶ καὶ μὴ μεθῆσθε μηδενί·
      εἰ δὲ μή, 'ν πέδαις παχείαις οὐδὲν ἀριστήσετε,   435
      ὡς ἐγὼ πολλῶν ἀκούσας οἶδα θρίων τὸν ψόφον.

Χο.   εἰ δὲ μὴ τοῦτον μεθήσεις, ἔν τί σοι παγήσεται.

Φι.   ὦ Κέκροψ ἥρως ἄναξ, τὰ πρὸς ποδῶν Δρακοντίδη,
      περιορᾷς οὕτω μ' ὑπ' ἀνδρῶν βαρβάρων χειρούμενον,
      οὓς ἐγὼ 'δίδαξα κλάειν τέτταρ' ἐς τὴν χοίνικα;   440

Χο.   εἶτα δῆτ' οὐ πόλλ' ἔνεστι δεινὰ τῷ γήρᾳ κακά;
      δηλαδή· καὶ νῦν γε τούτω τὸν παλαιὸν δεσπότην
      πρὸς βίαν χειροῦσιν, οὐδὲν τῶν πάλαι μεμνημένοι
      διφθερῶν κἀξωμίδων, ἃς οὗτος αὐτοῖς ἠμπόλα,
      καὶ κυνᾶς· καὶ τοὺς πόδας χειμῶνος ὄντος ὠφέλει,   445
      ὥστε μὴ ῥιγῶν γ' ἑκάστοτ'· ἀλλὰ τούτοις γ' οὐκ ἔνι
      οὐδὲν ὀφθαλμοῖσιν αἰδὼς τῶν παλαιῶν ἐμβάδων.

Φι.   οὐκ ἀφήσεις οὐδὲ νυνί μ', ὦ κάκιστον θηρίον,
      οὐδ' ἀναμνησθεὶς ὅθ' εὑρὼν τοὺς βότρυς κλέπτοντά σε

429 §§ S χ 189

429 χελάνας J   μακαρίζειν V   σε om. V   430 εἶα semel
q: bis a   νυν om. ΓΒ₂   ὀξυνόδιοι J   431 εἰπέτεσθ' R: εἰσπέσετ'
Γ   432 κεντεῖτε Flor. Chrest.: κεντεῖθ' οἱ δὲ a   καὶ om. RΓJ
433 βοήθει Bentley: βοηθεῖτε a   434 λάβεσθε q: βάλεσθε RΓJ:
βάλλεσθε V   τουτουί J   μεθεῖσθε Γ   435 μὴ 'ν Flor. Chrest.:
μὴν RVΓ: μὴ J   ταχείαις R   οὐδὲν] αὐτὸν Γ   437 Χο. V: om.
RΓJ   μεθήσῃς Γ   ἐν Farreus: ἔν a   τη τι J   σοι] σὶ Γ
439 περιοραοῖς V   440 οὓς] ὡς J   τεταγάρ R   441 Ἡμ. R
ἔν ἐστιν R   τᾶ J   442 Ἡμ. J   443-67 versuum initia habet Π
444 δε[ι]φθερων Π   κἀξομίδων J   ἠμπόλλα Γ   446 ῥιγῶν γ']
ῥιγόντ' R   οὐκ om. Γ₁   447 ουδ' εν Π   ἐμβάθων J   449 οὔτ' R
ὅτ' R   βρότρυς R   κλέπτοντας V

ΣΦΗΚΕΣ 69

προσαγαγὼν πρὸς τὴν ἐλάαν ἐξέδειρ' εὖ κἀνδρικῶς, 450
ὥστε σε ζηλωτὸν εἶναι; σὺ δ' ἀχάριστος ἦσθ' ἄρα.
ἀλλ' ἄνες με καὶ σὺ καὶ σύ, πρὶν τὸν υἱὸν ἐκδραμεῖν.

Χο. ἀλλὰ τούτων μὲν τάχ' ἡμῖν δώσετον καλὴν δίκην,
οὐκέτ' ἐς μακράν, ἵν' εἰδῆθ' οἷός ἐστ' ἀνδρῶν τρόπος
ὀξυθύμων καὶ δικαίων καὶ βλεπόντων κάρδαμα. 455

Βδ. παῖε, παῖ', ὦ Ξανθία, τοὺς σφῆκας ἀπὸ τῆς οἰκίας.

Ξα. ἀλλὰ δρῶ τοῦτ'.

Βδ.   ἀλλὰ καὶ σὺ τῦφε πολλῷ τῷ καπνῷ.

Ξα. οὐχὶ σοῦσθ'; οὐκ ἐς κόρακας; οὐκ ἄπιτε;

Βδ.   παῖε τῷ ξύλῳ.
καὶ σὺ προσθεὶς Αἰσχίνην ἔντυφε τὸν Σελλαρτίου.

Ξα. ἆρ' ἐμέλλομέν ποθ' ὑμᾶς ἀποσοβήσειν τῷ χρόνῳ. 460

Βδ. ἀλλὰ μὰ Δί' οὐ ῥᾳδίως οὕτως ἂν αὐτοὺς διέφυγες,
εἴπερ ἔτυχον τῶν μελῶν τῶν Φιλοκλέους βεβρωκότες.

Χο. ἆρα δῆτ' οὐκ αὐτὰ δῆλα τοῖς πένησιν,
ἡ τυραννὶς ὡς λάθρᾳ γ' ἐ-
λάμβαν' ὑπιοῦσά με, 465
εἰ σύ γ', ὦ πόνῳ πόνηρε καὶ Κομηταμυνία,
τῶν νόμων ἡμᾶς ἀπείργεις ὧν ἔθηκεν ἡ πόλις,
οὔτε τιν' ἔχων πρόφασιν

453-5 §§ † S ι 377   468-70 §§ S ε 3772

---

450 πρὸς σαγαγὼν J   ἐλαίαν V   454 εις Π   οἷον RΓJ   τρόπους V
456 παῦε R   τοὺς] τὰς Γ   457 Βδ. Bergk: om. Πα   458 Ξα.
MacDowell (Οι. β' Cantarella): par. ΠR: Σω. VΓJ   οὐκ (prius) om. J
ςις Π   Βδ. van Leeuwen: om. a: [Π]   459 Ξα. VΓJ: Οι. R:
om. Π   αἰσχύνην J   σελαρτίου VJ   460 Ξα. Bergk: par. ΠR: om.
VΓJ   461 Βδ. Brunck: par. ΠR: Χο. ΓJ: om. V   462 μελέων
VΓJ: [Π]   463 Ημ. RΓJ: par. Π   αὐτὰ δῆλα] signum verbi
compositi add. R: [Π]: αὐτόδηλα L. Dindorf   464 τυραννὶς J
464-5 ἐλάνθαν' VJ: ἐλάνθανεν Γ: [Π]   466 par. R: Ημ. Γ

οὔτε λόγον εὐτράπελον,
αὐτὸς ἄρχων μόνος;   470

Βδ. ἔσθ' ὅπως ἄνευ μάχης καὶ τῆς κατοξείας βοῆς
ἐς λόγους ἔλθοιμεν ἀλλήλοισι καὶ διαλλαγάς;

Χο. σοὶ λόγους, ὦ μισόδημε
καὶ μοναρχίας ἐραστὰ
καὶ ξυνὼν Βρασίδᾳ καὶ φορῶν κράσπεδα   475
στεμμάτων τήν θ' ὑπήνην ἄκουρον τρέφων;   476/7

Βδ. νὴ Δί' ἦ μοι κρεῖττον ἐκστῆναι τὸ παράπαν τοῦ πατρὸς
μᾶλλον ἢ κακοῖς τοσούτοις ναυμαχεῖν ὁσημέραι.

Χο. οὐδὲ μὴν οὐδ' ἐν σελίνῳ σοῦστιν οὐδ' ἐν πηγάνῳ·   480
τοῦτο γὰρ παρεμβαλοῦμεν τῶν τριχοινίκων ἐπῶν.
ἀλλὰ νῦν μὲν οὐδὲν ἀλγεῖς, ἀλλ' ὅταν ξυνήγορος
ταὐτὰ ταῦτά σου καταντλῇ καὶ ξυνωμότας καλῇ.

Βδ. ἆρ' ἄν, ὦ πρὸς τῶν θεῶν, ὑμεῖς ἀπαλλαχθεῖτέ μου;
ἢ δέδοκται καὶ δέρεσθαι καὶ δέρειν δι' ἡμέρας;   485

Χο. οὐδέποτέ γ', οὔχ, ἕως ἄν τί μου λοιπὸν ᾖ—
ὅστις ἡμῶν ἐπὶ τυραννίδ' ἐξεστάλης.

Βδ. ὡς ἅπανθ' ὑμῖν τυραννίς ἐστι καὶ ξυνωμόται,
ἤν τε μεῖζον ἤν τ' ἔλαττον πρᾶγμά τις κατηγορῇ.
ἧς ἐγὼ οὐκ ἤκουσα τοὔνομ' οὐδὲ πεντήκοντ' ἐτῶν·   490
νῦν δὲ πολλῷ τοῦ ταρίχους ἐστὶν ἀξιωτέρα,

473 (μισό- . . .)–477 §§ S μ 1125

469 εὐτραπέλου V   470 μόνος] χρόνον J   471 κατοξίας R
472 ἔλθωμεν RΓJ   474 ἐρασταί J   479 κακακοῖς R   480 Ἡμ.
RΓ: om. V   μήν γ' Γᵃᶜ λΣΓ: μέν γ' RVJΓᵖᶜ: γ' del. Hirschig   ποῦ
'στιν RΓJ   483 ταὐτὰ om. Γ   καταντλεῖ R: κανtατλῇ Γ   καλεῖ RV
484 Βδ. om. V   ἆρ' ἄν, ὦ] ἄρα γ' ἂν VΓJ   ἡμεῖς Γ   -θῆτέ VΓJ
μου ΓΒ₂: μοι RVJ   485 καὶ (prius) MacDowell: μοι a: τοι Platnauer
486–513 versuum fines habet Π   486 Χο. om. VJ   487 ὅστι Γ
ἐξεστάλης Meineke: ἐστάλης a: εσταλης Π   488 Βδ. om. RᵖᶜV
ἅπαθ' J   ἡμῖν RJ   ἡ τυραννὶς ΓΒ₂: τυρραννίς J   489 τ' ἤν τ' R
κατηγορεῖ VΓJ   490 πεντήκοτ' Γ

ὥστε καὶ δὴ τοὔνομ' αὐτῆς ἐν ἀγορᾷ κυλίνδεται.
ἢν μὲν ὠνῇταί τις ὀρφῶς, μεμβράδας δὲ μὴ 'θέλῃ,
εὐθέως εἴρηχ' ὁ πωλῶν πλησίον τὰς μεμβράδας·
"οὗτος ὀψωνεῖν ἔοιχ' ἄνθρωπος ἐπὶ τυραννίδι."   495
ἢν δὲ γήτειον προσαιτῇ ταῖς ἀφύαις ἥδυσμά τι,
ἡ λαχανόπωλις παραβλέψασά φησι θἀτέρῳ·
"εἰπέ μοι· γήτειον αἰτεῖς· πότερον ἐπὶ τυραννίδι;
ἢ νομίζεις τὰς Ἀθήνας σοὶ φέρειν ἡδύσματα;"

Ξα.   κἀμέ γ' ἡ πόρνη χθὲς εἰσελθόντα τῆς μεσημβρίας,   500
ὅτι κελητίσαι 'κέλευον, ὀξυθυμηθεῖσά μοι
ἤρετ' εἰ τὴν Ἱππίου καθίσταμαι τυραννίδα.

Βδ.   ταῦτα γὰρ τούτοις ἀκούειν ἡδέ', εἰ καὶ νῦν ἐγώ,
τὸν πατέρ' ὅτι βούλομαι τούτων ἀπαλλαχθέντα τῶν
ὀρθροφοιτοσυκοφαντοδικοταλαιπώρων τρόπων   505
ζῆν βίον γενναῖον ὥσπερ Μόρυχος, αἰτίαν ἔχω
ταῦτα δρᾶν ξυνωμότης ὢν καὶ φρονῶν τυραννικά.

Φι.   νὴ Δί', ἐν δίκῃ γ'· ἐγὼ γὰρ οὐδ' ἂν ὀρνίθων γάλα
ἀντὶ τοῦ βίου λάβοιμ' ἂν οὗ με νῦν ἀποστερεῖς.
οὐδὲ χαίρω βατίσιν οὐδ' ἐγχέλεσιν, ἀλλ' ἥδιον ἂν   510
δικίδιον σμικρὸν φάγοιμ' ἂν ἐν λοπάδι πεπνιγμένον.

497–8 § S γ 262   503 (εἰ . . .)–507 S § (1) ει 68   504 (ὁτιὴ . . .)–
507 (. . . δρᾶν) S § (2) ο 581   508 (ἐγώ . . .)–511 S § (1) λ 674
508 (ἐγώ . . .)–509 Apostol. 6. 48e   510 (. . . -λεσιν) Ath. 299 b;
§ Zonar. 601; ‡ An. Par. iv. 246. 28   510–11 S §§ (2) ο 818
511 (ἐν . . .) Ath. 396 a

492 κυκλ- J   493 ἢν] ἡ J   494 εὐλέως J   ὁ] ὡ J   πλησίου J
495 ἔοικ' ΓJ   496 -αιτεῖ RΓ   ἡδυσιμαί J   497 [φησιν] παρα-
βλείψασα Π : περιβλέψασα φησὶ Γ   498 αἰτεῖ γ' Γ   499 σὺ J
τρεφε[ι]ν Π   500 μεσομβρίας J   501 ἐξυ- J   503 ἡδέ' Dindorf :
ἡδέα a : [Π]   εἰ om. Γ   504 ὅτι S(1) : ὁτιὴ a S(1)ᵛ·ˡ·(2) : [Π]
505 ὀρθρο- Grynaeus : ὀρθο- a S(1)(2) : [Π]   506 ἔχω ΠVS(1) :
ἔχων RΓJS(2)   507 δρᾶιν R : δραύ J   τυραννικά ΠVS(1) : τυραννίδα
RΓJ   508 γ' om. ΓJ   γὰρ οὐδ' ἂν] γὰρ οὐδὲν Γ :]υδεν Π : μὲν οὖν
ἂν S(1)   509 τοῦ om. S(1)   ]ερης Π   510 οὐ χαίρω δὲ Ath. :
οὐ χαίρω An. Par. : οὐδὲ χαίρων S(2)ᵛ·ˡ·   -λεσιν Ath. Zonar. : -λεσι An.
Par. : -λισιν VS(2)ᵛ·ˡ· : -λυσιν RΓJS(1)(2) : [Π]   ]ϑιοπαν Π   511 μικρὸν S(1)   ἐν ολοπαδι Ath.ᵛ·ˡ· : ἐλοπάδι S(2)ᵛ·ˡ·   πεπηγ- R

Βδ.   νὴ Δί', εἰθίσθης γὰρ ἥδεσθαι τοιούτοις πράγμασιν.
ἀλλ' ἐὰν σιγῶν ἀνάσχῃ καὶ μάθῃς ἀγὼ λέγω,
ἀναδιδάξειν οἴομαί σ' ὡς πάντα ταῦθ' ἁμαρτάνεις.

Φι.   ἐξαμαρτάνω δικάζων;

Βδ.   καταγελώμενος μὲν οὖν   515
οὐκ ἐπαίεις ὑπ' ἀνδρῶν, οὓς σὺ μόνον οὐ προσκυνεῖς.
ἀλλὰ δουλεύων λέληθας.

Φι.   παῦε δουλείαν λέγων—
ὅστις ἄρχω τῶν ἁπάντων.

Βδ.   οὐ σύ γ', ἀλλ' ὑπηρετεῖς
οἰόμενος ἄρχειν· ἐπεὶ δίδαξον ἡμᾶς, ὦ πάτερ,
ἥτις ἡ τιμή 'στί σοι καρπουμένῳ τὴν Ἑλλάδα.   520

Φι.   πάνυ γε· καὶ τούτοισί γ' ἐπιτρέψαι 'θέλω.

Βδ.   καὶ μὴν ἐγώ.
ἄφετέ νυν ἅπαντες αὐτόν.

Φι.   καὶ ξίφος γέ μοι δότε·
ἢν γὰρ ἡττηθῶ λέγων σου, περιπεσοῦμαι τῷ ξίφει.

Βδ.   εἰπέ μοι, τί δ', ἤν—τὸ δεῖνα—τῇ διαίτῃ μὴ 'μμένῃς;

Φι.   μηδέποτε πίοιμ' ἄκρατον μισθὸν ἀγαθοῦ δαίμονος.   525

Χο.   νῦν δὴ τὸν ἐκ θἠμετέρου   στρ.
γυμνασίου λέγειν τι δεῖ καινόν, ὅπως φανήσει—   527/8

Βδ.   ἐνεγκάτω μοι δεῦρο τὴν κίστην τις ὡς τάχιστα.
ἀτὰρ φανεῖ ποῖός τις ὤν, ἢν ταῦτα παρακελεύῃ;   530/1

513 ἀγὼ] ἅπερ J   514 ἀναδειδ- Γ   οἴμαι σ' V: σ' οἴομ' J
516 ὑπαίεις V   ἐπ' ΓJ   519 ἐπιδίδαξον V   520 'στί] τι V
521 Φι. om. V   522 par. R   νυν] τοίνυν J   Φι. Bergler: om. a
γέ] δέ J   523 par. R   524 Βδ. Bergler: par. R: om. VΓJ
μήνμμένης R: μὴ 'μμείνης V   525 Φι. om. V: par. R   ἄκρατον
Richter: ἀκράτου a   526 δὲ RVΓ   θημέτρου J   527 γμμν- V
528 φανείσῃ J   529 κακίστην R   530 Χο. a: del. Dindorf
531 ταῦτα q: ταῦτ' αὐτὰ RΓJ: ταυτα αὐτὰ V

Χο.　—μὴ κατὰ τὸν νεανίαν
　　　τόνδε λέγειν. ὁρᾷς γὰρ ὥς σοι μέγας ἐστὶν ἀγὼν　533/4
　　　καὶ περὶ τῶν ἁπάντων,　535
　　　εἴπερ—ὃ μὴ γένοιτο—
　　　νῦν ἐθέλει κρατῆσαι.

Βδ.　καὶ μὴν ὅσ' ἂν λέξῃ γ' ἁπλῶς μνημόσυνα γράψομαι 'γώ.

Φι.　τί γάρ φαθ' ὑμεῖς, ἢν ὁδί με τῷ λόγῳ κρατήσῃ;

Χο.　οὐκέτι πρεσβυτῶν ὄχλος　540
　　　χρήσιμος ἔστ' οὐδ' ἀκαρῆ·
　　　σκωπτόμενοι δ' ἐν ταῖς ὁδοῖς θαλλοφόροι　542/3
　　　καλούμεθ', ἀντωμοσιῶν κελύφη.　544/5

　　　ἀλλ', ὦ περὶ τῆς πάσης μέλλων βασιλείας ἀντιλογήσειν
　　　τῆς ἡμετέρας, νυνὶ θαρρῶν πᾶσαν γλῶτταν βασάνιζε.

Φι.　καὶ μὴν εὐθύς γ' ἀπὸ βαλβίδων περὶ τῆς ἀρχῆς ἀποδείξω
　　　τῆς ἡμετέρας ὡς οὐδεμιᾶς ἥττων ἐστὶν βασιλείας.
　　　τί γὰρ εὔδαιμον καὶ μακαριστὸν μᾶλλον νῦν ἐστι δικαστοῦ,
　　　ἢ τρυφερώτερον ἢ δεινότερον ζῷον, καὶ ταῦτα γέροντος;
　　　ὃν πρῶτα μὲν ἕρποντ' ἐξ εὐνῆς τηροῦσ' ἐπὶ τοῖσι δρυφάκ-
　　　τοις　552
　　　ἄνδρες μεγάλοι καὶ τετραπήχεις· κἄπειτ' εὐθὺς προσιόντι
　　　ἐμβάλλει μοι τὴν χεῖρ' ἁπαλὴν τῶν δημοσίων κεκλοφυῖαν.
　　　ἱκετεύουσίν θ' ὑποκύπτοντες τὴν φωνὴν οἰκτροχοοῦντες·
　　　"οἴκτιρόν μ', ὦ πάτερ, αἰτοῦμαί σ', εἰ καὐτὸς πώποθ'
　　　ὑφείλου　556

532 Χο. om. RΓJ　　534 ἐστὶν q: ἔστ' a　　536 καὶ εἴπερ J
537 νῦν Wilamowitz: νῦν οὗτος a　　538 -μαι 'γώ q: -μ' ἐγώ a
542 σκοπ-J　　δ' Porson: δ' ἄν a: γὰρ ἂν q　　543 ταῖσιν RV　　ὁδοῖς
Porson: ὁδοῖς ἁπάσαις RΓJ: ὁδοῖσιν ἁπάσαις V　　544 καλλ- Γ
-ούμεθ' Porson: -οίμεθ' a　　ἀντωμουσιῶν R　　546 βασιλείας μέλλων
J　　548 γ' om. V　　549 ὡς om. J　　550 καὶ Porson: ἢ καὶ a
νῦν om. V　　552 πρῶτον R　　ἕρπον R　　τυροῦσ' Γ　　554 ἐμβάλει V
555 ὑποπίπτοντες R　　οἰατρο- J　　556 οἴκτιρόν van Herwerden:
οἴκτειρόν a

ἀρχὴν ἄρξας ἢ 'πὶ στρατιᾶς τοῖς ξυσσίτοις ἀγοράζων."
ὃς ἔμ' οὐδ' ἂν ζῶντ' ᾔδειν, εἰ μὴ διὰ τὴν προτέραν ἀπόφυξιν.

Βδ.   τουτὶ περὶ τῶν ἀντιβολούντων ἔστω τὸ μνημόσυνόν μοι.

Φι.   εἶτ' εἰσελθὼν ἀντιβοληθεὶς καὶ τὴν ὀργὴν ἀπομορχθεὶς 560
ἔνδον τούτων ὧν ἂν φάσκω πάντων οὐδὲν πεποίηκα,
ἀλλ' ἀκροῶμαι πάσας φωνὰς ἱέντων εἰς ἀπόφευξιν.
φέρ' ἴδω, τί γὰρ οὐκ ἔστιν ἀκοῦσαι θώπευμ' ἐνταῦθα
    δικαστῇ;
οἱ μέν γ' ἀποκλάονται πενίαν αὑτῶν, καὶ προστιθέασιν
κακὰ πρὸς τοῖς οὖσιν, ἕως ἂν ἰὼν ἀνισώσῃ τοῖσιν ἐμοῖσιν·
οἱ δὲ λέγουσιν μύθους ἡμῖν, οἱ δ' Αἰσώπου τι γέλοιον· 566
οἱ δὲ σκώπτουσ', ἵν' ἐγὼ γελάσω καὶ τὸν θυμὸν κατα-
    θῶμαι.
κἂν μὴ τούτοις ἀναπειθώμεσθα, τὰ παιδάρι' εὐθὺς ἀνέλκει
τὰς θηλείας καὶ τοὺς υἱεῖς τῆς χειρός, ἐγὼ δ' ἀκροῶμαι,
τὰ δὲ συγκύψανθ' ἅμα βληχᾶται, κἄπειθ' ὁ πατὴρ ὑπὲρ
    αὐτῶν   570
ὥσπερ θεὸν ἀντιβολεῖ με τρέμων τῆς εὐθύνης ἀπολῦσαι·
" εἰ μὲν χαίρεις ἀρνὸς φωνῇ, παιδὸς φωνὴν ἐλεήσαις·"
εἰ δ' αὖ τοῖς χοιριδίοις χαίρω, θυγατρὸς φωνῇ με πιθέσθαι.
χἠμεῖς αὐτῷ τότε τῆς ὀργῆς ὀλίγον τὸν κόλλοπ' ἀνεῖμεν.
ἆρ' οὐ μεγάλη τοῦτ' ἔστ' ἀρχὴ καὶ τοῦ πλούτου καταχήνη;

557 ξυνσίτοις RV   ἀκμάζων J   558–77 versuum fragmenta
(plerumque initia) habet Π   558 ὅς] ὡς R : ας Π   ἀπόφευξιν
H : [Π]   559 μοι om. Γ : [Π]   560 Φι. om. ΠR   ει γ' Π
561 φάσην J : [Π]   οὐδὲν πάντων Γ : [Π]   πεπόηκα RVΓ : [Π]
562 ἀπόφυξιν V : [Π]   564 ἀποκλαί- RV : αποκλοι- Π   -οντα R
565 κακο Π   ἂν ἰὼν ἀνισώσῃ Paley : ἀνιὼν ἀνισώσῃ V : ἂν ἰσώσῃ RΓJ :
α[Π   ἐμοίων J : [Π]   566 κύθους J   τὸ Γ : [Π]   567 σκώπτουσα
V : σκώπτουσιν J   ιν εγω Π : ἵνα ἐγὼ RV : ἢν ἐγὼ Γ : κἀγὼ J   568 -μεθα J
569 τοὺς] τὰς R   570 συ[γ]κηψαν- Π : συγκύπτον- RΓJ   -θ' ἄμαμα
R : -τ' απο- ΠV   βληχᾶτ' RV : βληχ[Π   571 θεὸς V   572 ἀρνὸς
φωνῇ] ἀνδρὸς φωνὴ J : α[++]ος φωνη[Π   ἐλαιησαις R : [Π]   573 αὖ
τοῖς Flor. Chrest. : αὐτοῖς RVΓ : αὐτοῖσι J : αυτο[Π : αὐταῖς B₂   χοι-
ρίοις R   574 κόλοπ' V : [Π]   575 [μεγ]αληι Π

Βδ.　δεύτερον αὖ σου τουτὶ γράφομαι, τὴν τοῦ πλούτου
　　　καταχήνην.　　　　　　　　　　　　　　　　576
　　　καὶ τἀγαθά μοι μέμνησ' ἄχεις φάσκων τῆς Ἑλλάδος
　　　ἄρχειν.

Φι.　παίδων τοίνυν δοκιμαζομένων αἰδοῖα πάρεστι θεᾶσθαι.
　　　κἂν Οἴαγρος εἰσέλθῃ φεύγων, οὐκ ἀποφεύγει πρὶν ἂν ἡμῖν
　　　ἐκ τῆς Νιόβης εἴπῃ ῥῆσιν τὴν καλλίστην ἀπολέξας.　580
　　　κἂν αὐλητής γε δίκην νικᾷ, ταύτης ἡμῖν ἐπίχειρα
　　　ἐν φορβειᾷ τοῖσι δικασταῖς ἔξοδον ηὔλησ' ἀπιοῦσιν.
　　　κἂν ἀποθνήσκων ὁ πατήρ τῳ δῷ καταλείπων παῖδ' ἐπί-
　　　　κληρον,
　　　κλαίειν ἡμεῖς μακρὰ τὴν κεφαλὴν εἰπόντες τῇ διαθήκῃ
　　　καὶ τῇ κόγχῃ τῇ πάνυ σεμνῶς τοῖς σημείοισιν ἐπούσῃ,　585
　　　ἔδομεν ταύτην ὅστις ἂν ἡμᾶς ἀντιβολήσας ἀναπείσῃ.
　　　καὶ ταῦτ' ἀνυπεύθυνοι δρῶμεν· τῶν δ' ἄλλων οὐδεμί' ἀρχή.

Βδ.　τουτὶ γάρ τοι σεμνόν· τούτων ὦν εἴρηκας μακαρίζω.
　　　τῆς δ' ἐπικλήρου τὴν διαθήκην ἀδικεῖς ἀνακογχυλιάζων.

Φι.　ἔτι δ' ἡ βουλὴ χὠ δῆμος, ὅταν κρῖναι μέγα πρᾶγμ'
　　　　ἀπορήσῃ,　　　　　　　　　　　　　　　　590
　　　ἐψήφισται τοὺς ἀδικοῦντας τοῖσι δικασταῖς παραδοῦναι·
　　　εἶτ' Εὔαθλος χὠ μέγας οὗτος Κολακώνυμος, ἀσπιδαπο-
　　　　βλής,
　　　οὐχὶ προδώσειν ἡμᾶς φασιν, περὶ τοῦ πλήθους δὲ μαχεῖ-
　　　　σθαι.
　　　κἂν τῷ δήμῳ γνώμην οὐδεὶς πώποτ' ἐνίκησεν, ἐὰν μὴ
　　　εἴπῃ τὰ δικαστήρι' ἀφεῖναι πρώτιστα μίαν δικάσαντας.　595

576 om. V: add. Vᵐᵍ　　Βδ. om. Π　　αὖ] ἄν RJ : [Π]　　ταυτί J :]ητι Π
γραφο[Π : γράψομαι a　　τοῦ om. J : [Π]　　πλούτου] οἴκου ℞ : [Π]
577 ἄχρις RVΓ : αχ[Π　　τὴν J : [Π]　　ἀρχὴν VΓ₁J : [Π]　　578 Φι.
om. V　　579 κἂν] καὶ J　　ὔαγρος Γ　　πρὴν J　　580 αὐτολέξας
V : ἀποτέξας J　　582 φορβιᾷ RV　　583 -λειπων B: -λιπὼν a
585 σημείοις J　　ἐπουσιν V　　586 ἀναπείθοι V　　587 ταῦθ' RV
588 τοι] τὸ V　　σεμνῶν ℞ : σε μόνον Reiske　　590 Φι. om. V　　ἔτη
Γ　　ταν J　　592 οὗτος ὁ J　　593 φασιν Bentley: φασι RVJ:
φησὶ Γ　　δὲ om. J　　595 -ρια φῆναι Γ

αὐτὸς δὲ Κλέων ὁ κεκραξιδάμας μόνον ἡμᾶς οὐ περιτρώγει,
ἀλλὰ φυλάττει διὰ χειρὸς ἔχων καὶ τὰς μυίας ἀπαμύνει·
σὺ δὲ τὸν πατέρ' οὐδ' ὁτιοῦν τούτων τὸν σαυτοῦ πώποτ'
ἔδρασας.
ἀλλὰ Θέωρος—καίτούστὶν ἀνὴρ Εὐφημίου οὐδὲν ἐλάττων—
τὸν σπόγγον ἔχων ἐκ τῆς λεκάνης τἀμβάδι' ἡμῶν περικωνεῖ.   600
σκέψαι μ' ἀπὸ τῶν ἀγαθῶν οἵων ἀποκλείεις καὶ κατερύκεις,
ἣν δουλείαν οὖσαν ἔφασκες καὶ ὑπηρεσίαν ἀποδείξειν.

Βδ.   ἔμπλησο λέγων· πάντως γάρ τοι παύσει ποτέ, κἀνα-
φανήσει
πρωκτὸς λουτροῦ περιγιγνόμενος, τῆς ἀρχῆς τῆς περισέμνου.

Φι.   ὁ δέ γ' ἥδιστον τούτων ἐστὶν πάντων, οὗ 'γὼ 'πελελήσ-
μην,   605
ὅταν οἴκαδ' ἴω τὸν μισθὸν ἔχων, κἄπειθ' ἥκονθ' ἅμα
πάντες
ἀσπάζωνται διὰ τἀργύριον, καὶ πρῶτα μὲν ἡ θυγάτηρ με
ἀπονίζῃ καὶ τὼ πόδ' ἀλείφῃ καὶ προσκύψασα φιλήσῃ
καὶ παππίζουσ' ἅμα τῇ γλώττῃ τὸ τριώβολον ἐκκαλαμᾶται,
καὶ τὸ γύναιόν μ' ὑποθωπεῦσαν φυστὴν μᾶζαν προσ-
ενέγκῃ,   610

609 (παπ- . . .) §§ S ε 341   610 §§ S φ 868

596 δὲ] δὲ ὁ RJ: δ' ὁ Γ   μόνον Flor. Chrest.: μόνους a   -τρώγοι V
597 χερὸς R   μύας RᵃᶜΓ   598 τὸν (secundum)] τῶν J   πώπερ J
599 καίπούστιν R   600 ἡμᾶς J   601 μ'] δὲ RΓJ   κατερύκεις J
602 οὖσαν om. VΓ   καὶ] αἱ J   ὑποδείξειν J   603 Βδ. om. V
604 περιγιγν- Brunck: περιγιν- a   605 Φι. om. R: par. V   'γὼ]
γὰρ V   'πελε- Meineke: 'πιλε- a   606 κᾶθ' V   ἦκ- B: εἰσήκ-
a   -ονθ' ἅμα]-ονθαμε V   607–25 versuum fines habet Π
607 -ζονται RJ   με] μεν Π   608 -νίζει J   τὼ om. Γ   ἀλείφει R
-κύσασα V   609 παππάζουσ' RΓJ   τὸ B: om. aS: [Π]   'κκαλα-
ματα Π   610 ἐπιθω- S   -έγκει R

κἄπειτα καθεζομένη παρ' ἐμοὶ προσαναγκάζῃ· "φάγε
   τουτί,

ἔντραγε τουτί." τούτοισιν ἐγὼ γάνυμαι· κοὐ μή με δεήσῃ
εἰς σὲ βλέψαι καὶ τὸν ταμίαν, ὁπότ' ἄριστον παραθήσει
καταρασάμενος καὶ τονθορύσας, ἀλλ' ἢν μή μοι ταχὺ
   μάξῃ,

τάδε κέκτημαι πρόβλημα κακῶν, "σκευὴν βελέων ἀλεωρήν".   615

κἂν οἰνόν μοι μὴ 'γχῇς σὺ πιεῖν, τὸν ὄνον τόνδ' ἐσκεκόμισμαι

οἴνου μεστόν, κᾆτ' ἐγχέομαι κλίνας· οὗτος δὲ κεχηνὼς
βρωμησάμενος τοῦ σοῦ δίνου μέγα καὶ στράτιον κατέπαρδεν.

ἆρ' οὐ μεγάλην ἀρχὴν ἄρχω καὶ τοῦ Διὸς οὐδὲν ἐλάττω,
ὅστις ἀκούω ταῦθ' ἅπερ ὁ Ζεύς;   620
ἢν γοῦν ἡμεῖς θορυβήσωμεν,
πᾶς τίς φησιν τῶν παριόντων·
"οἷον βροντᾷ τὸ δικαστήριον,
ὦ Ζεῦ βασιλεῦ."

κἂν ἀστράψω, ποππύζουσιν   625
κἀγκεχόδασίν μ' οἱ πλουτοῦντες
καὶ πάνυ σεμνοί.
καὶ σὺ δέδοικάς με μάλιστ' αὐτός·
νὴ τὴν Δήμητρα, δέδοικας. ἐγὼ δ'
   ἀπολοίμην εἰ σὲ δέδοικα.   630

Χο.   οὐπώποθ' οὕτω καθαρῶς   ἀντ.
     οὐδενὸς ἠκούσαμεν οὐδὲ ξυνετῶς λέγοντος.   632/3

611 -κάζει R   φεύγε J   612 τούτοισιν] τοῖσιν R Γ J :]ν Π   γάνυμι R : γάννυμαι J   κοὐ Dobree: καὶ Πα   δεησης Π   613 βλάψαι J παραθήσηι R[ac]   614 ἀλλ' ἢν ΠΓ: ἄλλην RVJ   616 'γχεῖς Γ: 'κχῆς J : [Π]   τόνδε κε- Γ   -κόσμιμαι J   617 ἐκχέομαι PH 618 δείνου R   619 οὐ] εὖ J   ἀρχὴ J   καὶ τῆς τοῦ q   Διους Π 620 ταῦθ' ὥσπερ R : ταῦτα ὅσπερ J   621 γοῦν] μὲν οὖν J   626 κἂν κε- J : και κέγχε- R   628 με om. V   μάλισθ' R   629 par. R : Βδ. Γ   δήμητραν R   δέδοικα σ' RΓ   633 ξυνεστῶς R

Φι.   οὐκ, ἀλλ' ἐρήμας ᾤεθ' οὕτω ῥᾳδίως τρυγήσειν·
         καλῶς γὰρ ᾔδειν ὡς ἐγὼ ταύτῃ κράτιστός εἰμι.   635

Χο.   ὡς δὲ πάντ' ἐπελήλυθεν
         κοὐδὲν παρῆλθεν, ὥστ' ἔγωγ' ηὐξανόμην ἀκούων,   637/8
         κἂν μακάρων δικάζειν
         αὐτὸς ἔδοξα νήσοις,   640
         ἡδόμενος λέγοντι.

Φι.   ὥσθ' οὗτος ἤδη σκορδινᾶται κἄστιν οὐκ ἐν αὑτοῦ.
         ἦ μὴν ἐγώ σε τήμερον σκύτη βλέπειν ποιήσω.

Χο.   δεῖ δέ σε παντοίας πλέκειν
         εἰς ἀπόφευξιν παλάμας.   645
         τὴν γὰρ ἐμὴν ὀργὴν πεπᾶναι χαλεπὸν
         μὴ πρὸς ἐμοῦ λέγοντι.

         πρὸς ταῦτα μύλην ἀγαθὴν ὥρα ζητεῖν σοι καὶ νεόκοπτον,
         ἢν μή τι λέγῃς, ἥτις δυνατὴ τὸν ἐμὸν θυμὸν κατερεῖξαι.

Βδ.   χαλεπὸν μὲν καὶ δεινῆς γνώμης καὶ μείζονος ἢ 'πὶ
            τρυγῳδοῖς   650
         ἰάσασθαι νόσον ἀρχαίαν ἐν τῇ πόλει ἐντετοκυῖαν.
         ἀτάρ, ὦ πάτερ ἡμέτερε Κρονίδη—

Φι.   παῦσαι καὶ μὴ πατέριζε.
         εἰ μὴ γάρ, ὅπως δουλεύω 'γώ, τουτὶ ταχέως με διδάξεις,
         οὐκ ἔστιν ὅπως οὐχὶ τεθνήσει, κἂν χρῇ σπλάγχνων μ'
            ἀπέχεσθαι.   654

Βδ.   ἀκρόασαί νυν, ὦ παπίδιον, χαλάσας ὀλίγον τὸ μέτωπον.

655 § S π 260

634 ᾤο*θ' R   οὕτως R   636 Χο. om. V   637/8 ἐγὼ γῆν
'ξανόμην J   642 Φι. om. V   αὑτῶι R : ἀστοῦ Γ   643 βλέπειν
σκυτη J   ποήσω RVΓ   644 Χο. om. V   647 νεανίᾳ μὴ Porson
648 ὅρα R   νεώ- V   -κοπον J   649 τι] τοι J   καρτ- V
650 καὶ μείζονος om. V   μείζωνος ἡ ἐπὶ τραγωδοῖς J   651 τῇδε V
652 κρονίδη J   Φι. om. R   παῦσε J   καὶ om. J   653 par. R :
Βδ. J   διδάξης J   654 σπλάγχνα J   655 Βδ. om. V : par. R :
Χο. J   παππίδιον S

καὶ πρῶτον μὲν λόγισαι φαύλως, μὴ ψήφοις ἀλλ' ἀπὸ
   χειρός, 656
τὸν φόρον ἡμῖν ἀπὸ τῶν πόλεων συλλήβδην τὸν προσιόντα,
κάξω τούτου τὰ τέλη χωρὶς καὶ τὰς πολλὰς ἑκατοστάς,
πρυτανεῖα, μέταλλ', ἀγοράς, λιμένας, μισθώσεις, δημιό-
   πρατα·
τούτων πλήρωμα τάλαντ' ἐγγὺς δισχίλια γίγνεται ἡμῖν.
ἀπὸ τούτου νυν κατάθες μισθὸν τοῖσι δικασταῖς ἐνιαυτοῦ, 661
ἐξ χιλιάσιν—"κοὔπω πλείους ἐν τῇ χώρᾳ κατένασθεν"·
γίγνεται ἡμῖν ἑκατὸν δήπου καὶ πεντήκοντα τάλαντα.

Φι.   οὐδ' ἡ δεκάτη τῶν προσιόντων ἡμῖν ἄρ' ἐγίγνεθ' ὁ μισθός.

Βδ.   μὰ Δί' οὐ μέντοι.

Φι.   καὶ ποῖ τρέπεται δὴ 'πειτα τὰ χρήματα τἄλλα; 665

Βδ.   ἐς τούτους τοὺς "οὐχὶ προδώσω τὸν Ἀθηναίων κολοσυρτόν,
ἀλλὰ μαχοῦμαι περὶ τοῦ πλήθους ἀεί". σὺ γάρ, ὦ πάτερ,
   αὐτοὺς
ἄρχειν αἱρεῖ σαυτοῦ τούτοις τοῖς ῥηματίοις περιπεφθείς.
κᾆθ' οὗτοι μὲν δωροδοκοῦσιν κατὰ πεντήκοντα τάλαντα
ἀπὸ τῶν πόλεων ἐπαπειλοῦντες τοιαυτὶ κἀναφοβοῦντες·
"δώσετε τὸν φόρον, ἢ βροντήσας τὴν πόλιν ὑμῶν ἀνα-
   τρέψω." 671

656 § S φ 147   659–60 (. . . -χίλια) §§ S π 2997   668 §§ S π
1246

---

656 πρῶτα JS   μὲν νῦν J   ὑπὸ S   658 τὰ om. J   λιμίας J
μισθώσεις Bergk : μισθούς aS : μισθοὺς καὶ q   660 πληρωμ' ἐγγὺς
τάλαντ' ἐγγὺς J   γίνετε J   661 τούτων VJ   μισθῶ κατάθες J
ἐνιαυτοῦ Bentley : τοῦ 'νιαυτοῦ a   662 κατένασθε J   663 τάλαντα
πεντήκοντα J   664 Φι. om. RV   ἐγίγνεθ' RVJ   665 Βδ. BAld :
par. R : Χο. J : om. VΓ   Φι. Liston : Βδ. Γ : om. RVJ   τὰ om. V
666 Βδ. Liston : par. R : Φι. ΓJ : om. V   ἀθηναῖον J   667 Βδ. σὺ ΓJ
668 ἄρχειν αἱρῆ σαυτοῦ post περιπεφθεὶς S   ἄρχει Γ   τουτος J   ῥηματίος
J : ῥήμασι S[v.l.]   περιπεμφθεὶς RVΓ' : παραπεμφθεὶς S[v.l.]   669 τάλας
V   670 ὑπαπ- V   671 βροντίσας ΓJ   ἡμῶν Γ   ἀναστρέψω RV

σὺ δὲ τῆς ἀρχῆς ἀγαπᾷς τῆς σῆς τοὺς ἀργελόφους περι-
τρώγων.

οἱ δὲ ξύμμαχοι, ὡς ᾔσθηνται τὸν μὲν σύρφακα τὸν ἄλλον
ἐκ κηθαρίου λαγαριζόμενον καὶ τραγαλίζοντα τὸ μηδέν,
σὲ μὲν ἡγοῦνται Κόννου ψῆφον, τούτοισι δὲ δωρο-
φοροῦσιν   675
ὕρχας, οἶνον, δάπιδας, τυρόν, μέλι, σήσαμα, προσκεφάλαια,
φιάλας, χλανίδας, στεφάνους, ὅρμους, ἐκπώματα, πλουθυγιείαν.
σοὶ δ', ὧν ἄρχεις " πολλὰ μὲν ἐν γῇ, πολλὰ δ' ἐφ' ὑγρᾷ
πιτυλεύσας",
οὐδεὶς οὐδὲ σκορόδου κεφαλὴν τοῖς ἑψητοῖσι δίδωσιν.

Φι.   μὰ Δί', ἀλλὰ παρ' Εὐχαρίδου καὐτὸς τρεῖς ἄγλιθας
μετέπεμψα.   680
ἀλλ' αὐτήν μοι τὴν δουλείαν οὐκ ἀποφαίνων ἀποκναίεις.

Βδ.   οὐ γὰρ μεγάλη δουλεία 'στὶν τούτους μὲν ἅπαντας ἐν
ἀρχαῖς
αὐτούς τ' εἶναι καὶ τοὺς κόλακας τοὺς τούτων μισθο-
φοροῦντας;
σοὶ δ' ἤν τις δῷ τοὺς τρεῖς ὀβολούς, ἀγαπᾷς, οὓς αὐτὸς
ἐλαύνων
καὶ πεζομαχῶν καὶ πολιορκῶν ἐκτήσω πολλὰ πονήσας. 685
καὶ πρὸς τούτοις ἐπιταττόμενος φοιτᾷς, ὃ μάλιστά μ'
ἀπάγχει,
ὅταν εἰσελθὸν μειράκιόν σοι κατάπυγον, Χαιρέου υἱός,

673–4 (. . . -μενον) S § (1) η 589   673 (ὡς . . .)–674 S § (2) λ 14

---

673 ᾔσθοντο RΓJ   μὲν et τὸν ἄλλον om. S(1)(2)   674 λαγαριζ-
λΣᴸ-AldCS(1)(2) : λαγαρυζ- aS(1)ᵛ·ˡ·(2)ᵛ·ˡ·   τραγαγήζοντα Γ   675 μὲν
οὖν J   δωροδοκοῦσιν RΓJ   676 δασπίδας V   σήμαμον Γ   678 σοὶ
Flor. Chrest. : σὺ a   ἄρχης R   680 Φι. om. V   τρεῖς γ' RVΓ
681 ἀποκλέεις V   682 Βδ. om. V   δουλεί' 'στι J   ἅπαντα J
αρˣ R   684 σοῦ V   διδῶ J   ὀβελοὺς J   οἷς R   αὐτὸς om. Γ
685 καὶ πολυορκῶν Γ : κοπολιορκῶν V

ὡδὶ διαβάς, διακινηθεὶς τῷ σώματι καὶ τρυφερανθείς,
ἥκειν εἴπῃ πρῲ κἂν ὥρᾳ δικάσονθ'· "ὡς ὅστις ἂν ὑμῶν
ὕστερος ἔλθῃ τοῦ σημείου, τὸ τριώβολον οὐ κομιεῖται."
αὐτὸς δὲ φέρει τὸ συνηγορικὸν δραχμήν, κἂν ὕστερος
    ἔλθῃ·   691
καὶ κοινωνῶν τῶν ἀρχόντων ἑτέρῳ τινὶ τῶν μεθ' ἑαυτοῦ,
ἤν τίς τι διδῷ τῶν φευγόντων, ξυνθέντε τὸ πρᾶγμα δύ'
    ὄντε
ἐσπουδάκατον, κᾆθ' ὡς πρίονθ' ὁ μὲν ἕλκει, ὁ δ' ἀντενέ-
    δωκεν·
σὺ δὲ χασκάζεις τὸν κωλακρέτην, τὸ δὲ πραττόμενόν σε
    λέληθεν.   695

Φι.   ταυτί με ποιοῦσ'; οἴμοι, τί λέγεις; ὥς μου τὸν θῖνα
        ταράττεις,
    καὶ τὸν νοῦν μου προσάγεις μᾶλλον, κοὐκ οἶδ' ὅ τι χρῆμά
    με ποιεῖς.

Βδ.   σκέψαι τοίνυν ὡς ἐξόν σοι πλουτεῖν καὶ τοῖσιν ἅπασιν
    ὑπὸ τῶν ἀεὶ δημιζόντων οὐκ οἶδ' ὅπῃ ἐγκεκύκλησαι,
    ὅστις πόλεων ἄρχων πλείστων ἀπὸ τοῦ Πόντου μέχρι
        Σαρδοῦς   700
    οὐκ ἀπολαύεις πλὴν τοῦθ' ὃ φέρεις ἀκαρῆ· καὶ τοῦτ' ἐρίῳ
        σοι
    ἐνστάζουσιν κατὰ μικρὸν ἀεὶ τοῦ ζῆν ἕνεχ' ὥσπερ ἔλαιον.
    βούλονται γάρ σε πένητ' εἶναι, καὶ τοῦθ' ὧν εἵνεκ' ἐρῶ σοι·

695 § S κ 2234   697 (οὐκ . . .)–699 (. . . -όντων) § S χ 477
699 (οὐκ . . .) S § (1) a 801 ; § (2) ε 88 ; § Zonar. 608   701–3 (. . .
εἶναι) § S a 801

---

688 διακινηθὴς Γ   τρυφερωθεὶς ΓΒ₂   689 ἡμῶν J   690 ἔλθοι J
692 κοινωνος V: κοινωνὸν J: κοινῶν ὄντων Γ   693 τι om. VΓJ   ξυν-
θέντες Γ   694 ἐσπουδάκαται J   πρίονθ' Reisig: πρίον' RV: πρίων J:
πρίονες Γ   ἀντεν- H : ἀνταν- a   695 κωλαγρέτην R : κολακρετὴν Γ
σε om. J   696 Φι. om. V: par. R   697 ποιεῖ J   698 Βδ.
om. RVS   699 ὅπῃ S(1)(2) Zonar.: ὅποι a   702 ἕνεκ' RVJ
ἔλαιον VS: ἄλευρον RΓJ   703 τοῦθ' ὧν Bentley: τούτων a   ἐρῶ
σοι] ἔρρωσο J

ἵνα γιγνώσκῃς τὸν τιθασευτήν, κᾆθ᾽ ὅταν οὗτός γ᾽ ἐπισίξῃ
ἐπὶ τῶν ἐχθρῶν τιν᾽ ἐπιρρύξας, ἀγρίως αὐτοῖς ἐπιπηδᾷς.
εἰ γὰρ ἐβούλοντο βίον πορίσαι τῷ δήμῳ, ῥάδιον ἦν ἄν.   706
εἰσίν γε πόλεις χίλιαι αἳ νῦν τὸν φόρον ἡμῖν ἀπάγουσιν·
τούτων εἴκοσιν ἄνδρας βόσκειν εἴ τις προσέταξεν ἑκάστῃ,
δύο μυριάδ᾽ ἂν τῶν δημοτικῶν ἔζων ἐν πᾶσι λαγῴοις
καὶ στεφάνοισιν παντοδαποῖσιν καὶ πυῷ καὶ πυριάτῃ,   710
ἄξια τῆς γῆς ἀπολαύοντες καὶ τοῦ 'ν Μαραθῶνι τροπαίου.
νῦν δ᾽ ὥσπερ ἐλαολόγοι χωρεῖθ᾽ ἅμα τῷ τὸν μισθὸν ἔχοντι.

Φι.   οἴμοι, τί ποθ᾽ ὥσπερ νάρκη μου κατὰ τῆς χειρὸς καταχεῖται;
καὶ τὸ ξίφος οὐ δύναμαι κατέχειν, ἀλλ᾽ ἤδη μαλθακός εἰμι.

Βδ.   ἀλλ᾽ ὁπόταν μὲν δείσωσ᾽ αὐτοί, τὴν Εὔβοιαν διδόασιν   715
ὑμῖν, καὶ σῖτον ὑφίστανται κατὰ πεντήκοντα μεδίμνους
πορεῖν. ἔδοσαν δ᾽ οὐπώποτέ σοι· πλὴν πρώην πέντε
μεδίμνους,
καὶ ταῦτα μόλις ξενίας φεύγων, ἔλαβες κατὰ χοίνικα
κριθῶν.
ὧν εἵνεκ᾽ ἐγώ σ᾽ ἀπέκλειον ἀεὶ
βόσκειν ἐθέλων καὶ μὴ τούτους   720
ἐγχάσκειν σοι στομφάζοντας.
καὶ νῦν ἀτεχνῶς ἐθέλω παρέχειν
ὅ τι βούλει σοι,
πλὴν κωλακρέτου γάλα πίνειν.

712 (ὥσπερ . . .) §§ S ε 742   713–14 (. . . -έχειν) § S ν 38
722–4 § S κ 1929

---

704 γιν- ΓJ   τιθασευτήν q : τιθασσευτήν a   ἐπισίζῃ RJ   705 par. R
τὸν ἐχθρόν ΓJ   ἐπιρύξας R   ἄγριος V   709 μυριάδ᾽ ἂν Dobree :
μυριάδες a   ἔζων om. R   ἐν] ἂν B   ἅπασι J   710 καὶ (tertium)
om. Γ   πυαρίτη J   711 τρόπαιον V   712 ἔλαιο- RΓJ   -λόχοι R
713 Φι. om. V   ποθ᾽] πέπονθα S   715 Βδ. om. V : par. R   με Γ
εὖβοι J   716 κατά] καὶ τὰ Γ   717 πρώην R   718 ἔλαβες
Ald : ἔλαβε a   724 πλὴν q : πλὴν τοῦ aS   κωλαγρετου R² : κωλα-
κρέντρου J : κολακρέτου S   μάλα V

Χο. ἦ που σοφὸς ἦν ὅστις ἔφασκεν· "πρὶν ἂν ἀμφοῖν μῦθον
        ἀκούσῃς,   725
     οὐκ ἂν δικάσαις." σὺ γὰρ οὖν νῦν μοι νικᾶν πολλῷ
        δεδόκησαι·
     ὥστ' ἤδη τὴν ὀργὴν χαλάσας τοὺς σκίπωνας καταβάλλω.
     ἀλλ', ὦ τῆς ἡλικίας ἡμῖν τῆς αὐτῆς συνθιασῶτα,

     πιθοῦ πιθοῦ λόγοισι, μηδ' ἄφρων γένῃ   στρ.
     μηδ' ἀτενὴς ἄγαν ἀτεράμων τ' ἀνήρ.   730
     εἴθ' ὤφελέν μοι κηδεμὼν ἢ ξυγγενὴς
     εἶναί τις ὅστις τοιαῦτ' ἐνουθέτει.
     σοὶ δὲ νῦν τις θεῶν   733ᵃ
     παρὼν ἐμφανὴς   733ᵇ
     ξυλλαμβάνει τοῦ πράγματος, καὶ δῆλός ἐστιν εὖ ποιῶν·
     σὺ δὲ παρὼν δέχου.   735

Βδ. καὶ μὴν θρέψω γ' αὐτὸν παρέχων
     ὅσα πρεσβύτῃ ξύμφορα, χόνδρον
     λείχειν, χλαῖναν μαλακήν, σισύραν,
     πόρνην, ἥτις τὸ πέος τρίψει
     καὶ τὴν ὀσφῦν.   740
     ἀλλ' ὅτι σιγᾷ κοὐδὲν γρύζει,
     τοῦτ' οὐ δύναταί με προσέσθαι.

Χο. νενουθέτηκεν αὐτὸν ἐς τὰ πράγμαθ', οἷς   ἀντ.
     τότ' ἐπεμαίνετ'. ἔγνωκε γὰρ ἀρτίως,
     λογίζεταί τ' ἐκεῖνα πάνθ' ἁμαρτίας   745

725–7 §§ † S σ 578   741–2 § S π 2648

---

725 Χο. om. V   σοφός τις J   ἀκούσας V   727 σκίπωνας VJB₂:
σκιπίωνας R : σκήπωνας ΓS   -βάλω VΓ   730 ἀγενὴς R   ἀτεράμ-
μων R   732 εἶναί τις] εἶν' αἴτιος R   ὅστις δὴ q   733 σοὶ] νῦν J
734 ἐστιν om. RΓJ   ποῶν RΓ   737 πρεσβύτης J   738 λείπειν V
741 γρέζει J   742 δύναμαί τε Γ   με om. ΓJ   743 εἰς Γ   πράγμαθ' Dindorf: πράγματα a   οἷς τότ'] οἶος τ' J   744 ἔγνωκεν RVΓ
745 λογίζονται V

ἃ σοῦ κελεύοντος οὐκ ἐπείθετο.
νῦν δ᾽ ἴσως τοῖσι σοῖς 747ᵃ
λόγοις πείθεται, 747ᵇ
καὶ σωφρονεῖ μέντοι μεθιστὰς ἐς τὸ λοιπὸν τὸν τρόπον
πειθόμενός τέ σοι.

Φι. ἰώ μοί μοι. 750

Βδ. οὗτος, τί βοᾷς;

Φι. μή μοι τούτων μηδὲν ὑπισχνοῦ.
κείνων ἔραμαι, κεῖθι γενοίμαν,
ἵν᾽ ὁ κῆρυξ φησι· "τίς ἀψήφιστος; ἀνιστάσθω."
κἀπισταίην ἐπὶ τοῖς κημοῖς 755
ψηφιζομένων ὁ τελευταῖος.
"σπεῦδ᾽, ὦ ψυχή—". ποῦ μοι ψυχή; "πάρες, ὦ σκιερά—".
μὰ τὸν Ἡρακλέα μή νυν ἔτ᾽ ἐγὼ 'ν τοῖσι δικασταῖς
κλέπτοντα Κλέωνα λάβοιμι.

Βδ. ἴθ᾽, ὦ πάτερ, πρὸς τῶν θεῶν ἐμοὶ πιθοῦ. 760

Φι. τί σοι πίθωμαι; λέγ᾽ ὅ τι βούλει πλὴν ἑνός.

Βδ. ποίου; φέρ᾽ ἴδω.

Φι. τοῦ μὴ δικάζειν. τοῦτο δὲ
Ἅιδης διακρινεῖ πρότερον ἢ 'γὼ πείσομαι.

Βδ. σὺ δ᾽ οὖν, ἐπειδὴ τοῦτο κεχάρηκας ποιῶν,

764 An. Ox. i. 252. 7

746–60 fragmenta habet Π 746 ἃ om. V παρακελεύοντος q
747 ἴσος V τοῖσι σοῖς Invernizi: τοῖς ἴσοις RVΓ:]ισοις Π: τοῖς ἴσοι
καὶ J 748 φρονεῖ J 751 τί ΠV: τί μοι RΓJ 752 Φι. om.
RV: [Π] 754 φησις Π: φασὶ V 756 τελευσταῖος J 757 σπένδ'
V σοι R: [Π] 758 ἐγὼ 'ν q: ἐγὼν ἐν a: [Π] 761 Φι. om.
V: par. R πίθωμαι Tyrwhitt: πείθομαι a Βδ. λέγ᾽ ΓJ λέγοντι (?) R
πλὴν] περὶ J 762 Βδ. Bergler: par. R: Φι. ΓJ: om. V Φι. Bergler:
dic. R: Βδ. ΓJ: om. V Φι. τοῦτο Γ: Φι. τουτί J 763 par. R
κρινεῖ J 764 Βδ. om. V: par. R ποῶν RVΓ

ἐκεῖσε μὲν μηκέτι βάδιζ', ἀλλ' ἐνθάδε   765
αὐτοῦ μένων δίκαζε τοῖσιν οἰκέταις.

Φι.   περὶ τοῦ; τί ληρεῖς;

Βδ.   ταῦθ' ἅπερ ἐκεῖ πράττεται.
ὅτι τὴν θύραν ἀνέῳξεν ἡ σηκὶς λάθρᾳ,
ταύτης ἐπιβολὴν ψηφιεῖ μίαν μόνην·
πάντως δὲ κἀκεῖ ταῦτ' ἔδρας ἑκάστοτε.   770
καὶ ταῦτα μὲν νῦν εὐλόγως, ἢν ἐξέχῃ
εἴλη κατ' ὄρθρον, ἡλιάσει πρὸς ἥλιον·
ἐὰν δὲ νείφῃ, πρὸς τὸ πῦρ καθήμενος·
ὕοντος εἴσει· κἂν ἔγρῃ μεσημβρινός,
οὐδείς σ' ἀποκλείσει θεσμοθέτης τῇ κιγκλίδι.   775

Φι.   τουτί μ' ἀρέσκει.

Βδ.   πρὸς δὲ τούτοις γ', ἢν δίκην
λέγῃ μακράν τις, οὐχὶ πεινῶν ἀναμενεῖς
δάκνων σεαυτὸν καὶ τὸν ἀπολογούμενον.

Φι.   πῶς οὖν διαγιγνώσκειν καλῶς δυνήσομαι
ὥσπερ πρότερον τὰ πράγματ' ἔτι μασώμενος;   780

Βδ.   πολλῷ γ' ἄμεινον· καὶ λέγεται γὰρ τουτογί,
ὡς οἱ δικασταὶ ψευδομένων τῶν μαρτύρων
μόλις τὸ πρᾶγμ' ἔγνωσαν ἀναμασώμενοι.

Φι.   ἀνά τοί με πείθεις. ἀλλ' ἐκεῖν' οὔπω λέγεις,
τὸν μισθὸν ὁπόθεν λήψομαι.

769 § S ε 2240; § Zonar. 800   771–2 S ε 1684   775 §§ S θ
266   783 § S a 1957; §§ Zonar. 202; Apostol. 11. 77a

767 Φι. om. V: par. R   ταῦτ' R   πράττετε Γ₂   768 συκὶς J
770 πάντες V   γε B   771 ἂν J   772 ἔλη R   ὀρθὸν νρΣΓ
ἡλιάσει MacDowell: ἡλιάσει VΓJ: ἐλιάσει R: ἡλιάσῃ S   773 νίφη
VΓJ   774 υἵοντας V   775 οὐδείς σ' q: οὐδεὶς VΓS: οὐδεὶσ' J:
οὐ δεῖ σ' R   ἀποκλείσῃ J   κιγκλήδι Γ   776 Βδ. om. R: dic. V
γ' om. J   777 μακακράν R   778 δάκνων J   779 Φι. om. V
διαγιν- ΓJ   781 Βδ. om. V   τουτουὶ V   783 ἀναμασσ- Sᵛ·ˡ·
Zonar. Apostol.   -όμενοι Zonar.   784 Φι. om. V

Βδ.   παρ' ἐμοῦ.

Φι.   καλῶς,   785
ὁτιὴ κατ' ἐμαυτὸν κοὐ μεθ' ἑτέρου λήψομαι.
αἴσχιστα γάρ τοί μ' ἠργάσατο Λυσίστρατος
ὁ σκωπτόλης. δραχμὴν μετ' ἐμοῦ πρῴην λαβὼν
ἐλθὼν διεκερματίζετ' ἐν τοῖς ἰχθύσιν,
κᾆπειτ' ἐνέθηκε τρεῖς λοπίδας μοι κεστρέων,   790
κἀγὼ 'νέκαψ'· ὀβολοὺς γὰρ ᾠόμην λαβεῖν.
κᾆτα βδελυχθεὶς ὀσφρόμενος ἐξέπτυσα·
κᾆθ' εἷλκον αὐτόν.

Βδ.   ὁ δὲ τί πρὸς ταῦτ' εἶφ';

Φι.   ὅ τι;
ἀλεκτρυόνος μ' ἔφασκε κοιλίαν ἔχειν.
"ταχὺ γοῦν καθέψεις τἀργύριον," ᾖ δ' ὃς λέγων.   795

Βδ.   ὁρᾷς ὅσον καὶ τοῦτο δῆτα κερδανεῖς.

Φι.   οὐ πάνυ τι μικρόν. ἀλλ' ὅπερ μέλλεις ποίει.

Βδ.   ἀνάμενέ νυν· ἐγὼ δὲ ταῦθ' ἥξω φέρων.

Φι.   ὅρα τὸ χρῆμα, τὰ λόγι' ὡς περαίνεται.
ἠκηκόειν γὰρ ὡς Ἀθηναῖοί ποτε   800
δικάσοιεν ἐπὶ ταῖς οἰκίαισι τὰς δίκας,
κἂν τοῖς προθύροις ἐνοικοδομήσει πᾶς ἀνὴρ

788 (δραχμὴν . . .)–789 Poll. 9. 89   792 §§ S ε 1227
794–5 (. . . -ριον) §§ S a 1117

785–6 Βδ. παρ' . . . λήψομαι om. J   785 Φι. om. R   786 par. R
787 ἠργ- Starkie : εἰργ- a   788 σκωπτόλις R : συνπτόλης J   δαρχμὴν R
πρώϊην R   789 διεκρεμ- J   -ατιζέμ' RΓJ   **790–808 fragmenta
habet Π**   790 κᾆπειτ' ἐνέθηκε Bergk : κάπειθεν ἔθηκεν V : κᾆπειτ'
ἐπέθηκε RJ : κᾆπειτ' ἀπέθηκε Γ :]εγεθ[Π   792 βδελυθεὶς J   ὀσφραι-
νόμενος R : ὀσφρώμενος Γ : [Π]   793 εἷλκον Γ Βδ. om. V ὁ om. J
794 ἀλεκτυ- J   -όνας Rᵃᶜ   795 γοῦν] γὰρ S   κατεψεῖς S   γ' αργ[Π
796 οσ ὅσον V   καὶ τοῦτο δῆτα ΠRΓ : καὶ τοῦτο V : δῆτα καὶ τοῦτο J
797 πόει RVΓ : [Π]   798 Βδ. om. V   801 δικάσειεν J   ]κειαισι Π
802 ἀνοικο- RΓ : [Π]

αὐτῷ δικαστηρίδιον μικρὸν πάνυ,
ὥσπερ Ἑκαταῖον πανταχοῦ πρὸ τῶν θυρῶν.

Βδ. ἰδού. τί ἔτ᾽ ἐρεῖς; ὡς ἅπαντ᾽ ἐγὼ φέρω,   805
ὅσαπέρ γ᾽ ἔφασκον κάτι πολλῷ πλείονα.
ἁμὶς μέν, ἢν οὐρητιάσῃς, αὑτηὶ
παρὰ σοὶ κρεμήσετ᾽ ἐγγὺς ἐπὶ τοῦ παττάλου.

Φι. σοφόν γε τουτὶ καὶ γέροντι πρόσφορον
ἐξηῦρες ἀτεχνῶς φάρμακον στραγγουρίας.   810

Βδ. καὶ πῦρ γε τουτί· καὶ προσέστηκεν φακῆ
ῥοφεῖν, ἐὰν δέῃ τι.

Φι.   τοῦτ᾽ αὖ δεξιόν.
κἂν γὰρ πυρέττω, τόν γε μισθὸν λήψομαι·
αὐτοῦ μένων γὰρ τὴν φακῆν ῥοφήσομαι.
ἀτὰρ τί τὸν ὄρνιν ὡς ἔμ᾽ ἐξηνέγκατε;   815

Βδ. ἵνα γ᾽, ἢν καθεύδῃς ἀπολογουμένου τινός,
ᾄδων ἄνωθεν ἐξεγείρῃ σ᾽ οὑτοσί.

Φι. ἓν ἔτι ποθῶ, τὰ δ᾽ ἄλλ᾽ ἀρέσκει μοι.

Βδ.   τὸ τί;

Φι. θηρῷον εἴ πως ἐκκομίσαις τὸ τοῦ Λύκου.

Βδ. πάρεστι τουτί, καὐτὸς ἄναξ οὑτοσί.   820

Φι. ὦ δέσποθ᾽ ἥρως, ὡς χαλεπὸν ἄρ᾽ ἦν σ᾽ ἰδεῖν.

Βδ. οἷόσπερ ἡμῖν φαίνεται Κλεώνυμος.

Φι. οὔκουν ἔχει γ᾽ οὐδ᾽ αὐτὸς ἥρως ὢν ὅπλα.

807–10 § S a 1590   819 ‡ Hdn. ap. *An. Ox.* iii. 253. 9

___

804 Ἑκατεῖον νρΣAld   805 dic. ante τί R   806 γ᾽ om. V
807 οὐρητιήσῃς V   808 ἠρεμήσεται S   810 ἐξηῦρες Meineke:
ἐξεῦρες aS   811 Βδ. om. RVJ   812 Φι.] dic. RV   813 par.
RV   περέττω J   **814–19 fragmenta habet Π**   815 ἐμὸν J
816 Βδ. om. R   817 αὐτοσί R   818 πυθῶ J   ἀλλ᾽ om. R
819 ἡρῷον εἴ πως μοι κομίσαιο τοῦ Λύκου Hdn.:]ει πως ε[Π   820 Βδ.
om. V   πάρεστη R   821 χαλεπὸς B   ἦν σ᾽ Post: ᾖσθ᾽ a   822 Βδ.
Bergk: om. a   823 Φι. Bergk: Οι. RΓJ: om. V   γ᾽ οὐδ᾽] δ᾽ J

D

Βδ.   εἰ θᾶττον ἐκαθίζου σύ, θᾶττον ἂν δίκην
      ἐκάλουν.

Φι.   κάλει νυν, ὡς κάθημ' ἐγὼ πάλαι.   825

Βδ.   φέρε νυν, τίν' αὐτῷ πρῶτον εἰσαγάγω δίκην;
      τί τις κακὸν δέδρακε τῶν ἐν τῇ οἰκίᾳ;
      ἡ Θρᾷττα προσκαύσασα πρώην τὴν χύτραν—

Φι.   ἐπίσχες, οὗτος· ὡς ὀλίγου μ' ἀπώλεσας.
      ἄνευ δρυφάκτου τὴν δίκην μέλλεις καλεῖν,   830
      ὃ πρῶτον ἡμῖν τῶν ἱερῶν ἐφαίνετο;

Βδ.   μὰ τὸν Δί' οὐ πάρεστιν.

Φι.   ἀλλ' ἐγὼ δραμὼν
      αὐτὸς κομιοῦμαι τό γε παραυτίκ' ἔνδοθεν.

Βδ.   τί ποτε τὸ χρῆμ'; ὡς δεινὸν ἡ φιλοχωρία.

Ξα.   βάλλ' ἐς κόρακας. τοιουτονὶ τρέφειν κύνα.   835

Βδ.   τί δ' ἐστὶν ἐτεόν;

Ξα.   οὐ γὰρ ὁ Λάβης ἀρτίως,
      ὁ κύων, παράξας εἰς τὸν ἱπνὸν ἁρπάσας
      τροφαλίδα τυροῦ Σικελικὴν κατεδήδοκεν;

Βδ.   τοῦτ' ἆρα πρῶτον τἀδίκημα τῷ πατρὶ
      εἰσακτέον μοι. σὺ δὲ κατηγόρει παρών.   840

Ξα.   μὰ Δί' οὐκ ἔγωγ', ἀλλ' ἅτερός φησιν κύων
      κατηγορήσειν, ἤν τις εἰσάγῃ γραφήν.

      838 §§ S τ 1059

---

824 Βδ. om. V   ἐκκαθίζου J   825–30 versuum initia habet Π
825–6 om. V   825 Φι. om. R   826 Βδ. om. R : par. Π   εἰσαγω
R   827 τίς τί J   δέδραχε V   828 πρώιην R   829 par. ΠR
830 μέλεις V : μέλλει J   831 κατεφαίνετο J   832 Βδ. om. V
Φι. Beer : om. a   833 γε] τε V   834 Βδ. ΣνΓ : par. R : om. VΓJ
835 Ξα. Brunck : Οι. a   836 par. R   Ξα. Brunck : Οι. ΓJ : dic.
V : om. R   838 σικελὴν RVJS   κατεδουσιν Γ₂ : om. Γ₁   839 Βδ.
om. V   841 Ξα. Brunck : Οι. ΓJ : par. R : dic. V

Βδ.   ἴθι νυν, ἄγ' αὐτὼ δεῦρο.

Ξα.   ταῦτα χρὴ ποιεῖν.

Βδ.   τουτὶ τί ἐστι;

Φι.   χοιροκομεῖον Ἑστίας.

Βδ.   εἶθ' ἱεροσυλήσας φέρεις;

Φι.   οὔκ, ἀλλ' ἵνα   845
ἀφ' Ἑστίας ἀρχόμενος ἐπιτρίψω τινά.
ἀλλ' εἴσαγ' ἀνύσας, ὡς ἐγὼ τιμᾶν βλέπω.

Βδ.   φέρε νυν, ἐνέγκω τὰς σανίδας καὶ τὰς γραφάς.

Φι.   οἴμοι, διατρίβεις κἀπολεῖς τριψημερῶν.
ἐγὼ δ' ἀλοκίζειν ἐδεόμην τὸ χωρίον.   850

Βδ.   ἰδού.

Φι.   κάλει νυν.

Βδ.   ταῦτα δή.

Φι.   τίς οὑτοσὶ
ὁ πρῶτός ἐστιν;

Βδ.   ἐς κόρακας. ὡς ἄχθομαι,
ὁτιὴ 'πελαθόμην τοὺς καδίσκους ἐκφέρειν.   853

Φι.   οὗτος σύ, ποῖ θεῖς;

Βδ.   ἐπὶ καδίσκους.

850 § S a 1324; § Zonar. 137

---

843 αὐτὼ *t*: αὐτῶι R: αὐτῶ VΓJ   Ξα. Brunck: Οι. ΓJ: om. RV
ποιεῖν RΓ   844 Βδ. Beer: par. R: dic. V: Φι. ΓJ   ἐστιν Γ   Φι.
Beer: dic. RV: Οι. ΓJ   χειρο- J   845 Βδ. Beer: par. R: dic. V:
Φι. ΓJ   Φι. Beer: dic. R: Οι. ΓJ: om. V   846 par. R   847 Φι. RΓJ:
dic. V: om. Beer   848 Βδ. om. R: dic. V: Οι. Γ   849 par. R: dic.
V   διατρίψεις VJ   851 Βδ. (prius) om. VJ: Οι. Γ   Φι. (prius) Bergler:
om. a   Βδ. (secundum) om. RΓ: dic. V   Φι. (secundum)] dic. RV
τιό J   852 dic. V   Βδ.] dic. RV: Οι. Γ   εἰς R¹: ἧς RˢVΓ
dic. ante ὡς V   853 par. R   ὅτι ὑπ- V   -ιλαθόμην RΓJ
854 dic. V   σύ] σοι V   Βδ.] dic. RV: Οι. Γ   καδίκους R

Φι.   μηδαμῶς·
    ἐγὼ γὰρ εἶχον τούσδε τοὺς ἀρυστίχους.   855

Βδ. κάλλιστα τοίνυν. πάντα γὰρ πάρεστι νῷν
    ὅσων δεόμεθα—πλήν γε δὴ τῆς κλεψύδρας.

Φι. ἡδὶ δὲ δὴ τίς ἐστιν; οὐχὶ κλεψύδρα;

Βδ. εὖ γ᾽ ἐκπορίζεις αὐτὰ κἀπιχωρίως.
    ἀλλ᾽ ὡς τάχιστα πῦρ τις ἐξενεγκάτω   860
    καὶ μυρρίνας καὶ τὸν λιβανωτὸν ἔνδοθεν,
    ὅπως ἂν εὐξώμεσθα πρῶτα τοῖς θεοῖς.

Χο. καὶ μὴν ἡμεῖς
    ἐπὶ ταῖς σπονδαῖς καὶ ταῖς εὐχαῖς
    φήμην ἀγαθὴν λέξομεν ὑμῖν,   865
    ὅτι γενναίως ἐκ τοῦ πολέμου
    καὶ τοῦ νείκους ξυνέβητον.

Βδ. εὐφημία μὲν πρῶτα νῦν ὑπαρχέτω.

Χο. ὦ Φοῖβ᾽ Ἄπολλον Πύθι᾽, ἐπ᾽ ἀγαθῇ τύχῃ

    τὸ πρᾶγμ᾽, ὃ μηχανᾶται   στρ. 870
    ἔμπροσθεν οὗτος τῶν θυρῶν,
    ἅπασιν ἡμῖν ἁρμόσαι
    παυσαμένοις πλάνων.

    ἰήιε Παιάν.

855 Ath. 424 c

---

854 Φι. (secundum)] dic. RV   855 par. R   τούσδε om. R
-ίκους Rᵃᶜ: -ίσκους Rᵖᶜ   856 par. R: dic. V: Οι. Γ   κάλιστα V
858 Φι. om. V: par. R   859 Βδ. om. V: par. R: Οι. Γ   γε
πορίζεις J   860 par. R: Φι. Γ   τίς πῦρ J   861 om. V
863–9 fragmenta habet Π   864 ταῖσπονδαῖς R: ται̣ς[Π
865 ἕξομεν RᵃᶜV:]μεν Π   867 ξυνεκτον V   868 par. R: [Π]
869 Χο. om. Γ: par. V: [Π]   πυθ᾽ ἡ ἐτ᾽ Γ: [Π]   870 δ] οὐ V
871 ἐνπ- R   873 πλάνου Γ

Βδ. ὦ δέσποτ' ἄναξ γεῖτον Ἀγυιεῦ, τοῦ 'μοῦ προθύρου προπύλαιε, 875
δέξαι τελετὴν καινήν, ὦ 'ναξ, ἣν τῷ πατρὶ καινοτομοῦμεν.
παῦσόν τ' αὐτοῦ τουτὶ τὸ λίαν στρυφνὸν καὶ πρίνινον ἦθος,
ἀντὶ σιραίου μέλιτος σμικρὸν τῷ θυμιδίῳ παραμείξας.
ἤδη δ' εἶναι τοῖς ἀνθρώποις ἤπιον αὐτόν,
τοὺς φεύγοντάς τ' ἐλεεῖν μᾶλλον τῶν γραψαμένων, 880
κἀπιδακρύειν ἀντιβολούντων,
καὶ παυσάμενον τῆς δυσκολίας
ἀπὸ τῆς ὀργῆς
τὴν ἀκαλήφην ἀφελέσθαι.

Χο. ξυνευχόμεσθα ταῦτά σοι κἀπᾴδομεν 885
νέαισιν ἀρχαῖς εἵνεκα τῶν προλελεγμένων.

εὖνοι γάρ ἐσμεν ἐξ οὗ ἀντ.
τὸν δῆμον ᾐσθόμεσθά σου
φιλοῦντος ὡς οὐδεὶς ἀνὴρ
τῶν γε νεωτέρων. 890

Βδ. εἴ τις θύρασιν ἡλιαστής, εἰσίτω·
ὡς ἡνίκ' ἂν λέγωσιν, οὐκ ἐσφρήσομεν.

Φι. τίς ἄρ' ὁ φεύγων οὗτος; ὅσον ἁλώσεται.

Βδ. ἀκούετ' ἤδη τῆς γραφῆς. "ἐγράψατο

880–1 §§ S φ 236   882 (παυ– . . .)–884 §§ S a 787; §§ Zonar. 102

875–8 fragmenta habet Π   875 Βδ. om. R : dic. V : [Π]   ἀγνεῦ
Γ : [Π]   προθύρου] προυπύλου V :]ρρ[Π   προπύλαιε Bentley : πρὸς πύλας
a : [Π]   877 αὐτὸ R : [Π]   πρίνιον J   878 σεραίου J : [Π]
μικρὸν RV : [Π]   -μείξας Starkie : -μίξας **Πα**   880 καὶ τοὺς RΓJ
τ' om. ΓS   882 -μένης J   884 ἀκαλήφου J   885 -μεθά Γ]
ταῦτά Dindorf : om. **a**   886 ἐν νέαισιν RΓJ   888 ἠδό- V   -μεθά
RΓJ   889 οὐδεὶς q : οὐδὲ εἷς **a**   890 γε νεωτέρων Reisig : νεωτέρων
ᵞᴾΣV : γενναιοτέρων **a** : νῦν γε σοῦ νεωτέρων q   891 θύραισιν Γ
892 εἰσ- J   893 ὅσον οὗτος J   894 Οι. RΓJ   ἀκούτ' Γ   γραφῆς
Bentley : γραφῆς ἧς **a**

Κύων Κυδαθηναιεὺς Λάβητ' Αἰξωνέα   895
τὸν τυρὸν ἀδικεῖν ὅτι μόνος κατήσθιεν
τὸν Σικελικόν. τίμημα κλῳὸς σύκινος."

Φι.   θάνατος μὲν οὖν κύνειος, ἢν ἅπαξ ἁλῷ.

Βδ.   καὶ μὴν ὁ φεύγων οὑτοσὶ Λάβης πάρα.

Φι.   ὦ μιαρὸς οὗτος. ὡς δὲ καὶ κλέπτον βλέπει.   900
οἷον σεσηρὼς ἐξαπατήσειν μ' οἴεται.
ποῦ δ' ὅ γε διώκων, ὁ Κυδαθηναιεὺς κύων;

ΚΥΩΝ

αὖ αὖ.

Βδ.   πάρεστιν.

Φι.   ἕτερος οὗτος αὖ Λάβης,
ἀγαθός γ' ὑλακτεῖν καὶ διαλείχειν τὰς χύτρας.

Βδ.   σῖγα, κάθιζε. σὺ δ' ἀναβὰς κατηγόρει.   905

Φι.   φέρε νυν, ἅμα τήνδ' ἐγχεάμενος κἀγὼ ῥοφῶ.

Κυ.   τῆς μὲν γραφῆς ἠκούσαθ' ἣν ἐγραψάμην,
ἄνδρες δικασταί, τουτονί. δεινότατα γὰρ
ἔργων δέδρακε κἀμὲ καὶ τὸ ῥυππαπαῖ.
ἀποδρὰς γὰρ ἐς τὴν γωνίαν τυρὸν πολὺν   910
κατεσικέλιζε κἀνέπλητ' ἐν τῷ σκότῳ.

Φι.   νὴ τὸν Δί', ἀλλὰ δῆλός ἐστ'· ἔμοιγέ τοι
τυροῦ κάκιστον ἀρτίως ἐνήρυγεν
ὁ βδελυρὸς οὗτος.

900 (ὡς . . .)–901 § S κ 1740

_____

895 Αἰξωνέα] ++ωνεα J   ¦896 τηρὸν Γ   900 Φι. om. V   καὶ
om. V   901 ἐξαναστήσειν ΓΒ₂   902 par. R   ὅ γε MacDowell:
ὄυ' Γ: οὐ VJ: ὁ R   -ναιὲς J   903 ΚΥΩΝ] Βδ. R   Βδ. om. R:
Φι. VΓ   Φι. Dobree: om. a   οὗτος semel VΓ: bis R: om. J
904 par. R   γ' om. Γ   905 Βδ.] κῆρυξ VJ   907 Οι. RΓJ
ἦν] ἦς ΓΒ₂   909 ἔργον J   ῥυπαπαὶ VJ   910 ἀποδρὰις R   εἰς J
911 κἀνέπληττ' J   912 Φι. om. V   914 βδελλυρὸς Γ

Κυ.　　　　　κοὐ μετέδωκ' αἰτοῦντί μοι.
κἀίτοι τίς ὑμᾶς εὖ ποιεῖν δυνήσεται,　　　915
ἢν μή τι κἀμοί τις προβάλλῃ, τῷ κυνί;

Φι.　οὐδὲν μετέδωκεν οὐδὲ τῷ κοινῷ γ', ἐμοί.
θερμὸς γὰρ ἀνὴρ οὐδὲν ἧττον τῆς φακῆς.

Βδ.　πρὸς τῶν θεῶν, μὴ προκαταγίγνωσκ', ὦ πάτερ,
πρὶν ἄν γ' ἀκούσῃς ἀμφοτέρων.

Φι.　　　　　ἀλλ', ὦ 'γαθέ,　　　920
τὸ πρᾶγμα φανερόν ἐστιν· αὐτὸ γὰρ βοᾷ.

Κυ.　μή νυν ἀφῆτέ γ' αὐτόν, ὡς ὄντ' αὖ πολὺ
κυνῶν ἀπάντων ἄνδρα μονοφαγίστατον,
ὅστις περιπλεύσας τὴν θυείαν ἐν κύκλῳ
ἐκ τῶν πόλεων τὸ σκῖρον ἐξεδήδοκεν.　　　925

Φι.　ἐμοὶ δέ γ' οὐκ ἔστ' οὐδὲ τὴν ὑδρίαν πλάσαι.

Κυ.　πρὸς ταῦτα τοῦτον κολάσατ' (οὐ γὰρ ἄν ποτε
τρέφειν δύναιτ' ἄν μία λόχμη κλέπτα δύο),
ἵνα μὴ κεκλάγω διὰ κενῆς ἄλλως ἐγώ·
ἐὰν δὲ μή, τὸ λοιπὸν οὐ κεκλάγξομαι.　　　930

Φι.　ἰοὺ ἰού.
ὅσας κατηγόρησε τὰς πανουργίας.
κλέπτον τὸ χρῆμα τἀνδρός. οὐ καὶ σοὶ δοκεῖ,
ὦ 'λεκτρυών; νὴ τὸν Δί' ἐπιμύει γέ τοι.
ὁ θεσμοθέτης· ποῦ 'σθ' οὗτος; ἀμίδα μοι δότω.　　　935

923-5 §§ S σ 621　　　935 § Sch. Aeschin. 3. 14

914 Κυ. Scaliger: om. a　　915 par. RV　ποεῖν Γ　917 Φι.
Tyrwhitt: par. V: Κυ. R: Οι. ΓJ　dic. ante οὐδὲ V: Κυ. J　κυνῶι R
918 Φι. RΓJ: par. V: del Bergk　919 -γίγνωσκ' Brunck: -γίνωσκ' a
920 ἄν ἀκούσῃς γ' J　921 γὰρ om. R　922 Κυ. Beer: Οι. RΓJ:
συνηγ V　923 ἄνδρα om. S　μου ὀφαγ- J　925 τό] τὸν R
σκίρρον S　927 Κυ. om. RV: Οι. Γ　τοῦτον] τοῦτο μὴ R　κολά-
σαντ' V　928 λόγχμη Rac J: λόγχη V　δύω RVΓ　929 δια-
κεκλάγγω V　930 οὐκ ἐκλαίξομαι J　932 ὅσα κατηγόρευσε J
933 κλέπτου J　σοί] σὺ R　934 -τρυόν R: -τυόν Γac　τοι] γοι J
935 θεσμότης J

Βδ. αὐτὸς καθελοῦ· τοὺς μάρτυρας γὰρ ἐσκαλῶ.
Λάβητι μάρτυρας παρεῖναι τρύβλιον,
δοίδυκα, τυρόκνηστιν, ἐσχάραν, χύτραν,
καὶ τἄλλα τὰ σκεύη τὰ προσκεκαυμένα.
ἀλλ' ἔτι σύ γ' οὐρεῖς καὶ καθίζεις οὐδέπω;   940

Φι. τοῦτον δέ γ' οἶμ' ἐγὼ χεσεῖσθαι τήμερον.

Βδ. οὐκ αὖ σὺ παύσει χαλεπὸς ὢν καὶ δύσκολος,
καὶ ταῦτα τοῖς φεύγουσιν, ἀλλ' ὀδὰξ ἔχει;
ἀνάβαιν', ἀπολογοῦ. τί σεσιώπηκας; λέγε.

Φι. ἀλλ' οὐκ ἔχειν οὗτός γ' ἔοικεν ὅ τι λέγῃ.   945

Βδ. οὔκ, ἀλλ' ἐκεῖνό μοι δοκεῖ πεπονθέναι,
ὅπερ ποτὲ φεύγων ἔπαθε καὶ Θουκυδίδης·
ἀπόπληκτος ἐξαίφνης ἐγένετο τὰς γνάθους.
πάρεχ' ἐκποδών· ἐγὼ γὰρ ἀπολογήσομαι.
χαλεπὸν μέν, ὦ 'νδρες, ἐστὶ διαβεβλημένου   950
ὑπεραποκρίνεσθαι κυνός, λέξω δ' ὅμως.
ἀγαθὸς γάρ ἐστι καὶ διώκει τοὺς λύκους.

Φι. κλέπτης μὲν οὖν οὗτός γε καὶ ξυνωμότης.

Βδ. μὰ Δί', ἀλλ' ἄριστός ἐστι τῶν νυνὶ κυνῶν,
οἷός τε πολλοῖς προβατίοις ἐφεστάναι.   955

Φι. τί οὖν ὄφελος, τὸν τυρὸν εἰ κατεσθίει;

Βδ. ὅ τι; σοῦ προμάχεται καὶ φυλάττει τὴν θύραν,
καὶ τἄλλ' ἄριστός ἐστιν. εἰ δ' ὑφείλετο,
σύγγνωθι· κιθαρίζειν γὰρ οὐκ ἐπίσταται.

946 (ἀλλ' . . .)–948 §§ S γ 323

936 Βδ.] θεσμο. VΓJ   937 τρυβλεῖον V   938 dic. V   τυρόκνυστιν J
939 dic. V   940 Φι. οὐδέπω J   941 Φι. om. J   τούτων V
942 αὖ] ἂν VJ   943 Φι. ἀλλ' Γ   944 Φι. RJ   945 par. R : Βδ.
J : om. Γ   λέγει Γ   946 Βδ. Brunck : par. RV : Φι. J : om. Γ
948 ἐξαίφνης om. S   949 par. R : Βδ. VΓJ : del. Brunck
950 -μένους RVJ   953 οὖν om. R   954 νῦν J

Φι.   ἐγὼ δ' ἐβουλόμην ἂν οὐδὲ γράμματα,   960
       ἵνα μὴ κακουργῶν ἐνέγραφ' ἡμῖν τὸν λόγον.

Βδ.   ἄκουσον, ὦ δαιμόνιε, μου τῶν μαρτύρων.
       ἀνάβηθι, τυρόκνηστι, καὶ λέξον μέγα·
       σὺ γὰρ ταμιεύουσ' ἔτυχες. ἀπόκριναι σαφῶς,
       εἰ μὴ κατέκνησας τοῖς στρατιώταις ἄλαβες.   965
       φησὶ κατακνῆσαι.

Φι.   νὴ Δί', ἀλλὰ ψεύδεται.

Βδ.   ὦ δαιμόνι', ἐλέει τοὺς ταλαιπωρουμένους.
       οὗτος γὰρ ὁ Λάβης καὶ τραχήλι' ἐσθίει
       καὶ τὰς ἀκάνθας, κοὐδέποτ' ἐν ταὐτῷ μένει.
       ὁ δ' ἕτερος οἷός ἐστιν. οἰκουρὸς μόνον·   970
       αὐτοῦ μένων γάρ, ἅττ' ἂν εἴσω τις φέρῃ,
       τούτων μεταιτεῖ τὸ μέρος· εἰ δὲ μή, δάκνει.

Φι.   αἰβοῖ, τί τόδε ποτ' ἔσθ' ὅτῳ μαλάττομαι;
       κακόν τι περιβαίνει με, κἀναπείθομαι.

Βδ.   ἴθ', ἀντιβολῶ σ', οἰκτίρατ' αὐτόν, ὦ πάτερ,   975
       καὶ μὴ διαφθείρητε. ποῦ τὰ παιδία;
       ἀναβαίνετ', ὦ πόνηρα, καὶ κνυζούμενα
       αἰτεῖτε κἀντιβολεῖτε καὶ δακρύετε.

Φι.   κατάβα, κατάβα, κατάβα, κατάβα.

Βδ.   καταβήσομαι.
       καίτοι τὸ "κατάβα" τοῦτο πολλοὺς δὴ πάνυ   980
       ἐξηπάτηκεν. ἀτὰρ ὅμως καταβήσομαι.

Φι.   ἐς κόρακας. ὡς οὐκ ἀγαθόν ἐστι τὸ ῥοφεῖν.

---

962 Κυ. R : par. V : om. J   964 ἀπόκρινε R   965 κατέκνισας V
ἄλαβαις V   966 Βδ. J   κατακνίσαι V   Φι. om. R : dic. V
967 τοὺς om. q   970 Φι. R   μόνος Rᵃᶜ : μόνος φύλαξ V
971 φένηι R : φέρει VᵃᶜΓᵃᶜ   973 Φι. om. V   τόδε MacDowell : τὸ
κακὸν a : κακὸν q   974 περβαίνει V : παραβαίνει J : περὶ μένει R
975 οἰκτίρατ' van Herwerden : οἰκτείρατ' a   978 αἰτεῖ R
979 Φι. om. R   κατάβα quater q : ter a   Βδ. om. V   980 ἤδη V
981 αὐτὰρ V   982 Φι. om. V   ἐς q : ἧς a   τὸ] τὸρ V

ἐγὼ γὰρ ἀπεδάκρυσα νῦν γνώμην ἐμὴν
οὐδέν ποτέ γ' ἀλλ' ἢ τῆς φακῆς ἐμπλήμενος.

Βδ. οὔκουν ἀποφεύγει δῆτα;

Φι.   χαλεπὸν εἰδέναι.   985

Βδ. ἴθ', ὦ πατρίδιον, ἐπὶ τὰ βελτίω τρέπου.
      τηνδὶ λαβὼν τὴν ψῆφον ἐπὶ τὸν ὕστερον
      μύσας παρᾷξον κἀπόλυσον, ὦ πάτερ.

Φι. οὐ δῆτα· κιθαρίζειν γὰρ οὐκ ἐπίσταμαι.

Βδ. φέρε νύν σε τῃδὶ τὴν ταχίστην περιάγω.   990

Φι. ὅδ' ἔσθ' ὁ πρότερος;

Βδ.   οὗτος.

Φι.   αὕτη 'ντευθενί.

Βδ. ἐξηπάτηται κἀπολέλυκεν οὐχ ἑκών.
      φέρ' ἐξεράσω.

Φι.   πῶς ἄρ' ἠγωνίσμεθα;

Βδ. δείξειν ἔοικεν. ἐκπέφευγας, ὦ Λάβης.
      πάτερ πάτερ, τί πέπονθας; οἴμοι. ποῦ 'σθ' ὕδωρ;   995
      ἔπαιρε σαυτόν.

Φι.   εἰπέ νυν ἐκεῖνό μοι·
      ὄντως ἀπέφυγε;

Βδ.   νὴ Δί'.

Φι.   οὐδέν εἰμ' ἄρα.

Βδ. μὴ φροντίσῃς, ὦ δαιμόνι', ἀλλ' ἀνίστασο.

---

984 ἐμπεπλησμένος J   986 Βδ. om. V   988 κἀπόλαυσον V
989 Φι. om. V   990 Βδ. om. V   τῃδὶ] τὴν δί J   991 Φι. (prius)
om. V   ὅδ' ἔσθ'] ἰδέσθ' V   Βδ. om. R   Φι. (secundum) om. J : dic.
RV   αὐτ'ηνθέν Γ : αὐτὴν στευθενί J   992 Βδ. om. RVJ   993 par.
R : Φι. ΓJ   ἐξετάσω Γᵃ   Φι. Dobree : om. a   γὰρ J   ἤτω- V
994 Βδ. om. R : par. V   ἔοικας R   995 Φι. οἴμοι J   996 Βδ. J
ἔπαιρ' ἔπαιρε RJ : ἔπαιρε ἔπαιρε Γ   Φι. om. V : dic. R   εἰπὲ 'κεῖνο q
997 par. R   πέφευγε R   Βδ. om. V : dic. R   Φι.] dic. RV

Φι.   πῶς οὖν ἐμαυτῷ τοῦτ' ἐγὼ ξυνείσομαι,
     φεύγοντ' ἀπολύσας ἄνδρα; τί ποτε πείσομαι;   1000
     ἀλλ', ὦ πολυτίμητοι θεοί, ξύγγνωτέ μοι·
     ἄκων γὰρ αὖτ' ἔδρασα κοὐ τοῦ 'μοῦ τρόπου.

Βδ.   καὶ μηδὲν ἀγανάκτει γ'. ἐγὼ γάρ σ', ὦ πάτερ,
     θρέψω καλῶς, ἄγων μετ' ἐμαυτοῦ πανταχοῖ,
     ἐπὶ δεῖπνον, εἰς ξυμπόσιον, ἐπὶ θεωρίαν,   1005
     ὥσθ' ἡδέως διάγειν σε τὸν λοιπὸν χρόνον·
     κοὐκ ἐγχανεῖταί σ' ἐξαπατῶν Ὑπέρβολος.
     ἀλλ' εἰσίωμεν.

Φι.   ταῦτά νυν, εἴπερ δοκεῖ.

Χο.   ἀλλ' ἴτε χαίροντες ὅποι βούλεσθ'. ὑμεῖς δὲ τέως,
     ὦ μυριάδες ἀναρίθμητοι,   1010
     νῦν μὲν τὰ μέλλοντ' εὖ λέγεσ-
        θαι μὴ πέσῃ φαύλως χαμᾶζ',
     εὐλαβεῖσθε. τοῦτο γὰρ σκαιῶν θεατῶν
     ἐστι πάσχειν, κοὐ πρὸς ὑμῶν.

     νῦν αὖτε, λεώ, προσέχετε τὸν νοῦν, εἴπερ καθαρόν τι
        φιλεῖτε.   1015
     μέμψασθαι γὰρ τοῖσι θεαταῖς ὁ ποιητὴς νῦν ἐπιθυμεῖ.
     ἀδικεῖσθαι γάρ φησιν πρότερος πόλλ' αὐτοὺς εὖ πεποιη-
        κώς·
     τὰ μὲν οὐ φανερῶς ἀλλ' ἐπικουρῶν κρύβδην ἑτέροισι ποι-
        ηταῖς,
     μιμησάμενος τὴν Εὐρυκλέους μαντείαν καὶ διάνοιαν, 1019

1019 Sch. Pl. *Sph.* 252 c; S ε 45; Apostol. 6. 46

---

999 ἐμαυτῷ] μεταυτῶ V   ξυνήσομαι ΓΒ₂   1001 ἐξύγγνωτέ J
1002 τρόπως J   1003 γ' om. J   1004 πανταχοῖ Brunck : πανταχοῦ a
1008 Φι. om. RV   1009 Χο. om. V   βούλειτε σθ' V   ταχέως ΓJ
1011 μὲν del. Burges   1012 χαμάξ V   1013 εὐλαβεῖσθαι V
1014 πάσχει Γ   ἡμῶν Γ   1015 αὖτ Γ   πρόσχετε B   1017 φησὶν
B : φησι a

εἰς ἀλλοτρίας γαστέρας ἐνδὺς κωμῳδικὰ πολλὰ χέασθαι,
μετὰ τοῦτο δὲ καὶ φανερῶς ἤδη κινδυνεύων καθ' ἑαυτόν,
οὐκ ἀλλοτρίων ἀλλ' οἰκείων μουσῶν στόμαθ' ἡνιοχήσας.
ἀρθεὶς δὲ μέγας καὶ τιμηθεὶς ὡς οὐδεὶς πώποτ' ἐν ὑμῖν,
οὐκ ἐκτελέσαι φησὶν ἐπαρθείς, οὐδ' ὀγκῶσαι τὸ φρόνημα,
οὐδὲ παλαίστρας περικωμάζειν πειρῶν· οὐδ', εἴ τις ἐρα-
     στὴς   1025
κωμῳδεῖσθαι παιδίχ' ἑαυτοῦ μισῶν ἔσπευσε πρὸς αὐτόν,
οὐδενὶ πώποτέ φησι πιθέσθαι, γνώμην τιν' ἔχων ἐπιεικῆ,
ἵνα τὰς μούσας αἷσιν χρῆται μὴ προαγωγοὺς ἀποφήνῃ·
οὐδ', ὅτε πρῶτόν γ' ἦρξε διδάσκειν, ἀνθρώποις φήσ' ἐπι-
     θέσθαι,
ἀλλ' Ἡρακλέους ὀργήν τιν' ἔχων τοῖσι μεγίστοις ἐπι-
     χειρεῖν,   1030
θρασέως ξυστὰς εὐθὺς ἀπ' ἀρχῆς αὐτῷ τῷ καρχαρόδοντι,
οὗ δεινόταται μὲν ἀπ' ὀφθαλμῶν Κύννης ἀκτῖνες ἔλαμπον,
ἑκατὸν δὲ κύκλῳ κεφαλαὶ κολάκων οἰμωξομένων ἐλιχ-
     μῶντο
περὶ τὴν κεφαλήν, φωνὴν δ' εἶχεν χαράδρας ὄλεθρον τε-
     τοκυίας,
φώκης δ' ὀσμήν, Λαμίας δ' ὄρχεις ἀπλύτους, πρωκτὸν δὲ
     καμήλου.   1035
τοιοῦτον ἰδὼν τέρας οὔ φησιν δείσας καταδωροδοκῆσαι,
ἀλλ' ὑπὲρ ὑμῶν ἔτι καὶ νυνὶ πολεμεῖ. φησίν τε μετ' αὐτοῦ
τοῖς ἠπιάλοις ἐπιχειρῆσαι πέρυσιν καὶ τοῖς πυρετοῖσιν,

1033 §§ Plu. *Mor.* 807 a   1034 (φωνὴν . . .) § S χ 86

1020 εἰς] ἧς V   κωμῳδία Γ   μάχεσθαι ΓΒ₂   1022 οἰκίων Γ
στόματ' RVJ   ἡνιχήσας Γ   1025 πειρῶν Brunck: περιῶν RΓJ:
περιών V   1026 ἑαυτῶν J   ἔσπευδε t   1027 πιθέσθαι B: πεί-
θεσθαι a   ἐποιεική Γ   1028 ἵνα τὰς] ἴκται J   αἴσειν R   προαγώ-
μενον Γ   1029 γ' ἦρξε B: ἦρξε RΓJ: φησὶν V   φησὶ πιθέσθαι R
1030 τοῖσι q: τοῖς a   1031 συστᾶς V   τῷ om. J   1032 κύνης
ἀκτῖν' J   1033 οἰμωζο- ΓᵃᶜPlu.   1034 εἶχε ΓJS   1035 δ'
(secundum) om. R   1036 -δοκήσειν Γ   1037 ὑμῶν B: ἡμῶν a
τε om. R   αὐτὸν Bentley   1038 πέροισιν R

οἳ τοὺς πατέρας τ' ἦγχον νύκτωρ καὶ τοὺς πάππους ἀπ-
  έπνιγον,
κατακλινόμενοί τ' ἐπὶ ταῖς κοίταις ἐπὶ τοῖσιν ἀπράγμοσιν
  ὑμῶν   1040
ἀντωμοσίας καὶ προσκλήσεις καὶ μαρτυρίας συνεκόλλων,
ὥστ' ἀναπηδᾶν δειμαίνοντας πολλοὺς ὡς τὸν πολέμαρχον.
τοιόνδ' εὑρόντες ἀλεξίκακον τῆς χώρας τῆσδε καθαρτὴν
πέρυσιν καταπρούδοτε καινοτάτας σπείραντ' αὐτὸν διανοίας,   1044
ἃς ὑπὸ τοῦ μὴ γνῶναι καθαρῶς ὑμεῖς ἐποιήσατ' ἀναλδεῖς.
καίτοι σπένδων πόλλ' ἐπὶ πολλοῖς ὄμνυσιν τὸν Διόνυσον
μὴ πώποτ' ἀμείνον' ἔπη τούτων κωμῳδικὰ μηδέν' ἀκοῦσαι.
τοῦτο μὲν οὖν ἐσθ' ὑμῖν αἰσχρὸν τοῖς μὴ γνοῦσιν παρα-
  χρῆμα·
ὁ δὲ ποιητὴς οὐδὲν χείρων παρὰ τοῖσι σοφοῖς νενόμισται,
εἰ παρελαύνων τοὺς ἀντιπάλους τὴν ἐπίνοιαν ξύνετριψεν.
ἀλλὰ τὸ λοιπὸν τῶν ποιητῶν,   1051
ὦ δαιμόνιοι, τοὺς ζητοῦντας
καινόν τι λέγειν κἀξευρίσκειν
στέργετε μᾶλλον καὶ θεραπεύετε,
καὶ τὰ νοήματα σῴζεσθ' αὐτῶν,   1055
ἐσβάλλετέ τ' εἰς τὰς κιβωτοὺς μετὰ τῶν μήλων.
κἂν ταῦτα ποιῆθ', ὑμῖν δι' ἔτους
τῶν ἱματίων
ὀζήσει δεξιότητος.   1059

ὦ πάλαι ποτ' ὄντες ἡμεῖς ἄλκιμοι μὲν ἐν χοροῖς,   στρ.
1060–4 Apostol. 18. 62c

1040 ἡμῶν J   1041 μάρτυρας J   1043 τοιοῦτον δ' V
1044 κάταπρούδοντε R   καινοτάτας et διανοίας Bothe: καινοτάταις et
διανοίαις **a**   σπαιροντ V: σπαίροντες Γ: σπαίροντας' J   1045 ἀναιδεῖς
R   1050 παρ- Σ^VΓ: -περ **a**   1053 λέγον J   1056 ἐσβάλλετέ
τ'] ἐσβάλλετ' ΓJ   ἐς Γ   1057 κἀνταῦθα J   ποῆθ' RVΓ
1060 Χο. V: Ἡμ. RJ   ὑμεῖς J: om. Apostol.

ἄλκιμοι δ' ἐν μάχαις,   1061
καὶ κατ' αὐτὸ τοῦτο μόνον ἄνδρες ἀλκιμώτατοι.
πρίν ποτ' ἦν πρὶν ταῦτα, νῦν
    δ' οἴχεται, κύκνου τε πολιώτεραι δὴ
    αἵδ' ἐπανθοῦσιν τρίχες.   1065
ἀλλὰ κἀκ τῶν λειψάνων δεῖ τῶνδε ῥώμην
νεανικὴν σχεῖν· ὡς ἐγὼ τοὐμὸν νομίζω
γῆρας εἶναι κρεῖττον ἢ πολλῶν κικίννους   1068/9
    νεανιῶν καὶ σχῆμα κεὐρυπρωκτίαν.   1070

εἴ τις ὑμῶν, ὦ θεαταί, τὴν ἐμὴν ἰδὼν φύσιν
εἶτα θαυμάζει μ' ὁρῶν μέσον διεσφηκωμένον,
ἥτις ἡμῶν ἐστιν ἡ 'πίνοια τῆς ἐγκεντρίδος,
ῥᾳδίως ἐγὼ διδάξω "κἂν ἄμουσος ᾖ τὸ πρίν".
ἐσμὲν ἡμεῖς, οἷς πρόσεστι τοῦτο τοὐρροπύγιον,   1075
Ἀττικοὶ μόνοι δικαίως ἐγγενεῖς αὐτόχθονες,
ἀνδρικώτατον γένος καὶ πλεῖστα τήνδε τὴν πόλιν
ὠφελῆσαν ἐν μάχαισιν, ἡνίκ' ἦλθ' ὁ βάρβαρος,
τῷ καπνῷ τύφων ἅπασαν τὴν πόλιν καὶ πυρπολῶν,
ἐξελεῖν ἡμῶν μενοινῶν πρὸς βίαν τἀνθρήνια.   1080
εὐθέως γὰρ ἐκδραμόντες "ξὺν δορὶ ξὺν ἀσπίδι"
ἐμαχόμεσθ' αὐτοῖσι, θυμὸν ὀξίνην πεπωκότες,

1064 (κύκνου . . .)–1070 S §§ (1) κ 2657   1067 (ὡς . . .)–1070
S § (2) κ 1597   1082 § S ο 415

1061 μάχαισιν q Apostol.   1062 κατ'] ταῦτ' R   αὐτὸ δὴ q Apostol.
ἀλκιμώτατοι Bentley: μαχιμώτατοι a Apostol.   1064 οἴχεταί γε q
Apostol.   τε om. S(1) Apostol.   -τερα RΓJ: -τεροι S(1) Apostol.
1065 οἱ δ' ἐπανθοῦσι VΓJS(1)   τρίχας VS(1)   1066 δεῖ] καὶ S(1)
γνώμην VB₂S(1)   1067 σχεῖν Reisig: ἔχειν aS(1)   1068 κρεῖττον
om. S(1)   1069 κίννους V: κοκκίνους J: κικίνους S(2)v.l.
1070 κεὐρυ- Kuster: κηὐρὺ- a: καὶ εὐρυ- S(1)(2)   1071 Χο. RJ
1072 θαυμάζειν V   ἐσφηκ- J   1073 ἥτις] ἢ τίς ΓJ   τῆσδε τῆς ΓJ
κεντρίδος V   1076 εὐγενεῖς J: εὐμενεῖς Vv17B   1078 ὠφελοῦσαν
ἐν Γ: ὠφελήσαμεν R   μάχεσιν R   ἦλθεν Γ: ἦνθ' R: ἦθ' J   1080 ὑμῶν
RΓ   μενοῖν J   1081 δουρὶ J   1082 πεπωκότος V

στὰς ἀνὴρ παρ' ἄνδρ', ὑπ' ὀργῆς τὴν χελύνην ἐσθίων.
ὑπὸ δὲ τῶν τοξευμάτων οὐκ ἦν ἰδεῖν τὸν οὐρανόν.
ἀλλ' ὅμως ἐωσάμεσθα ξὺν θεοῖς πρὸς ἑσπέραν·   1085
γλαῦξ γὰρ ἡμῶν πρὶν μάχεσθαι τὸν στρατὸν διέπτατο.
εἶτα δ' εἰπόμεσθα θυννάζοντες εἰς τοὺς θυλάκους,
οἱ δ' ἔφευγον τὰς γνάθους καὶ τὰς ὀφρῦς κεντούμενοι,
ὥστε παρὰ τοῖς βαρβάροισι πανταχοῦ καὶ νῦν ἔτι
μηδὲν Ἀττικοῦ καλεῖσθαι σφηκὸς ἀνδρικώτερον.   1090

ἆρα δεινὸς ἦ τόθ', ὥστε πάντα μὴ δεδοικέναι,   ἀντ.
καὶ κατεστρεψάμην
τοὺς ἐναντίους, πλέων ἐκεῖσε ταῖς τριήρεσιν.
οὐ γὰρ ἦν ἡμῖν ὅπως
ῥῆσιν εὖ λέξειν ἐμέλλομεν τότ' οὐδὲ   1095
συκοφαντήσειν τινὰ
φροντίς, ἀλλ' ὅστις ἐρέτης ἔσοιτ' ἄριστος.
τοιγαροῦν πολλὰς πόλεις Μήδων ἑλόντες
αἰτιώτατοι φέρεσθαι τὸν φόρον δεῦρ'   1099/1100
ἐσμέν, ὃν κλέπτουσιν οἱ νεώτεροι.

πολλαχοῦ σκοποῦντες ἡμᾶς εἰς ἅπανθ' εὑρήσετε
τοὺς τρόπους καὶ τὴν δίαιταν σφηξὶν ἐμφερεστάτους.
πρῶτα μὲν γὰρ οὐδὲν ἡμῶν ζῷον ἠρεθισμένον
μᾶλλον ὀξύθυμόν ἐστιν οὐδὲ δυσκολώτερον.   1105
εἶτα τἄλλ' ὅμοια πάντα σφηξὶ μηχανώμεθα.
ξυλλεγέντες γὰρ καθ' ἐσμοὺς ὥσπερ εἰς ἀνθρήνια

1083 §§ S χ 194   1085 ‡ An. Ox. i. 446. 4–5   1086 §§ Apostol.
5. 44b

1083 στὰς ἀνήρ] τὰς ἀνδρὶ J   παρ'] πρὸς R   χελώνην J   1084 τῶν]
τοῦ J   τοξοτῶν V   1085 ἐωσά- An. Ox.: ἀπεωσά- ΓJ: ἐπαυσά- R:
ἐσωζό- V   -μεθα τὸν στρατὸν An. Ox.   ἑσπέρας R: ἑσπέρα ΓJ
1086 γλὰξ J   1087 δ'] τ' Γ   ἐπό- VΓJ   θυννάζοντες J   1088 τὰς
(prius) om. Γ   1090 φηκὸς J   1091 ηι V: ἦν R   1093 πλέον Γ
1097 ὅστις Elmsley: ὅστις ἂν a   1102 Χο. R   εὑρίσετε Γ
1107 συλ- ΓJ   -λέγοντες RΓJ   κατ' Γ   ὥσπερ εἰς ἀνθρήνια Kock:
ὡσπερεὶ τἀνθρήνια a

οἱ μὲν ἡμῶν οὗπερ ἄρχων, οἱ δὲ παρὰ τοὺς ἔνδεκα,
οἱ δ' ἐν 'Ωιδείῳ δικάζουσ', ὧδε πρὸς τοῖς τειχίοις
ξυμβεβυσμένοι πυκνόν, νεύοντες εἰς τὴν γῆν, μόλις   1110
ὥσπερ οἱ σκώληκες ἐν τοῖς κυττάροις κινούμενοι.
ἔς τε τὴν ἄλλην δίαιτάν ἐσμεν εὐπορώτατοι·
πάντα γὰρ κεντοῦμεν ἄνδρα κἀκπορίζομεν βίον.
ἀλλὰ γὰρ κηφῆνες ἡμῖν εἰσιν ἐγκαθήμενοι
οὐκ ἔχοντες κέντρον, οἱ μένοντες ἡμῶν τοῦ φόρου   1115
τὸν γόνον κατεσθίουσιν οὐ ταλαιπωρούμενοι.
τοῦτο δ' ἔστ' ἄλγιστον ἡμῖν, ἤν τις ἀστράτευτος ὢν
ἐκροφῇ τὸν μισθὸν ἡμῶν, τῆσδε τῆς χώρας ὕπερ
μήτε κώπην μήτε λόγχην μήτε φλύκταιναν λαβών.
ἀλλά μοι δοκεῖ τὸ λοιπὸν τῶν πολιτῶν ἔμβραχυ   1120
ὅστις ἂν μὴ 'χῃ τὸ κέντρον μὴ φέρειν τριώβολον.

Φι.   οὗτοι ποτὲ ζῶν τοῦτον ἀποδυθήσομαι,
       ἐπεὶ μόνος μ' ἔσωσε παρατεταγμένον,
       ὅθ' ὁ βορέας ὁ μέγας ἐπεστρατεύσατο.

Βδ.   ἀγαθὸν ἔοικας οὐδὲν ἐπιθυμεῖν παθεῖν.   1125

Φι.   μὰ τὸν Δί', οὐ γὰρ οὐδαμῶς μοι ξύμφορον.
       καὶ γὰρ πρότερον ἐπανθρακίδων ἐμπλήμενος
       ἀπέδωκ' ὀφείλων τῷ γναφεῖ τριώβολον.

Βδ.   ἀλλ' οὖν πεπειράσθω γ', ἐπειδήπερ γ' ἅπαξ
       ἐμοὶ σεαυτὸν παραδέδωκας εὖ ποιεῖν.   1130

1127 Ath. 329 b

1108 οἱ (prius)] ὁ V   παραὶ J   1109 ἐν 'Ωιδείῳ] ἐνοδίωι R
ὧδε Starkie: οἱ δὲ a   1111 κατταροις R: κιττάροις Γ: κυτάροις V
1113 -ζόμενον VJ   1116 πόνον Bergk   1117–18 ἡμῖν ... μισθὸν
om. V   1117 ἔτ' Γ   ἡμῶν ΓJ   1118 ἐκροφῇ Reiske: ἐκροφῆ
RΓJ   1119 λόχμην VJ   1120 ἐνβραχὺ V   1122 οὔτι J
1125 ἀγάθ' RΓJ   παθεῖν om. Γ   1126 Φι. om. V   δαμῶς
J   1127 δὶς ἀνθρακίδων Ath.   ἐμπεπλησμενον J: ἅλμην πιών Ath.
1128 γναφεῖ J   1129 Βδ. om. RV   1130 ποεῖν RVΓ

Φι.   τί οὖν κελεύεις δρᾶν με;

Βδ.   τὸν τρίβων' ἄφες,
τηνδὶ δὲ χλαῖναν ἀναβαλοῦ τριβωνικῶς.

Φι.   ἔπειτα παῖδας χρὴ φυτεύειν καὶ τρέφειν,
ὅθ' οὑτοσί με νῦν ἀποπνῖξαι βούλεται;

Βδ.   ἔχ', ἀναβαλοῦ τηνδὶ λαβών, καὶ μὴ λάλει.   1135

Φι.   τουτὶ τὸ κακὸν τί ἐστι, πρὸς πάντων θεῶν;

Βδ.   οἱ μὲν καλοῦσι Περσίδ', οἱ δὲ καυνάκην.

Φι.   ἐγὼ δὲ σισύραν ᾠόμην Θυμαιτίδα.

Βδ.   κοὐ θαῦμά γ'· ἐς Σάρδεις γὰρ οὐκ ἐλήλυθας.
ἔγνως γὰρ ἄν· νῦν δ' οὐχὶ γιγνώσκεις.

Φι.   ἐγὼ   1140
μὰ τὸν Δί' οὐ τοίνυν, ἀτὰρ δοκεῖ γέ μοι
ἐοικέναι μάλιστα Μορύχου σάγματι.

Βδ.   οὔκ, ἀλλ' ἐν Ἐκβατάνοισι ταῦθ' ὑφαίνεται.

Φι.   ἐν Ἐκβατάνοισι γίγνεται κρόκης χόλιξ;

Βδ.   πόθεν, ὦ 'γάθ'; ἀλλὰ τοῦτο τοῖσι βαρβάροις   1145
ὑφαίνεται πολλαῖς δαπάναις. αὕτη γέ τοι
ἐρίων τάλαντον καταπέπωκε ῥᾳδίως.

Φι.   οὔκουν ἐριώλην δῆτ' ἐχρῆν αὐτὴν καλεῖν
δικαιότερόν γ' ἢ καυνάκην;

1137 Poll. 7. 59

1131 Φι. om. V: par. R   Βδ. om. RV   1132 par. R   ἀναβαλοῦ
B: ἀναλαβοῦ a   1133 Φι. om. V   παῖδα J   1135 Βδ. om. V
ἀναβαλοῦ R^{ac}VΓJ   1136 Φι. om. V   1137 Βδ. om. V   περσιδῆτ'
ὁ δε J   σκανδύκην Poll.^{v.l.}   1138 θριμαιτίδα V   1139 κού] καὶ J
1140 ἔγνωκας Γ   γιν- VJ   1141 par. R   1143 ἐν om. V
1144 Φι. om. RV   γίν- VΓJ   χόσιξ J   1145 Βδ. om. RV
1146 ποι R   1147 ταλάντων καταπέπτωκε J   1148 Φι. om. V:
par. R   ἐριάλην Γ   ταύτην RΓJ   1149 γ' om. VΓJ

Βδ.   ἔχ᾽, ὦ ᾽γαθέ,
καὶ στῆθ᾽ ἀναμπισχόμενος.

Φι.   οἴμοι δείλαιος.   1150
ὡς θερμὸν ἡ μιαρά τί μου κατήρυγεν.

Βδ.   οὐκ ἀναβαλεῖ;

Φι.   μὰ Δί᾽ οὐκ ἔγωγ᾽.

Βδ.   ἀλλ᾽, ὦ ᾽γαθέ—

Φι.   εἴπερ γ᾽ ἀνάγκη, κρίβανόν μ᾽ ἀμπίσχετε.

Βδ.   φέρ᾽, ἀλλ᾽ ἐγώ σε περιβάλω. σὺ δ᾽ οὖν ἴθι.

Φι.   παράθου γε μέντοι καὶ κρεάγραν.

Βδ.   τιὴ τί δή;   1155

Φι.   ἵν᾽ ἐξέλῃς με πρὶν διερρυηκέναι.

Βδ.   ἄγε νυν, ὑπολύου τὰς καταράτους ἐμβάδας,
τασδὶ δ᾽ ἀνύσας ὑπόδυθι τὰς Λακωνικάς.

Φι.   ἐγὼ γὰρ ἂν τλαίην ὑποδύσασθαί ποτε
ἐχθρῶν παρ᾽ ἀνδρῶν δυσμενῆ καττύματα;   1160

Βδ.   ἔνθες ποτ᾽, ὦ τᾶν, κἀπόβαιν᾽ ἐρρωμένως
ἐς τὴν Λακωνικὴν ἀνύσας.

Φι.   ἀδικεῖς γέ με
εἰς τὴν πολεμίαν ἀποβιβάζων τὸν πόδα.

Βδ.   φέρε, καὶ τὸν ἕτερον.

1149 Βδ. om. R: dic. V   1150 στῆθ᾽ ἀμπ- VΓJ: στῆθι γ᾽ ἀμπ- q
Φι.] dic. RV   1151 par. R   1152 Βδ. (prius) om. V: par. R
Φι. om. R: dic. V   ἐγώ V   Βδ. (secundum) van Leeuwen: om. a
ἀλλ᾽ om. Γ   1153 Φι. van Leeuwen: par. R: om. VΓJ   γ᾽ om. ΓJ
ἀπίσχετε J   1154 Βδ. om. V   Φι. σὺ γ᾽ Γ   ἴσθι J   1155 Φι.
om. VΓ   καταθοῦ RΓJ   Βδ. om. R: dic. V   1156 par. RV
1157 Βδ. om. V: par. R   ὑπολύου Hirschig: ὑποδύου RVΓ: ἀποδύον J
κατατράτους V   1159 Φι. om. R: par. V   1161 om. J   Βδ. om.
V: par. R   1162 Φι. om. V: dic. R   1163 τὴν] γῆν R
1164 Βδ. om. V

Φι.   μηδαμῶς τοῦτόν γ', ἐπεὶ
πάνυ μισολάκων αὐτοῦ 'στιν εἶς τῶν δακτύλων.   1165

Βδ.   οὐκ ἔστι παρὰ ταῦτ' ἄλλα.

Φι.   κακοδαίμων ἐγώ,
ὅστις ἐπὶ γήρᾳ χίμετλον οὐδὲν λήψομαι.

Βδ.   ἄνυσόν ποθ' ὑποδυσάμενος. εἶτα πλουσίως
ὡδὶ προβὰς τρυφερόν τι διασαλακώνισον.

Φι.   ἰδού. θεῶ τὸ σχῆμα, καὶ σκέψαι μ' ὅτῳ   1170
μάλιστ' ἔοικα τὴν βάδισιν τῶν πλουσίων.

Βδ.   ὅτῳ; δοθιῆνι σκόροδον ἡμφιεσμένῳ.

Φι.   καὶ μὴν προθυμοῦμαί γε σαυλοπρωκτιᾶν.

Βδ.   ἄγε νυν, ἐπιστήσει λόγους σεμνοὺς λέγειν
ἀνδρῶν παρόντων πολυμαθῶν καὶ δεξιῶν;   1175

Φι.   ἔγωγε.

Βδ.   τίνα δῆτ' ἂν λέγοις;

Φι.   πολλοὺς πάνυ.
πρῶτον μὲν ὡς ἡ Λάμι' ἁλοῦσ' ἐπέρδετο,
ἔπειτα δ' ὡς ὁ Καρδοπίων τὴν μητέρα—

Βδ.   μὴ 'μοιγε μύθους, ἀλλὰ τῶν ἀνθρωπίνων,
οἵους λέγομεν μάλιστα, τοὺς κατ' οἰκίαν.   1180

Φι.   ἐγῷδα τοίνυν τῶν γε πάνυ κατ' οἰκίαν
ἐκεῖνον ὡς "οὕτω ποτ' ἦν μῦς καὶ γαλῆ—"

Βδ.   ὦ σκαιὲ κἀπαίδευτε—Θεογένης ἔφη

1169 §§ S δ 743   1172 (δο- . . .) §§ S δ 1320   1173 §§ S σ
155

1164 Φι. om. V   1167 γήρῳ J : [V]   1168 Βδ. om. V
ὑποδησόμενος B   1169 διαλυκώνισον γρΣ^RVΓ : διαλακώνισον γρΣ^VΓ
1170 Φι. om. V   1172 σκορόδῳ S   1173 Φι. om. V   1174 Βδ.·
om. V   1176 τίνας B   1177 ἐπέρσετο J   1178 δ' om. Γ
ὁ om. Γ   1179 Βδ. om. V   1180 λέγω° Γ   1181 Φι. om. V
1183 Βδ. om. V   Θεαγένης Brunck

τῷ κοπρολόγῳ, καὶ ταῦτα λοιδορούμενος·
μῦς καὶ γαλᾶς μέλλεις λέγειν ἐν ἀνδράσιν;　　　　1185

Φι.　ποίους τινὰς δὲ χρὴ λέγειν;

Βδ.　　　　　　　　　　μεγαλοπρεπεῖς·
ὡς ξυνεθεώρεις Ἀνδροκλεῖ καὶ Κλεισθένει.

Φι.　ἐγὼ δὲ τεθεώρηκα πώποτ'; οὐδαμοῖ,
πλὴν ἐς Πάρον, καὶ ταῦτα δύ' ὀβολὼ φέρων.

Βδ.　ἀλλ' οὖν λέγειν χρή σ' ὡς ἐμάχετό γ' αὐτίκα　　　1190
Ἐφουδίων παγκράτιον Ἀσκώνδᾳ καλῶς,
ἤδη γέρων ὢν καὶ πολιός, ἔχων δέ τοι
πλευρὰν βαθυτάτην καὶ χέρας καὶ λαγόνα καὶ
θώρακ' ἄριστον.

Φι.　　　　　παῦε παῦ', οὐδὲν λέγεις.
πῶς ἂν μαχέσαιτο παγκράτιον θώρακ' ἔχων;　　　1195

Βδ.　οὕτως διηγεῖσθαι νομίζουσ' οἱ σοφοί.
ἀλλ' ἕτερον εἰπέ μοι· παρ' ἀνδράσι ξένοις
πίνων σεαυτοῦ ποῖον ἂν λέξαι δοκεῖς
ἐπὶ νεότητος ἔργον ἀνδρικώτατον;

Φι.　ἐκεῖν' ἐκεῖν' ἀνδρειότατόν γε τῶν ἐμῶν,　　　　1200
ὅτ' Ἐργασίωνος τὰς χάρακας ὑφειλόμην.

Βδ.　ἀπολεῖς με. ποίας χάρακας; ἀλλ' ὡς ἢ κάπρον
ἐδιώκαθές ποτ' ἢ λαγών, ἢ λαμπάδα
ἔδραμες, ἀνευρὼν ὅ τι νεανικώτατον.

Φι.　ἐγᾦδα τοίνυν τό γε νεανικώτατον·　　　　　1205

1185 γαλῆ R　μέλλεις λέγειν] λέγεις V　　　1186 Φι. om. V
-πρεπὲς J　　1187 -σθένη R¹　　1188 Φι. om. V　ἐγὼ δὲ] ἐγὼ t:
ἔγωγε B　οὐδαμοῖ Bekker: οὐδαμοῦ a　　1190 Βδ. om. RV　ἐμαί-
χετο Γ　　1191 ἐφουνδίων V　　1192 ὢν καὶ πολιός] ὢν πολιὸς ὢν V
1193 βαθυ- G: καθυ- V: βαρυ- RΓJ　λαγόνας RΓJ　　1194 παῦ' t:
παῦε a　　1195 par. R　πῶς δ' RΓJ　　1196 οὕτω V　νομίζουσι
σοφοὶ J　　1200 Φι. om. V　ἀνδρείοτατόν J　　1201-2 ὑφειλόμην
. . . χάρακας om. V　　1205 Φι. om. V

ὅτε τὸν δρομέα Φάυλλον ὢν βούπαις ἔτι
εἷλον διώκων λοιδορίας ψήφοιν δυοῖν.

Βδ.   παῦ'· ἀλλὰ δευρὶ κατακλινεὶς προσμάνθανε
ξυμποτικὸς εἶναι καὶ ξυνουσιαστικός.

Φι.   πῶς οὖν κατακλινῶ; φράζ' ἀνύσας.

Βδ.   εὐσχημόνως.   1210

Φι.   ὡδὶ κελεύεις κατακλινῆναι;

Βδ.   μηδαμῶς.

Φι.   πῶς δαί;

Βδ.   τὰ γόνατ' ἔκτεινε, καὶ γυμναστικῶς
ὑγρὸν χύτλασον σεαυτὸν ἐν τοῖς στρώμασιν.
ἔπειτ' ἐπαίνεσόν τι τῶν χαλκωμάτων,
ὀροφὴν θέασαι, κρεκάδι' αὐλῆς θαύμασον.   1215
ὕδωρ κατὰ χειρός· τὰς τραπέζας εἰσφέρειν·
δειπνοῦμεν· ἀπονενίμμεθ'· ἤδη σπένδομεν.

Φι.   πρὸς τῶν θεῶν, ἐνύπνιον ἐστιώμεθα;

Βδ.   αὐλητρὶς ἐνεφύσησεν· οἱ δὲ συμπόται
εἰσὶν Θέωρος, Αἰσχίνης, Φᾶνος, Κλέων,   1220
ξένος τις ἕτερος πρὸς κεφαλῆς, Ἀκέστορος.
τούτοις ξυνὼν τὰ σκόλι' ὅπως δέξει καλῶς.

Φι.   ἄληθες; ὡς οὐδείς γε διακρίων ἐγώ.

1206–7 § S φ 144   1208–9 Ath. 179 b   1214–15 Ath. 179 b
1216 Ath. 641 d

1206 φάυλον VJ   1208 Βδ. om. V   1209 ξυνποτικὸς R :
ξυμποτικὸς J   συνουσ- Γ¹   1210 Φι. om. V   Βδ. om. V : dic. R
1211 Φι. om. RV   ὡσὶ J   -κλιθῆναι RJ : -κλῖναι V   Βδ. om. V : dic.
R   1211–12 Βδ. μηδαμῶς . . . δαί; om. J   1212 Φι. om. V : par. R
δαί] δὲ V   Βδ. om. V : dic. R   ἔκκτ- Γ   -ειναι Γ²J   1213 χύτλαρον
V   1217 ἀπονενίμεθ' R : ἀπονενέμμεθ' V   σπένδοκεν R : σπένσοκε Γ
1219 Βδ. om. R   1220 αἰσχίνην V   1221 Ἀκέστορος CΣᴿⱽᴳ :
ἀκέστερος a   1222 δέξῃ Γ   1223–7 om. J   1223 ἐγώ von
Bamberg : δεδέξεται RVΓ

Βδ. ἐγὼ εἴσομαι. καὶ δὴ γάρ εἰμ' ἐγὼ Κλέων,
     ᾄδω δὲ πρῶτος Ἁρμοδίου, δέξει δὲ σύ.   1225
     "οὐδεὶς πώποτ' ἀνὴρ ἔγεντ' Ἀθήναις—"

Φι. "—οὐχ οὕτω γε πανοῦργος οὐδὲ κλέπτης."

Βδ. τουτὶ σὺ δράσεις; παραπολεῖ βοώμενος·
     φήσει γὰρ ἐξολεῖν σε καὶ διαφθερεῖν
     καὶ τῆσδε τῆς γῆς ἐξελᾶν.

Φι.   ἐγὼ δέ γε,   1230
     ἐὰν ἀπειλῇ, νὴ Δί' ἑτέραν ᾄσομαι.
     "ὦ 'νθρωφ', οὗτος ὁ μαιόμενος τὸ μέγα κράτος,   1232/3
     ἀντρέψεις ἔτι τὰν πόλιν· ἁ δ' ἔχεται ῥοπᾶς."   1234/5

Βδ. τί δ', ὅταν Θέωρος πρὸς ποδῶν κατακείμενος
     ᾄδῃ Κλέωνος λαβόμενος τῆς δεξιᾶς·
     "Ἀδμήτου λόγον, ὦ 'ταῖρε, μαθὼν τοὺς ἀγαθοὺς
     φίλει—"   1238/9
     τούτῳ τί λέξεις σκόλιον;

Φι.   ᾠδικῶς ἐγώ.   1240
     "οὐκ ἔστιν ἀλωπεκίζειν,
     οὐδ' ἀμφοτέροισι γίγνεσθαι φίλον."

Βδ. μετὰ τοῦτον Αἰσχίνης ὁ Σέλλου δέξεται,
     ἀνὴρ σοφὸς καὶ μουσικός, κᾆτ' ᾄσεται·
     "χρήματα καὶ βίαν   1245
         Κλειταγόρᾳ τε κἀ-
         μοὶ μετὰ Θετταλῶν—"

Φι. "—πολλὰ δὴ διεκόμπασας σὺ κἀγώ."

1225 δέξαι V   1226 ἔγεντ' Ἀθήναις Bentley : γένετ' ἀθηναῖος RVΓ
1227 Φι. B^(ac)Ald : Βδ. ΓB^(pc) : om. RV   οὐδὲ Hirschig : om. RVΓ
1229 φήσειν J   1232 Χο. VJ   ὦ 'νθρωφ'] ἄνθρωφ' J   1233 τὸ
μέγα κράτος om. J   1234 ἀντρ- Bentley : ἀνατρ- a   1236 Βδ. om.
VJ : par. R   ὁ θέωρος RJ   προ R   1237 ᾄδει RΓ : ᾄγει J
1240 τοῦτο R   Φι. om. RV   ᾠδικὸς Γ   dic. ante ἐγὼ R   1242 γίν-
Γ   1243 Βδ. om. V   1244 καταῖσεται R   1245 βίον Tyrwhitt
:246 κἀ-] καί R : κᾶν J   1248 Φι. om. V   διεκόμπασας Tyrwhitt :
διεκόμισας RΓJ : διεκόμισα V

Βδ.   τουτὶ μὲν ἐπιεικῶς σύ γ' ἐξεπίστασαι.
     ὅπως δ' ἐπὶ δεῖπνον εἰς Φιλοκτήμονος ἴμεν.   1250
     παῖ παῖ· τὸ δεῖπνον, Χρυσέ, συσκεύαζε νῷν
     —ἵνα καὶ μεθυσθῶμεν διὰ χρόνου.

Φι.   μηδαμῶς.
     κακὸν τὸ πίνειν. ἀπὸ γὰρ οἴνου γίγνεται
     καὶ θυροκοπῆσαι καὶ πατάξαι καὶ βαλεῖν,
     κἄπειτ' ἀποτίνειν ἀργύριον ἐκ κραιπάλης.   1255

Βδ.   οὔκ, ἢν ξυνῇς γ' ἀνδράσι καλοῖς τε κἀγαθοῖς.
     ἢ γὰρ παρῃτήσαντο τὸν πεπονθότα,
     ἢ λόγον ἔλεξας αὐτὸς ἀστεῖόν τινα,
     Αἰσωπικὸν γέλοιον ἢ Συβαριτικόν,
     ὧν ἔμαθες ἐν τῷ συμποσίῳ· κᾆτ' ἐς γέλων   1260
     τὸ πρᾶγμ' ἔτρεψας, ὥστ' ἀφείς σ' ἀποίχεται.

Φι.   μαθητέον τἄρ' ἐστὶ πολλοὺς τῶν λόγων,
     εἴπερ γ' ἀποτείσω μηδέν, ἤν τι δρῶ κακόν.
     ἄγε νυν, ἴωμεν· μηδὲν ἡμᾶς ἰσχέτω.

Χο.   πολλάκις δὴ 'δοξ' ἐμαυτῷ   στρ. 1265a
        δεξιὸς πεφυκέναι καὶ   1265b
        σκαιὸς οὐδεπώποτε,
        ἀλλ' Ἀμυνίας ὁ Σέλλου   1267a
        μᾶλλον, οὐκ τῶν Κρωβύλου,   1267b
        οὗτος ὅν γ' ἐγώ ποτ' εἶδον   1268a

1267–74 § S a 1677

1249 Βδ. om. V   ἐποιεικῶς Γ   1250 φιλοκτέμονος J   1251 σκεάζε V   1253 γίγν- Brunck: γίν- a   1254 πατάξαι γρΣΥΓ: κατάξαι a   1255 ἀποτείνειν RΓ: ἀναποτίνειν J   1256 γ' om. VΓJ   1257 -σατο Γ   1259 γελλοῖον V   1260 μέλων Γ   1261 ἀφείς σ'] ἀφείσ' J: ἀφεὶς Γ   1262 τἄρ' Hermann: γ' ἄρ' J: γ' ἄρα R: γ' ἄρ δ' Γ: ἄρα V   1263 γ' om. VΓ   εὐπο- J   -τείσω van Leeuwen: -τίσω RΓJ: -τισωμεν V   1264 Χο. R   1265 Χο. om. RV   'δοξα 'μαυτῷ VΓJ   1266 σκαιοὺς J   1267 κρωβύλων VS: κρωβυλας J   1268 ὅν] ὧν V   γ' om. VΓJS

ἀντὶ μήλου καὶ ῥοᾶς δειπ-   1268b
νοῦντα μετὰ Λεωγόρου· πει-
νῇ γὰρ ᾗπερ Ἀντιφῶν.   1270
ἀλλὰ πρεσβεύων γὰρ ἐς Φάρσαλον ᾤχετ'·
εἶτ' ἐκεῖ μόνος μόνοισι
τοῖς Πενέσταισι ξυνὴν τοῖς
Θετταλῶν, αὐτὸς πενέστης   1274a
ὢν ἐλάττων οὐδενός.   1274b

ὦ μακάρι' Αὐτόμενες, ὥς σε μακαρίζομεν.   1275
παῖδας ἐφύτευσας ὅτι χειροτεχνικωτάτους·
πρῶτα μὲν ἅπασι φίλον ἄνδρα τε σοφώτατον,
τὸν κιθαραοιδότατον, ᾧ χάρις ἐφέσπετο·
τὸν δ' ὑποκριτὴν ἕτερον ἀργαλέον ὡς σοφόν·
εἶτ' Ἀριφράδην πολύ τι θυμοσοφικώτατον,   1280
ὅντινά ποτ' ὤμοσε μαθόντα παρὰ μηδενὸς
[ἀλλ' ἀπὸ σοφῆς φύσεως αὐτόματον ἐκμαθεῖν]
γλωττοποιεῖν εἰς τὰ πορνεῖ' εἰσιόνθ' ἑκάστοτε.

.   .   .   .   ἀντ.

εἰσί τινες οἵ μ' ἔλεγον ὡς καταδιηλλάγην,
ἡνίκα Κλέων μ' ὑπετάραττεν ἐπικείμενος   1285
καί με κακίσας ἔκνισε, κᾆθ', ὅτ' ἀπεδειρόμην,
οἱ 'κτὸς ἐγέλων μέγα κεκραγότα θεώμενοι,

1275 Heph. 41   1275–6 S § (1) μ 53   1276–8 S § (2) κ 1591
1280–3 § S θ 576

1268 ῥοιᾶς RΓJS   1269 Λεωγόρου om. Γ   1270 ᾗπερ B:
ᾗπερ aS   1271–2 ᾤχετ'· εἶτ' ἐκεῖ om. Γ   1272 εἶτ' om. S
μόνοισι q: μόνοις aS   1273 πενέσταισιν R   ξυνεῖν R[1]: ξυνῶν S
1274 Θετταλοῖς S   1276 ἐμφυτεύσας J   1277 φῖνον V   1278 ᾧ]
αἴ V   ἐφέπετο RJ   1282 del. Bothe   φύσεος t   post 1283
lacunam ΣV   1284 par. R   κατηδιη- J   -άγειν ΓΒ₂   1285 ὑπερτά-
RVJ   1286 κακίσας Briel: κακίσταις a   1287 οἱ 'κτὸς q: ἐκτὸς a
θεώ- q: μ' οἱ θεώ- a

οὐδὲν ἄρ' ἐμοῦ μέλον, ὅσον δὲ μόνον εἰδέναι
σκωμμάτιον εἴ ποτέ τι θλιβόμενος ἐκβαλῶ.
ταῦτα κατιδὼν ὑπό τι μικρὸν ἐπιθήκισα·   1290
εἶτα νῦν ἐξηπάτησεν ἡ χάραξ τὴν ἄμπελον.

Ξα.   ἰὼ χελῶναι μακάριαι τοῦ δέρματος
      [καὶ τρισμακάριαι τοῦ 'πὶ ταῖς πλευραῖς]·
      ὡς εὖ κατηρέψασθε καὶ νουβυστικῶς
      κεράμῳ τὸ νῶτον, ὥστε τὰς πλευρὰς στέγειν.   1295
      ἐγὼ δ' ἀπόλωλα στιζόμενος βακτηρίᾳ.

Χο.   τί δ' ἐστίν, ὦ παῖ; παῖδα γάρ, κἂν ᾖ γέρων,
      καλεῖν δίκαιον ὅστις ἂν πληγὰς λάβῃ.

Ξα.   οὐ γὰρ ὁ γέρων ἀτηρότατον ἄρ' ἦν κακὸν
      καὶ τῶν ξυνόντων πολὺ παροινικώτατος;   1300
      καίτοι παρῆν Ἵππυλλος, Ἀντιφῶν, Λύκων,
      Λυσίστρατος, Θούφραστος, οἱ περὶ Φρύνιχον.
      τούτων ἁπάντων ἦν ὑβριστότατος μακρῷ.
      εὐθὺς γὰρ ὡς ἐνέπλητο πολλῶν κἀγαθῶν,
      ἀνήλατ', ἐσκίρτα, 'πεπόρδει, κατεγέλα,   1305
      ὥσπερ καχρύων ὀνίδιον εὐωχημένον·
      κἄτυπτε δή με νεανικῶς "παῖ παῖ" καλῶν.
      εἶτ' αὐτόν, ὡς εἶδ', ἤκασεν Λυσίστρατος·

1288–9 S § (1) μ 533   1288–90 S § (2) σ 687   1292–4 S
§ (1) ι 455   1294–5 S § (2) σ 1024   1297–8 § S π 835
1300–5 S §§ (1) π 735   1305–6 S § (2) ε 1309   1307 § S ν 111

1288 οἷον S(2)   1289 εἴπω τέ Γ   ἐκβάλλω J   1290 ταῦτα q:
ταυτὶ aS(2)   ἐπιθήκισα Rᵃᶜ: ἐπιθέκισον J: ἐπιθήκασα S(2)   1292 Ξα.
Brunck: Οι. a   μακάριαι χελῶναι S(1)   1293 om. Γ   πλευραῖς
ἐμαῖς q   1294–5 ὡς . . . πλευρὰς om. R₁: ὡς . . . στέγειν Rᵐᵉ
1294 κατηγέψ- Γ: κατηρίψ- Rᵐᵉ₂   1295 τὸν VJ   1296 par. R
1297 ᾖ qS: ᾗς a   1299 Ξα. Brunck: Οι. ΓJ: par. R: om. V   δέρων
ΓΒᵞᵖ   1300 καὶ γὰρ ἦν τῶν S(1)   ξυνόν V   1301 Ἵππυλος VΓJ:
ἱππόλυτος S(1)   1302 ὁ V   1304 ἐπέπλητο S(1)   1305 ἀν-
Lenting: ἐν- aS(1)(2)   -ήλλατ' J   πεπούρδει Γ   1307 κἄτυπτε R
δή om. RVJS

"ἔοικας, ὦ πρεσβῦτα, νεοπλούτῳ τρυγὶ
κλητῆρί τ' εἰς ἀχυρὸν ἀποδεδρακότι."   1310
ὁ δ' ἀνακραγὼν ἀντήκασ' αὐτὸν πάρνοπι
τὰ θρῖα τοῦ τρίβωνος ἀποβεβληκότι,
Σθενέλῳ τε τὰ σκευάρια διακεκαρμένῳ.
οἱ δ' ἀνεκρότησαν, πλήν γε Θουφράστου μόνου·
οὗτος δὲ διεμύλλαινεν, ὡς δὴ δεξιός.   1315
ὁ γέρων δὲ τὸν Θούφραστον ᾔρετ'· "εἰπέ μοι,
ἐπὶ τῷ κομᾷς καὶ κομψὸς εἶναι προσποιεῖ,
κωμῳδολοιχῶν περὶ τὸν εὖ πράττοντ' ἀεί;"
τοιαῦτα περιύβριζεν αὐτοὺς ἐν μέρει,
σκώπτων ἀγροίκως καὶ προσέτι λόγους λέγων   1320
ἀμαθέστατ' οὐδὲν εἰκότας τῷ πράγματι.
ἔπειτ', ἐπειδὴ 'μέθυεν, οἴκαδ' ἔρχεται
τύπτων ἅπαντας, ἤν τις αὐτῷ ξυντύχῃ.
ὁδὶ δὲ καὶ δὴ σφαλλόμενος προσέρχεται.
ἀλλ' ἐκποδὼν ἄπειμι πρὶν πληγὰς λαβεῖν.   1325

Φι.   ἄνεχε, πάρεχε.
κλαύσεταί τις τῶν ὄπισθεν
ἐπακολουθούντων ἐμοί.
οἷον, εἰ μὴ 'ρρήσεθ', ὑμᾶς,
ὦ πόνηροι, ταυτηὶ τῇ   1330
δᾳδὶ φρυκτοὺς σκευάσω.

ΑΝΗΡ

ἦ μὴν σὺ δώσεις αὔριον τούτων δίκην

1309 § S τ 1096   1310 § S κ 1795   1311–12 § S π 683
1315 § S δ 664

1309 τρύσιον J : Φρυγὶ Kock   1310 ἀχυρῶν' Γ₁J : ἀχυρῶνας Γ₂q
1311 ἀντείκασεν S   1312 θρία γε Γ₂q   1315 δι' ἐμύλαινεν V
1316 om. Γ   1317 κοσμᾷς J   -ποεῖ RV   1318 -λυχῶν Γ :
-τριχῶν J   1321 ἀμαθέστ' R   1323 ξυντύχοι J   1324 καὶ δὴ
Β : δὴ καὶ RΓ : καὶ VJ   1329 εἰ μὴ] ἐμοὶ Γ   'ρρήσεσθ' RVJ
1330 ταυτηὶ Bentley : ταύτῃ a   1332 ΑΝΗΡ MacDowell (simile suasit
Tyrwhitt) : Βδ. RJ : om. VΓ   αὔριον] δίκην J

ἡμῖν ἅπασιν, κεἰ σφόδρ' εἶ νεανίας.
ἀθρόοι γὰρ ἥξομέν σε προσκαλούμενοι.

Φι.   ἰὴ ἰεῦ, "καλούμενοι".   1335
       ἀρχαῖά γ' ὑμῶν. ἆρά γ' ἴσθ'
          ὡς οὐδ' ἀκούων ἀνέχομαι
          δικῶν; ἰαιβοῖ αἰβοῖ.
       τάδε μ' ἀρέσκει· βάλλε κημούς.
       οὐκ ἄπει; ποῦ 'στ' ἡλιαστής; ἐκποδών.   1340

       ἀνάβαινε δεῦρο, χρυσομηλολόνθιον,
       τῇ χειρὶ τουδὶ λαβομένη τοῦ σχοινίου.
       ἔχου· φυλάττου δ', ὡς σαπρὸν τὸ σχοινίον·
       ὅμως γε μέντοι τριβόμενον οὐκ ἄχθεται.
       ὁρᾷς ἐγώ σ' ὡς δεξιῶς ὑφειλόμην   1345
       μέλλουσαν ἤδη λεσβιεῖν τοὺς ξυμπότας·
       ὧν εἵνεκ' ἀπόδος τῷ πέει τῳδὶ χάριν.
       ἀλλ' οὐκ ἀποδώσεις οὐδ' ἐφιαλεῖς, οἶδ' ὅτι,
       ἀλλ' ἐξαπατήσεις κἀγχανεῖ τούτῳ μέγα·
       πολλοῖς γὰρ ἤδη χἀτέροις αὔτ' ἠργάσω.   1350
       ἐὰν γένῃ δὲ μὴ κακὴ νυνὶ γυνή,
       ἐγώ σ', ἐπειδὰν οὑμὸς υἱὸς ἀποθάνῃ,
       λυσάμενος ἔξω παλλακήν, ὦ χοιρίον.
       νῦν δ' οὐ κρατῶ 'γὼ τῶν ἐμαυτοῦ χρημάτων·
       νέος γάρ εἰμι. καὶ φυλάττομαι σφόδρα·   1355
       τὸ γὰρ ὑίδιον τηρεῖ με, κἄστι δύσκολον
       κἄλλως κυμινοπριστοκαρδαμογλύφον.

1346 § S λ 306   1348 §§ Eust. 1403. 16   1348–9 § S φ 282
1356–7 § S κ 2688

1333 *Bd.* Γ   ἅπασι J   θανίας J   1334 ἀθρόοι V   πρακαλ- J
1335 Φι. om. VΓ: par. R   1338 ἰαιβοῖ om. VΓ   1339 βάλε V
1340 ἄπει Weise: ἄπεισι a   'στ' MacDowell ('σθ' Flor. Chrest.): 'στιν a
1345 -οίμην R   1346 λεσβιεῖν om. V   1348 οὐδ' ἐφιαλεῖς Eust.:
οὐδὲ φιαλεῖς RVS: οὐδὲ φιαλῶς Γ: ἀλλὰ φιαλεῖς J   1349 -τήσης V
κἀγχανῇ ΓS   τούτῳ μέγα om. Γ   1350 ἠργ- Hall et Geldart: εἰργ-
RVJ: ἐργ- Γ   1356 τῶ J   ὑίδιον Γ: υἵδι J   καί τι S

ταῦτ' οὖν περί μου δέδοικε μὴ διαφθαρῶ·
πατὴρ γὰρ οὐδείς ἐστιν αὐτῷ πλὴν ἐμοῦ.
ὁδὶ δὲ καὐτός. ἐπὶ σὲ κἄμ' ἔοικε θεῖν.   1360
ἀλλ' ὡς τάχιστα στῆθι τάσδε τὰς δετὰς
λαβοῦσ', ἵν' αὐτὸν τωθάσω νεανικῶς,
οἵοις ποθ' οὗτος ἐμὲ πρὸ τῶν μυστηρίων.

Βδ.   ὦ οὗτος οὗτος, τυφεδανὲ καὶ χοιρόθλιψ,
      ποθεῖν ἐρᾶν τ' ἔοικας ὡραίας σοροῦ.   1365
      οὔτοι καταπροίξει μὰ τὸν Ἀπόλλω τοῦτο δρῶν.

Φι.   ὡς ἡδέως φάγοις ἂν ἐξ ὄξους δίκην.

Βδ.   οὐ δεινὰ τωθάζειν σε τὴν αὐλητρίδα
      τῶν ξυμποτῶν κλέψαντα;

Φι.   ποίαν αὐλητρίδα;
      τί ταῦτα ληρεῖς ὥσπερ ἀπὸ τύμβου πεσών;   1370

Βδ.   νὴ τὸν Δί', αὕτη πού 'στί σοί γ' ἡ Δαρδανίς.

Φι.   οὔκ, ἀλλ' ἐν ἀγορᾷ τοῖς θεοῖς δᾳς κάεται.

Βδ.   δᾳς ἥδε;

Φι.   δᾳς δῆτ'. οὐχ ὁρᾷς ἐσχισμένην;

Βδ.   τί δὲ τὸ μέλαν τοῦτ' ἐστὶν αὐτῆς τοὐν μέσῳ;

1364-5 S §§ (1) σ 790; §§ (2) σ 1263; §§ (3) τ 1209   1366-7 §§ S
ε 1803   1368-9 (. . . -αντα) §§ S τ 855   1370 (ταῦτα . . .)-1371
§§ S τ 172   1372 (ἐν . . .)-1375 §§ S δ 18

1358 ἐμοῦ RJ   διαφθερῶ J   1360 δὲ om. R   1361 δαίτας R
1363 οἴωε J: οἴως t   1364 Βδ. om. V: par. R   οὗτος semel S(1)(2)(3)
στυφεδανὲ S(2)   χαιρόθλιψ· R: χειρόθλιξ J   1365 ποθεῖς VΓS(1)
(2)(3): ποῖ θεῖς; van Herwerden   γ' Bothe   ὡραίαις J   σωροῦ
VS(3)ᵛˡ·   1366 par. R   -προίξῃ JS   ταὐτὸ VS: ταυτὶ Γ
1367 Φι. om. V: par. R   1368 Βδ. om. Γ: par. R: dic. V
1369 συμ- VΓS   Φι.] Βδ. Γ: dic. RV   1371 Φι. Γ: par. R: dic. V
σοί q: τοί aS   γ' ἡ] γε Γ: δ' ἡ γ' ἡ J   1372 Βδ. Γ: par. R: dic.
V   καίεται VΓS   1373 Βδ. om. RVΓ   Φι. q: Βδ. J: dic. RVΓ
ἐσχισμένην Meineke: ἐστιγμένην aS   1374 Βδ. q: par. RV: om. ΓJ
δὲ] δαί S   αὐτῆς om. V   τοὐν] ἐν VS

Φι. ἡ πίττα δήπου καομένης ἐξέρχεται. 1375

Βδ. ὁ δ' ὄπισθεν οὐχὶ πρωκτός ἐστιν οὑτοσί;

Φι. ὄζος μὲν οὖν τῆς δᾳδὸς οὗτος ἐξέχει.

Βδ. τί λέγεις σύ; ποῖος ὄζος; οὐκ εἶ δεῦρο σύ;

Φι. ἃ ἅ, τί μέλλεις δρᾶν;

Βδ. ἄγειν ταύτην λαβὼν
ἀφελόμενός σε καὶ νομίσας εἶναι σαπρὸν 1380
κοὐδὲν δύνασθαι δρᾶν.

Φι. ἄκουσόν νυν ἐμοῦ.
᾿Ολυμπίασιν, ἡνίκ' ἐθεώρουν ἐγώ,
᾿Εφουδίων ἐμαχέσατ' Ἀσκώνδᾳ καλῶς
ἤδη γέρων ὤν· εἶτα τῇ πυγμῇ θενὼν
ὁ πρεσβύτερος κατέβαλε τὸν νεώτερον. 1385
πρὸς ταῦτα τηροῦ μὴ λάβῃς ὑπώπια.

Βδ. νὴ τὸν Δί', ἐξέμαθές γε τὴν ᾿Ολυμπίαν.

ΑΡΤΟΠΩΛΙΣ

ἴθι μοι, παράστηθ', ἀντιβολῶ, πρὸς τῶν θεῶν.
ὁδὶ γὰρ ἀνήρ ἐστιν ὅς μ' ἀπώλεσεν
τῇ δᾳδὶ παίων, κἀξέβαλεν ἐντευθενὶ 1390
ἄρτους δέκ' ὀβολῶν κἀπιθήκην τέτταρας.

Βδ. ὁρᾷς ἃ δέδρακας; πράγματ' αὖ δεῖ καὶ δίκας
ἔχειν διὰ τὸν σὸν οἶνον.

Φι. οὐδαμῶς γ', ἐπεὶ

1375 *Φι.* om. VΓ: par. R δῆτ' οὐ J καομένοις Γ 1376 *Βδ.*
om. R^{pc}Γ: par. R^{ac}V ὁ δ'] οἶδ' Γ 1377 *Φι.* om. RV ὄζοων Γ₁
δᾳδὸς] +++++ R οὕτως J 1378 ὄζος om. V σύ (secundum)] σ Γ
1379 *Φι.* om. Γ: εταῖρα R: par. V *Βδ.* om. VΓ 1381 *Φι.*] dic.
R : +++++ Γ 1382 *Φι.* R 1383–4 om. Γ 1385 -βαλλε R
1386 ὑπώπιον V 1387 *Βδ.* om. Γ: par. V 1388 *ΑΡΤΟΠΩΛΙΣ*
om. RVΓ 1389 ἐστιν ἀνήρ J 1390 ἐντεῦθεν Γ 1391 ὁ
βαλὼν R -θηκαν V : -θήκεν Γ τέτταρας om. Γ 1392 *Βδ.* om. J
αὖ] ἂν V 1393 ἔγχεον Γ *Φι.* om. R

λόγοι διαλλάξουσιν αὐτὰ δεξιοί·
ὥστ' οἶδ' ὁτιὴ ταύτῃ διαλλαχθήσομαι.   1395

Αρ.   οὗτοι μὰ τὼ θεὼ καταπροίξει Μυρτίας
τῆς Ἀγκυλίωνος θυγατέρος καὶ Σωστράτης
οὕτω διαφθείρας ἐμοῦ τὰ φορτία.

Φι.   ἄκουσον, ὦ γύναι· λόγον σοι βούλομαι
λέξαι χαρίεντα.

Αρ.   μὰ Δία μὴ 'μοιγ', ὦ μέλε.   1400

Φι.   Αἴσωπον ἀπὸ δείπνου βαδίζονθ' ἑσπέρας
θρασεῖα καὶ μεθύσῃ τις ὑλάκτει κύων.
κἄπειτ' ἐκεῖνος εἶπεν· "ὦ κύον κύον,
εἰ νὴ Δί' ἀντὶ τῆς κακῆς γλώττης ποθὲν
πυροὺς πρίαιο, σωφρονεῖν ἄν μοι δοκεῖς."   1405

Αρ.   καὶ καταγελᾷς μου; προσκαλοῦμαί σ', ὅστις εἶ,
πρὸς τοὺς ἀγορανόμους βλάβης τῶν φορτίων,
κλητῆρ' ἔχουσα Χαιρεφῶντα τουτονί.

Φι.   μὰ Δί', ἀλλ' ἄκουσον, ἤν τί σοι δόξω λέγειν.
Λᾶσός ποτ' ἀντεδίδασκε καὶ Σιμωνίδης·   1410
ἔπειθ' ὁ Λᾶσος εἶπεν· "ὀλίγον μοι μέλει."

Αρ.   ἄληθες, οὗτος;

Φι.   καὶ σὺ δή μοι, Χαιρεφῶν,
γυναικὶ κλητεύεις ἐοικὼς θαψίνῃ
Ἰνοῖ κρεμαμένῃ πρὸς ποδῶν Εὐριπίδου;

1401-5 §§ S αι 335   1402 § Hdn. Philet. [Dain] 2   1406 (προ-
. . .)-1408 §§ S κ 1794   1413 §§ S θ 75

1394 par. R   λόγον διαλλέξουσιν Γ   1395 ὁτιὴ] οἱ τιὴ J
διαλεχθ- Γ: διαλλαθ- J   1396 Αρ. Ald: γυνή VJ: par. R: om. Γ
μὰ] νὴ J   -προίζει V   1397-1494 desunt in Γ   1397 ἀγγυ- J
1399 βουλήσομαι J   1400 Αρ. Ald: γυνή a   1401 Αἴσωπον] ἄσω
τὸν V   -ζονθ' qS: -ζοντ' a   1402 τις] τε Hdn.   1405 δοκῇς JS
1406 Αρ. Ald: γυνή VJ: om. R   προκαλ- S   1410 ἀνδίδασκε J
1411 μέλλει V   1412 Αρ. Tyrwhitt: Βδ. J: βδε η θερα R: om. V
Φι. Grynaeus: om. a   1413 Οι. J   κλητεύεις Β: κλητεύειν aS

Βδ. ὁδί τις ἕτερος, ὡς ἔοικεν, ἔρχεται   1415
     καλούμενός σε· τόν γέ τοι κλητῆρ' ἔχει.

ΚΑΤΗΓΟΡΟΣ

     οἴμοι κακοδαίμων. προσκαλοῦμαί σ', ὦ γέρον,
     ὕβρεως.

Βδ.   ὕβρεως; μὴ μὴ καλέσῃς, πρὸς τῶν θεῶν.
     ἐγὼ γὰρ ὑπὲρ αὐτοῦ δίκην δίδωμί σοι,
     ἣν ἂν σὺ τάξῃς, καὶ χάριν προσείσομαι.   1420

Φι. ἐγὼ μὲν οὖν αὐτῷ διαλλαχθήσομαι
     ἑκών· ὁμολογῶ γὰρ πατάξαι καὶ βαλεῖν.
     ἀλλ' ἐλθὲ δευρί. πότερον ἐπιτρέπεις ἐμοὶ
     ὅ τι χρή μ' ἀποτείσαντ' ἀργύριον τοῦ πράγματος
     εἶναι φίλον τὸ λοιπόν, ἢ σύ μοι φράσεις;   1425

Κα. σὺ λέγε. δικῶν γὰρ οὐ δέομ' οὐδὲ πραγμάτων.

Φι. ἀνὴρ Συβαρίτης ἐξέπεσεν ἐξ ἅρματος,
     καί πως κατεάγη τῆς κεφαλῆς μέγα σφόδρα·
     ἐτύγχανεν γὰρ οὐ τρίβων ὢν ἱππικῆς.
     κἄπειτ' ἐπιστὰς εἶπ' ἀνὴρ αὐτῷ φίλος·   1430
     "ἔρδοι τις ἣν ἕκαστος εἰδείη τέχνην."
     οὕτω δὲ καὶ σὺ παράτρεχ' εἰς τὰ Πιττάλου.

Βδ. ὁμοιά σοι καὶ ταῦτα τοῖς ἄλλοις τρόποις.

Κα. ἀλλ' οὖν σὺ μέμνησ' αὐτὸς ἀπεκρίνατο.

Φι. ἄκουε, μὴ φεῦγ'. ἐν Συβάρει γυνή ποτε   1435
     κατέαξ' ἐχῖνον.

1429 § S τ 953   1431 S §§ (1) ε 2913; § (2) ει 26   1435-40 §§
PSI xi. 1221. 4–13; § S ε 2289

1415 *Οι.* RJ   1417 *ΚΑΤΗΓΟΡΟΣ* Tyrwhitt: ἀνήρ τις J : par.
RV   ὤμοι R : ὤμοι J   κακοδαῖμον J   1418 εὐριπίδης ante versum J
Βδ. om. R dic. ante μὴ μὴ R : *Βδ.* R^{ms}   1419 δίδωμί σοι δίκην J
1420 προείσομαι J   1421 διαλεχθήσομαι R : διαλλαγήσομαι J
1423 πότερον Bentley : πρότερον a   1424 ἀποτείσαντ' van Leeuwen :
ἀποτίσαντ' a   τραύματος B   1426 par. R   1428 μεγάλ' RV
1431 εἰδοίη J   1433 σου VJ   1434 *Κα.* om. R   1435 *Φι.*
om. R   Συβάρει] βάρει R   γιωή J   1436 ἐχεῖ[νον] PSI

Κα.   ταῦτ' ἐγὼ μαρτύρομαι.

Φι.   οὐχῖνος οὖν ἔχων τιν' ἐπεμαρτύρατο.
      εἶθ' ἡ Συβαρῖτις εἶπεν· "εἰ ναὶ τὰν Κόραν
      τὴν μαρτυρίαν ταύτην ἐάσας ἐν τάχει
      ἐπίδεσμον ἐπρίω, νοῦν ἂν εἶχες πλείονα."   1440

Κα.   ὕβριζ', ἕως ἂν τὴν δίκην ἄρχων καλῇ.

Βδ.   οὗτοι μὰ τὴν Δήμητρ' ἔτ' ἐνταυθοῖ μενεῖς,
      ἀλλ' ἀράμενος οἴσω σε—

Φι.   τί ποιεῖς;

Βδ.   ὅ τι ποιῶ;
      εἴσω φέρω σ' ἐντεῦθεν· εἰ δὲ μή, τάχα
      κλητῆρες ἐπιλείψουσι τοὺς καλουμένους.   1445

Φι.   Αἴσωπον οἱ Δελφοί ποτ'—

Βδ.   ὀλίγον μοι μέλει.

Φι.   —φιάλην ἐπῃτιῶντο κλέψαι τοῦ θεοῦ.
      ὁ δ' ἔλεξεν αὐτοῖς ὡς ὁ κάνθαρός ποτε—

Βδ.   οἴμ', ὡς ἀπολεῖς αὐτοῖσι τοῖσι κανθάροις.

Χο.   ζηλῶ γε τῆς εὐτυχίας   στρ. 1450
      τὸν πρέσβυν, οἷ μετέστη
      ξηρῶν τρόπων καὶ βιοτῆς.
      ἕτερα δὲ νῦν ἀντιμαθὼν
      ἦ μέγα τι μεταπεσεῖται

1450–2 §§ S οι 2

_____

1436 Κα. q: dic. RV: Βδ. J   ταῦτ' ἐγὼ μαρτύρομαι om. S
1437 par. RV   1438 τὴν S   1439 τὰν PSI   1440 ἔχῃς S
1441 Κα. om. V: κλητ R   1442 δήμητραν V   εὐταυθοῖ J
1443 ἀἰράμενος R   γ' οἴσω σε q: γ' ἔγωγε B   ποεῖς RV   ποῶ RV
1444 par. R   δὲ μή] δεμὴς J   1445 ἐπικλητῆρες λείψουσι V
1446 Φι. om. V: Βδ. R   Βδ. om. V: dic. R   1447 Φι. L: par.
RV: om. J   1448 καύθαρός J   1449 par. RV   τοῖσι q: τοῖς a
1451 πρεσβύτην S   μετέστιν J   1454 μετα-] μέγα R: om. J
-πεσεῖται Dobree (-πεσεῖτ' Bentley): πείσεται a

ἐπὶ τὸ τρυφᾶν καὶ μαλακόν.   1455
τάχα δ' ἂν ἴσως οὐκ ἐθέλοι·
τὸ γὰρ ἀποστῆναι χαλεπὸν
φύσεως, ἣν ἔχοι τις, ἀεί.
καίτοι πολλοὶ ταῦτ' ἔπαθον·
ξυνόντες γνώμαις ἑτέρων   1460
μετεβάλοντο τοὺς τρόπους.

πολλοῦ δ' ἐπαίνου παρ' ἐμοὶ   ἀντ.
καὶ τοῖσιν εὖ φρονοῦσιν
τυχὼν ἄπεισιν διὰ τὴν
φιλοπατρίαν καὶ σοφίαν   1465
ὁ παῖς ὁ Φιλοκλέωνος.
οὐδενὶ γὰρ οὕτως ἀγανῷ
ξυνεγενόμην, οὐδὲ τρόποις
ἐπεμάνην οὐδ' ἐξεχύθην.
τί γὰρ ἐκεῖνος ἀντιλέγων   1470
οὐ κρείττων ἦν, βουλόμενος
τὸν φύσαντα σεμνοτέροις
κατακοσμῆσαι πράγμασιν;

Ξα.   νὴ τὸν Διόνυσον, ἀπορά γ' ἡμῖν πράγματα
      δαίμων τις εἰσκεκύκληκεν εἰς τὴν οἰκίαν.   1475
      ὁ γὰρ γέρων, ὡς ἔπιε διὰ πολλοῦ χρόνου
      ἤκουσέ τ' αὐλοῦ, περιχαρὴς τῷ πράγματι
      ὀρχούμενος τῆς νυκτὸς οὐδὲν παύεται

   1457–61 §§ S a 3556   1474–7 S § (1) ει 281   1476–9 S §§ (2)
δ 708   1478–9 S § (3) θ 283

────────

   1455 τὸ om. R   τρυφῶν Dindorf: τρυφὸν RJ: ρυφᾶν V: τρυφᾶν Bergk
1457 χαλεπὸν ἀεί S   1458 φύσεος q   ἔχει VJS   1461 -βάλλοντο
RV: -βαλον S   1464 ἄπεισιν t: ἄπεισι a   1471 οὐ] ὁ R
1473 κατακηλῆσαι ᵛᵖΣᵛ   1474 Ξα. Brunck: Οι. RJ: om. V   τὰ
πράγματα a: τὰ om. tS(1)   1475 εἰσκεκλήκηκεν J   ἐς S(1)
1476 ἔπινε J   1477 ἤκασέ R   -χαρὴς ἦν S(1): -χαρεὶς S(2)ᵛˡ
1478 παύσεται RJ

                                                          E

τάρχαῖ ἐκεῖν' οἷς Θέσπις ἠγωνίζετο·
καὶ τοὺς τραγῳδούς φησιν ἀποδείξειν κρόνους   1480
τοὺς νῦν διορχησάμενος ὀλίγον ὕστερον.

Φι. τίς ἐπ' αὐλείοισι θύραις θάσσει;

Ξα. τουτὶ καὶ δὴ χωρεῖ τὸ κακόν.

Φι. κλῇθρα χαλάσθω τάδε. καὶ δὴ γὰρ
σχήματος ἀρχὴ—   1485

Ξα. μᾶλλον δέ γ' ἴσως μανίας ἀρχή.

Φι. —πλευρὰν λυγίσαντος ὑπὸ ῥώμης.
οἷον μυκτὴρ μυκᾶται καὶ σφόνδυλος ἀχεῖ.

Ξα. πῖθ' ἐλλέβορον.

Φι. πτήσσει Φρύνιχος ὥς τις ἀλέκτωρ—   1490

Ξα. τάχα βαλλήσει.

Φι. —σκέλος οὐρανίαν ἐκλακτίζων.
πρωκτὸς χάσκει·—

Ξα.   κατὰ σαυτὸν ὅρα.

Φι. —νῦν γὰρ ἐν ἄρθροις τοῖς ἡμετέροις
στρέφεται χαλαρὰ κοτυληδών.   1495

     οὐκ εὖ;

Ξα. μὰ Δί' οὐ δῆτ', ἀλλὰ μανικὰ πράγματα.

1480–1 § S κ 2468

1481 τοὺς νῦν Bentley : τὸν νοῦν aS   -σόμενος S   1482 ἐπαυλείασι V
1483 Ξα. Brunck : Οι. RJ : Βδ. V   1484 par. RV   χαλασθίω J
dic. ante καὶ RV : Οι. J : del. Bentley   1486 Ξα. Brunck : Οι. R :
++ J : om. V   1487 Φι. om. RV   λυγίσαντος R^mg_2 VJ : τας R₁
ῥύμης Lobeck   1488 σφόνδυτος J   1489 Ξα. Brunck : Οι. J : par.
R : om. V   1490 Φι. om. V : par. R   πτήσει V   ὅς VJ
1491 Ξα. Brunck : Οι. J : par. R : om. V   βαλή- V   -σει Dindorf : -ση
R : -σεις VJ   1492 Φι. om. V : par. R   οὐρανίαν Meineke : οὐράνιον a   1493 Ξα. Brunck : Οι. RJ : dic. V   1494 Φι. Ald : om. a
1494 (τοῖς . . .)–1537 habet Γ   1495 κουτυ- J   -λιδῶν V
1496 Βδ. οὐκ RJ   Ξα. Beer : om. a

Φι. φέρε νυν, ἀνείπω κἀνταγωνιστὰς καλῶ.
εἴ τις τραγῳδός φησιν ὀρχεῖσθαι καλῶς,
ἐμοὶ διορχησόμενος ἐνθάδ' εἰσίτω.
φησίν τις, ἢ οὐδείς;

Ξα.   εἷς γ' ἐκεινοσὶ μόνος.   1500

Φι. τίς ὁ κακοδαίμων ἐστίν;

Ξα.   υἱὸς Καρκίνου
ὁ μέσατος.

Φι.   ἀλλ' οὗτός γε καταποθήσεται·
ἀπολῶ γὰρ αὐτὸν ἐμμελείᾳ κονδύλου.
ἐν τῷ ῥυθμῷ γὰρ οὐδέν ἐστ'.

Ξα.   ἀλλ', ὠζυρέ,
ἕτερος τραγῳδὸς Καρκινίτης ἔρχεται,   1505
ἀδελφὸς αὐτοῦ.

Φι.   νὴ Δί' ὠψώνηκ' ἄρα.

Ξα. μὰ τὸν Δί' οὐδέν γ' ἄλλο πλήν γε καρκίνους.
προσέρχεται γὰρ ἕτερος αὖ τῶν Καρκίνου.

Φι. τουτὶ τί ἦν τὸ προσέρπον; ὦτος ἢ σφάλαξ;

Ξα. ὁ πινοτήρης οὗτός ἐστι τοῦ γένους,   1510
ὁ σμικρότατος, ὃς τὴν τραγῳδίαν ποιεῖ.

Φι. ὦ Καρκίν', ὦ μακάριε τῆς εὐπαιδίας,
ὅσον τὸ πλῆθος κατέπεσεν τῶν ὀρχίλων.

1497 φέρω Γ   καταγ- V   1500 Ξα. Beer: Βδ. J: dic. VΓ: om. R
1501 Φι. om. VΓ: par. R   Ξα. Beer: Βδ. J: par. R: dic. Γ: om. V
1502 μεσαίτατος R: μέσσατος ⁿᵖΣΓ   Φι. om. V: par. R: dic. Γ   ἄλλον Γ
τε Γ   1503 ἀπολλῶ Γ   ἐμμελίαι R   κονδυλίου J   1504 Ξα.
Beer: Βδ. J: dic. RΓ: om. V   1505 καρκινίτις VΓ   1506 Φι.]
dic. RVΓ   ὠψ- Ald: ὀψ- a   1507 Ξα. Beer: Βδ. J: par. R: dic. V:
om. Γ   1508 dic. V   1509 Φι. om. VΓ: par. R   τουτὶ] τὸ τί Γ
ὦτος Borthwick: ὀξὶς a   σφάλαξ Borthwick: φάλαξ R: φάλαγξ VΓJ
1510 Ξα. Beer: Βδ. J: par. R: om. VΓ   1511 del. Hamaker
σμισκρ- J   ποεῖ RVΓ   1512 Φι. om. Γ: par. V

ἀτὰρ καταβατέον γ' ἐπ' αὐτούς μοι· σὺ δὲ
ἅλμην κύκα τούτοισιν, ἥν ἐγὼ κρατῶ.   1515

Χο. φέρε νυν, ἡμεῖς αὐτοῖς ὀλίγον ξυγχωρήσωμεν ἅπαντες,
      ἵν' ἐφ' ἡσυχίας ἡμῶν πρόσθεν βεμβικίζωσιν ἑαυτούς.

      ἄγ', ὦ μεγαλώνυμα τέκνα τοῦ θαλασσίοιο,   1518/19
      πηδᾶτε παρὰ ψάμαθον   1520
      καὶ θῖν' ἁλὸς ἀτρυγέτοιο, καρίδων ἀδελφοί·   1521/2
      ταχὺν πόδα κυκλοσοβεῖτε, καὶ τὸ Φρυνίχειον   1523/4
      ἐκλακτισάτω τις, ὅπως   1525
      ἰδόντες ἄνω σκέλος ὤζωσιν οἱ θεαταί.   1526/7
      στρόβει· παράβαινε κύκλῳ καὶ γάστρισον σεαυτόν·   1528/9
      ῥῖπτε σκέλος οὐράνιον· βέμβικες ἐγγενέσθων.   1530/1
      καὐτὸς γὰρ ὁ ποντομέδων ἄναξ πατὴρ προσέρπει   1532/3
      ἡσθεὶς ἐπὶ τοῖσιν ἑαυτοῦ παισί, τοῖς τριόρχοις.
      ἀλλ' ἐξάγετ', εἴ τι φιλεῖτ', ὀρχούμενοι θύραζε   1535
      ἡμᾶς ταχύ· τοῦτο γὰρ οὐδείς πω πάρος δέδρακεν,
      ὀρχούμενος ὅστις ἀπήλλαξεν χορὸν τρυγῳδῶν.

1517 § S β 236

1514 γ' om. J   μοι· σὺ δὲ Hermann : μ' ὦζυρέ RVΓ : ὦζυρὲ J
1516 ὀλίγον αὐτοῖς Γ₁ : αὐτοῖς ὀλίγου J   -σομεν Γᵃᶜ J   ἅπασιν J
1517 βεμβηκ- S   1518-20 om. R₁ : add. R₂ᵐᵍ   1518 Hμ. J
+++ τέκνα J   1519 θαλασσίοιο Burges : θαλασσίου ΓJ : θαλασίου
R₂ᵐᵍ V   1523 πόδα κυκλο- Dindorf : πόδ' ἐν κύκλῳ a   στροβεῖτε VΓ
1524 καὶ om. Γ   1526 Hμ. J   ἄδοντες J   ὠιζωσιν R : ὦσιν J
1528 par. R   1531 γενέσθων VΓ   1532 πουτο- J   1534 τοῖς
q : τοῖσι a   1537 ὀρχούμενον VJ   τις R   ἀπήλλαξε χορὸν Γ :
ἀπήλλαξεχθρὸν J   τραγωδόν J

COMMENTARY

HYPOTHESEIS

Most surviving Greek plays have one or more hypotheseis (introductions) prefixed to them in the manuscripts, composed not by the dramatist but some by Hellenistic, others by Byzantine scholars. They might more suitably be printed in an edition of the scholia, but since it is traditional to print them with the text, the hypotheseis of *Wasps* have been included here.

These two pieces, one in prose and one in verse, consist mainly of summaries of the plot of the play, which are of little interest to the reader of Aristophanes (as distinct from the student of Hellenistic scholarship) since we can make better summaries for ourselves. The only passage which might provide interesting information is the last paragraph of hyp. i, giving particulars of the contest in which the play was first performed, but unfortunately that paragraph appears to contain at least one mistake and cannot be treated as reliable evidence.

HYPOTHESIS I

5 περικειμένης: 'still available'. [περι- often means 'remaining', and so Zacher's emendation παρακειμένης is unnecessary.]

12 ἐξαίρειν: 'arouse'.

13 μηδαμῶς νουθετούμενος: 'refusing to be advised'. [Van Leeuwen emended the sentence to ὁ δὲ πρεσβύτης νουθετούμενος οὐδαμῶς μεθίει τοῦ πάθους.]

17–18 συνεχῶς μέλλων: 'intending throughout the trial'.

19–20 ἐκ τοῦ ποιητικοῦ προσώπου: 'through the character in the play'. In itself the phrase is obscure, but the following words show that what is meant is 'through the characterization of the chorus as wasps'.

[**21 τοῖς Πέρσαις** seems the only acceptable emendation of ταῖς δίκαις. Rogers proposed τοῖς Μηδικοῖς (neuter), but the Athenians in 490 and 480 were on the lookout for the enemy rather than for the war. Zacher's ταῖς Μηδικαῖς ἐφήδρευον ναυσίν is unsuitable because 1071–90 is about fighting on land, not at sea. H. Richards (*CQ* v [1911] 260) suggested a drastic and improbable rearrangement of the whole sentence.]

25 γελωτοποιεῖ τὸ δρᾶμα: 'the play turns to fun'. [Blaydes's πρᾶγμα is not essential.]

26 ὑποκειμένης: 'postulated', 'imaginary': the play is not based on a fantastic assumption contrary to the facts of real life (such as that a man may fly to heaven on the back of a beetle, or found a city in the sky among the birds), but consists of incidents which really could have happened.

32 ἐπὶ ἄρχοντος Ἀμεινίου: 423/2 B.C. [This arkhon's name is given as Ἀμεινίας in other authors (Diod. 12. 72. 1, Ath. 218 d, Σ Luc. *Tim.* 30), and since this was the usual Attic form (74 n.) it is probably right to restore it here. His name is not preserved in inscriptions.]

διὰ Φιλωνίδου: Philonides was a comic dramatist who wrote plays entitled Κόθορνοι, Ἀπήνη, and Φιλέταιρος. He is said also to have acted in some of Ar.'s plays, and to have produced for him his *Amphiaraos* and *Frogs* (*Birds* hyp. ii, *Frogs* hyp. i, Σ *Clouds* 531). But it cannot be true that, as the author of the hypothesis states here, he produced *Wasps* on Ar.'s behalf. The proof of this lies in 1017–22. That sentence is unintelligible unless the audience knows that the author is Ar. (It is different from *Akh.* 628–64, which would, I think, seem quite intelligible to spectators who thought that *Banqueters*, *Babylonians*, and *Akharnians* were all written by Kallistratos.) It also (especially 1018 κρύβδην) shows that, when a play by Ar. was produced by someone else, Ar.'s name was not publicly announced, and that the audience in general would assume that the play was written by the man who was announced as the producer. (*Knights* 512 does not contradict this, since there πολλούς may mean merely 'a number of his friends'.) Therefore Ar., not Philonides, must have been announced as the producer of *Wasps*, and this paragraph of the hypothesis may not be used as evidence that one man could produce two comedies at the same festival. [But it does not follow that διὰ Φιλωνίδου should be deleted from the text. The mistake is more likely to be due to the author of the hypothesis than to a later copyist.]

33 β′ ἦν: 'was second' in the competition. In my note on 1501 I suggest a possible reason why *Wasps* failed to come first. [The conjectures of Kanngiesser and Petersen would make *Wasps* first and *Proagon* second. They would also improve and clarify the arrangement of the various pieces of information in this passage. However, the author of the hypothesis is not so skilful a writer that we may rule out the possibility that he has presented his information in a muddled fashion.]

πρῶτος may seem superfluous, but it helps to clarify the distinction between the winners of the first and second places. Cf. Ath. 3 de Ἀλκιβιάδης δὲ Ὀλύμπια νικήσας ἅρματι πρῶτος καὶ δεύτερος καὶ τέταρτος, and *Knights* hyp. ii.

34 Προάγωνι: Ar. wrote a comedy with this title, of which some fragments survive (fr. 461–70). It seems likely that this was the play which Philonides produced in 422; but there is no evidence to prove it, and the possibility remains that Philonides produced a different *Proagon* written by himself or by some other person.

Λεύκων: Little is known about this dramatist, and nothing else about his *Ambassadors*. The only surviving fragments of his work are from a comedy called Φράτορες, which came third in the contest at the Dionysia in 421 (*Peace* hyp. iii). He also wrote a play called "Ονος ἀσκοφόρος (*Souda* λ 340).

HYPOTHESIS II

Aristophanes of Byzantion was a scholar at Alexandria at the beginning of the second century B.C. Each surviving play of Ar. except *Th.* has a hypothesis of ten iambic lines attributed to him. Some modern scholars, however, deny that he can have written them, mainly because the diction and versification are below the standard which might be expected of so distinguished a scholar.

1 ἄφνω: 'abruptly'; i.e. 'seized and shut up'. [Blaydes conjectured ἄνω, to be taken with αὐτός (cf. 68); this requires the omission of τ' in the next line.]

7-8 'Because of their ability to thrust a sting into people, showing considerable spirit.'

10. 'Since he has determined on judging by hook or by crook.'

DRAMATIS PERSONAE

The list on page 45 is the one presented by the manuscripts. It is not to be attributed to Ar. but to some Hellenistic or Byzantine scholar. It includes only speaking parts, not silent ones.

7 συμπότης is a double mistake. The compiler has thought that the man who speaks 1332-4 is identical with the one in 1417-41, and that this man is a drinking-companion of Philokleon's.

The list on page 46 is a fuller and more accurate list compiled by me.

THE PLAY

The scene represents a house with a door, at least one window at a higher level, and a flat roof. In front of the door stands, as usual, a small altar (used in 860-90, and perhaps at 820); cf. P. D. Arnott *Greek Scenic Conventions* (1962) 43-53. According to the dialogue there is a bar across the door (154), a net draped over the window (164, 367), and two εἰρεσιῶναι ('harvest-branches') hanging on the wall near the door (398-9); that these objects were physically present in the original performance is likely, but cannot be absolutely proved because we do not know to what extent an ancient audience was accustomed to use its imagination to supply such properties. In front of the door are two slaves; it emerges from the dialogue that their names are Xanthias (1, 136, 456) and Sosias (136). On the roof is a man asleep, who in due course is revealed to be the slaves' master, named Bdelykleon (67-8, 134).

1-53 *The play begins with dialogue between the two slaves. The opening lines show that they are supposed to be on guard, but in fact have been dropping off to sleep. Each then proceeds to relate a dream which he has had; both dreams turn out to be comic political allegories.*

The chief function of this passage is to provide a string of jokes to get the audience warmed up. Comic dramatists, modern as well as ancient, often find it advisable to delay action or explanation which is essential to the plot for a few minutes, to give late-comers in the audience time to arrive and settle down. But in order to arouse expectancy Ar. inserts one reference to the main theme very near the beginning: we hear that the slaves are guarding a 'monster' (4), and we are left wondering what the monster is. Ar. also takes an early opportunity to get in a hit at Kleon's loud rhetoric and hypnotic power over the Athenian people (31-41) and at the obsequious attitude towards him of his friend Theoros (42-6). The openings of *Knights* and *Peace* are similar; each of these plays begins with dialogue between two slaves, in which the main theme of the play is alluded to without, at first, being clearly explained (*Knights* 1-39, *Peace* 1-49).

In the first twelve lines the humour arises from the elaborate and indirect language which the slaves use to disguise the fact that they are falling asleep on duty; neither admits that he is doing anything wrong, but Xanthias is practising a difficult skill (2), Sosias is affected by a god (9), and so on. When they begin to relate their dreams, the basis of the comedy is twofold: the comparison of politicians to animals, and the series of puns (ἀσπίς/ἀσπίς, δῆμός/δῆμος, κόραξ/κόλαξ).

1 Sosias wakes first, and rouses Xanthias with words which evade admitting that he has been asleep himself.   **οὗτος**: 'Hi!' to attract attention, as often in Ar.   **τί πάσχεις;** 'What's the matter with you?' implying that the person addressed is not behaving as he ought; so also in *Birds* 1044, *Lys.* 880, etc.   **ὦ κακόδαιμον**: 'you silly fool', as in *Birds* 1569, 1604, etc. He means that Xanthias is stupid to go to sleep, because he will be punished for it.

2 **φυλακὴν καταλύειν**: 'to stop sentry-duty' before the proper time (not 'to go off duty' when relieved); cf. Pl. *Laws* 762 c, Dein. 1. 112, Arist. *Pol.* 1308ᵃ29. As a ridiculous excuse for his slumber, Xanthias pretends to be practising a difficult skill.

3 'You owe your ribs a heavy penalty then.'   **ἄρα**: 'in that case', as in 10, 20. For the 'broken tribrach' see page 23.   **πλευραῖς**: In the talk of slaves this word is always associated with a beating; cf. 1292-5. A πλευρά is a rib running round one side of the body from front to back. Greek slaves seem customarily to have been beaten on the upper or middle part of the back (cf. τὸ νῶτον in 1295, *Peace* 747); the belly and flanks are less usual and more painful alternatives (*Frogs* 662-3, Herodas 5. 34).   **προυφείλεις**: The point of προ- is just that owing will be followed by payment; cf. προμανθάνω, προδιδάσκω, with Dover's notes on *Clouds* 476, 966. For κακὸν προυφείλω meaning 'owe a penalty' cf. E. *IT* 523, Ant. 5. 61, D. 21. 77. The joke here is that Sosias talks as if Xanthias and Xanthias's ribs were two separate parties. Xanthias has enjoyed a snooze; Xanthias's ribs will as a consequence (an inevitable consequence, Sosias assumes) be beaten; therefore Xanthias ought, in fairness, to pay compensation to Xanthias's ribs. [Emendation from imperfect to present seems essential. There is no evidence that κακὸν προύφειλες could mean 'you owed a grudge', as some editors take it; and 'you owed a penalty' is unsuitable, because Xanthias has only just now incurred the debt to his ribs, by falling asleep. Besides, though metrically guaranteed examples are lacking, the imperfect should probably be προώφειλες: cf. προωφείλετο in Ant. 5. 61 and D. 21. 77. The emendation was first suggested by Elmsley in his note on E. *Hkld.* 241. The grammarian Phrynikhos (Bekker *Anecdota Graeca* 47. 29) has been adduced in support of it, but his wording is different and the reference is probably to some other passage.]

4 ἆρ' οἶσθά γ': 'Don't you realize . . .?' In this phrase γε more often comes directly after ἆρα: cf. 1336, *Birds* 668, 1221, and Denniston 50. Of course Sosias knows that Xanthias knows what they are guarding. But he is afraid that Xanthias has failed to realize what is implied, that a very careful watch needs to be kept.   **κνώδαλον**: 'monster'. The word properly denotes an animal, usually of a wild or strange variety. Then it is applied metaphorically to persons who behave in a strange or inhuman way; cf. *Lys.* 477.

5 [σμικρὸν: Here and in 878, where the mss. are divided and the metre is indecisive, I prefer σμικρὸν to μικρὸν on the assumption that scribes were more likely to corrupt the longer and less familiar form.]   **ἀπομερμηρίσαι**: 'to stop worrying'. For this sense of ἀπο- cf. ἀπαλγέω (Th. 2. 61. 4). Cf. Cassius Dio 55. 14. 2 ἔφη ποτὲ ἡ Λιουία "τί ἐστι τοῦτο, ὦ ἄνερ; διὰ τί οὐ καθεύδεις;" καὶ ὁ Αὔγουστος "καὶ τίς ἄν" εἶπεν, "ὦ γύναι, κἂν ἐλάχιστον ἀπομερμηρίσειε τοσούτους τε ἀεὶ ἐχθροὺς ἔχων . . .;" Σ^R says that μέρμηρα, besides meaning 'worry', also means 'sleep before dawn': μέρμηρα ἡ μέριμνα καὶ ἡ φροντὶς καὶ ὁ πρὸ ἕω ὕπνος. If he is right, the verb will mean 'to cast aside one's worries by sleeping before dawn'. But it is likely that he is only guessing from our passage. μερμηρίζω is a poetic verb (Lucian *How to Write History* 22 objects to its use in prose), and so it seems possible that Xanthias's language is comically high-flown: 'I will absent me from solicitude awhile'.

6-7 Sosias now admits feeling sleepy himself. 'You can take the risk, for all I care; for in fact something sweet is now pouring over *my* eyes too.'

σὺ δ' οὖν: permissive; cf. 764, 1154, *Clouds* 39, and Denniston 466–7. [ἤδη: ὕπνου is obviously a gloss on τι γλυκύ which has got into RV by mistake. Xanthias's question in 8 shows that it is not until 9 that Sosias mentions 'sleep' explicitly.] καταχεῖται γλυκύ: Both words are commonly used of sleep in Homer; e.g. *Odyssey* 2. 395, 11. 245. Thus the audience will be in no doubt that Sosias is speaking of sleep, and yet the circumlocution puzzles Xanthias, who asks if Sosias is having some sort of fit or trance.

8 ἀλλ' ἦ: 'what!' or 'why, . . .', introducing a surprised question; as Starkie says, ἦ asks the question and ἀλλά marks surprise. Cf. Denniston 27–8. ἐτεόν is used by Ar. to mark a question: 'tell me', 'pray'. So also in 184, 836.

κορυβαντιᾷς: The Korybantes were divinities associated with Kybele. Their origin is variously ascribed to Phrygia or Crete, but by the fifth century their worship had reached Athens and some respectable Athenians took part in it (Pl. *Euthd.* 277 d). The most notorious feature of the ritual was ecstatic dancing to the music of flutes and drums (*Wasps* 119, E. *Ba.* 123–9, Pl. *Kriton* 54 d, Men. *Theophoroumene* 27–8), which was thought to provide a cure for mental disorder or distress (Pl. *Laws* 790 d; cf. *Wasps* 119). While the fit was on them, the dancing worshippers reached a high pitch of frenzied excitement; they were possessed by the gods, their hearts pounded, and their eyes filled with tears (Pl. *Smp.* 215 e). In short they were 'mad', in the sense that they did not behave in a normal rational manner (Pl. *Ion* 533 e οἱ κορυβαντιῶντες οὐκ ἔμφρονες ὄντες ὀρχοῦνται). Thus κορυβαντιᾷς here is not very different in meaning from παραφρονεῖς: 'Are you out of your senses, or in a trance?' Cf. Men. *Sik.* 273–4 (Kassel) κορυβ[αντιᾷς,] μειράκιον;

For a discussion of the rites of the Korybantes in classical Athens see Ivan M. Linforth 'The Corybantic Rites in Plato' (*Univ. of California Publ. in Class. Philology* xiii [1946] 121–62). On the psychiatric function of the rites see E. R. Dodds *The Greeks and the Irrational* (1951) 77–80.

9 Σαβαζίου: This is the earliest reference to the god Sabazios. He was a Phrygian god (*Birds* 873 with Σ, fr. 566, Str. 470; Σ *Wasps* 9 says Thracian, perhaps by confusion with Dionysos), whose worship evidently reached Athens at the time of the Peloponnesian war (cf. E. R. Dodds in *Harv. Theol. Rev.* xxxiii [1940] 171–5). Ar. mentions him also in *Birds* 873, *Lys.* 388, fr. 566 (from *Seasons*). Cicero *De legibus* 2. 37 states that in one of Ar.'s plays Sabazios and other foreign gods are tried and expelled from the state; Meineke *Frag. Com. Gr.* ii 1170 conjectured that this play was *Seasons*.

Even in ancient times there was doubt whether Sabazios was a distinct god or merely Dionysos under a Phrygian name (Σ *Birds* 873). Practically nothing is known of his rites in classical Athens. Demosthenes describes some rites which Aiskhines assisted his mother to conduct (D. 18. 259–60), and these rites may have been partly Sabazian, for they include the cry σαβοῖ, and Str. 471 actually states that the rites described by Demosthenes are Σαβάζια καὶ Μητρῷα; but the description is a caricature and not necessarily accurate.

There is some late evidence for an Illyrian drink called *sabaia* made from grain: Ammianus Marcellinus 26. 8. 2 says 'est autem sabaia ex ordeo vel frumento, in liquorem conversis, paupertinus in Illyrico potus'. So it has been suggested by Jane Harrison *Prolegomena to the Study of Greek Religion* (1903) 420 that, whereas Dionysos was the god of wine, Sabazios was the god of beer. Can Sosias have been drinking beer? An Illyrian drink might be known in Thrace, and many slaves came from Thrace, and Sosias is a slave. However, I know of no other evidence that beer was drunk in classical Athens, and it seems more likely that Sosias means nothing more than 'the god of wine'. And next Xanthias confesses in the same style of humorous allusiveness that his sleepiness too has the same cause.

10 τὸν αὐτόν: not 'the same Sabazios' (as if there were several), but 'the same person, Sabazios'; i.e. 'you, like me, have been drinking wine'. **βουκολεῖς**: 'tend'. He just means 'honour', but this particular verb is used because Dionysos was a bull-god and his worshippers were sometimes called βουκόλοι (E. fr. 203, Arist. *Ath. Pol.* 3. 5, Lucian *On Dancing* 79).

11 ἐπεστρατεύσατο: used regularly of the Persian invasions of Greece; cf. 1124, And. 1. 107, Isok. 8. 77, 12. 157.

12 Μῆδός τις: 'A Persian sleep' means 'sleep behaving in a Persian fashion'. Cf. ταχύς τις, 'in a swift manner', in S. *Ai.* 1266, *OT* 618. The Persians are regarded as typical aggressors. **νυστακτής**: 'drowsy', 'dozing', used nowhere else in classical Greek, though νυστάζω is common enough.

13 εἶδον: In English we 'have' dreams or 'dream' them; Greeks regularly 'see' them. Cf. 25, and on the implications of this verbal usage for the Greek attitude to dreams see E. R. Dodds *The Greeks and the Irrational* 105.

14 Sosias inadvertently betrays that he has been asleep too, but Xanthias is too interested in his own dream to notice.

15 ἐδόκουν: 'I thought', 'I imagined'.

The joke of Xanthias's dream lies in the surprise ending. At first the subject seems to be serious: an eagle drops a snake which it is carrying in its talons, which is a traditional omen of failure in an enterprise (*Iliad* 12. 200–29; cf. *Knights* 197–210). But in 18 the word ἐπίχαλκον reveals that the ἀσπίς which is dropped is not a snake but a shield, and the climax is reached when in the very last word Kleonymos is unexpectedly substituted for the eagle.

16 καταπτάμενον: In Ar. the aorist of πέτομαι is usually ἐπτάμην, seldom ἐπτόμην. [There is no reason to remove the α form by emendation; cf.

E. Fraenkel *Beobachtungen zu Aristophanes* (1962) 98 n. 1.]   μέγαν:
Kleonymos is μέγας in 592, *Birds* 1477.

18 ἐπίχαλκον: 'covered with bronze', 'bronze-plated'. Ar. inserts this
word solely to indicate that ἀσπίδα means not 'asp' but 'shield'; therefore he has selected an adjective which is normally used of nothing
but shields. That ἐπίχαλκος is such a word is proved by Ameipsias 17,
where it is used alone for 'bronze-plated shield' with ἀσπίς unexpressed.

19 Κλεώνυμον: one of the favourite butts of Ar.'s earlier plays. Yet outside Ar. he appears remarkably seldom in Athenian history: only as
the proposer of two decrees of 426/5 concerning tribute (*IG* i² 57. 34,
65. 5) and of a decree offering a reward of 1,000 drachmas for information about the profanation of the Mysteries in 415 (And. 1. 27). He
may have died in 414 or soon after, since he is not mentioned in any
play later than *Birds* (of course the claim of a woman in *Th.* 605 to be
'the wife of Kleonymos' does not prove that he was living then).

Ar. satirizes him as gluttonous (*Knights* 956–8, 1290–9, *Birds* 289),
fat (*Akh.* 88, *Wasps* 592, *Birds* 1477), effeminate (*Clouds* 673–80), and
pushful (*Akh.* 844). He talked boldly when no action was required
(*Peace* 675, *Birds* 1478–9), but he did not keep his promises (*Clouds*
400), and was a useless coward in war. In particular there was
a notorious occasion on which he was said to have discarded his
shield in a battle, on which Ar. harps mercilessly (*Knights* 1369–72,
Clouds 353, *Wasps* 15–27, 592, 823, *Peace* 444–6, 670–8, 1295–1304,
Birds 290, 1480–1). It is not known when this occasion was, but since
it is not mentioned in *Akharnians* (Lenaia 425) but is referred to in
Knights (Lenaia 424), it was probably some time in 425. Throwing
away one's shield was (at least by 405) an offence for which the
penalty laid down by law was disfranchisement without loss of property (And. 1. 74); but Kleonymos does not seem to have suffered disfranchisement, and so probably his action, despite the fuss Ar. makes
of it, was not serious enough to be regarded as a legal offence.

20 γρίφου: 'riddle'. This is the earliest instance of the word, and the
earliest mention of the custom of posing riddles at drinking-parties.
Neither is heard of again until the middle of the fourth century, in
Antiphanes 74, 124, 194; these fragments of Middle Comedy are
preserved in Ath. 448 b–459 b, where riddles are discussed and quoted
at length.

21 πῶς δή; 'How do you mean?' asking for an explanation, as in
Clouds 673, 1442.   **προερεῖ**: 'will hold forth'. [This, the reading of
R, is preferable to προσερεῖ (VJ), which would require τοὺς συμπότας.
Green's προβαλεῖ, with the riddle understood as object, could be right;
for προβάλλω as 'pose' cf. *Clouds* 757, Antiphanes 74. 5, Pl. *Kharm.*
162 b.]

22 The original riddle is given in Ath. 453 b: τί ταὐτὸν ἐν οὐρανῷ καὶ ἐπὶ γῆς καὶ ἐν θαλάττῃ; The alternative answers are ἄρκτος καὶ ὄφις καὶ αἰετός καὶ κύων: each of these words is the name of an animal, a fish, and a constellation. [Hirschig's emendation "τί ταὐτόν ... is not essential, since riddles were often posed in positive form; cf. Antiphanes 196 and other instances in Ath. 448 b–459 b.]

24 Xanthias takes it for granted that his dream is a symbolic prophecy of misfortune in the future. This seems to be the normal attitude of ordinary Greeks to dreams; cf. 40–1, 47.

25 τοι- is scanned short, and the second foot is an anapaest with word-break after the first syllable; cf. page 23.

27 δεινόν γέ: 'It *is* a strange thing', contradicting a denial; cf. Denniston 132. πού: 'I think', 'surely'. ἄνθρωπος ἀποβαλών: Participle and noun combine to denote an act, and this act, not the noun alone, is the subject ('the *ab urbe condita* construction'); hence δεινόν is neuter. We might say 'a man's throwing away' or 'for a man to throw away'. ὅπλα: a pun, meaning not only 'armour' but also 'genitals' (LSJ ὅπλον V); cf. 823, *Akh.* 592.

28 αὖ: 'now', 'next'. In Ar. this word does not usually signify repetition, but marks transition to a fresh item in a series; so also in 57, 81, etc.

29 σκάφους: The 'ship of state' image is common; cf. J. Dumortier *Les Images dans la poésie d'Eschyle* (1935) 27–55, D. L. Page *Sappho and Alcaeus* (1955) 181–2. σκάφος is used for the image in D. 9. 69. It is introduced by Ar. here just for the sake of the pun in 30.

30 ἀνύσας τι: 'quickly', 'and hurry up'; so also in 202, 398, etc. τρόπιν: 'keel', keeping up the ship metaphor, with a pun on τρόπον, 'manner' (cf. S. *OT* 99 τίς ὁ τρόπος τῆς ξυμφορᾶς;). 'Tell me the hull story.'

31 Sosias's dream is longer than Xanthias's, but of the same kind: a combination of satirical allegory and puns. περὶ πρῶτον ὕπνον: a standard time-formula: not 'in my beauty sleep' (which would be ἐν τῷ πρώτῳ ὕπνῳ) but 'in the early part of the night'. Cf. Th. 2. 2. 1 ἐσῆλθον περὶ πρῶτον ὕπνον ξὺν ὅπλοις ἐς Πλάταιαν. Πυκνί: The Pnyx is the small hill on which meetings of the Athenian assembly were held, west of the Akropolis and the Areopagos.

32 πρόβατα: The Athenian citizens, Ar. implies, are sheep because they are stupid and easily led; so also in *Clouds* 1203, and cf. *Knights* 264, *Wasps* 955.

33 βακτηρίας: From this line and *Ek.* 74 it appears that it was customary for Athenian citizens to carry walking-sticks when they attended meetings of the assembly. Elsewhere we hear of sticks being used by old men (1296, *Akh.* 682, *Clouds* 541), countrymen (*Ek.* 276–9, *Wealth* 272), and beggars (*Akh.* 448, fr. 127). Otherwise Athenians did not usually carry sticks, whereas Spartans did; an Athenian who carried a stick all the time might be regarded as ostentatious or as an admirer of Sparta (*Birds* 1283, D. 37. 52). (The coloured stick which was a juror's badge of office in the fourth century was something quite different, and did not exist in Ar.'s time.)   τριβώνια: A τρίβων was a short cheap cloak, for which this disparaging diminutive form is often used. It was regularly worn by poor men who could afford nothing better (*Ek.* 850, *Wealth* 714, 842–6, 882, *Lys.* 32. 16) and by Spartans and ascetics (*Lys.* 278, D. 54. 34); cf. 116, 1131. Here Ar. implies that the ordinary citizens of Athens are poor, by contrast with greedy politicians.

35 φάλλαινα πανδοκεύτρια: 'a voracious whale'.

36 'A blazing sow' means 'an angry sow'. (Not 'a burnt sow'; live pigs seldom come into contact with fire, and Sosias's comparison must be to a reasonably familiar phenomenon.) Fire is a regular metaphor for anger; ἐμπίμπραμαι has this sense in Lucian *Kataplous* 12, Alkiphron 3. 7. 5, and cf. *Frogs* 859. A sow stands for anger in *Lys.* 684. For a full discussion of the interpretation of the phrase see Taillardat § 350. [The perfect passive of this verb has no σ in Attic (Photios σέσωται).]

37 αἰβοῖ: 'ugh!' This exclamation is used to express a number of different emotions, which seem to have no common factor except surprise: disgust at a bad smell (here, *Akh.* 189, *Peace* 15), other kinds of disgust (1338) sometimes inducing nausea (*Clouds* 906), dismay or annoyance (973, *Knights* 957, *Clouds* 102, 829, *Peace* 544, 1291, *Birds* 1055), the surprise of one favourably impressed (*Birds* 610), and even pleasurable anticipation (*Birds* 1342; this instance has not even the element of surprise in common with the others).   παῦε: When one character tells another to stop speaking or doing what he is doing at present, the verb is either παῦε (so also in 517, 1194, etc.) or παῦσαι (652, *Akh.* 1107, etc.), but not normally παύου or παῦσον. The distinction in meaning between the forms is hard to see, but tentatively I suggest that the following considerations may influence the choice of form: (*a*) since the meaning is reflexive ('Stop your own action') the middle voice is more suitable than the active; (*b*) since stopping is not (usually) a process either long-drawn-out or repeated, the aorist is more suitable than the present; (*c*) when the speaker urgently wants to stop the hearer as soon as possible, the shortest and most staccato word is preferable. Considerations (*a*) and (*b*) point to παῦσαι, but when (*c*) overrides them the result is παῦε or παῦ'. If this analysis is correct, παῦσαι is an unemotional 'Stop' and παῦε is an urgent 'Stop immediately!' παῦε is often (e.g. here, 1194, *Peace* 648) excitedly repeated, in anxiety that the person addressed should not say another word. (Cf. W. F. Bakker *The Greek Imperative* [1966] 43–66, especially 54. He sees that παῦε is urgent and emotional, but his explanation that the present means 'Begin here and now' cannot be the whole solution, partly because it does not explain why παῦε is preferred to παύου, and partly because 'Begin to stop speaking!' would be a very odd thing to say.)

38 'Your dream has a horrible smell of rotten leather.' ὄζει is intransitive, and the smell is defined by an adjective (internal accusative) and a noun (descriptive genitive) ; cf. *Knights* 892 βύρσης κάκιστον ὄζων. βύρσης: Kleon's father owned a tannery (*Knights* 44 with Σ), and so this word finally puts it beyond doubt that it is Kleon whom the whale represents. Most members of the audience will have guessed this while Sosias was still speaking 35–6, for Kleon was at this time the most prominent politician of all and his greed and loud voice were constant objects of Ar.'s satire. So the mention of leather enables the slow-witted to understand the allegory, and the quick-witted to feel complacent at having their guess confirmed.

40 ἴστη βόειον δημόν: 'began weighing some beef-fat'.   οἴμοι δείλαιος: 'Oh dear !' The αι is scanned short, as often; cf. page 22.

41 δῆμον: There is a similar pun between δημός, 'fat', and δῆμος, 'people', in *Knights* 954. The translation 'He began weighing up a bit of grease' . . . 'He wants to split up Greece into bits !' provides a similar pun; but it involves a political distortion, since τὸν δῆμον ἡμῶν means Athens only.

Kleon is also accused in *Knights* 817–18 of splitting (διατειχίζων) the Athenians. The two passages show that he was regarded by some Athenians as a cause of disunity in the city, presumably because he encouraged one social class to regard another as opponents. Some scholars have thought that *Wasps* 41 refers to a proposal by Kleon in 423/2 to exact a capital levy (εἰσφορά) ; but it is not, by itself, adequate evidence for such a proposal, since *Knights* 817–18 shows that this kind of accusation against Kleon was already current before 423/2.

42 Θέωρος was a hanger-on of Kleon (599, 1220, 1236–7) and a champion of the jurors (418–19). In about 426 he possibly went as an ambassador to king Sitalkes of Thrace (if *Akh.* 134–73 has any factual foundation). Ar. calls him a κόλαξ (45, 419), an impostor (*Akh.* 135), and a perjurer (*Clouds* 400). D. W. Bradeen (*Hesperia* xxxiii [1964] 48–50) identifies him with a Theoros who appears as ἄρχων τοῦ ναυτικοῦ on a casualty list of the Leontis tribe, suggesting that he died while a commander of the fleet at Samos in 409; but the evidence for this identification is rather slight.

43 χαμαί: There must be some comic or satirical point in saying that Theoros is sitting on the ground, but I do not know what it is.

44 Ἀλκιβιάδης: In 422 Alkibiades was probably about thirty, and had not yet become a leading politician. Ar.'s references here and in *Akh.* 716 show that he was already familiar to the Athenian public as a speaker in the assembly and in the law-courts; but the reason why Ar. has selected him for mention here is not his political importance but his lisp, which enables Ar. to make a pun. His lisp is said to have added to his charm (Plu. *Alk.* 1. 6) ; indeed his son lisped deliberately in order to be like him (Plu. *Alk.* 1. 8, quoting Arkhippos 45). From *Wasps* 45 it appears that the lisp took neither of the two forms which are common in English (*w* for *r*, and *th* for *s*) but a 'Chinese' form (*l* for *r*), which modern speech therapists call 'lambdacism'. τραυλίσας: 'lisping', an aorist participle used to refer to the same action as a past main verb, as in *Peace* 1199, *Ek.* 1046, etc.

45 ὁλᾷς; Θέωλος: lisping forms of ὁρᾷς; Θέωρος. Ar. has to make the beginning of the line contain one or two words in which λ is obviously substituted for ρ, to ensure that the audience sees the point of κόλακος when that word is reached. **κόλακος:** 'Crow' when lisped sounds like 'flatterer'. A κόλαξ is a 'flatterer' or 'parasite', one who makes himself agreeable to a rich or important man for selfish purposes. Eupolis wrote a comedy entitled Κόλακες, a fragment of which gives the best surviving description of the life of a κόλαξ (Eupolis 159). For Theoros as a κόλαξ, cf. 418–19. The man he flattered was Kleon; cf. 1033, 1220, 1237. For the play on κόλαξ and κόραξ cf. the witticism of the philosopher Antisthenes: κρεῖττον εἰς κόρακας ἢ εἰς κόλακας ἐμπεσεῖν· οἱ μὲν γὰρ νεκρούς, οἱ δὲ ζῶντας ἐσθίουσιν (D.L. 6. 4; attributed to Diogenes by Ath. 254 c).

46 'How right he was . . .!' The joke in 45 is not a very obvious one, and so this line is added to draw the audience's attention to it and make them think it out. **τοῦτ':** τραυλίζω is normally intransitive, but cf. Arist. *HA* 536ᵇ8 τραυλίζουσι τὰ πολλά.

47 'Well, now, isn't that a strange thing . . .?' Sosias carries straight on from his previous speech, beginning as it were a new paragraph. It is misleading to suggest (as Denniston 431 does) that οὔκουν here introduces an answer; for Sosias is talking about the κόραξ, but Xanthias's remark was about the κόλαξ. Sosias is quite unconscious of the secondary meaning of 45, and 46 is an aside, addressed by Xanthias not to Sosias but to himself or the audience.

48 [γιγνόμενος: It is pedantic to object to inconsistency between 43 (Theoros has a crow's head), 47–8 (he is turning into a crow as a whole), and 49 (he turned into a crow as a whole 'suddenly', without intermediate stages). Bothe's attempt to remove the inconsistency by emending to γενόμενος is useless, because it leaves 43 and 49 unaltered.] **ἥκιστ':** 'not at all'. **ὅπως;** '⟨You ask me⟩ in what way?' converting the direct question to a reported one; cf. ὅ τι; in 793, 957, 1443.

50 'Well, then, isn't this the obvious conclusion . . .?' (LSJ συμβάλλω III. 3). **οὔκουν,** besides being negative and interrogative, is inferential, drawing a conclusion from the previous sentence, as in *Lys.* 307. **ἐναργὲς** of logical plainness is rare; I know of no exact parallel. The infinitive is epexegetic: 'the obvious thing to conclude'.

51 ἐς κόρακας: i.e. colloquially 'to hell'. For the play on this common imprecation, cf. *Birds* 28, *Frogs* 187–9.

52 εἶτα: 'after that', explained by the participle in 53. **δύ' ὀβολὼ:**

the normal minimum payment for any small service in Athens; cf. *Frogs* 140-2. The line is evidence that a household slave could possess spending money of his own; this is probably implied also by 9-10 and 500.

53 ὑποκρινόμενον: 'interpreting', used of dreams also in *Odyssey* 19. 535, 555. Although the correct interpretation of dreams was considered important as early as Homeric times, it is not until Ar.'s time that we hear of anyone who charged fees for it: Lysimakhos, grandson of Aristeides, is said to have made a living in this way (Plu. *Arist.* 27. 4 quoting Demetrios of Phaleron = *FGrH* 228 F 45). So here Sosias is probably alluding to a topical novelty. [Since 'a man who interprets dreams so cleverly' clearly implies 'as you do', there is no need to insert σε by emendation. J. Geel (*Mn.* I i [1852] 423) proposed οὗτω σ', C. F. Schnitzer *Aristophanes: Werke* v (1852) 682 proposed οὗ σ' in 52.   **σαφῶς** (J), not σοφῶς (RV): the quality which Xanthias claimed for his reply was clarity (50), not subtlety or skill. Contrast *Akh.* 401 σοφῶς, where the slave has spoken epigrammatically and obscurely.]

54-135 *Xanthias addresses the audience, to tell them the subject of the play, which will strike a mean between the highbrow and the vulgar. The slaves' master has ordered them to guard his father, who is suffering from a strange disease. Xanthias challenges the audience to guess what it is, and Sosias pretends to hear various guesses, but they are all wrong, and in the end Xanthias gives the answer himself: the old man suffers from a passion for being a juror. A series of anecdotes shows how he thinks of nothing but law-courts, how his son has tried in vain to cure him and has finally confined him to the house, and how he shows extraordinary ingenuity in escaping. The father's name is Philokleon and the son's Bdelykleon.*

This passage is the real 'prologue' of the play, in the sense that it is the passage which introduces the main theme and characters. In Greek comedy such explanation is regularly given in a speech addressed directly to the audience, as here, though in some plays a passage of explanatory dialogue is substituted. *Knights* and *Peace* are especially like *Wasps*: each of these, after introductory dialogue between two slaves, has an explanatory speech addressed to the audience by one of the slaves about their master (*Knights* 40-72, *Peace* 50-81). Our passage is actually the longest monologue-prologue in an extant Greek comedy, but Ar. has taken several steps to prevent it from being tedious: there is some jocular dialogue before it (1-53) to get the audience into a good mood before the long exposition begins; the speech is broken in the middle by exchanges between Xanthias and Sosias and (supposedly) some members of the audience (so also the long prologue-speech of Strepsiades in *Clouds* 1-80 is interrupted by lines from Pheidippides and a slave); and the later part, instead of just stating the bare facts, gives some very amusing examples of the old man's behaviour.

At first the manner of expression is straightforward, even formal. The sense-pauses all come at the end of the line, the balanced negatives in 58–62 (οὔτε ... οὔθ' ... οὐδ' ... οὐδ') suggest rhetoric rather than conversation, and there is a rhyming antithesis in 65–6. In 74–83 the lines are naturally more conversational, and when Xanthias resumes his continuous speech his language becomes more lively and picturesque, with similes (96, 105, 107, 129), metaphors (91, 93, 110), and vivid description of the old man's activities. Such details as 'on the front bench' (90), 'shouted for his shoes' (103), and 'having wax plastered up under his nails' (108) are not essential information, but they bring the description to life, and transform a recital of facts into a fascinating and convincing picture.

54 φέρε νυν with a 1st person subjunctive: 'Well, now, let me . . .', announcing an intention of moving on to the next business, as in 826, 848, 1497, 1516.   κατείπω: 'reveal', a usual compound for making public some information which has previously been confined to a privileged few; cf. 283.   λόγον: 'theme' of the play, as in *Peace* 50, 148.

55 ὑπειπών: 'saying beforehand', 'prefacing'; cf. Th. 1. 35. 5, D. 18. 60. For the construction, with an accusative subsequently defined by a jussive infinitive, cf. E. *Supp.* 1171–2.

56 μέγα: 'ambitious'. Some have thought that Ar. here refers to the failure of the too highbrow *Clouds* in the previous year. But μέγα does not necessarily mean 'highbrow', and it is possible that he is not thinking of anything so specific.

57 αὖ: 28 n.   Μεγαρόθεν: The Megarians were traditionally rivals of the Athenians in the art of comedy, which they claimed to have invented (Arist. *Poet.* 1448ᵃ31). Consequently Athenian comic dramatists express contempt for Megarian comedy; cf. Eupolis 244 Ἡράκλεις, τοῦτ' ἔστι σοι τὸ σκῶμμ' ἀσελγὲς καὶ Μεγαρικὸν καὶ σφόδρα ψυχρόν, and Ekphantides 2. So also in our line Ar. implies that any joke must be a bad one if it comes from Megara. But this evidence is vague and tendentious, so that we cannot judge from it the real quality of Megarian comedy. For discussion of its earlier history see L. Breitholtz *Die dorische Farce* (1960) 31–82, *Dith. Trag. Com.*² 178–87; to me Ekphantides 2 seems acceptable evidence that Megarian comedy existed in the middle of the fifth century, but there is no firm evidence for its existence before that.   κεκλεμμένον: 'plagiarized'. [Σᴬˡᵈ says γράφεται δὲ κεκλαμμένον Δωρικῶς ἀπὸ μετοχῆς τῆς κλαπείς, ὡς τραφείς. ὥσπερ οὖν τεθραμμένον, οὕτω κεκλαμμένον ἔφη. This evidently means that the author of the note found κεκλαμμένον in a ms. But since the note does not appear in any earlier Σ, the ms. in which κεκλαμμένον appeared may have been only a fifteenth-century one, not necessarily a better authority than **a**.]

58 γὰρ has sometimes been taken to mean that the kinds of episode men-

tioned in this sentence were typical of Megarian comedy. But that is
not necessarily so; Euripides (61) cannot have been a common
character in Megarian comedy, and the episodes may all just be
examples of what is λίαν μέγα (56).   ἔστ': A pair of slaves is regarded as a single feature of a play. But even with indubitably plural
subjects ἔστι sometimes remains in the singular when it stands early
in a sentence and means 'there are' or 'I have'; e.g. Pl. R. 463 a ἔστι
μέν που καὶ ἐν ταῖς ἄλλαις πόλεσιν ἄρχοντές τε καὶ δῆμος, ἔστι δὲ καὶ ἐν
ταύτῃ; Euthd. 302 c, E. Hek. 1000–2.   κάρυ': Just as in modern
pantomimes a comedian used sometimes to scatter small presents
among the audience, so in Athenian comedies such eatables as nuts
and dried figs were sometimes thrown out; Ar. protests against the
practice in Wealth 797–801.

59 δούλω: In comedy slaves often appear in pairs (as in our present
scene); so the dual does not imply that Ar. has a particular play in
mind.

60 'Nor Herakles cheated of his dinner'. For the accusative cf. X. Kyr.
3. 1. 19 ἃ μὲν ἐβουλήθης ἐξαπατῆσαι αὐτόν. Herakles often appeared as
a glutton in comedy (e.g. Birds and Frogs; cf. Peace 741 with Σ), and
so here too there is no need to suppose that Ar. is referring to one play
specifically.

61 [οὐδ': Blaydes's emendation οὔτ' is unnecessary, since οὐδέ following
double οὔτε is quite common; cf. Denniston 193.]   αὖθις may be
'on the other hand', 'either', going with οὐδ'; cf. 57 αὖ. Or it may
equally well be 'yet again', 'as before', going with ἀνασελγαινόμενος.
ἀνασελγαινόμενος: 'being treated lewdly' (passive), or possibly 'behaving lewdly' (middle). This compound occurs nowhere else, but
ἀσελγαίνω is common enough; ἀνα- is just intensive (like 'up' in
English 'wake up', 'clean up', etc.), as in 670 ἀναφοβοῦντες. [Hermann
suggested ἐνασελ-, but that compound does not occur elsewhere in
Attic either.] The scene with Euripides in Akharnians is hardly lewd,
and Ar. would anyway not be likely to use such an opprobrious term of
his own play. So he is probably thinking of plays by other dramatists,
as in 58–60. One that he may well have in mind is Kallias's comedy
Men in Fetters, in which one of the characters seems to have been
Euripides in the guise of a woman (D.L. 2. 18, quoting Kallias com.
12); it is virtually certain that this play was performed before Wasps,
since Perikles was satirized in it (Σ Pl. Mx. 235 e).

62 οὐδ' . . . γ': 'and not . . . either'.   ἔλαμψε: 'shone', achieved
glory. εἰ indicates that Ar. does not necessarily mean to say that
Kleon has in fact gained any glory. Thus he may not have any one
particular incident in mind. If he does, it must be a recent one, possibly Kleon's successful attack on Thucydides (Markellinos Life of Th.
46), or else some other event in 423. It is not Kleon's success at
Pylos in 425; for Ar. has already attacked that in Knights, and now he

means that he will not make further attacks on the same man for further successes. **τῆς τύχης χάριν**: 'thanks to luck'. For this sense of χάριν cf. Pi. *P*. 3. 95 Διὸς χάριν. Ar. contemptuously assumes that any success of Kleon's must be due to luck.

63 αὖθις: as in *Knights* two years ago. **μυττωτεύσομεν**: 'we shall make mincemeat of'. μυττωτός was a mixture of cheese, garlic, leek, olive-oil, honey, and vinegar (*Knights* 771 with Σ, Σ *Wasps* 63). For the metaphor cf. *Peace* 247. In fact *Wasps* does attack Kleon, but less directly than *Knights*; he does not appear as one of the characters.

64 γνώμην ἔχον: probably just 'sensible'; cf. S. *Tr*. 389 οὐκ ἀπὸ γνώμης λέγεις, 'your advice is sensible'. Or perhaps 'with a purpose', i.e. 'with a moral'; cf. Th. 8. 90. 3 ἦν δὲ τοῦ τείχους ἡ γνώμη αὕτη, 'the purpose of the wall was this'.

65 'No cleverer than you are yourselves'. Ar. often uses δεξιός of an intelligent audience (e.g. *Clouds* 521); its opposite is σκαιός (1013). For its application to a good play cf. Strattis 1.

66 φορτικῆς: 'lowbrow', applied to Ar.'s successful rivals in *Clouds* 524, in contrast to σοφός, applied to *Clouds* itself in *Clouds* 522.

67 He points to the roof, the flat top of the scene-building. 'That man, asleep up there, is our master.'

72 ξυμβάλοι: 'understand' (cf. 50), i.e. 'diagnose'.

73 ἐπεὶ τοπάζετε: a quite common kind of ellipse with ἐπεί. The reason given for the preceding statement consists in a challenge to refute it; any attempt to take up the challenge will end in failure, and the failure will prove the original statement correct. 'Since ⟨if you guessed you wouldn't be right; if you don't believe me, go on,⟩ guess!' Cf. 519, S. *El*. 352, *OT* 390, *OK* 969, Lys. 12. 39, Pl. *Grg*. 473 e, D. 39. 32.

74–85 Now the two slaves pretend that various members of the audience are making guesses at the nature of the disease. Sosias pretends to hear the suggestions, and he repeats them aloud for Xanthias and the whole audience to hear. Probably Xanthias stands on the raised acting area (1341 n.), while Sosias walks around the edge of the orkhestra pretending to hear suggestions made by spectators sitting in the front two or three rows (cf. 78 ὁδί, 'down here, close to me'). Xanthias then says whether the suggestions are right or wrong; of course they are all wrong, and most of them serve simply as feed-lines for jokes.

The passage could hardly have been written or rehearsed if Ar. and his actors had not known in advance that the men named in 74–82 would be sitting near the front of the audience. Front seats at the theatre were reserved for holders of certain offices and other privileged persons, including priests of Dionysos and holders of certain other religious offices, arkhons, and generals; for a fuller list see *Dram. Fest.*[2] 268. So the passage proves, I think, that all the men named in 74–82 held offices of some sort in 423/2; and there is other evidence (74 n., 81 n.) that Amynias and Nikostratos were generals this year. (I have discussed this matter more fully in *CQ* xv [1965] 48-51.)

[All the mss. mark some changes of speaker in this passage, though not all in the same places. To give the whole passage to Xanthias has been thought preferable by some commentators, beginning with Σ^R, who writes τινὲς ἀμοιβαῖα. χαριέστερον δὲ λέγεσθαι αὐτὰ συνεχῶς πρὸς ἑνός. This shows that both views were already current in his time. I think that the distribution which I have given in the text is more likely, for the following reasons. (*a*) If the whole of 54-135 were spoken by Xanthias, his speech would be of unparalleled length. Nowhere else in Ar. does a single character speak continuously for more than 60 lines (*Akh.* 497-556). Intervention by Sosias adds variety to a passage which might otherwise become monotonous. (*b*) Xanthias is the man who gives information about the disease (cf. 54, 87), and so it is he who rejects the various suggestions, but these rejections (especially those beginning with οὔκ or οὐδαμῶς) are more naturally spoken by a different person from the reports of the suggestions themselves. If Xanthias were obviously in a position to hear what the members of the audience were saying, it might seem laboured for him to repeat all the suggestions; but if only Sosias can hear them, it is quite natural for him to repeat them to Xanthias.]

74 Ἀμυνίας: Amynias son of Pronapes seems to have been a general in this year, 423/2. (This appears from *Wasps* 74 and Hermippos 71. Cf. G. Kaibel in *Hermes* xxx [1895] 441-5 and my discussion in *CQ* xv [1965] 50-1.) He went on an embassy to Pharsalos in Thessaly (*Wasps* 1271-4; cf. Eupolis 209), presumably in the second half of 423, after he became general and shortly before *Wasps* was performed. 466-77 may possibly imply that on this occasion he was suspected of intriguing with Brasidas, the Spartan general, who was in northern Greece throughout 423; cf. Hermippos 71, where he is called a slave to the Spartans (εἰλωτισμένην). He was satirized by the comic dramatists as effeminate (he is spoken of in the feminine gender in *Clouds* 690-2 and Hermippos 71) and pretentious (Kratinos 212 Kock = 213 Edmonds); Ar. calls him 'son of Swank' in *Wasps* 1267 and probably also in 325 (cf. 325 n.). In 1267-74 it is said that he formerly had wealthy friends but is now poor. 74-6 probably means that gambling was how he lost his money. His period of notoriety was brief; almost all the references to him belong certainly or probably to the years 423 and 422. [Ἀμεινίας is a common Athenian name, but there seems to be no record of any other classical Athenian named Ἀμυνίας. Possibly we ought to emend υ to ει wherever he is mentioned. But, in face of unanimous support for υ in the mss., the argument from silence is perhaps not quite strong enough to justify emendation; even if it were certain that no other Athenian was named Ἀμυνίας,

that would not prove that our man was not so named. New names were invented sometimes; the name Ἀμυνίας did exist later, and somebody must have been its first holder.]

76 ἀφ': 'from the evidence of', because he is a gambler himself.

77 οὐκ: 'No'. This must be the beginning of an answer (cf. 634), and so one or more lines containing a fresh suggestion must have been lost between 76 and 77. From 77 it is plain that the lost suggestion began with φιλο-. Between gambling and drinking φιλογύνης or φιλόπαις is as likely as anything. [But there is another possibility. R has φιλόδικος wrongly inserted in 77, and though this is usually taken to be a mistaken anticipation of φιληλιαστής in 88, its meaning actually is not 'loving to be a juror' but 'loving to prosecute', 'litigious' (cf. E. G. Turner in CR lx [1946] 5–7), and it is conceivable that this is the lost suggestion to which 77 is the answer.] **ἀρχὴ τοῦ κακοῦ**: 'the beginning of the name of the disease'. Contrast Hdt. 5. 97. 3, where ἀρχὴ κακῶν means 'a source of trouble'. [ἀρχή, not ἀρχή, because it is the subject and the article is needed to show this. If it were the complement, "φιλο-" would be the subject and we should want τό "φιλο-". For crasis of ἡ ἀ- cf. Lys. 936.]

78 Σωσίας: It is not known who this Sosias was, though he could be the hellenotamias of that name mentioned in Ant. 5. 70. Lines 78–80 imply that he is an official sitting near the front of the audience and that he is vulnerable to attack as a toper. These two facts are enough to justify his mention, even if he was not otherwise prominent. [All the same, it is a little strange that Ar. chooses to mention a man of the same name as the character who speaks the line. It is true that the audience will not have noticed anything odd, since they do not yet know (until 136) that the character's name is Sosias. But another possibility is that Σωσίας has wrongly got into the text from the margin in place of the right name. Van Herwerden conjectured Σωσικλέης. An alternative, I suggest, is Νικίας; Nikias was a general in 423/2 (Th. 4. 129. 2, 133. 4) and so had a front seat. But the ousted name might be something totally different from Σωσίας.] **Δερκύλον**: Derkylos is evidently sitting next to Sosias in the audience. Who he was is unknown. (Σ says a comic actor, but this may be just a mistaken guess by someone who wrongly thought that the Sosias mentioned here was the character in the play.)

80 χρηστῶν ἀνδρῶν: 'of good chaps'. Fondness for drink is likewise jokingly adduced as a sign of merit in Frogs 739–40: πῶς γὰρ οὐχὶ γεννάδας, ὅστις γε πίνειν οἶδε καὶ βινεῖν μόνον; (Neither of these passages means that drinking is a sign of high social rank. Both χρηστός and γεννάδας are terms that may be applied to slaves, e.g. Frogs 179.)

81 Νικόστρατος: I have argued elsewhere (CQ xv [1965] 41–51) that this is Nikostratos son of Dieitrephes, who was a general this year (Th. 4. 129. 2, 133. 4). He took a prominent part in the Peloponnesian war as a general in the period from 427 (Th. 3. 75) to his death in 418 (Th. 5. 74. 3); on his skill and humanity see A. W. Gomme *The Greek Attitude to Poetry and History* (1954) 144-8. Line 82 implies that he was strikingly hospitable at sacrifices, or at least had been so on one well-known occasion. The reference to his deme may possibly mean that he had been very lavish in celebrating a sacrifice on behalf of his deme; but not necessarily so, since a man is sometimes identified by a demotic instead of a patronymic for no special reason (e.g. 233). **Σκαμβωνίδης**: The Skambonidai were a deme of the Leontis tribe, situated probably in the northern part of the city of Athens; cf. W. Judeich *Topographie von Athen* 2nd edition (1931) 172.

82 **φιλοθύτην** (cf. Ant. 2b. 12) and **φιλόξενον** are generally terms of praise, not blame. Ar. introduces them here not because he seriously regards such activities as faults but simply to provide an opportunity for comic comment on Nikostratos and Philoxenos.

83 **μὰ τὸν κύν'**: This oath, a favourite of Sokrates's, was, like 'by the goose' (cf. *Birds* 521), regarded as milder than an oath by the name of a god. Cf. Kratinos 231 οἶς ἦν μέγιστος ὅρκος ἅπαντι λόγῳ κύων, ἔπειτα χήν, θεοὺς δ' ἐσίγων. Its origin is unknown.

84 A pun on 'hospitable' and the man's name Philoxenos: the old man is not **φιλόξενος**, since Philoxenos is a catamite and the old man is certainly not that. Philoxenos son of Eryxis, of the deme Diomeia, was notoriously effeminate (cf. *Clouds* 686, Eupolis 235, Ath. 220 b). He is not to be confused with Philoxenos the dithyrambic poet and gourmand, who was only 55 years old when he died in 380/79 (*Marm. Par.* 69) and so was too young to be publicly mocked as a catamite in 423/2.

85 **ἄλλως φλυαρεῖτ'**: 'You're getting nowhere by talking this rubbish'.

86 **δὴ**: 'really'.   [**νυν**, not **νῦν**, because this particle often follows an imperative. Cf. S. *Ai.* 87 σίγα νυν, Kratinos 144 Kock = 137 Edmonds σίγαν νυν ἅπας ἔχε, in both of which νυν is guaranteed by the metre.]

87 **δεσπότου**: a loose expression. Strictly the son is now master of the household (67, 142); the father is only the former master (442). On the father's retirement from control, 613 n.

88 **φιληλιαστής**: 'fond of being a juror', a comic word invented by Ar. for the occasion: 'trialophile' or 'juromaniac'.

89 **τε**: probably prospective ('both') rather than connective ('and'); adequate connection is provided by τούτου, which refers back to φιληλιαστής.   **τούτου** suggests impatience (cf. 210): 'this judging business'.

90 **πρώτου ξύλου**: 'front bench' in the law-court.

91 'He doesn't have a grain of sleep all night.'   **πασπάλην**: literally 'finely ground meal', like παιπάλη (*Clouds* 260-2).

92 **ἦν δ' οὖν**: 'Or if (what is most unusual) . . .', admitting a supposition which has just been denied; cf. Denniston 464-5.   **κἂν ἄχνην**: 'for a speck, even if ⟨it is only that⟩'. κἂν is καὶ ἐὰν with a subjunctive

understood, as fairly often with expressions meaning 'only a little'. Cf. *Lys.* 672 κἂν σμικρὰν λαβήν, *Wealth* 126 κἂν σμικρὸν χρόνον, *Akh.* 1021, S. *Ai.* 1078, *El.* 1483, D. 2. 14.   ἐκεῖ: 'in the law-courts'; cf. 104, 765–70.

93 ὁ νοῦς πέτεται: cf. Theognis 1053 τῶν γὰρ μαινομένων πέτεται θυμός τε νόος τε.

κλεψύδραν: The water-clock was a device for measuring periods of time (not for telling the time of day), and it was used in Athenian law-courts to time the speeches of the litigants. It consisted of a vessel with one or more small holes in the bottom. At the beginning of a speech a certain quantity of water was put into it (varying according to the kind of case being tried); the speaker had to end his speech when all the water had run out.

The only surviving description of this kind of water-clock and its use in law-courts is a mutilated passage in Arist. *Ath. Pol.* 67, though there are plenty of passing references to it from *Akh.* 693 onwards, especially in the orators. A vessel found in the Agora has been identified as a water-clock; it has been described, with illustrations, by Suzanne Young (*Hesperia* viii [1939] 274–84). It is a pail-shaped pot some nine inches high, with a clay spout at the bottom which will drain it in six minutes. Many law-court speeches certainly lasted much longer than this; presumably there were water-clocks of various sizes, and one speaker might be allowed several in succession (or two in alternation) until his total allotted amount of water had run out.

The earliest occasion when we hear of a water-clock used elsewhere than in a law-court is in the first half of the fourth century: Euboulos wrote a comedy entitled Κλεψύδρα, in which the chief character was a woman who was nicknamed Klepsydra because she allowed each of her lovers to remain with her only until her water-clock ran out (Ath. 567 d). This implies that in the fourth century water-clocks were used in private houses, at least occasionally. But our line implies that they were not generally used in private houses in the fifth century: the water-clock is inseparably linked with the law-court in the old man's mind.

94 'From being in the habit of holding his vote'. For the construction cf. 1045.   δὲ . . . γ': 'Yes, and . . .' When δέ accompanies a phrase consisting of preposition, article, and noun, it usually precedes the article or follows the noun; 'the order preposition, article, particle, substantive seems to be rare' (Denniston 186). But perhaps this rule does not apply when, as here, an infinitive is used as a noun; cf. Pl. *Grg.* 490 c ἐν τῷ δὲ ἀναλίσκειν τε αὐτὰ καὶ καταχρῆσθαι, where the deletion of ἐν, proposed by Sauppe and accepted by Dodds, seems to be unnecessary.

ψῆφόν: An Athenian juror used for voting either a pebble (ψῆφος) or a mussel-shell (χοιρίνη in 333, 349, *Knights* 1332), which he brought with him to the court (109-10, 349). There is no evidence for the use of bronze votes before the fourth century. There were two voting-urns (καδίσκοι), one for condemnation and one for acquittal; the jurors filed past them, passing the urn for condemnation first and the urn for acquittal second (991, Phrynikhos com. 32). Each urn had a funnel (κημός) made of wicker-work placed on the opening (Σ *Knights* 1150, Σ *Wasps* 99). Presumably the juror could put his hand inside the funnel of each urn, so that no onlooker could see into which one he dropped his vote; thus the use of these urns ensured that the voting was secret (Lys. 13. 37, *Lex. Cant.* κημός). When all had voted, the votes were emptied out on to a flat stone to be counted (332-3, 993).

95 τοὺς τρεῖς: 'the first three': thumb, forefinger, middle finger. The thumb is a δάκτυλος (Hdt. 3. 8. 1).   **ἀνίσταται**: 'he gets up' out of bed; cf. 217.

96 ἐπιτιθείς: 'putting on' an altar, as in *Clouds* 426, *Frogs* 888.   **νουμηνίᾳ**: This and *Akh.* 999 show that the first day of the month was an occasion for religious festivity; cf. also Lys. fr. 53. Hermes and Hekate in particular were honoured with frankincense at the new moon (Porph. *Abst.* 2. 16).

97 καὶ . . . γέ: 'Yes, and . . .', just like 94 δὲ . . . γ'.

98 'Pyrilampes's son written on a door as handsome Demos.' The actual inscription would be ΔΗΜΟΣ ΚΑΛΟΣ, in the nominative. Here we have virtually an indirect-speech construction; in 99 by contrast we have a direct speech. In English we should be more likely to say 'the name of Pyrilampes's son written . . .'; for the telescoped construction omitting ὄνομα cf. Pl. *Tht.* 207 e Θεαίτητον γράφων. The expression Δῆμος καλός is equivalent to 'I love Demos'. This type of amatory scrawl on any convenient flat surface is parodied also in *Akh.* 144, where it is said that king Sitalkes of Thrace likes the Athenians so much that he writes on walls ΑΘΗΝΑΙΟΙ ΚΑΛΟΙ.

Pyrilampes was a prominent personality in Periklean Athens. He was the son of a man named Antiphon, and his sister married Glaukon (uncle of Kritias and grandfather of Plato). Demos was his son by his first wife. Subsequently he married his niece Periktione after the death of her first husband Ariston, and thus became Plato's stepfather. By this second marriage he had a son named Antiphon (not to be confused with the orator or sophist of that name). (These relationships are reconstructed from Pl. *Parm.* 126 bc, *Kharm.* 158 a, D.L. 3. 1, Plu. *Eth.* 581 d.) He was an outstandingly tall and handsome man (Pl. *Kharm.* 158 a). He was a friend of Perikles (Plu. *Per.* 13. 15), and he took some part in public life: he served as an Athenian ambassador to Persia and elsewhere (Pl. *Kharm.* 158 a). He also fought and was wounded in the battle of Delion in 424 (Plu. *Eth.* 581 d). In private

life he kept an aviary, in which the peacocks were particularly celebrated (Plu. *Per.* 13. 15, cf. Ath. 397 c). That he was prosecuted for
murder by Perikles and successfully defended by Thoukydides son of
Melesias (anon. *Life of Th.* 6) is improbable but not impossible.

Demos inherited his father's good looks, as *Wasps* 98 shows.
Kallikles was one of his admirers (Pl. *Grg.* 481 de). He also inherited
the aviary, which he guarded jealously, refusing to let anyone else
have any of the peacocks, and admitting visitors only on the first day
of the month; he seems to have been criticized for this restrictive
attitude in Antiphon's lost speech *Against Erasistratos* (Ath. 397 cd,
quoting Ant. fr. 57; cf. Plu. *Eth.* 833 d = *Life of Ant.* 20). Eupolis in
his *Cities* seems also to have criticized him by saying κυψέλη ἔνεστιν
which presumably means 'he has wax in his ears' (Σ^V *Wasps* 98,
quoting Eupolis 213), but the point of this satirical comment is obscure
(perhaps stupidity, if he was unable to understand what was said to
him; or perhaps haughtiness, if he pretended not to hear). Later in his
life he received a gold cup from the king of Persia (Lys. 19. 25), to
whom he possibly went as an ambassador like his father. The last
incident known of him is that in 390 he was appointed a trierarkhos,
which implies wealth, but he had some difficulty in finding the
necessary money, which may imply improvidence (Lys. 19. 25–6). He
was posted to Cyprus, his ship being one of a squadron of ten sent
under the command of Philokrates to assist Euagoras against the
Persians, but they were captured by the Spartans before reaching
Cyprus (Lys. 19. 25, X. *Hel.* 4. 8. 24).

Ar. selects Demos for mention here not only because he is notoriously
handsome but also because his name makes a good jingly parallel
with κημός.   [υἱὸν: τὸν (J) will not scan, because Πυ- is short.]

99 ἰὼν παρέγραψε πλησίον: 'he goes and writes next to it': aorist for
a regular occurrence, as in 574, 582, 586, 594, 618, 1257–61, 1278,
1459–61.   κημὸς: 94 n.

100 ἀλεκτρυόνα: A cock was the only kind of alarm-clock a Greek could
have. [B₂'s variant here is so absurd that it cannot be the result of
deliberate thought; so it is evidence that the contributions by this
hand should not be regarded as merely editorial conjectures.]   ἀφ'
ἑσπέρας: 'immediately after the evening', i.e. 'at the beginning of the
night', when everyone was just going to bed. Most people would
complain that such a cock was crowing much too early, but the old
man's complaint was just the opposite.

101 ἀναπεπεισμένον: 'because it had been bribed'. The old man is so
suspicious that he alleges bribery even in the most unlikely cases. This
compound of πείθω occurs often in *Wasps*, and has two uses; sometimes ἀνα- implies 'wrongly', so that the verb means 'seduce', 'mis-
lead', 'corrupt' (so here); sometimes ἀνα- implies 'back', 'in reverse',
so that the verb means 'win over', 'persuade to change one's mind',

'dissuade' (so in 116, 278, 568, 586, 784). In 974 it seems to have both senses at once.

102 ὑπευθύνων: 'officials undergoing examination'. This is the type of defendant most frequently mentioned in *Wasps*.

Every Athenian magistrate had to undergo an examination of his conduct in office. First his accounts were examined by the public auditors (λογισταί), chosen by lot from the members of the council (Arist. *Ath. Pol.* 48. 3); they were assisted by advocates (συνήγοροι of type *B*: 482 n.). They then referred his case to a law-court, where, if his accounts had seemed unsatisfactory, the advocates prosecuted him for embezzlement (κλοπή) or corruption (δῶρα) or 'malefaction' (ἀδίκιον) (*Ath. Pol.* 54. 2, cf. Ar. *Knights* 1358–61). At this trial it was possible also for anyone else to bring charges against him (Ais. 3. 23, D. 18. 117). A magistrate who had not handled public money had of course no accounts to be examined, but he had to give a written undertaking that he had neither received nor spent any money belonging to the state (Ais. 3. 22).

Next the ten examiners (εὔθυνοι), one chosen by lot from each tribe, and each assisted by two assessors (πάρεδροι), received any written complaints against his conduct in office (*Ath. Pol.* 48. 4). If a complaint was thought justified, he was condemned by the examiners and assessors, but their verdict was subject to ratification by a law-court, or by the deme-judges if the offence was one which fell within their jurisdiction (And. 1. 78, *Ath. Pol.* 48. 5).

The examination of accounts was called λόγος; the examination as a whole was usually called λόγος καὶ εὔθυναι or simply εὔθυναι (or εὔθυνα or εὐθύνη). Although the later part of the examination might also lead to a trial by jury, Ar. here probably has in mind primarily the financial examination; for that is the part which was always brought before a jury, and it is the part which is satirized later in the play (891–1008).

103 ἀπὸ δορπηστοῦ: 'directly after supper-time', when ordinary people would be going to bed; cf. X. *An.* 1. 10. 17, where ἀμφὶ δορπηστόν is the end of the day. κέκραγεν: The perfect of κράζω usually has a present sense. Here it and προκαθεύδει should be regarded as historic presents, referring to a single occasion in the past (the day when the cock crowed in the evening), not to a regular occurrence (for 91–6 shows that as a rule he goes to bed at night in the ordinary way). ἐμβάδας: 'Shouted for his shoes' means 'decided to go out'; Greeks did not wear shoes at home. An ἐμβάς was a cheap and austere kind of shoe (cf. 1157) made of leather (*Knights* 316–21, 868–70), normally worn only by men (*Ek.* 47, 314, 342, 507) and only by poor people (*Ek.* 850, Is. 5. 11). An external accusative is seldom used with κράζω, but cf. *Frogs* 426–7.

104 ἐκεῖσ': 'to the law-court'; cf. 92, 765–70. For fear of getting up too

late the next morning, he went straight to the court in the evening without going to bed at all. **προκαθεύδει πρῷ πάνυ**: 'had a sleep before the trial, in the very early morning'.

105 λεπάς: 'limpet'; cf. Thompson *Fishes* 147–8. The same simile is used in *Wealth* 1096. **τῷ κίονι**: 'The pillar' was evidently a feature of the law-courts. Perhaps each court had beside its entrance a pillar to which notices of the next day's cases were attached. [Not *τῳ κίονι*, 'a pillar'; the old man would have no reason for clinging to any pillar except a specially significant one.]

106 ἅπασι τιμῶν τὴν μακρὰν: 'because he awards the long line to all the accused'. For many kinds of offence the penalty was not fixed by law but was decided by the jury in each individual case: when an accused man was found guilty, the accuser proposed a penalty and the accused proposed a different (naturally lighter) penalty, and after each had spoken in support of his proposal the jury voted to decide between the two. For this purpose each juror had a tablet (*πινάκιον*) smeared with wax; a long line drawn in the wax was a vote for the severer penalty and a short line for the lighter (cf. 167, Pol. 8. 16, J. H. Lipsius *Das attische Recht* 927).

107 εἰσέρχεται: 'comes home', as in *Th.* 395, *Frogs* 981.

108 'Having wax plastered up under his nails' from drawing long lines on his tablet with them. **ἀναπεπλασμένος**: middle voice. [*πλάττω* and its compounds are used of kneading and shaping substances like wax, clay, and dough, and so *ἀναπεπλασμένος* is probably sound, even though not exactly paralleled. *ὑποπεπλασμένος* (J) is a compound which does not occur in classical Greek. Σ's gloss *πεπληρωμένος τοὺς ὄνυχας κηροῦ* is probably an explanation of *ἀναπεπλασμένος* and is not evidence that he read *ἀναπεπλη''μένος* as some have thought.]

109 'Because he got frightened that he might sometime run short of pebbles, for the purpose of being able to vote . . .'

110 ἔχοι: The optative shows that *τρέφει* denotes not only a present activity but also a past decision to undertake the activity: 'he decided to keep . . . in order to be able to vote, and is still keeping . . .'. Cf. *Frogs* 23 *τοῦτον δ' ὀχῶ, ἵνα μὴ ταλαιπωροῖτο μηδ' ἄχθος φέροι*, 'I decided to allow him to ride, in order that . . .'. **αἰγιαλὸν**: 'a whole beach'. **τρέφει**: He tends his collection of pebbles as carefully as if it were alive. [There is no reference here to the use of stones by bees for ballast, as R. E. White imagined (*CR* xii [1898] 209).]

111 τοιαῦτ' ἀλύει: 'Such is his frenzy'. Ar. is parodying a passage from Euripides's *Stheneboia* (fr. 665): *τοιαῦτ' ἀλύει· νουθετούμενος δ' ἔρως μᾶλλον πιέζει.*

113 μοχλοῖσιν: 'with bars'. The door visible to the audience has only one bar across it (154). Either we are meant to imagine bars across other doors and windows which are out of sight, or the plural is a vague and general one referring simply to the method of confinement. **ἐνδή-**

σαντες must here mean 'shut in', not 'bind'; 'imprison' is a normal meaning of δέω. [ἐγκλείσαντες may be a gloss which was intended to clarify this point and got into the text of J by mistake.]   ἂν with ὡς and the subjunctive in a final clause is fairly common in verse, though rare in prose; cf. 425.

115 λόγοισι: not otiose, but contrasted with the stronger action described in 118–24.

116 ἀνέπειθεν: 'tried to persuade': 101 n.   τριβώνιον: 33 n. The son wants his father to give up his life of poverty and wear warmer and more comfortable clothes. In this line Ar. prepares the way for the later scene in which the old man finally is persuaded to discard his old cloak (1122–56).

118 ἀπέλου κἀκάθαιρ': 'tried to cleanse and purify' by a religious ritual, in case the disease was caused by pollution of some kind (as in legend, for instance, disease afflicted the Thebans when they were polluted by Oedipus). Ceremonial washing was a method of purification from pollution. For the imperfect form of λούω/λόω cf. Wealth 657 ἐλοῦμεν. ὁ δ' οὐ μάλα: 'but he wouldn't', 'but not he!' There is no need to supply any one verb. Cf. Th. 846 ὁ δ' οὐδέπω.

119 ἐκορυβάντιζ': 'tried to make him celebrate the rites of the Kory-bantes' to cure his madness: 8 n.   αὐτῷ τυμπάνῳ: 'actually with a drum', 'drum and all'. It is idiomatic to use a dative of accom-paniment without σύν when it is reinforced by αὐτός; cf. 170, 1449.

120 εἰς τὸ Καινὸν ἐμπεσών: 'rushing into the New Court'. (Not 'the new court', alluding to a recently built court of which the official name was something different; the absence of δικαστήριον shows that 'the New' is a recognized proper name.) For a list of Athenian law-courts, 1108 n. The location of the New Court is unknown.

Later in the play it is implied that Philokleon is a juror of the court of the thesmothetai, not the New Court; and on one occasion he seems to belong to yet a third court (389). But Ar. does not care about this kind of inconsistency; by the time the later scenes are reached the audience will have forgotten the allusion to the New Court.

121 δῆτα: 'then', moving on to the next item in a series, as in Clouds 1058.

122 ξυλλαβών: Force has to be used to get the old man to spend the night out of reach of the law-courts.

123 εἰς Ἀσκληπιοῦ: 'in the temple of Asklepios'. For the omission of the accusative cf. 1250, Lys. 2, etc. Sleeping in a sanctuary of Asklepios was supposed to cure illness; cf. especially Wealth 633–748, and E. J. and L. Edelstein Asclepius (1945). The temple of Asklepios at Aigina is mentioned in Paus. 2. 30. 1; cf. IG iv² 126. 4. The reason why the temple at Aigina was the one to which the old man was taken is that in 422 no more convenient sanctuary of Asklepios was available. The famous temple at Epidauros was inaccessible to Athenians because

Epidauros was a member of the Peloponnesian League; the introduction of Asklepios to the city of Athens was not until 420/19 (*IG* ii² 4960), and the establishment of his sanctuary at Zea (east of Peiraieus) took place only very shortly before (cf. F. Robert in *Rev. Phil.* III iii [1929] 286–7, v [1931] 136).

124 κνεφαῖος: 'before dawn'.   ἐπὶ τῇ κιγκλίδι: 'at the court gate'. The general public were excluded from a law-court by railings (δρύφακτοι). (They could watch and listen from outside the railings.) The κιγκλίς was a gate in the railings through which the jurors were admitted to the court by the presiding magistrate; cf. 775.

125 ἐξεφρίομεν: 'we let out', imperfect. [This verb, found only in compounds, has the alternative present forms -φρέω and -πίφρημι. (For a list of instances see W. S. Barrett's note on E. *Hipp.* 867.) The imperfect from -φρέω would be -εφροῦμεν (cf. E. *Tro.* 652, D. 20. 53), from -πίφρημι would be -επίφραμεν (cf. Arist. *HA* 541ᵇ11 εἰσπιφράναι). If ἐξεφρίομεν (or ἐξεφρείομεν, the reading of J) is right, we must assume a third present form -φρίω (or -φρείω), for which there is no other evidence. If this assumption is intolerable, we must emend. ἐξεπίφραμεν may be possible, but it involves lengthening ι before φρ, which is uncommon in comic iambics (837 n.). Nauck conjectured ἐξεφρίεμεν, but this is no improvement on ἐξεφρίομεν, since there is no other evidence for a present -φρίημι (forms like -έφρηκα and -φρες may come from -πίφρημι). However, I do not feel sure that any emendation is necessary.]

The sentence runs comically on, with ὁ δέ and ἡμεῖς δέ alternating in ping-pong fashion, as the old man and his household try in turn to outwit each other.

126 διά τε τῶν: διὰ τῶν τε might be expected, but cf. Denniston 518. ὑδρορροῶν: 'gutters', to drain water from the floor of the house. (Not to drain rain from the roof, because rain-gutters would not lead out from the inside of the house, and because it is not until 129 that he climbs up a wall.)

127 ὀπῶν: 'holes', 'chinks' in the walls, under the door, etc.

128 κἀπακτώσαμεν: 'and made fast' the gaps, by filling them up; cf. Hdt. 2. 96. 2.

129 κολοιὸς: A tame jackdaw will hop up a ladder; cf. Thphr. *Char.*21. 6.

130 τοῖχον: the wall of the enclosed courtyard of the house (αὐλή), which is invisible to the audience. The audience must imagine (and presumably this was the usual lay-out of the larger Athenian houses; compare the Dema house described in *BSA* lvii [1962] 75–114) that the yard does not have rooms on all four sides of it, but on two or three sides. Its remaining side or sides are enclosed by a simple wall. The old man has the run of the yard, on to which the rooms of the house open, but to prevent his climbing over the wall huge nets have been stretched over the yard, from the wall to the roof of the house (131–2).

132 ἐν κύκλῳ: 'all round'.

133 Φιλοκλέων: i.e. 'Love-Kleon'. Kleon is the champion of the jurors; cf. 197, 242, *Knights* 255–6, and pages 3–4.

134 ναὶ μὰ Δία: 'yes, he is', retorting to the incredulous laughter of the audience at *Φιλοκλέων*. (Men are not usually named after the politicians whom they support.)   **δ' . . . γε**: 'and what's more'.   **τῳδί**: Bdelykleon, unlike Philokleon, is in full view (67–8).   **Βδελυκλέων**: 'Loathe-Kleon'. βδελυ- is not used elsewhere to form compound words, whereas μισο- is common (cf. 411, 473, 1165, and *Peace* 304 μισολάμαχος). Ar. might have named his character *Μισοκλέων*, but *Βδελυ*- is more vivid.

The two names which form the climax of Xanthias's long speech are a political joke. In the rest of the play they are used only occasionally (*Βδελυκλέων* in 137 and 372, *Φιλοκλέων* in 163 and 1466). It is convenient for us to use them in printing and discussing the play, but for the most part Ar. and his audience are more likely to have thought of the two characters as 'the old man' and 'the young man' or as 'the father' and 'the son'.

135 ἔχων: attracted from the dative by the proximity of *Βδελυκλέων*. **φρυαγμοσεμνάκους**: a comic invention, 'pomposnortical', meaning 'arrogant'; cf. Taillardat § 329.

136–229. *Philokleon attempts to escape from the house to get to the law-court. He tries a number of ingenious and comic methods in quick succession, but every time he is prevented by Bdelykleon and the slaves. Finally he gives up; but Bdelykleon warns Xanthias that soon his fellow jurors, who are like wasps when angered, will be coming to call for him.*

This is one of the best scenes of slapstick in Aristophanes. It is a model of 'jack-in-the-box clowning', by which I mean the type of slapstick in which someone keeps popping out and being pushed back inside out of sight. Every time the popper-out is pushed in, the audience experiences a feeling of satisfaction, and each fresh popping-out increases the hilarity. The richest effect is obtained if the popper-out does not always use the same route, so that the audience never knows just where he is going to appear next. Ar.'s appreciation of the potentialities of this type of slapstick is admirable; Philokleon's attempts to escape are all different, and each is more extraordinary and absurd than the one before. This is perhaps the best 'jack-in-the-box' scene ever written.

136 Bdelykleon shouts down from the roof.   **καθεύδετε**; suspicious or threatening; the slaves are supposed to be on guard.

137 οἴμοι: The meaning of this exclamation varies according to its context (and, no doubt, mode of utterance). Here perhaps the nearest English equivalent is 'ὄ-ὄ', implying 'Here comes trouble!', the usual comic attitude of an inferior to the approach of a superior.   **τί ἐστι**; Probably Sosias has not heard Bdelykleon's shout; he may have settled down to sleep again during Xanthias's long speech (86–135). Less probably he has heard the shout but does not understand why it worries Xanthias.

138 δεῦρ': not to where Bdelykleon is, but to a place to which he points, at the back of the house, out of sight of the audience.   **ἅτερος**: 'one or other'.

139 ἱπνὸν: 'kitchen'. The word means originally 'oven', 'furnace', and then the room or part of the house in which the oven is situated. Philokleon has gone out of his bedroom into the yard (ἐξελήλυθεν), across the yard, and into the kitchen. Bdelykleon has seen him crossing the yard. In a comic description of this kind it is unreasonable to press for further details by asking how he can subsequently see from the roof what Philokleon is doing inside the kitchen; in real life he could not.   [ἐξελήλυθεν (V) is preferable to εἰσ- (RJ) because the neighbouring εἰς τὸν ἱπνὸν is more likely to have caused corruption of ἐξ- to εἰσ- than of εἰσ- to ἐξ-.]

140 μυσπολεῖ τι: 'is doing some mouse-walking', i.e. 'is scurrying about like a mouse'. The verb occurs only here, and is probably a comic word invented by Ar. I see no reason for LSJ's statement that there is a play on μυστιπολεύω.   **καταδεδυκώς**: 'stooping down'. Philokleon is looking for escape-routes at floor level, such as mouseholes.

141 'See that he doesn't escape down the waste-hole of the sink.'

Sosias now runs off (round the side of the scene-building) to guard the outside of the kitchen, and does not reappear. (The duals in 191 and 381 show that there is subsequently only one slave on the stage with Bdelykleon, and 456 shows that he is Xanthias.)

142 σύ: Xanthias.   **πρόσκεισο**: 'keep close to', to guard; cf. E. *Ph.* 739 προσκεῖσθαι πύλαις.   **ταῦτ'**: 'yes', rather like northern English 'I will that'; so also in 851, 1008.

143 ἄναξ Πόσειδον: When ἄναξ or ὦ 'ναξ precedes a god's name in an exclamation, it marks surprise or annoyance at a sight or event which is unwelcome or unpleasant; cf. *Akh.* 94, *Peace* 180, 238, *Birds* 277, 295, *Lys.* 296, *Wealth* 438 (all of which have Ἄπολλον or Ἡράκλεις; there are no other instances in Ar. of ἄναξ Πόσειδον as an exclamation. When Poseidon is invoked in admiration, ἄναξ is always omitted; cf. ὦ Πόσειδον in *Knights* 144, *Peace* 564, *Frogs* 491, 1430.   **ἆρ'** 'does little more than add liveliness to the question' (Denniston 39); so also in 266, 273.   **κάπνη**: 'chimney'. According to Σ a kitchen chimney was a pipe (σωληνοειδές), not just a hole in the roof. But that does not necessarily mean that in this play the scenery included a realistic chimney. All that is essential in performance is that Philokleon's voice should be heard from any convenient aperture at roof level; since Bdelykleon calls it κάπνη, the audience then knows that Philokleon is in the chimney. Probably the flat roof of the scene-building had a trap-door which was used as the chimney here.

ψοφεῖ: 'is making a noise'. The noise is made by Philokleon climbing up inside the chimney. ψοφεῖ does not mean that the chimney has a trap-door which creaks when raised (as Starkie suggests), for 147 shows that the chimney's covering board is not attached to it.

144 οὗτος: addressed to the person inside the chimney. **καπνὸς ἔγωγ' ἐξέρχομαι**: 'I'm smoke coming out'. ἔγωγ' implies 'that's what *I* am'. Perhaps with these words Philokleon's head emerges into view.

145 φέρ' ἴδω: 'tell me', 'pray'. This phrase, which is common in Ar.'s early plays but disappears later (the last instance is *Th.* 630), is used only with questions. It does not necessarily mean that the speaker wishes to see anything. Cf. 563, 762. **ξύλου τίνος σύ;** 'what wood's smoke are you?' This question is asked in a perfectly straightforward tone of voice, and is funnier so. It would be beside the point to ask whether Bdelykleon really believes that some smoke is speaking or is only being sarcastic. **συκίνου**: 'of fig-wood', a pun on συκοφάντης, 'wrongly motivated accuser'; cf. 897. Ar. implies that gullible jurors like Philokleon accompany συκοφάνται as naturally as smoke accompanies burning wood. Various attempts have been made to translate the pun: 'medlar-wood' (Starkie), 'I'm peach wood' (Parker), 'de syco . . . more' (Van Daele).

146 νὴ τὸν Δί': 'yes . . .': Bdelykleon assents not to the first but to the second (punning) meaning of συκίνου. **γ'** indicates that the relative clause gives a reason for assent: 'yes, for that is . . .'. **δριμύτατος** keeps up the pun: the smoke of fig-wood is acrid, and the juror who supports συκοφάνται is fierce. (For δριμύς of an unrelenting juror cf. 277, *Knights* 808, *Peace* 349.) Translate 'sharpest'.

147 ἀτάρ breaks off the unprofitable discussion about smoke; Bdelykleon stops being jocular and becomes serious. **οὐκ ἐσερρήσεις γε;** 'get inside, damn you!' [This and *Th.* 657 refute the view that ἐς is not used before a vowel in comedy. Elmsley (page 115 of his edition of *Akh.*) was wrong to emend on this account. οὐκ ἐσερρήσεις was the reading in the text in the time of Σ (whose note is οὐκ εἰσελεύσει μετὰ φθορᾶς;), and is obviously right.] **τηλία**: 'chimney-cover', a lid put over the top of the chimney to keep out the weather when the fire is not alight. From Bdelykleon's words it is clear that it is not attached to the chimney but is left lying around on the roof when not in use. [This interpretation is clear enough from Bdelykleon's words, and so need not be doubted, even though Σ *Wealth* 1037 may well have no other ultimate authority than our passage for his note ἄλλοι δὲ τηλίαν τὸ τῆς καπνοδόχης πῶμα, ὅ ἐστι περιφερές. Σ *Wasps* 147 writes σανὶς βαθεῖα ἐν ᾗ τὰ ἄλφιτα ἐν τῇ ἀγορᾷ ἐπίπρασκον, but although τηλία sometimes means 'meal-board' it can hardly mean that here; why should Bdelykleon expect to find a meal-board ready to hand on the roof?]

148 δύου πάλιν: 'Go in again!' He pushes Philokleon out of sight down the chimney, and puts the chimney-cover on top. **ξύλον**: He puts

F

a heavy piece of wood on top of the chimney-cover to keep it in place. Presumably Greek householders often kept a lump of wood or stone on the roof for this purpose; or possibly, as J. Staquet suggested (*Revue Belge de Philologie et d'Histoire* x [1931] 590), Bdelykleon simply seizes a broad plank or other rudimentary bed on which he was sleeping until 136.

149 ἐνταῦθά νυν with imperative: 'There now!' spoken by the victor to the vanquished; so also in *Th.* 1001, *Wealth* 724.

151 'Because now I shall be called the son of Smoky'. Καπνίας was a nickname given to Ekphantides, a comic dramatist of the generation before Ar., because of the obscurity of his writing (Hskh. κ 716, cf. Σ^V *Wasps* 151). The joke is, perhaps, that Bdelykleon, being a character in Aristophanes, does not wish to be thought the product of an inferior dramatist. [νυνὶ (J) is more likely than νῦν (RV) because a short vowel is seldom scanned long before πν in iambic trimeters in comedy (though cf. 837).]

152 A shout and banging are heard from inside the door. The doors of Greek houses opened inwards (cf. W. Beare *The Roman Stage* Appendix G), but on this occasion Ar. assumes that the door opens outwards, because this gives a better visual jack-in-the-box effect: the audience sees Xanthias pushing and leaning against the door as if he were squashing Philokleon back inside. Since it is not actually opened until 178, most of the audience will not notice the inconsistency between its inward opening at 178 and the activities at 152–5. (Cf. A. M. Dale in *JHS* lxxvii [1957] 205–6.) παῖ: the usual call to a slave to open a door, e.g. *Akh.* 395, *Clouds* 132. Usually, of course, it is shouted from outside to a slave inside, but here the situation is comically reversed. [Most editors, assuming that the word must be spoken by Xanthias or Sosias, emend, e.g. ὅδε Hermann, νῦν Rogers. But attribution of παῖ to Philokleon, shouting from inside, makes further alteration unnecessary.] Bdelykleon, still on the roof, shouts down to Xanthias: 'Press hard against it then!' Xanthias leans against the door or engages in other comic activity to prevent Philokleon from bursting it open. [νυν: 86 n.]

154 κατάκλειδος: 'lock'. μοχλοῦ: 'bar' across the door, resting in sockets on each side of the doorway. As a rule a bar would be placed on the inside of a door to prevent intruders from opening it inwards, but on this occasion it is on the outside to prevent Philokleon from opening it outwards. A. M. Dale maintains (*JHS* lxxvii [1957] 205–6) that the bar does not exist physically but has to be imagined by the audience; this could be true, but there is no very cogent reason to believe it.

155 [φύλαττέ θ' ὅπως: For the metre in the second foot cf. 25; emendation is not required. (Elmsley conjectured φύλατθ' ὅπως.)] βάλανον: 'pin' put through the bar to keep it in place. But the word is a pun, since it also means 'acorn' or 'date', and so Bdelykleon expresses fear that Philokleon may eat it. (Town-gate βάλανοι are discussed by D. Barends *Lexicon Aeneium* 162–8, but domestic bars and pins may have been simpler.)   ἐκτρώξεται: 'eat out'. τρώγω is the normal verb for eating fruit or nuts. ἐκτρώγω is not used elsewhere in classical Greek; it is used here because the object of eating the pin would be to get it out of the bar.

Bdelykleon now disappears from the roof; a staircase or ladder leads down at the back of the scene-building, out of sight of the audience. At the same moment Philokleon's head appears at the window, behind the net which covers it.

156 δράσετ': The plural includes Bdelykleon and Sosias, even though they are at the moment out of sight behind the house.

157 Δρακοντίδης must have been awaiting trial when *Wasps* was performed. He cannot be identified with certainty. The following Athenians named Drakontides are known at this period:

A: a man belonging to the Antiokhis tribe, who was *epistates* (foreman of the *prytaneis*) on the day when the assembly ratified the treaty between Athens and Khalkis (*IG* i² 39. 2). This treaty is usually dated to the year 446/5.

B: a general in 433/2, who took part in the expedition to Kerkyra (*IG* i² 295. 20). J. M. Stahl (*Rh. Mus.* xl [1885] 439–43) identified *A* with *B* and also inserted his name by emendation in Th. 1. 51. 4, making him Drakontides son of Leogoras of the deme Thorai (in the Antiokhis tribe). On this identification see A. W. Gomme *Commentary on Thucydides* i 188–9, F. Jacoby *FGrH* IIIb Supp. i 52–3.

C: a man who attacked Perikles by proposing a decree that he should submit accounts for audit by a jury (Plu. *Per.* 32. 3). The date of this event is not clear. Usually it has been assigned to 432 or 430. F. J. Frost (*JHS* lxxxiv [1964] 69–72) prefers 438/7; he may be right, but his arguments do not amount to proof. This man could be the same as *A* and/or *B*.

D: a member of the Thirty in 404/3, of the deme Aphidna (Lys. 12. 73, X. *Hel.* 2. 3. 2, Arist. *Ath. Pol.* 34. 3). Since Aphidna belonged to the Aiantis tribe, *D* must be a different man from *A*.

The Drakontides in *Wasps* 157 and 438 could be any or none of these. H. B. Mattingly (*JHS* lxxxi [1961] 125) identifies him with *A*, *B*, and *C*, and uses this identification as evidence for his view that the treaty between Athens and Khalkis belongs to 424/3.

158 [Beer 150–1 shows that in 158–65 Philokleon's interlocutor is Xanthias. Bdelykleon does not leave the roof until the end of 155, and so cannot reach the front of the house in time to hear 157.]   τοῦτο: the acquittal of Drakontides.   γὰρ: 'Yes, for . . .'

160 ἀποσκλῆναι: 'that I should wither away'. S. *Tr.* 1160 likewise has an aorist infinitive (instead of a future) in the report of a prophecy.

We are expected to laugh at the very notion of such a prophecy, not to ask whether Philokleon has really visited Delphoi or has just invented the story.

161 'God help us! What a prophecy!' The exclamation implies horror (though the horror may be only pretended). Cf. *Birds* 61 Ἄπολλον ἀποτρόπαιε, τοῦ χασμήματος.

162 ἴθ': 'please'. This imperative is often used to introduce a request; cf. 760, 843, 975, 986, 1388. It does not necessarily mean that the person addressed is to go anywhere.   ἔκφρες: 'let out', from ἐκπίφρημι (125 n.). [ἔκφερέ (a), 'carry out', is unsuitable, because Philokleon is quite capable of walking.]   μὴ διαρραγῶ: 'or I shall burst' with passion; cf. *Knights* 340.

163 μὰ τὸν Ποσειδῶ: 'No, I won't'. This exclamation always accompanies or implies a future verb, expressing a strong refusal or defiance. So in *Knights* 338, 409, *Lys.* 1165, *Ek.* 748; a rule-proving exception is *Knights* 843, where the verb is present but the sense implied is 'No, he won't'.

164 δίκτυον: the net covering the window from which he is looking.

166 πῶς ἄν σ' ἀποκτείναιμι; looks like a tragic quotation or parody. Philokleon calls for a sword, as a tragic hero might (and cf. 522), but then thinks of an even deadlier weapon. For the repetition of πῶς cf. *Clouds* 79.

167 ὅπως instead of ὡς with a superlative for 'as . . . as possible' is uncommon in comedy, but occurs also in 365–6, *Peace* 207.   πινάκιον τιμητικόν: 'penalty tablet'; 106 n.

168 Bdelykleon, having descended from the roof, comes round the side of the house on to the stage just in time to hear Philokleon's melodramatic threat, and delivers a melodramatic response.   δρασείει: 'is minded to do'; the verb occurs nowhere else outside tragedy except in *Peace* 62, which is also paratragic.

169 Philokleon abruptly switches from melodrama to conversational tones. Throughout this scene half the fun is due to the bewildering speed with which he turns to a new method of escaping the moment the last one has failed.

170 αὐτοῖσι τοῖς κανθηλίοις: 'along with its panniers'; 119 n. It would not be usual to sell panniers with a donkey, but in this scene the donkey is made to wear panniers for the purely practical reason that in 179–91 Philokleon must have something to hang on to.

171 νουμηνία: The first day of the month was market-day; cf. *Knights* 43.   οὔκουν κἄν . . . δῆτ' ἄν; The pile of particles marks surprise: 'Surely *I* could do that, couldn't I?'

172–3 'Not as well as I could.' 'That's right; I should do it better.' Ar. several times uses this type of joke: one speaker negatives a statement as being too strong; another speaker confirms the negative (thus appearing to agree with the first), but then it turns out that he is negativing it as being too weak. Cf. *Wealth* 110–11 Χρ. εἰσὶ δ' οὐ πάντες κακοί. Πλ. μὰ Δί', ἀλλ' ἀπαξάπαντες, and *Peace* 6–7.

173 ἀλλά: 'still', 'anyway', giving way in the argument about superior salesmanship and dismissing it. [This shows that ἀλλὰ τὸν ὄνον ἔξαγε is spoken by Philokleon, who now gives up hope of being allowed out to lead the donkey to market himself (but has thought of the new trick which he tries in 179–91), not by Bdelykleon, who does not give way at all.] **ἔξαγε:** addressed to a slave inside the house (invisible to the audience). Philokleon disappears from the window, and Xanthias sets about removing the bar and unfastening the door to let the donkey out.

174 καθῆκεν: 'let down' like bait; cf. D. 29. 46 τοῦτον γὰρ τὸν λόγον καθεῖκεν. 'What a cunning excuse he dangled before you!' **εἰρωνικῶς:** 'disingenuously', 'hypocritically'.

175 ἐκπέμψειας: not 'send out', but 'let go out'; cf. Dein. 1. 25. **ἔσπασεν:** 'caught', as in *Th.* 928; Bdelykleon continues Xanthias's fishing metaphor.

177 Philokleon told a slave to bring out the donkey (173), but now Bdelykleon decides he cannot trust a slave to bring it out without letting Philokleon slip out at the same time, and so declares that he will bring it out himself. [Beer 151–2 attributed 177–82 to Xanthias, but it would be inappropriate for a slave to make a decision of this sort.] **μοι . . . δοκῶ:** 'I think I will'. The infinitive accompanying this phrase to express an intended action is sometimes present (cf. A. *Ag.* 16), sometimes future (e.g. 250, *Frogs* 1421), sometimes aorist (e.g. Pl. *Euthd.* 288 c, Men. *Dys.* 267).

178 παρακύψη: 'peep out'.

Xanthias has been unfastening the door since 174, and has now got it open. Bdelykleon goes in, and immediately reappears leading a donkey. (This does not mean that the donkey is supposed to have been led through the rooms of the house. The door visible to the audience leads into the yard, and the donkey's stable, like the rooms of the house, opens off the yard.) Philokleon is being carried along on the underside of the donkey, by holding on to the panniers (cf. 170). For the moment Bdelykleon and Xanthias do not notice him, though of course the audience would see him at once.

Although real animals were no doubt sometimes used in Greek plays, the donkey here must be a 'pantomime' one, played by two actors (just as the dogs in 899–1008 are played by men); for in 179–80 he has to bray on his cue to prompt Bdelykleon's questions. (So P. D. Arnott in *Greece & Rome* vi [1959] 178–9.) The pantomime donkey heehawing, with Philokleon hanging on underneath, would be a hilarious sight.

179 κάνθων: 'neddy'.

181 'Οδυσσέα τιν': 'some Odysseus', i.e. 'someone like Odysseus'. For τις added to a name cf. *Birds* 512, *Frogs* 912. Odysseus escaped from the cave of the Kyklops by clinging to the underside of a ram. In this passage Ar. gives us a comic parody of the legend, but there are no close verbal similarities to show that he is specifically parodying either *Odyssey* 9. 424–63 or Kratinos's play *'Οδυσσῆς*. The reason why Ar. uses a donkey instead of a ram is that sheep would not be kept in the yard of an Athenian house; besides it would be impossible in real life for a man to be carried on the underside of a sheep. (The Kyklops's sheep were doubtless giant-sized super-sheep.)

When Bdelykleon mentions Odysseus, he is simply making a joke; he does not yet suspect that anyone is actually clinging to the donkey. But now Xanthias takes a look underneath and discovers that someone is.   ἀλλά 'introduces the substantiation by the second speaker of an hypothesis or wish expressed by the first, confirming as actual what has hitherto been presented as imaginary' (Denniston 20).

182 τουτονί τιν': 'somebody here', pointing.   ὑποδεδυκότα: 'who has crept underneath'.

183 φέρ' ἴδωμαι: 'Let me look'. The middle of ὁράω is sometimes used as a synonym for the active in verse, e.g. Kratinos 138. [So Beer's φέρ' ἴδω. ναί (giving the whole line to Bdelykleon) is unnecessary. φέρ' ἴδω in the sense 'tell me' (145 n.) would here be less appropriate than 'let me look'.]   τουτὶ τί ἦν; 'Good heavens, what's this?' This phrase is idiomatically used to express surprise when the speaker catches sight of something for the first time; cf. 1509, *Akh.* 157, *Birds* 1495, *Frogs* 39. The reason for the imperfect is obscure. Possibly it is an assumption that the surprising object has been there for some time, even though the speaker has only just seen it. Or possibly there is a reference to a past thought resulting in the present surprising sight: 'What was this done for?' 'What was the point?'

184–5 Bdelykleon's questions are inserted by Ar. solely to introduce the jokes in Philokleon's answers. It is pointless to ask whether Bdelykleon is really incapable of seeing for himself that the man under the donkey is Philokleon.   Οὖτις: 'No-one'. In the legend Odysseus tells the Kyklops that his name is No-one, so that later when the Kyklops cries 'No-one is killing me' his friends do not come to his aid.   Ἀποδρασιππίδου: Odysseus's father is Laertes, but Philokleon substitutes a name more appropriate to his present situation, a comic compound of ἀποδράω and ἵππος with a patronymic ending: 'son of Fitzrunawayhorse'.

186 'You're a No-one who'll get no one advantage by it.' χαίρω means 'act with impunity'.

187 ὔφελκε: to Xanthias: 'Pull him out from underneath.'   θᾶττον: 'at once', without comparative force; so also in 824.   ὦ μιαρώτατος: 'the scoundrel!', exclamatory nominative; cf. 900.

188 ἵν' ὑποδέδυκεν: 'what a place he's crept under!' For ἵνα in an exclamation cf. S. *OT* 947, 1311.

189 κλητῆρος: a pun, meaning both 'donkey' (cf. 1310) and 'summons-witness'. In most kinds of prosecution no summons was issued by any official, and it was the duty of the accuser himself to give formal notice of his charge to the person he intended to prosecute. The notice was usually given orally. To preclude the possibility that an accused man might fail to appear for trial and subsequently defend his absence by claiming that he had not received a summons, an accuser delivering a summons took with him a friend who could afterwards testify that the summons had been properly delivered. 'Summon' is καλοῦμαι or προσκαλοῦμαι, 'witness a summons' is κλητεύω, and 'summons-witness' is κλητήρ. Cf. 1406-45, *Clouds*, 1217-22. **πωλίῳ** continues the pun, meaning both 'foal' and also metaphorically 'follower', 'worshipper'; for the metaphorical sense cf. Euboulos 84. 2 πώλους Κύπριδος.

190 ἥσυχον: 'in peace'. Xanthias is trying to drag him away from the donkey.

191 μαχεῖ: future. [μαχούμεθα shows that this, not μάχει, is required.] **ὄνου σκιᾶς**: Philokleon wants to be allowed to hide under the donkey, but 'a donkey's shadow' was a proverbial expression for something not worth fighting for. The joke is that an expression usually metaphorical is here used literally; for other jokes of this type cf. 783, 898. Σ relates the story from which the proverb was supposed to have originated: a man hired a donkey to carry some goods, and when taking a rest in the course of the journey sat in the donkey's shadow to avoid the heat of the sun; the owner objected that he had hired only the donkey and not the donkey's shadow, and they went to law about it. We cannot tell now whether the proverb really originated from this story or the story was invented to explain the proverb; J. S. L. de la Vega (*Emerita* xxviii [1960] 133-5) suggests that really the proverb originated from περὶ ὀνείρου σκιᾶς, but that is only a guess. Demosthenes made use of the story on a famous occasion in the Athenian assembly (Plu. *Eth.* 848 ab). Arkhippos wrote a comedy called ῎Ονου σκιά. The proverbial phrase occurs also in Ar. fr. 192, S. fr. 331, Pl. *Phdr.* 260 c, and is apparently parodied in D. 5. 25.

192 πόρρω τέχνης: partitive genitive: 'far advanced in skill'; cf. Pl. *Euthd.* 294 e πόρρω σοφίας, X. *Ap.* 30 πόρρω μοχθηρίας. **παράβολος**: 'fully grown', 'no chicken'. ἄβολος is a young horse, which has not yet shed its foal-teeth (S. fr. 408, Pl. *Laws* 834 c, etc.); παρ- is 'past' (as in παρακμάζω, etc.), and so παράβολος is 'past one's youth'. Bdelykleon means 'experienced', but Philokleon thinks he means 'deteriorating' and indignantly objects. (Cf. Taillardat § 29. I have found no other instance of παράβολος in this sense, but the alternative interpretation 'reckless' will not do because it is inconsistent with πόρρω τέχνης and irrelevant to 193-5.)

193-5 Philokleon continues to speak as if Bdelykleon were the Kyklops and intended to make a meal of him. He interprets 192 as an unfavourable comment on his quality for eating, meaning that he is old and going bad; and, indignant at the slur, forgets that he wants to avoid being eaten and actually invites Bdelykleon to see how good he tastes.   πονηρός means 'bad' not only of men but also of food; cf. 243, Pl. *Grg.* 464 e.   ἄριστον: 'in excellent condition'; it is unlikely that a pun is intended on ἄριστον meaning 'lunch', because that word has ᾱ and because 'lunch' is not the opposite of 'bad'.   ὑπογάστριον: a choice cut of an animal or fish for eating; cf. Ar. fr. 364. 'What, me? Gone bad? Certainly not; don't you realize I'm in prime condition now? Perhaps you will when you taste an undercut of old juror.' [The question-mark in 194 is due to me.   ἡλιαστικοῦ, rather than ἠ-: fifth-century inscriptions which show the aspirate correctly in other words never aspirate ἡλιαία (*IG* i² 39. 75, 63. 14, *ATL* D14. II. 7), and *Birds* 110 has ἀπηλιαστά (not ἀφ-); so *Lys.* 380 οὐκέθ' ἠλ- (ἡλ- R) should probably be emended to οὐκέτ' ἠλ-. Cf. H. T. Wade-Gery in *BSA* xxxvii (1940) 265 n. 3, and Dover's note on *Clouds* 863.]

196 ὤθει: 'push', addressed to Philokleon. But instead of obeying he shouts for help (197) while he and the donkey are pushed back into the house by Bdelykleon and Xanthias.

197 ξυνδικασταί: 'fellow jurors', a compound probably invented for this play. It is used again in 215, 233, 266, 430.

198 Philokleon and the donkey are now inside, and Bdelykleon shuts the door.

199 σύ: Xanthias.   τῶν λίθων: the stones that are lying about on the ground; cf. 222, *Akh.* 184, 319, *Peace* 225. The article does not mean that they have been specially prepared or collected.   πρὸς τὴν θύραν: 'against the door' to keep it shut.

200 βάλανον . . . μοχλόν: 154 n., 155 n.

201-2 'And, having put it ⟨the bar⟩ against the door, hurry up and roll the big mortar against it.' δοκός means a piece of wood used for building, a beam or board or plank (cf. *Clouds* 1496, Th. 4. 112. 2); here it seems to be the timber door, as distinct from the μοχλός which is probably iron. 'The big mortar' would be a large stone receptacle for grinding or crushing corn or other substances, and so would be the largest and solidest movable object which the household possessed. [Dobree conjectured τὴν δοκόν, meaning a beam set against the door to keep it shut, like the mortar.]

The object of laughter at this point is Xanthias. He is bombarded with orders without being given time to carry them all out; and then, to add injury to insult, he is hit on the head by something falling from above (203). He may have put the bar and pin in place, but he has certainly not had time to heap up a pile of stones or fetch the mortar. Thus we never discover how he would have solved the baffling problem of getting the mortar from inside the house without opening the door; we just laugh at the way in which he is interrupted each time he starts off to do anything.

203 τὸ βωλίον: 'this bit of dirt'. Xanthias rubs or wipes his head and looks upwards. The object is too small (note the diminutive ending) to be visible to the audience.

204 ἄνωθεν . . . ποθεν: 'from somewhere up above'. [Van Leeuwen transferred the last word to the next speech, giving πόθεν μῦς; But the change is unnecessary.]

205 μῦς; Xanthias's tone of voice conveys his incredulity and scorn at Bdelykleon's stupid suggestion.   οὑτοσί: 'there'. Xanthias points towards the roof, and Bdelykleon looks. Philokleon is not visible to the audience (if he were, Ar. would have given him some words to speak); in this passage attention and laughter are directed solely at the discomfiture and antics of Xanthias and Bdelykleon.

206 ὑπὸ τῶν κεραμίδων: 'under the tiles' of the roof. For ὑπό with the genitive meaning 'under' cf. *Th.* 281 ὑπὸ τῆς λιγνύος. Philokleon is supposed (absurdly) to be getting through a tiny hole between the roof and the top of the wall, and emerging under the eaves, where small animals and birds cling and nest.   ἡλιαστὴς ὀροφίας: 'a roof-juror'. The expression is meant to sound like a kind of animal; there was a kind of snake called ὀροφίας (Σ here, Hskh. ο 1299). [Not ἡ-: 195 n.]

208 ποῦ ποῦ: excited repetition, as in *Peace* 1197.   δίκτυον: 'hunting-net' for catching birds, as in *Birds* 1083. Bdelykleon is simply saying what is appropriate for someone trying to catch a bird; the net is not actually produced. (This is not a reference to the nets covering the yard and windows of the house.)

209 σοῦ: 'Be off with you !' 'Shoo!' The word is not just an exclamation but the passive imperative of σόω or σοέω, alternative forms of σεύω; cf. 458, A. *Th.* 31 σοῦσθε, S. *Ai.* 1414 σούσθω, A. *Pers.* 25 σοῦνται. πάλιν: 'go back!' Bdelykleon and Xanthias wave their arms in the direction of the roof, and the audience is to assume that Philokleon withdraws from under the tiles back into the house. In 197 physical force was needed to get him back inside; why are mere shouts and shooing enough this time? Because here the joke is precisely the idea that he can be treated just like a bird, and it would be less funny if he failed to react like a bird when shooed. Since his withdrawal is anyway not visible to the audience, the inconsistency with 197 will not be obtrusive to them (as it might be if they could actually see him turning round and going meekly in).   νὴ Δί' ἦ: 'really'; for ἦ following an oath cf. *Birds* 1397.   κρεῖττον ἦν: 'it would be better'. ἄν is omitted, as often with expressions denoting necessity, propriety, or possibility, because they contain an element of potentiality within themselves and so do not need ἄν to express it; cf. 478, *Clouds* 1215–16 κρεῖττον εὐθὺς ἦν τότε ἀπερυθριᾶσαι.

210 Skione (in Pallene, the south-western promontory of Khalkidike) revolted from Athens in the spring of 423, two days after Athens and Sparta had made a one year's truce, and the Athenians proceeded to besiege it (Th. 4. 120–2, 129–33, 5. 2. 2). Because of the truce this siege was the only fighting in which the Athenians were engaged at the time when *Wasps* was performed (cf. Th. 4. 134. 1). Skione eventually capitulated in the summer of 421 (Th. 5. 32. 1).

It has been suggested by R. Strömberg (*Classica et Mediaevalia* xxi [1960] 18–19) that Σκιώνην is a pun on ὄνου σκιά. But this is unlikely, because such a pun would be clear to an audience only if it immediately followed the reference to ὄνου σκιά in 191; by 210 this will no longer be fresh in their minds.

213 ἀπεκοιμήθημεν: This compound is used especially of soldiers going off duty to sleep; cf. Hdt. 8. 76. 3, X. *Kyr.* 2. 4. 22. The aorist implies that the action might have been taken before now, 'It's high time that . . .'; cf. *Lys.* 181–2 τί δῆτα ταῦτ' οὐχ ὡς τάχιστα, Λαμπιτοῖ, ξυνωμόσαμεν; **ὅσον ὅσον**: 'only just'; cf. *AP* 7. 472. 3–4 (Leonidas) ὅσον ὅσσον στιγμή. Doubled ὅσον does not occur elsewhere in Attic, but ὅσον μόνον does, e.g. 1288. **στίλην** obviously implies 'for a moment', but it occurs nowhere else and its literal meaning is uncertain. Σ^R says that it means 'a drop', Σ^V that Kallistratos (a scholar of the second century B.C.) said that it was a very small coin, 'a mite'.

214 ὦ πόνηρ': This vocative is regularly used to convey a mixture of sympathy and contempt: 'you poor fool!' So also in 223, *Clouds* 687, *Birds* 1648, etc.

215 παρακαλοῦντες: future participle to express purpose: 'to call for'.

216 ἀλλὰ νῦν γ': '⟨Perhaps they may later on,⟩ but *now* . . .'. He means 'It's much too early'. Previously he himself told us about Philokleon's habit of getting up ridiculously early (100–5), and so one might expect him to know also that the other jurors call for Philokleon early; but Ar. makes him ignorant of the fact in order to give Bdelykleon a pretext for explaining it for the audience's information. Ar. cares more that a passage should be convincing and effective in itself than that it should be consistent with passages in other parts of the play. **ὄρθρος βαθύς**: the first glimmer of light in the very early morning.

217 γοῦν emphasizing an exclamation: cf. 795, Denniston 455. 'They *have* got up late today!'

218 'For they regularly call for him any time after the middle of the night!' (My exclamation mark is intended to represent γε.) [The object is easily supplied from 215–16, and emendation to παραβάλλουσ', proposed by Wilamowitz 515, is unnecessary.]

220 'Ancient-honey-Sidon-Phrynikhos-lovely' is an appreciative comic adjective invented for the occasion. Phrynikhos wrote tragedies in the late sixth and early fifth centuries. His lyrics are compared to honey also in *Birds* 748–50: ἔνθεν ὡσπερεὶ μέλιττα Φρύνιχος ἀμβροσίων μελέων ἀπεβόσκετο καρπὸν ἀεὶ φέρων γλυκεῖαν ᾠδάν. One of his last and most famous tragedies was his *Phoenician Women*, which dealt with the defeat of Xerxes (A. *Per.* hyp.) and was performed in one of the years 478 to 473 (cf. *Dram. Fest.*² 236 n. 6). Σ^V says that it mentioned Sidon and quotes two phrases from it: καὶ Σιδῶνος προλιπόντα ναόν and Σιδώνιον ἄστυ λιποῦσα. Evidently the songs in this play, or one particular song about Sidon, were especially popular. For discussion of Phrynikhos see *Dith. Trag. Com.*² 63–5, H. Lloyd-Jones *Estudios sobre la tragedia griega* (1966) 19–33. For Philokleon's liking for Phrynikhos cf. 269, 1490. For -ήρατα (although 'lovely' is ἐρατός, not ἠρατός) cf. *Clouds* 301 πολυήρατον. [R makes ἀρχαῖα a separate word, but that is probably wrong; a scribe would be more likely to split up an unfamiliar compound than to lengthen it. Σ^V quotes a note by Aristarkhos that the compound is made ἀπὸ τοῦ μέλι καὶ τῆς Σιδῶνος καὶ τοῦ Φρυνίχου. This shows that Aristarkhos's text had -μελι-, not -μελη-, but not necessarily that it did not include ἀρχαιο- in the compound.]

222 ἤδη ποτ': 'straightaway'. ποτε following another temporal adverb just emphasizes it; cf. *Clouds* 346 ἤδη ποτ', *Birds* 1545 ἀεί ποτ', etc. **βαλλήσομεν:** This form of the future of βάλλω occurs only here and in 1491.

225 ἐκ τῆς ὀσφύος: 'coming out of their backs'. Cf. page 11 n. 2.

226 κεκραγότες: here 'buzzing'. κράζω is regularly used of loud harsh sounds made by animals as well as men, e.g. birds in *Birds* 307, frogs in *Frogs* 258.

227 βάλλουσιν: 'strike'.

229 Bdelykleon and Xanthias settle down on guard by the door, and immediately fall asleep.

Enter the chorus. They are old men who are in the habit of serving as jurors. They are dressed in ordinary long cloaks (408 ἱμάτια) ; at this stage there is nothing to make them look like wasps. They are accompanied by a number of boys, their sons, carrying lamps. [G. Hermann *De choro Vesparum Aristophanis* (1843), reprinted in his *Opuscula* viii (1877) 253–67, argued that the chorus consisted of twenty old men and four boys, and that all of them spoke individually; he distributed all the chorus's lines in 230–487 to individuals, giving 230–2 to the first chorister, 233–4 to the second, 235–9 to the third, 250 and 254–7 to the seventh (a boy), 262–3 to the tenth (another boy), and so on (the twenty-fourth got nothing but 309 ἀπαπαῖ φεῦ). However, the boys should not be reckoned among the twenty-four choristers, since that would leave the chorus below full strength after the boys' exit at 414. As for the old men, it is certainly possible that several of them speak different lines individually (and since Hermann various scholars have proposed different distributions), but it cannot be proved that they do so, since there is no point within the chorus's speeches at which a change of speaker is essential. I therefore prefer the conservative view that only the chorus-leader and one boy (his son) speak in 230–72 and 290–316, while 273–89 is a song by the whole chorus.]

230–72 *The old men have difficulty in walking along the street, which is dark and muddy. The leader urges on his companions, reminisces, has a dispute with his son about their lamp, talks about the weather, and finally expresses surprise that Philokleon is not there to meet them and suggests that they sing a song to call him out.*

The purpose of the passage is to show us the age, poverty, and helplessness of the old men. The ferocity described in 223–7 does not appear until later; here they are only peevish, nostalgic, and ineffective. The scene is not farcical (for the boy's threat in 254–7 to leave the old men floundering in the darkness and mud is not carried out). It combines pathos and gentle amusement in a manner similar to some scenes in Chekhov; the audience should not just laugh, but sympathize too. The effectiveness of the lines is enhanced by the skilful use of the metre; cf. notes on 230, 244, 246, 255.

230–47 *Metre*: iambic tetrameters; see page 24. In other early plays (*Akh.*, *Knights*, *Peace*) Ar. makes the chorus enter with trochaic tetrameters. Perhaps the iambic metre is considered more suitable than the trochaic for slow delivery, and is used here because the chorus consists of old men who are walking slowly and with difficulty. The only other extant plays in which Ar. uses this metre for the entrance of the chorus are *Lys.* and *Wealth*, in both of which also the chorus consists of old men.

230 Often in Ar.'s plays at the entrance of the chorus the chorus-leader begins by urging on his companions; cf. *Akh.* 204 τῇδε πᾶς ἕπου, *Peace* 301 δεῦρο πᾶς χώρει προθύμως, *Lys.* 254 χώρει, Δράκης, ἡγοῦ βάδην. Komias, Kharinades, and Strymodoros are other members of the chorus.

This line has the largest number of long syllables which the metre permits. This may mean that the line is spoken more slowly than an average iambic tetrameter, so that the metre helps to convey the impression that the old men are walking slowly. Alternatively, if the method of delivery used in the Athenian theatre (and perhaps a musical accompaniment) required the metrical beat to be maintained at a regular pace, the effect may be almost the opposite: the unusually large quantity of the syllables crammed into the line may convey the impression that the old men are trying to hurry but are having difficulty in doing so. Without knowing how lines were spoken in the Athenian theatre we cannot be sure which explanation is right; but at any rate it is clear that Ar. is in some way using the rhythm to reinforce the sense of the line.

231 'You *used* not to be, you know.' **μέντοι**: affirmative, not adversative. **γ'** emphasizes πρὸ τοῦ. The phrase recurs in 268; it is characteristic of old men to stress that the past was different from (and superior to) the present. **ἱμὰς κύνειος**: 'a dog-leash', i.e. tough and supple. *ἱμάς* means 'dog-leash' also in X. *Kyn.* 7. 6. It is unlikely that *κύνειος* has also the secondary meaning 'shameless', 'brazen', like *κύνεος* in *Iliad* 9. 373 and elsewhere, because the chorus-leader is praising the former physique of Komias, not criticizing his character.

233 **Στρυμόδωρε**: Ar. uses this name again for one of the chorus of old men in *Lys.* 259, and for a character mentioned in *Akh.* 273 who is perhaps meant to be an old man too. It looks as if he thought of this name as an old-fashioned one; the English equivalent might be something like 'Ebenezer'. **Κονθυλεῦ**: 'of Konthyle', a deme of the Pandionis tribe.

234 A rhetorical question; Euergides and Khabes are dead. (For if he had thought them both likely to be present, he would have used *καί* instead of *ἤ*.) **ἆρ'**: For interrogative *ἆρα* in a position later than first word in its sentence see Denniston 49. **Φλυεύς**: 'of Phlya', a large deme of the Kekropis tribe, situated north-east of Athens, just outside the city.

235 **δή**: regretful, as in 1064. **γ'** stresses *λοιπόν*. 'What's here is, I'm afraid, all that's left of . . .' **ἀππαπαῖ παπαιάξ**: an exclamation of sorrow; cf. 309. Yet elsewhere similar exclamations are used to express pleasure; e.g. *Th.* 1191 *παπαπαπαῖ*.

236 **ἥβης ἐκείνης, ἡνίκ'**: i.e. 'of those who were young when'. **Βυζαντίῳ**: The Greeks captured Byzantion from the Persians in 478 (Th. 1. 94. 2), and a year or two later the Athenians captured it from Pausanias (Th. 1. 131. 1). Anyone who took part in either of those operations will have been well over seventy years old in 422. Or perhaps Ar. has in mind an Athenian garrison stationed at Byzantion after its revolt from Athens in 440–39 (Th. 1. 115. 5, 1. 117. 3).

237 **περι-**: A long syllable resolved into two shorts (rare in this speech) helps to suggest haste and convey the meaning 'nipping round smartly'.

238 **ὅλμον**: The bread-seller's *ὅλμος*, unlike 'the big mortar' (201), was made of wood (239). So it must have been used for kneading dough rather than pounding grain into flour, which would need a stone receptacle. Translate 'bowl' rather than 'mortar'.

239 'And then we split it up and set about boiling some pimpernel.' They used the bowl for firewood, and made a kind of porridge out of pimpernel seeds. The genitive is partitive, as in Th. 1. 30. 2 *τῆς γῆς ἔτεμον*, 'they ravaged some land', etc.

The old man's reminiscence of his days of active service turns out not to be about any great military achievement, but a naughty escapade. So it is with Philokleon too (1200–1).

240 **ἀλλ'**: He breaks off his reminiscence and turns to action. **ἔσται...**: 'Lakhes will have it today', 'Lakhes will be for it today'.

Lakhes, son of Melanopos (Th. 3. 86. 1), of the deme Aixone (*Wasps* 895, Pl. *La.* 197 c), was a soldier rather than a politician. It is as a soldier that he appears in Plato's *Lakhes*, where he is presented as a bluff good-humoured man without intellectual pretensions. By now his age cannot have been much less than fifty, for he was older than Sokrates (Pl. *La.* 186 c). He went to Sicily as a general with a small Athenian force in the autumn of 427, and conducted operations against Syracuse and other cities with no conspicuous success or failure, until he was recalled to Athens in the spring of 425 (Th. 3. 86–115). In 424 he took part in the battle of Delion (Pl. *Smp.* 221 a, *La.* 181 b). Subsequently he was in favour of peace: in 423 he proposed the Athenian decree making a truce with Sparta for one year (Th. 4. 118. 11), and in 421 he was the chief supporter of Nikias in making peace (Th. 5. 43. 2). In 418 he was again a general, and was killed at the battle of Mantineia (Th. 5. 61. 1, 74. 3).

It may well be, though we have not enough evidence to be certain, that in 422 Lakhes, with Nikias, appeared to Kleon to be his chief rival. *Wasps* 240–4 and the trial scene later in the play (835–43, 891–1008) show that Kleon was hostile to Lakhes, was threatening to prosecute him, and said that he had made money out of his command in Sicily. The future tense in 240 shows that Lakhes had not yet been tried when *Wasps* was performed, and there is no evidence that he was ever tried. Probably the satire of the trial scene in *Wasps* persuaded Kleon not to prosecute. It is idle to speculate what the precise charge against him would have been; it could not have been misconduct as a general in Sicily, since his conduct in that term of office must have been examined by εὔθυναι in 425 (896 n.). Σ *Wasps* 240, referring to his recall from Sicily, says εἰκὸς γοῦν μετακληθῆναι αὐτὸν ἐπὶ τὴν κρίσιν, ἧς νῦν ὁ κωμικὸς μνημονεύει. The words εἰκὸς γοῦν show that this statement is only a conjecture, for which its author had no evidence except *Wasps*. The conjecture must be wrong, because *Wasps* was not performed until nearly three years later. Cf. F. Jacoby *FGrH* IIIb Supp. commentary on 328 F 127, H. D. Westlake in *Historia* ix (1960) 402 n. 67.

Whatever the charge brought or threatened against Lakhes by Kleon may have been in historical fact, in *Wasps* Ar. clearly assumes a charge of embezzlement. This implies that the chorus are jurors of the court of the thesmothetai, which was the court which tried cases of embezzlement (cf. 935). Kleon, we are meant to assume, spoke for the prosecution yesterday in another case of embezzlement, and in the course of his speech mentioned incidentally that Lakhes was likely to be accused in this court the next day. This does not mean that Kleon made the official announcement of the court's business: the order of trials was decided by the presiding magistrates (the thesmothetai), who might even decide that the court should not sit today at all (303–5). Later the chorus mention a man to be accused of treachery in the Thraceward region (288–9), and earlier Philokleon wanted to go to try Drakontides (157); if we wish to reconcile these allusions, we may say that several cases could be tried in one court on the same day, or that the jurors did not know for certain who would be tried each day, but anyway Ar. does not care about inconsistency between lines in different parts of a play.

241 σίμβλον χρημάτων: 'a hive of money'. A similar metaphor with βλίττω ('take the honey from') is used in *Knights* 794.

242–3 'So yesterday Kleon, our patron, ordered us to be there in good time with three days' rations of unwholesome anger.' Soldiers called up for a campaign were required to bring with them from home enough food for three days; cf. *Akh.* 197, *Peace* 312 σιτί' ἡμερῶν τριῶν. **πονηρὰν:** an adjective more naturally applied to food than to anger; cf. 193.

244 ἐπ' αὐτόν: 'to attack him', Lakhes. **κολωμένους:** The middle of κολάζω often has the same meaning as the active, e.g. 406, Pl. *Prt.* 324 c, *Mx.* 240 d. The future is usually κολάσω or κολάσομαι, but κολᾷ occurs in *Knights* 456. Hskh. κ 3409 gives a definition for κολω-μένους and so probably found it in a classical author, possibly but not necessarily in our line. **ὧν:** i.e. ἐκείνων ἅ: 'punish him for the crimes which he committed'. For the genitive of a crime with κολάζω cf. Th. 2. 74. 3, 6. 38. 4. **ἀλλὰ** is a repetition of ἀλλ' in 240; cf. Denniston 15. Its position at the end of the line deserves notice. In this metre sense-pauses commonly, though not always, come at the end of the line. Here the full stop comes slightly earlier than usual, and the effect is that the speaker seems to be trying to speed up and hurry on to the next thing; thus the rhythm reinforces the sense of ἀλλὰ σπεύσωμεν.

[245 σπεύσωμεν (RV): There is no objection to this reading; and since the subjunctives in 240 and 246 are present, corruption from present to aorist is less likely than from aorist to present. σπεύσωμεν occurs in *Lys.* 266, but σπεύδωμεν (J) nowhere else in Ar.]

246 ἅμα: a long syllable resolved into two shorts. The old man is trying to speed up and be brisk.

247 μή: 'in case'. διασκοπῶμεν has here the same construction as a verb of fearing; cf. *Th.* 396–7 σκοποῦνταί τ' εὐθέως μὴ μοιχὸς ἔνδον ᾖ τις. **λίθος:** Knocking the foot might be serious for an old man; cf. 275–7. [λίθος (V) or λαθών (RJ)? In favour of λαθών one may argue: (a) highwaymen and footpads (λωποδύται) were common in Athens and are often mentioned in Ar.; (b) ἐμποδών, an adverb, goes more naturally with a participle than with a noun; (c) to avoid stones one should not look in all directions (246 πάντη) but in front of one's feet. In favour of λίθος: (a) there are stones lying about in this street (199, 222), as there doubtless were in most Athenian streets; (b) the difficulty which the old men have in walking along the street is constantly stressed in this passage (230–2, 248, 256–7, 259); (c) since the old men's poverty is stressed, it would be inappropriate for them to fear thieves; (d) λαθών might be a gloss on λίθος written by someone who thought it necessary to explain that the old men would not be injured by a stone unless they failed to see it. The choice is difficult. λαθών is skilfully defended by Holzinger 7–10, but I think the balance of arguments favours λίθος.]

248–72 *Metre*: Euripidean fourteen-syllable. This consists of two iambic metra followed by an ithyphallic:

$$x - \cup - \quad x - \cup - \quad - \cup - \cup - -$$

A long syllable is resolved into two shorts only in 255 ἄπι-. The only lines without a diaeresis after the eighth syllable are 252 and 265.

This metre is virtually the same as the metre of 230–47 with the ninth syllable omitted; it could be called iambic tetrameter catalectic with syncopation at the beginning of the third metron. Thus the effect is that the rhythm continues almost unchanged, but with a slight increase in speed. This change is appropriately introduced at the point when the boy begins to take part in the conversation. [Here and there in even the oldest mss. (which seldom have metrical emendations) an extra syllable is interpolated in the middle of the line, evidently inserted by someone who thought the metre of these lines ought to be the same as of 230–47; e.g. σὺ in 248 and 249.]

248 ὤ: a cry of surprise (unreasonably deleted by editors).   **φύλαξαι**: i.e. 'avoid': 'Mind this mud!'

249 πρόβυσον: 'push forward' the wick, 'trim' the lamp, to make it burn more brightly and so enable him to see the mud. [There are no adequate grounds for emending to πρόμυξον in 249 (Scaliger) and προμύσσειν in 250 (Flor. Chrest.). (a) On 249 Σ^R says πρόμυξον, ἐκ τῆς μύξης προάγαγε, but here the word πρόμυξον may be not the lemma of the note but a synonym for πρόβυσον offered as part of the note. (b) In 250 Ald reads προβύσσειν and Σ^{Ald} (not, as some editors say, Σ^V) comments on προβύσσειν, but this may as easily be a mistake for προβύσειν as for προμύσσειν. (c) In Ar. one would not expect the form προμύσσειν for προμύττειν. (d) The grammarian Phrynikhos (Bekker *Anecdota Graeca* 59. 18–22) explains the phrase προβῦσαι φορτικὸν γέλωτα as a metaphor from pushing forward the wick of a lamp; this shows that προβύω was used for pushing forward the wick of a lamp. (e) Pol. 6. 103 says τὸ δὲ πρόμυξον τὸν λύχνον πρόβυσον λέγουσιν, which I take to mean 'For πρόμυξον they ⟨sc. classical writers⟩ say τὸν λύχνον πρόβυσον'; this may well be a reference to *Wasps* 249.]

250 τῳδί: The boy holds up his finger. To find a suitable twig or chip on the ground in the dark might involve a tedious search.   **προβύσειν**: For the tense, 177 n.; for the reading, 249 n.

251 τί δὴ μαθών: The English idiom is 'Who taught you to ...?' Cf. *Akh.* 826 τί δὴ μαθὼν φαίνεις ἄνευ θρυαλλίδος; *Clouds* 1506, *Lys.* 599, *Wealth*

908. The old man indignantly checks his son, and shakes his fist at him (cf. 254 κονδύλοις). τὴν θρυαλλίδ' ὠθεῖς: 'shove the wick about'. The further the wick is pushed forward, the faster it burns the oil and the brighter it shines. The old man wants it pushed forward far enough to enable him to see the mud, but no further for fear of wasting oil. To get it just right requires care and some small implement, such as a pin or a piece of wood of match-stick size, not a hasty jab at the burning wick with a finger.

252 'And that when oil is scarce, you idiot!' The Spartans destroyed many olive-trees in their invasions of Attica during the Peloponnesian war (Lys. 7. 6–7). This may be why Strepsiades too is short of oil (*Clouds* 56–9).

253 γὰρ: i.e. 'You do it because . . .'.   δάκνει: 'worry'; cf. *Clouds* 12–13 δακνόμενος ὑπὸ τῆς δαπάνης.   τίμιον: sc. oil, 'at a high price'.

255 ἄπι-: A long syllable resolved into two shorts helps to suggest a sudden burst of speed.

256 τουτουί: the lamp. After speaking of all the old men, boys, and lamps in 254–5, he reverts in 256–7 to himself and his own father and lamp in the singular.

257 ἀτταγᾶς: 'a francolin', a bird frequenting wet and marshy places, including the plain of Marathon (*Birds* 245–9); cf. Thompson *Birds* 59–61.

258 The boy's threats reduce the old man to impotence. He knows that the boy has the upper hand, but he tries to save his face by a pompous statement of his own importance in the law-courts. It would be interesting to know if Athenian boys and their fathers talked to each other like this in real life; Ar.'s picture of family manners may be comically distorted.   ἦ μὴν most often accompanies an oath or pledge, and so may be translated 'I swear' or 'I declare'; so also in 277, 643, 1332.   χἀτέρους: The καί implies 'not only you, but also . . .'.

[**259 βόρβορος:** Hermann's emendation μάρμαρος is unnecessary. 248 and 257 show that the ground is muddy; if there has been no rain lately (cf. 264–5), mud may still have been produced by the emptying of slops from the houses in the street. Cf. S. Srebrny in *Eos* l (1959–60) 43 n. 2.]

260–1 οὐκ ἔσθ' ὅπως οὐχ . . . ἀναγκαίως ἔχει: There is no redundancy, since the first phrase refers to the inference from evidence, the second to the performance of the action. 'It is undeniable that God is bound to send rain.'   ἡμερῶν τεττάρων τὸ πλεῖστον: 'within four days at the most'. For the adverbial accusative cf. D. 4. 21 πεντήκοντ' Ἀθηναίους τοὐλάχιστον, 'fifty Athenians at least'.

261 τὸν θεόν: For 'the god' as the author of the rain cf. *Peace* 1141. This probably just means 'the god who is responsible for rain' (i.e. Zeus), and is not evidence of monotheism. For the accusative and infinitive with ἀναγκαίως ἔχειν cf. *Peace* 334. [ποιῆσαι: ποι- or πο-? Plenty of Attic inscriptions give πο- where the next letter is ε or η, but none where the next letter is ο or ω; this is virtually proof that before ο or ω the Athenians always wrote ποι-, even where the syllable was scanned short (though it may possibly have been pronounced πο-). In *Wasps*, where the syllable is scanned short, RVΓ often (not always) give πο-, not only before ε or η but also before ο or ω (348, 734, 764, 1443); so some at least of their instances of πο- must be due to Hellenistic or Byzantine scribes who knew that πο- was sometimes written when the syllable was short but did not realize that it was avoided before ο or ω. On the other hand J always has ποι-; and this could be what Ar. wrote, since at least one fifth-century Attic verse inscription (*IG* i² 826) gives ποι- before ε or η where the metre demands a short syllable. Since, on this point, RVΓ cannot be right throughout but J may be so, I have followed J and put ποι- in the text everywhere. But it cannot be proved that Ar. never wrote πο-.]

262 γοῦν: 'at any rate', introducing evidence for the statement made in the previous sentence; so also in 391. μύκητες: 'fungus', 'snuff', produced on the wicks of the lamps by the damp atmosphere. Cf. Aratos 976–7 λύχνοιο μύκητες ἀγείρωνται περὶ μύξαν νύκτα κατὰ νοτίην, and Virgil *Geo*. 1. 390–2. [Hermann thought that this sentence should be spoken by one of the boys, since they are carrying the lamps. That may be right; but it is also possible that the boy is holding up the lamp next to the old man, and the old man peers at it and makes the remark.]

263 φιλεῖ: sc. ὁ θεός: 'he is accustomed'.

264 The old man rambles on into irrelevance. 'The crops need rain' is a typical old man's comment on damp weather, and does not imply that he possesses any crops himself. The comment is not appropriate to the time of year when *Wasps* is performed (January); we must imagine that it is early summer—or else that the old man's mind is wandering so far that he does not realize how unseasonable his remark is. [Pol. 7. 152, discussing words for 'early', says καὶ πρῷα δὲ κάρπια ὁ αὐτὸς (i.e. Ar.) εἴρηκεν. This shows that he had πρῷα in his text of Ar., but not necessarily that he had καρπίων, since he may just mean 'Ar. also calls crops πρῷα'.]

265 The accusative-and-infinitive clause is the object of δεῖται. 'Those of the crops which are not early require that rain should fall and then the north wind blow for them.' The north wind is dry in summer in Greece; cf. *Iliad* 21. 346–7. ἐπιπνεῦσαι: 'blow afterwards', as in Arist. *Prob*. 945ᵇ1. Crops need first rain to make them grow, and then dry weather to ripen them.

266 The chorus-leader has previously been walking along (around or across the orkhestra); he no doubt halted several times, but he must have been walking at 248 and at 259. Now he has finally come to

a stop (perhaps at the point of the orkhestra nearest to the house). He
expresses surprise that Philokleon has not come out of the house to
join them. Some nineteenth-century editors complained that this
passage was inconsistent with 112–32, on the ground that Philokleon's
friends must have known of his son's efforts to prevent him from going
to court; but Ar. does not care about minor inconsistencies between
different scenes, and it is dramatically effective that Philokleon's
friends should be surprised at his absence.   ἄρ': 143 n.

[It has been argued by S. Srebrny (*Eos* l [1959–60] 43–5) that 266–
89 belong between 316 and 317. C. F. Russo (*Belfagor* xxiii [1968]
317–24) supports this transposition with further arguments. Russo's
arguments are arithmetical: he maintains that 230–47 and 248–65 are
a symmetrical pair, finding similar pairs of 2 × 18 tetrameters in the
parodoi of *Peace* (301–18, 319–36) and *Wealth* (253–70, 271–89) and
less closely similar passages in other parodoi (*Knights* 247–83, *Frogs*
354–71); thus a break might be expected after 265. But it seems to me
doubtful whether Ar. intended symmetry here, since 248–65 are not in
the same metre as 230–47. Srebrny's arguments from the content of
the passage are stronger. Since 286–9 are an invitation to Philokleon
to leave the house, it is certainly odd for the chorus to decide to go on
(290) without either receiving any response from him or commenting
on the lack of response. It is also odd for Philokleon to wait for a space
of 27 lines listening to a quite irrelevant conversation before making
his reply (317–33). It is possible that an early manuscript of the play
had about 25 lines to a page, and the pages containing 266–89 and
290–316 got accidentally reversed. On the other hand the fact that
266–72 are in the same metre as 248–65 suggests that they should
form one continuous passage. So with some hesitation I have left the
lines in the traditional order; but I think it is quite possible that
Srebrny is right.]

267 ὡς: 'so that'.   πλῆθος: his fellow jurors.

268 πρὸ τοῦ γ': 231 n.   ἐφολκὸς: 'a laggard', as in A. *Supp.* 200.

269 ἡγεῖτ' ἄν: 'he would lead', the frequentative use of ἄν with the
imperfect to denote a regular past occurrence; so also in 279.   Φρυνίχου: 'a song of Phrynikhos': 220 n. For the ellipse of μέλος cf. 1225,
Men. *Dys.* 433 (with Handley's note).

270 μοι δοκεῖ: 'I think we ought to . . .'

271 ἦν τί πως: 'just in case', 'in the hope that he may'.

272 'μοῦ: 'My' is surprising after ᾄδοντας. But the idea that there is some
special point in the change from plural to singular (e.g. 'We shall all
sing, but I am the only singer good enough to give him pleasure') is
far-fetched; probably the change has no more significance than the
similar changes in 254–7, 465–7, 486–7, 1071–3, 1091–5, etc.   ἑρπύσῃ
suggests walking slowly and with difficulty. The chorus-leader is afraid
Philokleon may be hindered by illness or other impediments; cf. 275–7.

273–89 *The chorus sing a song in which they speculate on the reasons which may be keeping Philokleon indoors, and urge him to rouse himself.*

The song is a comic one. The reasons suggested for Philokleon's absence are all ludicrous or grotesque, and the last line ('make sure you pot him') produces an effect of bathos.

[*Metre*: This is metrically the most difficult passage in *Wasps*, and beginners had better not trouble with its analysis. My view is that it is best all regarded as ionic. An ionic metron is ∪∪ – –, but to maintain the view that this song is ionic throughout it is necessary to admit the following variations:

A: Sometimes the fourth syllable of the metron is suppressed, giving ∪∪ – (syncopation or catalexis). This is common elsewhere, e.g. 300 -θαρίου ∼ 313 παρέχῃς, *Frogs* 331 ποδὶ τὰν ∼ 350 ἱερᾶς, 332 φιλο-παίγ- ∼ 351 σὺ δὲ λαμ-, 335 ἱερὰν ∼ 352 δάπεδον, E. *Supp.* 45–7 ∼ 51–3, *Ba.* 64–8.

B: Sometimes the first syllable of the metron is treated as anceps, giving × ∪ – – or (with catalexis) × ∪ –; the syllable may be long in both the strophe and the antistrophe, or short anceps in the strophe may respond to long anceps in the antistrophe or vice versa. This also is common elsewhere, e.g. *Frogs* 324 -θάδε ναίων ∼ 340 -κει τινάσσων, 326 ἐλθὲ τόνδ' ∼ 342 νυκτέρου, 328 μὲν τινάσσων ∼ 345 -ται γερόντων, 336 -ταις χορείαν ∼ 353 μάκαρ ἧβαν, A. *Supp.* 1021 ∼ 1029. Cf. Dale² 125, especially n. 1.

C: Sometimes the fourth syllable of the metron is likewise treated as anceps. This is common elsewhere in the sequence ∪∪ – ∪ – ∪ – – (the 'anacreontic'), where short anceps at the end of one metron is immediately followed by long anceps at the beginning of the next; e.g. 297 ∼ 309/10, 298 ∼ 311, *Frogs* 327 ὁσίους εἰς θιασώτας ∼ 344 φλογὶ φέγγεται δὲ λείμων. But 281a διὰ τὸν χθεσινὸν ἄνθρω- (∪∪ – ∪ ∪∪ – –) is much more unusual; there is however one parallel, 314 ἀνόνητον ἄρα σ', ὦ θυ-. Thus in this song, I suggest, Ar. regards the ionic simply as × ∪ – × so that any metron (not only one whose successor begins –) may be ∪∪ – ∪ or – ∪ – ∪ (276b τὸ σφυρὸν γέ-, 286 -τω σεαυτόν).

D: Sometimes a choriamb (– ∪ ∪ –) is used in place of an ionic. This occurs among ionics elsewhere, e.g. A. *Ag.* 689 -ανδρος ἐλέπ- ∼ 707 ὃς τότ' ἐπέρ-, E. *Hipp.* 732 ἠλιβάτοις ∼ 742 'Εσπερίδων, *Ph.* 1515 ἢ δρυὸς ἢ. Cf. Dale² 129–30.

E: The third period of the strophe and of the antistrophe, following a pause, begins with a single long syllable: 277b ἢ ∼ 286 ἀλλ'. This may be paralleled by E. *Ba.* 72 ∼ 88, though the metrical analysis of that passage has been disputed.

Some scholars have tried to get rid of some of these variations by emendation, e.g. 281a χθιζινὸν Hermann, 282 τε λέγων θ' Richter; but this is the wrong approach, for we do not have enough certainty about

the metre of this song to be able to condemn on metrical grounds
readings which in sense are unobjectionable. Others deny that the
whole song is ionic, and analyse parts of it in dactylo-epitrite or other
metres; cf. Dale² 189–90. It is certainly true that some parts can be
scanned as dactylo-epitrite (most easily 277b–9b ~ 286–8b). But I prefer (though this is really only a personal preference) to treat the whole
passage as ionic, with an exceptionally free use of variations as described above, for two reasons: (a) some parts cannot be made dactylo-
epitrite, and it seems more plausible and intelligible to treat a song as
ionic throughout than as ionic and dactylo-epitrite mixed; (b) the
next song (291–316) is plainly ionic, and Ar. shows some tendency to
use the same or similar metres for two or more passages in one play.
But, I stress, neither of these reasons is conclusive, and alternative
analyses remain possible.

My analysis in ionics is shown below. Here I use *ion* to mean
× ∪ – × and *ion*ʌ to mean × ∪ –. Where the scheme shows ⊻ or ⊽, the
upper symbol refers to the strophe and the lower to the antistrophe.
The strophe and the antistrophe each fall into three periods, separated
by pauses; this is shown by the hiatus at the end of 275b and 277a.

273, 281a	∪∪ – ∪∪ – ⊽ ∪∪ – –	*ion*ʌ *ion ion*
274, 281b	∪∪ – – ∪∪ – ⊽	*ion ion*
275a, 282	– ∪∪ – ⊻ ∪ – – ∪∪ – ∪∪ – –	ch *ion ion*ʌ *ion*
or	– ∪∪ – ⊻ ∪ – – ∪∪ – ∪∪ – –	ch *ion*ʌ ch *ion*
275b, 283a	– ∪ – – – ∪ – – ‖	*ion ion*
276a, 283b	⊽ ∪ – ⊽ ∪ – –	*ion*ʌ *ion*
276b, 284	– ∪ – ⊻ – ∪ – –	*ion ion*
277a, 285	– ∪ – – – ∪ – – ‖	*ion ion*
277b, 286	– – ∪∪ – ∪∪ – – – ∪ – ⊽	– ch *ion ion*
278, 287	– ∪∪ – ∪∪ – ⊻	ch *ion*
279a, 288a	– ∪∪ – ∪∪ – –	ch *ion*
279b, 288b	– ∪ – – – ∪ – –	*ion ion*
280, 289	∪∪ – – ∪∪ ◠	*ion ion*ʌ]

273 θυρῶν: A double door may be called either θύρα or θύραι.   **ἄρ'**:
143 n.

274 ὑπακούει with dative: 'answer'. With a genitive it means 'hear',
e.g. 318.

275 ἐμβάδας: 103 n.   **προσέκοψ'** . . . **τὸν δάκτυλόν**: 'stubbed his toe'.

276a ἐφλέγμηνεν: 'became swollen' as a result of stubbing his toe.

277a For the idea that swollen groins may result from knocks or other
strains on the feet cf. *Lys.* 987–8 ἦ βουβωνιᾷς ὑπὸ τῆς ὁδοῦ; *Frogs* 1280
ὑπὸ τῶν κόπων γὰρ τὼ νεφρὼ βουβωνιῶ. Dirt in an abrasion of the foot
might lead to blood-poisoning, and so to swelling of the lymph-nodes
in the groin.

277b δριμύτατός: 146 n.   **τῶν παρ' ἡμῖν**: 'of our company', i.e. of jurors.

278 ἀνεπείθετ': 'was persuaded to relent': 101 n.

279b κάτω κύπτων: 'putting his head down' in obstinacy and hostility, like a bull; cf. *Frogs* 804 ἔβλεψε γοῦν ταυρηδὸν ἐγκύψας κάτω. **ἂν**: frequentative: 269 n. **οὕτω**: 'like this'; the chorus imitate him.

280 'You are boiling a stone' is a proverbial expression for trying to persuade someone who cannot be persuaded. It occurs also in [Pl.] *Eryx.* 405 b.

281 τάχα δ' ἂν with ὀδυνηθείς: 'perhaps he may have felt sore . . ., and . . .'. For τάχα ἄν with a participle cf. S. *OT* 523–4, Th. 6. 2. 4, Pl. *Phdr.* 265 b. **χθεσινὸν**: i.e. 'tried yesterday'. [Hermann conjectured χθιζινόν on metrical grounds. From Phryn. *Ekl.* 295 Rutherford = p. 323 Lobeck it appears that Phrynikhos had χθεσινόν somewhere in his text of Ar. In *Frogs* 987, where the mss. present χθεσινόν, the metre indisputably shows it to be false; so Phrynikhos's reference may well be to our passage.] **ἡμᾶς διεδύετ'**: 'slipped through our fingers', i.e. was acquitted.

282 φιλαθήναιος is a word used not of patriotic Athenians but of foreigners friendly to Athens; cf. *Akh.* 142 (Sitalkes), Pl. *Ti.* 21 e (the people of Sais in Egypt), Is. 19. 308 (Philip). [-αι- is probably short (cf. page 22, under 3(*a*)), responding to 275a προσ-. But it could be long, if the first syllable of the ionic metron is anceps.] **ἦν** (not ἐστι): 'he had always been'.

283a τὰν Σάμῳ: 'the affair in Samos'. Σ says that at the time of the revolt of Samos from Athens in 440 a plan of the Samians was revealed to the Athenians by a man named Karystion, and he was afterwards rewarded with Athenian citizenship: . . . Σάμιοι μηχανήν τινα κατεσκεύασαν κατ' αὐτῶν, ἣν μαθόντες Ἀθηναῖοι ὑπό τινος Καρυστίωνος ἐφυλάξαντο, καὶ Σαμίους μὲν κακῶς διέθηκαν, τὸν δὲ Καρυστίωνα ἐτίμησαν σφόδρα μετὰ τοῦ γένους καὶ τῆς αὐτῶν πολιτείας ἠξίωσαν. This may well be true. If it is, then we may conclude that shortly before the performance of *Wasps* either Karystion himself was tried in Athens on some charge and was acquitted, or else some other man, when tried on some charge, claimed that he and not Karystion had been the first to give information about the Samian plan in 440, and was acquitted. **κατείποι**: 54 n.

283b διὰ τοῦτ': the man's acquittal; the words sum up διὰ τὸν χθεσινὸν ἄνθρωπον, ὅς . . . ὀδυνηθείς: For the use of this verb for mental distress or sorrow rather than physical pain cf. *Akh.* 3.

284 εἶτ': 'then', as a result; cf. 276.

286–7 σεαυτὸν ἔσθιε: i.e. sulk in annoyance at yesterday's event; the chorus are assuming that their guess in 281–5 is correct. 'Bite one's lip' or 'bite oneself' is a common expression for anger; cf. 778, 1083, *Odyssey* 1. 381, E. *Ba.* 621, etc.

288 παχὺς: i.e. wealthy; cf. *Peace* 639 τοὺς παχεῖς καὶ πλουσίους. (But in *Clouds* 842 παχύς is 'stupid'.) **τἀπὶ Θρᾴκης**: 'the Thraceward region', the usual phrase for the part of the Athenian empire consisting of towns on the northern side of the Aegean and islands near it. The greatest recent blow to the Athenians in this area was the capture of Amphipolis by Brasidas in the winter of 424/3 (Th. 4. 102–8). Thucydides was the commander of the Athenian fleet in that area at the time, and he was subsequently attacked by Kleon (Markellinos *Life of Th.* 46) and exiled. But the reference here is probably not to the trial of Thucydides, which must have been held nearly a year before *Wasps* was performed; there had been other fighting in that area more recently (210 n.), and anyway Ar. does not necessarily have a particular real individual in mind.

289 'Make sure you pot him', a metaphor from cookery; the English idiom is 'cook his goose'. The line is discussed and correctly explained by Karl Holzinger *De verborum lusu apud Aristophanem* (1876) 48–50, Taillardat § 600.

290–316 *The chorus-leader calls to his son to move on. But instead the boy starts putting questions to his father, and the two of them sing a duet. The boy asks for a present of dried figs, which his father indignantly refuses. In the antistrophe they lament the fact that they will have nothing to eat if the court does not sit today.*

The song illustrates once again the jurors' poverty. It is possible to see pathos in the earlier part of each stanza, but the later lines are undoubtedly meant to be funny: in 297–302 the old juror displays comic indignation, and in 312–16 the boy's lines are a burlesque of melodramatic grief.

Metre: ionics, with fewer variations than in 273–89. The basic metron ∪ ∪ − − is far the commonest. Occasionally the first syllable is lengthened, or the fourth shortened or suppressed, not always at the same point in the antistrophe as in the strophe. Responsion of × ∪ − × to × ∪ − occurs in 296 ~ 308 and 301 ~ 314; the two instances defend each other against emendation, and cf. *Birds* 1560 ~ 1701, *Frogs* 1486 ~ 1495. 314 also contains the unusual sequence ∪ ∪ − ∪ ∪ ∪ − −; cf. 281*a*. The strophe and antistrophe end with ∪ ∪ − ∪ − −, a catalectic ionic clausula found elsewhere, e.g. E. *Ba.* 385 ~ 401, 536 ~ 555; cf. Dale² 128, especially n. 2. In 309 the antistrophe is a metron shorter than the strophe; cf. 309 n. In 315 the exclamation ἐέ is outside the metre. 290 is a longer exclamatory utterance outside the responsion system; cf. 874.

290	∪ ∪ − − ∪ ∪ ∧ ‖	*ion ion*∧
291, 303	∪ ∪ − − ∪ ∪ − −	*ion ion*
292, 304	∪ ∪ − − ∪ ∪ − −	*ion ion*
293, 305	∪ ∪ − − ∪ ∪ − −	*ion ion*
294, 306	∪ ∪ − − ∪ ∪ − −	*ion ion*
295, 307	∪ ∪ − − ∪ ∪ − −	*ion ion*

{296	∪∪--	-∪--			ion ion
{308	∪∪--	∪∪⌒‖			ion ion⌃
{297	∪∪--	∪∪--	∪∪-∪	-∪--	ion ion ion ion
{309/10	∪∪--		∪∪-∪	-∪--	ion ion ion
298, 311	∪∪-∪	-∪--			ion ion
299, 312	∪∪--	∪∪--	∪∪-⌒‖		ion ion ion
300, 313	∪∪--	∪∪--	∪∪-		ion ion ion⌃
{301	∪∪-	∪∪--	∪∪--	∪∪--	ion⌃ ion ion ion
{314	∪∪-∪	∪∪--	∪∪--	∪∪-⌒‖	ion ion ion ion
315	έέ				
302, 316	∪∪-∪	--			ionic clausula

290 ὕπαγε: 'go on', 'forward!' παῖ may be followed by hiatus because it is much like an exclamation; so also in *Clouds* 1145, 1165, *Frogs* 37.

The chorus-leader calls to his son to lead the way with the lamp, apparently giving up hope of seeing Philokleon. But instead the boy starts asking questions, and so they are still outside the house when Philokleon eventually looks out at 317.

291 'Will you give me something?' For the omission of the infinitive cf. *Frogs* 1279 εἰς τὸ βαλανεῖον βούλομαι.

295 ἀστραγάλους: 'knucklebones', used much like dice for various games. The context shows that they were very cheap.

297 ἰσχάδας: 'dried figs'. σῦκα (302) is a more general word for figs, whether dried or not. Figs were one of the commonest kinds of sweet. παπία: 'papa', 'daddy'. [πάπας, παπίας, and παπίδιον (all with ā) are alternative spellings to παππ-. They are given by mss. in a number of passages (cf. 655, *Ek.* 645, Men. *Dys.* 194), and there is no need to remove them by systematic emendation.] οὐκ ἄν: sc. πριαίμην ἰσχάδας. The chorus-leader is so shocked that he brusquely interrupts before the boy has finished his sentence and metron—a striking example of the use of a metrical effect to point up the sense.

298 εἰ ... γ' after a negative: 'even if'; cf. Denniston 126.

299 τἄρα: τοι is 'certainly'; ἄρα is 'in that case', i.e. 'if you don't buy me some figs'.

300 γὰρ introduces the reason for the refusal in 297-8. μισθαρίου: the juror's fee of three obols. The diminutive is disparaging.

301 τρίτον αὐτὸν: 'with two others'. This use of αὐτός with an ordinal number does not occur elsewhere in Ar., but is regular in other authors, e.g. Th. 1. 46. 2, X. *Hel.* 2. 2. 17, D. 28. 16. Its purpose is not to indicate that the individual named is superior to others, but to stress that he is accompanied by others; cf. K. J. Dover in *JHS* lxxx (1960) 61-77, especially 70. Here the two others are his wife and son; he is too poor to have a slave as well. ἄλφιτα: 'groats', grain roughly crushed, not ground into flour. They were used for making a kind of cake (μᾶζα, cf. 614), which was the Athenians' staple food. Although ἄλφιτα were not necessarily made from barley (see L. A. Moritz in *CQ* xliii [1949] 113–17), in Ar.'s time they were usually so, because wheat, if available (wheat was less plentiful and more expensive than barley; cf. 715–18), would be used for making bread. The old jurors evidently cannot afford bread. ξύλα: firewood. ὄψον is practically any kind of food except cereals, anything eaten with a μᾶζα to make it more palatable, such as fish, meat, vegetables, or fruit.

302 'And you ask me for figs!', an indignant climax. Figs were normally common and cheap in Athens (cf. *Wealth* 798). During the Peloponnesian war the devastation of Attica no doubt reduced the supply of figs, as of oil (cf. 252); all the same, the fact that the old juror regards them as an expensive luxury is a sign that he is very poor indeed.

303–5 'If the magistrate does not hold a sitting of the court today'. The chorus are jurors of the court of the thesmothetai (240 n.); so ἄρχων does not mean the chief arkhon. The sentence shows that the jurors are making for one particular court, which is evidently the court to which they have been allocated for the year, and thus that the later practice by which jurors were allocated to courts each morning by lot (Arist. *Ath. Pol.* 64) had not yet been introduced. It shows also that the jurors did not always know before they reached the court whether any trial would be held that day or not.

308 πόρον: 'way', 'means', 'provision' of money. But πόρος can also mean 'strait' of water, and so the boy absurdly slips into a quotation from Pindar (fr. 189 Schroeder = 179 Bowra) in which Ἕλλας πόρον ἱερόν means 'holy strait of Helle', i.e. the Hellespont. 'Have you any way "—to Tipperary"?'

309 ἀπαπαῖ φεῦ: 235 n. [At this point one metron is lacking, by comparison with 297. There are several other passages in Ar. where an antistrophe has one metron less (or more) than its strophe; cf. 544 ∼ 647, *Akh.* 216 ∼ 231, *Knights* 306 ∼ 386, *Clouds* 953–6 ∼ 1028–31, *Peace* 464 ∼ 491, *Frogs* 536 ∼ 592, *Ek.* 487 ∼ 498. How these passages were performed is quite uncertain. Cf. Dale² 207.]

311 γε following an interrogative: see Denniston 124–5. [There is no need for Cobet's emendation τό.]

312 This melodramatic question is a quotation from Euripides's lost tragedy *Theseus*, in which it was uttered by children condemned to be eaten by the Minotaur (Σ *Wasps* 312 = E. fr. 385). But the boy's father gives a down-to-earth and cynical answer, producing a comic effect of bathos. ἔτικτες: For the imperfect cf. A. *Eu.* 321 μᾶτερ, ἅ μ' ἔτικτες, Hes. *Th.* 45 (with West's note), etc.

313 πράγματα βόσκειν: 'trouble to feed'. For the epexegetic infinitive cf. X. *Kyr.* 4. 5. 46 πράγματα δὲ παρέξουσιν ἐπιμέλεσθαι, Pl. *Phd.* 115 a.

314 'A useless ornament then art thou, O shopping-bag, which I have brought.' Σ says that in *Theseus* Hippolytos spoke the line ἀνόνητον ἄγαλμα, πάτερ, οἴκοισι τεκών (E. fr. 386). There seems to be some confusion, since for chronological reasons Hippolytos can hardly have appeared as a character in a play in which Theseus killed the Minotaur. Nevertheless there need be no doubt that the boy is parodying a tragic line in a melodramatic tone.   ἄρα with imperfect implies 'as I now realize'; so also in 451, 821, 1299.   γ' immediately after a vocative is unusual, but here it emphasizes the whole expression σ', ὦ θυλάκιον.

315–16 ἐὲ . . . στενάζειν: more parody of tragedy.

317–33 *Philokleon looks out of the window and sings a solo. He laments his inability to leave the house to join his friends, and in despair he prays to Zeus to turn him into smoke, strike him with a thunderbolt, or turn him into stone.*

The song is a burlesque of tragic songs—or possibly of some particular tragic song, sung for example by Danae shut up in her tower, as B. L. Gildersleeve suggested (*AJP* i [1880] 457–8). Characters in tragedy often pray to be freed from the troubles of life by being turned into smoke (e.g. A. *Supp.* 779), struck by a thunderbolt (e.g. S. *Tr.* 1086–8), or turned into stone (e.g. E. *Her.* 1397), but each of Philokleon's prayers leads to an unexpected and ridiculous conclusion. Cf. H. Kleinknecht *Die Gebetsparodie in der Antike* (1937) 64–6, Peter Rau *Paratragodia* (1967) 150–2.

Metre: After an introductory line of two bacchiacs, the early part of the song is in aeolic metre, built on the choriamb (– ◡ ◡ –). A pherecratean or reizianum is here, as often, used for the close of each period, followed by a pause. (Where the presence of a pause is proved by hiatus, I mark it ||.)

317a	◡ – – ◡ – –	ba ba
317b	◡ – ◡◡ – ◡ –	telesillean
318a	– – ◡◡ – –	reizianum
318b	– ◡◡ – ◡ – –	aristophanean
319a	– – ◡◡ – –	reizianum
319b	– – – ◡◡ – ◡ –	glyconic
320	– ◡ – ◡◡ – ◡ –	glyconic
321	– – – ◡◡ – ◡ –	glyconic
322	– ◡ – ◡◡ – – ||	pherecratean
323	– – – ◡◡ – – ||	pherecratean

At 324 the metre changes to anapaests (see pages 26–7) : a short run in 324–6 and a longer run in 327–33. (For change of metre in mid sentence after an invocation cf. 728–9, 869–70.) The reason why the metre changes in the middle of the song is that there is a change of mood which the metre subtly reflects. Aeolics are often used for pathos, but anapaests (a marching rhythm) are more often used for action. Philokleon begins by deploring his situation in aeolics. A series of glyconics (319b–21) is brought to a close by a pherecratean (322), a common practice in aeolic verse. We might then expect a fresh series of glyconics or other aeolic lines, but instead there is a pause (observe the hiatus ποιῆσαι. ἀλλ'), and then comes another pherecratean, invoking Zeus the thunderer (323). Again there is a pause (observe the hiatus -βρόντα, ἤ), and then finally Philokleon launches himself into anapaests with a call for action. A bridge between the two metres is provided in 323–4. 323 is a pherecratean; yet this form of phere-cratean (− − − ∪ ∪ − −) is identical with a sequence which can close an anapaestic run (. . . − − − ∪ ∪ − −). 324 is anapaestic (− ∪ ∪ − − ∪ ∪ − − −); yet it is so arranged that the first eight syllables are identical with two choriambs (− ∪ ∪ − − ∪ ∪ − . . .). Thus both lines give the impression that Philokleon is not quite sure whether to ven-ture into anapaests or keep to aeolics; the metre helps to convey that he only gradually, and with hesitation, emerges from his tone of self-pity into an urgent plea.

317 τήκομαι: 'I have been pining', a common expression in tragedy (e.g. E. *Andr.* 116, *El.* 208), but rare in comedy (but cf. *Wealth* 1034). **ὀπῆς**: presumably the window from which he now looks.

318 ὑπακούων: 274 n. [Van Herwerden's ὅπ' ἀκούων is unnecessary.] **ἀλλὰ γάρ**: 'but since'. When the chorus sang, they expected Philo-kleon either to come out of the house to meet them or to sing in answer to them (273–4). Now he explains why he has done neither: he cannot sing because of his distress, and he cannot leave the house because he is guarded. At the top of his voice he sings 'I can't sing'—a joke of the type in which a character obviously does precisely what he says he is not doing, much like Polonius's long-winded 'Brevity is the soul of wit . . . I will be brief . . . I swear I use no art at all . . . I will use no art' (*Hamlet* 2. 2. 90–9). [Some editors miss the joke and emend ᾄδειν to some word meaning 'come out', thus wrongly anticipating the point of the next sentence.]

319b τῶνδ': Bdelykleon and Xanthias, in full view asleep in front of the door.

321 καδίσκους: 94 n.

322 'To do some mischief'; i.e. to condemn somebody, but he comically uses the kind of expression which would be used by an impartial critic more naturally than by himself. Cf. 340, 418.

323 ἀλλ': regularly used to introduce a prayer; cf. Denniston 16.

324 'Turn me into smoke', so as to be able to escape easily. But 'smoke' is used colloquially of people who are all talk and no action. (Cf. 459. *Σ Birds* 822, referring to Eupolis 122 Kock = 94 Edmonds, says about Theagenes ἐκαλεῖτο δὲ καπνός, ὅτι πολλὰ ὑπισχνούμενος οὐδὲν ἐτέλει. And *Σ Birds* 1126 says about Theagenes and Proxenides καπνοὶ ἦσαν καὶ κομπασταὶ καὶ μόνον ὑπόσχεσις.) So Philokleon absurdly goes on to mention as alternatives two Athenians who are 'smoke' in this colloquial sense.

325 Proxenides is satirized as a boaster also in *Birds* 1126, where he is called ὁ Κομπασεύς ('Bragger by deme') and is paired off with Theagenes (1183 n.). Σ *Birds* 1126 says that he was satirized by Telekleides (fr. 18) as παρειμένον τῷ σώματι, but this expression probably means only 'relaxed', 'at ease' (cf. E. *Ba.* 683), and so tells us nothing more about his character or activities.   τὸν Σέλλου: 'the son of Swank'. The noun σέλλος does not occur except in the expression ὁ Σέλλου in this play (where it comes again in 1243 and 1267; cf. also 459), but its meaning 'boaster' is clear from the use of the verb σελλίζομαι in Phrynikhos com. 10 ἄγαμαι, Διονῦ, σοῦ στόματος, ὡς σεσέλλισαι. 'Son of Swank' is not a nickname of one particular individual, but may be applied to any boastful man; in 1243 it is Aiskhines (and cf. 459), in 1267 Amynias. Who is it in 325? Philokleon must have made the reference clear by a gesture on the word τοῦτον. Far the easiest gesture would have been to point to Amynias, whom we know to have been sitting at the front of the audience (74). I conclude that in 325 'the son of Swank' is probably Amynias (74 n.). For this type of invented patronymic cf. 1267 τῶν Κρωβύλου, *Akh.* 1131 Λάμαχον τὸν Γοργάσου.

326 ψευδαμάμαξυν: For the type of compound cf. *Knights* 630 ψευδατραφάξυος. An ἀμάμαξυς or ἁμάμαξυς was a kind of vine, and several interpretations of the compound seem possible; perhaps *A* is the likeliest.

A: The most important feature of the vine is that it produces grapes; it was the Athenians' most valuable fruit-tree. So to call a man 'a sham vine' may mean that he gives an impression that he will produce something valuable, but fails to do so; that is, he is an empty boaster, whose talk is unfruitful.

B: The second characteristic of the vine is that it climbs up a pole or another tree by twining itself round (περιπλέκεσθαι). So Taillardat § 391 suggests that ψευδαμάμαξυν means 'devising lies' (ψευδεῖς λόγους πλέκοντα). This is possible, but it gives a less satisfactory image, because a vine twines itself, but a liar devises not himself but lies; Taillardat does not distinguish πλέκειν from πλέκεσθαι.

C: Σ^V says that the wood of the vine makes a loud noise when burning. But this is a less distinctive feature of the vine than grapes and poles are, and so is less likely to be the basis of the image here.

D: Hskh. α 3425 says that ἁμάμαξυς is applied to a lame man walking on two crutches (presumably by a metaphor from a vine supported on poles). Thus Ar. might be abusing Amynias as a cripple or in some way physically unsound. However, Hesykhios more probably means that this metaphor was used on one particular occasion, not that it was a regular meaning of ἁμάμαξυς.

327 τόλμησον: 'deign', 'be so good as to'.

329 διατινθαλέῳ: 'boiling'.   σπόδισον: 'bake', as in Pl. *R.* 372 c.

Philokleon moves gradually from the language of prayer to the language of cooking, until he reaches the absurd conclusion 'dip me in vinegar sauce'. Cf. 194–5.

330 ἀποφυσήσας: 'after blowing off the ashes'.

332–3 The conventional prayer to be turned to stone becomes a prayer to be turned into a particular stone for which Philokleon has a special affection (94 n.).

334–402 *The chorus question Philokleon, and he tells them who has confined him to the house and why. After a burst of indignation they discuss with him how he may escape. Eventually he decides to gnaw through the net and descend from the window by a rope, but while he is doing so Bdelykleon and Xanthias wake up and rush to prevent him.*

The passage is one of gradually mounting excitement as the escape is planned, working up towards a climax of farcical activity. The sense of excitement is enhanced by the metre, with its rapid trochees and vigorous anapaests.

Metre: trochaic and anapaestic tetrameters, interspersed with continuous runs of trochees and anapaests (see pages 24–9). The scene is approximately symmetrical: 334–45 and 365–78 are trochaic, 346–64 and 379–402 anapaestic. But the correspondence between 346–64 and 379–402 is not exact: the first anapaestic passage contains 12 tetrameters (346–57) and a continuous run (358–64), but the second contains 24 tetrameters (379–402) and no continuous run. T. Gelzer *Der epirrhematische Agon bei Aristophanes* (1960) counts this scene as an agon. It does possess some of the features of an agon, but not all.

334 γάρ in a question asking for further information about the subject of the previous speaker's remarks: see Denniston 82. **ταυτά**: adverbial accusative, 'in this way', as in *Akh.* 385, *Clouds* 131. [So Meineke's οὐνταῦθά is unnecessary.] 'Shutting you away by means of the door' means 'shutting you up indoors'.

337 πρόσθεν: in front of the house, beside the door. From the window he points down at Bdelykleon. **ὕφεσθε τοῦ τόνου**: 'lower yourselves from your ⟨present⟩ tone of voice', i.e. 'lower your voices'.

338 τοῦ ἔφεξιν: 'on what pretext', like τοῦ χάριν in *Frogs* 1418, *Wealth* 53. E. W. Handley (*Eranos* li [1953] 133–4) suggests that the use of two -σις nouns makes 338–9 sound 'poetic'; but since πρόφασις is a common prose word the inference is doubtful. **ὦ μάταιε**: 'you silly man'. The chorus are impatient because he fails to explain the situation clearly to them.

339 If we had this line by itself we might call it anapaestic, but the trochaic context shows, I think, that Ar. intended it as a kind of trochaic verse: ∪∪∪∪ ∪∪– instead of –∪–× –∪–; see pages 27–9. One might expect closer responsion to 370 –∪∪∪ –∪–, but this licence of responsion is paralleled by *Birds* 335 πολέμιον ἐτράφη ∼ 351 τῷδ' ἀποφυγόντε με: cf. Dale² 57.

340 κακόν: 322 n.

341 It is not from financial necessity that Philokleon is a juror, since his son is able and willing to entertain him sumptuously at home. Here Ar. is not only characterizing Philokleon, but also preparing the way for the festivity in the last part of the play.   **βούλομαι:** the passive εὐωχεῖσθαι must be understood.

342 χανεῖν implies contempt for what was spoken (cf. S. *Ai.* 1227): 'bluster'.   **Δημολογοκλέων:** 'Soapbox-Kleon', an abusive distortion of Bdelykleon's name. For similar distortions cf. 459, 466, 592. δημολόγος is a contemptuous word for a public speaker; cf. Pl. *Sph.* 268 b, where δημολογικός stands in the same relation to πολιτικός as σοφιστικός to σοφός. Δημολογοκλέων sounds as if it might be an insult to Kleon, who is the jurors' friend, and Starkie maintains that this is the joke: in attempting to abuse Bdelykleon the chorus inadvertently abuse their own patron Kleon. But this is perhaps over-subtle for an audience to appreciate. Another possibility is that the word means 'an inferior Kleon', a man who tries to make speeches as good as Kleon's but fails. [At any rate the word does not present enough difficulty to justify emendation. Many emendations have been suggested; the latest, proposed by S. Srebrny in *Aus der altertumswissenschaftlichen Arbeit Volkspolens* ed. J. Irmscher and K. Kumaniecki (1959) 21–4, is . . . χανεῖν ὅδ'; ἦ μάλα γ', ὦ Κλέων, ⟨ἔσθ'⟩ ὅ τι λέγεις ⟨σὺ⟩—τὸ περὶ τῶν νέων—ἀληθές.]   **-τι λέγεις τι:** a metron reduced to ∪ ∪ – ∪; so also 343 περὶ τῶν νε-. The responding syllables in 374–5 are – ∪ – – in each case. See pages 27–9, and cf. 339 n.

343 νεῶν: Since triremes were paid for by the richer citizens through *leitourgiai*, complaints about the condition of ships or suggestions to send them out were unpopular with the rich; cf. *Ek.* 197–8. The chorus take it for granted that Bdelykleon is rich and anti-democratic, and that it is in some such way as this that Philokleon has provoked his anger. [Bentley's νέων is not preferable. In the earlier part of the play Philokleon and the chorus show no special antagonism to young men as such; they are taken in by young upstart orators (e.g. 687). Only after being convinced by Bdelykleon do they express hostility to young politicians (e.g. 1101).]

345 ξυνωμότης: For the tendency in Athens during the Peloponnesian war to accuse a political opponent of 'conspiracy' or 'tyranny' with little or no justification cf. 417, 463–507, 953, *Birds* 1074, *Lys.* 619, 630, *Th.* 338, 1143, And. 1. 36, Th. 6. 27. 3, 28. 2, 53. 3, 60. 1. In the fourth century, after the regime of the Thirty, the vocabulary of political abuse changed, and the charges were of 'oligarchy' or κατάλυσις τοῦ δήμου; cf. And. 3. 1–12, Isok. 7. 57, 8. 51, D. 13. 14.

346 ἀλλ' sometimes marks the conclusion of a speaker's remarks by a request for speech or action by someone else, implying 'But I've said enough; now *you* . . .'. So it is used in an agon when the chorus, after singing an ode, bids a character speak (κατακελευσμός). Cf. 379, 546, 728.   ἐκ τούτων ὥρα: 'in view of this it is time'.

348 πᾶν: 'anything'.

349 κιττῶ: 'crave'.   σανίδων: 'notice-boards', pieces of wood inscribed with notices of pending trials; so also in 848.   χοιρίνης: 94 n.

350 ὀπή: 'a chink', as in 127, not as in 317.   [ἔνδοθεν: A dactyl in this position in an anapaestic tetrameter is uncommon, but cf. 397, *Clouds* 326.]   διορύξαι: 'dig through'. This compound normally has as its object the thing which is penetrated (e.g. a wall), not the space which is created (e.g. a hole, a trench); cf. *Clouds* 714, *Wealth* 565. So it is here: the chorus want Philokleon to find an existing chink and dig through it, so as to make a large hole.

351 During the Greek siege of Troy Odysseus on one occasion entered the city disguised in rags (*Odyssey* 4. 244–50, E. *Hek.* 239–41), and on another occasion entered it through a drain (S. fr. 367, Servius on Virgil *Aen.* 2. 166). Ar. has here combined the two legends.

352 ὀπῆς: partitive genitive: 'enough of a hole'.   οὐδ' εἰ is the negative of κἄν (92 n.): 'not for a gnat, even if I were only a gnat'. σέρφος εἴην is understood.

353 ὀπίαν: 'cheese'. Fig-juice (ὀπός) was used as a rennet for curdling milk to make cheese (*Iliad* 5. 902, E. *Kyk.* 136, Ath. 658 c, etc.). Cheese does not generally slip through small holes; Philokleon is just making an absurd pun on ὀπή. 'There isn't a way . . . ; I can't turn myself into whey.'

354 ἐπὶ is temporal: 'on active service', 'when we were in the army'; so also in 557, *Lys.* 100. The chorus-leader reminisces, as in 236–9, but here the reminiscence leads to a suggestion which is meant to be practical. We are to imagine that at Naxos Philokleon stuck some stolen skewers into the wall, and fastened a rope to them so as to lower himself to the ground. If the feat sounds improbable, that is no doubt as Ar. intended.

355 The subjugation of Naxos by the Athenians occurred in the late 470s or early 460s (Th. 1. 98. 4).

356 'Yes, but what about it? This situation is nothing like that one.'

357 ἐμαυτοῦ: an extension of the genitive of comparison, as with verbs meaning 'rule'. 'I was in control of myself' means 'I was physically fit'. Cf. Pl. *R.* 571 d ὅταν ὑγιεινῶς τις ἔχῃ αὐτὸς αὑτοῦ καὶ σωφρόνως.

359–60 Philokleon exaggerates shamelessly and laughably. His guards, Bdelykleon and Xanthias, are lying fast asleep in full view, and in 364 they have no weapons better than household skewers.   διαταξάμενοι: 'drawn up for battle'.

361 'Are keeping a watch over the passes.' He speaks as if he had to cross a range of mountains.

363 ὥσπερ: with γαλῆν; for the order of words cf. *Clouds* 257 ὥσπερ με τὸν Ἀθάμανθ' ὅπως μὴ θύσετε.   γαλῆν: literally 'weasel' or 'ferret', but

as it was a household animal the best English equivalent is 'cat'. For
its thievish character cf. *Peace* 1151, *Th.* 559.

364 ἔχοντ': i.e. ἔχοντε: 'with skewers', which might be suitable weapons
for attacking a cat, but come as rather an anticlimax after 359–60. Ar.
puts them in just for the amusing bathos; Bdelykleon and Xanthias do
not really have skewers visible to the audience. (In 221–9 it seemed
they had no weapons except the stones on the ground, and in 398–9
Xanthias is told to use the harvest-branches for lack of other weapons.)
Perhaps an echo of 354 is intended: 'if anyone uses skewers today, it
won't be me'.

365 [καὶ νῦν: Dobree conjectured καινὴν, which could be right. But καὶ
νῦν, 'now too ⟨as in Naxos⟩', is satisfactory.]   **ὅπως**: 167 n.

366 ἕως: 'it is dawn'. In 216 dawn had not yet broken.   **ὦ μελίττιον**:
'my little honey-bee', or possibly 'honey', as van Herwerden suggests
(*Mn.* II xxi [1893] 444–5); μέλισσα means 'honey' in S. *OK* 481.
This term of endearment is found nowhere else, but it may well have
been in colloquial use; it is natural enough to connect sweet people
and honey. It may be intended by Ar. to sound comic when addressed by old men to another old man. It is unlikely to have any
connection with the insect guise of the chorus, since they are not bees
but wasps; perhaps Starkie, writing in Dublin, was thinking of some
Irish wasps when he wrote: 'It is natural for the Wasps to call their
comrade "a bee".'

367 δίκτυον: the net covering the window from which he is looking. In
165 he was toothless, so that Xanthias might make an amusing retort;
now he has teeth, so that the audience may laugh at him chewing the
net; Ar. does not care (and the audience probably does not notice)
that the two passages are incompatible.

368 Δίκτυννα: 'the goddess of nets'. Diktynna was a goddess of hunting
who originated in Krete, and was subsequently identified with Artemis
(cf. *Frogs* 1359, E. *Hipp.* 145, *IT* 127). Her name may well have been
derived in fact from Dikte, a mountain in Krete, but since nets were
used for hunting it was assumed later that it came from δίκτυον, and
etymological myths grew up on this basis (Kall. *Hymn* 3. 189–203,
D.S. 5. 76. 3–4, Paus. 2. 30. 3); cf. M. P. Nilsson *Geschichte der griechischen Religion* i 2nd edition (1955) 311–12. Thus Ar. may well have
believed that Diktynna meant 'goddess of nets', and is not necessarily
making a pun. But the way in which Philokleon utters a pious prayer
before attacking the net with his teeth is certainly meant to be funny.
τοῦ δικτύου: i.e. 'for damaging the net'.

**369 '*That* shows a man making his way to safety ⟨whereas your previous
shilly-shallying . . .⟩'; the contrast implied by μὲν is left unexpressed.

370 'Come on, apply your jaw!' The first metron is reduced to − ∪ ∪ ∪;
see pages 27–9 and 339 n. Philokleon makes a show of chewing at
the net for a few moments, and then pushes it aside. In performance

he cannot chew it for long, since the audience would get bored; therefore the actor does not actually gnaw it in half, but just creates an
impression of doing so.

373 ὦ τᾶν: a polite form of address; but it often has a slightly condescending
tone, implying that the speaker is somehow superior or knows better;
cf. 1161 and other instances discussed by G. J. de Vries (*Mn*. IV xix
[1966] 225–30). In various strata of English society 'my dear fellow',
'my good man', 'old boy', 'chum', and 'mate' are similarly used. The
chorus are slightly patronizing in their promise to protect Philokleon.

375 δακεῖν τὴν καρδίαν: i.e. 'feel miserable'; for the metaphor cf. 287,
Akh. 1 δέδηγμαι τὴν ἐμαυτοῦ καρδίαν.

376 'Run a race for his life'; cf. *Iliad* 22. 161, Hdt. 8. 74. 1, 9. 37. 2,
Pl. *Tht.* 172 e.

377 εἰδῇ μὴ: 'know not to', as in E. *Hipp.* 729.   **πατεῖν**: 'trample on',
a common metaphor for 'treat with contempt'; cf. S. *Ant.* 745 τιμάς
γε τὰς θεῶν πατῶν.

378 ψηφίσματα is generally used only of political decrees, but cf.
Empedokles 115 θεῶν ψήφισμα παλαιόν. The chorus regard their way
of life as divinely ordained; cf. 158–60. [Not τοῖν θεοῖν (Hirschig),
referring to Demeter and Kore; accusations of profanation of the
Eleusinian Mysteries did not become fashionable until 415.]

379 ἀλλ': 346 n.   **τῆς** is not evidence that the house has only one
window; it is just 'the window which you're looking out of'.   **τὸ
καλῴδιον**: Although the article is used, this is the first we have heard
of a rope. He must have produced a rope from inside the house during
373–8. Now he fastens one end of it to something out of sight inside the
window and the other end to himself.

380 'Filling your heart with Diopeithes'; i.e. 'putting your trust in
God'. For the use of a notorious man's name in place of a quality or
substance cf. 325, 459. Just as in those lines 'Proxenides' or 'Aiskhines' is a jocular synonym for 'smoke', so here 'Diopeithes' stands for
'religion', partly because the etymological meaning of the name is
'trust in Zeus', but mainly because Diopeithes was a notorious hot-
gospeller. He is satirized as a religious maniac and fanatical dis-
penser of oracles in *Knights* 1085, *Birds* 988, Telekleides 6, Phrynikhos
com. 9, Ameipsias 10. Some years previously he proposed a decree for
the impeachment of atheists and astronomers, which was thought to
be directed against Anaxagoras and through him against Perikles
(Plu. *Per.* 32. 2). He is said to have been a friend of Nikias (*Σ Knights*
1085).

381 ἄγε is a standard exclamation for 'come!' 'well now', and so is
often used in this singular form even when addressed to more than one
person; so also in 1518, and cf. εἰπέ μοι (403 n.).   **τούτω**: Bdelykleon
and Xanthias.   **ἐσκαλαμᾶσθαι**: 'to get me hauled in'. Philokleon
hanging at the end of the rope will be like a fish at the end of a rod and

line. The middle voice here and the circumlocution with ποιεῖν in 382 imply that Bdelykleon and Xanthias, who are outside, will call to slaves inside to come to the window and pull up the rope.

383 πρινώδη: 'tough as holm-oak'; for the metaphor cf. 877.   καλέσαντες: 'summoning up'.

385 μανθάνετ': imperative: 'take notice', 'let me tell you'. [Lenting made μανθάνετ'; a parenthetical question, but Philokleon can hardly ask the chorus 'Do you understand?' before he has given them his instruction.]   τι πάθω: i.e. 'die'; so also in 387, *Peace* 169–70, *Ek.* 1105, etc.

386 θεῖναί μ': 'you are to bury me'. A jussive infinitive (the subject, if it is not the person addressed, being in the accusative) is often used instead of an imperative in formal contexts such as laws, proclamations (e.g. 937), and prayers (e.g. 872, 879–84), and sometimes in other contexts (e.g. 1216). Here Philokleon is giving a solemn instruction. δρυφάκτοις: the railings which excluded the general public from a law-court; 124 n. Philokleon has a great affection for them because they are a physical symbol of the privileged position of jurors; cf. 830–1. But his request to be buried under them is absurd; no one could really be buried in a law-court. The joke implies that a request to be buried in a particular place was not unusual in classical Athens, but I have not found any other instance.

389 Lykos was an Athenian hero. (He is generally identified with Lykos son of Pandion, and since Pandion was an Athenian hero this identification may be accepted, despite the lack of clear evidence for it.) But the reason why Philokleon chooses this hero for his prayer is that next to the principal shrine of Lykos in Athens there was a law-court, called 'the court at Lykos' (τὸ ἐπὶ Λύκῳ, Pol. 8. 121). Presumably the image of Lykos was visible from inside the court, and so Philokleon assumes that Lykos listens to the trials. Juvenal has a similar joke about the statue of Apollo in the forum at Rome: 'forum iurisque peritus Apollo' (Juv. 1. 128).   γείτων (to suit the metre, in place of γείτον; contrast 875): Philokleon regards Lykos as his neighbour because he regards a law-court as his second home. For the purpose of this joke only, he is a juror of 'the court at Lykos', though elsewhere in the play he belongs to other courts (120 n.). For further fun about the shrine of Lykos cf. 819–23; for a list of Athenian courts, 1108 n. [Lykos and the court near his shrine have been discussed by A. L. Boegehold (*Hesperia* xxxvi [1967] 111–20), who is rightly sceptical towards late evidence about them. But I disagree with his interpretation of *Wasps* 389. He thinks that the audience is at first led to believe that Philokleon is invoking Apollon; but in fact the addressee is made clear from the start by the vocative Λύκε. (I see no reason to suppose that an audience could not distinguish Λύκε from Λύκειε or Λύκιε.) He also thinks that γείτων means that Lykos is a neighbour of

Apollon; but in fact Apollon has not been mentioned and Philokleon must mean that Lykos is a neighbour of his own. So there is no basis for Boegehold's conclusion that the law-court (if that is what it is) of which remains have been found near the precinct of Apollon Patroos in the Agora is 'the court at Lykos' rather than any other court.]

γάρ: i.e. '⟨I address you⟩ because'. It is common in a Greek prayer to mention some of the god's qualities before making the request; cf. 875, *Frogs* 875–8, *Ek.* 1–5, etc.   κεχάρησαι: The middle and passive forms of χαίρω have the same meaning as the active, and the perfect often has the same meaning as the present; cf. 764. 'You take pleasure in the same things as I do.'

390 τῶν φευγόντων ἀεί: 'those who are on trial each day'; cf. D. 21. 223 οἱ ἀεὶ δικάζοντες, 'those who are jurors on any given occasion', and *Wasps* 1318, And. 1. 91, Pl. *Ap.* 25 c, etc.

391 γοῦν: 262 n.   ἵνα combines its local and final senses: 'where you might hear'.

392 μόνος is common in prayers; a god is praised especially for those qualities or functions which no other god has. Cf. *Peace* 590, *Birds* 1546, *Th.* 1141, *Ek.* 12.   παρά has the accusative because previous motion is implied; cf. 1083, 1108. It would be normal for a distressed person to sit beside a shrine, as a suppliant. But in this case the situation is comically reversed: Philokleon assumes that Lykos shares his enthusiasm for trials and so has deliberately taken up a position beside the court to be near distressed defendants.

393 πλησιόχωρον: 'neighbour'; cf. 389 γείτων.

394 οὐ μή with the aorist subjunctive denies (οὐ) any fear or suspicion that (μή) an event may happen (subjunctive) on any single occasion (aorist), and thus makes a strong 'never'; so also in 612.   κάννας: 'wicker fence', surrounding the shrine; cf. Pherekrates 63 σκηνὴ περίερκτος περιβόλοις κάνναισι.   οὐρήσω μηδ' ἀποπάρδω: As often in Ar. (cf. 323–33) the prayer ends in comic bathos. Philokleon is so poor that he cannot promise Lykos any more expensive kind of honour. Urination against something shows a lack of respect for it; cf. *Frogs* 95, D. 54. 4. Breaking wind is often mentioned in Aristophanic comedy; it is one of the author's devices for expressing a character's attitude to a situation. Sometimes it denotes fear (e.g. 1177). More often it indicates that the character is pleasing himself, not exercising self-control in consideration for others; thus it may mean simply enjoyment (e.g. 1305, *Peace* 335), or contempt for someone else (often in the compound καταπέρδομαι with a genitive, e.g. 618, *Peace* 547, *Wealth* 618), or it may be a symptom of the simple straightforward behaviour of a countryman (ἀγροικός) as opposed to the refined restraint of a city-dweller (e.g. *Wealth* 705). So here Philokleon means that he will put himself under restraint out of respect for Lykos. For a full discussion of breaking wind in Ar. see R. Hošek *Lidovost a lidové*

motivy u Aristofana (1962, in Czech with summaries in Russian and German) 160–74.

At the end of his prayer he at last climbs out of the window and begins to let himself down the rope. Meanwhile Bdelykleon wakes and, without looking upwards, calls to Xanthias.

395 ὥσπερ: 'it seems as if'. Since the chorus and Philokleon have been speaking and singing for 165 lines, this remark is as comic as the Major-General's 'I thought I heard a noise' in *The Pirates of Penzance*. **ἐγκεκύκλωται**: 'has been floating round'.

396 Xanthias looks up and sees Philokleon coming down the rope. His negative contradicts Bdelykleon's διa-: 'No, he's not slipping *through*; he's coming *down*.' Bdelykleon then looks up and sees Philokleon.

397 [-τατε, τί ποι-: 350 n. Ar. generally avoids ∪∪∪∪ in anapaests (except in lyrics: 1010 n.), but it occurs also in 1015, *Knights* 503, *Clouds* 916, *Peace* 169, *Birds* 688, *Th.* 822, *Frogs* 1525. These instances are few enough to show that he prefers to avoid ∪∪∪∪, but numerous enough to refute the view that he never allows it. Thus emendation of these lines on metrical grounds is not justified.] **τί ποιεῖς;** not a genuine question (he can see what Philokleon is doing), but an expression of indignation; so also in 1443, *Clouds* 723, 1495, etc.

οὐ μή with the future indicative is used for strong negative future statements and prohibitions. The origin of the usage has been much disputed and cannot be discussed in detail here, but in my opinion the two likeliest explanations are these:

A: Because οὐ μή with the aorist subjunctive is equivalent to a negative future statement (394 n.), it may have been felt appropriate to use οὐ μή with any future statement to make it strongly negative.

B: Because a negative future question (e.g. οὐ μενεῖς;) is equivalent to a command or request, it may have been felt that the addition of another negative made a question equivalent to a prohibition ('Won't you not . . .?').

Instances like *Frogs* 508–9 οὐ μή σ' ἐγὼ περιόψομαι 'πελθόντ' favour explanation *A*. Instances like *Clouds* 505 οὐ μὴ λαλήσεις, ἀλλ' ἀκολουθήσεις ἐμοί; (where οὐ may be taken with both verbs and μὴ with the first only) favour *B*. Probably *A* and *B* both influenced the development of the idiom, and it is a mistake to plump for one explanation to the exclusion of the other. Here οὐ μὴ καταβήσει may be regarded as partly statement and partly interrogative-imperative, a mixture of 'You're certainly not going to come down' and 'Will you stay up there!'

398: addressed to Xanthias. **κατὰ τὴν ἑτέραν**: 'the other way'. The feminine noun to be understood is probably not ὁδόν but the abstract noun corresponding to the verb, i.e. ἀνάβασιν. Cf. 1231 ἑτέραν ᾄσομαι (sc. ᾠδήν), *Frogs* 191 νεναυμάχηκε τὴν περὶ τῶν κρεῶν (sc. ναυμαχίαν). Xanthias is to unbar the door and go into the house and up the stairs to the window from which Philokleon has emerged.

φυλλάσι: branches with leaves on them, i.e. the εἰρεσιῶναι (399).
An εἰρεσιώνη was a branch dedicated in honour of the harvest. It was
a branch of olive, or possibly of laurel, adorned with wool, figs and
other fruits, small loaves or cakes, and small jars of olive-oil, wine, and
honey. The members of a household would dedicate one or more of
these harvest-branches on the occasion of the Pyanopsia, a festival in
honour of Apollon celebrated on the 7th day of Pyanopsion (approximately October). (Whether εἰρεσιῶναι were dedicated also at the
Thargelia, in early summer, is doubtful.) Offerings were made to the
sun and the seasons (Ἥλιος and Ὧραι). A boy sang these words:

εἰρεσιώνη σῦκα φέρει καὶ πίονας ἄρτους
καὶ μέλι ἐν κοτύλῃ καὶ ἔλαιον ἀποψήσασθαι
καὶ κύλικ' εὔζωρον, ὡς ἂν μεθύουσα καθεύδῃ.

The harvest-branches were hung up outside the door of the house and
left there, becoming gradually dry and withered, until replaced by
new harvest-branches a year later. Cf. *Knights* 729 and *Σ*, *Wealth* 1054
and *Σ*, Lykourgos fr. 4. 2 (Burtt p. 142, Malcovati p. 172), Plu. *Thes.*
22. 6–7, *Souda* ει 184, and also M. P. Nilsson *Geschichte der griechischen
Religion* i 2nd edition (1955) 122–7.

Bdelykleon wants Xanthias to take one of the harvest-branches
hanging on the wall beside the door and beat Philokleon with it.
Evidently these are the only things conveniently to hand which can be
used as weapons for beating him—which goes to show how he was
exaggerating in his talk of weapons in 359–64. During 399–402
Xanthias unbars the door and disappears inside, taking with him one
of the two harvest-branches, while Bdelykleon takes the other harvest-
branch and tries to hit Philokleon from below. (I assume here and in
the following notes that real branches are used in the performance.
But the alternative possibility that there are no actual branches cannot
be disproved; cf. 208, where there is no actual bird-net.)

399 ἤν πως: 'in case', 'to see if', 'in the hope that'.   πρύμναν ἀνακρούσηται: 'back water'. The phrase is used in a literal sense of oars-
men in Hdt. 8. 84. 1. For the metaphorical use cf. *Birds* 648 δεῦρ'
ἐπανάκρουσαι πάλιν, E. *Andr.* 1120 χωρεῖ δὲ πρύμναν. [πρύμναν here has
ᾱ, as in S. *Ph.* 482. The two passages defend each other against
emendation.]

400 'Won't you help me, all you who have trials coming on this year?'
Philokleon calls out to those members of the audience who are
prosecutors in forthcoming cases: surely none of them will acquiesce in
the loss of a juror so certain to vote for condemnation.

401 These four men are evidently all likely prosecutors. Probably they
were all regarded as συκοφάνται. We know nothing else about them,
but they must all be real persons, not fictional. Σμικυθίων and Τεισιάδης
are normal Athenian names. Χρήμων and Φερέδειπνος are comic

inventions (the first is either 'Money-man', from χρήματα, or 'Needy',
from χρή; the second is 'Dinner-carrier' or 'Dinner-getter', from φέρω
and δεῖπνον), and are probably distortions of the men's real names,
which may have been for example Χρέμων and Φερεκλείδης. For this
kind of comic distortion cf. 459, 466, 592, 895. [Τεισ- was restored by
H. van Herwerden (*Mn.* II xxi [1893] 445). It is not clear that Dindorf's Χρῆμον is required, since the invented name may have a stem in
-ων-, not -ον-; even if it has -ον-, cf. 389 γείτων.]

402 μᾶλλον: 'instead ⟨of going to court to vote for you⟩'.

At this point, or soon afterwards, Xanthias appears at the window.
While the chorus sing 403–14 Philokleon, now half-way down the
rope, is comically belaboured by the leafy and ornamented harvest-
branches simultaneously by Xanthias from above and by Bdelykleon
from below. In performance this should be an amusing piece of
clowning.

403–62 *The chorus now show their waspish character. They accuse Bdelykleon of
treason and tyranny, and threaten to attack him with their stings unless he
releases Philokleon. Bdelykleon calls out more slaves to hold Philokleon while he
and Xanthias fetch weapons for beating off the wasps; Philokleon and the
chorus express indignation at his being consigned to the custody of slaves.
Bdelykleon and Xanthias return with sticks and smoke; then the wasps attack
and are driven off.*

It is in this passage that the double character of the chorus is most
clearly displayed. They are spoken of as wasps, able to fly and sting
and to be repelled by smoke. Yet they are also men (e.g. 454 ἀνδρῶν),
and they continue to speak as Athenian jurors.

The anger and excitement are built up gradually to the climax of the
battle. First the chorus strip for action (408); then their stings are seen
and frighten Xanthias (420–7). Philokleon calls on them to attack
(430–2), and Bdelykleon calls out more slaves (433–6). At the end
comes the actual fight (456–9). But it is strange that before the fight
begins there is an interval of nineteen lines (437–55) during which
Bdelykleon and Xanthias are not seen at all, while Philokleon and the
chorus do nothing but threaten three unresponsive slaves. These lines
relax the tension just at a time when it ought not to be relaxed. Ar.
seldom misjudges the structure of a scene, but he appears to have done
so at this point, unless 437–55 has some further significance which
escapes us.

[O. Musso (*Stud. Ital.* xxxvi [1964] 86–9) suggests that 437–55
parodies Euripides's *Kresphontes*, but I am not convinced that he is
right. The old man Kresphontes cannot have been shown in the
hands of his slaves in that play, since its action occurred after his
death. The new fragments of it (*P.Oxy.* 2458), which Musso quotes,
do not resemble anything in *Wasps* 437–55; and this passage contains a number of comic or colloquial expressions (e.g. 455 βλεπόντων

κάρδαμα) which can hardly be borrowed from a tragedy. Really the only evidence in favour of Musso's view is a fragment from *Kresphontes* which runs αἰδὼς ἐν ὀφθαλμοῖσι γίγνεται, τέκνον (E. fr. 457). This clearly resembles *Wasps* 447; yet, since the phrase was proverbial (447 n.), Ar. did not necessarily get it from *Kresphontes*.]

403–525 *Metre*: trochaic tetrameters, but in 405–29 and 463–87 the chorus have some trochaic runs, and their lines include some reduced metra (see pages 26–9). They are shown in the following scheme; all lines omitted from the scheme are ordinary trochaic tetrameters.

```
405    – ∪ – ∪   – ∪ – ∪
406    – ∪ – ∪   – ∪ – ∪
407    – ∪ – ∪   – ∪ ∪ – ⌒ ‖      (407 n.)

410    – ∪ – ∪   – ∪ – –
411    – ∪ – ∪   – ∪ ∪ ∪
412    – ∪ – ∪   – ∪ ∪ ∪ ∪
413    – ∪ ∪ ∪   – ∪ –
414    – ∪ –     – ∪ –

418    – ∪ –     – ∪ –    – ∪ –    – ∪ –
419    – ∪ –     – ∪ –    – ∪ –    – ∪ –

428    – ∪ –     – ∪ –    – ∪ –    – ∪ –
429    – ∪ –     – ∪ ∪ ∪  – ∪ –    – ∪ ⌒ ‖

463    – ∪ – –   – ∪ – ∪  – ∪ – ∪
464    – ∪ – ∪   – ∪ – ∪
465    – ∪ ∪ ∪   – ∪ ⌒ ‖

468    – ∪ ∪ ∪   – ∪ ∪ ∪
469    – ∪ ∪ ∪   – ∪ ∪ ∪
470    – ∪ –     – ∪ ⌒ ‖

473    – ∪ – –   – ∪ – ∪
474    – ∪ – ∪   – ∪ – ∪
475    – ∪ –     – ∪ –    – ∪ –    – ∪ ⌒ ‖
476/7  – ∪ –     – ∪ –    – ∪ –    – ∪ –

486    – ∪ ∪ ∪   – ∪ –    – ∪ –    – ∪ – ‖
487    – ∪ –     – ∪ ∪ ∪  – ∪ –    – ∪ –
```

This scene, like the previous one, is approximately symmetrical:

403–29   Trochaic, with some reduced metra.
430–60   Trochaic tetrameters, without reduced metra.
461–87   Trochaic, with some reduced metra.
488–525   Trochaic tetrameters, without reduced metra.

But metrical correspondence between 403–60 and 461–525 is not exact, and one should hesitate to emend the text merely to make it exact (411 n.).

The vigorous trochaic rhythm makes the whole passage seem energetic and fast-moving. The reduced metra in some of the chorus's lines perhaps convey the impression that they get out of breath and are unable to keep up the pace; see pages 28–9. In 403–14 one may imagine them at first rushing to and fro pugnaciously, and then beginning to stagger slowly and gasp from their exertions.

403 εἰπέ μοι: a standard interjection, remaining in the singular form even when more than one person is addressed; cf. *Akh.* 319, 328, *Peace* 383, etc., and ἄγε (381 n.).   κινεῖν: more often used of arousing someone else's anger, but cf. E. *Med.* 98–9 μήτηρ κινεῖ κραδίαν, κινεῖ δὲ χόλον. 'Why do we hesitate to show the wrath which we show when . . .?'

404 ἡμῶν: with τὴν σφηκιάν, not with τις.

405 The repetition, with alternating long and short vowels separated always by single consonants, produces a very strong rhythmical effect; the wasps are limbering up for action.

406 τοὐξύθυμον: ὀξύθυμος, 'sharp-spirited', is used elsewhere of men (e.g. A. *Eu.* 705, E. *Ba.* 671), but it is specially appropriate to wasps and their stings, since for them ὀξυ- has a literal as well as a metaphorical sense. It recurs in 455, 1105; cf. 430 ὀξυκάρδιοι.

407 ἐντέτατ': perfect passive of ἐντείνω: 'is on the stretch', i.e. 'is braced for action'; cf. X. *Oik.* 21. 9 προθύμους καὶ ἐντεταμένους παρέχεσθαι εἰς τὸ ἔργον. [– ∪ ∪ in place of – ∪ is rare in a trochaic run, but occurs also in *Birds* 396; cf. *Wasps* 496, where it occurs in a trochaic tetrameter. One might expect a catalectic metron here to conclude the run 405–7, as in 465 -οῦσά με. Yet, since the sense is satisfactory and the metre not impossible, I hesitate to emend.]   ὀξύ: The position of the adjective makes it predicative. 'Now the sting is braced and sharp' does not mean that it was not sharp before, but that now its sharpness may be seen and felt.

408 A ἱμάτιον is a long cloak worn out of doors. The chorus now take off their cloaks and hand them to the boys, who go off with them at 414. Taking off one's cloak is a normal preparation for a fight; cf. *Th.* 568. Under their cloaks, and therefore seen by the audience now for the first time, the chorus are wearing costumes which make them look like wasps: stings projecting from their rumps (420, 1073–5), narrow waists (1072), and perhaps black-and-yellow tunics. [B₂'s βαλόντες would mean that the boys, instead of taking their fathers' cloaks, were to throw off their own cloaks in order to run faster. This would litter the orkhestra with the cloaks of all the chorus and all the boys. λαβόντες clears all the cloaks out of the way of the action, and so is preferable.]

409 For 'Fetch Kleon!' as a cry from someone who feels outraged or victimized cf. *Frogs* 569–78. These passages show that he was regarded, by some people at least, as a champion of the weak against oppression and injustice.

411 ὡς ἐπ': 'to face'. [L. P. E. Parker (*CQ* xviii [1968] 263) wishes to obelize 411–12 on two grounds: (*a*) lack of responsion between 410–14 and 468–70, (*b*) 'split resolution' in 412 -νον, ὅ- (i.e. a long syllable is resolved into two shorts and there is word-break between them). But I leave it unobelized, because (*a*) I am not convinced that Ar. intended 410–14 and 468–70 to respond closely (405–7 and 463–5 do not respond closely either), (*b*) there are parallels in Ar. for split resolution at this point in a trochaic metron (*Knights* 284 αὐτίκα μάλα and perhaps *Lys.* 1262 -ροκτόνε, μόλε), and the chorus, bursting with indignation, probably do not pause at all between ἀπολούμενον and ὅτι.]

413 λόγον: 'theory', 'rule'.

[**414 ὡς χρὴ** (**a**) is unnecessary for the sense 'this rule, not to judge cases', and impossible for the metre. It is a gloss inserted to explain the infinitive, as in D. 20. 155.]

By now Philokleon has come right down the rope, or perhaps has fallen off it. Bdelykleon seizes him and holds him firmly despite his struggles to get away. Xanthias disappears from the window, re-emerges from the door, and by 420 has restored both harvest-branches to their places on the wall, or else has dumped them out of the way inside the house.

415 τὸ πρᾶγμ': 'the facts'. [**κεκράγατε:** There is doubt about the perfect imperative form. In *Akh.* 133 the mss. have κεχήνατε, but Herodian quoted that line as an instance of -ετε (Bekker *Anecdota Graeca* 1287). For another possible instance of -ατε see Men. *Dys.* 173 with Handley's note. Perhaps emendation to -ετε is not essential.]

416 νὴ Δί' . . . γ': 'Oh yes we will!' **εἰς τὸν οὐρανόν:** i.e. very loudly. **ὥς:** sc. ἴσθι: 'I assure you that . . .', as in *Clouds* 209, *Lys.* 499, etc. [**τόνδ':** Elsewhere the middle μεθίεμαι takes a genitive, in the sense 'let go one's hold of'. But Bdelykleon may mean not 'I will not stop holding on to him with my own hands' but 'I will not release him from confinement by me', and so emendation to τοῦδ' is probably unnecessary.]

417 τυραννίς: 345 n.

418 ὦ πόλις: 'Oh Athens!' 'Oh my country!' The patriotic exclamation seems to be proceeding καὶ θεοί, but suddenly turns to bathos. **Θεώρου:** 42 n. **θεοισεχθρία:** 'devilry'. The jurors are so wrong-headed that they admire bad qualities; 322 n.

419 [**ἡμῶν**, regarded by most editors as a conjecture, is in fact the reading of J.] **κόλαξ:** 45 n.

420 Ἡράκλεις: an exclamation of surprise or shock, as in *Akh.* 284, *Birds* 814, etc.   καὶ: 'actually'. Since the chorus removed their cloaks at 408, Xanthias has been inside the house or attending to the harvest-branches, so that it is only now that he notices their stings.

421 γ': 'yes'.   Φίλιππον τὸν Γοργίου: Gorgias, of Leontinoi in Sicily, was a famous teacher of rhetoric. He came to Athens on an embassy in 427, and afterwards stayed in Greece or made frequent visits, so that he was a well-known figure in Athens. Two of his rhetorical compositions (*Helen* and *Palamedes*) survive in full, with fragments of others; and he is a leading character in Plato's *Gorgias*. But about Philippos not much is known. I see no need to deny that τὸν Γοργίου means that he was Gorgias's son, but some have preferred to take it as 'disciple of Gorgias'. In *Birds* 1701–5 he and Gorgias are mentioned together as men who live by their tongues.   ἀπώλεσαν ἐν δίκῃ, 'demolished in a trial', means that he had recently lost a case in an Athenian court (not that he had been condemned to death, since *Birds* 1701–5 shows that he was still alive in 414). ἐν δίκῃ can mean 'justly', but it is unlikely that Ar. intends that meaning here; in this play he wants to stress that some condemnations are unjust, not that some are just.

422 ἅπας ἐπίστρεφε δεῦρο: 'every man wheel this way'. The leader gives orders in military fashion to the other members of the chorus. [Dindorf emended to ἀλλὰ πᾶς. But ἅπας with an imperative is proved right by the metre in *Ek.* 502, Kratinos 144 Kock = 137 Edmonds.]

423 ἵεσο: 'charge'; cf. Hdt. 6. 112. 1 (the battle of Marathon).

424 ξυσταλείς: probably 'close together', 'shoulder to shoulder'. It is less likely to mean 'with clothes tucked up ready for action', since the chorus have already removed their cloaks at 408. Cf. *Lys.* 1042, where a similar ambiguity arises.   ἐμπλήμενος: aorist middle of ἐμπίμπλημι (not passive as LSJ say); so also in 603, 911, 984, 1127, 1304. 'After filling yourself with anger and passion.'

426 μέντοι: 'really'.

427 ὡς: exclamatory: 'How frightened I am!' Contrast 228; it is a shrewd touch of characterization that Xanthias cannot imagine a danger before he sees it.   ἐγκεντρίδας: 'stings', just a synonym for κέντρα, as in 1073. [Pol. 8. 16 says that ἐγκεντρίς was the name of the stylus with which a juror drew the line on his tablet for imposing a penalty (106 n.). But this does not mean that the chorus's stings are styluses which they flourish in their hands in this scene, for 1075 shows that their stings projected from their rumps. Nor is Xanthias making a pun on 'sting' and 'stylus'; he is afraid only of a physical attack by weapons which are plainly visible, and there is no possibility that he (a slave) may be tried in a law-court. So ἐγκεντρίς here does not mean 'stylus'. There is in fact no evidence in classical Greek for this meaning, and no likelihood that jurors would have a special piece of equipment for drawing one line on a tablet; and it seems possible that Polydeukes has just made a false deduction from *Wasps*.]

429 'You will think tortoises lucky in their shells.' For the genitive of cause cf. 588, 1292, 1512.

430 Since 415 Philokleon has been looking on helpless in Bdelykleon's grasp. Now he shouts to the chorus to attack.   εἶά: 'come on!'

432 κύκλῳ: 'all over'; cf. Pl. *Phdr.* 251 d πᾶσα κεντουμένη κύκλῳ.

433 Bdelykleon shouts for three slaves to hold Philokleon, and they come running out of the house. Athenians often named slaves simply from their nationality (so here Φρύξ; cf. 828 Θρᾷττα, 1371 Δαρδανίς) or by names common in their own countries (so here Μίδας, a Phrygian name; cf. Str. 304); for a list of instances of such names see Headlam and Knox's note on Herodas 1. 1. Μασυντίας seems to mean 'chewer', from μασάομαι.   βοήθει: For the singular cf. *Ek.* 293–4 ὦ Χαριτιμίδη καὶ Σμίκυθε καὶ Δράκης, ἕπου. [Bentley's conjecture is acceptable; a scribe who did not understand metre thought the plural preferable with three vocatives. The singular does not mean that we must accept the far-fetched suggestion of W. M. Ramsay (*CR* xii [1898] 335–7) that ὦ Μίδα καὶ Φρύξ means 'thou Midas, who art also Phryx' and is an elaborate address to Sosias; line 8 is not adequate evidence that Sosias is a Phrygian. Objections to Prato's βοηθεῖτ' εὐθύ have been stated by K. J. Dover (*Lustrum* ii [1957] 84).]

435 εἰ δὲ μή is a stereotyped phrase for 'otherwise', so that after the preceding negative it means 'if you *do*'; cf. *Clouds* 1433, *Peace* 384, *Birds* 133, *Frogs* 629.   πέδαις παχείαις: 'heavy fetters'. For the threat to put a slave in fetters cf. *Wealth* 275–6.

436 'Since I'm well acquainted with the sound of a lot of fig-leaves.' This is evidently a metaphor for meaningless noise or empty threats. Σ quotes a proverb in an iambic trimeter: πολλῶν ἐγὼ θρίων ψόφους ἀκήκοα. The line gives Bdelykleon's reason for being merciless to the slaves if they let Philokleon go: the wasps will not really hurt them. [A. Y. Campbell (*CR* xliv [1930] 216) wanted to give this line to the chorus. But the chorus has no particular reason for thinking that Bdelykleon's threat to fetter and starve the slaves is idle. Campbell was misled by a belief that a fight actually took place at 432.]

Bdelykleon now goes into the house, accompanied by Xanthias, while Philokleon is held by Midas, Phryx, and Masyntias (or by two of them; cf. 442, 452–3). Meanwhile the chorus continue to make threatening remarks and gestures from the orkhestra.

437 ἔν τί σοι παγήσεται: 'something will be stuck into you', i.e. 'I shall sting you'. ἐμπαγήσεται is split (tmesis); cf. 784 ἀνά τοί με πείθεις. [ἕν (a) is impossible, because it means not 'something' but 'one thing', i.e. 'only one thing'.] This threat is probably addressed to one of the slaves holding Philokleon, or possibly to Bdelykleon as he disappears through the doorway.

438 Kekrops, the mythical first king of Athens, is appealed to as a champion of Athenians against foreigners. τὰ πρὸς ποδῶν: The accusative limits the application of Δρακοντίδη: 'as far as the parts towards the feet are concerned', i.e. 'below the waist'. As a symbol of having been born from the soil of Athens, Kekrops is regularly represented as being a serpent below the waist, i.e. δράκων or δρακοντοειδής. Here Δρακοντίδη (157 n.) is substituted, apparently from no other reason than to make the audience laugh from surprise. There is no implication that Drakontides is a friend of the jurors, for in 157 Philokleon was hoping to condemn him.

439 περιορᾷς: For this kind of prayer, asking a god not to allow something which is already happening, cf. Ek. 369–70 ὦ πότνι' Εἰλείθυια, μή με περιίδῃς διαρραγέντα, Akh. 55.

440 'Four to the quart' means tears of a κοτύλη each (about half a pint). He implies that this was a great favour he did them; cf. 450–1.

441 εἶτα δῆτ': 'Well, really!'

442 τούτω: Evidently only two of the slaves who were called at 433 are now holding Philokleon (cf. 452). The third is perhaps standing by to ward off attacks by the chorus. παλαιὸν: 'old' in the sense 'former'; on Philokleon's retirement from control of the household, 613 n.

444 διφθερῶν κάξωμίδων: cheap and hard-wearing kinds of clothes. The διφθέρα was a leather coat, worn especially by herdsmen (Clouds 72, Ek. 80). The ἐξωμίς was a tunic which left the right arm and shoulder bare.

445 κυνᾶς: a fresh object for ἡμπόλα: the construction with μεμνημένοι is now forgotten. κυνῆ is a general word for 'hat', not necessarily of dogskin. τοὺς πόδας ὠφέλει: i.e. 'gave them shoes'.

446 ἑκάστοτ': often added at the end of a sentence to indicate that an event occurred a number of times; we might say 'regularly'. Cf. 770, 1283.

446–7 'But there's no respect at all in their eyes.' οὐδὲν: 'not at all'. [οὐδ' ἐν, 'not even in', is not likely to be right, since the eyes are a normal place to show αἰδώς. Indeed the expression is proverbial: Arist. Rhet. 1384ª34 mentions ἡ παροιμία τὸ ἐν ὀφθαλμοῖς εἶναι αἰδῶ, and more or less the same words are found in Theognis 85–6, E. fr. 457.] ἐμβάδων: a surprise, in place of δεσποτῶν: 103 n.

448 He addresses one of the two slaves holding him. οὐκ . . . οὐδὲ . . . οὐδ': 'Won't you release me even now, even remembering . . .?'

449 βότρυς: not specially valuable produce (as they would be in northern Europe). Grapes, olives, and figs were the commonest crops in Attica; thus in the next line, when the slave was tied to the nearest tree to be beaten, it was an olive-tree. Cf. V. Ehrenberg The People of Aristophanes 2nd edition (1951) 73–4.

451 ζηλωτὸν: The joke is that the slave ought to have been pleased because what was done to him was done well (εὖ κάνδρικῶς). ἄρα: 314 n.

452 καὶ σὺ καὶ σύ: both the slave addressed in 448–51 and the other one holding him.

453 τούτων: 'for this', i.e. failure to release Philokleon.

454 οὐκέτ' ἐς μακράν: 'quite soon now'; cf. D. 18. 36 μετὰ ταῦτ' εὐθύς, οὐκ εἰς μακράν.

455 βλεπόντων κάρδαμα: 'looking mustard', with a sharp, fierce expression. For the metaphor and the internal accusative cf. 643, *Knights* 631 κἄβλεψε νᾶπυ, *Akh.* 254 βλέπουσα θυμβροφάγον, *Peace* 1184 βλέπων ὀπόν, *Frogs* 603 βλέποντ' ὀρίγανον, *Ek.* 292 βλέπων ὑπότριμμα.

With these words the chorus begin their attack (at last; they have been getting ready and uttering threats ever since 403) by trying to climb up from the orkhestra on to the raised area in front of the house (1341 n.). At the same moment Bdelykleon reappears through the doorway with Xanthias, and now we discover why it was they went inside: to fetch implements for shooing the wasps away. Xanthias has a big stick or cudgel, and Bdelykleon has something which produces smoke—presumably damp burning material of some kind which he carries in a cauldron or other large container, and bellows for blowing the smoke in any desired direction.

457 σύ: probably the extra slave who is not holding Philokleon (442 n.). [But throughout 457–60 it is impossible to be certain who speaks which words. Perhaps the likeliest guess is that all the orders are given by Bdelykleon and all the other words are spoken by Xanthias. But it is quite possible that the other slaves join in the shouting, and that the slaves call out orders and encouragement to one another. It is also possible that one or more further slaves, Sosias for instance, appear at 455, and indeed V*ΓJ* attribute 458 to Sosias; but there is no clear indication in the text that this is right.]

The chorus are now attacking, but they are quite ineffective. Since they do not actually sting anyone, there is no need to ask how they use the stings which are part of their costume, nor to assume, with Paul Mazon *Essai sur la composition des comédies d'Aristophane* (1904) 71, that they charge back-first. Xanthias beats them back with his stick, and another slave blows smoke at them; Bdelykleon possibly also uses a stick against them. Meanwhile Philokleon is still held by the other two slaves.

458 οὐχὶ σοῦσθ'; 'shoo, won't you!': 209 n.

459 προσθείς: 'applying'. **Αἰσχίνην:** Aiskhines is equivalent to smoke; cf. 324–6. Ar. ridicules him as a boaster, and especially for talking about wealth which he did not possess; cf. 1243–8. In *Birds* 823 it is suggested that his wealth is in Cloudcuckooland. Nothing else is known about him; there is no special reason to identify him with the Aiskhines who was a member of the Thirty in 404/3 (X. *Hel.* 2. 3. 2). **ἔντυφε:** 'engulf them in smoke'. **τὸν Σελλαρτίου:** 'son of Swank-artios', a mixture of Σέλλου (325 n.) and the real name of Aiskhines's father, which must have ended in -άρτιος. Compare the comic distortions of names in 342, 466, 592, 836.

460 The battle is now over (no doubt there are pauses between lines in 457–60), and the chorus have been driven back into the orkhestra. ἆρ' ἐμέλλομέν: 'You see, we were sure to . . .' This sentence can hardly be taken as a question; but can non-interrogative ἆρα stand first? Instances in New Comedy (Denniston 48 n. 2) are not quite parallel. But an Aristophanic parallel is perhaps provided by *Birds* 797 ἆρ' ὑπόπτερον γενέσθαι παντός ἐστιν ἄξιον. This is usually taken as a question, but παντός does not show the 'studious moderation' usual when ἆρα (without οὐ) expects a positive answer (Denniston 581), and the line is probably best taken as a statement, 'So you see . . .!' τῷ χρόνῳ: 'eventually'.

462 μελῶν βεβρωκότες: For the partitive genitive with βιβρώσκω cf. *Odyssey* 22. 403 βεβρωκὼς βοός. For the metaphor cf. *Clouds* 924 γνώμας τρώγων Πανδελετείους. **Φιλοκλέους**: Philokles, son of Philopeithes and Aiskhylos's sister (Σ *Birds* 281), was a writer of tragedies good enough to win the first prize in the contest in which Sophokles competed with *OT* (S. *OT* hyp. ii). He seems to have continued writing at least until 411 (*Th.* 168). He is satirized by the comic dramatists as being ugly and having a harsh and bitter style of writing, because of which he was called ὁ Ἁλμίωνος, 'son of Briny' (*Birds* 281 with Σ, *Th.* 168 with Σ; cf. Kratinos 292, Telekleides 14). That is why Bdelykleon suggests that a diet of his songs would have made the chorus harsher and fiercer. We heard before (220, 269) that they prefer sweeter songs of an earlier date. 'Lucky for you they've been training on Phrynichus and not on some of these modern songs. You'd have been overcome by the fumes!' (David Barrett's translation).

463–525 *The chorus continue to accuse Bdelykleon indignantly of tyranny and conspiracy. In reply he scornfully comments on the contemporary tendency to accuse of tyranny any person who does anything out of the ordinary, and says that he only wants to give his father a comfortable life. Philokleon retorts that he prefers a life of judging. He claims that it makes him a ruler, but Bdelykleon says it makes him a slave; and so they agree to discuss the question and let the audience decide which of them is right.*

The chief purpose of the passage is to provide a transition from the fight in 456–62 to the orderly debate in 526–724. But it is saved from being merely a mechanical link-passage by the eloquent defence of individuality in 488–507. For the metre see pages 189–90.

463 οὐκ αὐτὰ δῆλα: 'isn't it clear by itself?' i.e. without further demonstration. [In R αὐτὰ δῆλα has a curved line underneath showing that the copyist thought it should be taken as one word, and L. Dindorf conjectured αὐτόδηλα. But the change is unnecessary.]

464 τυραννὶς: 345 n.

465 ἐλάμβαν': 'was getting me in its grip'. [*ἐλάνθαν'* (VJ) would be tautologous with *λάθρạ*. The presence of *λάθρạ* made corruption to *ἐλάνθαν'* easy.]   **ὑπιοῦσά**: 'creeping up on me'.

466 σύ: Bdelykleon.   **πόνῳ πόνηρε**: literally 'troublesome with trouble', i.e. 'you scoundrelly scoundrel'; cf. *Lys.* 350.   **Κομηταμυνία**: 'Long-hair-Amynias'. For Amynias, 74 n. For the type of compound cf. 342, 459, 592. In Athens long hair was worn especially by cavalrymen (*Knights* 580, 1121, *Clouds* 14, *Lys.* 561); by others it was regarded as a sign of wealth and ostentation, and of a man who thought himself superior (1317, *Clouds* 545, *Birds* 911, *Wealth* 572). But long hair was also worn generally by Spartans (*Birds* 1282, Hdt. 1. 82. 8), and in view of the political context here (especially 473–7) the chorus probably mean not (or not primarily) that Amynias and Bdelykleon are arrogant, but that they favour the Spartans.

467 'You exclude us from our legal rights.'   **ὧν**: Ar. sometimes employs this attraction of the relative pronoun from the accusative to the genitive (so also in 561, 588), but more often avoids it (cf. 440, 444, 516, 907, 1458).

471 τῆς: 'this', such as there has just been.

472 ἔλθοιμεν: 'we could come'. In this sense the optative is normally accompanied by *ἄν*. But in verse *ἄν* is sometimes omitted, provided that the clause is of such a kind (e.g. a question or a relative clause) that there is no danger of its being mistaken for a wish. Cf. E. *Alk.* 52 ἔστ' οὖν ὅπως Ἄλκηστις ἐς γῆρας μόλοι; A. *Pr.* 292, *Ag.* 620, *Kho.* 172, 595, S. *Ant.* 605. [Not *ἔλθωμεν* (RΓJ): the subjunctive is impossible in this kind of clause, which is not deliberative but potential.]

473 σοὶ λόγους: 'To you? Talk?' One might supply *λέγωμεν*, but really the words are exclamatory and no particular verb need be understood. [Bothe's conjecture σοὶ 'ς λόγους is hardly necessary.] The chorus's attitude here is just like that in *Akh.* 292–3: Δι. . . . . ἀλλ' ἀκούσατε. Χο. σοῦ γ' ἀκούσωμεν;

475–7 Brasidas was the leading Spartan general of this period. His name is similarly used in an accusation of treason in *Peace* 640.   **κράσπεδα στεμμάτων**: 'woollen fringes'. This seems to imply that wearing clothes with woollen fringes was a Spartan habit, and *Σ* states that this was so, though it is not clear whether he had any independent evidence or merely made the deduction from this passage. For στέμματα meaning 'wool' cf. E. *Or.* 12.   **ὑπήνην**: 'beard', including moustache. The Spartans let their beards, like their hair (466 n.), grow long, whereas Athenians generally trimmed theirs. Cf. *Lys.* 1072.   **ἄκουρον**: 'uncut', 'untrimmed' (not 'unshaven').

478 κρεῖττον: sc. *ἦν*: 209 n.   **ἐκστῆναι**: 'abandon', 'give up as hopeless'.

479 ναυμαχεῖν: a striking metaphor which I have not found elsewhere.

480 The second οὐδέ is adverbial ('not even'), the first and third are connective.

ἐν σελίνῳ . . . ἐν πηγάνῳ: obviously a proverbial expression for being at the very beginning of something (corresponding to such English phrases as 'scratching the surface'), but the origin is obscure. Σ offers two explanations:

A: Celery and rue were planted at the edges of gardens; therefore a person who was among the celery and rue had hardly entered the garden.

B: New-born babies were placed among celery; therefore being among the celery means being at the very beginning of life. Rue is irrelevant, and is added by Ar. as a joke.

Of these, *A* looks like a weak invention to explain the proverb, but *B* seems too extraordinary to have been invented. Furthermore celery is one of several kinds of leaf used for strewing a couch in Theok. 7. 68. *B* is therefore preferable.

481 παρεμβαλοῦμεν: For the future tense referring to words which have just been spoken cf. *Knights* 249 καὶ πανοῦργον καὶ πανοῦργον· πολλάκις γὰρ αὖτ' ἐρῶ.   τριχοινίκων means both that the previous line contained references to vegetables (since vegetables were measured by the χοῖνιξ, e.g. *Peace* 1144), and that it was a sesquipedalian expression for 'at the beginning' (since three quarts are a large quantity). 'We will slip in this sample of our market-gardening vocabulary.' Cf. *Peace* 521, where a ῥῆμα μυριάμφορον is required for addressing Peace, the giver of wine.

482 ἀλλ' ὅταν: 'but you will when'.

ξυνήγορος: 'advocate'. Several different types of person were called συνήγοροι in Athens:

A: men, normally relatives or friends, who were invited by an accused person to speak in his support at a trial; e.g. D. 21. 127, 59. 14, Hyp. 1. 11, 4. 12.

B: ten men who acted as official prosecutors at the examination of magistrates' accounts (102 n.). They were chosen by lot (Arist. *Ath. Pol.* 54. 2), and were paid one drachma a day (691). The advocates in 687–95 and *Knights* 1358–61 are clearly of this type, and so perhaps are those in *Akh.* 676–718 (if σπουδάσας ξυνηγορεῖν in *Akh.* 685 can mean 'who has put himself forward as a candidate for choice by lot'; or if the use of lot, mentioned only in *Ath. Pol.* 54. 2, had in the fifth century not yet been introduced for these officials).

C: men specially appointed to assist the prosecution in a case of treason. Plu. *Eth.* 833 f (= *Life of Ant.* 23) quotes the decree of Andron, passed in 411, providing for the prosecution of the oligarchs Arkheptolemos, Onomakles, and Antiphon: the generals are to select up to ten members of the council as advocates to take part in the prosecution. Perikles was probably an advocate of this type when he prosecuted Kimon for taking bribes from the Makedonian king (Plu. *Per.* 10. 6 ὑπὸ τοῦ δήμου προβεβλημένος, cf. Plu. *Kimon* 14. 3–5; but Arist. *Ath. Pol.* 27. 1 rather suggests type *B*).

D: five men elected to speak in defence of laws whose repeal was proposed (D. 24. 23, 24. 36). But there is no evidence that this type of advocate existed before the fourth century.

In our line the reference is plainly to type *C*.

483 ταὐτὰ ταῦτά: 'these same charges'. [ταὐτὰ ταῦτά or ταῦτα ταὐτά? Ar. wrote simply ταυτqταυτα, and breathings and accents in medieval mss. are not evidence of his intentions. But in the singular we have ταὐτὸ τοῦτο (*Clouds* 234, 1281, *Peace* 972, *Wealth* 153), never τοῦτο ταὐτό, and this shows which order he preferred.]   **σου καταντλῇ**: 'pours over you'; for the metaphor cf. Pl. *R* 344 d, 536 b, *Ly.* 204 d.   **ξυνωμότας καλῇ**: 'issues a summons to conspirators'. For the generalizing plural cf. 488. 'Summon', with a prosecutor as subject, is usually καλοῦμαι or προσκαλοῦμαι in the middle voice, but the active is used in 1418. [483 and 1418 defend each other against emendation.]

484 ἄν with an optative in a question may express a wish: 'I do wish you would . . .'. Cf. A. *Ag.* 1448–53, S. *Ai.* 388–91, *OK* 1100–1.

485 [δέδοκται καὶ is my conjecture for δέδοκταί μοι. μοι is retained by some editors and defended by H. Weber *Aristophanische Studien* (1908) 132; he takes it as a 'dative of disadvantage', to give the meaning 'Have you decided that I . . .?' But the dative with δέδοκται is too common for a hearer to take δέδοκταί μοι in any sense except 'I have decided'. I assume that καὶ was lost by haplography after -ται, and μοι subsequently inserted in an attempt to mend the metre. Platnauer (*CR* lxiii [1949] 6) suggests τοι.]   **δι' ἡμέρας**: 'all day'.

486 οὐδέποτέ γ': 'Never!' answering 484 and ignoring the sarcasm of 485.   **τί μου**: partitive genitive, as in *Clouds* 725: 'any bit of me'. The English idiom is 'Over my dead body!'

487 'A man who set out to be a tyrant over us!' The obvious antecedent is left unexpressed (as in 518). For the objective genitive with τυραννίς cf. D. 2. 30, 18. 66. [486–7 are so obviously meant as another pair of 'cretic' lines, like 418–19, 428–9, 475–7, that emendation to restore that metre here is justified, even though the sense would be satisfactory without it.]

488–507 is a splendid example of Ar.'s rhetoric. First Bdelykleon states his point in one line (488), and then clarifies it (489–92). Next follow three examples, taking three or four lines each, the third being a comic one interjected by Xanthias (493–502). Finally comes Bdelykleon's own case, explained in five lines (503–7), clearly introduced by καὶ νῦν ἐγώ, boiling up in the middle into a magnificently indignant compound adjective, and ending with a restatement of the main point in the last line. The key words are ξυνωμόται and τυραννίς. These words were used by the chorus at the conclusion of their last two speeches (483, 487). Bdelykleon inserts both in his first line (488), repeats τυραννίς in each example (495, 498, and Xanthias in 502), and, so as not to bore by exact repetition, concludes with the slightly different phrase ξυνωμότης ὢν καὶ φρονῶν τυραννικά.

For other references to τυραννίς and ξυνωμόται as political accusations at this period, 345 n. The twentieth-century English equivalents would hardly be 'tyranny' and 'conspirators', but rather 'dictatorship' and 'subversive'.

490 οὐδὲ: 'not even'; i.e. 'for as long as fifty years I have not . . .'. He means 'I have never heard it mentioned in talk about the last half-century' (roughly what we call the Pentekontaetia); the line is not evidence that he is fifty years old.

491 τοῦ ταρίχους ἀξιωτέρα: 'cheaper than kippers'.

492 καὶ δή: 'Look at the way . . . !'   **κυλίνδεται**: 'is bandied about'; cf. Pl. *Phdr.* 275 e κυλινδεῖται μὲν πανταχοῦ πᾶς λόγος.

493 ὀρφῶς: 'perch' (Thompson *Fishes* 187–8). [On the accent see pages 272–3 of Rogers's edition of the play.]   **μεμβράδας**: 'sprats' (Thompson *Fishes* 32).

494 εἴρηχ': 'says': perfect for a regular occurrence, as in 561, 591, 616, 626, 694–5.   **πλησίον**, together with the use of οἱ ἰχθύες to refer to a single place (789 n.), shows that fishmongers all had their stalls near one another in one part of the Agora. The rudeness of Athenian fishmongers is a common topic in fourth-century comedy (e.g. Amphis 30, Alexis 16).

495 ἐπὶ denotes purpose: 'with a view to tyranny'. The rival fishmonger, annoyed at not making a sale, suggests that a man who is not content with the cheapest and most ordinary kind of fish evidently thinks himself better than other people and so is no true democrat. The anecdote is a comic exaggeration, and yet it is based on the true observation that ordinary people are often suspicious or hostile towards those whose actions or tastes are unusual. A striking example of the suspicion which Ar. here satirizes is the case of Alkibiades, who was accused of aiming at tyranny not because of any political plan for establishing a tyranny but because his general behaviour implied that he thought himself superior to other people; cf. R. Seager 'Alcibiades and the charge of aiming at tyranny' (*Historia* xvi [1967] 6–18).

496 προσαιτῇ: 'asks for in addition'. In this second anecdote a fishmonger's customer expects the fishmonger to provide an onion free of charge to go with his fish; evidently this was sometimes done in Athens. (In *Knights* 676–9 the Sausage-seller gains popularity by giving people onions to go with their fish.) A woman selling vegetables overhears, and is indignant at losing a sale. Since greengrocers' stalls were probably not mixed up with fishmongers' stalls (494 n.), the passage suggests that a greengrocer might walk with a basket of vegetables among the sellers and buyers of meat and fish.   ταῖς ἀφύαις ἥδυσμά τι: 'as a flavouring for his fish'. ἀφύαι is a general term for small fish (Thompson *Fishes* 21-3). [The substitution of – ∪ ∪ for – ∪ in a trochaic tetrameter is uncommon, but it occurs in *Akh.* 318, *Knights* 319; cf. also *Wasps* 407 and note. These instances defend one another, and wholesale emendation, suggested by Platnauer (*CR* i [1951] 132-3), is not justified.]

497 παραβλέψασα θἀτέρῳ: 'after looking askance with one eye', i.e. 'with a suspicious look'; cf. *Ek.* 498 παραβλέπουσα θἀτέρῳ.

498 πότερον ἐπὶ τυ-: a metron with both long syllables resolved, making ∪ ∪ ∪ ∪ ∪ ∪, perhaps to suggest nagging or chattering.

499 φέρειν: 'produce as tribute'. The verb is regularly used of land producing food (LSJ φέρω V), but also of payment by subjects to a ruler (LSJ φέρω IV. 5).

500 γ': 'yes'. As often in Ar., when one character has made a serious or semi-serious statement, another adds a supporting comment or illustration at a more vulgar level of humour.   πόρνη implies that a slave could possess spending money: 52 n.   τῆς μεσημβρίας implies that Xanthias thought that the posture which he demanded would be cooler.

501 κελητίσαι: 'to take a ride'. The verb is sometimes used literally of horse-riding, but more often, as here, of a sexual posture in which the woman is above the man. 500-2 and Makhon 360-9 (Gow), where the verb is καθιππάσθαι, both imply that the use of this less usual posture is a favour which a woman might choose to withhold from a lover.   μοι: for the dative with ὀξυθυμέομαι cf. *Th.* 466-7.

502 τὴν Ἱππίου τυραννίδα: 'a tyranny like Hippias's', with a pun on ἵππος, continuing the equestrian sense of κελητίσαι. Hippias was the last tyrant of Athens, expelled in 510.

503 ταῦτα: words like 'tyranny' and 'conspiracy'.   γάρ: 'yes, . . .', introducing a generalized explanation of the preceding individual instances.   τούτοις: people like the chorus, the sprat-seller, the vegetable-seller, and Xanthias's girl.   εἰ: 'since', introducing a further individual instance to support the general statement (LSJ εἰ B. VI).

504-5 Bdelykleon's indignation is bubbling over and running away with his tongue. Consequently (*a*) there is no pause between 504 and 505, so that τῶν stands in one line and the words which it defines in the next, (*b*) the adjectives in 505 are all run together into a single word. The features of Philokleon's life are going about at crack of dawn (ὀρθροφοιτο-), addiction to malicious accusations (-συκοφαντο-) and trials (-δικο-), and hardship (-ταλαιπώρων). [ὀρθρο- (Grynaeus), rather than ὀρθο- (*a*), must be right, because we have already been told in the prologue and seen in the parodos that Philokleon and the other jurors habitually go out very early in the morning. It is not true, though some editors say so, that Σ has ὀρθρο-; the note says παρὰ τὸ ὀρθεύειν καὶ φοιτᾶν καὶ . . ., but ὀρθεύειν may well be a corruption of ὀρθρεύειν.]

506 Μόρυχος, mentioned also in 1142, was notorious as a gourmand (*Akh.* 887, *Peace* 1008, Pl. com. 106) and thus represents the opposite extreme to Philokleon's present life. He had a house near the Olympieion in south-east Athens (Pl. *Phdr.* 227 b with *Σ*), an area where wealthy people seem to have lived (cf. C. Wachsmuth *Die Stadt Athen* i 683). He is said also to have written tragedies (*Σ Akh.* 887, *Σ Peace* 1008). The statement that he went as an envoy to Persia (*Σ Akh.* 61) may be based on a misunderstanding of *Wasps* 1142.

508 ἄν is so placed as to emphasize an important word at the beginning of the sentence, and is later repeated with the verb; so also in 510–11. **ὀρνίθων γάλα:** 'birds' milk', a proverbial expression for an extreme luxury or delicacy; cf. *Birds* 734, 1673, Mnesimakhos 9, Men. fr. 892 Koerte. Similarly in Petronius 38. 1 Trimalchio is so rich that he has everything: 'lacte gallinaceum si quaesieris, invenies.'

510 βατίσιν: 'skate' (Thompson *Fishes* 26–8). **ἐγχέλεσιν:** a delicacy; Morykhos is associated with eels in *Akh.* 887, *Peace* 1008.

511 δικίδιον: The diminutive is affectionate: 'a nice little trial'. **φάγοιμ':** For the metaphor cf. 1367. **λοπάδι:** a shallow earthenware pot with a lid, 'casserole'; cf. B. A. Sparkes in *JHS* lxxxii (1962) 130 (with plate). **πεπνιγμένον:** cooked in an enclosed vessel, 'baked' or 'stewed'.

515 μὲν οὖν: 'More than that: . . .'

516 μόνον οὐ: 'all but', perhaps the earliest instance of it.

518 ὅστις has no expressed antecedent, as in 487.

519 ἐπεὶ δίδαξον: 73 n.

520 τιμή: 'profit'. **καρπουμένῳ:** 'reaping the fruits of', 'exploiting', referring to the tribute paid to Athens by the Athenian empire.

521 τούτοισί: the audience. (Not the chorus, who are Philokleon's supporters in the contest; cf. 526–47. It is true that in 726 the chorus declare Bdelykleon the winner; but that is because (*a*) Bdelykleon's victory is more effective dramatically if even his opponent's supporters acknowledge it, (*b*) it is impracticable in performance to make the audience declare who has won, (*c*) by the time 726 is reached 521 has been forgotten anyway.) **ἐπιτρέψαι:** 'to refer the question', for them to judge.

522 ἅπαντες: the slaves, all of whom (including Xanthias) now go into the house, taking with them the wasp-fighting equipment which was brought out at 455. **ξίφος γέ μοι δότε:** a melodramatic utterance, of which nobody takes any notice; cf. 166. [καὶ ξίφος . . . τῷ ξίφει was first attributed to Philokleon by Bergler in his note on 714 (712 by his numbering).]

524 δ': The position of a particle is not affected by a vocative, exclamation, or exhortatory interjection at the beginning of a sentence; cf.

563.   τὸ δεῖνα: For a moment Bdelykleon cannot think of the right legal term. 'What if you don't—what do you call it?—abide by the arbitration?' In this exclamatory use τὸ δεῖνα is not declined. Cf. *Peace* 268, *Birds* 648, *Lys.* 921, 926, 1168, fr. 4. The usage has been discussed by A. C. Moorhouse (*CQ* xiii [1963] 23).

525 Philokleon solemnly and melodramatically invokes a curse on himself if he breaks his word. At the end of a dinner, before the rest of the drinking began, it was customary to pour a libation and to drink in honour of 'good fortune' (ἀγαθὸς δαίμων). For this purpose undiluted (ἄκρατος) wine was used, whereas for subsequent drinking wine was usually mixed with water. (Cf. *Knights* 85, 105-6, Theopompos com. 76, Nikostratos com. 20, Antiphanes 137, D.S. 4. 3. 4.) So this drink was the climax of the dinner, and the most welcome part of the whole proceedings. Philokleon's favourite activity is judging, and for him the climax and most welcome moment is the time when he gets paid at the conclusion of a trial; in his life this event corresponds to the drink to good fortune at the end of a dinner in the life of an ordinary person. So he comically adapts the normal phrase ἄκρατον οἶνον ἀγαθοῦ δαίμονος (*Knights* 85) by substituting 'pay' for 'wine'. Cf. *Peace* 300, where a metaphor from drinking to good fortune is used for a welcome climax.

526-724 The debate (ἀγών), symmetrically arranged in the order song, speech, song, speech. The agon, as found in six of Ar.'s surviving plays (*Knights, Clouds, Wasps, Birds, Lys., Frogs*), can be analysed into the following parts (the names are those used by scholars, not by Ar.): ode (here 526-45), katakeleusmos (546-7), epirrhema (548-619), pnigos (620-30), antode (631-47), antikatakeleusmos (648-9), antepirrhema (650-718), antipnigos (719-24). For full discussion of this form of scene see T. Gelzer *Der epirrhematische Agon bei Aristophanes* (1960).

526-45 *The chorus sing a short song of encouragement to Philokleon. They tell him that the reputation of old men depends on him.*

The song is in Ar.'s usual lyric style, with two characteristically heavy, and therefore slightly comic, metaphors (527, 545). At two points it is interrupted by lines from Bdelykleon and Philokleon.

526-45 and 631-47 *Metre*: The lines sung by the chorus are iambo-choriambic; that is, each metron may be either iambic ($\times - \cup -$) or choriambic ($- \cup \cup -$). Sometimes, especially at the end of a period, an iambic metron is syncopated or catalectic ($\cup - -$, a bacchiac). Occasionally *ch* in the strophe responds to *ia* in the antistrophe or vice versa. In 636 the eight syllables are arranged with *ch* in the middle to make a glyconic ($- \cup - \cup \cup - \cup -$); responsion of a glyconic to *ch ia* seems not to occur elsewhere, but responsion of a glyconic to *ia ch* does (e.g. E. *Supp.* 1000 ∼ 1023), and so there is no need to doubt the text here (cf. Dale[2] 135). At 544/5 ∼ 647 the antistrophe has a metron less than the strophe: 309 n.

526	*ia ch*	631	*ia ch*
527/8	*ch ia ch ba* ‖	632/3	*ch ch ch ba* ‖
532	*ch ia*	636	glyconic
533/4	*ch ia ch ba*	637/8	*ia ia ch ba*
535	*ch ba*	639	*ch ba*
536	*ch ba* ‖	640	*ch ba*
537	*ch ba*	641	*ch ba* ‖
540	*ch ia*	644	*ch ia*
541	*ch ch*	645	*ch ch*
542/3	*ch ia ch*	646	*ch ia ch*
544/5	*ia ch ba*	647	*ch ba* ‖

The spoken lines interjected by Bdelykleon and Philokleon are iambic tetrameters.

526 The opening of the agon in *Knights* 756 is similar: νῦν δή σε πάντα δεῖ κάλων ἐξιέναι σεαυτοῦ . . . [δή (J) is preferable to δὲ (RVΓ) because a connective particle has little point at the beginning of a song. Cf. *Knights* 756, just quoted, where δή is guaranteed by the metre.]

527–8 γυμνασίου: For the metaphor cf. Pl. *Grg.* 493 d. The corresponding English metaphor is 'school', but to a Greek an ἀγών naturally suggests athletics; cf. 548 βαλβίδων. ὅπως φανήσει: 'to make sure you appear'. The chorus are addressing Philokleon. [But that does not necessitate Brunck's insertion of σὲ in 526 in place of δή.]

529 Bdelykleon shouts into the house. τὴν κίστην: 'my box'. Cf. *Akh.* 1098 παῖ παῖ, φέρ' ἔξω δεῦρο τὴν κίστην ἐμοί. Greek clothes being short of pockets, a man (or woman) would have a small box containing things which he might need while away from home (especially food, e.g. *Akh.* 1085–6, *Knights* 1211–20), and when he went out he (or his slave) would carry the box with him; it served purposes much like those of a modern lady's handbag. For the moment Bdelykleon does not say what he now wants to get out of his box. [Nor is there any particular reason why he should say at this point. So it is unnecessary to follow Willems 520–4 in rearranging the lines; he placed 538 before 529, and in compensation moved 530–1 to follow 537.]

530–1 He turns to address the chorus-leader. ἀτὰρ marks resumption of the conversation after a line addressed to someone else, as in *Wealth* 1111. He interrupted the chorus in the middle of a sentence, and so now invites them to complete it. φανεῖ comes first, before the interrogative word, because he is picking up the chorus's φανήσει— and asking for a continuation of it. 'Well, he'll show that he's *what* sort of a man, if you give him this exhortation?' [S. Srebrny (*Eos* 1 [1959–60] 45–8) wishes to read εἰ (with indicative) instead of ἤν (with subjunctive), on the ground that the exhortation is being given now, not in the future. But it can be regarded as being in the future, since it is not yet complete.]

532 The chorus resume their interrupted sentence: '⟨. . . that you appear⟩ to be a better speaker than this young man'.　κατά: 'like' (LSJ κατά B. IV. 3), so that μὴ κατά is 'better than'; cf. D. 21. 169 οὐ κατὰ τὰς Μειδίου λητουργίας.

535 περὶ τῶν ἁπάντων: 'everything is at stake'. A whole way of life depends on the result of the debate. Cf. *Clouds* 955–8 (also in the song introducing an agon) νῦν γὰρ ἅπας ἐνθάδε κίνδυνος ἀνεῖται σοφίας, ἧς πέρι τοῖς ἐμοῖς φίλοις ἐστὶν ἀγὼν μέγιστος.

536 δ: The antecedent is ἐθέλει. 'If he's really determined to win—which God forbid'.　-το: *brevis in longo* at the end of a catalectic metron.

[**537** οὗτος, which does not fit the metre, may be a gloss inserted by someone who thought it necessary to make clear that Bdelykleon was the subject of ἐθέλει. It was deleted by Wilamowitz *Isyllos von Epidauros* 137. Deletion of νῦν (Bentley) and addition of σ' (Porson), giving γένοιθ'—οὗτός σ' ἐθέλει, is less satisfactory, because the catalectic metron should give a pause and word-end at the end of 536.]

538 Since 529 a slave has brought Bdelykleon's box out of the house, and now we discover why he wants it: he opens it, gets out writing materials, and prepares to take notes (sitting, for example, on the steps leading up from the orkhestra: 1341 n.). The slave probably goes back into the house and shuts the door.　καὶ μὴν . . . γ': 'Yes indeed ⟨I am determined to win⟩, and . . .'; cf. 548.　δσ' . . . ἁπλῶς: 'absolutely everything'; cf. *Akh.* 873 δσ' ἐστὶν ἀγαθὰ Βοιωτοῖς ἁπλῶς (followed by a list).　μνημόσυνα: 'to remind me'; he wants to be sure that when his turn comes to speak he answers every point which Philokleon has made.　γράψομαι: The middle voice here and in 576 is probably 'write for my own use', but possibly 'get written' (implying that the slave who brings the box stays to act as secretary).

539 γάρ: Philokleon, ignoring Bdelykleon's last remark, asks the chorus for an explanation of their last words. 'What do you say will happen if he wins?'

540 πρεσβυτῶν ὄχλος: 'all the old men', 'the many old men'.

541 ἔστ': ἔσται elided: 'will be' meaning 'will have been shown to be'.

542–5 θαλλοφόροι καλούμεθ': 'we shall be called olive-bearers'. Specially selected old men were appointed to carry olive-shoots in the procession at the Panathenaia (X. *Smp.* 4. 17). Selection would be meant as an honour; but our phrase implies that, because only the very old were selected, calling an old man 'olive-bearer' was a regular sarcastic joke implying that he was no longer fit to do anything else. [Porson's conjectures seem the best for restoring the metre. ἄν may have originated by dittography of ἐν, and καλούμεθ' may then have been altered to the optative to suit ἄν. ἁπάσαις is possibly a gloss intended to make clear that ταῖς ὁδοῖς are not any particular streets; in fact Ar. elsewhere uses ἐν ταῖς ὁδοῖς without ἁπάσαις for 'in the streets' generally (*Knights* 348, *Clouds* 362, 964, *Lys.* 523, *Ek.* 773).] **ἀντωμοσιῶν**: oaths sworn by an accuser that the accused was guilty, and by the accused that he was not guilty. These oaths were sworn when the formal accusation was made, and were recorded in writing; when the trial took place, the written record of the oath was often read out to the jury (e.g. Is. 3. 7, 5. 2). **κελύφη**: 'containers', 'shells'. Jurors metaphorically take in legal documents; but the metaphor is disparaging, because shells of peas, eggs, or crabs have no value apart from their contents.

546–630 *Philokleon defends his claim that a juror's life and power are as good as a king's. He argues that* (1) *rich and important defendants are subservient to him,* (2) *various kinds of entertainment are provided for him in court,* (3) *his decisions are not subject to examination,* (4) *leading politicians take good care of him,* (5) *at home his family show him affection, and he is not dependent on his son for a living. He concludes by comparing himself to Zeus.*

Philokleon makes no attempt to argue that the jury system is right or just, or even that it is beneficial to Athens. His sole concern is to show that the jurors themselves get pleasure and power from it. Likewise Bdelykleon (648–724), accepting Philokleon's purely selfish attitude, argues simply that the jurors do not enjoy as much power and profit as they might. The subject of the whole debate is not moral but materialistic: not justice, but money and power.

Though comic points are interspersed, this defence is on the whole serious, full, and fair. It is not a mere Aunt Sally; Ar. has genuinely tried to put the best case that he thinks can be put for Philokleon. The effect is that when this case is subsequently demolished by Bdelykleon the refutation is fully convincing.

The lively manner in which the case is put is admirable. Philokleon's speech does not consist of dull generalizations, but of individual examples vividly described; it is easy for the audience to imagine the accused men standing at the court entrance (552–8), or the cringing attitude of Theoros (599–600), or the daughter coaxing her father (607–9). Much of it is arranged in the form of a narrative of a typical day in a juror's life. Now and then the long speech is interrupted by a line or two from Bdelykleon; this helps to prevent the audience getting tired of Philokleon's voice.

In many respects the language and style are like those of Attic prose, such as one might find in a discussion in Plato. But they are distinguished by several features: there are some lively metaphors (e.g. 596 περιτρώγει, 609 ἐκκαλαμᾶται), an epic quotation (615), some comic compounds (592 Κολακώνυμος, 596 κεκραξιδάμας), and some snatches of quoted conversation (556–7, 572, 611–12, 623–4). And the whole thing is expressed in neat and (seemingly) effortless anapaests, which gives it impetus and vigour.

Metre: anapaestic tetrameters (546–619), ending with a run of twenty anapaestic metra (620–30). In the agon in some plays (*Clouds* 949–1104, *Frogs* 895–1098) Ar. uses anapaestic lines only for the case with which he sympathizes, and iambic lines for the case which he dislikes (possibly because anapaests have a more dignified and solid sound); so the fact that Philokleon's speech is anapaestic may be a further indication that Ar. is trying to present his case without prejudice.

546 ἀλλ', ὦ with participle: 'you who . . .', as often when the chorus invite a character to speak in an agon; cf. 346 n., and for the use of a participle cf. *Knights* 333, *Clouds* 959, *Frogs* 1004.

547 'Try all your tongue' means 'Try your utmost in speaking'; cf. 562, S. *El.* 596 πᾶσαν ἴης γλῶσσαν. **πᾶσαν** echoes πάσης in 546: 'since all our dominion is at stake, all your eloquence must be used'. **βασάνιζε**: 'Test' here evidently just means 'exert fully', but I have found no exact parallel.

548 καὶ μὴν . . . γ': 'Yes, indeed I will, and . . .'; cf. 538.   **εὐθὺς ἀπὸ βαλβίδων**: 'right from the starting-line'. For the metaphorical use of βαλβίς cf. E. *Med.* 1245, *Her.* 867, and also *Akh.* 483 γραμμή: 527 n.

549 οὐδεμιᾶς ἥττων: 'as good as any'.

551 δεινότερον: 'more awe-inspiring'.

552 ἕρποντ': perhaps just 'come', as often in tragedy; or perhaps 'stroll', stressing that he receives attentions without making any physical effort.   **τηροῦσ'**: 'look out for'.   **δρυφάκτοις**: 124 n., 386 n.

553 τετραπήχεις: 'six feet tall'. For tallness admired as a virtue cf. *Frogs* 1014 γενναίους καὶ τετραπήχεις καὶ μὴ διαδρασιπολίτας.

554 'He puts his hand in mine.' For accused men shaking the hands of arriving jurors to ingratiate themselves cf. [X.] *Ath. Pol.* 1. 18 ἀντιβολῆσαι ἀναγκάζεται ἐν τοῖς δικαστηρίοις καὶ εἰσιόντος του ἐπιλαμβάνεσθαι τῆς χειρός. Demosthenes accuses Aiskhines and Meidias of accosting jurors before their trials (D. 19. 1, 21. 4).   **ἐμβάλλει**: When describing something which happens regularly, Ar. sometimes switches abruptly to and fro between the singular (referring to any one occasion) and the plural (referring to all occasions). Here he reverts to the plural in 555, and back to the singular in 558; cf. 564–8, 705, *Clouds* 973–5, etc.   **ἁπαλὴν** in the predicative position: 'which is soft ⟨having had to do no manual work⟩ because it has . . .'.   **τῶν δημοσίων**: 'some public money'; cf. *Knights* 827, *Th.* 812. The accused man is evidently ὑπεύθυνος.

555 ὑποκύπτοντες: 'bowing'.   **οἰκτροχοοῦντες**: 'pouring out pitifully'; the compound occurs nowhere else.

556 ὦ πάτερ: 'sir', a respectful address to an older man, as in *Knights* 725.   **καὐτὸς**: 'you, like me'.   **ὑφείλου**: ὑφαιρέομαι is a usual verb for keeping back money which is due to be paid over; e.g. *Frogs* 148.

557 ἀρχὴν: any kind of office, not necessarily as one of the nine arkhons. **᾽πὶ στρατιᾶς**: 354 n. **τοῖς ξυσσίτοις ἀγοράζων**: 'when buying food for your mess'. This shows that in the Athenian army each group of soldiers (ξύσσιτοι) arranged its own meals, one or more individuals being appointed and given money to buy food for the whole group.

558 ἔμ᾽ οὐδ᾽ ἂν ζῶντ᾽ ᾔδειν corresponds roughly to the English 'wouldn't have known me from Adam'; cf. D. 21. 78 τοῦτον οὐδ᾽ εἰ γέγον᾽ εἰδώς. **ἀπόφυξιν**: 'acquittal'. Only this final word in the sentence reveals that this is not the first time the man has been accused; he remembers seeing Philokleon in the jury which acquitted him last time, and is evidently a habitual thief. [ἀπόφυξις is an earlier, ἀπόφευξις a later form (Homer has φύξις and φύξιμος, not φεύξ-). Ar.'s mss. sometimes give one, sometimes the other; cf. 562, 645. Since both were probably in use in his time and we have no evidence that he was consistent in his usage, I see no reason to remove either form by emendation.]

559 Bdelykleon with a flourish finishes writing his note on Philokleon's last remarks. The line is inserted by Ar. solely to make a break in Philokleon's speech. The same purpose is served by 576–7, 588–9, 603–4, 664–5, 680–1, 696–7, 713–14; and other lines whose function is partly or solely to break up a long speech are *Clouds* 984–5, 1000–1, *Lys.* 1136, 1147–8, *Ek.* 189–92, 204, 213, *Wealth* 499, and the wife's lines in *Wealth* 653–763.

560 εἰσελθὼν ἀντιβοληθεὶς: No καί links these two participles because ἀντιβοληθεὶς καὶ . . . ἀπομορχθεὶς refer to earlier events than εἰσελθών. **τὴν ὀργὴν ἀπομορχθεὶς**: 'after having my anger wiped away'. He speaks as if anger were like tears or sweat; cf. the similar metaphor in E. *Ba.* 344 μηδ᾽ ἐξομόρξῃ μωρίαν τὴν σὴν ἐμοί, Ar. *Akh.* 843.

561 Before entering the court, we are to understand (it is not stated explicitly), Philokleon promises to favour the accused man who entreats him; but 'inside I do none of the things I say' and he treats the speeches just as entertainment. **πεποίηκα**: 494 n.

562 πάσας φωνὰς ἱέντων: 'men talking as hard as they can'; cf. 547, *Knights* 522 πάσας δ᾽ ὑμῖν φωνὰς ἱείς. **εἰς**: 'to obtain', as in 1112.

563 φέρ᾽ ἴδω: 145 n. **τί οὐκ**: 'every'.

565 ἰὼν: 'each man, as he goes on'. For the singular, 554 n. For the metaphorical use of εἶμι, 'proceed ⟨verbally⟩', cf. *Clouds* 1058 ἄνειμι, 1075 πάρειμι', 1408 μέτειμι, *Frogs* 920 τὸ δρᾶμα δ᾽ ἂν διῄει, but there seems to be no parallel without a prepositional prefix. [The separation of ἀνιὼν (V) into ἂν ἰὼν was suggested by Paley in his note on *Frogs* 259, and again by L. Siegel (*Wien. Stud.* xxxv [1913] 196–8). Platnauer (*CQ* iii [1953] 53–4), to avoid the singular and the unusual use of εἶμι, proposes ἄν πως ἀνισῶσιν. Dover (*Lustrum* ii [1957] 84), while approving of πως, suggests that ἰσώσῃ might be intransitive with κακά as subject. Other emendations suggested are more drastic. But I think ἰὼν can probably stand.] **ἐμοῖσιν**: a comic surprise ending: 'builds them up as high as—mine'. Philokleon inadvertently makes a point against his own case. Starkie says that the sigmatism of this line is 'due to the bitterness of the tone'; but Philokleon is not bitter but delighted, and so the sigmatism is probably accidental.

566 The speakers try to win the jurors' favour by inserting irrelevant bits of entertainment into their speeches. **Αἰσώπου**: Aesop, who lived in the first half of the sixth century, was known by everyone to have been a composer of fables; but it is doubtful whether he left any fables in writing, and it is likely that by Ar.'s time it was customary to attribute any short amusing fable to Aesop, in much the same way as it was customary to attribute any traditional Athenian law to Solon. Cf. 1259, 1401, 1446.

567 θυμὸν: 'anger'. Demosthenes complains that jurors acquit guilty men who tell them a few jokes: τοὺς τὰ μέγιστ' ἀδικοῦντας καὶ φανερῶς ἐξελεγχομένους, ἂν ἐν ἢ δύ' ἀστεῖ' εἴπωσιν καὶ παρὰ τῶν φυλετῶν τινες ἠρημένοι σύνδικοι δεηθῶσιν, ἀφίετε (D. 23. 206).

568 ἀναπειθώμεσθα: 101 n. [The absence of a diaeresis at the end of the second metron is unusual in anapaestic tetrameters, but there are a few other instances (*Akh.* 645, *Clouds* 987, *Birds* 600, Kallias com. 5) and this is not an adequate reason for emending the line; cf. J. W. White *The Verse of Greek Comedy* 126–7.] **ἀνέλκει**: 'brings up' on to the platform in the court; so also in *Akh.* 687. For the use of children to arouse a jury's pity, 976 n.

569 τῆς χειρός: 'by the hand' (LSJ χείρ II. 3).

570 συγκύψανθ': 'cowering together'. **ἅμα βληχᾶται**: 'wail in chorus'. βληχάομαι is generally used of the bleating of sheep and goats, but βληχή is used of children in A. *Th.* 348. [A short vowel before βλ is usually scanned long (e.g. 613), but there are exceptions (A. *Supp.* 761, *Kho.* 589, S. *El.* 440, *OT* 717, and perhaps Ar. *Lys.* 384, Eupolis 105, Theopompos com. 5); so we need not emend. ἀποβληχᾶται (*ΠV*) could conceivably be right, meaning 'bleat in his defence', a comic variation of ἀπολογεῖται: but the rest of the sentence, especially ὑπὲρ αὐτῶν, implies that the father is trying to protect the children, not the children to defend the father.]

571 τῆς εὐθύνης ἀπολῦσαι: 'to acquit him in his examination': 102 n.

572 For the sudden switch to direct speech cf. 689. [It is not necessary to emend to obtain indirect speech, as some have done, e.g. Platnauer (*CR* lxiii [1949] 6–7).] **ἀρνὸς**: a pun: the children are bleating like sheep (570), and one of them is—not ἀρήν ('lamb') but ἄρρην ('male'). **ἐλεήσαις**: The optative is proper in a prayer; cf. 571 ὥσπερ θεόν. For -αις, instead of -ειας, cf. 726, *Clouds* 776, *Peace* 405. 'Pity the voice' means 'have pity when you hear the voice'; cf. *Peace* 400 ἐλέησον αὐτῶν τὴν ὄπα.

573 χοιριδίοις: another pun, meaning both 'piglets' and 'private parts' of a girl; cf. 1353, 1364, *Akh.* 769–96.   **με πιθέσθαι**: sc. ἀντιβολεῖ.

572–3 does not necessarily imply that the accused man takes Philokleon to be a countryman. Townsmen too may like young animals,
and anyway Ar.'s overriding purpose just here is simply to make two
puns of his favourite type.

574 κόλλοπ': 'peg', round which the string of a lyre was twisted to keep
it tight. The metaphor means 'relax the intensity'.   ἀνεῖμεν: aorist
for a regular occurrence; 99 n.

575 καταχήνη: 'snub'. Philokleon enjoys his power over rich men, but
fails to realize that he would snub them better by not giving in to their
blandishments.

576 γράφομαι: 538 n.

577 μέμνησ': 'mention', imperative. Philokleon has explained how he is
superior to other men, but has yet to show what advantages he gets
from his superiority.   ἄχεις: crasis for ἃ ἔχεις.

578 τοίνυν: 'Well . . .', responding to an invitation to speak, as in 1181,
1205; cf. Denniston 571.   δοκιμαζομένων: When a young Athenian
citizen reached the age of eighteen, his name was entered by the
members of his deme on their register. To ensure that no one was
admitted to the register before that age, newly registered youths were
reviewed by the council. This review was called δοκιμασία. Since
Athenians had no birth certificates, the councillors evidently must
have inspected the youths in the nude to judge from their physical
development whether they were adult. If they thought that any of
them was younger than eighteen, they imposed a fine on the deme
which had registered him (Arist. *Ath. Pol.* 42. 2). The members of the
deme could then appeal to a law-court (as *Wasps* 578 shows; cf. Arist.
Ath. Pol. 45. 1), where the jurors would have to inspect the youth for
themselves to decide the case. Cf. W. K. Lacey *The Family in Classical
Greece* (1968) 95. Philokleon's interest here is homosexual, in 1341–81
heterosexual; so Ar. does not regard the combination of both interests
in one man as unnatural.

579 Another example of irrelevant entertainment added to a defence
speech. Oiagros was evidently a tragic actor. Nothing else is known
of him, but 579–80 would have little point if it did not have some sort
of basis in fact. It may therefore be assumed that he had recently been
accused of some offence, that in the course of his speech in his own
defence he quoted some lines from *Niobe*, and that he was acquitted.
Ar. mischievously implies that the jurors were influenced more by
Oiagros's histrionic art than by the strength of his case.   εἰσέλθῃ:
This verb is regularly used for 'come to court', the subject being either
the accused or the accuser or both, or the case, or (less often; e.g.
And. 1. 29, D.18. 210) the jury.   φεύγων: 'accused'.   ἀποφεύγει:
'is acquitted'.

580 Aiskhylos's *Niobe* was still remembered in Ar.'s time (cf. *Frogs* 912),
and so that is probably the play meant here. But Sophokles also wrote

a *Niobe*, and possibly it may be meant, if it was performed shortly before
Wasps was written.   τὴν καλλίστην ἀπολέξας: 'selecting the finest one'.
581 ταύτης ἐπίχειρα: 'as payment for it'.
582 ἐν φορβειᾷ: 'wearing his harness'. A player of the αὐλός sometimes
wore an arrangement of leather straps around his mouth and the
mouthpiece of the instrument, fastened behind his head. Cf. Plu.
Eth. 456 bc, quoting Simonides 177:

κaὶ ὁ Μαρσύας, ὡς ἔοικε, φορβειᾷ τινι καὶ περιστομίοις τοῦ πνεύματος τὸ
ῥαγδαῖον ἐγκαθείρξε καὶ τοῦ προσώπου κατεκόσμησε καὶ ἀπέκρυψε τὴν
ἀνωμαλίαν,

χρυσῷ δ' αἰγλήεντι συνήρμοσεν ἀμφιδασείας
κόρσας καὶ στόμα λάβρον ὀπισθοδέτοισιν ἱμᾶσιν.

It must have served one or more of the following purposes: to support
the instrument, leaving both hands free to move up and down; to
support the cheeks and lips, relieving the pressure of breath on them;
to prevent loss of breath round the sides of the mouthpiece, making
possible a longer note (cf. A. A. Howard in *HSCP* iv [1893] 29–30).
Sophokles (fr. 768, quoted by Cicero *Att.* 2. 16. 2) seems to regard
playing without this harness as a louder and more violent kind of
playing: φυσᾷ γὰρ οὐ σμικροῖσιν αὐλίσκοις ἔτι, ἀλλ' ἀγρίαις φύσαισι
φορβειᾶς ἄτερ. But in *Wasps* 582 the implication of ἐν φορβειᾷ is different: not 'softly', but 'with the proper professional equipment'.
Birds 861 ἐμπεφορβειωμένον is similar.   ἔξοδον: 'an exit-tune',
music for the jurors as they leave the court. The word is a metaphor
from drama; at the end of a play the αὐλητής played as the chorus
withdrew. Cf. Kratinos 276 τοὺς ἐξοδίους ὑμῖν ἵν' αὐλῶ τοὺς νόμους.
(This is a distinct sense from the one in Arist. *Poet.* 1452ᵇ21, where
ἔξοδος is the whole final scene of a play.)   ηὔλησ': aorist for
a regular occurrence; cf. 99.
583 ἐπίκληρον: 'heiress', or more strictly 'daughter accompanying an
inheritance'. If a man died leaving a daughter but no sons, his
property passed to the husband of his daughter. If she was not yet
married, he might nominate an heir in his will, or otherwise his
nearest surviving male relative might claim the inheritance; but in
either case the property and the daughter went together, so that
whoever inherited the property had also to marry the daughter (or
alternatively, in some cases, to provide her with a husband and a
dowry); cf. W. K. Lacey *The Family in Classical Greece* (1968) 139–46.
If the inheritance was disputed, a law-court judged between the rival
claimants by the process called διαδικασία; cf. A. R. W. Harrison
The Law of Athens i (1968) 158–62. The case envisaged by Philokleon
is one in which the dead man has left a will specifying the man who is to
have his daughter and property, but the interpretation or validity of
the will is disputed by another claimant.

584 κλαίειν μακρὰ τὴν κεφαλήν: 'go hang', 'go and boil its head'. The same phrase is used in *Wealth* 612 and similar phrases elsewhere, but of course they are normally addressed to persons, and κεφαλὴν is comically inappropriate for a will. 'We send the will off with a flea in its ear.' [Should κλαίειν be emended to κλάειν? Though there is no inscriptional evidence and we have only manuscripts to go by, there seems no reason to doubt that both forms were used in Athens in the fifth century. Both appear in mss. of Ar.; in *Wasps* a has κλα- in 179, 392, 440, κλαι- in 584, and is divided in 564. Hellenistic and Byzantine scribes are more likely to have altered κλα- to κλαι-, which was the more familiar form to them; and if Ar. always used the same form it was probably κλα-. But it cannot be demonstrated that his usage was consistent, and on the evidence which we have I doubt whether automatic emendation of κλαι- is justified.]

585 κόγχῃ: literally 'shell', but here evidently a small case enclosing the seals to protect them from damage, either made from a sea-shell or else shaped like one. σεμνῶς: 'pompously'. The seals and case are almost personified. This is a variation of the type of joke in which an important man is treated rudely; many people sometimes wish they could ignore or tear up a legal or official document. σημείοισιν: Like the English 'seal' σημεῖον is used both for a piece of metal or jewel engraved with a special device, often on a finger-ring (e.g. *Knights* 952), and also for the piece of wax or other soft material stamped with such a device (so here; cf. X. *Hel.* 5. 1. 30, D. 42. 2). In the second sense the plural is usual; presumably it was customary to make several impressions of a seal on a single document. The soft material used for sealing is called 'dirt' (ῥύπους) in *Lys.* 1198, which suggests clay (like the Egyptian γῆν σημαντρίδα in Hdt. 2. 38. 3) rather than wax; but there it is boxes which are sealed, and so that does not prove that wax was not used for sealing documents in Athens in Ar.'s time. For the sealing of a will cf. Is. 7. 1, D. 45. 17.

586 'We give her to whoever . . .'

587 τῶν δ᾽ ἄλλων οὐδεμί᾽ ἀρχή: 'no other office is ⟨immune from examinations of official conduct⟩'. Being a juror was not strictly an ἀρχή at all; cf. Lykourgos 79 τρία γάρ ἐστιν ἐξ ὧν ἡ πολιτεία συνέστηκεν, ὁ ἄρχων, ὁ δικαστής, ὁ ἰδιώτης, and Pl. *Laws* 767 a. But sometimes it is loosely called so; the point is discussed in Arist. *Pol.* 1275ᵃ23–32.

588 'Yes, that *is* impressive; I congratulate you on what you've said.' Bdelykleon acknowledges that Philokleon's response to his request in 577 has been a good one. [Reiske emended σεμνόν to σε μόνον without a stop after it. Σ says λείπει ἡ κατά. κατὰ τοῦτό σε, φησί, μακαρίζω, τὸ ἀνεγκλήτως πράττειν. This shows that he recognized no stop in the middle of the line and took τουτὶ with μακαρίζω, but it does not prove that he read σε μόνον, since his note may be an attempt to explain τουτὶ σεμνὸν μακαρίζω. Since σεμνόν followed by a colon gives a satisfactory sense, I have let it stay in the text, but it is still possible that σε μόνον is right; the double accusative with μακαρίζω is not exactly paralleled, but it is similar to the double accusative with τιμωρέομαι in E. *Kyk*. 695, *Alk*. 733.]

589 ἀνακογχυλιάζων: 'removing the seal-cap of'. But there is a pun, since κόγχη also means 'vagina' (see LSJ Supp.) and διαθήκη 'physical condition' (e.g. Demokritos 9). 'It's wrong of you to interfere with the heiress's condition.'

591 The Athenian legal code was not comprehensive; whereas we generally regard any act as legal if it is not specifically forbidden by law, the Athenians might regard an act as an offence even if no law applied to it. In such a case the council or assembly might decree that the offender should be brought before a law-court and tried. Instances are provided by the affairs of the mutilation of the Hermai and the profanation of the Mysteries in 415 (And. 1. 17, 28, 66) and the overthrow of the oligarchs in 411 (Plu. *Eth*. 833 f = *Life of Ant*. 23). **ἐψήφισται:** perfect for a regular occurrence: 494 n. **ἀδικοῦντας:** present, instead of aorist or perfect, because ἀδικέω can mean 'am guilty' as well as 'do wrong'; so also in 896, 1017.

592 The fact that Euathlos and Kleonymos are mentioned immediately after the occasions when the council or the assembly sent a case to a law-court, instead of with Kleon and Theoros (596–600), suggests that they had recently been concerned in such cases. Euathlos held the office of συνήγορος (482 n.) and prosecuted Thoukydides son of Melesias shortly before 425 (Ar. fr. 411, *Akh*. 710; cf. 947 n.). He may be identical with the Euathlos who was a pupil of Protagoras (Quintilian 3. 1. 10, D.L. 9. 56). **Κολακώνυμος:** 'Flatter-onymos', a comic compound of κόλαξ and Κλεώνυμος. For this type of compound cf. 342, 459, 466; for κόλαξ, 45 n.; for Kleonymos, 19 n. **ἀσπιδαποβλής:** crasis for ὁ ἀσπ-: 'the shield-discarder', a compound invented by Ar. [The mss. have ἀσπ-, but O. Bachmann (*Philol*. Supp. v [1889] 247) pointed out that ἀσπ- is more likely; cf. 596 ὁ.]

593 περὶ τοῦ πλήθους: 'in defence of the people'.

594–5 'And no one ever carries a proposal in the assembly unless he proposes to adjourn the courts after they have first tried one case.' A juror was paid three obols for any day on which he sat, regardless of the number of cases tried, but he received no fee if no cases were tried. Normally a court could try several cases in one day. Thus a proposal that the courts should try one case and then adjourn was in effect a proposal that the jurors should have a half-holiday with a full day's pay. Cf. *Knights* 50 πρῶτον ἐκδικάσας μίαν: that passage shows that this means of winning popularity was used by Kleon. *Wasps* 594–5 does not necessarily mean that the meeting of the assembly at which the politician wanted the jurors' votes took place on the same day as the courts' early adjournment; D. 24. 80 shows that, in the fourth century at least, the courts never sat on a day when the assembly met. For the form of words in 594 cf. *Clouds* 432 ἐν τῷ δήμῳ γνώμας οὐδεὶς νικήσει πλείονας. **δικάσαντας**: The gender is ungrammatical, but natural because τὰ δικαστήρι' refers to persons; cf. 688, 711, 1342.

596 αὐτὸς: Philokleon regards Kleon as the greatest man of them all. **κεκραξιδάμας**: 'shout-conqueror', a comic compound coined after the manner of poetic epithets; cf. Pindar's ἀνδροδάμας, λεοντοδάμας. Shouting is regarded by Philokleon as a merit, by Ar. as a fault. **μόνον**, if right, goes closely with ἡμᾶς ('only us') and is used only because μόνους does not fit the metre. **περιτρώγει**: 'takes bites out of'. The metaphor means that, although Kleon attacks others who receive money from the state, he never proposes a reduction of the jurors' pay; cf. *Frogs* 367 τοὺς μισθοὺς τῶν ποιητῶν ῥήτωρ ὢν εἶτ' ἀποτρώγει.

597 διὰ χειρὸς ἔχων: 'keeping hold of us', suggesting not just protection but control as well; cf. Th. 2. 13. 2. **τὰς μυίας ἀπαμύνει**: like an assiduous attendant; cf. *Knights* 60, where the Paphlagonian slave (Kleon) is so attentive to his master Demos (the people) that he shoos away the—politicians.

599 Θέωρος: 42 n. **καἰτοὐστὶν**: crasis for καίτοι ἐστὶν. 'And yet he's a man just as important as Euphemios.' Philokleon is impressed by Theoros's condescension. Euphemios was evidently a person of no importance at all, yet well enough known to the audience for his name to raise a laugh; perhaps he behaved as if he were important when he was not. We know nothing else about him.

600 'With his sponge he blacks our shoes from his bowl.' The idea of the obsequious servant (cf. 597) is developed. The line is not a metaphor but just a comic invention; the audience is expected to laugh at the thought of the high and mighty Theoros performing so menial a task. **περικωνεῖ** occurs only here. It seems to mean 'cover with pitch' (from κῶνος, 'pine-cone' or 'pine'), and if so it appears to be the earliest reference to the use of blacking for shoes. The purpose would presumably be just to keep the stitches dry, not to produce a shine.

601 'See what kind of good things these are, from which . . .!' For the order cf. *Clouds* 1071–2 σκέψαι . . . ἡδονῶν θ' ὅσων μέλλεις ἀποστερεῖσθαι. [Hall and Geldart suggest emending to ἀφ' ὅσων ἀγαθῶν οἵων τ', but this is probably unnecessary. **μ'** (V): not δ' (following RΓJ), because he is not moving on to a fresh point but summing up the points which he has made since 577.]

602 ἦν: attracted from ἃ to the gender and number of the complement.

603–4 'Have your fill of talking; for in any case you will stop eventually, and you'll turn out to be a rump which defeats washing, which is what that grand rulership of yours is'; i.e. 'I shall show that your degradation is too squalid to be cleaned away by talk about power'. **ἔμ-**

πλησο: 424 n.   **τῆς ἀρχῆς τῆς περισέμνου,** in apposition to λουτροῦ, refers to the boast in 548-9.

605 'And what is pleasantest of all . . . is when . . .'

[**606 κἄπειθ' ἥκονθ' ἅμα:** B's correction of the unmetrical reading of RΓJ is no doubt right; εἰσ- originated from dittography of -ειθ'. The alternative κᾆτ' εἰσήκοντά με is unlikely, despite the reading of V; how would either of the thetas have got into the mss. except from aspirated elisions?]

608 τὼ πόδ' ἀλείφῃ: Anointment after washing was normal, to protect the skin against the sun. This applied to all (or all exposed) parts of the body; the reason for mentioning the feet in particular is that it requires slightly more effort to reach one's own feet, and Philokleon enjoys the homely luxury of having someone to do it for him.

609 Philokleon has his money in his mouth (cf. 791); his daughter fishes it out with her tongue, to his enjoyment. It is notable that Ar. regards the idea of καταγλωττισμός between father and daughter as amusing, not disgusting.   [**παππίζουσ':** Eust. 565. 32 says that παππίζω is the comic form, παππάζω the Homeric.]

610 γύναιον: The diminutive is affectionate here, like the English 'little woman'; elsewhere it is usually contemptuous (And. 1. 130, D. 19. 305, 25. 57).   **φυστὴν μᾶζαν:** presumably something like 'puff-pastry', from φυσάω. Σ says it was made from barley-meal and wine.

611 προσαναγκάζῃ: verbal persuasion, as in Pl. *Smp.* 217 d.

612 οὐ μή με δεήσῃ: 'I shall never need': 394 n. [The mss.' καὶ μή με δεήσῃ is not acceptable, since 'may it never be necessary', though it might be subjunctive in Homer, should be optative in Attic.]

613 εἰς σὲ βλέψαι implies 'be dependent on you'.   **τὸν ταμίαν:** 'your steward', a slave who looks after the supplies of food for the household and dispenses them on Bdelykleon's orders.   **ὁπότ' ἄριστον παραθήσει:** indirect question dependent on βλέψαι: 'to see when he will serve lunch'.

This passage is important evidence for the retirement of elderly Athenians from control of their households. Bdelykleon is now master of the house and controls the slaves (cf. 67, 142), of whom Philokleon is only 'the former master' (442). But Bdelykleon is legally required to support (τρέφειν) his father (cf. 736, 1004; the law is mentioned in Is. 8. 32, X. *Apom.* 2. 2. 13, D. 24. 107, etc.). Presumably the date at which a father handed over control of his household was the date after which his son was required to support him, but there is no evidence to show clearly when this was; it may have been when the father reached a certain age (perhaps sixty), or it may have been any date chosen by the father or mutually agreed between father and son. Cf. W. K. Lacey *The Family in Classical Greece* (1968) 116-18.

614 τονθορύσας: This verb is used of a grumbling slave also in *Frogs* 747, Herodas 6. 7.   [**ἀλλ' ἦν:** ἄλλην (RVJ), with a full stop after μάξῃ,

H

gives a slightly more awkward construction, but cannot be ruled out as impossible. Then the participles imply fear and μᾶζαν is understood with ἄλλην: 'for fear that he may soon have to knead me another'. But after this we should expect a connective particle, either 'but' or 'for', in 615.] **μάξῃ**: 'knead a cake', here used with the object unexpressed—like English 'bake', but barley-cakes (μᾶζαι, cf. 301 n.) were eaten uncooked.

615 τάδε: used rather vaguely to refer to the juror's pay and what it will buy. **πρόβλημα κακῶν**: 'as a shield against trouble'; for the genitive cf. Pl. *Ti.* 74 b. **σκευὴν βελέων ἀλεωρήν**: 'equipment which is a protection against missiles'. The warlike metaphor πρόβλημα leads Philokleon on to absurdly inappropriate military language: the same type of joke as in 194–5. The poetic ending of βελέων and the non-Attic ending of ἀλεωρήν shows that the phrase is a quotation, probably the end of an epic hexameter, but its source is unknown; Homer has only δηίων ἀνδρῶν ἀλεωρήν (*Iliad* 12. 57, 15. 533).

616 'γχῆς refutes the statement of LSJ s.v. χέω that -έη is never contracted in this verb. **πιεῖν**: an explanatory infinitive often added to ἐγχέω, e.g. X. *Kyr.* 1. 3. 9. **ὄνον**: some kind of vessel for holding wine. C. Robert ('Εφ. Ἀρχ. [1892] 251–3) suggests that the reference is to the kind of ὄνος which was a piece of pottery shaped to fit over a woman's knee when she was spinning, and that Philokleon gets this, filled with wine, from the women's apartments because the women are so fond of him (607–12). But this can hardly be right, because (a) the knee-covering ὄνος would be a very awkward receptacle for wine, · (b) it would be too large for him to have had it hidden under his cloak ever since his appearance on the stage, so as to produce it with a flourish at this line (τόνδ'), (c) ἐσκεκόμισμαι, 'I bring home for myself' (frequentative perfect; 494 n.), shows that the wine comes from outside the house, not from the women's apartments. So I think that the ὄνος must be a very small jar or flask. It probably has two handles looking like donkey's ears (hence the name) and a narrow neck (cf. 618). Philokleon carries it around all the time (e.g. on a string round his neck), and uses his juror's pay to replenish it when necessary.

617–18 κλίνας: 'tipping it up'. Now comes the pun: he speaks of his ὄνος (flask) as if it were an ὄνος (donkey). 'It opens its mouth and brays, and gives a loud warlike fart at your goblet.' The wine makes a 'glob-glob-glob' noise when poured through the narrow opening, and Philokleon interprets this as a rude noise made by the little flask at the cup provided by Bdelykleon. **κατέπαρδεν** implies contempt: 394 n.

620 ἀκούω ταῦθ': 'have the same things said about me'.

623 βροντᾷ: This passage indicates that the metaphor 'thunder' for the noise made by a crowd was in fairly regular use, even though there seems to be no other surviving instance. In 671 and *Akh.* 531 the metaphor is different, referring to an individual's authoritarian conduct.

625 ποππύζουσιν: an onomatopoeic word for a sound ('popopopop' or something similar) uttered on seeing lightning, to avert the bad omen. Possibly the modern Greek exclamation πωπώ may be descended from it. Cf. Plin. *Nat.* 28. 25: 'fulgetras poppysmis adorare consensus gentium est'.

626 ἐγκεχόδασίν μ': 'have the willies at me', frequentative perfect (494 n.). An accusative is added because the verb is treated as equivalent to 'fear'; cf. D. 4. 45 οἱ δὲ σύμμαχοι τεθνᾶσι τῷ δέει τοὺς τοιούτους ἀποστόλους. Philokleon assumes that all rich men have got rich by dishonest methods.

631–47 *The chorus sing a short song congratulating Philokleon on his speech, and telling Bdelykleon that he will find it hard to answer.*

This song corresponds to 526–45, and is part of the symmetrical structure of the agon. It has no special distinction, but it serves the useful purpose of providing a musical interlude after Philokleon's long speech and arousing expectancy for Bdelykleon's. Philokleon's spoken interruptions (634–5, 642–3) are particularly boastful. For the metre see pages 203–4.

631 καθαρῶς: 'clearly', with λέγοντος.

634 'Indeed you didn't; yet he thought he'd be picking unwatched vines', i.e. that he would win by default. **ἐρήμας:** sc. ἀμπέλους. Cf. *Ek.* 885–6 ᾤου δ' ἐρήμας οὐ παρούσης ἐνθάδε ἐμοῦ τρυγήσειν. **οὕτω ῥᾳδίως:** 'so easily', referring to Bdelykleon's confidence in 513–25. [Dawes *Miscellanea Critica* 233 conjectured οὗτος (cf. 642), but the reference to Bdelykleon is clear enough without it.]

635 καλῶς γὰρ ᾔδειν: '⟨otherwise he wouldn't have challenged me,⟩ for he knew very well . . .' **ταύτῃ:** 'in this respect', 'in this line'. Bdelykleon, says Philokleon (but Ar. does not mean us necessarily to believe him), when he made his challenge in 519, knew that Philokleon was a good speaker, but thought that he would not take the trouble to speak in defence of his way of life.

636 'How thorough his treatment has been!' **ἐπέρχομαι** is 'go over', 'explain', as in *Knights* 618–19. [Porson emended to ὡς δ' ἐπὶ πάντ' ἐλήλυθεν to avoid the glyconic in this iambo-choriambic passage. But ἐπὶ πάντ' ἔρχομαι has the unsuitable meaning 'try everything', 'leave nothing untried', implying that most of the attempts fail; cf. S. *OT* 265, E. *Hipp.* 284, X. *An.* 3. 1. 18.]

638 ηὐξανόμην: 'grew taller' with pride and pleasure. Cf. Pl. *Euthd.* 300·d ὁ Κλεινίας πάνυ ἥσθη καὶ ἐγέλασεν, ὥστε ὁ Κτήσιππος ἐγένετο πλεῖον ἢ δεκαπλάσιος.

639–40. According to the conventional Greek belief, men when they die normally proceed to a colourless and unsubstantial kind of half-existence as shades in the realm of Hades; but some individuals specially favoured by the gods, instead of dying, are transferred to a perfectly happy life in a land on the edge of the world, beside the Ocean. This land is sometimes called Elysion, sometimes the Islands (or Island) of the Blessed. Its situation and pleasures are described in *Odyssey* 4. 561–9, Hes. *Works* 166–73, Pi. *O*. 2. 68–77; for discussion see M. P. Nilsson *Geschichte der griechischen Religion* i 2nd edition (1955) 324–9. Hence to think that one is in the Islands of the Blessed is to be perfectly happy; cf. Pl. *Mx*. 235 c, *R*. 519 c. We expect the verb to be 'live', but to the chorus 'live' and δικάζειν are synonymous.

642 Philokleon's success and his supporters' glee discomfort Bdelykleon. [So Dindorf's emendation ὡς is unnecessary.] So Philokleon says, at least; but does Bdelykleon really show signs of worry at this point? I think it would be out of character for him to do so. More probably he calmly scratches his head or performs some other business which Philokleon comically misinterprets as a sign of intense agitation. σκορδινᾶται: 'fidgets' from annoyance; cf. *Frogs* 922 τί σκορδινᾷ καὶ δυσφορεῖς; οὐκ ἐν αὑτοῦ: The metaphor 'not at home' implies 'passionate', 'unable to control himself'; cf. Pl. *Kharm*. 155 d ἐφλεγόμην καὶ οὐκέτ' ἐν ἐμαυτοῦ ἦν, S. *Ph*. 950, Men. *Sam*. 125 (Koerte).

643 σκύτη βλέπειν: 'look whips', i.e. 'look whipped': 455 n., and cf. Eupolis 282 ἀτεχνῶς μὲν οὖν τὸ λεγόμενον σκύτη βλέπει.

644 σε: Bdelykleon.

645 εἰς ἀπόφευξιν: 'to obtain acquittal'. The chorus are so much in the habit of showing favour to the accuser, who speaks first, and disfavour to the accused, who speaks second, that they have forgotten that in this debate the second speaker, to whom they are showing disfavour, is not on trial.

646 πεπᾶναι χαλεπόν: 'it is hard to soften'; for the metaphor cf. X. *Kyr*. 4. 5. 21. [After χαλεπόν Porson added νεανίᾳ to obtain exact responsion to the strophe. But cf. 309 n.]

647 πρὸς ἐμοῦ: 'on my side', 'in my favour' (LSJ πρός A. III. 2).

648–724 *Bdelykleon gives his reasons for saying that Philokleon's power is an illusion. His argument is mainly financial: the jurors, and ordinary Athenians generally, receive only a small part of the profits from the Athenian empire, though it was acquired by their efforts. Much larger profits go to the demagogic politicians, who order the people about and deceive them; they say they do what is best for the people, but really do what is best for themselves. Philokleon, to his own amazement and dismay, finds himself being gradually convinced by what Bdelykleon says.*

It is this passage which makes clear that the real object of Ar.'s attack in this play is not the jurors themselves, who are merely foolish and mistaken, but the self-seeking politicians who wield excessive influence over them. It is doubtful whether the details of Bdelykleon's calculations would stand up to critical auditing, but in comic verse one can hardly expect arithmetical precision. What is more important is whether in general terms the allegation is true that leading politicians were making large personal profits from the Athenian empire by dishonest methods. Unfortunately this question is unanswerable, because good non-Aristophanic evidence about it is lacking. All one can do therefore is to praise the presentation of the case: contrasts are effectively made between the poor jurors and the rich politicians, and between what the politicians say and what they do; lively examples are given; calculations and lists are cleverly used to make the Athenians' mouths water at the thought of wealth which is diverted from them. (Gelzer *Der epirrhematische Agon* 100–6 points out that the epirrhema of the agon contains evidence, the antepirrhema argumentation. But he rather exaggerates the distinction; Bdelykleon uses arguments, but he gives evidence and examples too.)

Metre: like Philokleon's speech, anapaestic tetrameters ending with an anapaestic run.

648 The metaphor of πεπᾶναι (646) is continued: if the chorus's anger is not softened by skilful speaking, it will be hard to grind down by any other means. **νεόκοπτον**: 'A newly cut millstone' is probably not a new stone, but one on which the striations enabling the stone to grip and cut the grain have been recut after wear (like retreading a tyre); cf. L. A. Moritz *Grain-mills and Flour in Classical Antiquity* (1958) 37–8.

649 τι: 'something sensible', as in 1409.

650 Philokleon has now sat down to listen, and Bdelykleon stands in a central position. He begins formally, as if making a speech in a law-court, but Philokleon does not let him continue long in this manner. μέν is common at the opening of a speech; cf. 907 and Denniston 383. **δεινῆς γνώμης**: 'a task requiring exceptional intellect'. **μείζονος ἢ 'πὶ τρυγῳδοῖς**: 'above the scope of comedians'. Bdelykleon, a character in the play, comments on the play, like Xanthias in 54 ff. The comment implies that comedy normally deals with trivial subjects, not with subjects of fundamental importance to the state; Ar. regards this part of his play as being above the normal level of comedy.

651 ἐντετοκυῖαν: 'inborn'. The perfect passive form of τίκτω is not used in Attic, and here instead the active form is used intransitively. [Although there is no other instance of τέτοκα used intransitively, the parallel uses of γέγονα and πέφυκα show that no emendation is needed.]

652 ὦ πάτερ ἡμέτερε Κρονίδη: a regular form of address to Zeus in Homer (e.g. *Iliad* 8. 31); observe the epic lengthening of -ε before Κρ-. μὴ πατέριζε: 'don't "father" me'; cf. Shakespeare *Richard II* 2. 3. 86–7 'My gracious uncle!' 'Tut, tut! Grace me no grace, nor uncle me no uncle.'

Philokleon impatiently interrupts before Bdelykleon can complete the anapaestic line. Thus the metre enhances the characterization; in

548–630 Bdelykleon never interrupted a line of Philokleon's. But the
line remains hard to interpret. There appear to be three alternative
interpretations:

A: Bdelykleon is beginning a prayer to Zeus to make his speech
successful, in the formal manner of an orator beginning a public
speech (e.g. D. 18. 1). Philokleon tells him not to waste time on such
formalities, but go straight to the main point.

B: Bdelykleon sarcastically addresses Philokleon as Zeus because
Philokleon compared himself to Zeus (619–30). Philokleon thinks it is
a piece of flattery intended to win him over.

C (a compromise between *A* and *B*): Bdelykleon is praying to
Zeus, but Philokleon wrongly imagines that he himself is being
addressed.

Most editors favour *B*, but the most recent translators (Parker,
Barrett) adopt *C*, perhaps rightly.

653 τουτί refers to the preceding clause; cf. *Clouds* 1262 ὅστις εἰμί, τοῦτο
βούλεσθ' εἰδέναι;

654 τεθνήσει: 'you'll be dead'. This future form occurs also in *Akh.* 590.
[Elmsley emended it to τεθνήξεις. But since τεθνάναι existed as well as
τεθνηκέναι, τεθνήσομαι may have existed as well as τεθνήξω. Its existence is confirmed by Σ *Akh.* 590, who writes Ἀττικοὶ δὲ διὰ τοῦ σ φασὶ
τεθνήσει.] σπλάγχνων: 'sacrificial feasts', as in *Knights* 410. A person accused of homicide was excluded from religious places and
ceremonies; cf. D. 20. 158 and my *Athenian Homicide Law* (1963) 25.

655 παπίδιον: 'daddy', like 297 παπία; Bdelykleon abandons the for-
mality of 650–2. χαλάσας: 'relaxing', ceasing to frown; cf. E. *Hipp.*
290 στυγνὴν ὀφρῦν λύσασα.

656 'And first calculate roughly, not with counters but on your fingers.'
This implies that for exact calculations counters would normally
be used.

657 The tribute paid by the subject cities of the Athenian empire is
mentioned first, because it was far the largest source of Athenian
revenue at this time. συλλήβδην: 'altogether'.

658 τέλη: 'taxes', a general term covering most of the other items mentioned in 658–9. χωρὶς: 'besides'. ἑκατοστάς: 'one-per-cents'.
[X.] *Ath. Pol.* 1. 17 mentions a one-per-cent tax levied at Peiraieus,
presumably some kind of harbour tax. For the one-per-cent purchase
tax see note on 659 ἀγοράς. πολλὰς shows that there were other one-
per-cent taxes of which we know nothing.

659 πρυτανεῖα: 'court dues'. πρυτανεῖα (the term is always plural, even
for a single payment) had to be paid to the state by the prosecutor in
certain kinds of case in which he claimed money from the accused, e.g.
prosecution for debt (*Clouds* 1131–1200), for loss of property (Isok.
18. 12), or for destruction of an olive-tree (D. 43. 71). The payment
had to be made at the time when the written notice of prosecution was

given, on the last day of the month (*Clouds* 1197). The amount paid was 3 drachmas if the sum claimed was over 100 and not more than 1,000 drachmas, 30 drachmas if the sum claimed was over 1,000 drachmas (Pol. 8. 38; cf. Isok. 18. 3, D. 47. 64). If the prosecutor won his case, his convicted opponent had to refund to him the amount he had paid in πρυτανεῖα, besides paying the debt or other money owed (D. 47. 64, Pol. 8. 38). It is stated by Harp. s.v. πρυτανεῖα, Pol. 8. 38, that πρυτανεῖα had to be paid also by the accused, but there is no earlier evidence for this, and payment by the accused seems not to be envisaged in *Clouds* 1131–1200. The revenue derived by the state from this source was used for the jurors' pay ([X.] *Ath. Pol.* 1. 16, Pol. 8. 38). For a more detailed discussion see J. H. Lipsius *Das attische Recht* 824–7; for speculation about the origin of the name see R. J. Bonner and G. Smith *The Administration of Justice from Homer to Aristotle* i 63–5.

μέταλλ᾽: The silver mines at Laureion (south-east of Athens) belonged to the state but were leased to private individuals. Leases were allocated according to the vote of the council by the officials known as πωληταί (sellers of state property); the leases were normally for three years, or in some cases for ten years (Arist. *Ath. Pol.* 47. 2). Such, at least, was the system in the fourth century, and there is a fair amount of literary and epigraphical evidence about leases and rents from 367 onwards, which has been discussed by R. J. Hopper (*BSA* xlviii [1953] 200–54). But it is impossible to say how much revenue the state obtained from the mines in Ar.'s time. In 483/2 there was a surplus of 100 talents from this source (Arist. *Ath. Pol.* 22. 7; cf. Hdt. 7. 144. 1), but that was exceptional, and anyway conditions may easily have changed sixty years later. But the mines remained an important source of revenue until the Spartan occupation of Dekeleia at the end of the Peloponnesian war (Th. 6. 91. 7, X. *Poroi* 4. 25), and large profits were made from them also by some individuals in this period, especially Nikias and Hipponikos (X. *Poroi* 4. 14–15).

ἀγοράς: It is not known what kinds of market tax are covered by this term, but they probably include the purchase tax called ἐπώνιον, which at this time seems to have been one per cent (*IG* i² 329).

λιμένας: This term may cover taxes on ships using the harbours, on persons arriving or departing by sea, and on goods imported and exported. But details are not known. Possibly the one-per-cent tax mentioned in [X.] *Ath. Pol.* 1. 17 (658 n.) is included.

μισθώσεις: 'rents' for land and property owned by the state. For example, an Athenian decree of 418/7 authorizes the lease of the precinct of Kodros and Neleus and Basile for twenty years for the growing of olives, and lays down full details of the procedure to be followed (*IG* i² 94). [μισθούς (a) does not scan, and is probably a more familiar word substituted for a less familiar one. καί is *q*'s conjecture to restore the metre, but this still leaves an unsatisfactory sense: μισθός is 'pay', and is a type of state expenditure, not revenue (cf. 661).]

δημιόπρατα: 'goods confiscated and sold'. Certain kinds of offenders, especially those convicted of intentional homicide (Lys. 1. 50, D. 21. 43), had their property confiscated. It was then sold by the πωληταί in the presence of the council (Arist. *Ath. Pol.* 47. 2). There exist a number of inscriptions recording details of such sales, most notably of the goods confiscated from those condemned for mutilation of the Hermai and profanation of the Mysteries in 415 (*SEG* xiii 12–22, xvi 13).

It should not be assumed that the items mentioned individually in 657–9 are meant to be a complete list of Athenian sources of revenue; they are just some important examples.

660 'We get a total of nearly 2,000 talents.' No other evidence enables us to check the accuracy of this figure for the total annual revenue of Athens. It is discussed in *ATL* iii 344–5, but the calculations there are over-exact; cf. Gomme *Commentary on Thucydides* iii 503–4. γίγνεται: 'comes to', the normal verb for an arithmetical result.

661 ἀπὸ τούτου: 'out of this total'. [τούτων (VJ), referring to τάλαντ' ἐγγὺς δισχίλια, is also possible.] κατάθες: 'set aside', 'put into a category of its own', as in X. *Oik.* 9. 8; not 'pay down in cash', nor 'put down in writing'. ἐνιαυτοῦ with μισθὸν: 'a year's pay'.

662 ἐξ χιλιάσιν: the total number of jurors appointed for each year (Arist. *Ath. Pol.* 24. 3). κατένασθεν: 'dwell', a poetic verb in an epic form (for Attic κατενάσθησαν), indicating that the whole clause is an epic quotation or parody. Therefore its application to our context must not be pressed strictly; for example οὔπω, 'not yet', must not be taken to imply that an increase in the number of jurors was expected.

663 6,000 jurors each paid 3 obols a day would receive 150 talents only if they all sat on 300 days, which is, approximately, the largest possible number; for the courts did not sit on the forty or more days in the year when the assembly met (D. 24. 80), nor on festival days ([X.] *Ath. Pol.* 3. 8). Bdelykleon is giving the maximum amount, and does not necessarily mean that all the jurors in fact sat on so many days in every year.

664–5 ἄρ' marks an inference from the previous speaker's words, and μέντοι marks assent to the inference. 'So the pay we've been getting is less than a tenth of the revenue!' 'It is indeed.' Cf. *Birds* 1667–8, Pl. *La.* 190 c, X. *Oik.* 1. 8. In all these passages the inclusion or omission of a question-mark is a matter of taste and makes no difference to the meaning. The position of 'connective' ἄρα is exceptionally late here, but it is almost as late in *Clouds* 1359, *Wealth* 1047, fr. 150. καὶ ... δὴ in a question implies surprise; cf. Denniston 211. ποῖ τρέπεται: 'to what use is it put?' 'what's done with it?'; cf. *Clouds* 858 τὰς δ'

ἐμβάδας ποῖ τέτροφας; 'πειτα: 'in that case', also implying surprise.
[The correct attribution of this sentence to Philokleon and the next to
Bdelykleon was made by 'H. L.' (*Classical Journal* xxxii [1825] 44-5),
kindly identified for me by the present Minister of Ecclesmachan as
his predecessor Henry Liston (father of Robert Liston the surgeon).]

666 'To those ⟨men who say⟩ "I shall never betray . . ." '. Bdelykleon
quotes Philokleon's words in 593, and probably uses the same tone
of voice and gesture; but he distorts the quotation by introducing
τὸν Ἀθηναίων κολοσυρτόν, 'the Athenian rabble', which reflects what
(as he claims) the demagogues thought, not what they said.

668 ἄρχειν αἱρεῖ σαυτοῦ: 'choose to rule over you'. Many Athenian
officials were appointed by lot; but some were elected by vote,
including ambassadors, military and naval officers, and perhaps συνήγοροι (type *B*: 482 n.). Kleon and other manipulators could not
control the lot, but they could win elections, especially if only their
partisans took the trouble to vote; cf. *Akh.* 598 Λα. ἐχειροτόνησαν γάρ
με— Δι. κόκκυγές γε τρεῖς.   ῥηματίοις: 'phraselets', a term fashionable in the years 425-1 for the modes of expression of the latest style of
oratory; cf. *Akh.* 444, 447, *Knights* 216, *Clouds* 943, *Peace* 534. περιπεφθείς: literally 'baked round', but all extant instances of περιπέττω
are metaphorical. Usually it means 'disguise', but here clearly it is
'bamboozle'. 'You've been led up the garden path' is a corresponding
English expression seldom used literally.

669 The cities of the Athenian empire might give bribes to Athenian
politicians to dissuade them from proposing increases of tribute or
other measures. The allegation of taking bribes from the allied cities is
made against Kleon in *Knights* 801-2; Th. 3. 11. 7, without mentioning bribes, confirms that allied cities paid court to leading Athenian
politicians.   κατὰ πεντήκοντα τάλαντα: 'fifty talents at a time',
a ridiculously large round number; cf. *Th.* 811.

671 For the general tone of this passage cf. *Knights* 65-9 (where the
Paphlagonian represents Kleon and the other slaves the victims of his
alleged bullying; ἀναπείσετ' means 'bribe'): Παφλαγὼν δὲ περιθέων
τοὺς οἰκέτας / αἰτεῖ, ταράττει, δωροδοκεῖ λέγων τάδε· / "ὁρᾶτε τὸν Ὕλαν
δι' ἐμὲ μαστιγούμενον; / εἰ μή μ' ἀναπείσετ', ἀποθανεῖσθε τήμερον." /
ἡμεῖς δὲ δίδομεν.   τὸν φόρον: 'your tribute to me', i.e. a bribe (corresponding to μ' ἀναπείσετ' in *Knights* 68).   βροντήσας: Philokleon
thought himself equal to Zeus (619-30), but Bdelykleon implies that
it is really the demagogue who behaves like Zeus. (This verb is used of
Perikles 'the Olympian' in *Akh.* 531, but it is wrong to see a reference
to Perikles in *Wasps* 671, for here Ar. is attacking contemporary
politicians.)

672 ἀργελόφους: Σ says this word means the feet of a sheepskin. It is
clearly a metaphor for odd scraps of little value. 'You're content to
nibble the scrag-end of your empire.'

673 μέν has no answering δέ-phrase about the demagogues; instead the sentence runs straight into the main clause with a fresh μέν and δέ (675). **σύρφακα**: 'rubbish', 'litter', a contemptuous expression for the ordinary Athenians. This is how the allies, not Bdelykleon, think of them.

674 κηθαρίου: κήθιον means 'dice-box' (Hermippos 27, Ath. 477 d), but κηθάριον does not occur elsewhere. Σ preserves two alternative explanations:

A: a basket-work container on top of a voting-urn. This explanation makes κηθάριον synonymous with κημός (94 n.).

B: a saucer, which would hold only small quantities of food.

B may be a mere guess from λαγαριζόμενον. *A* suits ψῆφον in 675, and so is preferable. ἐκ κηθαρίου will then be 'by means of the voting-urn', referring to the way in which Philokleon earns a living; for this use of ἐκ cf. Isok. 15. 152 ἐκ τῶν ἰδίων τρέφειν ἐμαυτόν. **λαγαριζόμενον**: 'getting thin', a comic substitution for τρεφόμενον. [This is obviously the meaning required here, and -ιζ- is obviously the correct form to express this meaning. In Pherekrates 121, quoted by Σ^V, a different meaning seems to be required, and so possibly the form too may be different there; the ingenuity of Σ^V in searching for a single explanation to cover both passages is misplaced.] **τραγαλίζοντα** occurs nowhere else, but is evidently connected with τράγημα and τρωγάλια. It suggests delicious food, so that τὸ μηδέν is, like λαγαριζόμενον, an anticlimax: 'feasting on nothing'.

675 Κόννου ψῆφον: According to Σ, Κόννου θρῖον was a proverbial expression for something worthless. Since this is stated on the authority of the Alexandrian scholar Kallistratos, and since it appears too odd to have been invented, it should be accepted; but the origin of the expression remains unknown. There is no special reason to connect it with the Konnos who taught Sokrates to play the harp (Pl. *Euthd.* 272 c, *Mx.* 235 e), and no way of telling whether it is true that Konnos was a dumb lyre-player (*Souda* κ 2048). Because the line is addressed to Philokleon, ψῆφον is comically substituted for θρῖον.

676 ὕρχας: two-handled jars used for preserved fish (*PSI* 4. 428. 8, 84, Σ *Wasps* 676). The bribes are of course the contents, not just empty jars. [This is easily understood, and there is no need to seek a defining genitive. Pol. 10. 74 attributes the phrase ὕρχας οἴνου to Ar.'s Ὁλκάδες, but this is not evidence that the same phrase should be read in *Wasps* 676, where the other items in the list are all single words.] **δάπιδας**: 'rugs', for sleeping on or in, a kind of luxury which a rich man would have but a poor man would not; cf. *Ek.* 840, *Wealth* 528, 542. **τυρόν**: Cheese was not plentiful in Athens and was often imported, especially from Sicily; cf. 838, 896–7. **σήσαμα**: Sesame oil was widely used in Asia (Hdt. 1. 193. 4, 3. 117. 4, X. *An.* 4. 4. 13), but in Athens it must have been dearer than olive oil. Sesame cakes are provided for special feasts in *Akh.* 1092, *Peace* 869. προσκεφάλαια: 'cushions' or 'pillows', a luxury used for reclining at dinner (e.g. *Akh.* 1090) or for sleeping at night (e.g. *Wealth* 542).

677 φιάλας: cups made of gold or silver, used for religious ceremonies; cf. 1447, *Peace* 431, *Birds* 975.　χλανίδας: There is little or no difference between a χλανίς and a χλαῖνα (738, 1132). Each is a large piece of woollen cloth which may be used either as a blanket or as a cloak, warmer and more luxurious than a τρίβων.　στεφάνους: On festive occasions everyone wore a crown (even slaves, e.g. *Wealth* 21). Ordinary people's crowns would be made merely of flowers or leaves, and therefore thrown away after use. Richer people might have crowns made of gold or other permanent material. So to say of someone that he possesses crowns is to imply that he is well off (e.g. 710, *Ek.* 606). A gold crown was sometimes formally conferred as an official honour, even on foreigners (e.g. Th. 4. 121. 1), but *Wasps* 677 does not mean that cities of the Athenian empire formally honoured Athenian politicians in this way; the crowns here are just ordinary presents, like the other items in 676-7. ὅρμους: 'necklaces', generally of gold, worn by women; e.g. *Lys.* 408-10, E. *El.* 176-7. ἐκπώματα: cups made of gold or other valuable material, but (unlike φιάλαι) used for ordinary drinking purposes; cf. *Akh.* 74, *Ek.* 447. πλουθυγιείαν: 'health-and-wealth', generally conferred only by the gods; cf. *Knights* 1091, *Birds* 731.

678 The argument is that the ordinary Athenians whose exertions in the army and navy built up the Athenian empire ought to receive the benefits accruing from it. For the emphasis on military and naval service as the qualification cf. 684-5, 1117-21. ἐφ' ὑγρᾷ: 'on the deep'; ὑγρά as a noun for 'sea' is Homeric, and indicates that we have here an epic quotation or parody. πιτυλεύσας: 'rowing', making a zeugma with ἐν γῇ. For a detailed discussion of πίτυλος, which denotes a rhythmical movement, see W. S. Barrett's note on E. *Hipp.* 1464.

679 τοῖς ἑψητοῖσι: 'for your boiled fish'.

The contrast drawn by Bdelykleon in this passage is at variance with the picture given by 'the Old Oligarch', who claims that, because the allies' legal disputes are tried in Athenian courts, they do pay attentions to ordinary Athenian citizens as well as to the generals and other leaders ([X.] *Ath. Pol.* 1. 18).

680 When Bdelykleon says 'not even a head of garlic', he just means 'not even a very cheap present'. But Philokleon takes him literally, and proceeds to corroborate that no one has, as a matter of fact, given him any garlic. It is a common type of Aristophanic joke for a speaker to take the previous speaker's words more literally than they were intended. Εὐχαρίδου: doubtless a well-known greengrocer. καὐτὸς: Although Bdelykleon's remarks were in the 2nd person singular,

Philokleon has taken them to refer to jurors generally, and so uses αὐτός to mark his individual example. [Zacher's κἀχθὲς is therefore unnecessary.]

681 αὐτήν: i.e. 'my actual *slavery*'; to show that he does not rule others is not enough to show that he is himself ruled.   **ἀποκναίεις:** 'you're wearing me out', i.e. 'I'm getting tired of waiting'.

682 γὰρ: '⟨I *am* demonstrating it,⟩ for . . .'   **ἀρχαῖς** must refer to officials elected by vote, not those appointed by lot: 668 n.

684 ἐλαύνων: 'rowing'.

686 ὅ has the previous clause as antecedent: 'you run about at their beck and call, a thing which . . .'.   **ἀπάγχει:** 'infuriates', as in *Clouds* 988.

687 Nothing is known about the son of Khaireas, not even his name. 691–3 shows that he was one of the ten advocates who acted as official prosecutors. (The idea that the name is chosen for the sake of a pun—'son of Mr. Joyous'?—is not plausible. Khaireas was an ordinary Athenian name, and the son of Khaireas must have been a well-known figure in the courts. The reason for using his father's name here may be that his own name will not scan conveniently, or that it is shared by a well-known namesake, so that it would be ambiguous without the patronymic.)   **εἰσελθὸν:** 'coming into court'. While speaking for the prosecution in one case, the son of Khaireas incidentally urges the jurors to be punctual for tomorrow's case, just as Kleon does (242–4). [Rogers takes εἰσελθὸν as 'came forward in the assembly' and 689 εἴπῃ as 'moved a resolution'; but this is wrong, because ὅταν must refer to an event which happened several times, whereas a resolution would be a once-for-all event.]

688 ὡδὶ διαβάς: 'standing with his legs apart, like this'. Bdelykleon gives a comic demonstration. For the masculine after μειράκιον, in accordance with sense rather than grammar, cf. Pl. *La.* 180 e.   **δια-κινηθείς:** probably 'with extravagant gestures', but there seems to be no exact parallel.   **τρυφερανθείς:** 'daintified'. [Neither τρυφερανθείς (RVJ) nor τρυφερωθείς (ΓΒ₂) occurs elsewhere, and either may be right here.]

689 ἥκειν εἴπῃ: 'tells you to arrive'. σε is understood (not σοι, for the -ι of δικάσαντι cannot be elided); for this accusative cf. S. *Ph.* 101 λέγω σ' ἐγὼ δόλῳ Φιλοκτήτην λαβεῖν.

690 ὕστερος τοῦ σημείου: 'after the signal'. No one knows what the signal was. A signal, which may or may not have been the same, was used to mark the beginning or end of a meeting of the assembly or council; it was something visible which was put up and taken down, but exact details are not known (*Th.* 278 with Σ, And. 1. 36). For the rule that jurors who arrived late were excluded from the court cf. 774–5, 891–2. It would obviously have been wrong to allow a man to take his place on a jury when he could not hear the whole case. But if an advocate was late (691), it would be worth while to delay the opening of the trial until he arrived, rather than proceed with no advocate or with one not fully conversant with the details of the case.

691 τὸ συνηγορικὸν: 'the advocate's fee'. The son of Khaireas was evidently an advocate of type *B* (482 n.), prosecuting magistrates on the examination of their accounts. This line proves that such advocates were paid one drachma a day.

692-3 'And sharing with one of his fellow officials (i.e. the other nine advocates) whatever any accused man gives him, the two of them, arranging the affair between them . . .' κοινωνῶν . . . ἑτέρῳ is ungrammatically but naturally regarded as a dual subject; cf. *Birds* 203-4 ἀνεγείρας τὴν ἐμὴν ἀηδόνα καλοῦμεν αὐτούς.

694 In this sentence perfect and present tenses are used quite indiscriminately for regular occurrences (494 n.). ἐσπουδάκατον: 'are very serious', meaning that they look and speak seriously, though they are not really in earnest; so also in X. *Smp.* 2. 17. ὡς πρίονθ': 'like a pair of sawyers' at each end of a two-handled saw. Naturally not all ten advocates would speak in the same prosecution, but this sentence shows that it was common for two to do so. The simile means that the son of Khaireas and his colleague co-operate by both speaking in such a way as to conceal important evidence, so that the corruption of the one is not revealed by the speech of the other. (R. J. Bonner and G. Smith *The Administration of Justice from Homer to Aristotle* ii 31-3 suggest that Ar. means that the son of Khaireas co-operates with an undersecretary. But this view is refuted by 692, which implies that both partners hold the same kind of office.)

695 The jurors are so busy thinking about their pay that they do not give enough attention to the case. χασκάζεις: 'keep gasping for' in expectation; cf. *Akh.* 10. κωλακρέτην: 'treasurer'. The kolakretai were the officials in charge of the state treasury (τὸ δημόσιον), and so paid out the fees to persons who performed various kinds of service to the state; *Wasps* 695 and 724 (and cf. *Birds* 1541) are the evidence that they paid jurors.

696 θῖνα: mud or sand under water, and so metaphorically 'depths'.

697 προσάγεις μᾶλλον: 'you are bringing nearer to ⟨your point of view⟩'. [The application of προσ- is not very easily understood, and possibly the verb ought to be emended to προάγεις (which according to Blaydes is the reading of G, a late ms. of no independent authority, which I have not collated) or the middle προσάγει (conjectured by Blaydes).]

698 τοῖσιν ἅπασιν: 'the whole population', as explained in 706-11.

699 δημιζόντων: 'people-izing', claiming to set the δῆμος above all other considerations. The verb is formed by analogy with μηδίζω, etc. οὐκ οἶδ' ὅπῃ: 'somehow or other', 'sort of'. ἐγκεκύκλησαι: a rare compound, here used metaphorically. The literal use is probably of a number of men standing round another to prevent his getting away; cf. Plu. *TG* 5. 3. 'You've been hemmed in.'

700 ὅστις, not ὅς, because this clause gives the evidence or explanation for the preceding statement. **ἀπὸ τοῦ Πόντου μέχρι Σαρδοῦς**: This definition of the extent of the Athenian empire is exaggerated. In the north-east Byzantion and Khalkedon certainly paid tribute, but they are nearly twenty miles short of the Black Sea. In the reassessment of tribute made in 425/4 some places on the Black Sea were included, and in 424 Lamakhos, in command of tribute-collecting ships, went to the Black Sea (Th. 4. 75), but it is dubious whether tribute was actually paid by these places. In the west Ar.'s exaggeration is greater: Athens had founded a colony at Thourioi and had alliances with several cities in Sicily and southern Italy, but no city in this area paid tribute, and there is no other evidence of any Athenian influence over Sardinia. There is a similar exaggeration in *Knights* 173–4, where Athenian influence is said to extend from Karia to Carthage.

701–2 'You don't get any advantage from them at all, except your pay; and this they always drip into you with wool like oil a little at a time, to keep you alive.' Two explanations of the simile seem possible:

A: If a person has an aching ear, drops of oil are put into it by means of a small lump of wool (as we may use cotton wool). This is the explanation of *Σ*.

B: If a person is ill and eats little food, it prevents him from dying but does not give him strength, and this kind of feeding resembles Athenian politicians' treatment of poor citizens. Cf. D. *Prooimia* 53. 4 νῦν δὲ δραχμῇ καὶ χοῖ καὶ τέτταρσιν ὀβολοῖς ὥσπερ ἀσθενοῦντα τὸν δῆμον διάγουσιν, ὁμοιότατ', ὦ ἄνδρες Ἀθηναῖοι, τοῖς παρὰ τῶν ἰατρῶν σιτίοις διδόντες ὑμῖν. καὶ γὰρ ἐκεῖν' οὔτ' ἰσχὺν ἐντίθησιν οὔτ' ἀποθνῄσκειν ἐᾷ.

A does not suit τοῦ ζῆν ἔνεχ', and *B* does not suit ἐρίῳ. Ar. seems to have combined, or confused, two ideas.

703 'They want you to be poor, and that for the following reasons.' ὧν εἴνεκ' is abridged from ἐκείνων εἴνεκα ἅ. [The mss.' καὶ τούτων εἴνεκ', ἐρῶ σοι, 'and for the following reasons, as I shall tell you', makes ἐρῶ σοι very weak.]

704 τιθασευτήν: 'tamer'; for the application of this metaphor to Athenian politicians' treatment of the people, cf. D. 3. 31 ὑμᾶς ἐπάγουσ' ἐπὶ ταῦτα καὶ τιθασεύουσι χειροήθεις αὐτοῖς ποιοῦντες. **γ'** stresses οὗτός: Philokleon acts on *his* orders and no one else's. [Meineke suggested σ', but ἐπισίξῃ is intransitive and would require σοι; cf. Theok. 6. 29. γιγνώσκῃς implies distinguishing the tamer from others, and justifies γ'.] **ἐπισίξῃ**:.For hissing to set a dog on someone cf. Theok. 6. 29 σίξα δ' ὑλακτεῖν νιν καὶ τᾷ κυνί, 'I hissed to the dog too to bark at her'.

705 ἐπιρρύξας: 'setting you on', according to *Σ*. But there is no parallel; the simple ρύζω means 'bark' or 'growl'. **αὐτοῖς**: For the sudden switch to the plural, 554 n.

707 χίλιαι: The number of cities assessed for tribute at this time was a little over 300; fewer actually paid it. This shows that Ar. (and probably most of his audience too) had no exact knowledge of Athenian revenues, and casts doubt on his figure in 660.

709 δύο μυριάδ': 20,000 may have been approximately the total number of Athenian citizens (adult males) of the lowest class (thetes) at this period (after the Plague); but there is no definite evidence. Cf. F. Jacoby *FGrH* IIIb Supp. i 464–6 and especially ii 378 n. 19, A. H. M. Jones *Athenian Democracy* (1957) 9, A. French *The Growth of the Athenian Economy* (1964) 137–8. [Dobree's emendation assumes the corruption of the dual to the more familiar plural. It seems the best way of restoring ἄν to the line. ἄν is needed because here (a) it cannot be understood from an ἄν earlier in the sentence, (b) ἔζων is not a verb which by itself conveys a potential meaning, (c) ἔζων cannot be regarded as a rhetorical exaggeration by which a possibility is stated as a fact, since that would require ζῶσιν.] **τῶν δημοτικῶν:** 'the ordinary people' as opposed to the rich; so also in D. 21. 209 ὑμῶν τῶν πολλῶν καὶ δημοτικῶν.   **ἐν πᾶσι λαγῴοις:** 'surrounded by hare's meat', apparently a comic distortion of ἐν πᾶσιν ἀγαθοῖς or some such phrase; cf. *Akh.* 1025–6 ὥπερ μ' ἐτρεφέτην ἐν πᾶσι βολίτοις. Hare was a delicacy, eaten on festive occasions, e.g. *Akh.* 1006, *Peace* 1196.

710 στεφάνοισιν: 677 n.   **πυῷ καὶ πυριάτῃ:** πυός is 'beestings', the first milk after birth, and πυριάτη is beestings heated and curdled. These, like hare, were delicacies; cf. *Peace* 1150, Kratinos 142. We might say 'cream and cream-cheese'.

711 A striking illustration of the Athenians' view that they were superior to other Greeks, and that their greatest achievement was the victory of Marathon. Cf. Th. 6. 82–3, especially 83. 2 τὸν βάρβαρον μόνοι καθελόντες εἰκότως ἄρχομεν.   **τῆς γῆς:** 'our country'. The use of γῆ for the people rather than the land seems to be poetic; e.g. E. *Tr.* 868.   **ἀπολαύοντες:** δύο μυριάδ' (709) is feminine dual, but the masculine plural suits the sense and the change is natural; cf. 595, 688, 1342.   **'ν Μαραθῶνι:** Elsewhere Ar. usually omits ἐν with Μαραθῶνι (*Akh.* 696–7, *Knights* 781, *Th.* 806), but in fr. 413 διὰ τοὺν Μαραθῶνι τροπαῖον is guaranteed by the metre.   **τροπαίου:** a marble column bearing a statue (doubtless of Nike), of which fragments have been found (cf. E. Vanderpool in *Hesperia* xxxv [1966] 93–106). It may have been the first Greek victory monument to be erected in stone; if so, the innovation shows the extraordinary importance attached to the battle of Marathon (cf. W. C. West in *Class. Phil.* lxiv [1969] 7–19).

712 ἐλαολόγοι: Olive-pickers would be temporary hired labourers (like English hop-pickers), whose chief object was to earn over a short period extra money to supplement their regular income.   **ἅμα:** 'Go along with' here means 'take orders from'; cf. Th. 7. 57. 6 τοὺς ἅμα Γυλίππῳ, 'the men under the command of Gylippos'.

713 [τί ποθ': τί πέπονθ'; (*Souda*), 'What has happened to me? A kind of numbness . . .', may possibly be right, but it means removing something else from the line to make it scan. Kuster deleted -περ (leaving ὡς as 'for'), Blaydes μου, Meineke κατά.] **ὥσπερ νάρκη**: 'like numbness'. (Not 'electric ray', to which καταχεῖται would be inappropriate.) **καταχεῖται**: 'is creeping over'; cf. 7.

714 Philokleon finds that he is gradually being convinced. He expresses his dismay melodramatically, with a military metaphor: he is no longer able to carry on the fight. (Starkie thinks that he is giving a cunning excuse for not committing suicide, but that cannot be right. 522–3 has long since been forgotten, and anyway no one actually gave him a real sword at that point.) **μαλθακός**: not 'cowardly', but 'weak', 'flabby'.

715 **αὐτοί**: 'the masters'; for this use of αὐτός cf. *Clouds* 219, Pl. *Prt.* 314 d, etc., and also Latin 'ipse' and Irish-English 'himself'. **Εὔβοιαν**: Two explanations are possible. (*a*) Euboia was a principal source of imported grain, and so here 'Euboia' may be a comic way of saying 'huge quantities of grain' (cf. Euphanes 1, where τὸν Πάρνηθ' ὅλον seems to mean 'huge quantities of timber'); then 716 is an explanation of the metonymy. (*b*) Euboia was an area in which many allotments of land were held by Athenian settlers (κληροῦχοι), and so Bdelykleon may mean 'allotments of land in Euboia'; then the offer in 715 is quite distinct from the one in 716. **διδόασιν**: 'offer', i.e. 'say that they will make a proposal to give'.

Σ says that an Athenian military expedition to Euboia in 424/3 was recorded by Philokhoros (*FGrH* 328 F 130). But even if this expedition did take place (and it is not mentioned by either Thucydides or Diodoros), its purpose is unknown, and there is no way of telling whether the demagogues' offers (whether of corn or of allotments) had any connection with it. The expedition and its historical context have been discussed by A. E. Raubitschek (*Hesperia* xii [1943] 33) and H. B. Mattingly (*JHS* lxxxi [1961] 124–32), but both tend to draw more definite conclusions than the meagre evidence warrants.

716 'And they undertake to provide grain in instalments of fifty medimnoi.' Fifty medimnoi would be an absurdly large quantity of grain to give to one citizen. Ar. is ridiculously exaggerating the demagogues' promises: 'when they're frightened, they offer you the earth'. (Σ takes it to mean allotments of land in Euboia each producing fifty medimnoi of grain a year, but σῖτον πορίειν cannot mean this.)

717 **πρώην** shows that the distribution of five medimnoi of barley to each citizen was recent. It therefore has no connection with the distribution of Egyptian grain in 445/4 recorded by Philokhoros (*FGrH* 328 F 119, Plu. *Per.* 37. 4), as Σ seems to have realized, though some modern scholars have confused the two; cf. G. Nenci in *Riv. Fil.* xcii (1964) 173–80. *Wasps* 717–18 is proof of a distribution of barley in 423/2.

718 **καὶ ταῦτα** with participle, as in 252, 1184, 1189, etc.: 'and that with difficulty, facing prosecution for being an alien'. ταῦτα refers to the whole clause πρώην πέντε μεδίμνους ἔλαβες . . . [Previous editors have punctuated so as to make ταῦτα the object of ἔλαβες, in defiance of the gender of μεδίμνους.]   ξενίας φεύγων: A man suspected of exercising any of the rights of an Athenian citizen when not entitled to them could be prosecuted by the procedure called γραφὴ ξενίας. (For this procedure see J. H. Lipsius *Das attische Recht* 416.) Ar.'s words here imply that the dole of five medimnoi of barley was distributed to citizens only, and that some people who claimed it were accused of not being citizens and were prosecuted by γραφὴ ξενίας, but were acquitted (acquittal is implied not by φεύγων, which means 'being prosecuted', but by ἔλαβες). The 2nd person singular refers to Philokleon, but here Philokleon is simply being taken as a typical ordinary Athenian; Ar.'s intention is not to give biographical information about Philokleon, but to indicate that ordinary Athenians were subjected to prosecution before being allowed to draw the dole. The implication is that this happened to 'everybody'; but since allowance must be made for comic exaggeration, Ar.'s words do not prove that the number of persons prosecuted was very large in actual fact. The ground of prosecution for ξενία will have been, in most cases at least, that one or both of a man's parents were not Athenian. (W. K. Lacey *The Family in Classical Greece* 282 n. 15 infers from the chorus's stress in 1076 on their indigenous origin that the ground of prosecution cannot have been non-Athenian parentage. But this inference is not valid, not just because 718 does not refer particularly to the chorus, but because it refers to acquittal; the complaint is that accusations of non-Athenian parentage were brought unjustifiably against genuine Athenians.) κατὰ χοίνικα: 'by the quart'. A khoinix of grain was regarded as a minimum ration for one man for one day; a more generous ration was two khoinikes (Hdt. 6. 57. 3, 7. 187. 2, Th. 4. 16. 1). There were 48 khoinikes in a medimnos, so that Ar.'s words imply that the dole was given out in 240 instalments—clearly comic exaggeration. But the phrase does prove that the dole was distributed in instalments, not all at once; the reason was no doubt that the authorities did not know in advance how many citizens were entitled to it, or would apply for it, and so did not know how large each citizen's total share could be until everyone had come at least once.   κριθῶν: Barley was quite usually eaten in Athens, but it would be a disappointment when σῖτος had been promised, since σῖτος might be wheat. (In Ar.'s time σῖτος was a general word for 'grain', and might always mean either wheat or barley; see L. A. Moritz in *CQ* v [1955] 135-41.) The sentence is so arranged that the disappointments build up to a climax: πέντε μεδίμνους—ξενίας φεύγων—κατὰ χοίνικα—κριθῶν. κριθῶν is the last straw, and to enable it to be the final word Ar. has moved the καὶ—ταῦτα-participle phrase forward from its usual position at the end of the sentence.

721 ἐγχάσκειν: 'laugh' in the sense of 'play a trick and get away with it'. It resembles χαίρω in the sense of 'act with impunity', except that ἐγχάσκω always has a hostile or disparaging tone. The person tricked is sometimes, as here, expressed in the dative. Cf. 1007, 1349, *Akh.* 221, *Knights* 1313, *Clouds* 1436, *Lys.* 272. 'And that they should not get away with tricking you by their ranting.'   **στομφάζοντας**: using pompous long-winded language. Aiskhylos is called a στόμφαξ in *Clouds* 1367.

724 ὀρνίθων γάλα (508 n.) is comically distorted to fit Philokleon. For the kolakretai, 695 n.

725–59 *The chorus declare that Bdelykleon has won the debate, and sing a strophe urging Philokleon to take his advice. Bdelykleon says he will give his father everything an old man wants, but still Philokleon remains ominously silent. In their antistrophe the chorus optimistically sing that he sees the error of his ways and will do as his son says. But instead he breaks out into paratragic lamentation, and like a bereaved hero expresses yearning for his life in the law-courts.*

The passage forms a musical conclusion to the agon, at first serious, but turning to comedy when Philokleon bursts into melodramatic lamentation. A conflict between reason and sentiment is revealed. Everyone (even Philokleon) agrees that Bdelykleon is right, and yet Philokleon feels that sitting on juries is his only pleasure in life, so that he is lost without it.

Metre: 725–8 are anapaestic tetrameters, delivered probably by the chorus-leader only. (Cf. *Knights* 457–60, *Birds* 627–38. Tetrameters at the end of an agon, giving the chorus's verdict, are sometimes called a σφραγίς.) They serve as a transition from the preceding anapaestic dialogue to the song which follows (just as 546–7 and 648–9 serve as transitions from songs to anapaestic dialogue). The song begins in mid sentence: the chorus-leader invokes Philokleon (728) and then his colleagues join him in singing the plea (729 πιθοῦ πιθοῦ . . .); cf. 869–70.

729–35 and 743–9 are a strophe and antistrophe, sung no doubt by the whole chorus (or each by half of it) and not by the leader alone. The metre is iambo-dochmiac (cf. 870–3 ~ 887–90). An iambic metron ×–∪– is sometimes shortened to –∪– (*cr*). A dochmiac is ×––∪– or ×∪∪–∪– (other forms of dochmiac exist but are not used in this song). Dochmiacs are not common in comedy; if there is a special reason for their use here, I do not know what it is.

729, 743	*ia ia ia*
730, 744	*doch doch*
731, 745	*ia ia ia*
732, 746	*ia cr ia* ‖
733*a*, 747*a*	*cr cr*

733*b*, 747*b*   doch
734, 748   ia ia ia ia
735, 749   doch ‖

736–42 and 750–9 are anapaests.

725 A sententious comment, typical of choruses in Greek plays.   ἢ που
σοφὸς . . .: cf. A. *Pr.* 887–8 ἢ σοφὸς ἢ σοφὸς ἦν ὃς πρῶτος . . .   πρὶν
ἂν ἀμφοῖν . . .: The original saying was a hexameter, which Σ quotes:
μηδὲ δίκην δικάσῃς πρὶν ἂν ἀμφοῖν μῦθον ἀκούσῃς. The author is
unknown. Almost the same line appears at Ps.-Phok. 87, but is
probably out of place there. E. *Hkld.* 179–80 adapts it a little more
freely: τίς ἂν δίκην κρίνειεν ἢ γνοίη λόγον, πρὶν ἂν παρ' ἀμφοῖν μῦθον
ἐκμάθῃ σαφῶς;

726 ἂν with optative for a polite command or request: 'do not judge'.
δικάσαις instead of -ειας: 572 n.   γὰρ οὖν: 'for in fact'.

727 'I throw down the sticks' is not meant literally (for καταβάλλω is
singular and one member of the chorus will not be carrying more than
one stick); it must be a set phrase for surrender, like the English
'throw up the sponge'. But I have found no other instance or evidence
to show to what circumstances the phrase originally belonged (perhaps some kind of fencing-match, in which each opponent had
a staff in each hand?).

728 συνθιασῶτα: 'member of our θίασος' metaphorically. Since a θίασος
was really a religious association, the best English equivalent here will
be not 'comrade' (which suggests politics), nor 'partner' (which
suggests commerce), nor 'fellow' (which suggests scholarship), but
'brother'. For the metaphorical use cf. *Wealth* 508 ξυνθιασώτα τοῦ
ληρεῖν καὶ παραπαίειν. But whereas in *Wealth* 508 the genitive is partitive, denoting the activity in which the brothers share, in *Wasps* 728
ἡλικίας is not partitive (since the activity shared by the brothers is
sitting on juries) but just descriptive: 'O brother of the same age as
ourselves'.

732 'To give me such good advice.'   ὅστις is commonly used with the
future indicative to express purpose, but past tenses of the indicative
are normal in final clauses expressing purposes which, being dependent on unfulfilled conditions or wishes, cannot now be accomplished;
cf. 961.

733–4 'Now some god clearly is coming forward and assisting you in
your difficulty.' For the genitive with συλλαμβάνω cf. S. *Ph.* 281–2, E.
Med. 946.

735 'Come forward and receive his help.'   παρὼν echoes παρὼν in
733*b*, and means that Philokleon is to respond to the god's generous
act, and not to spurn it by withdrawing or showing any other kind of
resistance or rejection. This participle often implies assistance or
co-operation; e.g. *Birds* 548 ἀλλ' ὅ τι χρὴ δρᾶν, σὺ δίδασκε παρών.

737–8 χόνδρον λείχειν: 'gruel to drink'. The implication is that an old man is toothless (cf. 165) and can take only soft or liquid food. **χλαῖναν:** see note on 677 χλανίδας. **σισύραν:** also a rug used as a cloak or as a blanket, like a χλαῖνα or χλανίς. But the difference was that a σισύρα was made from the skin of goats or sheep with the hair or wool left on it, whereas a χλαῖνα was made of wool which had been sheared, spun, and woven. Thus a χλαῖνα would be softer, a σισύρα rougher and more windproof.

739–40 'A whore to indulge in comprehensive below-the-belt massage' (Parker).

741 κοὐδὲν γρύζει: 'and doesn't utter a sound' of agreement or approval. Peter Rau *Paratragodia* (1967) 152–3 takes Philokleon's silence in 741–9 as a parody of the silence of some characters in tragedies. But could an audience distinguish a paratragic silence from an ordinary silence?

742 προσέσθαι: 'please' (LSJ προσίημι II. 4).

743–4 'He's been scolding himself about the activities which he was mad on before.' **ἐπεμαίνετ᾽:** For the metaphor cf. 1469. **ἔγνωκε:** 'he has understood'.

745 ἁμαρτίας: 'as errors'.

746 οὐκ ἐπείθετο: 'he previously would not believe ⟨to be errors⟩'.

748 σωφρονεῖ μέντοι: 'he's really being sensible'.

749 πειθόμενός: the third instance of the verb in five lines, placing strong emphasis on the idea of submission. It occurs another three times in 760–3. Philokleon's submission to Bdelykleon is a turning-point of the plot. [Brunck's πιθόμενός is unnecessary, because the first syllable of a dochmiac may be either short or long, and the antistrophe need not respond to the strophe in this respect; cf. 730 ∼ 744.]

750 ἰὼ μοί μοι: an exclamation of grief, typical of tragedy; cf. *Clouds* 1259–61, where it is comically taken to be the utterance of a character in a tragedy. ἰ- is here scanned long (as sometimes in tragic anapaests, e.g. A. *Ag.* 1455, E. *Alk.* 741), and μοι is not shortened before οὗτος, so that the cry is a long-drawn-out wail.

752 τούτων: the items listed in 737–40.

753 κείνων: the features of his former life as a juror. He is still speaking in the manner of a character lamenting in a tragedy; notice the shorter forms of ἐκείνων and ἐκεῖθι, the poetic deponent form in place of ἐρῶ, and the Doric form of γενοίμην. Possibly Ar. has in mind Admetos's lament in E. *Alk.* 866–7: ζηλῶ φθιμένους, κείνων ἔραμαι, κεῖν᾽ ἐπιθυμῶ δώματα ναίειν. Cf. also S. *Ai.* 1217 γενοίμαν ἵν᾽ . . ., E. *Hipp.* 732 ἠλιβάτοις ὑπὸ κευθμῶσι γενοίμαν, ἵνα . . ., etc.; songs of longing to be somewhere else are common in tragedy.

754 'Where the herald says . . .', i.e. in a law-court. Evidently the words which follow were regularly pronounced by the herald at the end of the jury's voting. It may be because Ar. wants to fit in the exact formula that he has twice consecutively abandoned the diaeresis usual in anapaests, dividing φησι and ἀψήφιστος between metra.

755 κἀπισταίην: 'and I long to stand over . . .'.   **κημοῖς**: 94 n.

756 He likes to save up his pleasure until the last possible moment.

757 He now utters a couple of tragic quotations. These quotations have no real relevance to his own situation and are meaningless without their contexts, but this does not matter; the purpose of his using tragic words, gestures, and tones of voice is simply to convey the impression that he is in a tragic situation. It is as if a character in an English farce suddenly struck attitudes and cried 'Woe is me! To be or not to be! O that this too too solid!'   **σπεῦδ', ὦ ψυχή**: The source is unknown, but it may be Euripides; cf. ὦ θυμέ, parodying Euripides, in *Akh.* 450, 480, 483. But Philokleon absurdly thinks that if his ψυχή can be addressed it ought to be visible, and so he looks round for it and can't find it: 'Where's my soul got to?'   **πάρες, ὦ σκιερά—**, 'Allow me, O shadowy—', is from Euripides's *Bellerophon* according to Σ, who quotes the whole passage (E. fr. 308):

> πάρες, ὦ σκιερὰ φυλλάς, ὑπερβῶ
> κρηναῖα νάπη· τὸν ὑπὲρ κεφαλῆς
> αἰθέρ' ἰδέσθαι σπεύδω τίν' ἔχει
> στάσιν Εἰνοδία (Valckenaer: εἰοδίας V: ἐνοδίας Γ).

758–9 'Then I'd better not find Kleon guilty of theft in future!' A threat is implied. Philokleon is convinced by Bdelykleon's arguments that politicians like Kleon are thieves, though he has not yet been persuaded to give up being a juror.   **νυν** is 'in that case', 'if what you say is so'.   **'ν τοῖσι δικασταῖς**: 'in court', 'at a sitting of the court', just as ἐν τῷ δήμῳ means 'at a meeting of the assembly'.   **κλέπτοντα**: The theft is past, but the present tense of κλέπτω, as of ἀδικέω, can have a perfect sense: 'being guilty of theft'. So also in *Frogs* 611.

760–859 *Since Philokleon cannot bear to give up judging, Bdelykleon suggests that he should have a private court at home, trying members of the household, with greater convenience than in the public law-courts. He agrees, and they proceed to set up a court, including various special arrangements for his comfort. He demands to have certain characteristic features of the real law-courts, and comic substitutes are found for them. Meanwhile Bdelykleon wonders what case to bring before his father. Xanthias opportunely reports that the dog Labes has stolen and eaten a Sicilian cheese, and Bdelykleon decides that the dog shall be tried.*

The dramatic purpose of the scene is to prepare the way for the satirical trial in 891–1008. But it is not just a mechanical transition. The whole idea of setting up a private court is interesting in itself, and the comic features of the court are brilliantly worked out, to make the scene one of the most amusing in the play.

760 ἴθ': 'please'; 162 n.

761 τί σοι πίθωμαι; 'What am I to do at your request?' πείθομαι takes an accusative (usually a neuter pronoun or adjective) of the thing which one is prevailed on to do or believe; so also 762 τοῦτο. Cf. *Clouds* 87 Στ. . . . ὦ παῖ, πιθοῦ. Φε. τί οὖν πίθωμαι δῆτά σοι;

762 φέρ' ἴδω: 145 n.

763 'Hades shall decide between us' means 'I will fight you to the death'. He recurs to the tragic style which he adopted in 750–7. He may have in mind, as Σ suggests, a line of Euripides's *Cretan Women* which began Ἅιδης κρινεῖ ταῦτ' (E. fr. 465).

764 σὺ δ' οὖν: 6 n.   κεχάρηκας: 389 n.

765 ἐκεῖσε: to the law-courts. ἐκεῖ in 767 and 770 is similar.   μὲν . . . ἀλλ': This combination of particles suggests a compromise. (Denniston 6 perhaps goes too far when he says that the proposed course of action, though represented as a bargain, is really a surrender.)   ἐνθάδε αὐτοῦ are used together for emphasis: 'right here', at home. So also in *Wealth* 1187 and in other authors.

766 δίκαζε τοῖσιν οἰκέταις: 'try the slaves'.

767 περὶ τοῦ; 'for what offence?'   ταῦθ' is governed by some unexpressed idea such as 'I mean' or 'you will do'. For the 'broken tribrach' see page 23.

768 ὅτι: 'because', but in English we should say 'if' or 'when'.   ἀνέῳξεν: aorist (of ἀνοίγνυμι) because the event will be past at the time to which the main verb (ψηφιεῖ) refers.   σηκίς: 'servant-girl', 'maid', strictly one born in the household, not bought (Pol. 3. 76). This line shows that female slaves would not be allowed to go out without specific permission.

769 'You'll vote for just a single imposition on her.'   ἐπιβολήν: a pun: 'fine' and 'sexual violation'. There is a similar pun on ἐπιβάλλω in *Birds* 1215–16.   μίαν μόνην implies that for more serious offences more than one will be imposed.

770 'Anyway that's what you used to do *there* regularly'; i.e. 'in the law-courts you used to impose fines'.   δὲ where one might expect γάρ: cf. Denniston 169. [But B's γε could be right.]   ἑκάστοτε: 446 n.

771 ταῦτα: internal accusative with ἡλιάσει: 'and this judging you'll naturally do in the sunshine now'. [Platnauer (*CQ* iii [1953] 54) prefers to put a colon after εὐλόγως and understand 'you will be doing'; that is possible, but it is perhaps a little easier to take the words with the verb which is expressed.]   ἐξέχῃ: 'comes out', regularly used of the sun (LSJ ἐξέχω I. 2. b).

772 εἵλη: 'warmth'. [εἵλη, εἴλη, or ἕλη? Two notes in Σ point the way to the right spelling. One says ἡ τοῦ ἡλίου αὐγή, δασέως· ληφθέντος δὲ διὰ τοῦ ι, ψιλῶς: this means that the two alternative forms were ἕλη and εἵλη, not εἴλη. The other, quoted from Didymos, says οὕτως δὲ οἱ Ἀττικοὶ διὰ τοῦ ι: this shows that the Attic form was εἵλη, not ἕλη.]

κατ' ὄρθρον: 'before dawn'. When Philokleon gets up in the morning, he will decide whether to sit indoors or outdoors that day. [If ΣΓ's variant κατ' ὀρθὸν is right, as it may be, it should be taken with ἡλιάσει πρὸς ἥλιον, meaning 'correctly', 'as the word implies you should'. ἡλιάσει rather than ἡ-: 195 n.]   πρὸς: 'facing', 'in view of'; cf. 773 πρὸς τὸ πῦρ 'in front of the fire', *Clouds* 198 πρὸς τὸν ἀέρα 'in the open air', *Peace* 692 πρὸς λύχνον 'by lamplight'. The jingle εἱλ- . . . ἡλ- . . . ἡλ- is probably intended to sound funny, even though the pronunciation of the three syllables will not have been identical.

774 ὕοντος: genitive absolute, as in *X. Hel.* 1. 1. 16: 'if it begins to rain' on a day when he has decided to sit outdoors.   **μεσημβρινός**: not precisely 'at noon', but in the middle part of the day, when the morning is already well advanced, i.e. very late; cf. *Akh.* 40. For the rule that a juror who arrived late was excluded from the court cf. 690, 891–2.

775 θεσμοθέτης: The thesmothetai were six of 'the nine arkhons', the others being the ἄρχων (ἐπώνυμος), the βασιλεύς, and the πολέμαρχος. The duties of the thesmothetai were almost entirely judicial; they presided over various kinds of case in their court, called ἡ ἡλιαία τῶν θεσμοθετῶν (1108 n.). The kinds of case for which they were responsible included prosecutions for embezzlement (cf. 935). 775 shows that one of them would control the admission of jurors to their own court. It does not necessarily mean that they controlled the admission of jurors to all the courts, and since several courts would sit simultaneously in different parts of Athens (cf. 1107–9) it is unlikely that they did so; probably the admission of jurors to each court was controlled by the magistrate presiding in that court.   **κιγκλίδι**: 124 n.

776 δίκην: 'speech', as in *X. Apom.* 4. 8. 1, Demetrios *On Style* 229.

778 δάκνων: 'to the annoyance of'; 286–7 n. The jurors in court would be annoyed because they had to wait for their meal, the speaker because the jurors were inattentive. But there is also a play on the word: the hungry jurors bite themselves because they have nothing else to bite, but in his private law-court Philokleon will be able to eat his dinner while the case continues.

779–80 διαγιγνώσκειν τὰ πράγματ': 'decide the cases'.   **ἔτι μασώμενος**: 'while still chewing'.

781 γ': 'yes, you will', contradicting an implied denial; cf. 27.   **καὶ λέγεται γὰρ**: 'for in fact people sometimes say . . .'.   **τουτογί**: When the deictic suffix -ί is added to οὗτος or ὅδε or νῦν, the particle γε or δέ or μέν may be inserted before the -ί.

783 ἀναμασώμενοι: 'chewing it over', 'ruminating'. The joke is that a common metaphorical expression will in Philokleon's case be true literally. For other jokes of this type cf. 191, 898.

784 ἀνά . . . πείθεις: tmesis (cf. 437) for ἀναπείθεις. For the order of words cf. E. *Or.* 1047 ἔκ τοί με τήξεις.

785 καλῶς: 'Good!' Although the word is classed as an expression of thanks by J. H. Quincey (*JHS* lxxxvi [1966] 139), Philokleon is here more concerned with expressing his own satisfaction than his gratitude to Bdelykleon.

786 κατ' ἐμαυτὸν: 'individually'. As the following lines show, one drachma (equivalent to six obols) would be given to each pair of jurors, who had then to make their own arrangements to get it changed into obols and divide it between themselves.

787 μ' (i.e. με, not μοι): 'to me'. With ἐργάζομαι, as with ποιέω, a second accusative is regularly used for the person affected by the action. The dative is unusual, but occurs in 1350, S. *OT* 1373. [In Attic ἐργάζομαι has ἠργ- in the imperfect and aorist, but εἰργ- in the perfect (Meisterhans *Grammatik der attischen Inschriften*³ 171).]

Lysistratos, a Kholargeus by deme (*Akh.* 855), was a well-known man-about-town, often satirized in comedy (cf. *Knights* 1267). According to Ar. he was always cold and hungry (*Akh.* 856–9). He was renowned for his jokes and sarcasm (*Wasps* 788, 1308–10, *Akh.* 854, fr. 198). He was probably the same person as Lysistratos son of Makareus, who was mocked as a catamite (Σ *Wasps* 787 distinguishes them, but cf. *Lys.* 1105). He moved in high-class society: he was a member of 'Phrynikhos's set' (1302), and he was also a friend of Andokides the orator (And. 1. 122). At some date he was attacked by Philinos (probably a brother of Kleophon; cf. A. E. Raubitschek in *Hesperia* xxiii [1954] 68–71), who brought a charge of homicide against him in an attempt to prevent him from taking some sort of legal or political action (Ant. 6. 36). In 415 he took part in the mutilation of the Hermai; he was denounced by Andokides and fled into exile, but returned to Athens sometime later (And. 1. 52–3, 67–8). (Antiphon and Andokides only say 'Lysistratos' without further identifying him, and so they may possibly mean different men. But on the whole it seems likely that the references are all to the same man, because they all suit a man belonging to a superior social set with political interests; see note on 1302 οἱ περὶ Φρύνιχον. Besides, the mere fact that they think it unnecessary to say which Lysistratos they mean suggests that there was only one well-known Lysistratos at this period.)

789 'He went to get it changed in the fish-market.' It is an Attic idiom to use the names of goods sold for the places where they are sold; cf. *Frogs* 1068 περὶ τοὺς ἰχθῦς, Antiphanes 125 ἐν τοῖς ἰχθύσι, and for instances with other kinds of goods *Clouds* 1065, *Birds* 13, *Lys.* 557, *Ek.* 303, Eupolis 304, Lys. 23. 6, D. 19. 245, Thphr. *Char.* 11. 4. The existence of the idiom proves that in the Agora shops or stalls selling the same kind of goods were grouped together.

790 ἐνέθηκε . . . μοι: probably 'put in my hand'. The alternative 'put in my mouth' (as in *Knights* 717) is less probable, for although money was often carried in the mouth (cf. 791) it can hardly have been customary to make payments in this way, and the point of the joke is lost unless Lysistratos follows the usual procedure for handing over money. [ἐπέθηκε (RJ) would mean 'laid down', i.e. placed on a table or something similar for Philokleon to pick up. This is less probable, since if Philokleon had picked up the 'obols' himself he would have been more likely to notice what they really were. There is no evidence that ἐπέθηκε could mean 'palmed off on me', as Starkie suggests.] λοπίδας . . . κεστρέων: 'scales of mullet'. On the grey mullet see Thompson *Fishes* 108–10. It has silvery scales, and an obol is a very small silver coin; so a mullet-scale might be mistaken for an obol at a superficial glance.

791 νέκαψ': 'popped them in my mouth', 'snapped them up'. Greeks had neither pockets nor a sense of oral hygiene, and so it was common to carry small change in the mouth; cf. 609, *Birds* 503, *Ek.* 818, fr. 3, 48. (What must the effect have been in an epidemic!) For the use of ἐγκάπτω in this connection cf. Alexis 128. 7; that line and *Wasps* 791 prove that the verb does not mean 'gulp down' (as LSJ and others say), for Philokleon did not wish to swallow his money. Contrast *Birds* 503, where ὀβολὸν κατεβρόχθισα does mean 'I swallowed an obol'.

792 βδελυχθείς: 'in disgust'.

793 εἷλκον: i.e. 'I tried to catch hold of him ⟨to stop him going away⟩', 'I collared him'.   δ τι; 48 n.

794 We should say 'the digestion of an ostrich'. Lysistratos expressed mock surprise that Philokleon had put the mullet-scales in his mouth, and pretended to think that he was trying to eat them.

795 ' "You do digest your money quickly!" said he.'   γοῦν: 217 n. καθέψεις: literally 'boil down'; there is no parallel for 'digest', but the extension of the verb to this sense is easy (cf. Latin 'concoquo'). For the redundant λέγων cf. *Birds* 472 ἔφασκε λέγων.

796 τοῦτο: the advantage of being paid individually.

797 Philokleon finally gives his consent to Bdelykleon's suggestion. μέλλεις: 'you intend'.

798 ταῦθ': Both here and in 806 Bdelykleon speaks as if he had mentioned some specific articles. Actually, although he has spoken vaguely of food and a fire, he has not given a precise list; we just have to assume from his general description of the private law-court that 'these things' means the equipment needed for the court. Neuter plural pronouns are sometimes used vaguely, referring to nouns which have to be understood from the context; cf. 859. [It is therefore probably unnecessary to postulate, as do P. J. Hoekstra *Quaestiones de Aristophanis Vespis* (1878) 73 and Wilamowitz 516, a lacuna either before or after ἀνάμενέ νυν. Reiske emended ταῦθ' to πάνθ', but that does not help 806.] Bdelykleon now goes into the house.

799 ὅρα τὸ χρῆμα: 'Just look at that!' The imperative is not addressed to any specific person; cf. E. Fraenkel 'Anreden an nur gedachte Zuhörer' (*Museum Helveticum* xxiv [1967] 190–3). λόγι': Predictions by oracles or prophets were commonly recorded or remembered, and circulated in writing or (as here) orally. Some men, called χρησμο-λόγοι, systematically collected them (or unscrupulously invented them), so as to make a living by revealing them to purchasers. (A comparison with modern sellers of racing tips may be suggestive, but must not be taken too seriously.) The outbreak of the Peloponnesian war increased the demand for such prophecies; cf. Th. 2. 8. 2 καὶ πολλὰ μὲν λόγια ἐλέγετο, πολλὰ δὲ χρησμολόγοι ᾖδον ἔν τε τοῖς μέλλουσι πολεμήσειν καὶ ἐν ταῖς ἄλλαις πόλεσιν. Ar. makes fun of prophecies and credulous acceptance of them in *Knights* (61, etc.), and of χρησμολόγοι in *Peace* 1043–1126, *Birds* 959–91 ; clearly he for one had little respect for them. For the distinction between λόγιον and χρησμός, which is minimal, see R. A. Neil's note on *Knights* 120. The prophecy in 800–4 is not a real and familiar one, but one invented by Ar. for Philokleon.

800 ἠκηκόειν: For the 1st singular pluperfect the mss. of Ar. present both the older termination -η (*Akh.* 10, *Birds* 511) and the newer -ειν (here, *Peace* 616, *Ek.* 32, 650). [There is no reason to impose consistency by emendation.]

802 προθύροις: the space in front of the door of a house. For the plural, used of the space before a single house, cf. Hdt. 6. 35. 2. **ἐνοικο-δομήσει:** For variation between future indicative and optative within a single indirect statement cf. Th. 2. 80. 1. [ἀνοικο- (RΓ) is unlikely to be right, since this compound usually means 'rebuild'.]

804 Ἑκαταῖον: A shrine or image of Hekate or Hermes or Apollon Agyieus (cf. 875) was often set up in the street in front of a house, because these were the deities of roads and travelling.

805 Bdelykleon, helped by some slaves (the verb in 815 is plural), brings various articles out of the house, and during the next few lines they are arranged to give an impression of a law-court. There is a seat for the presiding magistrate (Bdelykleon) and a seat for the jury (Philokleon). There may also be seats for the accuser, the accused, and the witnesses; alternatively these persons, when they enter, may stand or sit on the ground. There may be a platform or stand for speakers (905 n.) There are also some smaller items: a chamber-pot (807), a fire in a brazier (811), a bowl or saucepan of soup (811) with two cups (855, 906), and a cock in a cage (815, 934). When everything is in place, the slaves probably stand at the back or sides of the stage to watch the proceedings. **ἰδού:** 'There you are!' So also in 851, 1170. **τί ἔτ' ἐρεῖς;** i.e. 'what more can you want?' **ὡς:** 'since', explaining why Philokleon will have no more to say; or possibly 'I assure you', as in 416.

806 γ' shows that the relative clause is an explanation or amplification of ἅπαντ'; cf. 1268 and Denniston 138–40.

808 παρὰ σοί shows that Philokleon now takes his seat in some central position (or at least that it is now clear where he is going to sit). **ἐπὶ τοῦ παττάλου**: Bdelykleon hangs the pot on a peg projecting from the wall of the house (or possibly on a peg attached to one of the pieces of furniture just brought on). But there is a pun: ἐπί means both 'on' and 'near', and πάτταλος means both 'peg' and 'penis'; cf. *Ek.* 1020 and Karl Holzinger *De verborum lusu apud Aristophanem* (1876) 50–2.

811 προσ-: 'near' the fire, to keep warm.   **φακῆ**: 'soup' made from lentils (φακοί); this was regarded as a homely treat, enjoyed by ordinary people though despised by rich ones (*Wealth* 192, 1004, fr. 23).

812 ῥοφεῖν: the regular verb for eating soup from a bowl; cf. 814, 906, 982, *Peace* 716, etc.

815 ὄρνιν: a cock (934). A slave (not Bdelykleon; the verb is plural) brings it in a cage and hangs it on the wall or in some other elevated position (cf. 817 ἄνωθεν) near Philokleon.

816 γ': 'Why, . . .'; cf. Denniston 133.

818 τὸ τί; 'What is it?' as in *Clouds* 775, *Frogs* 7, 40, etc. The origin of the idiom is perhaps that the questioner, in his eagerness to hear the answer, himself supplies the article which is expected to be the beginning of it and then invites the other speaker to supply the noun: 'The —what?' In *Peace* 693 we find τὰ τί; That means that the noun is expected to be plural, but τί remains singular because the noun is expected to be a single word or expression (cf. *Clouds* 200 τί γὰρ τάδ' ἐστίν; 'What is the name of these things?'). (The alternative explanation, that τό is a demonstrative pronoun, so that the phrase means 'What is that?' seems less likely to be right, since then one would expect, sometimes at least, the order τί τό;)

819 Λύκου: 389 n. Philokleon thinks his court would look even more like a real one if the shrine of Lykos stood beside it. [Little attention need be paid to Herodian's version of this line; he attributes it to Eupolis, which shows that either he was only quoting from memory or his notes were confused in some way.]

820 Caught napping by Philokleon's unforeseen request, Bdelykleon has to improvise. He points to the altar (τουτί) which stands permanently in front of the house (cf. page 125); then he beckons (οὑτοσί) to one of the slaves who came out of the house at 805 and have been arranging the equipment (not Xanthias or Sosias, but a mute character), and makes him sit on the altar. Such, at least, is my guess; an improvised solution of this sort seems likelier than that Ar. had specially constructed for the occasion either a herm, as suggested by H. Comfort (*AJP* lii [1931] 362–9), or a shrine of Hekate, as suggested by L. A. Post (*AJP* liii [1932] 266).

821 'How hard it was to see you!' Philokleon falls to his knees in

reverence in front of the altar (cf. 824).   ἆρ' with imperfect (314 n.)
suggests that 'Lykos' has been present for some time but Philokleon
had not recognized him. Cf. *Peace* 819 ὡς χαλεπὸν ἐλθεῖν ἦν ἆρ' εὐθὺ
τῶν θεῶν. [The conjecture of L. A. Post (*AJP* liii [1932] 266) is preferable to B's conjecture χαλεπὸς ἆρ' ἦσθ', from which corruption to
χαλεπὸν would be unlikely.]

822 'He looks just like Kleonymos to *me*', i.e. he is very big (cf. 592) and
not at all hard to see. Presumably the slave impersonating Lykos is
very fat (i.e. the actor is grotesquely padded).   Κλεώνυμος: 19 n.

823 'Well admittedly, even though he is a hero, he too is unarmed.'
ὅπλα: a pun, as in 27 : the slave is wearing no phallos, and Kleonymos
threw away his shield. Philokleon, who is on his knees, looks up
between the legs of the slave sitting above him. [The attribution of
822–3 to speakers is muddled in the mss. The respectful address to
Lykos in 821 is clearly Philokleon's; so 822, which is a retort to the
statement that Lykos was hard to see, is Bdelykleon's; so 823, where
γ' implies that the line is a comment on 822 by a different speaker, is
Philokleon's again. There is no reason for making a slave speak here.]

825 ἐκάλουν: Either καλέω (cf. 851, 1441) or εἰσάγω (826, 840, 842, 847)
may be used of a presiding magistrate bringing a case before a court.
κάθημ' ἐγὼ πάλαι: another instance of the kind of joke in which
a character's words are exactly contrary to his actions (cf. 318–19).
Philokleon was seated at 808, but at 821 he left his seat to make his
obeisance to 'Lykos', so that at 824 he is not sitting, as Bdelykleon's
remark clearly shows. Now he rushes back to his seat.

826 αὐτῷ: Philokleon. Bdelykleon is soliloquizing.

828 Θρᾷττα: a slave named from her nationality (433 n.). Other slaves
called Θρᾷττα are mentioned in *Akh.* 273, *Peace* 1138, *Th.* 279–94, and
in other authors.

829 'Hi! Stop! You nearly killed me!' or as we say 'You'll be the death
of me!'   ὀλίγου as an adverb is simply an abbreviation of ὀλίγου
δεῖν, 'to lack little'; so also in *Akh.* 348, *Clouds* 722, etc.

830 δρυφάκτου: 386 n.

831 'Which was the first of our mysteries to be revealed'. At some
religious festivals, such as the Eleusinian Mysteries, part of the
ceremony consisted of the showing of certain sacred things to initiated
or privileged persons. Cf. *Th.* 628–9 (a test whether a person was
present at the Thesmophoria) σὺ δ' εἰπέ μοι ὅ τι πρῶτον ἡμῖν τῶν ἱερῶν
ἐδείκνυτο, and Pl. *Euthd.* 277 e (a metaphor from Korybantic initiation); those two passages show that πρῶτον does not mean 'most
important' but refers to the order of events in the ritual. Philokleon
regards the railing as the first of his sacred things because it was the
one he came to first when approaching the court.

834 'What's all the fuss? What a strange thing fondness for a place is!'
Philokleon has rushed into the house, leaving Bdelykleon soliloquizing.

This line covers the slight interval between Philokleon's exit and the slave's entrance (it would be awkward if both had to pass through the doorway in opposite directions at the same moment).

835 A slave comes out of the house, shouting over his shoulder at the dog, which remains out of sight inside. He is not named in the dialogue; I assume that he is Xanthias, but the audience would hardly care about his name or identity. The device of having a character shout back to someone inside when emerging from the house became common in New Comedy, e.g. Men. *Dys.* 206, 456, 546. βάλλ' ἐς κόρακας: i.e. 'Go to hell!' βάλλω is used intransitively. τρέφειν: infinitive of exclamation: 'Fancy keeping a dog like that!' Cf. *Clouds* 819 τὸν Δία νομίζειν ὄντα τηλικουτονί.

836 ἐτεόν: 8 n.   οὐ γὰρ . . .; 'Because, of course, . . .', 'Why, . . .', showing real or assumed surprise that the previous question needed to be asked. γάρ shows that this sentence explains why Xanthias is cursing and exclaiming (not, *pace* Denniston 79, why Bdelykleon asked his question), while οὐ . . .; (a question expecting the answer 'yes') implies that the explanation is obvious. Cf. 1299, *Akh.* 576, *Knights* 1392.   Λάβης: an invented name, a mixture of Λάχης and λαβεῖν. It implies that the dog represents Lakhes and that Lakhes is a thief, though the audience will hardly understand the full implication until Xanthias reaches the end of the sentence. Σ quotes Telekleides 23 for the similar dog's name Δάκης, from δακεῖν. For Lakhes, 240 n.

837 ὁ κύων: inserted only to make things clear to the audience; Bdelykleon would not really need to be told that Labes was the name of his own dog.   ἰπνὸν: 139 n. [The ι is short by nature (cf. 139, *Birds* 436, *Wealth* 815), and in comic iambic trimeters a naturally short vowel followed by a mute and a liquid consonant is usually scanned short, unless tragedy is being parodied. But there are exceptions (cf. *Birds* 45 καθιδρυθέντε, 820 ἀτεχνῶς), and so the lengthening here is not proof either that the line is meant to sound tragic or that it should be emended.]   ἁρπάσας: often used of dogs and other animals, e.g. *Akh.* 1160–1 κύων ἁρπάσασα φεύγοι.

838 τροφαλίδα: 'a cheese', from τρέφω in the sense 'curdle'.   Σικελικὴν: At this point the brighter members at least of the audience will realize that the dog's theft represents the peculation of which Lakhes was accused in Sicily. Cheese was regularly imported from Sicily; cf. Hermippos 63. 9, Antiphanes 236, Philemon 76.

839 ἄρα: equivalent to ἄρα, 'in that case', 'then'.

841 κύων: Those members of the audience who have already realized that Λάβης stands for Lakhes will no doubt realize here that κύων stands for Kleon. To the duller spectators all will become clear at 895. It is slightly forced that at this point the dog should already have expressed to Xanthias his willingness to prosecute; but Ar. and the

audience are both eager for the trial to begin without long-winded preliminaries.

842 τις: not 'anyone', implying doubt or ignorance of the person's identity, but the appropriate magistrate; in English we should probably use a passive verb. Cf. D. 21. 3 κατηγορήσων, ἐπειδή τις εἰσάγει, πάρειμι, where τις is the man actually presiding while Demosthenes is speaking. **εἰσάγη:** The aorist subjunctive might be expected for a single act, but cf. 847 εἴσαγ'. [Bergk's conjecture εἰσαγάγη is rightly rejected by C. W. Peppler (*AJP* liv [1933] 53).] **γραφήν:** 'prosecution', an ordinary public case.

843 ταῦτα χρὴ ποιεῖν: accepting the order: 'very good'. Xanthias goes into the house. Philokleon has just come out carrying a short piece of fence.

844 χοιροκομεῖον 'Εστίας: 'the household pig-pen'. One or more pigs would be kept in a pen in the yard for domestic use, and when one was slaughtered it would be a sacrifice to Hestia, the goddess of the household. Cf. Kallimakhos 6. 108 καὶ τὰν βῶν ἔφαγεν, τὰν 'Εστίᾳ ἔτρεφε μάτηρ. It might seem enough for Philokleon to say χοιροκομεῖον, but 'Εστίας is added to lead to the joke in 845–6. (This interpretation, which is that of Wilamowitz 518 n. 1, seems likelier than the view that pigs wandered freely into the house and had to be kept off the hearth by a fence.)

845–6 Bdelykleon suggests that it is an insult to Hestia to remove her pen. But Philokleon retorts that his intention is, on the contrary, to pay her a compliment. **ἀφ' 'Εστίας ἀρχόμενος:** a proverbial metaphor for beginning from the beginning, because in a prayer to a number of gods it was customary to pray to Hestia first; cf. *Birds* 865 for the order of a prayer, and Pl. *Euthph.* 3 a for the metaphorical use. Philokleon is making a kind of pun, by using the expression at the same time metaphorically and literally. **ἐπιτρίψω:** 'squash' by condemnation.

847 τιμᾶν βλέπω: 'I have my eye on awarding a penalty.' For the infinitive with βλέπω cf. *Akh.* 376 οὐδὲν βλέπουσιν ἄλλο πλὴν ψηφηδακεῖν, Alexis 97 ὀρχεῖσθαι μόνον βλέποντες.

848 σανίδας: 349 n. **γραφάς:** 'notices of prosecution', 'charge statements'. γραφή is more often the abstract 'prosecution'; for its use for the physical document cf. D. 18. 53.

849 Bdelykleon goes into the house once more, while Philokleon addresses his departing back. **διατρίβεις κἀπολεῖς:** 'You're wasting time, and you'll be the death of me.'

850 'I've been longing to make a furrow in my space.' He is playing on the words; they could mean 'plough my farm', but Philokleon has no farm; his 'space' (LSJ χωρίον 5) is the space on his voting-tablet (106 n.) and his furrow is a long line in the wax. Cf. *Th.* 782, where αὖλαξ, 'furrow', is used of a line drawn on a wax-tablet. [Bentley's conjecture κηρίον reduces the ambiguity, but is perhaps unnecessary. Philokleon may make his point clearer to the audience than it appears to the reader, by making a gesture of drawing a line.]

851 ἰδού: 'Here they are!' Bdelykleon returns with some flat pieces of wood, on which notices of prosecution are supposed to be written, and hangs them up on the wall.   κάλει: 'Call the case!'   ταῦτα δή: 'Very well'; cf. 142, 1008. Philokleon peers at the notices on the wall, but before he has made out the first name Bdelykleon's next remark distracts him. [The attribution of 851–62 to speakers has been satisfactorily established by J. C. B. Lowe (*Hermes* xcv [1967] 53–6). Bdelykleon is the person who is expected to provide all the equipment, and Philokleon the one who is impatient to begin the proceedings.]

852 ἐς κόρακας: not, as usually, 'To hell with you!' but just 'Dash it!' Bdelykleon is annoyed only with himself.

853 καδίσκους: 94 n. He starts hurrying towards the house again.

854 ἐπί: 'to fetch'.

855 εἶχον: imperfect because he has had them on the stage since 805, but we should say 'have' or 'have got'.   ἀρυστίχους: small jugs or cups, used for drawing (ἀρύω) liquids from larger containers; they were brought with the bowl of soup (811, cf. 906).

856 κάλλιστα τοίνυν: 'That's fine, then.'

857 πλήν γε δή: Bdelykleon suddenly notices another omission, and in his annoyance combines two emphasizing particles. This is the only instance in Ar. of γε δή together (though γέ τοι δή also occurs). κλεψύδρας: 93 n.

858 ἡδί: the pot (807): when it is full, the case will have lasted long enough.   τίς: One would expect τί. If τίς is right, it has been attracted to the gender of the preceding ἡδί.

859 αὐτά: 'the things' generally, not just the voting-urns and water-clock. For the vague use of the pronoun cf. 798. [Meineke's πάντα is unnecessary.]   ἐπιχωρίως: 'in the Athenian manner'; cf. *Clouds* 1173–6. The Athenians thought themselves shrewd and quick-witted.

860–90 *A sacrifice is made to Apollon as a prelude to the trial. The chorus pray for the success of the private court, and Bdelykleon prays that his father may become less hard-hearted and more lenient to accused men.*

The interruption of the action by a sacrifice at this point is surprising. J. H. Lipsius *Das attische Recht* (1915) 904 drew the conclusion that a sacrifice always preceded the introduction of cases in an Athenian court. But there is no other evidence for such a ceremony in the ordinary courts (the Areopagos and the other special homicide courts, with their religious connections, are a different matter), while 824–5, 851, 891–2 imply that normally nothing intervened between the arrival of the jurors and the introduction of the first case. So it seems possible that Ar., after writing the rest of 760–1008, decided that such a long scene needed a musical interlude in the middle to entertain those members of the audience who preferred song to talk, and thought that a sacrifice was the most convenient way of providing it.

The effect of the prayer is comic, because formal religious language (e.g. 875) is used to introduce quaint requests like 'Mix a bit of honey in his dear little heart' (878). Cf. H. Kleinknecht *Die Gebetsparodie in der Antike* (1937) 52–3.

Metre:

860–2: iambic trimeters, providing a transition from the preceding dialogue.

863–7: anapaests.

868–9: iambic trimeters. In 869 the chorus-leader invokes Apollon in a spoken line, and in 870, continuing the same sentence, his colleagues join him in singing the plea; cf. 728–9. (869 must be a spoken trimeter, not part of the following lyric iambics, because the responding line 886 is spoken: 886 contains two anapaests, which would be very unusual in lyric iambics.)

870–3: a very short iambo-dochmiac song; see the scheme below.

874: a ritual cry to Apollon, outside the metre.

875–84: four anapaestic tetrameters, followed by a run of anapaests.

885–6: iambic trimeters.

887–90: iambo-dochmiac antistrophe to 870–3.

The iambo-dochmiac metre of 870–3 and 887–90 is similar to that of 733–5 and 747–9. In the following scheme *ba* means an iambic metron shortened to ∪ – – (i.e. catalectic, with a pause after it; observe the hiatus between 870 and 871).

$$
\begin{array}{lll}
870, 887 & ia\ ba\ \| \\
871, 888 & ia\ ia \\
872, 889 & ia\ ia \\
873, 890 & doch
\end{array}
$$

860 ἀλλ' marks a breaking off from the preceding conversation. Bdelykleon speaks to the slaves standing at the back of the stage. The slave sitting on the altar (820 n.) will naturally take this opportunity of getting off it.   **πῦρ**: The sacrifice will consist of burning incense on the altar; cf. *Frogs* 871–2 ἴθι νυν λιβανωτὸν δεῦρό τις καὶ πῦρ δότω, ὅπως ἂν εὔξωμαι. The fire might have been obtained from the brazier near Philokleon (811), but in a performance of the play it would be quicker and more practical to have a flame ready off-stage for a slave to bring it straight out of the house to the altar.

861 μυρρίνας: Bdelykleon will wear a myrtle-wreath while making the sacrifice, and perhaps Philokleon, the chorus, and the slaves too. Cf. *Th.* 36–8 ἐξέρχεται θεράπων τις αὐτοῦ πῦρ ἔχων καὶ μυρρίνας προθυσό-μενος.   **τὸν** means that the slave is to bring the household stock of incense, in its box or jar.

862 εὐξώμεσθα τοῖς θεοῖς: probably an exact quotation from the regular language of ritual; cf. *Birds* 903, Makhon 136 (with Gow's note).

During 863–7 one or more slaves bring the fire and incense to Bdelykleon at the altar, and distribute myrtle-wreaths.

864 ἐπί: 'for', 'in connection with'. **σπονδαῖς**: 'reconciliation' between Philokleon and Bdelykleon; cf. 866–7.

865 φήμην ἀγαθήν: 'an auspicious utterance', i.e. a prayer. [**λέξομεν**: ἔξομεν (R^{ac}V) may possibly be right, with the meaning 'we shall make', as in S. *Ai.* 564 δυσμενῶν θήραν ἔχων and similar periphrastic expressions.]

868 A call for silence was the usual beginning of a religious ceremony. [Dindorf gave this line to the chorus in his earliest edition, and this was followed by some other editors, though he himself later rightly restored it to Bdelykleon. Bdelykleon is conducting the sacrifice, and so is clearly the person to call for silence. Cf. *Akh.* 237, *Birds* 959, *Th.* 295.] During 869–90 Bdelykleon performs the ceremony of burning the incense on the altar.

869 ἐπ': 'for', 'to bring'.

870 τὸ πρᾶγμ': the holding of a private law-court.

872 ἁρμόσαι: 'guide', jussive infinitive; 386n.

873 παυσαμένοις πλάνων: The jurors who form the chorus hope all to have their own private courts, so that they may stay at home while trying cases, like Philokleon.

875 γεῖτον: Apollon is Bdelykleon's neighbour because the altar stands near his house. Cf. Plautus *Bacchides* 172–3 'saluto te, uicine Apollo, qui aedibus propinquus nostris accolis'.

Ἀγυιεῦ: 'god of streets'. Apollon Agyieus, like Hermes and Hekate (cf. 804), was frequently represented in front of houses in the streets of Athens by a pointed stone pillar (Σ *Wasps* 875 κίονας εἰς ὀξὺ λήγοντας ὡς ὀβελίσκους, Σ E. *Ph.* 631). There are also references to altars (βωμοί) to Apollon Agyieus in front of houses (S. fr. 370, *IG* ii² 4719, Phot. Λοξίας), and some authorities mention both the altar and the pillar, but without making clear what was the connection between them (Harp. ἀγυιᾶς, *Souda* a 383, Eust. 166. 22–5). But two are explicit. Hskh. a 856 says that the pillar and the altar were the same thing: ἀγυιεύς· ὁ πρὸ τῶν θυρῶν ἑστὼς βωμὸς ἐν σχήματι κίονος. Helladios, as reported in Phot. *Bibl.* cod. 279. 535b (Migne *Patrologia Graeca* civ 324), clearly distinguishes the altar from the image of Apollon: τὸν Λοξίαν γὰρ προσεκύνουν, ὃν πρὸ τῶν θυρῶν ἕκαστος ἱδρύοντο, καὶ πάλιν βωμὸν παρ' αὐτῷ στρογγύλον ποιοῦντες. Either Hesykhios or Helladios must be wrong. The fact that incense was burnt (*Wasps* 861, S. fr. 370) seems to show that there was a horizontal surface. C. A. Rhomaios (*BCH* xlix [1925] 212) argues that the conical pillar had a flat top; but such pillars could not be called κίονας εἰς ὀξὺ λήγοντας ὡς ὀβελίσκους. It therefore seems likely that the

I

flat-topped altar was a separate object from the pointed pillar, as Helladios says. But Helladios is perhaps wrong in calling the altar round, since a quadrangular shape is indicated by *IG* ii² 4850, Σ Ar. *Th.* 489.

In the theatre the altar standing on the stage was regularly regarded as an altar of Apollon Agyieus; cf. Pol. 4. 123 ἐπὶ δὲ τῆς σκηνῆς καὶ ἀγυιεὺς ἔκειτο βωμὸς ὁ πρὸ τῶν θυρῶν, and P. D. Arnott *Greek Scenic Conventions* 45. But there is no evidence that the stage house, as distinct from real houses, also had a pointed pillar in front of it.

τοῦ 'μοῦ προθύρου προπύλαιε: No distinction in meaning between θύρα and πύλη is intended here. 'The standing-before-the-door god of the space before *my* door' is simply 'the god standing before my door'.

876 τελετήν: 'rite', a religious metaphor for Philokleon's private trials. καινοτομοῦμεν: 'open up', a metaphor from mining. This seems to be its earliest instance, but it recurs in *Ek.* 584–6 and becomes common in the fourth century.

877 [λίαν: There is no other place in Ar. where the ι must be short. But since it is sometimes short in tragedy, and this is a solemn (or mock-solemn) religious passage, there is no need to emend.]   πρίνινον: cf. 383 πρινώδη.

878 ἀντὶ σιραίου: 'instead of in condensed wine', 'as in condensed wine'. σίραιον was new wine boiled down. It was sweet anyway (cf. Pol. 6. 16 σίραιον δ' ἐκάλουν τὸν ἐκ γλεύκους ἡψημένον γλυκύν) ; adding a little bit of honey would make it very sweet indeed—and that is how sweet Bdelykleon wants Philokleon to be. For ἀντί meaning 'just like' cf. *Knights* 364, *Ek.* 1111, D. 17. 3 δουλεύειν ἀντὶ τῶν ἀργυρωνήτων. The phrase has been fully discussed by V. Coulon (*Rev. Ét. Gr.* xlix [1936] 419–26).   [σμικρὸν (ΓJ) rather than μικρὸν (RV): 5 n.]   θυμιδίῳ: 'dear little heart'; this diminutive form occurs nowhere else and may have been invented by Ar. for comic effect.

879–81 'Let him now be gentle to people, and pity the defendants rather than the prosecutors, and weep when they entreat him.' The accusative and infinitives are jussive; 386 n.   ἀντιβολούντων: genitive absolute.

884 ἀκαλήφην: 'nettle', or possibly 'sea-anemone' (as in *Lys.* 549), but in either case a metaphor for 'sting', 'prickliness'.

885–6 'We join in this prayer with you, and we sing a song for your new government, because of what you have said.'

[890 γε νεωτέρων: γενναιοτέρων (a) will not match the metre of 873. Σᵛ comments εἰ μὲν γενναιοτέρων, τῶν σπουδαίων· εἰ δὲ νεωτέρων, τῶν ὁμηλίκων, showing awareness of both readings.]

By the end of the song the sacrifice is finished. The slaves collect the myrtle-wreaths; perhaps one of them takes the wreaths back into the house while the others continue to stand or sit at the back or sides of the stage.

891–1008 *The trial of the dog Labes is held. A speech for the prosecution is made by a dog of Kydathenaion. When the time comes for Labes to defend himself he can say nothing, and so instead Bdelykleon speaks in his defence, and calls a cheese-grater to give evidence and Labes's puppies to arouse the sympathy of the jury—that is, of Philokleon. Philokleon remains hostile to Labes, but when the time comes for him to vote Bdelykleon tricks him into putting his vote into the wrong urn, and so Labes is acquitted. Philokleon is overcome with consternation, but Bdelykleon consoles him.*

This masterly scene achieves several different objects simultaneously: it satirizes the conduct of Athenian trials; it satirizes the dispute between Kleon and Lakhes; it provides some entertaining farce; and it advances the story of the cure of Philokleon.

The principal weakness of Athenian trials, the prejudice and irresponsibility of the jurors, is shown by Philokleon's attitude and comments. Even before the parties appear, he has made up his mind that the accused will be convicted (893); he judges Labes's guilt from his facial expression (900); he believes all that is said against the accused and disbelieves all that is said in his favour. The motives of prosecutors are attacked too: the dog's speech reveals that his motives in bringing the case are not patriotic but selfish. But the best part of the satire of the Athenian legal system is the speech for the defence, making fun of a whole series of tricks which were the stock-in-trade of Athenian forensic orators: the recounting of past services to the state as reasons for excusing the present offence (952–9); the completely irrelevant excuse (959); the personal attack on the prosecutor (970–2); the attempts to arouse pity, culminating in calling up the accused's weeping children (976–8).

In the satirical treatment of Kleon and Lakhes, the dog of Kydathenaion, representing Kleon, comes off far the worse. He is represented as a loud barker: his very first utterance is a meaningless bark (903), and it is significant that he is able to present his own case, whereas Labes is not. He claims to do good service to Athens (915), but in fact the only service he performs is that of a watch-dog who leaves the hard work to others (929–30, 970–2), and he is really just as selfish and thieving himself as he accuses his opponent of being (903–4, 928). Lakhes is more leniently treated. He is a good soldier and general, who fights in defence of Athens (952–7), and if he is not good at defending himself verbally, that is not to be held against him (946–8). But Ar. does not believe him to be innocent; he plainly regards him as guilty of theft (958; cf. 836–8).

Ar. is very careful to ensure that even the dullest members of the audience do not fail to follow the political allegory throughout the trial. Sometimes the accuser and the accused are actually called 'men' (918, 923, 933, 1000), and constantly, among all the talk of dogs and cheese, words like 'the state' (917), 'the soldiers' (965),

'sailing round' (924), and 'make out his accounts' (961) are slipped in
to remind us to think also of the politician and the general.

Yet, with all this, the scene is not overweighted by its serious
political implications, since plenty of comic relief is provided by
Philokleon's interruptions and antics, culminating in his horrified
collapse (995). And the plot of the play is forwarded at the same time;
for the domestic trial, and especially the involuntary experience of
voting for an acquittal, is a further stage in the process of curing
Philokleon of his disease.

891 Bdelykleon acts as the presiding magistrate, and pretends that there
is a full-size jury, instead of just Philokleon; so also in 894, 907–8, etc.
[ἡλιαστής rather than ἡ-: 195 n.]

893 ἆρ': equivalent to ἄρα, just adding liveliness to the question, like ἄρ'
in 143, 266. (Denniston 45–6 is muddled; in *Peace* 1240 there is an
inferential connection, but not in *Wasps* 893.)   ὁ φεύγων οὗτος:
'this defendant', meaning the defendant in this case, for whom all
these preparations have been made. [The line has been well explained
by J. C. B. Lowe (*Hermes* xcv [1967] 56–9). Dobree suggested making
οὗτος Bdelykleon's answer to τίς ἆρ' ὁ φεύγων; but that cannot be
right. It is only in 899 that Labes appears and Bdelykleon points him
out. The question in 893 is answered adequately by 894–7.]

894 ἐγράψατο: 'prosecuted', aorist because referring to the time when
the charge was made. This verb takes an external accusative of the
person prosecuted. The charge may be added as an internal accusative (e.g. 907–8), or the offence may be expressed by an infinitive, as
by ἀδικεῖν here; cf. *Peace* 107–8 γράψομαι Μήδοισιν αὐτὸν προδιδόναι τὴν
Ἑλλάδα. The same range of constructions is used with other verbs of
prosecution; e.g. D. 21. 1 προυβαλόμην ἀδικεῖν τοῦτον, 21. 28 τοῦτο γὰρ
αὐτὸν ἐγὼ προυβαλόμην.

For the general form of this document cf. the ἀντιγραφή read out in
D. 45. 46, which begins: Ἀπολλόδωρος Πασίωνος Ἀχαρνεὺς Στεφάνῳ
Μενεκλέους Ἀχαρνεῖ ψευδομαρτυρίων. τίμημα τάλαντον.

895 Κύων: 'Dog' is treated as a proper name to make a pun on 'Kleon'.
Κυδαθηναιεὺς: Kleon belonged to Kydathenaion (cf. *IG* ii² 1138.
23–6), a deme of the Pandionis tribe, situated near the centre of
Athens. Since all the audience will have known that, this reference
finally makes clear to the dullest that the prosecuting dog represents
him.   **Λάβητ'**: For the comic name, 836 n. For Lakhes and his dispute with Kleon, 240 n.   **Αἰξωνέα**: Lakhes belonged to Aixone (Pl.
La. 197 c), a deme of the Kekropis tribe. It was situated on the coast
eight miles south of Athens, south-west of mount Hymettos; cf.
C. W. J. Eliot *Coastal Demes of Attika* (1962) 6–21.

896 ἀδικεῖν: Officials undergoing examination of their financial conduct
could be accused of three kinds of offence: embezzlement (κλοπή),
corruption (δῶρα), and 'malefaction' (ἀδίκιον). ἀδίκιον is a **vague**

term, but since the penalty specified for it in Arist. *Ath. Pol.* 54. 2 (simple restitution of the amount of the offence) is much less than for the other two (tenfold restitution), it probably means only depriving the state of money by culpable neglect or inadvertence, as opposed to deliberate deception. But that does not suit the case of Labes, who is accused of deliberately stealing the cheese. Therefore the charge against him, if it were strictly defined, would be one of κλοπή, not of ἀδίκιον, and ἀδικεῖν here should not be regarded as a technical term. For the present tense, 591 n. Translate: '. . . accused Labes of Aixone of an offence in that he ate up the Sicilian cheese . . .'.

Even if Dog's prosecution of Labes is a γραφὴ κλοπῆς (and Ar. does not say this explicitly), that does not prove that Kleon prosecuted Lakhes by a γραφὴ κλοπῆς. In fact Lakhes's εὔθυναι for his generalship in Sicily must have been completed at least two years before the performance of *Wasps*, and since he was not a general in 424/3 he cannot have been ὑπεύθυνος in 423/2 (cf. 240 n.). But Ar. does not care about this kind of legal detail; since Kleon often prosecuted men who were ὑπεύθυνοι, and since he had recently been saying that Lakhes made money out of his generalship in Sicily, it is fun to imagine him prosecuting Lakhes in this way.

μόνος: Dog's motive for complaint is that Labes did not give him a share of the booty; cf. 914.

897 'Penalty: a fig-wood collar.' A collar, because that is an appropriate penalty for a dog; fig-wood, to make a pun on συκοφάντης (cf. 145), implying that Kleon prosecuted for malicious or selfish reasons.

898 μὲν οὖν: 'No, . . .'; Philokleon thinks he can improve on the penalty proposed. 'A dog's death' is a phrase for a horrible death (Hskh. κ 4571), and the joke is that an expression usually metaphorical is here applied literally to a dog. For other jokes of this type cf. 191, 783.

899 καὶ μὴν . . . οὑτοσί . . . πάρα: 'And here is . . .' An actor dressed as a dog comes out of the house. Whether he also has something in his dress or mask to suggest Lakhes, I do not know. This actor is just a super; he has no lines to speak.

900 ὦ μιαρὸς οὗτος: exclamation, not vocative (cf. 187): 'What a scoundrel he is!'   καί is used in an exclamation or question to stress the following word; cf. Denniston 316. 'What a *thieving* look he has!' κλέπτον βλέπει: Instead of a noun (as in 455, 643) the internal accusative is here a neuter participle; cf. E. *Alk.* 773 πεφροντικὸς βλέπεις. [Some editors read κλεπτόν, which may be right; but there is no evidence for an adjective κλεπτός except this line and 933, and adjectives in -τός are usually passive.]

901 σεσηρὼς: This perfect (from σαίρω) regularly has a present sense. 'How he grins and . . .!' (C. H. Whitman *Aristophanes and the Comic Hero* 154 suggests that the verb can mean 'make a clean sweep'. σαίρω does mean 'sweep' literally, but I know no parallel for this metaphorical sense.)

902 γε, if right, emphasizes ὁ διώκων, in contrast to the accused: 'But where's the *prosecutor*?' [Other possible emendations: ποῦ δ' ἔσθ' ὁ Toup, ποῦ 'στὶν ὁ Dobree, ποῦ ποῦ 'σθ' ὁ Dobree, ποῦ μοὐ (crasis for μοι ὁ, as in *Knights* 1237) Dindorf. ποῦ δ' οὐκδιώκων, proposed by Flor. Chrest., is attractive, but there is no parallel for ἐκδιώκω in the sense 'prosecute'. Reiske's ποῦ δ' αὖ ὁ involves either hiatus or correption or synizesis of a type not exactly paralleled in iambic trimeters.]

903 With loud barks the prosecuting dog (Dog of Kydathenaion) comes out of the house and takes up a position on the opposite side of the court to Labes. This dog must be played by a speaking actor.   **ἕτερος . . .:** 'This is a second Labes', referring to the derivation from λαβεῖν, i.e. 'This dog is just as thievish as the other'.

904 'Very good at barking and at licking pots clean' is sarcastic, implying 'Good for nothing except . . .'.   **διαλείχειν:** cf. *Knights* 1034, also referring to Kleon. [Coulon (*Rev. Ét. Gr.* xlix [1936] 408 n. 5) and Lowe (*Hermes* xcv [1967] 59–65) rightly give the whole line to Philokleon, for whom the cynical sarcasm is in character. γ' just emphasizes ἀγαθός and does not mark a change of speaker. David Barrett in his translation makes Philokleon pat Dog and give him a plate of soup, and then say 'There, there now, quite a different kind of dog. Not like nasty Labes, eh? Knows how to bark and lick the plates, doesn't-um?' This interpretation is attractive, because it gives more point to διαλείχειν τὰς χύτρας and to 906 κἀγώ, but its drawback is that it must involve (though Barrett does not say so) emendation of αὖ in 903 to ἦ or οὐ.]

905 σίγα, κάθιζε: addressed to Philokleon. κάθιζε shows that he has left his seat and has been walking around looking at the two dogs.   **σὺ:** Dog of Kydathenaion.   **ἀναβὰς:** ἀναβαίνω is the regular word for mounting a platform or stand to deliver a speech, just as leaving it at the end of a speech is καταβαίνω (cf. 979). Something to stand on may have been brought on to the stage at 805; but not necessarily, since Bdelykleon may be just pretending that the private court has the same equipment as a real one.

906 τήνδ': the soup (811). Philokleon has resumed his seat, and while the dog is speaking he pours some soup into one of the cups (855) and eats it.   **κἀγώ:** καί reinforces ἅμα: 'while *he* is speaking, let *me* have my soup'.

907 [In some mss. this and subsequent speeches of Dog are attributed to a slave speaking on Dog's behalf. This must be wrong, because in 916 the speaker calls himself the dog, and in 841–2 Xanthias said that the dog would conduct the prosecution.]   **μὲν** has no corresponding δέ, as often at the beginning of a speech; cf. Denniston 383.

909 τὸ ῥυππαπαῖ: 'the yo-ho-ho'. ῥυππαπαῖ was a sailors' cry (cf. *Frogs* 1072), which Ar. has here turned into a comic collective noun for 'sailors'; cf. Alexis 206 τῶν βαβαὶ βαβαί. The Athenian navy was manned by citizens of the poorest class, and it was they who gave Kleon the most support.

910 τὴν γωνίαν: the corner of the kitchen. (Attempts to show that Sicily is in a corner of the Greek world are far-fetched and misguided.)

911 κατεσικέλιζε: 'he began to Sicilize down', a comic coinage.

913 'He just gave a horrible belch of cheese over me.' This shows that Labes is standing or sitting somewhere near Philokleon. ἐνερεύγομαι is given an internal accusative (cf. 1151) and descriptive genitive, like ὄζω (38).

914 κοὐ μετέδωκ' αἰτοῦντί μοι: Ar. alleges that Kleon demanded bribes from other politicians, threatening with punishment those who refused; cf. Knights 65–9 (671 n.).

916 προβάλλῃ: the usual verb for throwing scraps of food to dogs or other animals; e.g. Birds 626, Hdt. 9. 112. The sentence implies 'I'm the only competent watch-dog you have; if I'm not fed you'll have no one to look after you at all'. In Knights 1017–24 also Ar. makes Kleon claim to be a dog who barks for the people and so deserves their protection in return.

917 τῷ κοινῷ γ', ἐμοί: 'to the state—that is, to me'. Philokleon identifies himself with the δῆμος, because an Athenian jury was regarded as equivalent to the whole nation; this is illustrated by the way in which speakers in law-court cases use ὑμεῖς for 'Athens' even when referring to events in which no member of the present jury took part. [That is one reason why Tyrwhitt was right to allot this line to Philokleon. Another is that οὐδέ, 'and not ... either', shows that ἐμοί here must be someone different from μοι in 914. οὐδὲν μετέδωκεν must go with οὐδὲ ... ἐμοί; taken by itself, or appended to 914–16, it would be a pointless repetition of κοὐ μετέδωκ' in 914.]

918 'The man's hot-headed—as hot as this soup.'

921 αὐτὸ γὰρ βοᾷ: 'the case speaks for itself', needing no advocate or witness; cf. Knights 204 αὐτό που λέγει, D. 19. 81 τὰ πεπραγμέν' αὐτὰ βοᾷ. Here 'shouts' is specially appropriate because of Dog's (Kleon's) loud voice.

922 ὡς ὄντ' αὖ: 'since he is, secondly'. αὖ (28 n.) provides an amusing touch of satire of speakers who produce the same argument over again as if it were a new one.

923 κυνῶν ... ἄνδρα: The literal and allegorical aspects of the trial are comically confused. Some words in the sentence apply to Lakhes (ἄνδρα, περιπλεύσας, πόλεων), others only to Labes (κυνῶν, μονοφαγίστατον, θυείαν, σκῖρον, ἐξεδήδοκεν). **μονοφαγίστατον:** 'most solitary-eating', 'lone-eating-est'. The superlative occurs nowhere else and may be a comic invention; but ὀψοφαγίστατος was a normal Attic word (X. Apom. 3. 13. 4, Pol. 6. 37).

924 θυείαν: 'bowl', a large receptacle for mixing food. On the difference between θυεία and ὅλμος see L. A. Moritz *Grain-mills and Flour in*

Classical Antiquity (1958) 22. It would be one of the biggest and least moved objects in an ordinary Athenian kitchen, and so is regarded as a fixed point in the account of the dog's tactical movements. [Some have wanted to give the word a second sense, applying to Lakhes. Σ^Γ takes it as a pun on θάλασσαν, which is far-fetched. Some modern editors say it stands for Sicily because Sicily is shaped like it: a 'mortar' with a narrow base and a wide top might look triangular in profile, and Athenians, even if ignorant of geography, knew that Sicily was triangular, for Τρινακρία was another name for it. But this is over-subtle. θυείαν has no more application to Lakhes than πόλεων to Labes; the sentence is a comic combination of words applicable only to one or the other.]

925 ἐκ τῶν πόλεων implies that Lakhes received payments from Sicilian cities, perhaps as contributions to the maintenance of the Athenian fleet; cf. H. D. Westlake in *Historia* ix (1960) 394 n. 37. σκίρον: 'cheese-rind'; the reason why Ar. uses this word instead of another for 'cheese' is to make the rather feeble pun in 926, since σκίρος means 'cement', 'plaster of Paris'.

926 'Yes, but I haven't enough even to mend my water-jar.' πλάσαι: consecutive infinitive: 'mend', not 'make', because τὴν shows that the jar already exists.

928 κλέπτα: substituted for 'robins' in the proverb οὐ τρέφει μία λόχμη δύο ἐριθάκους (quoted by Σ).

929 κεκλάγγω: 'bark'; the perfect of κλάζω often has a present sense. διὰ κενῆς ἄλλως: 'in vain and to no purpose'; cf. Pl. com. 174. 20–1 μάτην . . . διὰ κενῆς.

930 is intended by Dog as a dreadful threat, but Ar. means it to be comic; he would be delighted if Kleon did stop barking. Dog here concludes his speech and sits down.

931 ἰοὺ ἰού: 'Whew!'

933 'What a thieving thing the man is!' τὸ χρῆμα is common in exclamations; cf. 799, *Birds* 826 λιπαρὸν τὸ χρῆμα τῆς πόλεως, *Clouds* 2 (with Dover's note), and L. Bergson in *Eranos* lxv (1967) 79–117.

934 For the cock cf. 815. ἐπι- implies agreement, as in ἐπινεύω.

935 ὁ θεσμοθέτης: nominative instead of vocative, as often when someone is formally called on to perform an official duty; e.g. *Akh.* 54 οἱ τοξόται. For the thesmothetai, 775 n. At this trial the presiding thesmothetes is Bdelykleon, but evidently he has left his seat at the end of Dog's speech to organize the appearance of the witnesses; he is probably at the door of the house. ἀμίδα: cf. 807. After 936 Philokleon leaves his seat, takes the pot down from its peg, and uses it.

937 Bdelykleon now resumes his seat and formally (in a jussive accusative and infinitive: 386 n.) orders the witnesses to appear. They come out of the house and take their places in the court as he names them:

a cup, a pestle, a cheese-grater, a fireplace, and a kitchen-pot, followed by other kitchen utensils. The most effective way of handling this passage in performance would clearly be to have them all played by mute actors; and since in this play and other plays Ar. used human performers for dogs, birds, clouds, and so on, there is no reason why he should not have used human performers for kitchen utensils. The alternative is to suppose that the various objects are carried into the court by slaves, but that would make the performance, especially of 963–6, more awkward and less effective.

938 ἐσχάραν: 'fireplace'. In *Akh.* 888 the word means a portable brazier, and it could do so here, but need not; if the pestle and the cheese-grater can stand up and walk out of the kitchen, it is pedantic to object to the fireplace's doing so too.

939 προσκεκαυμένα: 'burnt'. But there is a pun: we expect προσκεκλη-μένα, 'summoned' (this verb is used of summoning witnesses in D. 29. 20, 43. 38, Pl. *Laws* 936 e), but instead Bdelykleon substitutes a word appropriate to kitchen utensils.

940 καθίζεις: He means 'Haven't you resumed your place?' but Philokleon, still using the pot, misinterprets him.

941 '⟨No, I'm not sitting,⟩ but I think *he*'ll be suffering from nervous diarrhoea very shortly.'   τοῦτον: Labes, stressed by γ' to make a contrast with the previous line.

943 καὶ ταῦτα implies that it is worse to be hostile to accused men, who are being attacked anyway, than to accusers.   ὀδὰξ ἔχει: 'are you holding on to them with your teeth?'

944 As Philokleon returns to his seat he makes some contemptuous gesture by way of reply to Bdelykleon. So Bdelykleon sighs or shrugs his shoulders, and he next turns to Labes and calls on him to make his defence. Labes takes up his position (on the platform, if there is one), but then says nothing at all.

947 Thoukydides son of Melesias was a leading opponent of Perikles until he was ostracized in 443. The trial referred to here is obviously the same as the one described in *Akh.* 703–12, where Thoukydides's inability to defend himself adequately against Kephisodemos and Euathlos is given as an example of the unfairness of the prosecution of old men by young men. (The inability to defend himself links the two passages, and makes it reasonable to rule out the possibility that *Wasps* 947 refers to the trial of Thucydides the historian in 424/3.) Euathlos (592 n.) and Kephisodemos were συνήγοροι (*Akh.* 705, 715: cf. fr. 411), presumably of type *B* (482 n.), and so probably Thoukydides had held some office and was convicted of financial misconduct. Since he was old at the time, the trial must have been not before his ostracism but after his return in 433; but it was before *Akh.* was performed at the Lenaia of 425, and so it may be assigned to one of the years 432–426.

948 τὰς γνάθους limits ἀπόπληκτος: 'paralysed in the jaws', 'struck dumb'.

949 πάρεχ': 'make way', as in 1326. Labes leaves the speaker's place, which is taken by Bdelykleon; his speech in defence of Labes lasts from 950 tυ 981. In real Athenian courts it was common for an accused person to have one or more others to speak in his support, but such supporters did not speak until the accused himself had spoken first.

950 διαβεβλημένου: 'slandered', 'falsely accused', a common word in speeches for the defence.

953 μὲν οὖν: 'on the contrary'.   ξυνωμότης: 345 n.

955 'Able to take charge of many sheep.'   τε has usually been regarded as connective. But elsewhere Ar. uses οἷός τε, not οἷος alone, with an infinitive, and so it seems preferable here to take οἷός τε together as 'able'; then the reason for the absence of a connective particle will be that οἷός τε . . . ἐφεστάναι is an amplification of ἄριστος, not a fresh point.   προβατίοις: cf. 31–6.

958 εἰ δ' ὑφείλετο: 'if he did steal'. Here 'if' is virtually equivalent to 'although'; Bdelykleon admits that Labes is guilty, but asks for pardon nevertheless. A modern jury would be bound to find a man guilty if they believed him to have stolen. But in Athens, if a jury believed that a man had committed an offence and yet for some reason did not deserve to be punished, their proper course was to acquit him. And past services to the state were often accepted as compensation for an offence; it was possible, as we see from surviving speeches, for an accused man to argue that the good which he had done to the state in the past was greater than the harm which he had done it on this occasion. (Lys. 12. 38 comments critically on this practice.) Nevertheless in real life a speaker would not admit guilt quite so explicitly as Bdelykleon does by ὑφείλετο; his words are not an exact copy of real speeches but a parody of them.

959 κιθαρίζειν: Learning to play the lyre was part of the traditional education of an Athenian gentleman (cf. *Knights* 987–96, *Clouds* 964). It is a symbol of artistic and intellectual activity; the opposite is digging, which symbolizes physical labour (cf. *Birds* 1432 σκάπτειν γὰρ οὐκ ἐπίσταμαι, fr. 221, and E. K. Borthwick in *CQ* xviii [1968] 199 n. 1). Speeches for the defence would often point out the disadvantages and handicaps from which the accused suffered. But inability to play the lyre, or even lack of education generally, is a comically inadequate excuse for theft. Again Ar. is ridiculing a type of excuse made in real courts.

960–1 'I wish he didn't even know how to write, so that he couldn't have made out his accounts for us dishonestly.'   ἐνέγραφ': A past tense of the indicative is normal for a final clause expressing a purpose which cannot now be fulfilled, because the action or event on which it depends has not been fulfilled. The compound ἐγγράφω is regularly used for the writing of official documents; it is used of official accounts also in Lys. 30. 5, D. 24. 199, Ais. 3. 20.

963 The cheese-grater (cf. 938) comes and stands next to Bdelykleon (in 966 only he hears its answer). For the questioning of a witness in a real court cf. And. 1. 14; there, as here, the orator puts propositions to the witness, and the witness simply assents. μέγα: 'loudly', for the whole court to hear. [L. A. Post (*AJP* liii [1932] 265–6) suggests that the cheese-grater represents the Sicilian city Katane, and takes this passage as evidence that representatives of Katane gave evidence for Lakhes at a trial. The evidence for the identification is a remark made by Kallippos on losing Syracuse and capturing Katane, ὅτι πόλιν ἀπολωλεκὼς τυρόκνηστιν εἴληφεν (Plu. *Dion* 58. 4). I do not know what was the point of Kallippos's joke; but I think that ταμιεύουσ' in 964 makes it impossible that Ar.'s cheese-grater is Katane, for Katane cannot have been Lakhes's ταμίας. The reason why Ar. makes a cheese-grater the chief witness is simply that it is the kitchen utensil most obviously connected with cheese.]

964 ταμιεύουσ': A general would have a treasurer (ταμίας) to look after the public money under his control, used for such purposes as paying for the soldiers' food (hence τοῖς στρατιώταις in 965; cf. 557 n.). For real generals' treasurers see D. 49. 6, Ais. 1. 56. It is not clear whether such treasurers were public officials or privately appointed by each general. The cheese-grater is like a ταμίας because it doles out the amount of grated cheese used in cooking.

965 κατέκνησας: 'grated'; some such verb as κατένειμας, 'distributed', is comically adapted to suit the τυρόκνηστις. ἄλαβες: crasis for ἃ ἔλαβες. Bdelykleon pauses and pretends to hear an answer spoken very quietly in his ear by the cheese-grater.

966 The cheese-grater returns to its place at the back or side of the court. The other kitchen utensils never give evidence; the joke of calling them as witnesses was made sufficiently in 937–9, and it would be tedious now for them all to give evidence individually.

967 [-μόνι' ἐλέ-: Either (*a*) this is a proceleusmatic (∪ ∪ ∪ ∪); but there is no certain instance of this in comic iambic trimeters; other possible instances (notably *Wealth* 1011, Pl. com. 188. 1, Nikostratos com. 15. 2) are open to the alternative scansion ∪ ∪ ∪ ∪ ∪ — (if it is accepted, as it must be, that word-break between the second and third syllables of a tribrach is allowed). Or (*b*) -έει is scanned as one long syllable; this kind of contraction is common enough with εα (1067 n.), εου, and εω, but parallels with εει are lacking. Or (*c*) the text must be emended; *q* emended by omitting τοὺς. H.-J. Newiger (*Hermes* lxxxix [1961] 179), following Wilamowitz, prefers (*b*), perhaps rightly; but (*a*) remains a possible alternative.] τοὺς ταλαιπωρουμένους: 'the distressed'; the appeal is made in general terms, as in 942–3.

968 τραχήλι': 'giblets'.

969 ἀκάνθας: 'bones'.   **κοὐδέποτ' ἐν ταὐτῷ μένει:** he has to wander from place to place in search of food.

970 'But the other one—what a creature he is! He's nothing but a house-guard.' I take **οἷός** as exclamatory. To take it as relative gives the sense 'such as he is', which is practically meaningless. To take it as indefinite, modifying οἰκουρὸς, with the sense 'a sort of house-guard' (cf. LSJ οἷος II. 7), is awkward, because it is separated from οἰκουρός. To call Dog (Kleon) a house-guard might seem to be a compliment; but the point is that this work is less arduous than the outdoor work undertaken by Labes (cf. 952, 955).

972 τὸ μέρος: 'his share'.   **εἰ δὲ μή:** 'otherwise', i.e. 'if he doesn't get it'.

973 αἰβοῖ: 37 n. As in 713–14 Philokleon with dismay feels himself being gradually convinced. [The reading of **a** will not scan. The reading of *q* is just a conjecture to restore the metre, and so has no more authority than later conjectures, e.g. αἰβοῖ, τί τὸ κακόν; ἔσθ' Hamaker, αἰβοῖ (*extra metrum*). τουτὶ τὸ κακὸν τί ποτ' ἔσθ' Reisig. My emendation assumes that τὸ κακόν was a gloss on τόδε which ousted it from the text. κακόν τι in 974 suggests that τὸ κακόν was not mentioned in 973. For τόδε of an inward feeling cf. E. *Supp.* 609; for ὅστις following this pronoun cf. E. *Hipp.* 943.]

974 περιβαίνει με: 'is encircling me'. For the metaphor cf. E. *Supp.* 609 τόδε μοι θράσος ἀμφιβαίνει, A. *Th.* 834 κακόν με καρδίαν τι περιπίτνει κρύος.

975 οἰκτίρατ' . . . **ὦ πάτερ:** a comic confusion of the pretence that there is a full-size jury and the fact that there is only Philokleon.

976–8 Ar. parodies yet another custom of the Athenian courts, by which an accused man might bring in his children to arouse the jury's sympathy. Lys. 20. 34 comments that sometimes a jury acquits a guilty father out of pity for his children without even knowing whether they will be good citizens or not; cf. also And. 1. 148, Pl. *Ap.* 34 c, D. 21. 99, 186–8. Labes's puppies (played by actors) now come out of the house; they say nothing, but perhaps they weep noisily. **ὦ πόνηρα:** 'you poor creatures'.   [**αἰτεῖτε:** Hirschig conjectured αἰτεῖσθε, thinking the middle preferable for supplication; but cf. S. *OT* 216.]   **δακρύετε** adds the finishing touch to the satire: they weep when told to, not of their own accord.

979 is the only iambic trimeter containing five trisyllabic feet. Philokleon wants Bdelykleon to stop speaking because he feels himself being won over against his will. He wipes away a few tears (cf. 983).

981 ἐξηπάτηκεν: They thought that the cry 'Go down!' meant that the jury was convinced by the speech, but afterwards they received an adverse verdict. This passage shows that in Athenian courts jurors sometimes called out κατάβα when they wanted to hear no more from a speaker.

Bdelykleon leaves the speaker's platform or position, and the puppies withdraw to sit or stand with the other witnesses. Meanwhile Philokleon has been taking some more soup, and blames it for his tears, which are really due to emotion. Perhaps now Bdelykleon collects the two cups (855) from beside the soup, so as to have them ready for the voting.

983 'I wept away my resolution.'

984 οὐδέν: a limiting accusative, but by Ar.'s time οὐδὲν ἀλλ' ἤ had developed into a regular adverbial expression for 'only': 'only because I'm full of soup'.   ποτέ just strengthens οὐδέν (like the much commoner ποτε following τίς or τί), and coheres with it so closely that the two are treated as a single word and γ' follows ποτέ instead of being placed immediately after οὐδέν.

985 'So he's not being acquitted, then?' (i.e. 'Your tears are not tears o pity after all?'). 'It's hard to tell.' Philokleon absurdly maintains the pretence that there is a full-size jury, so that he cannot forecast which way the majority will go.

986 πατρίδιον: a wheedling diminutive; cf. *Clouds* 223 ὦ Σωκρατίδιον, *Frogs* 582 ὦ Ξανθίδιον.   ἐπὶ τὰ βελτίω τρέπου: 'change your mind for the better'.

987 ψῆφον: Presumably this pebble was brought on at 805 with the other equipment. Now Bdelykleon picks it up and gives it to Philokleon. For the voting procedure in real courts, 94 n.   τὸν ὕστερον: 'the second urn'. The whole passage shows that the second urn is the urn for acquittal, and that it was normal for the jurors in a court to pass the urn for condemnation first and the urn for acquittal afterwards. We may imagine now the two cups standing in some central position (possibly on a table brought on with them at 805, or possibly on the altar which stands on the stage permanently), and Philokleon holding his vote and standing at one end, with Bdelykleon beside him. There is a similar situation in Phrynikhos com. 32, where οὗτος is 'the further' and ὁδί 'the nearer': ἰδού· δέχου τὴν ψῆφον. ὁ καδίσκος δέ σοι ὁ μὲν ἀπολύων οὗτος, ὁ δ' ἀπολλὺς ὁδί.

988 μύσας παρᾷξον: 'shut your eyes and dash past', to avoid being tempted by the sight of the urn for condemnation.   ἀπόλυσον: 'acquit him'.

989 Since Philokleon has no good reason for refusal, he gives an absurd one, copying the absurd excuse given by Bdelykleon for Labes in 959. It is a regular type of joke for one character to learn a trick from another and later use it against the very person from whom he learned it. One might call it 'a boomerang joke'. There are jokes of this type in 1383 and 1446; examples from other plays have been listed by H. W. Miller (*AJP* lxv [1944] 27–9).

990 τῃδί: 'this way'. Bdelykleon leads Philokleon by a long detour round the back of the urns (cups) until he comes to the one for acquittal without having passed the one for condemnation. Philokleon, unrealistically, is supposed not to notice which way he is going, and when he comes to an urn asks whether it is the first, meaning the urn for condemnation; Bdelykleon says it is, meaning the first one he has come to.

991 [An equally good distribution of the words would be *Βδ. . . . ὅδ' ἔσθ' ὁ πρότερος. Φι. οὗτος;* suggested by Beer 154. The passage could be effectively played either way, and we cannot tell which Ar. intended.] **αὕτη 'ντευθενί:** 'It's off!' 'Away it goes!' Philokleon says goodbye to his precious vote as he lets go of it and it falls into the cup. [This explanation of *ἐντευθενί*, 'hence', seems satisfactory, so that Dobree's conjecture *'νταῦθ' ἔνι* is not needed.]

992 is inserted in case some members of the audience were not quick enough to follow the business of 987–91; Bdelykleon addresses it to the chorus or the audience, or perhaps just to himself. Meanwhile Philokleon goes back to his seat.

993 φέρ' ἐξεράσω: 'Now, let me pour them out.' Bdelykleon turns each of the cups upside down; no votes fall out of the first, and one out of the second. He makes a show of counting them. **πῶς ἄρ' ἠγωνίσμεθα;** 'What's the result of our trial, then?' *ἀγών* and *ἀγωνίζομαι* are regularly used of legal trials.

994 δείξειν ἔοικεν: 'I think it will be clear.' The absence of a word for 'very soon' is odd. For the impersonal use of *δείξει* cf. *Frogs* 1261 *δείξει δὴ τάχα*, D. 2. 20 *δοκεῖ δ' ἔμοιγ', ὦ ἄνδρες Ἀθηναῖοι, δείξειν οὐκ εἰς μακράν.* **ἐκπέφευγας:** 'you've got away': not the regular term for 'be acquitted', which is *ἀποφεύγω*. On hearing the news Philokleon faints. Labes and the witnesses possibly cheer, or at least look gleeful. Bdelykleon rushes to Philokleon and lifts him off the ground.

997 οὐδέν εἰμ': 'There is no hope for me', 'I am undone'. This use is common in tragedy, and may be meant to sound tragic here; so also in *Knights* 1243. But in 1504 *οὐδέν ἐστ'* is 'he's no good', 'he's useless'; so also in *Ek.* 144. Cf. A. C. Moorhouse 'A Use of *οὐδείς* and *μηδείς*' (*CQ* xv [1965] 31–40).

999 'How shall I live with this on my conscience?'

1001 ὦ πολυτίμητοι θεοί: Philokleon is uttering a prayer, but elsewhere this phrase is used just as an exclamation (*Th.* 594, Men. *Dys.* 202, 381, 479).

1002 οὐ τοῦ 'μοῦ τρόπου: sc. *ὄν*: 'uncharacteristically'.

1005 ἐπὶ θεωρίαν: 'to the theatre'.

1007 ἐγχανεῖταί: 721 n. Hyperbolos may have been still a young man at this time, for he entered politics at an unusually early age (Kratinos 262, Eupolis 238). He was the son of Antiphanes, of the deme Perithoidai (*FGrH* 324 F 42; cf. the ostraka in *Hesperia* viii [1939] 246, xvii [1948] 186), though his enemies alleged that his father was a foreign slave called Khremes (And. fr. 5, *FGrH* 115 F 95, Pl. com.

166–7, 170, Polyzelos 5, *Σ Peace* 681 ; cf. A. E. Raubitschek in *Phoenix* ix [1955] 124–5). He had wealth, which of course he was said by some to have obtained dishonestly (*Clouds* 1065–6 ; cf. Pl. com. 169). He was a lampmaker by profession (*Clouds* 1065, *Peace* 690, And. fr. 5, etc.), but he gained notoriety by a series of successful prosecutions in the law-courts (*Akh.* 846–7, *Knights* 1363, *Clouds* 876, *Wasps* 1007). At some time he is said to have prosecuted Nikias (Himerios 36. 18 [ed. Colonna, page 152]). His earliest known political act is his proposal in 425/4 to send a hundred ships to Carthage (*Knights* 1303–4), but the purpose of this proposal is obscure, and indeed it has been suggested that it was never really made (cf. Gomme *Commentary on Thucydides* iii 524). His appointment as a hieromnemon (*Clouds* 623–4) and as a councillor (Pl. com. 166–7) was due merely to lot; but the power of his oratory is proved by the fact that after Kleon's death in 421 he became the dominant figure in the assembly (*Peace* 679–84). There are two surviving decrees of this period of which he is the proposer (*IG* i² 84, 95). He is said to have been a general at some time too (*Σ Akh.* 846, *Σ Peace* 1319). But Nikias and Alkibiades soon emerged as his rivals, and by a combined effort they succeeded in getting him ostracized ; this was the last ostracism ever held (Th. 8. 73. 3, *FGrH* 324 F 42, 328 F 30, Plu. *Arist.* 7, *Nik.* 11, *Alk.* 13). He went to live in Samos, where in 411 he was murdered by a group of Athenian oligarchs and his body was thrown into the sea (Th. 8. 73. 3, *FGrH* 115 F 96, *Σ Peace* 681). He was constantly attacked in comedy (*Clouds* 551–9 with *Σ*), and Thucydides is exceptionally severe on him, severer even than on Kleon : μοχθηρὸν ἄνθρωπον, ὠστρακισμένον οὐ διὰ δυνάμεως καὶ ἀξιώματος φόβον, ἀλλὰ διὰ πονηρίαν καὶ αἰσχύνην τῆς πόλεως (Th. 8. 73. 3). But after his death he was remembered, like Kleon, as a champion of the oppressed (*Frogs* 570) ; and his ascendancy after Kleon's death (*Peace* 679–84) proves that he possessed both popularity and power, whatever Thucydides may say.

1008 ταῦτά: 'very well'; cf. 142, 851. **εἴπερ δοκεῖ:** 'if you like', acquiescing; cf. *Clouds* 11, *Th.* 216, E. *Hipp.* 507 (with Barrett's note).

Philokleon and Bdelykleon go into the house, followed by the dogs and witnesses. The slaves clear all the law-court impedimenta from the stage during the next few lines, taking it into the house. Only the chorus then remain in view.

1009–1121 The parabasis : a passage, occurring usually about half-way through a comedy, in which the chorus 'come forward' (παραβαίνειν) and address the audience in the absence of the actors. The names which are traditionally given to its parts by scholars (though probably not by Ar.) are : kommation (here 1009–14), parabasis (1015–50) (Ar. himself calls this part ἀνάπαιστοι; cf. *Akh.* 627, *Knights* 504, *Peace* 735, *Birds* 684), pnigos (1051–9), ode or strophe (1060–70),

epirrhema (1071–90), antode or antistrophe (1091–1101), antepirrhema (1102–21).

1009–59 *The chorus present the author's complaint at the Athenian audience's
treatment of him. He had served them well, both in plays which he wrote for
production by others and in plays produced openly by himself, and he made no
improper use of his success. The first objects of his attacks were not ordinary men
but 'the jagged-toothed monster' (Kleon) and 'the shivers and fevers' (συκοφάνται). But despite these services the audience last year rejected his best and
most novel comedy. Originality deserves a more favourable reception.*

In Ar.'s early plays the first half of the parabasis is regularly devoted
to a defence by the author of some aspect of his work, with a criticism
of the attitude of the Athenian audience; cf. *Akh.* 628–64, *Knights* 507–
50, *Clouds* 518–62, *Peace* 734–74. Our passage is an interesting survey
by Ar. of his career as a comic dramatist so far. His comments on the
failure of *Clouds* are a striking example of the indignation of the *avant-
garde* intellectual dramatist at the failure of unintellectual audiences
to understand the merits of his work; parallels abound in the modern
theatre.

The chief stylistic feature of the passage is its profusion of metaphors:
in his youth Ar. poured out comedies from inside other men's bellies
(1020); his muses are horses in a chariot-race (1022), in which his
idea is the chariot (1050); Kleon is a jagged-toothed monster (1031),
with flatterers for hair (1033) and with the voice of a deadly torrent
(1034); prosecutors are fevers (1038), strangle their fathers in the
night (1039), and are nightmares to inoffensive citizens (1040); and so
on. Yet the meaning is never obscured by the images, because Ar.
takes care to make the point of each metaphor clear: for example,
'bellies' (1020) is prepared for by the reference to Eurykles (1019),
and the chariot-crash is made intelligible by the fact that the object of
the verb is not 'chariot' but 'idea' (1050).

Metre: The rhythm of the kommation is first anapaestic (1009–10),
then iambic (1011–12), and then trochaic (1013–14). The reason for
changing the rhythm twice in so short a passage is not apparent.
[Burges deleted μὲν in 1011 in order to make the iambic passage
trochaic; cf. 1011 n.] Then follow the ἀνάπαιστοι, presumably recited
by the chorus-leader alone. 1015–50 are anapaestic tetrameters, and in
1051–9 the passage concludes with a run of eighteen anapaestic metra.

1009 The chorus bid a temporary farewell to the actors. Cf. *Knights* 498,
Clouds 510, *Peace* 729, in each of which the parabasis begins ἀλλ' ἴθι
χαίρων, and *Akh.* 1143 ἴτε δὴ χαίροντες. τέως: while the actors are
away; so also in *Peace* 729.

1010 A quotation or traditional phrase, appearing also in Pl. *Laws* 804 e
and (with intervening words) Pl. *Tht.* 175 a. [-ριάδες ἀναρί- is ∪ ∪ ∪
∪ ∪ ∪. In non-lyric anapaests Ar. usually avoids having more than two
successive short syllables (397 n.), but in lyrics he sometimes has

longer series (twenty-two in *Lys.* 481–3). So it seems best to accept the series of short syllables here, making a catalectic anapaestic line. Some editors make the line acatalectic by regarding -δες and -ρί- as long. But it is unlikely that -δες would be allowed to stand for a long syllable when no pause in the sense follows it; no parallel is provided by *Birds* 212 *Ἴτυν*, since this word may have ῡ anyway (cf. S. *El.* 148).]

1011–14 'Take care that the good words now to be uttered do not fall to the ground unheeded. For that is what happens to a stupid audience, and is not characteristic of you.'   μὲν implies a contrast with lighter parts of the play, which require less close attention, though no δέ-clause is added to express this. [Burges deleted μὲν to make 1011–12 trochaic, and from the point of view of sense it would be no great loss. But its intrusion, if it is not genuine, is hard to explain.]   φαύλως: 'lightly', receiving little attention.   χαμᾶζ᾽: For the metaphor cf. Pl. *Euthph.* 14 d οὐ χαμαὶ πεσεῖται ὅ τι ἂν εἴπῃς.   σκαιῶν: 65 n.

1015 The chorus-leader now requests the audience's attention in speech, as if the whole chorus had not already done so in song.   αὖτε: 'next': 28 n. αὖτε is an old-fashioned form, used elsewhere by Ar. only in lyrics (*Clouds* 595, *Lys.* 1296) and in an epic quotation (*Peace* 1270). It is not clear why he uses it here.   λεῴ: the usual vocative in proclamations; cf. ἀκούετε λεῴ in *Akh.* 1000, *Peace* 551, *Birds* 448. προσέχετε τὸν νοῦν occurs similarly near the beginning of the parabasis in *Knights* 503, *Birds* 688; cf. *Clouds* 575 τὸν νοῦν προσέχετε, 1122 προσεχέτω τὸν νοῦν. [For ∪ ∪ ∪ ∪ in anapaests, 397 n. The instances listed there show that emendation to πρόσσχετε is not essential on metrical grounds, though it is true that the ligatures for εχ and σχ are easily confused in mss. Since attention is to be sustained for some time, the present is the more suitable tense.]   καθαρόν: 'frank'.

1017 ἀδικεῖσθαι: For the present tense, 591 n.   πρότερος: 'although he gave no provocation'.

1018 τὰ μὲν: adverbial accusative: 'partly'. Instead of τὰ δέ, 1021 has μετὰ τοῦτο δὲ. No connective particle links 1018 with 1017 because it is not an addition but only an amplification of it (i.e. there is asyndeton in place of γάρ). φησιν is understood, governing χέασθαι, to which all the participles in 1018–22 are subordinate. 'For (he says) he poured out lots of comedy, partly not openly but helping other poets in secret . . . but afterwards openly too . . .' [Thus the syntax does not demand emendation. Starkie changed εἰς to ὥστ᾽ in 1020, with no colon at the end of 1017. Cf. 1020 n.]

ἐπικουρῶν κρύβδην ἑτέροισι ποιηταῖς: *Knights* was the first play which Ar. produced himself. *Banqueters* in 427, *Babylonians* in 426, and *Akh.* in 425 were all produced by Kallistratos (*Knights* 512–16, *Clouds* 528–31, Σ *Wasps* 1018, *Akh.* hyp. i, anon. *On Comedy* 11, Phot. Σαμίων). But why is ἑτέροισι ποιηταῖς plural? Several answers have been suggested:

A : 'The plural is generic, "another poet" ' (Starkie). Then the reference is to Kallistratos only. This is possible, but not entirely convincing, since there is nothing in the context to make this type of plural natural.

B : Perhaps Ar. is thinking not only of the plays which preceded *Knights* but also of *Clouds*, produced in 423 by Philonides. But even if it is true that Philonides produced *Clouds* (which is implied by anon. *On Comedy* 11 but contradicted by Σ *Clouds* 510), still 1021 μετὰ τοῦτο makes it likely that 1018–20 refers only to the plays before *Knights*.

C : Perhaps Ar. wrote another play before *Knights*, in addition to *Banqueters*, *Babylonians*, and *Akh.*, and it was produced (say at the Lenaia of 426) by Philonides or someone else other than Kallistratos and Ar. himself. This is the view of C. F. Russo *Aristofane, autore di teatro* (1962) 26. Russo's other argument for the hypothesis is weak, but he may well be right in regarding it as the best explanation of the plural in *Wasps* 1018.

1019 Eurykles was a prophet whose voice came from the bellies of other people; in other words, besides being a prophet he was a ventriloquist. Cf. Pl. *Soph*. 252 c οἵκοθεν τὸν πολέμιον καὶ ἐναντιωσόμενον ἔχοντες, ἐντὸς ὑποφθεγγόμενον ὥσπερ τὸν ἄτοπον Εὐρυκλέα περιφέροντες ἀεὶ πορεύονται, Plu. *Eth*. 414 e εὔηθες γάρ ἐστι καὶ παιδικὸν κομιδῇ τὸ οἴεσθαι τὸν θεὸν αὐτὸν ὥσπερ τοὺς ἐγγαστριμύθους Εὐρυκλέας πάλαι νυνὶ δὲ Πύθωνας προσαγορευομένους ἐνδυόμενον εἰς τὰ σώματα τῶν προφητῶν ὑποφθέγγεσθαι τοῖς ἐκείνων στόμασι καὶ φωναῖς χρώμενον ὀργάνοις. Ar., Plato, and Plutarch all make it quite clear that what happened was that the voice of Eurykles came from the belly of someone else; consequently those scholars (from Σ Pl. *Soph*. 252 c onwards) who say that the voice came from the belly of Eurykles are mistaken. Plutarch's use of the plural shows that the name was applied to a number of people; presumably the original Eurykles had subsequent imitators. *Wasps* 1019 does not necessarily mean that the original Eurykles lived in Ar.'s time. **διάνοιαν** : 'device'.

1020 εἰς : ἐνδύω more often has a direct accusative, but εἰς is found in X. *Kyr*. 8. 1. 12, Arist. *HA* 609ᵇ21. [So Starkie's ὥστ' (1018 n.) is not needed on this account.]

1021 κινδυνεύων : taking the risk of failure at the dramatic festivals. καθ' ἑαυτόν : 'on his own responsibility', the opposite of acting as a subordinate to someone else; cf. *Knights* 513 χορὸν αἰτοίη καθ' ἑαυτόν.

1022 Sc. exercising full control over his own artistic activities, instead of merely assisting other people's. Ar. did not control the performances of which Kallistratos had charge (cf. *Knights* 541–4). 1022 simply states the converse of 1018, and a comparison of the two shows that there is a slight ellipse in each: in 1018 we should understand something like 'acting independently' with φανερῶς, and in 1022 something like 'assisting' with ἀλλοτρίων. For the idea that each artist has his own muse or muses cf. *Frogs* 1306, where the *Μοῦσ' Εὐριπίδου* appears as a character. **στόμαθ' ἡνιοχήσας:** The metaphor is of driving horses in a chariot; for its application to drama cf. *IG* ii² 6626 ἡνίοχος τέχνης τραγικῆς.

1023 μέγας: proleptic, 'raised to greatness'; cf. D. 2. 8 ἤρθη μέγας. Ar. refers primarily to the success of *Knights*, with which he won the first prize at the Lenaia of 424.

1024 ἐκτελέσαι: 'end up', 'turn out', 'become', as perhaps in Simonides 81 Bergk; cf. LSJ τελέω I. 8. Coulon (*Rh. Mus.* ciii [1960] 122–3) takes this infinitive as adverbial, meaning 'completely'; but the sequence οὐκ ἐκτελέσαι . . ., οὐδ' ὀγκῶσαι . . ., οὐδὲ . . . περικωμάζειν shows that it must be an ordinary indirect-speech infinitive like the others. **ἐπαρθείς:** 'over-confident' (as in *Frogs* 777), with a play on ἀρθείς in 1023: 'though raised to the skies he didn't get above himself'. **ὀγκῶσαι τὸ φρόνημα:** 'get big-headed'.

1025 πειρῶν: 'looking for a pick-up', taking advantage of his popularity; cf. *Peace* 762–3 οὐχὶ παλαίστρας περινοστῶν παῖδας ἐπείρων.

1026 'Urged him that a favourite of his, with whom he was annoyed, should be satirized', to punish him and make him more amenable in future. (Not 'pleaded with him, in annoyance that his favourite should be satirized', because of 1028: mere omission to satirize someone could not be called προαγωγεία.) The view, based on *Σ*, that Ar. is here criticizing Eupolis for satirizing Autolykos is probably a mistake, since Eupolis's *Autolykos* was not performed until 420 (Ath. 216 d), and Eupolis 215, sometimes thought to refer to Autolykos, more probably refers to his mother (τὴν Λύκωνος being Lykon's wife, not his effeminate son).

1027 γνώμην: 'purpose'.

1028 προαγωγούς: 'procurers'.

1029 ἦρξε: 'began' with *Knights* in 424. This use of the active of ἄρχω instead of the middle is unusual; generally in Attic the active is used for 'begin' only in the sense 'be the first to'. [So perhaps the text is corrupt. γ' (B) is only a conjecture to restore the metre. πρῶτον ἦρξε may be a gloss on some less obvious expression for 'began'.] **ἀνθρώποις:** 'ordinary human beings'. Kleon, the chief object of attack in *Knights*, is regarded as an inhuman monster. [L. Siegel (*Wien. Stud.* xxxv [1913] 198–9) prefers R's reading φησὶ πιθέσθαι, 'says he didn't give in to people'. But this makes 1029 a weak repetition of 1027.]

1030–7 are repeated, with a few variations, in *Peace* 752–9. This does not mean that the lines are out of place in either play, but only that Ar. was pleased with them. The past tenses in 1032–4 refer to the time of *Knights*, and do not imply that Kleon was dead when the lines were written.

1030 ὀργήν: 'spirit', 'courage', as in Hdt. 6. 128. 1. **τοῖσι μεγίστοις:** neuter: 'the greatest monsters'. [Merry's conjecture θῆρσι is unnecessary. The mss. have τοῖσι in *Peace* 752 also.]

1031 καρχαρόδοντι: 'jagged-toothed'. Kleon called himself a watch-dog; so Ar. identifies him with Kerberos, the watch-dog of hell, one of the monsters with whom Herakles had to deal. Cf. other references to Kleon: *Knights* 1017 κύνα καρχαρόδοντα, 1030 κύνα Κέρβερον ἀνδραποδιστήν, *Peace* 313 ἐκεῖνον τὸν κάτωθεν Κέρβερον.

1032 Κύννης: Kynna was a prostitute (*Σ* here, *Σ Knights* 765), but here her name is used merely as a comic distortion of κυνός, which can be kept in English only by a similar distortion of 'canine': 'from whose Kynnine eyes shone terrible rays'. Ar. may have been thinking of the Homeric phrase κυνὸς ὄμματ' ἔχων (*Iliad* i. 225).

1033 κύκλῳ goes with περὶ τὴν κεφαλήν, and the force of οὗ continues from 1032 (as μὲν and δὲ show): 'and all around whose head licked a hundred heads of damned flatterers'. The alliteration with κ gives a suitably harsh sound to the line. **κολάκων:** a surprise for ὄφεων. Ar. seems to combine Kerberos (1031 n.) with two other monsters: the Hydra, which had a hundred heads and was killed by Herakles; and Typhoeus, a giant with snakes instead of hair, described in Hes. *Th.* 825 as having ἑκατὸν κεφαλαὶ ὄφιος. Kleon is called 'Typhoeus' in *Knights* 511.

1034 χαράδρας: For the comparison of Kleon's voice to a torrent cf. *Akh.* 381, *Knights* 137, *Peace* 314, fr. 636. For χαράδρα used of speech cf. Pherekrates 51. **ὄλεθρον τετοκυίας:** 'death-dealing'.

1035 The rhythm of this line is perhaps meant to suggest the Homeric description of the Chimera: πρόσθε λέων, ὄπιθεν δὲ δράκων, μέσση δὲ χίμαιρα (*Iliad* 6. 181). For the unpleasant smell of seals cf. *Odyssey* 4. 442 φωκάων ἁλιοτρεφέων ὀλοώτατος ὀδμή. **Λαμίας:** According to legend Lamia was a Libyan woman loved by Zeus; Hera from jealousy destroyed her children, and Lamia from envy went around destroying and eating other women's children. So nurses used to threaten children with Lamia as a kind of bogy or man-eating ogress, one of whose peculiarities was that she removed her eyes to go to sleep and replaced them when she went out. Ar.'s reference to testicles shows that she was hermaphroditic. This is confirmed by a comparison of *Wasps* 1177 and *Ek.* 76–8; these two passages refer to the same incident, but whereas *Wasps* 1177 has ἡ Λάμι', *Ek.* 77 has τοῦ Λαμίου, showing that the masculine name Lamias was regarded as interchangeable with the feminine Lamia. (*Ek.* 76–8 is an obscure passage, but evidently refers to a well-known Athenian named Lamios; thus Λαμίου is a kind of pun, since it may be the genitive of either Λάμιος or Λαμίας. The passage is discussed by R. G. Ussher in *Hermes* xciv [1966] 376–7.) Plays entitled *Lamia* were written by Euripides and Krates; 'the unwashed testicles' may be an allusion to an unsavoury passage in one of these. Cf. 1177 n. on the escapade of Lamia mentioned there.

1036 κατα- implies action against someone, here the Athenian public: 'take bribes to betray you'.

1037 μετ' αὐτοῦ: i.e. 'as well as attacking Kleon'. For μετά linking an additional indirect object to a dative cf. 1247.

1038 The relationship between ἠπίαλος and πυρετός is shown by fr. 332: ἠπίαλος πυρετοῦ πρόδρομος. The 'shivers and fevers' here are the συκοφάνται, as 1041 shows; the original audience will have realized this at once, without waiting for 1041, by remembering Ar.'s play from last year. A συκοφάντης was a man who habitually prosecuted others not because he himself had suffered any injury or loss, nor even necessarily because he believed them guilty, but to gain a financial profit or a political or oratorical reputation.

πέρυσιν: at the Lenaia of 423, since *Clouds* followed (cf. 1043–4) at the Dionysia of 423. It is not known which play this was. Platnauer (*CR* lxiii [1949] 7), following Meineke, maintains that it was *Merchant-ships* (Ὀλκάδες), the evidence being in *Peace* hyp. iii: οὐ τοῦτο δὲ μόνον ὑπὲρ εἰρήνης Ἀριστοφάνης τὸ δρᾶμα καθῆκεν, ἀλλὰ καὶ τοὺς Ἀχαρνεῖς καὶ τοὺς Ἱππέας καὶ ⟨τὰς⟩ Ὀλκάδας, καὶ πανταχοῦ τοῦτο ἐσπούδακεν, τόν τε Κλέωνα κωμῳδῶν τὸν ἀντιλέγοντα καὶ Λάμαχον τὸν φιλοπόλεμον ἀεὶ διαβάλλων. But this evidence is inadequate, for the following reasons: (*a*) *Peace* hyp. iii says that *Akh.*, *Knights*, and *Merchant-ships* all favoured peace, but not that each of them attacked both Kleon and Lamakhos, and since we know for a fact that Lamakhos is not mentioned in *Knights* it is possible that Kleon was not mentioned in *Merchant-ships*; (*b*) *Wasps* 1037 μετ' αὐτοῦ does not necessarily mean that Kleon was attacked in the play at the Lenaia of 423, but may refer to *Knights*, since in 1038 πέρυσιν may modify τοῖς ἠπιάλοις . . . only, i.e. 'besides attacking Kleon ⟨in 424⟩, he last year attacked . . .'; (*c*) the plays mentioned in *Peace* hyp. iii are not necessarily in chronological order; (*d*) even if my objections (*a*), (*b*), and (*c*) were all refuted, it would still remain possible that *Merchant-ships* was performed at the Dionysia of 422. So Ar.'s play attacking συκοφάνται at the Lenaia of 423 was possibly *Merchant-ships*, but not certainly; another possibility is *Farmers* (suggested by Willems 571; it is often assigned to the Dionysia of 424, but Plu. *Nik.* 8. 4 is no proof of that date; O. Musso, in *Stud. Ital.* xxxvi [1964] 80–9, prefers 421, but resemblances between *Farmers* and *Peace* are not proof that both were written in the same year); or it may have been some other play.

1039 is simply a way of saying 'were utter scoundrels', since attacking one's parents, and especially parricide by strangling, is a cliché for the worst kind of crime. Thus one of the bad characters who flock to Cloudcuckooland is a πατραλοίας (*Birds* 1337–71); cf. also *Wasps* 1134, *Clouds* 911, 1327, *Frogs* 149, 773, *Ek.* 638–40.

1040 ἐπὶ ταῖς κοίταις is 'on the beds', but the following ἐπὶ is more vaguely 'in relation to': 'lying down on the beds of those among you who keep out of politics'.   **ἀπράγμοσιν** is a term of praise, like the

English 'minding one's own business', 'peaceful', as opposed to the unfavourable words πολυπράγμων and 'busybody'. When it is desired to criticize someone for taking no part in public affairs, ἀπράγμων is avoided; cf. Th. 2. 40. 2 τόν τε μηδὲν τῶνδε μετέχοντα οὐκ ἀπράγμονα ἀλλ' ἀχρεῖον νομίζομεν. The whole concept has been discussed in detail by V. Ehrenberg (*JHS* lxvii [1947] 46–67).

1041 ἀντωμοσίας: 545 n. προσκλήσεις καὶ μαρτυρίας: 'summonses and statements of evidence'. All three nouns here refer to documents rather than activities. Ar. means that an ἀπράγμων man, who possibly could not read and certainly could not understand legal documents, would often be overwhelmed with them by an experienced accuser who understood all the intricacies of the law. συνεκόλλων: 'put together', used of assembling a written document also in Pl. *Mx.* 236 b; cf. *Clouds* 446 ψευδῶν συγκολλητής.

1042 The 'shivers and fevers' cause their victims to have nightmares or become delirious. ἀναπηδᾶν: 'jump up and hurry to . . .', as in *Birds* 490. πολέμαρχον: The polemarkhos was the third in importance of the nine arkhons. At this period he no longer commanded the army; his chief functions were religious and legal. His legal functions concerned cases involving persons who were not Athenian citizens; so Ar.'s statement that Athenians afflicted by συκοφάνται rush to the polemarkhos is evidence that many συκοφάνται were not citizens but metics. (Arist. *Ath. Pol.* 43. 5 confirms that it was possible for metics to be συκοφάνται.) A citizen prosecuting a non-citizen would go to the polemarkhos to demand sureties for the accused's subsequent appearance in court (κατεγγυᾶν πρὸς τὸν πολέμαρχον, e.g. D. 32. 29, Isok. 17. 12). This does not mean that the polemarkhos had charge of the trial; in fact the magistrates responsible for the trial of a γραφὴ συκοφαντίας were the thesmothetai (Arist. *Ath. Pol.* 59. 3).

1043 ἀλεξίκακον: an epithet of Herakles (*FGrH* 4 F 109, Luc. *Alex.* 4), to whom Ar. is still comparing himself. καθαρτὴν: For Herakles as a purifier, because he freed men from monsters and pests, cf. S. *Tr.* 1012, E. *Her.* 225.

1044 *Clouds* was awarded only the third prize when performed at the Dionysia of 423. Ar.'s sense of injury at this rebuff receives fuller expression in *Clouds* 518–62 (written for the second edition of the play). καινοτάτας . . . διανοίας: 'brand-new ideas'. Ar. prides himself on his originality and avoidance of repetition; cf. 57–63, *Clouds* 546–7. [Bothe's emendation seems necessary. I have found no parallel for σπείρω with the dative of the thing sown.]

1045 'Which you made fruitless, from not understanding them clearly.' Ar. was convinced that *Clouds* was a subtle play, requiring an intelligent audience for its appreciation; cf. *Clouds* 521.

1046 σπένδων: Libation makes an oath more solemn and binding (e.g. *Akh.* 148), but in the present case we can hardly believe that Ar.

is actually making repeated libations; the word seems hardly more than a metaphor for 'solemnly'. πόλλ' ἐπὶ πολλοῖς: 'many libations upon many'; i.e. 'he swears solemnly and repeatedly by Dionysos that no one ever heard . . .'. Dionysos is the god of drama.

1050 παρελαύνων: a metaphor from chariot-racing: 'while overtaking his rivals he crashed his idea'. [The correct reading is restored from ΣΥΓ, who in the course of discussing the line remarks πρὸς τὸ "παρελαύνων" ἐπήνεγκε τὸ "ξυνέτριψε".]

1056 Ar. gives a comic final twist to a serious sentence by suggesting that the Athenians store up good ideas in boxes like clothes. Citrons (μῆλα Μηδικά or μῆλα Περσικά) were used, like lavender or mothballs in modern times, to preserve clothes (Thphr. *HP* 4. 4. 2, Plin. *Nat.* 12. 15, Ath. 84 a).

1058 ἱματίων: Cloaks would be worn in winter and stored away in summer.

1059 ὀζήσει: impersonal, with a descriptive genitive (cf. 38) and a genitive of source, as in *Peace* 529. 'There will be a smell of cleverness coming from your cloaks.'

1060–1121 *The chorus discuss their own character. They are old now, but in their youth they were strong and lusty. They are true Athenian wasps, because they fought for Athens against the Persians, and they resemble wasps in other ways too. They think that drones who have not served in the army or navy should not receive the juror's pay of three obols.*

In Ar.'s early plays the second half of the parabasis is regularly devoted to a discussion of the chorus's character as knights, clouds, or whatever they may be, with a defence of their point of view; cf. *Akh.* 665–718, *Knights* 551–610, *Clouds* 563–626. Our chorus have a double character, as old jurors and as wasps, and it is in this passage that Ar. explains most fully what it is about the jurors which makes him regard them as wasps. Three features may be distinguished: jurors look like wasps, because they are crowded together in law-courts like wasps in nests (1107–11); jurors behave like wasps, because they are quick-tempered and hurt men whom they dislike (1104–5, 1113); and the old jurors are like worker-wasps, because they have fought for Athens, by contrast with younger men, who are like drones without stings. This last feature is the one on which Ar. mainly concentrates, with the result that there is a strong resemblance to the tone of the second half of the parabasis of *Akh.* (in which the old Akharnians contrast themselves with younger men) and of *Knights* (in which the knights discuss military exploits). The passage throws a more favourable light on the old jurors than any other part of the play. From the scenes between Philokleon and Bdelykleon, especially 650–724, it might seem that they were stupid and contemptible, but now it is shown that they deserve respect for the services which they have done Athens in the past.

The opening lines (1060–5) are nostalgic in tone, and this is marked by features of style: repetition of words (ἄλκιμοι, πρίν), which suggests harping on a single theme; metrical pauses (see next paragraph), which suggest reluctance to move on; language of a kind suitable to epic or lyric poetry (ἄλκιμοι and the imagery of κύκνου . . . ἐπανθοῦσιν τρίχες). After 1065 these features disappear; the tone becomes brisker and the language plainer—except for the Herodotean tinge of the lines about the Persian wars (1079–88; see notes on those lines).

Metre: The whole passage is trochaic. 1060–70 and 1091–1101 (presumably sung) are runs of trochees, and 1071–90 and 1102–21 (presumably spoken) are trochaic tetrameters. The trochaic metre has a vigorous and rapid rhythm, which suits the military and waspish subject-matter. But in 1060–5 the subject-matter has a different tone (see previous paragraph), and so Ar. has slowed down the rhythm of these lines by reducing some of the metra to $-\cup-$ or $-\cup\cup\cup$ (see pages 27–9). Presumably because 1060–5 and 1091–6 were sung to the same music, he has also included reduced metra in most (all but two) of the same places in the antistrophe, though there is nothing in the subject-matter of 1091–6 to make slowness appropriate.

```
1060, 1091   -∪-∪  -∪-⏒  -∪-∪  -∪-
1061, 1092   -∪-   -∪-
1062, 1093   -∪-∪  -∪⏠∪  -∪-∪  -∪⏞ ‖
1063, 1094   -∪--  -∪-
1064, 1095   -∪--  -∪⏠∪  -∪-∪
1065, 1096   -∪--  -∪⏝ ‖
```

1060 'Once upon a time we were . . .!' For ὤ with a 1st person pronoun and participle cf. And. 1. 51. Ar. has adapted the wording of a proverb applied to men past their best: πάλαι ποτ' ἦσαν ἄλκιμοι Μιλήσιοι (*Wealth* 1002 with *Σ*, 1075, Ath. 523 f; the men of Miletos were said to have declined from strength in the seventh century to slackness in the sixth).

1062 κατ' αὐτὸ τοῦτο: 'as far as *this* is concerned'. Each member of the chorus points to his phallos. There are no adequate grounds for denying that in Old Comedy a chorus representing men wore phalloi (cf. *Dram. Fest.*[2] 222), and our line is good evidence that they did so. μόνον: 'above all' (LSJ μόνος A. II. 4). [The second syllable of a trochaic metron must be short, and so ἄνδρες μαχιμώτατοι (a) will not scan. ἀλκιμώτατοι (Bentley) makes a suitable climax after 1060–1.]

1063–5 Didymos said (according to *Σ*) that this passage was adapted from Timokreon of Rhodes. For the comparison of the white hairs of age to the plumage of a swan cf. E. *Her.* 692–4, *Ba.* 1365. ἐπανθοῦσιν: For the metaphor cf. *Ek.* 13 τὴν ἐπανθοῦσαν τρίχα, X. *Kyn.* 4. 8.

1066 τῶνδε ῥώμην: The normal rule is that initial ῥ counts as a double consonant, so that a short vowel at the end of the preceding word is scanned long. But here -ε remains short. This is the only exception to the rule in Ar., but there are others in Pherekrates 152. 2, Hermippos 82. 8, Pl. com. 138, and in tragedy.

1067 νεανικήν: εα is scanned as a single long syllable; so also in 1070 νεανιῶν. Other words in which Ar. scans εα as one syllable are θέασαι (*Peace* 906, *Th.* 280) and έα (*Th.* 176, *Ek.* 784). σχεῖν is aorist because it denotes an act rather than a state: 'summon up', not 'possess'.

1069 κικίννους: 466 n. on criticism and resentment of long hair.

1070 σχῆμα: 'appearance'. The word covers both dress (e.g. *Knights* 1331) and posture (e.g. *Frogs* 539).

1071 φύσιν: 'appearance', 'shape', meaning natural physique, not (like σχῆμα) deliberately adopted.

1072 μέσον διεσφηκωμένον: with a narrow waist. This effect was obtained presumably by padding the members of the chorus above and below the waist and giving them tight belts.

1073 ἡ 'πίνοια τῆς ἐγκεντρίδος: 'the purpose of the sting'. With ἐπίνοια a genitive is often used for the person who has the intention, or occasionally for the object intended (e.g. E. *Med.* 760), but I have noticed no other Attic passage in which it is used for an instrument acquired for carrying out the intention. For ἐγκεντρίς, 427 n. [To object to 'wonders, on seeing my wasp-waist, what is the purpose of our sting', on the ground that the sting is something different from the waist, is pedantic.]

1074 κἂν ἄμουσος ᾗ τὸ πρίν: The quotation is from Euripides's *Stheneboia* (fr. 663) : ποιητὴν δ᾽ ἄρα "Ερως διδάσκει, κἂν ἄμουσος ᾗ τὸ πρίν. Later it became hackneyed; cf. Pl. *Smp.* 196 e, Men. fr. 229 Koerte, [Longinos] *On the Sublime* 39. 2, Plu. *Eth.* 405 e, 622 c, 762 b.

1076 'We are the only Athenians who are really indigenous natives.' The old jurors who fought in the Persian wars are contrasted with younger Athenians who did not. There was a tradition that the Athenians were indigenous while other Greeks were later immigrants (cf. *Lys.* 1082, E. *Ion* 589–90, fr. 360. 7–10, Th. 1. 2. 5, etc.), but here the chorus deny that younger Athenians deserve the traditional title.

1078–88 is not a historical account of one particular battle, but a medley of memories of various occasions during the Persian wars (cf. N. G. L. Hammond in *JHS* lxxxviii [1968] 50–1). The language is reminiscent of Herodotos's account, published not long before; see the following notes.

1079 The Persians burned Athens in 480, and smoke may be used for attacking a wasps' nest; cf. 457. **πυρπολῶν:** cf. Hdt. 8. 50. 1.

1080 ἐξελεῖν: 'to destroy', a sense common in Herodotos. **τἀνθρήνια:** 'our nests', 'our hives'. Strictly σφῆκες should live in a σφηκιά and ἀνθρῆναι in an ἀνθρήνιον, but evidently Ar. is not interested in the distinction between the two kinds of insect; cf. 1107.

1081 ἐκδραμόντες: The Athenians at Marathon were reputed to have been the first Greeks ever to charge an enemy at a run (Hdt. 6. 112. 3). But this line hardly amounts to a statement that the members of the chorus fought in a battle 67 years ago; cf. page 10 n. 2.   **ξὺν δορὶ ξὺν ἀσπίδι**: The quotation, which appears again in *Peace* 356, is from a tragedy named *Momos* by Akhaios (fr. 29): Ἄρης ὁ λῃστὴς ξὺν δορὶ ξὺν ἀσπίδι (Σ⁰ *Wasps* 1081, Σ⁰ *Peace* 356). [Khoiroboskos *In Theod.* 1. 346. 15–16 is probably wrong to ascribe it to Sophokles. He gives the form σὺν δόρει σὺν ἀσπίδι, but that is less likely to have been the original; probably in some copies of Akhaios and Ar. ξὺν was supplanted by the more familiar σὺν (thus in *Peace* 356 the mss. have σὺν δορὶ σὺν ἀσπίδι), and subsequently some editor changed δορὶ to δόρει in an attempt to restore the metre. Cf. Platnauer's note on *Peace* 356.]

1082 θυμὸν: a pun. Most wasps drink from thyme (θύμον) which is sweet, but these Athenian wasps drank in a spirit (θυμός) which was bitter.

1083 στὰς ἀνὴρ παρ' ἄνδρ': 'each man standing beside the next'. The nominative singular is in partitive apposition to the plural subject, as is regular with words meaning 'each' or 'one . . . another'. The accusative is used with παρά because previous motion is implied; cf. 392, 1108, E. *Hel.* 1072 ἀνὴρ παρ' ἄνδρα στήσεται ξιφηφόρος.   **τὴν χελύνην ἐσθίων**: 286–7 n.

1084 Before the battle of Thermopylai the Spartans were told that when the Persians shot arrows they were so numerous that they hid the sun, to which Dienekes replied that it would be good to fight in the shade (Hdt. 7. 226).

1086 An owl was a good omen for the Athenians because it was Athena's symbol. Plu. *Them.* 12. 1 says that it was before the battle of Salamis that an owl was seen.   **διέπτατο**: 16 n.

1087 θυννάζοντες: 'harpooning', a variation for 'stinging'. Cf. A. *Per.* 424–6 (the battle of Salamis) ὥστε θύννους . . . ἔπαιον: but there the Greeks hit drowning Persians (like tunny caught in nets) with broken oars and wreckage, whereas Ar. appears to be thinking of spears and arrows in a land battle.   **θυλάκους**: 'bags': a contemptuous term, used also in E. *Kyk.* 182, for trousers, which the Persians wore in battle (Hdt. 5. 49. 3, 7. 61. 1).

1088 τὰς γνάθους: 'in the face', a limiting accusative.

1091 ἆρα: 'so', introducing a conclusion; cf. 839.   **δεινὸς ἦ**: 'I was terrible'. [ἦν could be right. Both forms of the first person singular were in use in Ar.'s time; ἦν is guaranteed by the metre in *Wealth* 29, E. *Alk.* 655, *Ion* 280, etc. It has been discussed by E. Harrison (*CR* lvi [1942] 6–9).]   **πάντα μὴ δεδοικέναι**: 'to fear nothing'.

1093 ἐκεῖσε: to the enemy's territory.

1095 ἐμέλλομεν: past indicative in a final clause expressing an unfulfilled purpose; cf. 961. The unfulfilled act on which it depended is οὐ γὰρ ἦν ἡμῖν φροντίς. 'We took no care in order to be ready to make a good speech . . .' (Not an indirect question, which would require a present or future tense.)

1097 ἀλλ' ὅστις . . .: The construction changes to an indirect question.

1098 τοιγαροῦν: 'That is why'. Ar. uses τοιγαροῦν only here, τοιγάρτοι only in *Akh.* 643. **πόλεις:** Greek cities in Asia Minor and the Aegean which were overrun by the Persians before 479 and subsequently became part of the Athenian empire and paid tribute to Athens; cf. 657.

1099–1100 'We are chiefly responsible for the tribute's being brought to Athens.' **φέρεσθαι:** the normal verb for the annual payment of tribute, not (as has been supposed) a reference to the transfer of the Delian League's treasury from Delos to Athens.

1101 The chorus have accepted the view put forward by Bdelykleon in 655–724.

1102 πολλαχοῦ: probably 'in many details', 'thoroughly'; or possibly 'in various circumstances'. **εἰς ἅπανθ':** 'in all respects' (LSJ εἰς IV. 2).

1103 The accusative nouns limit ἐμφερεστάτους.

1106 ὅμοια: adverb, not adjective: 'in a similar way to wasps'. Cf. Hdt. 3. 8. 1 σέβονται δὲ Ἀράβιοι πίστις ἀνθρώπων ὅμοια τοῖσι μάλιστα.

1107 καθ' ἐσμούς: 'by the swarm' (LSJ κατά B. II. 1). Each courtful of jurors is like a swarm of wasps. **ἀνθρήνια:** 1080 n. [Kock's conjecture was made in *Jahrbücher für classische Philologie* Supp. vi (1872) 188–9. H. Weber *Aristophanische Studien* (1908) 154–5 defends ὡσπερεὶ τἀνθρήνια (a) as meaning 'like troops of ἀνθρῆναι'. But there is no other evidence that ἀνθρήνιον can have this sense; a form in -ιον should mean a place or structure rather than a group or collection.]

1108 οὗπερ ἄρχων: 'where the arkhon sits', i.e. the chief arkhon. This sentence, in which the courts of the arkhon and the Eleven are distinguished from the Odeion, implies that each of the magistrates presiding over trials sat always in the same court (and this is implied by other passages too, e.g. Ant. 6. 21, fr. 42, And. 1. 28, D. 59. 52). Therefore the later system, by which courts were allocated to magistrates each day by lot (Arist. *Ath. Pol.* 66. 1), was not yet in use (and D. 59. 52 shows that it did not come into use before the second half of the fourth century). But which was the arkhon's court? Ten courts are known which were certainly or probably in use before the middle of the fourth century (excluding the Areopagos and the other special courts for homicide cases):

1. The court of the thesmothetai (ἡ ἡλιαία ἡ τῶν θεσμοθετῶν) (*IG* i² 39. 75, Ant. 6. 21, And. 1. 28). It is likely, though not certain, that at the time of *Wasps* this court was in the Metiokheion (τὸ Μητιοχεῖον or τὸ Μητιόχου), so called because it was built by Metiokhos. The identity

of the Eliaia with the Metiokheion is suggested by a comparison of *Lex. Rhet.* 310. 29–30, which explains ἡλιαία as μέγα δικαστήριον καὶ οἱ χίλιοι δικασταί, with Pol. 8. 121 and Hskh. μ 1290, where, although both passages suffer from corruption, the Metiokheion seems to be described in similar terms. The view that the Metiokheion was built before the time of *Wasps* is favoured by *Lex. Rhet.* 309. 18 and Phot. Μήτιχος; these too suffer from corruption, but they seem to say that Metiokhos was a politician as well as an architect, which means probably that he was the Metiokhos who was a friend of Perikles (Plu. *Eth.* 811 f, quoting *Com. adesp.* 1325). Since the Eliaia was the court which tried cases of impeachment (εἰσαγγελία) and other cases requiring exceptionally large juries (a thousand jurors or more), and it was perhaps in 462/1 that it took over this kind of case from the Areopagos, it may well have been found necessary to construct a specially large building for it in the time of Perikles. So the identification of the Eliaia with the Metiokheion is plausible, though the evidence for it falls far short of conclusive proof.

2. The Odeion (τὸ Ὠιδεῖον); cf. 1109. Phot. Ὠιδεῖον says that the arkhon's court was in the Odeion, and this conclusion is accepted by F. Jacoby *FGrH* IIIb Supp. ii 151. But in fact *Wasps* 1108–9, with its οἱ μὲν . . ., οἱ δὲ . . ., οἱ δ᾽ . . ., shows clearly that the arkhon's court was somewhere different from the Odeion, and Photios's statement must be wrong, at least for Ar.'s time. The suggestion that the five eisagogeis sat in the Odeion (J. H. Lipsius *Das attische Recht* 137 n. 11) is also unlikely to be right for Ar.'s time, since those officials probably did not yet exist (L. Gernet *Droit et société dans la Grèce ancienne* 173–8).

3. The Inserted Court (τὸ Παράβυστον), where the Eleven sat (Harp. Παράβυστον, giving Ant. *Against Nikokles* as his authority). Paus. 1. 28. 8 says that it was situated in an obscure part of the city, but he does not otherwise locate it, and his statement may be a mere guess from the name, which suggests that it was constructed in a confined space between other buildings.

4. The New Court (τὸ Καινόν); 120 n.

5. The Court at Lykos (τὸ ἐπὶ Λύκῳ); 389 n.

6. The Kallion (τὸ Κάλλιον), apparently so called because it was built by Kallias (*FGrH* 324 F 59, *Lex. Rhet.* 269. 33, Phot. Κάλλιον). Jacoby *FGrH* IIIb Supp. i 167 suggests that it was built in the time of Perikles by the Kallias who went as ambassador to Persia, but that is doubtful; Kallias was a common name.

7. The Triangular Court (τὸ Τρίγωνον) (Harp. Τρίγωνον, giving Lykourgos *Against Aristogeiton* as his authority, Σ *Wasps* 120, Paus. 1. 28. 8, *Lex. Rhet.* 309. 25).

8. The Greater Court (τὸ Μεῖζον) (Pol. 8. 121, referring to Lysias).

9. The Middle Court (τὸ Μέσον) (Pol. 8. 121, Σ *Wasps* 120, Phot. Μέσον).

10. The Painted Portico (ἡ στοὰ ἡ ποικίλη). An inscription of the middle of the fourth century shows that this was used as a law-court (*IG* ii² 1641. 28–30).

Only the first five of these were certainly in use as courts at the time of *Wasps*, but any or all of the others may have been so, and may therefore have been the court of the arkhon. The Eliaia (Meti-okheion), the Odeion, and the Inserted Court are the only ones which were certainly or probably not the arkhon's court. For a fuller dis-cussion of all these courts see Jacoby *FGrH* IIIb Supp. i 164–7, ii 146–53 (commentary on 324 F 59); but I do not agree with his interpreta-tion of *Wasps* 1108–9.

τοὺς ἕνδεκα: The Eleven were the officials in charge of the Athenian police, and were also the presiding magistrates for certain types of criminal trial. They sat in the Inserted Court (see above, no. 3). For the accusative cf. 392, 1083.

1109 The Odeion was a large hall south-east of the Akropolis, built by Perikles for musical performances. This is the earliest reference to its use as a law-court (1108 n.).   ὧδε . . .: 'packed in tight against the walls, like this'. The speaker huddles himself up, as if he were being squashed. [With οἱ δὲ (a) it is necessary to take πρὸς τοῖς τειχίοις as the name of another court, 'the Court at the City Walls'. But there is no other evidence for such a court, and if it existed its name ought to be ἐπὶ τοῖς τείχεσιν. The view of Willems 550–3 that οἱ δὲ means the audiences in the courts already mentioned is not plausible, because it is unlikely that the audiences in courts consisted mainly of jurors excluded from the day's juries.]

1110 νεύοντες: It is not clear why the jurors were 'bending to the ground'. Perhaps they sat on low backless benches which induced a crouching posture. To say that they stooped with age would be inappropriate to this context, where the subject is the conditions in the courts.

1111 'Like larvae moving in their cells.'

1112 'We are very resourceful in making a living too.'

1113 κἀκπορίζομεν βίον: 'and we provide a livelihood ⟨for our families⟩'. καί seems to suggest that there is a connection between stinging and obtaining a livelihood, without saying exactly what the connection is; it is not precisely true that wasps gain a livelihood by stinging or jurors by condemning, but (Ar. implies) it often seems like it.

1114 ἀλλὰ γάρ: 'But ⟨our efforts are wasted,⟩ for'.   κηφῆνες: Drones have no sting and do no work in a wasps' nest. The 'drones' whom Ar. is attacking here are Athenians who do not serve in war (οὐκ ἔχοντες κέντρον), but evade military service by one means or another. They are not the politicians and orators whom Bdelykleon accused of making themselves rich at the jurors' expense (655–724), but jurors who have not fought for Athens as the chorus have; this is proved by 1121 τριώβολον. The underlying idea is that the pay of a juror, which is obtained without hard work, should be regarded as a kind of pension for veterans, a reward for past services in war; cf. 678, 684–5.

1115 μένοντες: 'staying in Athens'; cf. *Akh.* 1052, *Peace* 341. [φόρου: J. T. Allen (*Univ. of California Publ. in Class. Philology* xi [1930] 97–100) proposes πόρου, to mean 'of our providing', with an echo of 1112–13. He argues that the jurors' livelihood comes not only from the tribute but also from court fees and fines, and that this is implied by 1113. However, the jurors' pay did come partly from the tribute (cf. 657), and 1117–21 must refer to military and naval expeditions made to assert Athenian control over the Aegean and ensure the tribute's continuation. So a reference to tribute in 1115 is not out of place, but is needed to clarify the point of 1117–21.]

1116 γόνον: 'produce', 'yield'; for this sense of the word cf. A. *Eu.* 946 γόνος ⟨δὲ γᾶς⟩ πλουτόχθων, referring to the produce of the silver-mines. The wasps' produce is honey. (Actually honey is not produced by wasps. Here and in *Lys.* 475 Ar. seems to confuse wasps with bees. This does not necessarily mean that he really thought them identical, but only that he was more interested in composing a striking metaphor than in observing entomological precision.) The Athenians' 'honey' is the money which they gain from the allies' tribute each year. τοῦ φόρου is added to τὸν γόνον to make the allegory clear. [With Bergk's πόνον the meaning is 'our work, namely the tribute'; cf. Pi. *P.* 6. 54 μελισσᾶν τρητὸν πόνον, meaning 'honeycomb'. Some editors have maintained that Σ had πόνον in his text, but this cannot be demonstrated. True, he says that drones τὰ τῶν μελισσῶν ἔργα ἐσθίουσιν, and Σ^Ald quotes Hes. *Works* 304–6, including the words μελισσάων κάματον τρύχουσιν, but all this is simply fair comment on 1114 κηφῆνες, and proves nothing about the reading which Σ had in 1116. The only note on 1116 is Σ^R's ὡσανεὶ ἔφη τὸν γόνον τῶν μελισσῶν. So πόνον should be regarded simply as a conjecture—plausible, but without manuscript authority.]

1118 ἐκροφῇ: 'gulps down'; for the metaphor cf. *Knights* 905 μισθοῦ τρύβλιον ῥοφῆσαι. [ἐκφορῇ (all mss. except V, which omits part of 1117–18 by haplography) would give the inappropriate meaning 'carry out'. Cantarella's ἐκφέρῃ, 'carry off', is possible.]

1119 φλύκταιναν: Blisters may be produced either by rowing (cf. *Frogs* 236) or by marching. There is a slight zeugma with λαβών, which means 'taking' with its first two objects and 'receiving' with the third. [This is understandable, and the bathos is even mildly amusing. It is not necessary to adopt μήτε κώπης μήτε λόγχης μηδὲ φλύκταιναν λαβών, conjectured by E. S. Thompson (*CR* ix [1895] 307).]

1120–1 'But in future I think that any citizen at all who doesn't have his sting should not be paid three obols.' [ἀλλά contrasts the future with the present, as in 1051, not the chorus's opinion with someone else's; so Brunck's ἀλλ' ἐμοὶ is unnecessary. Cf. 270.]

1122–1264 *Bdelykleon dresses Philokleon in a new cloak and boots. He instructs him in the art of polite conversation, gives him practice in singing drinking-songs (skolia), and explains how to tell a funny story to avoid trouble after a drunken prank; and they both go off to a party.*

This scene is of crucial importance for the development of the plot, because it is the central part of Philokleon's conversion from his old way of life to his new one. It is no mere mechanical link between earlier and later scenes. It is the earliest extant example of a major comic theme: the attempt to teach a simple ignorant person how to behave in superior society without betraying his origin or ignorance. From its best-known instance one may call this 'the *Pygmalion* theme', and Philokleon can be regarded as a distant ancestor of Eliza Doolittle. One thing is missing, inevitably: in Athens there seems to have been no difference of dialect between different social classes (Ar. fr. 685 and D. 37. 52–5 probably refer to vocabulary or tone of voice, not dialect), and so there can be no jokes about accent or pronunciation. But there is still a great deal of variety in the fun: comments on clothes, and slapstick in putting them on; parody of different types of conversation; comic miming of the actions of a guest at dinner; sarcastic comment on the facility with which 'gentlemen' avoid punishment for their misdeeds. The climax of the scene is the singing of the drinking-songs. In the original performance, before an audience familiar both with the words and tunes of the traditional songs and with the characters of Kleon, Theoros, and Aiskhines, it must have been a delightfully witty entertainment.

1122 When Philokleon and Bdelykleon come out of the house, they are followed by a slave (cf. the plural verb in 1153), who carries a thick woollen cloak of a type called κaυνάκης (1137) and a pair of Lakonian boots (1158). Philokleon is wearing the short τρίβων and ordinary shoes which he has been wearing throughout the play. Gestures, more than words, make clear at once that Bdelykleon is trying to get him to take off his τρίβων and put on the κaυνάκης, and he is refusing to do so. **τοῦτον**: For the accusative with the passive ἀποδύομαι cf. Lys. 10. 10.

1123 μόνος: Being poor (or parsimonious) he, like Sokrates (X. *Apom.* 1. 6. 2), wears no tunic; his τρίβων is his only garment.   παρατε-ταγμένον: 'when I was in the ranks'. The comic implication is that he has been wearing the same garment for over fifty years, ever since the Persian wars. [Wilamowitz 520 conjectured παρατεταγμένος, 'at my side', but the change is not essential, and is rejected by Willems 571.]

1124 βορέας: a comic surprise for βασιλεύς, the king of Persia: 11 n.

1127 ἐμπλήμενος: 424 n. 'Once, after filling myself with sprats . . .'

1128 'I had to pay three obols to the cleaner.' Last time Philokleon had a good meal he soiled his cloak (while sleeping in it; cf. *Ek.* 347); better not to have had the meal at all! (I see no need to deny that the debt was the result of the meal. But Wilamowitz 520–1 suggests that the sentence is comically illogical: 'When one has some good luck, some bad luck always follows', and on this occasion the bad luck was that he had to pay a debt.) [γναφεῖ: Emendation to κν- is unnecessary, because (despite Σ Wealth 166) γν- was certainly used in Attic (*IG* ii² 1638. 28).]

1129 'But still, just try it, now that you *have* . . .' The perfect tense means 'let it have been tried ⟨before you reject it⟩'.

1130 εὖ ποιεῖν: 'to treat you well'. An infinitive of purpose is common with παραδίδωμι.

1131 Philokleon acquiesces sulkily, making Bdelykleon repeat what he has already said (inside the house, before 1122). τρίβων': 33 n. ἄφες: 'let me take off'.

1132 χλαῖναν: 677 n. ἀναβαλοῦ: 'throw over yourself'. [ἀναλαβοῦ (a) is less likely to be right here and in 1135, because ἀναβάλλομαι is certainly used in 1152.] τριβωνικῶς: 'in a practised manner', an adverb invented for the sake of a pun on the two meanings of τρίβων, 'short cloak' and 'practised'. 'Give up your cape, and put on this cloak capably.'

1133 ἔπειτα: 'so', 'then', introducing an indignant question, as in *Akh.* 126, *Clouds* 1249, etc. Here a ὅτε-clause is added to clarify the ground of indignation. 'Why do we have to have children anyway, since . . . ?'

1134 ἀποπνίξαι: 'suffocate'. He grumblingly pretends that the woollen cloak will stifle him. Choking one's father was proverbially wicked; cf. 1039.

During 1133–4 Bdelykleon has got the τρίβων off Philokleon, leaving him naked (i.e. the actor wears only his comic padding and phallos). Now the slave offers him the woollen cloak.

1135 ἔχ': 'Here!', calling attention and followed by another imperative, as in *Akh.* 1121, *Peace* 1193, etc.

1136 Philokleon examines the cloak distastefully without putting it on. πρὸς πάντων θεῶν: 'I *ask* you', more emphatic than the usual πρὸς θεῶν.

1137 shows that Περσίς and καυνάκης are synonyms. They are a kind of cloak woven (1143) from wool (1147), with woollen tufts or tassels hanging from it (1144). Statuettes and reliefs show that the tufts were not just a fringe along the edge but were arranged in horizontal rows all over the cloak, making it very thick and warm (cf. 1146–56). For detailed discussion of this type of garment, with illustrations showing the archaeological evidence, see Léon Heuzey 'Une étoffe chaldéenne, le kaunakès' (*Rev. Arch.* III ix [1887] 257–72), and Émile Cherblanc *Le Kaunakès* (1937); but Cherblanc's interpretation of *Wasps* 1122–56 is wrong at some points, and his attempt to emend 1144 is unnecessary and misguided.

The καυνάκης which Bdelykleon offers Philokleon is not just a Greek imitation of a Persian cloak, but is actually imported from Persia

(1143). Philokleon's ignorance of it must be laughable, yet credible; so the passage shows that such cloaks were worn by some Athenians, but only rarely. It is the earliest evidence for the use in Athens of textiles imported from the East. Possibly such imports had only begun at the time of the negotiations between Athens and Persia in 424/3 (1139 n.); possibly a καυνάκης had notoriously been brought home by one of the Athenian envoys on that occasion.

1138 σισύραν: 738 n.   **Θυμαιτίδα**: 'Thymaitian', from the Athenian village of Thymaitadai, which was near Peiraieus (Pol. 4. 105). The joke must be that a Thymaitian σισύρα looked totally different from a καυνάκης. Philokleon is so ignorant about clothes that he cannot tell a luxurious Persian cloak from a rough Attic one.

1139 Σάρδεις: Ar. must have in mind some person or persons who have recently enjoyed a trip to Sardis—possibly Epilykos and his colleagues who went as envoys from Athens to the king of Persia in 424/3 (cf. H. T. Wade-Gery *Essays in Greek History* 207–11). In *Akh.* 599–619 the complaint is made that only leading politicians are appointed to such well-paid embassies; cf. too *Wasps* 1188. So 1139 implies 'You haven't had the same opportunities as *some* people'.

1140 νῦν: 'as it is', i.e. 'since you haven't been to Sardis'. [Wilamowitz 521–2 makes this sentence a question. But Bdelykleon, who has just been saying that Philokleon cannot be expected to recognize the type of cloak, cannot now ask whether he does recognize it.]

1141 τοίνυν is regularly used when a speaker admits his ignorance of a piece of information just given to him; cf. *Peace* 615, *Birds* 511. 'I don't, I must admit.' [Emendation, such as Wilamowitz's οὐδὲ νῦν, is unnecessary.]

1142 ἐοικέναι: often εἰκ- in the infinitive and participle in Attic, but cf. 1413 ἐοικώς, fr. 646 ἐοικέναι.   **Μορύχου**: 506 n.   **σάγματι**: 'pack', some sort of bag or container for armour and other equipment (*Akh.* 574, E. *Andr.* 617). It is not clear what was distinctive about Mory-khos's pack or why Philokleon thinks that the καυνάκης looks like it. But in view of 1144 I suggest that Morykhos, who was notoriously fond of food, may recently have attracted attention by having some sausages hanging from his pack when he came on duty for some military expedition; citizens reporting for military duty were required to bring their own food for the first three days (243 n.), and the woollen tassels of the καυνάκης look like sausages (1144). The alterna-tive view that Morykhos had a cloak which was thought to be like a shield-case because Morykhos was round has been discussed and supported by H. L. Crosby (*Class. Phil.* x [1915] 326–30); but he fails to explain why it is funny to compare a καυνάκης to Morykhos's cloak.

1143 Ekbatana was the capital of Media and the summer residence of the kings of Persia.

K

1144 Philokleon points to the woollen tassels. 'Do they make wool-sausages in Ekbatana?' If I am right in suggesting that he was already thinking of sausages in 1142, the point of 1144 is to make the joke clear to those members of the audience who did not see it before.

1145 πόθεν: 'What!' 'Nonsense!' as in *Frogs* 1455, etc. In full the idea would be something like 'Where did you get that idea from?'

1147 τάλαντον: value, not weight (as 1146 proves) : 'a thousand pounds' worth', a wild exaggeration.   καταπέπωκε: 'has swallowed up'; for the metaphor cf. *Frogs* 1466.

1148 ἐριώλην really means 'hurricane', but Philokleon pretends that it is derived from ἔριον and ὄλλυμι, so as to mean 'consuming wool'. In English it would be an equivalent joke to say 'Shouldn't you have called it a waste-coat rather than a cloak?' Dionysios I of Syracuse is said to have used the same pun in a tragedy (Phot. *Bibl.* cod. 279. 532 b [Migne *Patrologia Graeca* civ 313] = Dionysios fr. 12).

1149 ἔχ': 'Keep still!' The slave, at a sign from Bdelykleon, now tries to put the cloak on Philokleon. (Not, at this point, Bdelykleon himself; 1154 ἐγώ marks a contrast with previous efforts.)

1150 στῆθ': 'stop moving about!' Philokleon is walking away.   ἀναμπισχόμενος: 'while being dressed up', or perhaps 'while being re-dressed'. This compound does not occur elsewhere. [But that does not prove that it needs emendation. Wilamowitz 522, comparing 1135, wishes to delete καὶ and read στῆθ' ἀτρέμας ἀμπισχόμενος. But this is not necessary, since ἔχω can mean 'keep still'; cf. LSJ ἔχω B. I. 1, Willems 573.]

1151 'What a hot puff the wretched thing belched at me!'

1153 'If you must ⟨make me wear hot clothes⟩, dress me in an oven instead.' The joke is that an oven would be cooler.

1154 φέρ', ἀλλ' ἐγώ: 'Well then, let *me* . . .' [φέρε often introduces an aorist subjunctive, seldom a future indicative; so περιβάλω is preferable to περιβαλῶ.]   δ' οὖν: permissive, as in 6, 764: 'you can go'. Bdelykleon takes the cloak from the slave, hands him Philokleon's τρίβων, and dismisses him into the house. The slave leaves the Lakonian boots (1158) behind on the ground.

1155 γε: grudging acquiescence: 'but at least put a meat-hook near by'. τιὴ τί δή; cf. *Peace* 1018, *Th.* 84. Since τιή and τί δή both mean 'why?' the expression is redundant.

1156 πρὶν διερρυηκέναι: 'before I have been cooked to rags'. During 1155–6 Bdelykleon has got the cloak on to Philokleon.

1157 ὑπολύου: the usual verb for taking off shoes. [ἀποδύου (cf. the reading of J) may be right, but is less likely, because this verb is more often used of clothes than shoes; cf. 1122.]   ἐμβάδας: 103 n.

1158 ὑπόδυθι: 'get into'. ὑποδύομαι is used of putting on shoes or boots only here and in 1159 and 1168; the usual verb is ὑποδέομαι. [Some editors therefore emend all three lines; and indeed in 1159 and 1168

-δησ- might easily be accepted, since η and υ were often confused in the
Byzantine period, when both were pronounced alike. But emendation
of 1158 is a more drastic matter: ὑπόδησαι will not scan. The use of
ὑποδύομαι may be justified if Λακωνικαί were boots; see next note.]
Λακωνικάς: a type of footwear regularly worn only by men, not
women (*Th.* 142, *Ek.* 74, 269). They were red (Pol. 7. 88), and
fastened by leather straps (*Ek.* 508). Our passage shows that they
were regarded as superior to ἐμβάδες, and probably that they were
warmer, just as the καυνάκης is warmer than the τρίβων; this, combined with the use of ὑποδύομαι, 'get down into', and of ἔνθες (1161),
'put in', instead of ὑποδέομαι, 'fasten under the feet', suggests that they
were boots, not shoes or sandals.

1159 γάρ introduces a scornful question (cf. Denniston 77–8) : 'Because
⟨you think⟩ . . .?' but in English we should say 'What!'   **τλαίην**:
not 'dare', but 'bear'; Philokleon is chauvinistic, not cowardly. His
objection is absurd, since 'Lakonian' means only that the boots are of
a certain style, not that they are imported from Sparta. It is as if
a Cambridge man refused to wear 'Oxford' shoes, or a Lancastrian to
eat Yorkshire pudding.

1160 is tragic in manner, but Starkie's suggestion that it parodies E.
Hkld. 1006 ἐχθροῦ λέοντος δυσγενῆ (δυσμενῆ Stephanus) βλαστήματα is
far-fetched.

1161 Bdelykleon holds one of the boots ready in front of Philokleon. His
action makes **ἔνθες** clear without τὸν πόδα.   **ποτ'**: 'eventually', 'after
all this delay'; so also in 1168.   **ὦ τᾶν**: 373 n.; used by a son to his
father also in *Clouds* 1432. Bdelykleon is polite, but still implies that he
knows better than Philokleon.   **ἀπόβαιν'**: 'step out', a suitable
expression for one who, while standing, puts one foot forward into
a boot; it has a similar sense in Hp. *Mokhlikon* 20.   **ἐρρωμένως**:
'firmly', to push the foot down to the bottom of the boot.

1162–3 As Philokleon puts his foot into the boot he continues to grumble.
He misinterprets ἀπόβαιν' ἐς τὴν Λακωνικήν, which sounds like 'dis-
embark in Lakonia'. 'But you *are* doing me wrong, landing my foot on
enemy territory.'

1164 τὸν ἕτερον: sc. ἔνθες πόδα. (Or possibly φέρε with no comma may
mean 'put out'; cf. *Th.* 1115 φέρε δεῦρό μοι τὴν χεῖρ', ἵν' ἄψωμαι,
Herodas 7. 113 φέρ' ὧδε τὸν ποδίσκον. But with this one would expect
δεῦρο or some similar word.) Bdelykleon holds out the second boot, but
now Philokleon turns sharply away.

1165 'One of its toes is very anti-Spartan.'   **μισολάκων**: The compound is found only here and may have been invented for the
occasion, but it is of a common and easily formed type; e.g. 411
μισόπολιν, 473 μισόδημε, *Peace* 304 μισολάμαχος.

1166 'There is no other way but this.' The same sentence is used in *Clouds*
698 (where it evokes the same response, κακοδαίμων ἐγώ) and *Peace* 110.

1167 He comically regards lack of chilblains as a deprivation. ἐπὶ
γήρᾳ: 'in my old age', or more strictly 'arising from my old age': not
purely temporal, but denoting the circumstances which give rise to
chilblains.

1168–9 εἶτα . . .: 'Now, stepping forward in an opulent manner, like this,
. . .' Philokleon has at last put on the second boot; this is shown by
ὡδί, since Bdelykleon cannot demonstrate a rich man's walk while still
holding out the boot for him. During the demonstration Philokleon
may be fastening the straps of the boot.   τρυφερόν τι: adverbial
(internal) accusative: 'a voluptuous strut', 'luxuriously'.   διασαλακώνισον: 'swagger'. The compound is not found elsewhere, but
σαλάκων, meaning 'pretentious', occurs several times in Aristotle (e.g.
in *Rhet*. 1391ᵃ2 rich men are called τρυφεροὶ καὶ σαλάκωνες), and
σαλακωνίζομαι in Hermippos 71. δια- will mean 'with legs apart'; cf.
688 διαβάς. [This reading, given by all mss. and recognized by Σ,
makes good sense, and so may be accepted. But Σ's two variants
would also give good sense: διαλυκώνισον, from an effeminate man
named Lykon (cf. 1301); or διαλακώνισον, 'walk in a Lakonian
manner', because Philokleon is wearing Lakonian boots.]

1170 ἰδού: 'There!' He has finished fastening the boots, and stands up.
Except for his head he is completely enveloped in the cloak and boots.
σχῆμα: his manner of holding himself and moving. 'Now, watch my
bearing, and see which rich man I most resemble in my walk.' He
hobbles a few steps in a ridiculously awkward manner.

1172 'A man who has put a garlic dressing on a boil', who cannot walk
properly because he has a boil on his foot. A garlic poultice is used for
suppurating a boil. (Not 'a boil dressed in garlic' meaning that
Philokleon is red-faced in a white cloak, because the matter now under
consideration is not how hot he is in the cloak but how he can walk in
the boots. The line is fully discussed and rightly explained by Holzinger 29–34.)

1173 'Actually I'm *trying* to do the waggle-bottom.'
These antics can continue *ad lib*., as long as the audience is laughing.
When the actor playing Bdelykleon judges that the joke is wearing
thin, he breaks in to introduce a new topic: how to conduct a polite
conversation. We now begin to realize that the object of dressing
Philokleon up is not just to let him live in warmth and luxury but to
enable him to mix with high society.

1174 σεμνούς: 'impressive'.

1177 Λάμι': 1035 n.   ἐπέρδετο: 394 n. The occasion when Lamia/
Lamias broke wind is referred to also in *Ek*. 76–8, and Σ there quotes
from a play called *Lamia*: σκυτάλην ἔχουσ' ἐπέρδετο. (The quotation is
attributed to Pherekrates by Σ, but the name is generally emended to
Krates, and the fragment listed as Krates 18, because Krates is
known to have written a *Lamia* and Pherekrates is not.) Together the

three passages tell us that Lamia/Lamias was caught, holding a stick, and broke wind in fright. They do not explain how the incident fitted into the rest of the legend about this person. Presumably in Ar.'s time the incident had become notorious because it had been represented in a recent play (either Krates's or another; Euripides also wrote a *Lamia*, which may have been a satyr-play).

1178 Καρδοπίων: unknown. The verb would be a vulgar one, if Philokleon had a chance to get it out; the joke is that he suggests vulgar topics when serious ones are required. (Theok. 1. 105 οὐ λέγεται τὰν Κύπριν ὁ βουκόλος; is different. There the verb is omitted from delicacy or prudery or archness; but Philokleon has none of these qualities, and it is better to suppose that he is about to utter the verb when Bdelykleon hastily interrupts him.)

1179 μὴ 'μοιγε: sc. εἴπῃς or λέγε, as in 1400, *Clouds* 84, etc. Although γε follows the pronoun, as in English we may say 'Don't tell *me* that!', it does not really imply that Philokleon should relate legends to anyone else; cf. Denniston 122. **τῶν ἀνθρωπίνων**: partitive genitive, sc. λόγων: 'some human stories', not legends about gods. [Phrynikhos (Bekker *Anecdota Graeca* 21. 14) says ἀνθρωπικὸς μῦθος· ὁ περὶ ἀνθρωπείων πραγμάτων, and Meineke *Fragmenta Comicorum Graecorum* ii 241 wanted therefore to emend to ἀνθρωπικῶν in our line. Van Leeuwen (*Mn.* II xxxvii [1909] 124) in support argues ingeniously that Photios attributed the phrase ἀνθρωπικὸς μῦθος to *Wasps*. But this depends on an emendation of Photios, and it remains doubtful whether either Photios or Phrynikhos was referring to our passage.]

1180 τοὺς κατ' οἰκίαν: 'fireside stories'. He means 'stories that we tell at home', but Philokleon misunderstands him to mean 'stories about things which happen at home'.

1181 τοίνυν: 'All right, then', complying with the request; so also in 1205. **τῶν γε πάνυ κατ' οἰκίαν**: partitive genitive, with ἐκεῖνον· 'a *very* fireside story'.

1182 οὕτω: used to introduce fables; cf. *Lys.* 785, Pl. *Phdr.* 237 b. **γαλῆ**: 363 n. 'Once upon a time there was a mouse and a cat . . .'

1183 ὦ σκαιὲ κἀπαίδευτε: Bdelykleon loses his temper, but then pulls himself up and pretends that he was merely quoting a remark made by someone else: '—as Theogenes said to . . .'.

Θεογένης, who belonged to the deme Peiraieus (Σ *Peace* 928) but lived at Akharnai (*Lys.* 61–4), was a prominent politician. In 425 he was appointed with Kleon to Pylos on a fact-finding commission (Th. 4. 27. 3). In 421 he was one of the seventeen Athenians who took the oaths to observe the Peace of Nikias and the alliance with Sparta (Th. 5. 19. 2, 24. 1). At this period he was often satirized in comedy as a fat, greedy, dirty man, who engaged in business and liked to be thought rich, who talked a lot but whose actions often failed to match his words (*Peace* 928, *Birds* 822, 1127, 1295, with Σ on all these passages; cf. Eupolis *Demes* fr. 110a Edmonds). In 411 he was perhaps associated with the Four-hundred, and on their fall had to withdraw from politics, and possibly from Athens; at any rate he is not heard of again (if it is true that the Theogenes in X. *Hel.* 1. 3. 13 was a different man) until he became a member of the Thirty in 404 (X. *Hel.* 2. 3. 2). [I have discussed this man more fully elsewhere (*Rh. Mus.* civ [1961] 229–36), giving reasons for thinking that all these allusions are to the same man, and suggesting that on the whole the weight of manuscript evidence favours Θεα- rather than Θεο-. If Θεα- is right, εα is scanned as one long syllable; cf. 1067 and note. But Θεο-, given by all mss. in *Wasps* 1183, cannot be proved wrong. Different views about the man's identity have been put forward by S. Srebrny (*Eos* xxviii [1925] 79–86) and by A. Andrewes and D. M. Lewis (*JHS* lxxvii [1957] 178–9).]

It is not likely that Theogenes really said these words to a dung-collector. Probably the two points of the joke are that he often delivered pompous reproofs, and that it was for some reason funny to mention dung in connection with him. According to Σ, Ar. made another joke about Theogenes and dung in *Seasons* (fr. 571).

1184 καὶ ταῦτα λοιδορούμενος: Bdelykleon is still trying to explain away his outburst; ὦ σκαιὲ κἀπαίδευτε was said only by that very rude man Theogenes, and only in a quarrel (the participle may be either middle or passive).

1185 ἀνδράσιν: grown men, as opposed to children; so also in *Clouds* 823, *Peace* 51, 766.

1186 μεγαλοπρεπεῖς: 'impressive'. Philokleon is to try to make himself appear an important person.

1187 ὡς: '⟨e.g.⟩ how . . .'; cf. *Clouds* 659.   **ξυνεθεώρεις**: 'you were on a sacred embassy with'. θεωροί were men appointed to go as official representatives of the state to attend one of the great international festivals (Olympia, Pythia, Isthmia, Nemea) or to consult an oracle. This line means, I think, that Androkles and Kleisthenes had recently been appointed to go on a sacred embassy, and that some people, including Ar., thought it disgraceful or laughable that such men should be chosen to represent Athens. Thus the sentence ends in anticlimax: to say that one had been a colleague of these men would not be an impressive boast at all.

Androkles was a demagogic politician. (Arist. *Rhet.* 1400^{a}9–14 gives a sample of his eloquence.) He was often satirized in comedy as penniless and immoral (Σ *Wasps* 1187, alluding to Kratinos, Telekleides, and Ekphantides; cf. Kratinos 208, 263, 458 Kock = 209a Edmonds, *Com. adesp.* 48, 51). In 415 he was prominent in the discussions of the profanation of the Mysteries and was largely responsible for driving Alkibiades into exile, and it was for this reason that he was murdered by oligarchs in 411 (Th. 8. 65. 2, And. 1. 27, Plu. *Alk.* 19. 1–3).

Kleisthenes is ridiculed for effeminacy in every other surviving fifth-century play of Ar. except *Peace*, and most notably as a character in *Th*. Besides his appointment to a sacred embassy in 423/2 (*Wasps* 1187), he was a commander in the navy in 406 (*Frogs* 48), but nothing else is known about him. (In Lys. 25. 25 a Kleisthenes is said to have got rich by accusing men who had taken part in the oligarchic revolution in 411. But that may be a different man; and Schwartz, in *Rh. Mus.* xliv [1889] 121 n. 1, suggested that Κλεισθένην there should be emended to Κλειγένην, referring to the Kleigenes of *Frogs* 709 and And. 1. 96.)

1188 Philokleon ridicules the suggestion. 'What? *Me* on a sacred embassy?' Again Ar. implies that ordinary Athenians never get a chance to travel abroad at the state's expense: 1139 n.

1189 Πάρον: This must mean that at some date an Athenian sacred embassy had gone to Paros, but there is no evidence to show when or why.   φέρων: 'earning'. The point must be that he went to Paros in the humblest possible capacity, as a rower. At this period the rate of pay for a rower seems usually to have been one drachma a day (Th. 3. 17. 4, 6. 8. 1, 6. 31. 3, 8. 45. 2). Our line is evidence that at an earlier period, when Philokleon would have been young enough to row, the rate was two obols a day.

1190 ἀλλ' οὖν . . . γ': 'Well, in that case, at least . . .', introducing a second-best suggestion, that he should talk about an achievement by another old man instead of himself.   αὐτίκα: 'for example'.

1191 The contest between Ephoudion and Askondas must be a real incident, but nothing is known of either except Σ's statement (partly confirmed by Hskh. ε 7567) that an Ephoudion from Mainalia (in Arkadia) was a victor at the 79th Olympic games (in 464). This identification fits well: I suggest (though this is only a guess) that Ephoudion was a young man in 464, and that twenty or more years later (within the memory of many of Ar.'s audience), when growing old, he fought a contest at the Olympic games (cf. 1382) against one of the leading athletes of the younger generation, named Askondas, and did surprisingly well. (Bdelykleon does not say that he won.)   παγκράτιον: The pankration was one of the regular events at the Olympic games and other athletic meetings. It was a kind of wrestling, in which punching and kicking were allowed. Cf. H. A. Harris *Greek Athletes and Athletics* (1964) 105-9.

1193 πλευρὰν . . . λαγόνα: singular for plural, as is common in such descriptions in English too. The Greek discusses an athlete in much the same way as an Englishman discusses a horse. 'A very deep side ⟨i.e. chest⟩, and arms, and a flank, and . . .' Commendation for χέρας and λαγόνα is understood partly from the commendation of πλευρὰν and partly from the tone of voice; one might say, 'And his arms! And his flank!' [βαρυτάτην (RΓJ) is possible as a complimentary adjective applied to a warrior or athlete; cf. Pi. *I.* 4. 55 συμπεσεῖν δ' ἀκμᾷ βαρύς, Philostr. *Gym.* 31. But this should refer to the body as a whole; for πλευρὰν a more suitable epithet is βαθυτάτην, evidently the reading of V's predecessor, as the scribe of G (a copy of V) realized. Further emendation in this line is unnecessary: χέρας may be used for χείρας to suit the metre, even in comedy, cf. *Lys.* 1317, *Frogs* 1142; the singular λαγόνα is defended by the singular πλευρὰν; for καὶ at the end of an iambic trimeter cf. *Akh.* 143, *Lys.* 1176, *Wealth* 752.]

1195 θώρακ': The list in 1193–4 has been leading up to this pun. Bdely-kleon means 'chest', but Philokleon misunderstands him to mean 'breastplate' and objects that in a pankration the contestants are unarmed. θώραξ in the sense 'chest' or 'torso' was an anatomical term, not yet in general use (cf. 1196 and H. Weber *Aristophanische Studien* 165–6); that is why Philokleon misunderstands it. The pun cannot be preserved exactly in English; Rogers in his translation uses 'a chest of iron' and 'an iron chest'. (Starkie and others take θώρακ' ἔχων to mean 'having had a drink'. But although θωρήττομαι has this meaning in *Akh.* 1135 and *Peace* 1286, there is no instance of θώρακ' ἔχω in this sense. And a drink would be less out of place at a pan-kration than a breastplate.)

1196 νομίζουσ': 'are accustomed to', 'are in the habit of'.

1198 σεαυτοῦ: with ἔργον. He makes a fresh attempt to get Philokleon to tell an impressive story about himself.

1199 ἐπὶ νεότητος: with ἔργον: 'done in your youth'.

1200 ἐκεῖν' ἐκεῖν': repeated in eagerness to answer the question; so also in *Clouds* 657.   **ἀνδρειότατόν**: The variation from ἀνδρικώτατον is merely to fit the metre; there is no distinction of meaning.

1201 The great achievement of Philokleon's youth turns out to be no more impressive than the chorus-leader's (237–9).   **Ἐργασίωνος**: a fictional name, formed from ἐργασία. We might say 'Farmer Giles'.

1202 ποίας: ποῖος with a noun repeated from the previous speech signifies scornful rejection: 'Posts indeed!': so also in 1369, 1378. **ὡς**: 'tell how': λέγε is easily understood from the context.

1203 λαμπάδα: 'torch race'. Torch races were held in Athens at certain festivals, particularly the Hephaistia, the Prometheia, and the great Panathenaia. They were relay races; a torch was handed on by each runner to his successor, and had to be kept burning.

1204 ἀνευρὼν: 'recalling', not 'inventing'.

1206 Phayllos, like Ephoudion (1191), was a distinguished athlete of the previous generation, referred to also in *Akh.* 214. He came from Kroton (in south Italy), and at the Pythian games was a victor twice in the pentathlon and once in the stadion, i.e. running 200 yards (Paus. 10. 9. 2. Pausanias says he was never an Olympic victor; so the state-ment of Σ *Akh.* 214 that he was is probably a mistake. This does not mean that he was defeated at Olympia; a man living in Italy might seldom compete at the Greek festivals). An epigram (*App. Anth.* 297) imaginatively and alliteratively attributes to him a long jump of 55 feet and a discus throw of 95 feet:

πέντ' ἐπὶ πεντήκοντα πόδας πήδησε Φάυλλος,
δίσκευσεν δ' ἑκατὸν πέντ' ἀπολειπομένων.

At the battle of Salamis in 480 he commanded the only ship which came from Italy; either for this reason or because of his Pythian victories a statue of him was erected at Delphoi (Hdt. 8. 47. 1, Plu. *Alex.* 34, Paus. 10. 9. 2). Also there survives the base of a monument to him on the Athenian Akropolis (*IG* i² 655). Cf. E. N. Gardiner 'Phayllus and his Record Jump' (*JHS* xxiv [1904] 70–80).

βούπαις: 'big boy', 'youth'. Because bulls and horses were the Greeks' largest animals, βου- and ἱππο- were used as prefixes meaning 'great'; e.g. βουκόρυζα 'severe cold', βουλιμιάω 'am very hungry', ἱπποτυφία 'great pride', ἱππόκρημνος 'very steep'. So in English 'horse-chestnut', 'horse-laugh', etc. Cf. L. J. D. Richardson's discussion of βου- (*Hermathena* xcv [1961] 53–63).

1207 εἶλον διώκων: a pun. At first we think he means 'I ran after Phayllos and caught him', which would be a great athletic achievement. But from the next words we find that he means 'I prosecuted Phayllos for using abusive language, and got him convicted by two votes'. διώκω and αἱρέω are regular legal terms. λοιδορίας: genitive of accusation; cf. 1407, 1418.

1208 κατακλινείς: 'reclining', as the Greeks did at meals. προσμάνθανε: 'learn now'. προσ- only means 'in addition to what you already know', 'and so become wiser'. It does not imply that Philokleon has just learned another lesson; the lesson is only now about to begin. [Cf. *Th.* 20, where προσμαθών, referring to the first lesson, is defended by the metre. So Dobree's προμάνθανε is unnecessary.]

1209 ξυνουσιαστικός occurs nowhere else before the Hellenistic period. Possibly Ar. has invented it to satirize, while talking about fashionable society, the current fashion for adjectives in -ικός; cf. 1259, *Knights* 1378–81, *Clouds* 1172–3, and C. W. Peppler's discussion of -κός (*AJP* xxxi [1910] 428–44).

1211 ὡδί: He flops down on to the ground in some ridiculously clumsy way.

1212 Philokleon stands up again. During 1212–17 Bdelykleon demonstrates the actions which he describes and Philokleon comically tries to imitate him, all in mime; of course there are no actual rugs, ornaments, water, and so on. δαί: 'then', after the rejection of a suggestion; so also πῶς δαί; in E. *Kyk.* 450, *Hel.* 1246, and τί δαί; in *Clouds* 656, *Birds* 1640, etc.

1213 'Pour yourself out fluidly on the rugs.' The affected language gives good scope for comic business by Philokleon. στρώμασιν: For a luxurious party (but hardly for an ordinary meal) rugs were spread over the (unupholstered) couches or benches on which the guests reclined.

1214 χαλκωμάτων: objects hung on the walls or disposed about the room as ornaments; not plates or cups used for the meal, since they do not arrive until 1216. Several surviving fifth-century cups have pictures of drinking parties at which cups and jugs are hanging on the wall; cf. T. B. L. Webster in *Bulletin of the John Rylands Library* xlv (1962) 266.

1215 ὀροφὴν θέασαι: Philokleon gazes upwards. The phrase shows that in a rich Athenian's house there would be painting or other ornamentation on the ceiling. Archaeological evidence for the interior painting of Greek houses dates only from the fourth century and later; for a summary see Webster *ibidem*. κρεκάδι' occurs nowhere else, but presumably it is derived from κρέκω in the sense 'weave' and means 'tapestries' or 'curtains' hanging against the wall. If so, this is the earliest evidence for the use of textile hangings to decorate a Greek room. Hdt. 9. 82 seems to imply that such decoration was unknown in Greece at the time of the Persian wars. For other evidence for textiles decorating rooms, all later than *Wasps*, see W. K. Pritchett in *Hesperia* xxv (1956) 248–9, Webster op. cit. 262–5. (Wilamowitz 523–4 suggests a connection with the bird called κρέξ, but that is far-fetched. There is no reason why this species of bird should be associated with grand dining-rooms.) αὐλῆς: 'hall'. An αὐλή is a large space surrounded by walls. Any house may have an open-air courtyard; e.g. 131. But here the αὐλή has a ceiling (ὀροφὴν); only a very grand house would have an interior room large enough to be called an αὐλή.

1216 ὕδωρ κατὰ χειρός: 'Water for our hands!' He enlivens his description by pretending to address the waiters. Greeks used no forks for eating, but washed their hands both before a meal and after it. The method was that the diner held his hands over a bowl and a slave poured water over them from a jug; so κατὰ means 'down on to', 'over'. Cf. *Birds* 463–4 Πε. καταχεῖσθαι κατὰ χειρὸς ὕδωρ φερέτω ταχύ τις. Ευ. δειπνήσειν μέλλομεν; ἢ τί; and fr. 502. The expression κατὰ χειρός is used only of washing before a meal, ἀπονίψασθαι of washing after it (Ath. 408 f); cf. 1217. τὰς τραπέζας εἰσφέρειν: 386 n.: 'Bring in the tables!' At a Greek dinner there was one small table for each two or three diners. The food was put on the tables outside the dining-room, and when the meal was to begin slaves carried in the tables and placed them in front of the couches on which the diners were reclining. So 'Bring in the tables!' means 'Serve dinner!' Cf. *Frogs* 518 ἡ τράπεζ' εἰσῆρετο, 'dinner was just being served' (a single table for two diners only).

1217 σπένδομεν: After the dinner wine was brought, and the diners poured out a little in honour of a god before drinking the rest. These libations marked much the same stage in the proceedings as the loyal toast at a British dinner.

1218 ἐνύπνιον: adverbial (internal) accusative, as in Men. *Dys.* 407, *Perik.* 169 (and the similar use of ὄναρ is common): 'is our feast a dream?' Since the food and everything else are imaginary, he is bemused by Bdelykleon's rapid description.

1219 αὐλητρίς: crasis for ἡ αὐλ-. The flute-girl would begin to play immediately after the libations (cf. Pl. com. 69. 4-6). She would be a slave (cf. 1353), hired for the party by the host from her proprietor. In the fourth century it was forbidden to charge more than two drachmas a time for the hire of a flute-girl (Arist. *Ath. Pol.* 50. 2), but no fifth-century price is known.   **ἐνεφύσησεν**: 'has begun to play'. [This compound seems to occur nowhere else, but that does not prove that we must emend to ἀν-.]

1220 Θέωρος: 42 n.   **Αἰσχίνης**: 459 n.   **Φᾶνος**: evidently another friend of Kleon. In *Knights* 1256 he is called ὑπογραφεὺς δικῶν, which seems to mean that he helped Kleon with prosecutions. [Not Φανός: cf. Hdn. Gr. (Lentz) i 175.]

It is a little surprising that Bdelykleon names Kleon and his friends as the guests at a typical high-class party. Ar. may have been in-fluenced by any or all of these considerations: (*a*) He has had the brilliant comic idea of adapting drinking songs into abuse of Kleon, Theoros, and Aiskhines; so these men should be named in 1220 to prepare for the jokes in 1224-48. (*b*) Although these men claimed to protect the rights of ordinary Athenians, they were not themselves regarded as ordinary Athenians but as important men (that is why in 596-600 Philokleon is so impressed by their condescension); so they were not out of place in high-class society. (*c*) Since Bdelykleon won the agon, he and Philokleon no longer hold different views about Kleon; their names are really out of date (except for a single mention in 1466 they are in fact never used after the agon); now the son represents familiarity with high society (such as Kleon) and the father represents ignorance of it.

1221 ξένος τις ἕτερος: 'a foreigner as well'.   **πρὸς κεφαλῆς**: 'at your head', reclining next to Philokleon. Bdelykleon points to the spot where each guest is imagined to be reclining, as he names them in order round the circle: Theoros at Philokleon's feet (1236), and so on round to Akestor's son at Philokleon's head.   **Ἀκέστορος**: crasis for ὁ Ἀκ-: 'Akestor's son', in apposition to ξένος. [This reading is clearly implied by Σ's note: ἐπεὶ καὶ αὐτὸν τὸν Ἀκέστορα ξένον κωμῳδοῦσι . . .] Akestor was a tragic dramatist, who was said not to be of Athenian birth (cf. ξένος) but claimed Athenian citizenship (*Birds* 31-2) and eventually obtained it (Metagenes 13). Because of his alleged foreign origin the comic dramatists often called him Σάκας and 'Mysian' (Σ *Wasps* 1221 and Σ *Birds* 31, quoting Kratinos 85, Kallias 13,

Metagenes 13, Theopompos 60; the Sakai lived east of the Caspian sea, the Mysians in north-west Asia Minor), and also a slave and a parasite (Eupolis 159). Nothing is known about his son.

1222 σκόλι': A skolion was a type of song sung at an Athenian drinking-party. One guest held a sprig of myrtle and sang a line or more; then he passed the sprig to another, who was said to 'receive' or 'take up' (δέχεσθαι) the song and had to sing the next line or more; and so on. The song might be either traditional or extemporized. A collection of twenty-five skolia, each of two or four lines, is preserved in Ath. 694 c–695 f. Some of them, perhaps all, seem to belong to the second half of the sixth century or the beginning of the fifth, and that period was probably the heyday of skolia. But *Wasps* 1222–49 shows that they were sung in the late fifth century, and Antiphanes 85 seems to show that they were still current in the middle of the fourth. For the texts of surviving skolia see D. L. Page *Poetae Melici Graeci* (1962) nos. 884–917; for a discussion of them see C. M. Bowra *Greek Lyric Poetry* 2nd edition (1961) 373–97.   **ὅπως δέξει καλῶς**: 'make sure you take up the songs well'. [Some editors give καλῶς to Philokleon and ἄληθες; to Bdelykleon, but that is not an improvement. It makes ὅπως δέξει weak; Bdelykleon is more likely to be worried about the quality of Philokleon's singing than about whether he will sing at all.]

1223 ἄληθες; implies 'Why say such a thing? The answer is obvious'. So also in *Clouds* 841, *Birds* 174, etc. Elsewhere ἄληθες; (often ἄληθες, οὗτος;) shows anger, implying 'How dare you say such a thing?'; so in 1412, *Birds* 1048, *Frogs* 840, etc.   **ὡς οὐδείς γε διακρίων ἐγώ**: 'I'll do it better than any hillman'. Singing in alternation was a pastime of ancient shepherds; cf. Theokritos, and Virgil's *Eclogues*. Some have seen a reference here to the hillmen of north-east Attika (διάκριοι in Arist. *Ath. Pol.* 13. 4, Plu. *Sol.* 29. 1, ὑπεράκριοι in Hdt. 1. 59. 3) who supported the tyrant Peisistratos, notably Bowra *Greek Lyric Poetry*² 376–80; but this suggestion is only speculative, and it does not receive adequate support from the *Admetos* song (1238 n.). [Flor. Chrest. proposed οὐδείς διακρίων δέξεται. But δεδέξεται (RVΓ) may be a gloss added to supply οὐδείς with a verb. The verb in fact can easily be understood from δέξει in the previous line, but 'I' is desirable to point the comparison with οὐδείς γε διακρίων. So ἐγώ is probably right. It was proposed by A. von Bamberg *De Ravennate et Veneto Aristophanis codicibus* (1865) 22–4.]

1224 ἐγὼ εἴσομαι: 'I'll find out'; cf. *Lys.* 750 εἴσομαι δ' ἐγώ. -ὼ εἴ- is scanned as one syllable by synizesis; cf. S. *Ph.* 585 ἐγώ εἰμ'.   **καὶ δή**: 'suppose that'. This idiom is not used elsewhere by Ar., but it is common in some other authors; e.g. E. *Med.* 386 καὶ δὴ τεθνᾶσι· τίς με δέξεται πόλις;

1225 As the Euripidean example just quoted shows (and cf. Denniston 253), after καὶ δή meaning 'suppose that' the next clause usually has no connective particle, where in English we might say 'then' or 'in that case'. So **δέ** means that the whole line is governed by καὶ δή: 'Suppose that I'm Kleon, and I sing . . . and you're going to take up the song'. [Thus the imperative δέξαι (V) is not likely to be right, since with it we should expect asyndeton.] **Ἀρμοδίου**: sc. μέλος (cf. 269). A song entitled *Harmodios* may be referred to as Ἀρμόδιος (*Akh.* 980, Antiphanes 85) or as Ἀρμοδίου μέλος (Ar. fr. 430) or just as Ἀρμοδίου (so here; cf. *Lys.* 1236–7 εἰ μέν γέ τις ᾄδοι Τελαμῶνος, Κλειταγόρας ᾄδειν δέον). Harmodios and Aristogeiton killed Hipparkhos, brother of the tyrant Hippias, in 514, and were afterwards honoured as heroes. Their exploit was a favourite subject for skolia. Four skolia about them survive complete (Page *Poetae Melici Graeci* nos. 893–6), but not the one of which Bdelykleon now sings the first line. Probably the title *Harmodios* was used indifferently for any of them. In *Akh.* 1093, to specify one particular skolion about Harmodios, the opening words are quoted: τὸ "*φίλταθ' Ἀρμόδι', οὔ*". There has been some speculation about the date and authorship of these Harmodios skolia, but there is no clear evidence (except of course that they cannot be earlier than 514); the most recent discussion is by A. J. Podlecki (*Historia* xv [1966] 139–40), but his arguments for 477 are no more cogent than other scholars' for other dates.

1226 ἔγεντ': a contraction for ἐγένετο, not infrequent in lyrics. The metre of this and the next line is hendecasyllabic: − × − ∪ ∪ − ∪ − ∪ − − (the 'phalaecean', familiar to us from Catullus). One of the commonest metres for skolia is a four-line stanza of which the first two lines are hendecasyllabic (Page *Poetae Melici Graeci* nos. 884–90, 893–6, 907). Philokleon therefore gets the right metre but the wrong words. The proper words, which presumably were familiar to most members of the audience, must have been something like 'so brave and patriotic', but instead he uses words which (Ar. means us to think) are appropriate to Kleon.

1228 τουτὶ σὺ δράσεις; 'Is that what you'll do?' [Emendation to introduce ᾄσει is unnecessary; cf. *Ek.* 887.]   **παρ-**: 'amiss', 'miserably'. **βοώμενος**: 'being shouted at'; for the loudness of Kleon's voice cf. 36, 1034. Bdelykleon is not saying that Kleon is powerful, only that he is raucous.

1231 ἑτέραν: ᾠδήν is understood from ᾄσομαι: 398 n.

1232–5 is adapted from Alkaios. The original lines are (following the restored text of Lobel and Page *Poetarum Lesbiorum Fragmenta* no. 141):

> ὦνηρ οὗτος ὁ μαιόμενος τὸ μέγα κρέτος
> ὀντρέψει τάχα τὰν πόλιν· ἁ δ' ἔχεται ῥόπας.

Philokleon has converted the lines to the second person, substituting ὦ 'νθρωφ' for ὦνηρ (Aeolic for ὁ ἀνήρ). If our text is right (but this is a type of change often made by copyists), he has also substituted Attic forms for Aeolic ones, except that α stands for Attic η in τὰν, ἀ, and ῥοπᾶς. The substitution of ἔτι for τάχα may be just a mistake by Ar. The metre is the fourteen-syllable sapphic (a kind of extended glyconic) : − − − ∪ ∪ − ∪ ∪ − ∪ ∪ − ∪ −. Alkaios's lines may have been addressed to Pittakos, who became ruler of Mytilene at the beginning of the sixth century. The point of using them against Kleon is that since his success at Pylos in 425 he had become the dominant figure in Athens. ἀ δ' ἔχεται ῥοπᾶς: 'she is close to the crisis', the moment which will decide whether the city will survive. A partitive genitive is regular with verbs meaning 'touch' or 'take hold of'; so also 1237 τῆς δεξιᾶς.

1236 πρὸς ποδῶν: 'at your feet': 1221 n. If I am right in thinking that 1220–1 named the imaginary guests in order round the circle, Theoros is opposite Kleon and would have to reach across the circle to take his hand; but perhaps the audience is expected to have forgotten by now that Kleon was not next to Theoros.

1238–9 The first line of another well-known skolion. Its metre is the greater asclepiad : − − − ∪ ∪ − − ∪ ∪ − − ∪ ∪ − ∪ −. Σ quotes the second line, τῶν δειλῶν δ' ἀπέχου γνοὺς ὅτι δειλῶν ὀλίγα χάρις, and says that, although some thought it was composed by Alkaios or Sappho, it was really by Praxilla of Sikyon (Page *Poetae Melici Graeci* no. 749) ; cf. Eust. 326. 38–41. If this attribution is right (and there is no firm evidence to set against it), it refutes the suggestion of Bowra *Greek Lyric Poetry*² 376–9 that the song is connected with the Peisistratids. Admetos is the legendary king of Pherai in Thessaly, husband of Alkestis. Σ quotes two lines from Ar. *Storks* (fr. 430) about the singing 'to the myrtle' of this skolion and *Harmodios*: ὁ μὲν ᾖδεν ''Ἀδμήτου λόγον'' πρὸς μυρρίνην, ὁ δ' αὐτὸν ἠνάγκαζεν Ἁρμοδίου μέλος. He quotes also a line from Kratinos (236) about a man trying to sing *Kleitagora* (for which cf. 1245–7) when the flautist played *Admetos*: Κλειταγόρας ᾄδειν, ὅταν Ἀδμήτου μέλος αὐλῇ. This quotation shows that the singing of skolia was accompanied by the flute, at least sometimes. At the imaginary party which Philokleon is attending there is an imaginary flautist (1219). But the real flautist, who accompanied other songs in the play from behind or beside the stage, may also have played to accompany the singing of skolia in this scene.

1240 λέξεις: λέγω may be used of any method of oral utterance, including singing; cf. Anakreon 402 (c) Page. ᾠδικῶς: 'lyrically'. This probably means that 1241–2 are not part of a skolion but come from a lyric poem or from a song in a play. This view is supported by their aeolic metre, which is different from that of any extant skolion: 1241 is − − ∪ ∪ − ∪ − −, which is common in tragedy (e.g. E. *Med.* 151–3), and 1242 is the same with the addition of − ∪ − (e.g. E. *Med.* 158). They must have been a well-known quotation, which Philokleon sings because they are the only lines he can think of on a theme similar to 1238–9; but Ar. means the audience to take them as a satirical comment on Theoros, the κόλαξ, whose song is turned against himself just as Kleon's was in 1226–7.

1241 ἀλωπεκίζειν: 'to be foxy', i.e. to be cunning and unscrupulous. D. M. Lewis (*Historia* xii [1963] 23) suggests that the word refers also to the deme Alopeke, which he regards as the headquarters of the 'coast' party (παράλιοι) in the middle of the sixth century, and he assigns the song to that period; but this is highly speculative.

1242 ἀμφοτέροισι: 'to both sides'.

1243 Αἰσχίνης: 459 n.   ὁ Σέλλου: 325 n.

1244 κᾆτ': εἶτα is 'next after Theoros', so that it just repeats μετὰ τοῦτον. [κατάσεται (perhaps indicated by R's καταίσεται) would suggest an incantation or spell. The point of 1245–7 is not clear enough for us to be sure that this sense would not be appropriate, but the asyndeton would be hard to explain. Dobree suggested κἀντάσεται, perhaps rightly.]

1245–7 The song *Kleitagora* was another well-known skolion, mentioned in other passages (*Lys.* 1237, fr. 261, Kratinos 236), but no other lines of it are quoted. Σ here says that Kleitagora was a Thessalian poetess, Σ *Lys.* 1237 that she was a Lakonian poetess, but these may be just guesses, and nothing else is known about her or the song. It is not even clear what were the real subject and verb of the sentence quoted here. The metre is dochmiac: $- \cup \cup - \cup -$. [Tyrwhitt 53 emended to βίον, 'means'. This would certainly be a more suitable object for boasting (1248) than 'force'. However, the verb in the original song will not have been διεκόμπασας but something else to which, for all we know, 'force' may have been appropriate. Ar. has distorted the song to introduce διεκόμπασας, and possibly did not worry that this verb really fitted only the first of the two objects.]

1248 διεκόμπασας: δι- implies competition, as in 1481, 1499. For Aiskhines's boasting, 325 n. This line is probably invented by Philokleon (like 1227) rather than quoted from any real song (like 1232–5, 1241–2). The metre is hendecasyllabic, like 1226–7; for all we know, this may have been the correct metre of the next line of *Kleitagora*. [διεκόμπασας (Tyrwhitt) is preferable to διεκόμισας because (*a*) boasting was the notorious feature of Aiskhines's character, and the point of this whole passage is that the songs begun by Kleon, Theoros, and Aiskhines are turned against themselves; (*b*) Σᴸ says τοῦτο, φησὶν, ἐπάξω πρὸς τὸ σκόλιον Αἰσχίνου ἐπεὶ κομπαστὴς ἦν, which implies that he had something about boasting in his text. One might add (*c*) διεκόμισας would not fit the metre; however, that is doubtful, because we have no evidence except the line itself to show what the metre was supposed to be.]

1249 ἐπιεικῶς: 'reasonably well'. Since Philokleon has actually not changed his approach to skolia since 1227–8, when Bdelykleon condemned his efforts, the line seems unconvincing. Ar. seems to cut short the episode abruptly because he feels it has lasted long enough.

1250 ὅπως ἴμεν: 'we must go'. ὅπως with the future indicative, with no governing clause, is generally used for urging another person to do something. But sometimes the verb is 1st person plural, because 'we' includes 'you' (so here, *Ek.* 297, E. *IT* 321, *Or.* 1061), and occasionally even 1st person singular (E. *Hek.* 398, *Tro.* 147, Antiphanes 177). **Φιλοκτήμονος**: 'Philoktemon's house'; cf. 123. The man is an imaginary rich friend, 'Mr. Acquisitive', from κτάομαι (though in the fourth century some real Athenians of this name existed).

1251 He shouts to a slave inside the house, no doubt the steward (cf. 613). They are going to take their own dinner with them to the party. Though the evidence is sparse, it seems likely that in Ar.'s time this was a more usual type of party than that in which all the food was provided by the host. Cf. Pherekrates 52 Kock = 248b Edmonds: συσκευασάμενος δεῖπνον ἐς τὸ σπυρίδιον ἐβάδιζεν ὡς πρὸς Ὠφέλην. **Χρυσέ**: presumably a name regularly given to slaves with blond hair. [Wilamowitz 483 conjectured Κροῖσε, a name known to have been given to slaves. But it cannot be proved that a slave could not be called Χρυσός.]

1252 διὰ χρόνου: 'after an interval', 'for the first time for some time', as in *Peace* 570, 710, *Lys.* 904, *Wealth* 1055; διὰ πολλοῦ χρόνου is used in 1476, *Wealth* 1045. This clause is addressed to Philokleon, not to the slave.

1253 γίγνεται: 'results', with the infinitives as subjects, a construction commoner with συμβαίνει.

1254 θυροκοπῆσαι must be an offence; so not just 'knocking at doors', but 'breaking down doors'. Cf. Antiphanes 239 θυροκοπῶν ὦφλεν δίκην, Herodas 2. 50–1 ἦν θύρην δέ τις κόψῃ, μνῆν τινέτω.   **πατάξαι καὶ βαλεῖν**: used together also in 1422, like English 'assault and battery'. [κατάξαι is used often of hitting someone on the head, but generally κεφαλήν is expressed with it.]

1255 ἐκ κραιπάλης: κραιπάλη can mean either 'drinking-bout' or 'hangover'. ἐκ can mean either 'after' (time) or 'with' (manner). ἐκ κραιπάλης is 'after the drinking-bout' in *Akh.* 277 and Alexis 9. 8, and so this is probably the meaning here, though here 'with a hangover' would give equally good sense.

1257–61 The aorists denote habitual actions, not past time; 99 n.

1259 Αἰσωπικὸν: 566 n.   **Συβαριτικόν**: Σ (if we accept a transposition of Αἰσωπικοὶ and Συβαριτικοὶ) says that Sybaritic stories were about human beings, by contrast with Aesop's about animals. Σ *Birds* 471 repeats this information and adds, referring to Mnesimakhos (fr. 6), that short concise stories were called Συβαρίτιδες. But these statements may be mere guesses, and nothing else is known about stories from Sybaris. (1427–40 are not genuine examples.) For -κός, 1209 n.

1262 τἄρ': cf. 299. [τοι emphasizes the whole sentence, γε would emphasize μαθητέον only. The correction was suggested by Hermann in his note on Orph. *A.* 1176.]   τῶν λόγων: 'of these stories'; the article means 'the ones which you mention'.

1264 In 1252–5 Philokleon was reluctant to go out to dinner, but the news that he will be able to misbehave without penalty has made him change his mind, and now he is as keen as Bdelykleon.   ἄγε νυν suggests that he wants Bdelykleon to hurry; probably in the course of 1256–63 a slave (Xanthias, I assume; 1292 n.) comes out of the house with a basket containing their dinner (1251) and Bdelykleon is now inspecting it. [Bergk unnecessarily transferred the line to Bdelykleon.] μηδὲν ἡμᾶς ἰσχέτω: The same words are used in *Knights* 724.

Bdelykleon and Philokleon go off, followed by Xanthias carrying their dinner.

1265–91 The second parabasis: a passage like the parabasis (1009–1121), but shorter, in which the chorus address the audience in the absence of the actors. In form it is like the second half of the main parabasis: ode or strophe (1265–74), epirrhema (1275–83), antode or antistrophe (missing), antepirrhema (1284–91).

Sarcastic compliments are paid to Amynias, who has been ingenious enough to discover some people who are his own social equals, and to Automenes, whose third son has shown great originality by inventing a new kind of sexual perversion. Then the author declares that it was a mistake to imagine that he had ended his attacks on Kleon.

The earlier part of the passage (1265–83) has no connection with the general theme of the play. It is simply an interlude, in which Ar. amuses the audience by satirical comments on well-known personalities; this is just like the whole of the second parabasis of *Knights* (1264–1315), which even includes a passage about some of the same men, the sons of Automenes. Ar. successfully sustains his sarcastic tone throughout 1265–83, and in addition 1265–74 is an excellent comic lyric. The trochaic rhythm trips quickly along and is impeccably neat; every sentence seems to fit into the metre without effort and without any awkward distortion of the word-order. The four little stanzas are neatly arranged. The first (1265–6, six metra) shows that the theme is to be cleverness. The second, the shortest of all (1267, four metra), names Amynias as the man whose cleverness is to be (sarcastically) praised. The third, rather longer (1268–70, eight metra), tells us that he has become poor, preparing the way for the final stanza, the longest and most important (1271–4, eleven metra), which leads to the pun with which the song triumphantly concludes.

The final speech (1284–91) presents Ar.'s comments on part of his own career and the Athenians' attitude to him, like the first part of the main parabasis (1009–59), but much more briefly. As in that passage, the style is marked by a number of striking metaphors: Kleon has jabbed at him, flayed him, and squeezed him (1286, 1280):

Ar. has behaved like an ape (1290), and like a stake failing to support a vine (1291).

Metre: The song (1265–74) is trochaic, which suggests that the music may have been brisk and bright. The final line of each of the two speeches is a trochaic tetrameter (1283, 1291), but the other lines (1275–82, 1284–90) are: – ∪ ∪ ∪ – ∪ ∪ ∪ – ∪ ∪ ∪ – ∪ –. One may call this 'paeonic tetrameter', or one may regard it as a trochaic tetrameter with ∪ in place of – for the third syllable of the metron (see pages 27–9); in any case it clearly has close affinities with the trochaic lines.

1267 Ἀμυνίας: 74 n. **ὁ Σέλλου:** 325 n. **μᾶλλον:** sc. σκαιὸς πεφυκέναι ἔδοξεν. (The words understood are not δεξιὸς πέφυκεν, because γὰρ in 1270 introduces the evidence for this statement. Hunger and poverty may be evidence of stupidity but cannot be evidence of cleverness.) **οὐκ τῶν Κρωβύλου:** 'descended from the sons of Chignon'. A κρωβύλος was a kind of bun in which long hair was fastened at the back of the head. (Cf. Gomme *Commentary on Thucydides* i 101–3; he gives references to earlier discussions.) It is frequently illustrated in vase-paintings of the late sixth and early fifth centuries, but by Ar.'s time it was no longer fashionable and Athenian men generally kept their hair short. So the jocular patronymic is used to mock Amynias's long hair, for which cf. 466. For the same reason, presumably, Hegesippos is called ὁ Κρωβύλος ἐκεῖνος in Ais. 3. 118. [The singular Κρωβύλου is defended by the analogy of ὁ Σέλλου. After τῶν corruption from the singular to the plural is likelier than the reverse.]

1268 ποτ': 'formerly'. 'Instead of an apple and a pomegranate' implies that these fruits are very cheap and common, and are what Amynias has to eat now. The accusative meaning 'expensive food' is left unexpressed, but is implied by 'with Leogoras'.

1269 Leogoras was the father of the orator Andokides. His father, also named Andokides, was a colleague of Perikles as general (*IG* i² 1085, *FGrH* 324 F 38; cf. Th. 1. 51. 4). Leogoras was friendly with the king of Makedonia and led an Athenian embassy to him in 426 (*IG* i² 57. 51, And 2. 11). In 415, as his son relates in his speech *On the Mysteries*, he was accused of participation in the profanation of the Mysteries and the mutilation of the Hermai, but in the end escaped punishment on both charges. He was well known for his wealth, and was satirized by the comic dramatists for spending his money on pleasures and luxurious living (*Clouds* 109 with Σ, Pl. com. 106, Eupolis 44, Ath. 387 a); so the point here is that a dinner with Leogoras would be a very lavish one. For further discussion of Leogoras see my edition of And. *On the Mysteries* (1962), especially pages 1–2, 206–7.

1270 'For now he's as hungry as Antiphon.' This is why Amynias seemed stupid (γὰρ introduces a reason for the previous statement): he used to associate with rich men, but now he has lost all his wealth, no doubt by gambling (cf. 74–6). Antiphon was a common name in Athens; but since Ar. seems to assume that the audience will know which Antiphon is meant here without further explanation, it is reasonable to conclude that he means the famous Antiphon, the orator, who at this period was reaching the peak of his oratorical career. He is mentioned again in 1301. There is no other evidence for his hungriness. It is unlikely that he was poor, since he was a successful orator and a leader of the oligarchic government in 411 (membership of which was based, at least in part, on property). So Ar. probably means that Antiphon has a big appetite; Amynias however is hungry not because he has a big appetite but because he is poor.

1271 'Yet ⟨he's not stupid after all⟩ for he went as an ambassador to Pharsalos and . . .' Pharsalos was one of the chief cities in Thessaly. Σ quotes three lines from Eupolis *Cities* (fr. 209) which he says also refer to Amynias's embassy, but nothing else is known about it. It has been conjectured that its purpose was to seek Thessalian troops to help Athens in the war (H. D. Westlake *Thessaly in the Fourth Century* B.C. 37) or to combat an attempt by Brasidas to gain control of Thessaly by intrigue with the Penestai (J. S. Morrison in *CQ* xxxvi [1942] 64). [It is not necessary to emend to produce an even number of metra, since a trochaic run may contain an odd number; cf. *Lys.* 1052, 1056, 1066, 1070.]

1272 μόνος μόνοισι: a regular idiom for 'all on their own', used in *Ek.* 448 and in other authors. [μόνοις (a) may be right, but a catalectic metron is less likely where there is no pause in the sense.]

1273 Πενέσταισι: πενέστης is a general word for 'poor man' or 'labourer', but in particular it is used virtually as a proper name for the serfs in Thessaly. These Penestai were people without citizen rights, and are often compared to the Spartans' Helots, but seem to have been less harshly treated. The point of the sentence is a pun: 'He visited the Poor Men of Thessaly, being himself as poor a man as any of them'. It also forms the climax (or anticlimax) of the whole passage about Amynias, since this is how he showed himself to be clever: although almost everyone is superior to him, he was ingenious enough to discover some friends with whom he could associate on equal terms, so as to get a meal out of them. The song, which seemed at first to be paying a compliment to Amynias, turns out to be an insult after all. (The Penestai are mentioned only for the sake of the joke. The passage does not prove that Amynias really intrigued with them when he was in Thessaly.)

1274 ἐλάττων οὐδενός: 'inferior to none of them', 'just as good as any of them'; cf. 599. [Bentley's ἔλαττον is unnecessary.]

1275 Αὐτόμενες: not otherwise known.

1276 ὅτι χειροτεχνικωτάτους: 'as skilful as can be'.

1278 The musical brother of Ariphrades is named as Arignotos in

Knights 1278, Ath. 220 b.   κιθαραοιδότατον: 'outstanding lyrist'. The word is usually contracted to -ρῳδ-, but Σ quotes another instance of the longer form, Eupolis 293. Both there and here probably this form is used merely to suit the metre.   ᾧ χάρις ἐφέσπετο: 'whom charm accompanies', aorist for a regular occurrence; 99 n. For the metaphor cf. Phokylides 4. 2 οἷς οὔτ᾽ ἐν μύθοις ἕπεται χάρις οὔτ᾽ ἐνὶ βουλῇ. But here Ar. is being sarcastic, and so χάρις is probably meant *à double entente*, hinting at homosexuality.

1279 τὸν δ᾽ ὑποκριτὴν ἕτερον: 'and next the actor'. This second son of Automenes is not otherwise known.   ἀργαλέον ὡς: 'awfully' (literally 'it's awful how'). Cf. ἄφατον ὡς in *Birds* 428, *Lys.* 198, 1148.

1280 The notorious thing about Ariphrades was his peculiar taste for female secretion, referred to here (1283) and in *Peace* 885, and fully described in *Knights* 1280–7. He is said to have been a pupil of Anaxagoras (Ath. 220 b). There are passing references to an Ariphrades in *Ek.* 129 and fr. 63, but perhaps not the same one. There was a comic dramatist named Ariphrades (Arist. *Poet.* 1458[b]31); if this is the same man, Ar. may have disliked him as a rival. Ariphrades has been discussed at length by E. Degani (*Maia* xii [1960] 190–217), who argues that Ar. disliked Ariphrades because of his philosophical (Anaxagorean) and political opinions; this is possible, but the evidence for Ariphrades's opinions is really very thin. [Inscriptions prove that third-declension names in -ης could have either -η or -ην in the accusative in the fourth century. No inscription proves that -ην was used in the fifth century, but it is given by mss. in many passages, and it is not certain that it ought to be removed by emendation.]

1281 ὤμοσε: sc. Αὐτομένης. It is now forgotten that at the beginning of the sentence Automenes was addressed in the 2nd person.   μαθόντα παρὰ μηδενὸς: 'without any teaching from anyone'. [This phrase clearly qualifies γλωττοποιεῖν; it is intolerably clumsy to make μαθόντα qualify ἐκμαθεῖν. 1282 must have been concocted from a gloss on μαθόντα παρὰ μηδενός. The form φύσεως, which will not scan, might be altered to φύσεος, which is the reading of L and Vv17; but another reason for removing the line is that its deletion makes 1275–83 the same length as 1284–91. Two speeches forming a pair in a parabasis normally have the same number of lines.]

1283 γλωττοποιεῖν: 'lick', referring to *cunnilinctus*; cf. *Knights* 1284–5. ἑκάστοτε: 446 n.

At this point there should be a song, corresponding to 1265–74. The form of the second parabasis in Ar.'s earlier plays is always song, speech, song, speech. (Cf. *Akh.* 971–99, *Knights* 1264–1315, *Peace* 1127–90, *Birds* 1058–1117. In *Clouds* 1115–30 there is only a speech, with no songs at all; but this passage may have been altered for the second edition of the play, and anyway is not evidence that a second parabasis could contain one song without a second song to correspond.)

This song probably contained another satirical attack on some individual, like 1265-74.

1284-91 Whereas in 1015-50 Ar. is spoken of in the 3rd person, now he speaks for himself, through the chorus-leader, in the 1st person. The same thing happens in *Clouds* 518-62. The parabaseis of *Akh.* and *Peace* seem even odder, since in them he switches from 3rd to 1st half-way through (*Akh.* 659, *Peace* 754). There are also passages in *Akh.* where he (or perhaps rather Kallistratos, if he was regarded as the author; cf. note on hyp. i 32) seems to speak in the 1st person through the leading character, Dikaiopolis (*Akh.* 377-82, 502-3). The likeliest explanation (though it is admittedly speculative) is that in the earliest comic performances the author took the only solo part himself, and consequently it later remained an accepted convention that either the chorus-leader or the leading character could speak as the author to the audience, even when the author was not actually performing the part.

When was this quarrel between Ar. and Kleon? The passage proves, I think, that they had a quarrel after the performance of *Knights* in 424. There is no other evidence of a quarrel between them at this date (since Σ *Wasps* 1284 does not quote independent evidence of it, but only makes a conjecture from this passage), but it would have been natural for Kleon to try to retaliate for Ar.'s onslaught in *Knights*. The course of the affair was that Kleon attacked Ar. by an abusive speech and other unspecified methods, perhaps a legal prosecution or a threat of one (1285-6); Ar. received no support from the general public (1287-9); so he gave way, perhaps by making some kind of public apology (1290), which was thought by some people to be a sincere reconciliation (1284); but later, in *Wasps*, he renewed his attacks on Kleon (1291). [It is not possible to make the passage refer to Kleon's prosecution of Ar. after the performance of *Babylonians* in 426 (Σ *Akh.* 378), which would mean that 1291 referred to *Knights*, since νῦν could not be used of a play performed two years previously. The view of van Leeuwen *Prolegomena ad Aristophanem* 44-5, followed by S. Srebrny in his contribution to *Charisteria T. Sinko* (1951), is that it was after *Knights*, not after *Babylonians*, that Kleon impugned Ar.'s status as an Athenian citizen with a prosecution, or threat of prosecution, by γραφὴ ξενίας, and that *Wasps* 1284-91 refers to that; this is possible, but the evidence does not prove it. I disagree with the comments on the passage made by V. Steffen (*Eos* xlvii [1954] 18); he overlooks 1291 νῦν.]

1284 καταδιηλλάγην: 'I made peace'. This double compound occurs only here, but does not differ in meaning from διαλλάττω and καταλλάττω.

1286 κακίσας ἔκνισε: 'stung with abuse'. The aorist perhaps implies that there was one occasion when Kleon delivered a particularly abusive speech against Ar., whereas the imperfect verbs imply that other kinds of attack, such as legal action or threats of it, lasted for some time. [So it is not certain that the aorist must be removed by emendation. Other emendations of κακίσταις (a) are more violent than Briel's. Van Leeuwen posited the loss of a whole line at this point, in order to make 1284–91 equal to 1275–83, keeping 1282.] ἀπεδειρόμην: 'I was being flayed', not generally used of verbal or legal attacks, but used here as a joke because Kleon was a tanner. δέρω is usual in Attic, but δείρω is used to suit the metre in *Clouds* 442, *Birds* 365, Kratinos 361.

1287 οἱ 'κτὸς: 'those who were not involved'.

1288 ἄρ': 'after all'.   μέλον: accusative absolute. μέλει may have either a genitive or an infinitive; here both are used. 'Caring nothing for me, but only to know . . .'   ὅσον μόνον: The same duplication for 'only' is used in *Lys.* 732, Pl. *R.* 607 a, etc.; cf. 213 ὅσον ὅσον.

1289 θλιβόμενος ἐκβαλῶ: 'produce when squeezed', an unusual metaphor, perhaps from fruit squeezed for juice.

1290 ὑπό τι: 'a bit', as in Pl. *Phdr.* 242 d, *Grg.* 493 c, Xenarkhos 2. 1, etc. ἐπιθήκισα: 'I played a trick'. πίθηκος and its derivatives are regularly used of a man engaged in trickery (not in comic behaviour); cf. *Akh.* 907, *Knights* 887, *Peace* 1065, etc. The trick which Ar. played was to pretend to give up attacking Kleon; cf. 1284.

1291 'The stake deceived the vine': Kleon thought he could depend on Ar., but now Ar. has attacked him again in *Wasps*. The change of metre in the final line helps to suggest the idea of an unexpected outcome. (The line cannot mean that the Athenian public let down Ar., because εἶτα shows that it refers to a later event than 1287–9. Outsiders laughed; after that—1290 ταῦτα κατιδών—Ar. played a trick; and after that—1291 εἶτα—the pole let down the vine.)

1292–1325 *Xanthias describes Philokleon's conduct at the party: he became drunk and skittish, thrashed Xanthias, made insulting remarks to the other guests, and is now on his way home, hitting everyone he meets.*

The chief purpose of this passage is to prepare the way for Philokleon's appearance in a state of comic intoxication, but the opportunity is also taken to make satirical comments on Lysistratos and Theophrastos. The description of the party is very skilfully written. Interest is aroused from the start; the passage begins not with plain statements but with an exclamation about tortoises. Soon afterwards comes the list of guests; all of them were presumably well known to the audience, who would therefore be agog to hear more about them. Later parts of the account are enlivened by a vivid series of verbs (1305), elaborate comparisons (1306, 1309–13), and direct speech (1309–10, 1316–18). Before anyone has time to become bored, the description comes to an end and Philokleon appears in person.

1292 Xanthias appears, running and shouting. I assume, for simplicity, that Xanthias is the slave who accompanies Bdelykleon and Philokleon to the party (appearing at 1264 and 1292–1325), and that

Xanthias is also the slave who watches Philokleon dancing (1474–1515). But this cannot be proved. It is possible that one or both of these scenes may be performed by Sosias, or even by some other slave; 433 and 1251 show that there are other slaves in the household.

This type of entrance was apparently very popular with ancient audiences, and in later comedy it became a convention to have an entrance by a running slave; but in Ar.'s time it was not yet conventional. δέρματος: 429 n. The whole of 1292 is very similar to 429, but the situation is different, and probably the similarity has no special point but is just accidental.

[1293 is not long enough for a complete iambic trimeter, and must have originated from glosses on 1292. Bentley added τέγους to make a complete line, but this labours the point quite adequately made in 1294–5. R has στεγειν after πλευραῖς, because the scribe's eye jumped from πλευραῖς to πλευρὰς in 1295, thus omitting all the rest of 1294–5; these two lines (including στέγειν) are added at the foot of the page by a later hand.]

1294 κατηρέψασθε: This seems to be the only Attic instance of κατερέφω, but it does not differ in meaning from ἐρέφω.

1295 κεράμῳ: 'tiles', a collective noun, as in Clouds 1127, Th. 2. 4. 2, etc. πλευρὰς: 3 n.

1296 στιζόμενος: literally 'tattooed', but here metaphorical for 'beaten black and blue'.

1297–8 παῖ is a normal way of addressing a slave (cf. 152, 1251), but Ar. plays on the ambiguity of the word by proceeding with the sense 'child'; children are customarily beaten (cf. Clouds 1416). A similar remark is made in Th. 582–3: τί δ' ἐστίν, ὦ παῖ; παῖδα γάρ σ' εἰκὸς καλεῖν, ἕως ἂν οὕτως τὰς γνάθους ψιλὰς ἔχῃς. In both passages the metre suggests tragedy. Evidently Ar. is parodying a notorious occasion in a tragedy when the chorus-leader delivered a couplet beginning τί δ' ἐστίν, ὦ παῖ; παῖδα γάρ . . . We do not know what tragedy it was, but there are several passages in surviving tragedies in which similar explanations of vocatives are given; e.g. E. Andr. 64 ὦ φιλτάτη σύνδουλε—σύνδουλος γὰρ εἶ . . .

1299 'Why, don't you see, the old man's turned out to be a most outrageous nuisance!' οὐ γὰρ . . .; 836 n. ἄρ': 314 n. ἀτηρότατον: ἄτη and ἀτηρός are solemn poetic words, used seldom in prose and never elsewhere in comedy; but possibly this particular phrase had passed into common speech, as in English 'bane' is archaic and poetic but 'the bane of my life' is colloquial. Cf. E. Andr. 353 γυναῖκές ἐσμεν ἀτηρὸν κακόν. Peter Rau Paratragodia (1967) 165 takes our line as paratragic; but this seems less probable, since the audience's attention here should be concentrated on Philokleon's actions, and a melodramatic manner would tend to distract attention from the content of Xanthias's description.

1300 παροινικώτατος: 'most drunk and disorderly'. The word occurs only here.

1301 καίτοι: 'and yet', as if the men named were notorious for drunkenness and riotous behaviour. Ἵππυλλος (or, according to the *Souda*, Ἱππόλυτος): not known. Ἀντιφῶν: 1270 n. Λύκων: Lykon, of the deme Thorikos (Σ Pl. *Ap.* 23 e), was a politician, but little is known of his political activities. In 405 he was alleged to have betrayed Naupaktos to Sparta for a bribe (Metagenes 10). In 399 he supported Meletos and Anytos in their accusation of Sokrates (Pl. *Ap.* 23 e, 36 a, D.L. 2. 38). His wife Rhodia was the object of rude comments in several comedies (*Lys.* 270 with Σ, Eupolis 215, 273); his son Autolykos was a handsome and athletic boy who, with his father, is the chief guest of Kallias in X. *Smp.* (According to Ktesias *Pers.* 52, an Athenian named Lykon assisted Pissouthnes, satrap of Lydia, to rebel against the king of Persia and afterwards betrayed him, but there is no special reason to suppose that this was the same Lykon.)

1302 Λυσίστρατος: 787 n. Θούφραστος: unknown. His character is described in 1315–18. Φρύνιχον: The association with other politicians (Antiphon, Lykon, and probably Lysistratos, if Ant. 6. 36 refers to him: 787 n.) makes it reasonably certain that this is Phrynikhos the politician, not Phrynikhos the comic dramatist. (Phrynikhos the tragic dramatist, referred to in 220, 269, 1490, 1524, lived at a much earlier date.) Phrynikhos, who was the son of Stratonides (Σ *Lys.* 313), of the deme Deiradiotai (Plu. *Alk.* 25. 6), was alleged to have been a shepherd-boy in his youth, but later came to the city and engaged in political and legal activities (Lys. 20. 11–12, 25. 9); he must have been at this stage of his career at the time of *Wasps*. Otherwise our knowledge is confined to the last year of his life, 412 and 411 (described in Th. 8): he was one of the generals in command of the Athenian force at Samos, he was one of the leaders of the oligarchy of Four-hundred, and he was assassinated in the late summer of 411. Thucydides comments particularly on his shrewdness and on his courage (Th. 8. 27. 5, 68. 3).

The expression οἱ περὶ Φρύνιχον shows that in 422 Phrynikhos was generally known to be a leading member of a group of friends which included all the men listed in 1301–2, 'Phrynikhos's set'. What kind of a group was it? Since several of the members were politicians and orators (Phrynikhos, Antiphon, Lykon, and Lysistratos, if I have identified them correctly), it may be concluded that all or most of the group had political interests. There are also indications that some of them were men of an undemocratic turn of mind, who considered themselves better than common Athenians: Antiphon and Phrynikhos were leaders of the oligarchic revolution in 411; Lysistratos seems to have been associated with Andokides and the mutilators of the Hermai (787 n.), who had oligarchic tendencies (see my *Andokides: On the*

Mysteries 190–3); Theophrastos was 'a most superior person' (1315–18). But to conclude from this that Phrynikhos's set was an oligarchic ἑταιρεία is to go too far. It is not clear from the text that any oligarchic revolution was being planned as early as 422, nor that the members of the group held oligarchic views at this time: Lykon's later association with Anytos (1301 n.) makes it unlikely that he was ever an oligarch, and Phrynikhos himself is said to have opposed oligarchy as late as 412/11 (Th. 8. 48. 4–7). So Phrynikhos's set should be regarded simply as a group of men with similar tastes and interests, whose purpose in meeting was more social than political. And it is because of their social prestige, not for any political significance, that Ar. has chosen this group to be the one whose dinner Philokleon has attended: they are an outstanding and well-known part of Athenian high society. Ar. regards them as snobs, who treat too contemptuously those whom they regard as their inferiors (1303 implies that they are all ὑβρισται). That is why it is funny to hear that Philokleon has discomfited them.

1303 ὑβριστότατος: 'rudest'.

1305 ἀνήλατ': 'he jumped up' from where he was reclining. [He would only do this once, so that there is no need to emend the aorist to an imperfect. But ἐνήλατ' would mean 'jumped in' or 'jumped on'.] ἐσκίρτα: 'he pranced about'. Cf. *Clouds* 1078, where Wrong tells Pheidippides to enjoy himself: χρῶ τῇ φύσει, σκίρτα, γέλα, νόμιζε μηδὲν αἰσχρόν. 'πεπόρδει signifies enjoyment: 394 n. Here the pluperfect of πέρδομαι is used in an imperfect sense. Cf. *Peace* 335, where the perfect form has a present sense: ἥδομαι γὰρ καὶ γέγηθα καὶ πέπορδα καὶ γελῶ.

1306 καχρύων: barley which has been roasted in order to free the grains from their husks; this would be a luxury for a donkey. The genitive is used by analogy with verbs meaning 'fill' (e.g. 1304): 'feasted on barley-grains'.

1307 δή stresses ἔτυπτε, showing that it is (from Xanthias's point of view) the most important part of the account. [κἄτυπτεν ἐμέ, proposed by Elmsley in his note on *Akh.* 127, throws too much stress on 'me', as if Philokleon would have been more likely to hit someone else; but if he hit anyone his own slave would be the expected victim.]   νεανικῶς: 'vigorously', 'lustily', as in *Peace* 897. The beating came as an unpleasant shock all the more because the call of παῖ παῖ, the ordinary way of attracting a slave's attention (cf. 152, 1251), led Xanthias to expect just an order to perform a service or go on an errand. 'He called me over, and then *beat* me!' (Possibly there is a pun, if παῖ is an alternative form of παῖε, 'Hit!' However, this shortened imperative is found in only one passage, X. *Kyn.* 6. 18, and even there it is not certain; there is a variant reading παῖε, and a copyist may easily have been confused by παῖς which comes immediately before. And if παῖ really meant both 'Slave!' and 'Hit!' it would be such an obvious pun for comedy, in which the beating of slaves is often mentioned, that one would expect to meet it more often. So I think it is doubtful whether there is any pun here.)

1308-13 In conversation at a party or elsewhere, to provide amusement, one man would compare another to something funny, and his victim would then compare him to something in return. In Pl. *Men.* 80 c, when Menon has compared Sokrates to an electric ray, Sokrates says γιγνώσκω οὗ ἔνεκά με ἤκασας. . . . ἵνα σε ἀντεικάσω. In Pl. *Smp.* 215 a Alkibiades carefully explains that the comparison which he is about to make is not, as Sokrates would naturally assume, just for amusement. Cf. also *Birds* 804-8, X. *Smp.* 6. 8-10, and G. Monaco *Paragoni burleschi degli antichi* (1963).

1309 τρυγὶ: literally 'new, unfermented wine', and so metaphorically of a raw, immature youth; we might say 'a green young man'. Cf. *Wealth* 1085-6, where there is a pun on 'youth' and another meaning of τρύξ, 'dregs': Khremylos, referring to the Old Woman, says to the Young Man 'You must drink the τρύξ (dregs) too', and the Young Man replies ἀλλ' ἔστι κομιδῇ τρὺξ παλαιά, 'She's very old to be called τρύξ (youth)'. (LSJ τρύξ II. 4 wrongly say that it means 'an old man or woman'; there is no evidence for that.) Lysistratos means that Philokleon is like a young man who has just inherited property, including slaves, and has not yet learned how to treat his slaves properly, but enjoys the novelty of beating them. [Kock's conjecture Φρυγὶ has often been adopted, but is unnecessary, because τρυγὶ is satisfactory.]

1310 κλητῆρι: 'donkey'; cf. 189.   ἀχυρὸν: 'bran-heap', proverbial for having a thoroughly good time, like English 'in clover'; cf. fr. 76 εἰς ἄχυρα καὶ χνοῦν, Philemon 188 ὄνος βαδίζεις εἰς ἄχυρα τραγημάτων. [The neuter ἄχυρα ('bran') has ῠ, but the masculine ἀχυρός ('bran-heap') has ῡ; cf. *Com. adesp.* 783 Kock = Ar. fr. 222a Edmonds, *App. Prov.* 1. 71. So Dindorf's coinage ἀχυρμὸν need not be accepted.]

1312 θρῖα: The ordinary meaning of θρῖον is 'fig-leaf'. A locust's 'fig-leaves' are presumably its wings (which do look rather like leaves), although there is no parallel for this use.   τοῦ τρίβωνος: defining genitive: 'which are its cloak'.

1313 Sthenelos was a tragic dramatist, whose poetry, according to Aristotle, was lucid but undignified (Arist. *Poet.* 1458ᵃ18-21). Other allusions to him in comedy tell us no more (Ar. fr. 151, Pl. com. 70, 128). One surviving iambic line is doubtfully attributed to him (Nauck *TGF*² 762).   σκευάρια: 'equipment', probably costumes and properties for his plays; cf. *Akh.* 451. Σ says that poverty forced him to sell it.

Philokleon's two comparisons of Lysistratos, to a locust without its wings and to Sthenelos without his equipment, clearly mean that he looked in some way naked or lacking in some essential. In *Akh.* 857 he is said to be always cold, and so probably the point is that he was in the habit of going about inadequately dressed. Perhaps he wore, even in winter, only a tunic and no cloak; if so, that is the reason for calling the locust's wings its τρίβων in 1312.

1314 ἀνεκρότησαν: 'clapped'. With this verb 'hands' is sometimes inserted (e.g. *Wealth* 739, Ais. 2. 42), sometimes omitted (e.g. *Knights* 651).

1315 διεμύλλαινεν occurs only here. Σ says it means ὑπερηφάνως τὰ χείλη διέστρεφεν, and if that is right we may translate 'grimaced', 'made a wry face'. It probably comes from δια- meaning 'in different directions' and μύλλον meaning 'lip' (Pol. 2. 90), rather than μυλλός meaning 'crooked' (Hskh. μ 1858). Photios (under σιλλαίνει) defines μυλλαίνει as διὰ τῶν ὀφθαλμῶν σκώπτει, which would give the meaning 'winked'; but this interpretation fits our context less well.   **ὡς δὴ**: 'as being', implying that Theophrastos thinks himself clever but Xanthias does not necessarily agree. Cf. E. *Andr.* 234–5 τί σεμνομυθεῖς κεἰς ἀγῶν' ἔρχῃ λόγων, ὡς δὴ σὺ σώφρων;

1317 ἐπὶ τῷ: 'why?'   **κομᾷς**: 466 n.

1318 κωμῳδολοιχῶν: 'clown-licking', a lively compound found nowhere else and perhaps invented by Ar. Evidently it means that Theophrastos tries to gain the favour of important men by talk and behaviour intended to make them laugh (perhaps like Philippos ὁ γελωτοποιός in X. *Smp.*).   **τὸν εὖ πράττοντ' ἀεί**: 'whoever is successful at the moment': 390 n.

1319 περι- means 'over and above what was to be expected', 'gratuitously'. One accusative is internal and one external, as in *Th.* 535–6 τοιαῦτα περιυβρίζειν ἡμᾶς.   **ἐν μέρει**: 'one after another', as in A. *Ag.* 1192. Elsewhere in Ar. it always means 'taking one's turn' (*Birds* 1228, *Lys.* 540, *Frogs* 32, 497).

1320 ἀγροίκως: 'stupidly'; cf. *Clouds* 628, 646.

1321 οὐδὲν εἰκότας τῷ πράγματι: 'inappropriate', 'not suitable to the circumstances'. Philokleon's conversation has evidently been of the same kind as in 1174–85.

1324 καὶ δὴ: 'Look!', often used to mark a character's entrance on the stage, and sometimes, as here, preceded by a demonstrative pronoun with the deictic -ί; cf. 1483, *Lys.* 77 ἡδὶ δὲ καὶ δὴ Λαμπιτὼ προσέρχεται, *Birds* 268.   **σφαλλόμενος**: middle voice: 'tripping himself up', 'stumbling'.

1325 Xanthias rushes into the house, looking apprehensively over his shoulder, and shuts the door behind him.

1326–40 *Philokleon returns from the party, belligerently drunk, defying the threats of men whom he has attacked on the way home.*

Philokleon is intoxicated from here to the end of the play, but Ar. makes skilful variations in his mood. Here he is pugnacious and noisy. In this mood he may be amusing to the audience for a minute or two, but would soon become tiresome; so the passage is kept very short.

Metre: mostly trochaic. This rapid rhythm is made even faster at some points by the resolution of a long syllable into two shorts (1326 ἄνε-, πάρε-, 1328 ἐπα-, 1339 τάδε). In 1332–4 a man intervenes in iambic trimeters, the metre of ordinary conversation, trying to make Philokleon sober up. He succeeds in so far as he gets him to speak, if not in trimeters, at least in iambics for a few moments (1335–8). But the calmer rhythm does not last long; a resolution (1337 ἀνέ-) and an exclamation (1338) prepare the way for another burst of trochaics (1339–40). (For a more elaborate contrast between fast trochaics and slower iambics, compare the argument between Dionysos and the Frogs in *Frogs* 209–67.)

1326 Philokleon appears comically drunk (staggering about, belching, slurring his words, etc.). In one hand he carries a burning torch (1331, 1361). His other arm is around a flute-girl, whose name is later said to be Dardanis (1371). She is a slave (1353, cf. 1219 n.), and she is stark naked, as 1373–7 shows; that is, the male actor wears a skin costume padded to a female shape. (Wilamowitz, in his note on *Lys.* 1114, thought that her nakedness proved that the part was played by a woman; but clearly it does not. There is no positive evidence that women acted in plays in classical Athens; and since female speaking parts were played by men, it may be presumed that female silent parts were played by men too.) Behind them follow several angry men, shaking their fists.   ἄνεχε, πάρεχε: 'Stand up! Make way!', a shout addressed to anyone who may be in the way (actually no one is). For the meaning of πάρεχε cf. 949. The whole phrase is used also in E. *Kyk.* 203, *Tro.* 308. It has been thought that it means 'Raise the torch! Hold it near!' with φῶς or φλόγα understood. But that interpretation will not fit *Wasps* 1326, where Philokleon is himself carrying the torch (1331); nor E. *Tro.* 308, where Kassandra is carrying the torch (and φῶς φέρω should be read; cf. 348); nor E. *Kyk.* 203, where no one is carrying a torch, and if anyone were the Kyklops would be telling him to put it down, not to raise it (cf. 204–5).

1327 κλαύσεται: 'will be sorry for it', a threat, as in *Clouds* 933, *Lys.* 436, etc.

1329 οἷον: exclamatory: 'How I'll . . .!'

1331 φρυκτούς: 'fried fish'; cf. Anaxandrides 33. 11, Alexis 155. 3. σκευάσω: the normal verb for preparing food: 'I'll make fried fish out of you'. Cf. *Knights* 372 περικόμματ' ἐκ σοῦ σκευάσω, 'I'll make mince out of you'.

1332 One of the men following Philokleon speaks. The words show that they are men whom he has attacked on meeting them in the street on his way home; cf. 1322–3. [In the list of characters in the mss. at the beginning of the play the man is called συμπότης, but in 1299–1321 it does not appear that Philokleon has committed any legal offences against any of the guests at the party. Tyrwhitt 54 correctly says 'Hic autem loquitur aliquis ex turba, quam Senex variis contumeliis excitavit'.] **ἦ μὴν**: 258 n.

1333 **κεἰ σφόδρ' εἶ νεανίας**: 'even if you *are* a young man'. For the form of expression cf. *Clouds* 1492. Farcically, Philokleon's wild youthful behaviour has made the man believe that he is really young, despite his aged appearance. Youth was commonly accepted as an excuse for rash conduct; cf. Dodds's note on E. *Ba.* 973–6.

1334 **προσκαλούμενοι**: 'to summon'.

1335 'Hoo hoo, "summon"!', derisively repeating the end of the previous line. The prepositional prefix is omitted in repetition, as in *Knights* 95–8, 365–6, *Frogs* 306, etc.

1336–8 'Your talk *is* out-of-date. Don't you know I can't endure even a mention of law-suits?' **ἀρχαῖα**: 'out-of-date', derogatory, as in *Clouds* 984, 1357, etc. For **γε** stressing a comment after the repetition of a word from the previous speech cf. Denniston 129. **ἆρά γ' ἴσθ'**: 4 n. **ἰαιβοῖ αἰβοῖ**: 37 n. The addition of ἰ- makes no apparent difference; ἰαιβοῖ expresses disgust at a smell in *Knights* 891, just as αἰβοῖ does elsewhere. For the combination of an exclamation with ἰ- and the same one without cf. *Th.* 223 ἀτταταῖ ἰατταταῖ.

1339–40 **τάδε**: i.e. 'what I'm doing at present'. **βάλλε**: 'away with'. **κημούς**: 'voting-funnels': 94 n. His attitude now is the exact opposite of what it was when he used to write up κημὸς καλός (99). [The suggestion of Wilamowitz 525 that κημός here has its sense of 'muzzle', and that Philokleon as he speaks pulls off the flute-girl's φορβειά (cf. 582), does not suit the context so well, and is rightly rejected by Willems 580–1 and Holzinger 36–7.] **ποῦ 'στ' ἡλιαστής**; a rhetorical question implying 'There's no juror here'. ['στ' ἠ- rather than 'σθ' ἠ-: 195 n.] **ἐκποδών**: 'Get out of it!' He chases all the men away, brandishing the torch. There may be a considerable amount of horse-play, with the men running in different directions to avoid him. When they are all gone, he lands up at some point above ground level (1341 n.), to which he invites Dardanis to come up.

1341–87 *Philokleon tries to persuade the flute-girl to gratify his desire for her. He pretends that he is young and Bdelykleon old; he says that he will come into money later, but at present is kept short of money by his son. When Bdelykleon arrives and accuses him of stealing away the flute-girl, he first pretends that she is a torch, and then tries to distract attention by a conversational gambit of the kind which Bdelykleon himself earlier recommended.*

Here Philokleon's mood changes; he ceases to be pugnacious, and becomes amorous, and then mischievous. The passage has some notable punning and *double entendre* (1342–4, 1373–7). But its most remarkable section is that in which the old man talks as if he were young, so that the words 'father' and 'son' appear to have exchanged meanings. For a moment we seem to have got into a kind of Looking-glass Land, where life is lived backwards. But these lines are not just an elaborate verbal joke. They imply a comment on the plot of the play as a whole: Philokleon's change to a new way of life has rejuvenated him.

1341 ἀνάβαινε is one of the chief pieces of evidence commonly quoted in favour of the view that the theatre had a raised stage: Philokleon is taken to be on the stage, while Dardanis is down in the orkhestra. 1342 confirms that she is to take at least one step up. Other instances of ἀναβαίνω and καταβαίνω which are used as evidence are in 1514, *Akh.* 732, *Knights* 149, 169, *Ek.* 1152; cf. P. D. Arnott *Greek Scenic Conventions* (1962) 33–4. These passages undoubtedly prove that there was some raised area, but they do not show how extensive it was; it may have been only a small rostrum, or a couple of steps leading up to the house door or to the altar in front of it.   **χρυσομηλολόνθιον:** 'my dear little golden cockchafer'. The diminutive noun is neuter, but in 1342 he lapses naturally into the feminine gender; cf. 595, 688, 711.

1342 σχοινίου: 'cord'. He holds out to her, to pull herself up by, the phallos which was a normal part of the costume of an actor in a comedy.

1343–4 'Hold on! But be careful, because the cord's rotten! All the same, it doesn't mind being rubbed.'   **σαπρὸν:** virtually a pun. Applied to a rope it means 'rotten', but applied to a person it means 'too old for sexual activity'; cf. 1380, *Ek.* 1098, *Wealth* 1086, Makhon 185 Gow.

After 1344 there is a tug of war, perhaps extended by comic business, by the end of which Dardanis has been pulled up the step or steps to the upper level.

1346 λεσβιεῖν: 'titillate' by *fellatio*, which the Lesbians were supposed to have invented (as *Σ* says, quoting Strattis 40, 41, Theopompos com. 35); cf. *Frogs* 1308. [There the word is ἐλεσβίαζεν and so in *Wasps* 1346 Blaydes emends to λεσβιᾶν, the future infinitive of λεσβιάζω. But verbs in -ίζω are often formed from place-names, e.g. λακωνίζω, μεγαρίζω, and so λεσβίζω may have existed as well as λεσβιάζω.]

1348 ἐφιαλεῖς: 'carry out', 'do it' as opposed to mere talk. For this sense of ἐφιάλλω cf. *Peace* 432 ἔργῳ 'φιαλοῦμεν, *Odyssey* 22. 49 οὗτος γὰρ ἐπίηλεν τάδε ἔργα. [On the form of the word see Platnauer's note on *Peace* 432. But his explanation of the construction is incorrect, as *Odyssey* 22. 49 shows.]   **οἶδ' ὅτι:** inserted parenthetically after the first few words of a sentence: cf. *Akh.* 555, *Clouds* 1175, etc. εὖ οἶδ' ὅτι and εὖ ἴσθ' ὅτι are similarly used.

1349 κάγχανεῖ: 721 n.

1350 For the dative and the form ἠργ-, 787 n.

1352 υἱὸς: Whereas usually a wild son is checked by a severe father, in this case a wild father is checked by a severe son. So throughout 1352–9 there is a comic paradox: υἱός appears where we should normally expect πατήρ, and vice versa.

1353 λυσάμενος: buying her freedom from her owner. This shows that she is a slave.   **χοιρίον**: 573 n. We may translate 'piglet', but strictly Philokleon is using the figure of speech known as 'synecdoche' (part for whole).

1354 οὐ κρατῶ: When a man died, his property normally passed to his son or nearest male relative. If the heir was still a minor, the property was looked after by his father or guardian until he came of age. Philokleon, still pretending to be a wild youth, claims that he has property of which he has not yet obtained control because he has not yet come of age. κρατῶ is the normal legal term for control as distinct from ownership, e.g. Isaios 8. 2. Notice that 1354–5 is not consistent with 1352: in 1352 the event he is awaiting is his son's death, i.e. the money belongs to the son and only when he dies will it be inherited by the father; in 1354–5 the event awaited is his own coming of age, i.e. the money belongs to himself, and he will gain control of it when he comes of age, whether his son is dead or not. The situation is not meant to be a real one; he is simply flinging out youthful boasts one after another, regardless of consistency.

1357 κἄλλως: 'and besides'.   **κυμινοπριστοκαρδαμογλύφον**: 'Splitting cummin' is a regular expression for parsimony, e.g. Arist. *EN* 1121ᵇ27, Theok. 10. 55. 'Paring cress' seems not to be mentioned elsewhere. We might say 'skin-flint-cheese-paring'.

1358 ταῦτ': 'therefore' (LSJ οὗτος C. VIII. 1).   **διαφθαρῶ**: 'go to the bad'.

1360 ὁδὶ δὲ καὐτός: 'And here he is, in person!' So also in *Akh.* 1189, *Birds* 1718.

1361 δετάς: 'sticks bound together', i.e. 'torch'; cf. *Iliad* 11. 554 καιόμεναι τε δεταί.

1362 τωθάσω: 'play a trick on'; cf. 1368.   **νεανικῶς**: 'like a young man', 'as young men do'.

1363 οἴοις: 'by such means as those by which', i.e. 'in the same way as'. **πρὸ τῶν μυστηρίων**: The 'great' Eleusinian Mysteries were the central feature of an annual festival in honour of Demeter and Kore. The rites of the Mysteries were secret, and could be attended only by those who had been initiated; the admission of new initiates was an important part of the festival each year. The point of *Wasps* 1363 is not very clear, but a plausible explanation is that candidates for initiation generally had to endure jokes and ridicule from their relatives and friends who were already initiated. Normally a father would have been initiated years earlier than his son, but Philokleon is still pretending to be younger than Bdelykleon. (It is less likely that there is here a specific reference to the γεφυρισμός, the 'abuse at the bridge' during the Eleusinian procession, since that seems to have been an occasion for insults rather than leg-pulling. *Frogs* 416–30, which may be intended to suggest the γεφυρισμός, is very different in content and tone from *Wasps* 1369–77).

Philokleon thrusts the torch into Dardanis's hand and makes her stand up straight and still, probably in front of the altar which stands before the house. Bdelykleon comes running up, shouting to him.

1364 τυφεδανὲ καὶ χοιρόθλιψ: 'you sex-maniac!' Neither compound occurs elsewhere, and both may have been invented for the occasion.

1365 ποθεῖν ἐρᾶν τ': 'Desire' is stressed in order to increase the effect of the unexpected word σοροῦ. [ποῖ θείς; ἐρᾶν γ', suggested by H. van Herwerden *Studia Thucydidea* (1869) 164, is attractive but not essential.] σοροῦ: a surprise for κόρης. A ὡραία κόρη is a young girl; a ὡραία σορός is a timely coffin, for a person in ripe old age.

1367 Contrast 510–11. Philokleon now attributes to Bdelykleon the tastes which he used to have himself.   **ἐξ ὄξους**: 'dipped in vinegar'.

1368–9 'Isn't it dreadful, that you played a trick by stealing the flute-girl from the other men at the party!'

1369 ποίαν: 1202 n. For the 'broken anapaest' see page 23.

1370 ἀπὸ τύμβου πεσών: Cf. *Clouds* 1273 τί δῆτα ληρεῖς ὥσπερ ἀπ' ὄνου καταπεσών; In Pl. *Laws* 701 cd the phrase ἀπό τινος ὄνου πεσεῖν is quoted as a proverb, to illustrate the danger of being carried along by an argument without checking each step in it. Although the origin of the expression is unknown (the explanations in *Souda* a 3459 being only inept guesses), it is clear that ἀπ' ὄνου πίπτω is a phrase for 'talk nonsense'. Philokleon, still pretending that he is very young and Bdelykleon very old, has substituted 'tomb' for 'donkey', with absurd effect.

1371 γ' stresses 'ὅτι rather than σοί. 'Yes, I think this *is* Dardanis whom you've got here.'   [τοί can hardly be right. When γε and τοι are used together, γε normally precedes.]   **Δαρδανίς**: The name implies that she is a slave from Dardania, the area around Troy: 433 n.

[**1372 κάεται** or καίεται? There is no adequate epigraphical evidence (Meisterhans *Grammatik der attischen Inschriften*[3] 178), but probably usage in this verb ran parallel to that in κλάω/κλαίω (584 n.).]

1373 δῆτ': 'that's right', with a word repeated from a preceding question, as in *Lys.* 848 Λυ. ἀνήρ; Κι. ἀνὴρ δῆτ', etc.   **ἐσχισμένην**: 'split'. A torch would be made of several pieces of split wood bound together (cf. 1361 δετάς). Philokleon points to the place where her body divides into two legs; for this meaning of ἐσχισμένην cf. *AP* 11. 262 τεμνομένην. Bdelykleon proceeds to inspect it. [ἐστιγμένην cannot be right, because 'tattooed' applied to a torch means nothing. Σ[R] has διεστιγμένης, διερρηγμένης περὶ τοῦ γυναικείου αἰδοίου, which looks like an attempt to say that ἐστιγμένη means 'split', which is nonsense; but possibly this note was concocted out of an earlier note explaining ἐσχισμένην.]

1374 μέλαν: 'black thing'; he points to the pubic hair.

1375 πίττα: 'pitch'. Torches were most often made of pine-wood, from which pitch would run out when it became hot.

1376 ὁ δ' ὄπισθεν οὑτοσί: 'this thing behind', attracted from the neuter to the gender of the complement πρωκτός.

1377 'No, that's a branch of the torch sticking out.'

1378 ποῖος: 1202 n.   οὐκ εἶ δεῦρο σύ; 'Come this way, you!' He starts taking Dardanis towards the door of the house.

1379 ἁ: 'Hey!', a cry of protest, as in *Th.* 689, *Wealth* 127, 1052.

1382 ἐθεώρουν: 1187 n. Now he tries to follow the advice which Bdely-kleon gave him then, in order to get the better of—Bdelykleon. For the boomerang joke, 989 n.

1383 1191 n.

1385 Philokleon suits the action to the word, and knocks Bdelykleon down (cf. 1436). Dardanis probably makes her escape by running out of sight at this point, taking the torch with her.

1386 ὑπώπια: 'black eyes'.

1387 'You've certainly learned up Olympia!' Bdelykleon, as he scrambles to his feet, ruefully reflects that Philokleon has made unexpectedly effective use of his lesson. But before he can do anything about it he is distracted by the appearance of a new character.

1388–1449 *Two persons whom Philokleon has attacked on his way home come in turn to deliver summonses to him. He tries to put them off by telling them stories, but he only makes them angrier. Finally Bdelykleon, ignoring an attempt to soothe him by yet another fable, takes the old man into the house to keep him out of trouble.*

Most of Ar.'s earlier plays have a scene near the end in which several visitors are repulsed in turn. *Wasps* 1388–1449 has an especially close resemblance to *Clouds* 1214–1302, in which two debtors come to claim their money from Strepsiades, receive unsatisfactory answers, and retreat threatening legal action. The main sources of amusement in these scenes are the pompous indignation of the complainants when they receive treatment which they regard as unsatisfactory and disrespectful, and the comic muddle made by the main character (Philokleon or Strepsiades) of the advice which he received earlier about dealing with such situations. *Wasps* 1388–1449 contains the comic pay-off for which 1253–63 prepared.

1388 A woman bread-seller hurries up; her name, we hear later (1396), is Myrtia. She is carrying her bread-basket, and she shouts loudly and indignantly; ἀρτοπώλιδες had a reputation for being abusive (*Frogs* 857–8), and so were especially suitable for the kind of scene which Ar. gives us here. In his *Old Age* a passage, of which three lines are pre-served, showed a bread-seller remonstrating indignantly when her loaves were snatched from her (Ath. 109 f, quoting Ar. fr. 125); this may mean that *Wasps* 1388–1414 was so successful in performance that Ar. decided to repeat the effect.

She is accompanied by a man with a yellow face, who turns out to be Khairephon (1408). She has evidently met him in the street while she was chasing Philokleon; for as they enter she is still asking him for his support. **παράστηθ'**: 'stand by me', i.e. 'help me'.

1390 ἐντευθενὶ: from her basket.

1391 δέκ' ὀβολῶν: 'worth ten obols'. It is not known how much bread this was. D. 34. 37, mentioning a dole of bread 'by the obol' in the fourth century, implies that an obol's worth of bread was a small amount, but by then the value of the obol had decreased. **κἀπιθήκην τέτταρας**: 'and four loaves besides'. [Dobree's conjecture *τετ-τάρων*, 'and loaves worth four obols besides', is pointless. The reason for mentioning the four loaves separately is that they did not come to an exact number of obols. If the extra loaves had come to four obols, the woman would have said 'fourteen obols' in the first place.]

1392 πράγματ': legal business; so also in 1426. 'Now we must have trouble and law-suits.'

1394 διαλλάξουσιν αὐτά: 'will settle them'. In the sense 'reconcile' this verb normally has a personal object, but cf. Hdt. 1. 61. 2 *κατηλλάσσετο τὴν ἔχθρην*, 7. 145. 1. In the following passage Philokleon tries to act on Bdelykleon's advice in 1256–61.

1395 ταύτῃ: 'with this woman'. (If it meant 'in this way', 1395 would be a mere repetition of 1394.)

1396 τὼ θεὼ: 'the two goddesses', Demeter and Kore. Only women swore by them (*Ek.* 155–8). (The Spartan oath *ναὶ τὼ σιώ*, in *Peace* 214 and elsewhere, probably refers to Kastor and Polydeukes.)

1397 She recounts her name and parentage to sound impressive, and perhaps to show that she is a native Athenian, not an immigrant or freedwoman. (Herodas 1. 76 is similar.) The names are ordinary Athenian ones. **θυγατέρος** instead of *θυγατρός* to fit the metre, as in E. *Or.* 751.

1401 Αἴσωπον: 566 n. In 1259 Bdelykleon meant that Philokleon might tell a story by Aesop. But Philokleon muddles the advice, thinks that *Αἰσωπικόν* means 'about Aesop', and invents a story of his own which has an all-too-pointed application to Myrtia. **ἐσπέρας**: 'one evening', as in *Peace* 228, *Birds* 1054, *Lys.* 409.

1402 Aesop's fables are regularly about animals, but Philokleon is hinting that Myrtia is a human 'bitch'. **μεθύσῃ**: Myrtia is not really drunk, but he is trying to convey the impression that it is she and not himself who is at fault. **ὑλάκτει**: imperfect, because it has *ῡ*.

1404 ἀντὶ: 'in exchange for', 'selling'.

1405 πυροὺς: The application of the fable to Myrtia becomes more and more obvious as it goes on. Dogs do not have any use for wheat, but bakers do.

1406 καὶ: 'as well', adding insult to injury. **προσκαλοῦμαί σ'**: 'I summon you'; 189 n. She is now formally issuing a summons; this line proves that, although a woman could not conduct her own case in court (but had to have it conducted by her husband or nearest male relative), she could deliver her own summons. In real life a summons, besides naming the offence alleged and the magistrates before whom the accused was to appear, also had to specify the date on which he was to appear (cf. *Clouds* 1222).   ὅστις εἶ: She does not know his name.

1407 ἀγορανόμους: 'market-controllers'. The agoranomoi were officials appointed by lot; in Aristotle's time there were five for the market in Athens and five for the market in Peiraieus (Arist. *Ath. Pol.* 51. 1), but in the fifth century probably only three for each (*Akh.* 723–4). They had to enforce the law against fraud in the market, by ensuring that the goods offered for sale were of proper quality and of full size or weight (Arist. *Ath. Pol.* 51. 1; the law is mentioned in D. 20. 9, Hyp. 3. 14); their supervision covered all kinds of goods except corn (Lys. 22. 16; corn was the responsibility of the σιτοφύλακες), but including bread (*Wasps* 1407, X. *Smp.* 2. 20). They were responsible for seeing that good order was kept in the Agora (*Akh.* 968; cf. Arist. *Pol.* 1299ᵇ16–17, 1321ᵇ12–14), and for keeping out persons legally excluded from it (*Akh.* 824–5), such as persons accused of homicide (D. 20. 158), Megarians after Perikles's Megarian decree (Th. 1. 139. 1), and persons guilty of impiety after the decree of Isotimides (Lys. 6. 24). They were responsible also for collecting taxes payable by the persons selling goods (if that is a fair deduction from the statement of Σ *Iliad* 21. 203 that taxes were specified in the ἀγορανομικὸς νόμος); taxes were certainly paid by non-Athenians using the Athenian market (*Akh.* 896, D. 57. 34), and may have been paid by Athenians too. *Wasps* 1407 shows that they were the officials before whom accusations of market offences were made. There is some evidence that they could punish offenders on the spot by whipping in a pillory (Pol. 10. 177), but probably this punishment was imposed only on non-citizens, and the usual procedure when citizens were accused will have been for the agoranomoi to preside over a trial in a law-court. **βλάβης**: 'for damage', genitive of accusation; cf. 1207, 1418.

1408 κλητῆρ': 189 n.; 1408, 1416, and *Clouds* 1218 show that in Ar.'s time one summons-witness was sufficient, though in the fourth century two seem to have been required (D. 40. 28, 53. 14).

Khairephon was a friend and follower of Sokrates, and is frequently mentioned as such in *Clouds*. He belonged to the deme Sphettos (*Clouds* 156). He became attached to Sokrates in his youth (Pl. *Ap.* 21 a), sometime before the Peloponnesian war (Pl. *Kharm.* 153 b), and it was he who put to the Delphic oracle the famous question 'Is there anyone wiser than Sokrates?' (Pl. *Ap.* 21 a, X. *Ap.* 14). The only other known event in his life is that in 404/3 he joined the democratic party in exile; he returned to Athens with them in 403, but was dead by 399 (Pl. *Ap.* 21 a). The distinctive feature of his appearance was a sallow complexion (1413, Eupolis 239), which made him look like a corpse

(*Clouds* 503–4), and it was a joke to call him a bat (*Birds* 1296, 1564; cf. fr. 573); perhaps this means simply that he was not sunburnt because intellectual pursuits kept him indoors in the daytime. He had a wild and enthusiastic temperament (Pl. *Ap.* 21 a, *Kharm.* 153 b), less amicable than that of his younger brother Khairekrates (X. *Apom.* 2. 3. 14).

But why does Ar. select him to be the Bread-seller's summons-witness? There must have been something funny about linking him with a bread-seller or with a summons. (The alternative explanation that this is not the well-known Khairephon is ruled out by the reference to his yellowness in 1413.) Although he says nothing, a good deal may be made of his appearance and behaviour. No doubt the actor wears a grotesque yellow mask, and he may ape the Bread-seller's gestures or perform other antics not mentioned in the dialogue.

1409 ἦν: 'to see if'.   τί: 'something sensible', as in 649.

1410 Lasos of Hermione was a poet who lived in the second half of the sixth century. He composed dithyrambs, and was associated with the establishment of dithyrambic contests in Athens; cf. *Dith. Trag. Com.*[2] 13–15. He disliked the sound of the letter σ, and wrote a *Hymn to Demeter* in which it was entirely avoided (Ath. 455 c). He detected a forgery inserted by Onomakritos in his collection of oracles of Mousaios, as a result of which Hipparkhos expelled Onomakritos from Athens (Hdt. 7. 6. 3); and he is said to have written the first book on music (*Souda* λ 139). For the surviving fragments of his poetry see Page *Poetae Melici Graeci* nos. 702–6; for a detailed discussion see G. A. Privitera *Laso di Ermione* (1965).   ἀντεδίδασκε: 'was directing in a competition', presumably a dithyrambic contest. Σιμωνίδης: the poet of Keos. In an elegiac epigram (145 Bergk = 79 Diehl) he claims to have won fifty-six prizes in dithyrambic contests.

1411 ὀλίγον μοι μέλει is not a proverbial gem of sixth-century conversation; the joke is that, after an impressive build-up, Philokleon attributes to the famous poet a perfectly commonplace remark (cf. *Knights* 1195, *Clouds* 1142, *Birds* 1636, etc.) as a rebuff to the Bread-seller. As he says it he makes some rude gesture at her (whatever was the ancient equivalent of snapping the fingers or thumbing the nose).

1412 ἄληθες: 1223 n. The Bread-seller indignantly turns to stalk away, but she turns so suddenly that she collides with Khairephon, who has been standing beside or behind her, and sends him sprawling at her feet.

1413 'Are you acting as a summons-witness for a woman? You're like a yellow Ino . . .' Philokleon indulges in another comparison; cf. 1308–13.   [ἐοικώς: In view of the parallel in 1142 Dobree's emendation κλητεύων ἔοικας is unnecessary. κλητεύειν ἔοικας is impossible, because then θαψίνῃ 'Ινοῖ would be in apposition to γυναικί, but it was Khairephon who was notoriously yellow.]   θαψίνῃ: He does not mean that Ino was yellow but that Khairephon is (1408 n.): 'You look like a yellow Ino' means 'You look like Ino, but yellower'.

1414 'Ino hanging on to the feet of Euripides' in supplication. There must have been a scene in Euripides's *Ino* in which Ino abased herself by hanging on to the feet of another character. Since we do not know what happened in that play, we cannot guess whose feet; but one of the surviving fragments of it is clearly part of a plea for mercy and may well come from that scene: μὴ σκυθρωπὸς ἴσθ' ἄγαν πρὸς τοὺς κακῶς πράσσοντας ἄνθρωπος γεγώς (E. fr. 406). Evidently the scene struck Ar. and others as ridiculous, because Ino's undignified posture seemed unsuitable for a tragic heroine, as undignified as Khairephon's present situation grovelling at the Bread-seller's feet. Εὐριπίδου, because of its position, must go with ποδῶν, not with 'Ινοῖ. Ar. has mischievously substituted the author's own name for the name of his character before whom Ino grovelled. This is the type of joke in which the last word of a sentence is the name of a contemporary Athenian unexpectedly substituted for some other noun, as in 19. (For a different interpretation see Taillardat § 383. But his equation Εὐριπίδου = 'son of the Euripos' = 'raging madman' = Athamas, Ino's husband, is too complicated for an audience to work out.)

As the Bread-seller and Khairephon depart, another accuser comes into view. He is a man showing all the signs of having been beaten. He has wounds on his head and elsewhere, and he hobbles along groaning loudly. Another man holds his arm and helps him along. [J, followed by t, has ἀνήρ τις εὐριπίδης against 1417–18, and the older editors took this to mean that the accuser was Euripides. But this must be wrong. There is nothing in the dialogue to suggest that he is Euripides; he does not speak in the tragic language which Ar. puts into Euripides's mouth when he brings him on as a character in other plays. Somehow the name must have got from 1414 into the margin in some earlier ms.; perhaps some muddled reader thought that 1414 meant that Euripides was standing on the stage. (Cf. *Clouds* 1478–85, where some words are mistakenly attributed to Hermes in some mss.) Tyrwhitt 54–5 corrects the attribution of lines.]

This passage shows that Ar. must have had at least four speaking actors for *Wasps*. It is impossible for the Bread-seller and the Accuser to be played by the same actor, since there is no interval at all between the departure of the one and the arrival of the other.

1416 τόν: the one whom he needs to deliver a summons. 'At any rate, he's got his summons-witness.'

1418 ὕβρεως: 'for assault'. Though this legal term is used also of wrongful confinement (D. 53. 16) and of sexual violation (Ais. 1. 15), its commonest use is, as here, of wrongfully striking a person. It is distinct from αἰκία: αἰκία is simply hitting someone, but ὕβρις is hitting him wantonly or insultingly (Arist. *Rhet.* 1374ᵃ13–15, *Souda* υ 16; cf.

L

D. 21. 72). To accuse someone of ὕβρις, the legal procedure was that of γραφή; the penalty was not fixed by law, but was decided by the jury in each case. The law laying down the procedure is preserved in D. 21. 47. **καλέσης**: 483 n.

1419 δίδωμί σοι: 'I am willing to pay you'.

1420 χάριν προσείσομαι: 'I shall be grateful too'; cf. Pl. *Ap.* 20 a, S. *OT* 232.

1421 ἐγὼ μὲν οὖν: 'No, *I* will'. Philokleon thinks he can arrange the settlement better himself.

1423 ἐλθὲ δευρί: He leads the Accuser to one side, as if to say something very confidential. But Bdelykleon follows and stands behind him, and so overhears the whole conversation (cf. 1433–4). [**πότερον**: πρότερον (a) could be taken with ἐλθὲ δευρί: 'come and listen to me, before going to court'. But the next sentence really needs Bentley's πότερον to indicate from the start that alternatives are being proposed.]

1423–5 'Will you leave to me the question how much money I must pay for the affair before being your friend for the future, or will you tell me how much?' For ἐπιτρέπω introducing an indirect question cf. *Akh.* 1115–16; here it does not refer to a formal arbitration, which could not be conducted by the accused. **πράγματος**: genitive of crime, as with 'prosecute', 'be convicted', etc.; cf. *Ek.* 663 τῆς αἰκείας οἱ τύπτοντες πόθεν ἐκτείσουσιν; (where emendation to τὴν is shown by *Wasps* 1424 to be unnecessary).

1427 Συβαρίτης: cf. 1259. Since his 'Aesopic' story failed to make a favourable impression, he now tries a couple of 'Sybaritic' ones.

1428 κατεάγη τῆς κεφαλῆς: 'he was hurt in the head'. In this phrase the part concerned is expressed sometimes in the genitive (e.g. *Akh.* 1180, Pl. *Grg.* 469 d), sometimes in the accusative (e.g. And. 1. 61, Lys. 3. 14). It is sometimes said that the genitive is partitive; thus it would mean that only part of the man's head was hurt, and the accusative that the whole of it was hurt. But there is nothing in the contexts of the instances to indicate such a distinction; even if this was the original distinction, the two forms of expression have become interchangeable. **μέγα σφόδρα**: 'very seriously'. [These two adverbs are not combined elsewhere, and since RV have μεγάλ' σφόδρα there may be some corruption in the text. But no convincing emendation has been suggested.]

1429 τρίβων ἱππικῆς: sc. τέχνης: 'skilled in horsemanship'. τρίβων usually takes a genitive (e.g. *Clouds* 869, E. *Ba.* 717), but sometimes an accusative (e.g. E. *Med.* 686, *Rh.* 625), without distinction of meaning.

1430 ἐπιστάς: 'standing over him' as he lay on the ground.

1431 'Each man should practise whichever art he knows', a proverb of unknown origin. ἔρδω is not used in Attic prose or comedy, nor is the optative usual for a command in Attic. The proverb was still familiar in the time of Cicero, who expects Atticus to recognize it from the first two words alone: 'o illud uerum *"ἔρδοι τις"*!' (Cic. *Att.* 5. 10. 3). It was translated into a Latin iambic line, and is quoted in that form by Cic. *Tusc.* 1. 41: 'quam quisque norit artem, in hac se exerceat'. Horace *Ep.* 1. 14. 44 and Propertius 2, 1. 46 adapt it to their own metres.

1432 παράτρεχ': 'run along!', 'be off!', as in Alexis 16. 11.   **τὰ Πιττάλου:** 'Pittalos's'; i.e. 'Pittalos's house', or more strictly 'Pittalos's property', since the plural would cover any land or buildings which Pittalos owned. For the form of expression cf. D. 54. 7 ἐγγὺς τῶν Πυθοδώρου, Herodas 5. 52 τὰ Μικκάλης, Theok. 2. 76, etc.; and without a name Lys. 12. 12 εἰς τὰ τοῦ ἀδελφοῦ τοῦ ἐμοῦ, Hdt. 1. 63. 2, D. 43. 62, etc. Pittalos is mentioned in *Akh.* 1032, 1222, and was evidently a doctor, but nothing else is known about him.

The implication of this story is 'It's no use complaining about your injuries'. The Accuser is understandably indignant.

1433 'This talk of yours is just like your previous behaviour' to the Bread-seller.   [σοι: σου (VJ) would make little effective difference to the meaning, but it would grammatically have to be taken as a possessive genitive with τρόποις, from which it is rather widely separated. σοι (R) is a vaguer 'dative of the person concerned', to be taken with the sentence as a whole, and so may naturally stand near the beginning.]

1434 ἀλλ' οὖν: 'Well, in that case', resorting to a second best (cf. 1190), that Philokleon's answer should be used as evidence against him at his trial.   **σὺ:** Bdelykleon. 'Remember for yourself the answer which he gave ⟨so that you will be ready to accept my evidence about it at the trial, without argument or dispute⟩.' [Editors who make σὺ the summons-witness deprive αὐτός of point and have to emend it.]

1435 The Accuser begins to walk away, accompanied by his summons-witness. At μὴ φεῦγ' they stop and turn round, only to find that Philokleon wants to tell another 'Sybaritic' story.

1436 ἐχῖνον: 'jar', a large wide-mouthed vessel (Erotianos p. 41. 18 Nachmanson). Once again (as in 1385) Philokleon suits the action to the word; as he says 'broke a jar' he knocks the Accuser down, as if to break him by way of illustration. This provokes the cry ταῦτ' ἐγὼ μαρτύρομαι, 'I call on you ⟨the summons-witness, or anyone else who may be within hearing⟩ to witness this', a standard phrase when someone claims that an offence is being committed against him. For the accusative of the act to be witnessed cf. *Clouds* 1297, *Frogs* 528, *Wealth* 932. In Ar. the simple verb is used to perform the act of calling to witness, the compound ἐπιμαρτύρομαι to refer to it (1437, *Clouds* 495), but this distinction is not always observed by other authors.

1438 ναὶ τὰν Κόραν: Doric for νὴ τὴν Κόρην. Kore is the daughter of Demeter, also called Pherrhephatta or Persephone. An oath by her alone is much rarer than an oath by Demeter and Kore (cf. 1396), but it is likewise a woman's oath (cf. Epikrates 9, Herodas 1. 32; it is only for the sake of a pun that Plautus makes a man use it in *Captiui* 881).

1440 ἐπίδεσμον: 'bandage'. This story is made to fit the Accuser's situation even more clearly than the previous one.

1441 ὕβριζ': defiant and ironical, as in S. *El.* 794 ὕβριζε· νῦν γὰρ εὐτυχοῦσα τυγχάνεις, A. *Pr.* 82, E. *Med.* 603.   ἄρχων: 'the magistrate', i.e. one of the thesmothetai (as in 304), since they were the magistrates responsible for cases of ὕβρις (D. 21. 47).   καλῇ: 825 n.

1442 The Accuser departs with his summons-witness, and Bdelykleon turns angrily to Philokleon.   ἐνταυθοῖ: 'here', not implying motion but just a synonym for ἐνταῦθα, as in *Clouds* 814 and *Th.* 225 (both almost identical with *Wasps* 1442), and *Akh.* 152, *Clouds* 843, *Frogs* 273.

1443 As Bdelykleon speaks he picks Philokleon up and begins to carry him towards the door of the house (slowly, for they do not get inside until 1449). [B emends οἴσω σε to ἔγωγε, unnecessarily. Even when Philokleon knows that Bdelykleon is carrying him away, he may still ask indignantly 'What are you doing?'] ὅ τι: 48 n.

1445 'There soon won't be enough summons-witnesses for all the people who want to summon you.'

1446 Philokleon tries another Aesopic story, this time a genuine one. The legend is that, when Aesop visited Delphoi, the Delphians took a dislike to him; so they hid a sacred bowl in his luggage, and when he left they ran after him, accused him of stealing it, and condemned him to death. Before dying he related to them the fable of the beetle and the eagle, implying that they would not escape revenge (1448 n.). For a detailed discussion of the legend see Anton Wiechers *Aesop in Delphi* (1961); he suggests that the Sacred War in the early sixth century was later regarded as revenge for the killing of Aesop.   ὀλίγον μοι μέλει: Bdelykleon deliberately uses against Philokleon the words which Philokleon used against the Bread-seller in 1411. For the boomerang joke, 989 n.

1448 The fable of the beetle and the eagle was evidently well known, since Ar. assumes that the words ὁ κάνθαρός ποτε— are enough to enable the audience to see the point. It is referred to also in *Peace* 129–34, *Lys.* 695, and related in full by Σ *Peace* 130. The eagle stole the young of the beetle, and the beetle in revenge rolled away the eagle's eggs. The eagle appealed to Zeus and was invited to nest in his bosom, but the beetle came and flew round Zeus's head, causing him to jump up and break the eggs. The moral is that the wicked have no refuge from vengeance, not even in the bosom of Zeus; and so Philokleon means to imply 'I'll get my own back on you somehow or other'.

1449 'Oh! You'll be the death of me, you and your beetles too!' αὐτοῖσι: 119 n.; here the implication is 'You'd be quite bad enough on your own, but with beetles added—!' [Reiske, to obtain a more usual context for αὐτοῖσι . . ., conjectured ἀπολῶ σ'. But the rude threat would be less in character for the patient Bdelykleon, and οἴμοι suits self-pity better. Cf. Pherekrates 108. 20 οἴμ᾽, ὡς ἀπολεῖς μ᾽ ἐνταῦθα διατρίβουσ᾽ ἔτι.] They disappear into the house.

1450-73 *The chorus congratulate Philokleon on the change which he is making in his way of life, and Bdelykleon on his wise and kind treatment of his father.*

This simple and pleasant little song serves two purposes. The first is to provide a short interlude, letting the audience and the actor playing Philokleon draw breath before the hectic final scene. The second is to round off the main theme of the play by a concluding comment on the persuading of Philokleon to give up his old way of life as a juror.

The song describes his transformation as begun but not yet completed. Past tenses are used to say that he has departed from his previous habits (1451-2) in consequence of Bdelykleon's arguments (1470-1); but the completion of his re-education is still in the future (1453-5), and there is still room for doubt whether he will go right through with it (1456) so as to devote himself to more dignified pursuits (1472-3). All this is in full accord with what we have seen of his behaviour in the preceding scene, in which it was obvious that he had given up his old way of life but had not yet learned to behave in the way Bdelykleon wished.

[It is therefore surprising that some editors have thought this song out of place or inconsistent with the previous scene. Rogers (pages xiv-xv), for example, uses it as evidence for his view that 'the scenes which appeal to the lower tastes of the audience were added by an afterthought, and formed no part of the original scheme of the Play'. Several editors, following a suggestion by Zielinski, even go so far as to transfer it to a different part of the play, exchanging it with the second parabasis (1265-91). These suggestions are quite unacceptable, and result from a failure to see that Philokleon's re-education is a slow process, as Ar. says quite plainly: τὸ γὰρ ἀποστῆναι χαλεπὸν φύσεως, ἣν ἔχοι τις, ἀεί (1457-8). The process has not been completed in 1292-1449, and the song is not meant to be a comment on that scene alone. It is a brief reflection on the theme of the whole play and on Philokleon's probable development in years to come. Its proper place therefore is near the end of the play; Bdelykleon makes his final exit, and the chorus bid him farewell (cf. 1464 ἄπεισιν) by reviewing his achievement.]

Metre: The rhythm suggests a gaily-tripping little dance. The first half of each dimeter is either iambic (× – ∪ –, with the second and/or fourth syllable sometimes resolved to ∪ ∪) or the unit o o – × (the symbol o o means a position which may be occupied by – – or – ∪ or ∪ –; the first syllable is sometimes resolved to ∪ ∪). This is one form of the 'base' found in aeolic verse, but in our passage it may be regarded not just as four introductory syllables but as the first metron of each dimeter in which it occurs; cf. *Clouds* 518-62, where it forms the first

and third metron in each eupolidean tetrameter. The second half of
each dimeter is either a choriamb (− ∪ ∪ −) or, to make a catalectic
verse, a bacchiac (∪ − −, following *ia*) or a cretic (− ∪ −, following the
unit o o − ×, as in *Clouds* 518–62).

1450, 1462	*ia ch*	
1451, 1463	*ia ba*	
1452, 1464	*ia ch*	
1453, 1465	*ia ch*	
1454, 1466	*ia ba* ‖	
1455, 1467	*ia ch*	
1456, 1468	*ia ch*	
1457, 1469	∪∪ ∪ − −	and *ch*
1458, 1470	∪͞∪ ᴐ − ∪	and *ch*
1459, 1471	− − − −	and *ch*
1460, 1472	∪ − − ᴐ	and *ch*
1461, 1473	∪∪ ∪ − ∪	and *cr*

1450–1 'I do congratulate the old man on the comfortable life to which
he has changed from . . .'   τῆς εὐτυχίας: genitive of cause, regular
with ζηλῶ (e.g. *Akh.* 1008, *Knights* 837).   οἷ: For the metaphorical
use, referring not to a place reached but to a degree of success achieved,
cf. *Akh.* 836.

1452 For the omission of ἐκ with the genitive after μεθίσταμαι cf. *Wealth*
365.   ξηρῶν qualifies both nouns. Literally 'dry', it here means
'austere', 'frugal', lacking the normal comforts of life; so also in
Antiphanes 16. The opposite is λιπαρός, meaning 'oily', 'comfortable'.
The Greeks regarded oil for the hair and body as one of the most
important comforts of life; cf. 608 n. and Denniston's note on E.
El. 239.

1453 ἕτερα: 'still more lessons' in the art of living luxuriously.

1454 μέγα τι: internal accusative: 'he will undergo a great alteration'.
[Emendation of this phrase on metrical grounds is unnecessary, since
ἢ μέγα τι μετα- may be regarded as an iambic metron and so responds
adequately to the iambic metron ὁ παῖς ὁ Φιλο- in 1466. But -πείσεται
cannot be right, because it fails to respond to -κλέωνος.]

1455 The neuter participle and adjective are used as abstract nouns:
'luxury and softness'. [τρυφᾶν (Bergk) may be right, but it seems more
natural to have an adjectival form parallel to the adjective μαλακόν.]

1457–8 'It's always hard to depart from the natural character which
a man has.'   ἔχοι: One might expect ἂν ἔχῃ. But the optative is
commonly used in an indefinite relative clause in primary sequence
when two conditions are fulfilled: (*a*) the sentence is a general maxim,
applicable at all times and not only in the present; (*b*) the main
clause is a statement of obligation, propriety, or possibility with an
infinitive, as here τὸ ἀποστῆναι χαλεπόν; presumably this statement is

regarded as equivalent to a potential optative, such as χαλεπῶς ἄν τις ἀποσταίη, which would require historic sequence in the relative clause. Cf. S. *Ant.* 666 ὃν πόλις στήσειε, τοῦδε χρὴ κλύειν, *OT* 315, 979, X. *Kyr.* 1. 6. 19, 2. 4. 10.

1459 ταῦτ' ἔπαθον: 'have this experience'. The aorist denotes a regular occurrence here and in 1461; cf. 99. ταῦτα is used for a single action, as in 843, etc. [So Dindorf's τοῦτ' is unnecessary.]

1464 τὴν may here perhaps be regarded as the last word of a verse, for the song is otherwise entirely in dimeters. A sentence ends at the corresponding point in the strophe. Cf. 504.

1465 φιλοπατρίαν: 'love for his father'.

1467 ἀγανῷ: 'kindly', 'benign', a poetic word.

1468–9 'I was never so entranced or so carried away with a man's behaviour.' **ἐπεμάνην:** For the metaphor cf. 744. **ἐξεχύθην:** There seems to be no exact parallel to this metaphor, but Pi. *I.* 1. 4 Δᾶλος, ἐν ᾷ κέχυμαι is similar.

1470–3 'For in every point he was superior in the argument, in his wish to provide his father with more dignified pursuits.'

1474–1515 *Philokleon, still drunk, declares that the old tragic dances are the best. He demonstrates some movements from them, and then challenges to a dancing-match anyone who thinks he can dance better. The sons of Karkinos come forward to take up the challenge.*

The purpose of this passage is simply to introduce the dancing which concludes the play (which is a novelty; cf. 1536–7). But it is enlivened by Philokleon's antics in 1482–95 and by jokes about the sons of Karkinos (especially the pun and comparisons in 1507–15).

1474 Xanthias (or possibly Sosias or another slave: 1292 n.) bursts out of the house to tell the audience excitedly what is going on inside. The speech is a 'messenger's speech', like 1299–1325, to introduce the ensuing scene. [This does not mean, as Rogers thinks, that 1474–81 is an alternative account of Philokleon's behaviour at the party, showing that Ar. has re-modelled the play incompetently. It describes Philokleon's behaviour in his own house; cf. 1475 τὴν οἰκίαν. He was drunk when he returned from the party; Bdelykleon took him indoors to prevent him from assaulting members of the public, but there is no reason why that should have made him instantly sober.] **νὴ τὸν Διόνυσον:** a usual oath, but perhaps it has special point in a description of a drunk man. **ἀπορά:** 'baffling'; the household does not know what to do with Philokleon.

1475 εἰσκεκύκληκεν: 'has wheeled in'. This is not a reference to the theatre's ἐκκύκλημα, since Philokleon did not enter the house by that means, but simply a metaphor for 'has put in'. [There is a similar metaphor in *Th.* 651, where the reading of R, the only ms., is εἰς οἷ' ἐμαυτὸν εἰσεκύλησα πράγματα. The corrupt εἰσεκύλησα is usually emended to εἰσεκύλισα, but in view of *Wasps* 1475 it might be better to read εἰσεκύκλησα. At any rate *Th.* 651 is not sufficient evidence to justify altering *Wasps* 1475 to εἰσκεκύλικεν.]

1476 διὰ πολλοῦ χρόνου: 1252 n.

1477 ἤκουσέ τ' αὐλοῦ: This shows that the music of an αὐλός was not generally heard except on festive occasions.

1478 ὀρχούμενος: 'the natural result of intoxication for a Greek', as Starkie says, quoting Eriphos 1, Alexis 222, Thphr. *Char.* 6. 3, 12. 14, and other passages.

1479 'Those old dances with which Thespis competed' in tragic contests. According to Athenian tradition Thespis was the first man to write a tragedy with an actor separate from the chorus. For Philokleon's taste for old-fashioned music, cf. his liking for Phrynikhos (220, 269, 1490). Xanthias is amazed that anyone should revive such old-fashioned dances nowadays. (1480–1 shows beyond doubt that the Thespis meant here is the early tragedian, and so Σ^Ald's note ὁ κιθαρῳδός· οὐ γὰρ δὴ ὁ τραγικός [cf. *Souda* θ 283] must be a mistake.)

1480 τραγῳδούς: not 'tragedians', but 'performers in tragedy', 'tragic dancers'. Thespis is presumed to have performed in his own plays. **κρόνους:** Kronos was superseded by his son Zeus, and so his name became a term for anyone who was out of date or behind the times, 'fogy'; cf. *Clouds* 398, 929, 1070, *Wealth* 581, Pl. *Euthd.* 287 b, Hyp. fr. 252. Philokleon paradoxically maintains that the new dances are out of date and the old ones are not.

1481 [τοὺς νῦν: τὸν νοῦν (a) adds nothing significant to κρόνους, and τοὺς νῦν is needed to show that Philokleon is not condemning old tragedians like Thespis. Bentley made the conjecture in his *Dissertation upon Phalaris* 2nd edition (1713) 265.] **διορχησάμενος:** 'by dancing against them'. δι- implies competition, as in 1248, 1499.

1482–95 *Metre:* A run of anapaests accompanies Philokleon's re-entrance and dancing.

1482 Philokleon appears in the doorway. The door is probably standing open (left open by Xanthias when he came out at 1474), so that his elaborate command to open it is just a piece of showing-off. (Cf. A. M. Dale in *JHS* lxxvii [1957] 206 n. 1.) **θάσσει** is a tragic word, and the whole line is probably a quotation from some unknown tragedy.

1483 'There you are! Here comes the nuisance!' The same words are used in *Clouds* 906–7, and (in a different order) in *Frogs* 1018. **καὶ δή:** 1324 n.

1484 κλῇθρα χαλάσθω: possibly another tragic quotation; cf. χαλᾶτε κλῇθρα in E. *Hipp.* 808, *IT* 1304, *Hel.* 1180. **καὶ δή:** 'Look!' He performs the movements clownishly as he describes them in 1484–95. The various movements must be ones which were thought typical of dances in tragedies of an earlier generation. Although Thespis is mentioned in 1479, the movements are not necessarily all ones which were used by Thespis himself; indeed it is not clear that Athenians in Ar.'s time knew much about the details of Thespis's performances. He is mentioned merely as a representative figure of old-fashioned tragedy, and what 1478–81 shows is simply that the movements in 1484–95 are ones which Athenians of Ar.'s time believed were used by Thespis and other early tragedians.

It has sometimes been denied that Philokleon's dances are old tragic ones. The subject has been very thoroughly discussed by Ervin Roos *Die tragische Orchestik im Zerrbild der altattischen Komödie* (1951), with full references to earlier discussions. He maintains that the dances are ones customarily performed by ἐταῖραι, which Philokleon has seen at the party. No doubt some of the individual movements mentioned in 1484–95 may sometimes have been performed by ἐταῖραι, but that does not prove that they were not performed in early tragedies too; and Roos's thesis (like the suggestion of some earlier scholars that Philokleon dances the κόρδαξ or the σίκιννις) is untenable because it is contrary to what Ar. says. 1478–81 proves beyond doubt that Philokleon's movements are meant to be in the style of the dances in early tragedies. These lines cannot be explained away as a joke or a mistake by Xanthias; they are not funny in themselves, and they are completely pointless unless they are an introduction and explanation of what Philokleon actually does in 1484–95.

1485 σχήματος: 'figure' of a dance, as in *Peace* 323, X. *Smp.* 7. 5, etc.

1487 λυγίσαντος agrees not with σχήματος but with τινος understood: 'the figure of one bending his torso', i.e. 'the figure of bending one's torso'. πλευρὰν λυγίζω means bending forwards, backwards, or sideways. This kind of movement was a feature of the dance called ἴγδις (Antiphanes 127, Ath. 629 f) or ἰγδισμα; cf. *EM* 464. 51–2 ἔστι δὲ καὶ εἶδος ὀρχήσεως ἰγδίσματα, ἐν ᾗ ἐλύγιζον τὴν ὀσφῦν ἐμφερῶς τῷ δοίδυκι. Possibly that is the dance which Philokleon begins to perform here (this suggestion is made by Meineke *Fragmenta Comicorum Graecorum* iii 69 and supported by Roos *Die tragische Orchestik* 21–76). However, bending may well have been included in other dances besides the ἴγδισμα, and we do not know whether the ἴγδισμα was used by Thespis and other early tragedians. ὑπὸ ῥώμης: 'vigorously'. [This gives adequate sense, and so need not be emended. But ὑπὸ ῥύμης, 'with a swing', gives excellent sense, and may be right. It was proposed by Lobeck on page 404 of his edition of Phryn. *Ekl.*]

1488 μυκτὴρ μυκᾶται: a comic jingle: 'How my snout snorts!' The dancing makes him breathe heavily. (The character is an old man; the actor, however, must be very fit physically to dance and speak simultaneously.) σφόνδυλος ἀχεῖ: 'my backbone sounds', i.e. cracks; ἀχεῖ, with Doric α for η, is another tragic expression.

1489 πῖθ' ἐλλέβορον implies 'You're mad'. Hellebore is a kind of plant (the 'Christmas rose' is a familiar variety of it), and a drink made from it, acting as a strong purge, was supposed to cure madness, which was thought to be caused by an excess of black bile in the body. Our line is the earliest mention of hellebore as a cure for madness, and it may only recently have come into use; cf. A. O'Brien-Moore *Madness in Ancient Literature* (1924) 30–9. For the use of 'Drink hellebore!' as a way of saying 'You're mad' cf. D. 18. 121 τί σαυτὸν οὐχ ἐλλεβορί-ζεις; and Men. fr. 63 Koerte Α. ἐλλέβορον ἤδη πώποτ᾽ ἔπιες, Σωσία; Σω. ἅπαξ. Α. πάλιν νῦν πῖθι· μαίνει γὰρ κακῶς.

1490 Φρύνιχος: 220 n. Since the dance movements which Philokleon is performing are old ones (1478–81), the reference must be to Phrynikhos the early tragedian, not to the Phrynikhos of 1302 or any other Phrynikhos of Ar.'s time. He was especially associated with dancing (Plu. *Eth.* 732 f, Ath. 22 a), and particularly with a high kick (1524), so that the audience will have had no difficulty in knowing which Phrynikhos is meant here. In *Frogs* three different men named Phrynikhos are mentioned, the tragic dramatist (910, 1299), the comic dramatist (13), and the politician (689), and in each case the audience is expected to recognize from the context alone which Phrynikhos is meant.

[There is some evidence that there was a fourth Phrynikhos who acted and danced in tragedy. Σ *Birds* 750 distinguishes Phrynikhos the actor, son of Khorokles, from Phrynikhos the tragic poet, son of Polyphradmon. Σ *Wasps* 1302 mentions 'Phrynikhos the tragic actor' and Σ *Clouds* 1091 'Phrynikhos the tragic dancer'; and a list of names compiled in the year 415 and quoted in And. 1. 47 includes Φρύνιχος ὁ ὀρχησάμενος, 'Phrynikhos who used to be a dancer'. Putting these pieces of evidence together one might suppose that a Phrynikhos acted and danced in tragedy in the generation before Ar., so that in *Wasps* 1490 he is regarded as an old-fashioned dancer, and in And. 1. 47 the aorist tense is used because he has retired from dancing. But I think this is unlikely. The tragedian Phrynikhos will have acted and danced in his own plays, so that 'the tragic actor' or 'the tragic dancer' is not necessarily a different person from the dramatist; and although Σ *Clouds* 1091 and Σ *Wasps* 1302 seem to assume that he is contemporary with Ar., that may mean only that they did not know his date. The patronymic 'son of Khorokles', meaning 'famous for choruses', sounds too good a coincidence to be true, and may be the invention of some compiler who did not know Phrynikhos's real patronymic. Thus Σ *Clouds* 1091, Σ *Wasps* 1302, and Σ *Birds* 750 can all be explained as containing garbled references to Phrynikhos the tragic dramatist, not to another tragic performer named Phrynikhos. In And. 1. 47 the text may well be corrupt; see my note there.]

'Phrynikhos is cowering like a cock' means that Philokleon is pretending to be Phrynikhos, dancing one of Phrynikhos's dances. The movement which he now tries to perform consists of bending forwards,

like a cock cowering before a winning opponent in a cock-fight, and
then straightening up and kicking up one leg as high as possible.
Plutarch quotes three times (*Alk.* 4. 3, *Pel.* 29. 11, *Eth.* 762 e) a tragic
line ἔπτηξ' ἀλέκτωρ δοῦλος ὡς κλίνας πτερόν, without naming the
author; probably it was a well-known line of Phrynikhos which Ar. is
here parodying (so Nauck, who lists it as fr. 17 of Phrynikhos). Cf.
Roos *Die tragische Orchestik* 76–88, E. K. Borthwick in *CQ* xviii (1968)
44–6. [But Borthwick's references here to Pyrrhic dances are misleading. Pyrrhic dances were not obsolete in Ar.'s time, but were
regularly performed at the Panathenaia (*Clouds* 988–9, *Frogs* 153,
Lys. 21. 1) ; and their chief features were manipulation of a shield and
leaps in the air (cf. Borthwick in *JHS* lxxxvii [1967] 20), not high
kicks. So Philokleon's old-fashioned tragic dance is not a Pyrrhic.]

1491 τάχα βαλλήσει: 'You'll soon be pelted' with stones by passers-by. It
was customary to throw stones at madmen; cf. *Birds* 524–5 ὥσπερ
δ' ἤδη τοὺς μαινομένους βάλλουσ' ὑμᾶς. Thus Xanthias is using yet
another form of words to say again what he said in 1486 and 1489.
For βαλλήσ- cf. 222. [There is no objection to the use of the future
middle form with a passive meaning, which occurs in many verbs; cf.
especially *Clouds* 1379 τυπτήσομαι. Platnauer (*CQ* i [1951] 167), dis-
liking it, suggests βαλλήσει σ' (with οὐράνιον σκέλος in the next line),
but this is rightly rejected by Roos (*Eranos* l [1952] 142–3). Borthwick
(*CQ* xviii [1968] 46) thinks the verb is active and means that Philokleon will next perform throwing movements, as in a Pyrrhic dance;
but this is wrong, not only because Philokleon's dance is not a Pyrrhic,
but also because Xanthias throughout this passage (1486, 1489, 1491,
1493, 1496) is exclaiming at Philokleon's madness, not knowledge-
ably describing his choreography.]

1492 οὐρανίαν: 'skywards', adverbial accusative: 398 n. Ar. is using the
vocabulary of a ball game, in which οὐρανίαν and οὐρανιάζω were used
of throwing the ball high in the air; one might get a similar effect in
English translation by using a verb like 'lob' or 'punt'. Cf. Hskh. o
1830 οὐρανίαν· ὅταν τὴν σφαῖραν ἀναβάλωσιν. καὶ τὴν τοιαύτην δὲ καθόλου
παιδιὰν οὐρανίαν καλοῦσι καὶ οὐρανιάζειν. παρὰ τοῦτο οὖν ἔπαιξεν
Ἀριστοφάνης. [The last words of Hesykhios's explanation make it
practically certain that he is referring to our passage, and so confirm
Meineke's emendation of οὐράνιον, which will not scan.]   **ἐκλακτίζων:** 'Kicking out' was evidently a distinctive feature of Phrynikhos's
dances; cf. 1524–5. Pol. 4. 102 says that ἐκλακτίσματα were women's
dances, and this statement is taken by Roos as evidence for his view
that Philokleon performs dance movements appropriate to ἑταῖραι;
but it cannot apply to our passage, since Philokleon is now imitating
Phrynikhos and Phrynikhos was not a woman.

1493 πρωκτὸς χάσκει: i.e. 'I'm doing the splits', by kicking his leg so
high.   **κατὰ σαυτὸν ὅρα:** 'Look after yourself!', i.e. 'Take care you

don't injure yourself!' [Lenting gave προωκτὸς χάσκει to Xanthias and κατὰ σαυτὸν ὅρα to Philokleon, with the sense 'Mind your own business!' But κατὰ σαυτὸν ὅρα suits Xanthias's attitude better: 1491 n.]

1495 κοτυληδών or κοτύλη strictly means the socket of the hip-joint, and ἄρθρον is often used for the ball of a joint. But here ἐν makes these interpretations impossible. So Ar. is evidently not using the precise technical terms of anatomy, and we should translate more vaguely 'in my limbs each joint is moving supply'.

1496 οὐκ εὖ; 'Wasn't that good?' The change of metre shows that he ends his dance before asking this question. [These two words must be a question by Philokleon, because μὰ Δί' οὐ δῆτ' regularly comes at the beginning of a speech rejecting a suggestion by the previous speaker, and should not be preceded by other words in the same sentence; cf. 169, 396. But who is it who replies to this question? J makes Bdelykleon Philokleon's interlocutor throughout 1496–1515. Σ's reference to ὁ παῖς is ambiguous, since it may mean either 'son' or 'slave'. The decisive argument against Bdelykleon is that in 1496 the speaker declares that Philokleon's activity is mad; if Bdelykleon thought his father was behaving insanely, he would not stand by and watch but would try to stop him; but in the following lines Philokleon continues unimpeded; therefore Bdelykleon does not speak 1496 and is not on the stage in this scene.]

1497 ἀνείπω: 'let me make a proclamation'.

1499 ἐμοὶ δι-: 'against me'; cf. 1481.

1500 γ': 'yes'. Philokleon is looking round the audience. Xanthias sees a man entering the orkhestra from the side.

1501 Karkinos son of Xenotimos, of the deme Thorikos, was one of the three generals commanding an Athenian fleet which made attacks on the Peloponnesian coast in 431 (Th. 2. 23. 2, IG i² 296. 30–40). On this or another occasion some comic dramatist unkindly remarked that in an emergency even Karkinos obtained office (Com. adesp. 52), but it may possibly have been because of his success as an admiral that he was nicknamed θαλάττιος (1519, Pl. com. 134). He was also a dancer like his sons (Peace 781–4) and a dramatist (Peace 791–5). It is not clear what kind of plays he wrote: in Clouds 1259–61 a loud lament is thought to sound like one of his gods, which suggests that he wrote tragedies; but one of his plays is said to have been called Mice (Σ Peace 794), which sounds like a comedy. (Dover in his note on Clouds 1261 takes that line as a reference to Karkinos's son; but this is not the natural interpretation, since Karkinos was himself a dramatist.)

The sons of Karkinos are referred to as dancers in Peace 781–90, 864. The best-known of them was Xenokles, who wrote tragedies (Th. 169, Frogs 86) and defeated Euripides at the Dionysia in 415 (Ael. VH 2. 8). One of his lines is parodied in Clouds 1264 (according to Σ on that line). He was called δωδεκαμήχανος (Pl. com. 134), which may mean that he made much use of stage machinery; alternatively it may just mean 'versatile' (cf. *Frogs* 1327). He seems also to have had a reputation as a clever orator (*Th.* 440–2). Another son of Karkinos was named after his grandfather, Xenotimos; we hear of him conveying a letter from the king of Bosporos to Athens in the 390s (Isok. 17. 52). The third son was called either Xenarkhos (Σ *Peace* 781) or Xenokleitos (Σ *Frogs* 86).

[There are some statements that Karkinos had four sons, one of whom was called Datis and was a tragedian (Σ *Wasps* 1502, Σ *Peace* 289, Σ *Frogs* 86). But *Wasps* 1502 ὁ μέσατος implies that there were not four, and 1511 (if genuine) that only one of them wrote tragedies. Perhaps 'Datis' was a nickname of Xenokles, and they were later assumed wrongly to have been different persons; so van Leeuwen argued (*Mn.* II xvi [1888] 435–8), maintaining that the Datis in *Peace* 289 was Xenokles. However, there is some contemporary evidence for a fourth son: Pherekrates 14, quoted by Σ^{VΓ} *Wasps* 1509. This fragment is from *Savages*, performed in 420 (Ath. 218 d). It will not scan and must be corrupt, but it seems to say first that Karkinos has three sons and then to make a correction, presumably spoken by a different character: μὰ τὸν Δί' οὐ τρεῖς [τε ἐκεῖνοί] εἰσιν ἀλλὰ (Meineke: οἱ VΓ) τέτταρες. So probably Karkinos had four sons but one of them for some reason (for example, because he was still a boy, or because he was not a dancer) was not known to the general public in 422, but did become known to them later.]

We may assume, I think, that the sons of Karkinos appeared in person in the original performance of *Wasps*. It is not so likely that their parts were played by three mute actors who were dressed as the sons of Karkinos and parodied their dancing. Nothing in the scene (certainly not Philokleon's boastful bantering, which merely reveals his own character) suggests that Ar. intends any kind of parody or attack here; 1518–34 is complimentary. But a year later we find Ar. saying 'If Karkinos asks you to dance with his sons, don't!' (*Peace* 781–6). This means, I suggest (modifying the view of J. Nicole in *Mélanges Graux* [1884] 163–7), that their participation in *Wasps* was a failure, and Ar. regretted allowing them to take part. If their performance was in some way unsatisfactory, spoiling the play's spectacular ending, that may possibly explain why it failed to win the first prize (hyp. i 33).

1502 μέσατος: 'midmost', an unusual superlative. [μεσαίτατος (R) is a more usual form, and may be right here. But the existence of μέσατος is certified by the metre in Theok. 7. 10, 21. 19, and preference may be given to it as the more difficult reading.] **καταποθήσεται:** For καταπίνω used metaphorically for 'defeat' cf. *Knights* 693.

1503 ἐμμελείᾳ κονδύλου: 'with a fist-dance'. He does not mean that he will actually punch his opponent, but only, as the next sentence shows, that he will win easily because he is the better dancer. 'I shall thrash him' is a similar metaphor in English. ἐμμέλεια is the regular word for a dance in a tragedy, as opposed to other kinds of drama (Ath. 20 e).

1504 οὐδέν: 997 n.   **ᾦζυρέ:** crasis for ὦ οἴζυρέ. The only instances of οἴζυρός in Attic are four of the vocative in Ar.; the others are *Clouds* 655, *Birds* 1641, *Lys.* 948. The contexts of these passages show that it does not mean 'you wretch', as it is sometimes translated, but simply implies disagreement. So here Xanthias means 'No, you won't walk away with a victory so easily'. At this point another dancer is seen entering the orkhestra, and soon (1508) he is followed by a third.

1505 Καρκινίτης: 'Karkinite', a noun formed by analogy with such words as Ἀβδηρίτης and Συβαρίτης, as if the family of Karkinos were a separate nationality.

1506 ὠψώνηκ' ἄρα: 'What a tasty meal I've got, then!', continuing the metaphor of 1502.

1507 καρκίνους: 'crabs', an obvious pun, for which Ar. has prepared the way by making Philokleon use metaphors from eating in 1502 and 1506. [Some have emended the line to remove one γε or both. But there is no valid objection to having γε twice in one sentence; e.g. *Peace* 19, 675.]

1509 τουτὶ τί ἦν: 183 n. For the shape of the line, suggesting alternative comic answers, cf. *Birds* 1203, *Lys.* 982.   **ὦτος ἢ σφάλαξ:** 'an owl or a mole'. The third son of Karkinos makes his appearance performing a few steps of the 'owl dance' or 'look-out dance'. This type of dance, named σκώψ or σκώπευμα or σκοπός, is mentioned by Pol. 4. 103, Ath. 629 f (quoting A. fr. 79), Hskh. ὑπόσκοπον χέρα (quoting A. fr. 339), and Photios under σκοπός (referring to Eupolis 446) and σκώπευμα. The dancer turned his head from side to side (Pol. 4. 103 εἶδος ὀρχήσεως ἔχον τινὰ τοῦ τραχήλου περιφοράν) and peered with his hand above his eyes (Ath. 629 f τῶν ἀποσκοπούντων τι σχῆμα ἄκραν τὴν χεῖρα ὑπὲρ τοῦ μετώπου κεκυρτωκότων). Philokleon thinks that Karkinos's son, performing this peering movement, looks like a nocturnal creature dazzled by daylight. (The statement of Arist. fr. 355 that the ὦτος or long-eared owl is not nocturnal is incorrect; contrast *HA* 597ᵇ23.) This ingenious emendation of the mss.' unintelligible readings has been proposed with full discussion by E. K. Borthwick (*CQ* xviii [1968] 47–51). The owl dance has been discussed by Lillian B. Lawler (*Trans. Am. Phil. Ass.* lxx [1939] 482–502).

1510 πιννοτήρης: 'pinna-guard', a very small species of crab, so called because it lives inside the shell of a kind of shell-fish called 'pinna', and when it sees an octopus or other enemy approaching it nips the pinna to prompt it to close its shell; cf. Thompson *Fishes* 202 and

Rogers's note on *Wasps* 1510. Xanthias here calls the third son of Karkinos 'pinna-guard' or 'look-out crab' because he is the καρκίνος (continuing the pun of 1507) who is performing the look-out dance (1509 n.), and also because he is the smallest member of the family (if 1511 is genuine).

1511, if genuine, shows that the third dancer is Xenokles (1501 n.). [But it is a mere explanation of 1510, adding nothing to the joke, and it may be right to delete it as a gloss.]

1512 For the genitive, 429 n.

1513 κατέπεσεν: 'has alighted', 'has dropped in on us'.   ὀρχίλων: 'wrens'; cf. Thompson *Birds* 219-20. The metaphor is used because the sons of Karkinos were small (cf. Pherekrates 14) and musical; cf. *Peace* 787-90, where they are called 'quails'. There is no pun on ὀρχησταί or on ὄρχεις, as Σ suggests.

1514 καταβατέον μοι: not necessarily 'I must go down from the stage to the orkhestra', though he may well do so at this point, but 'I must enter the contest' (LSJ καταβαίνω I. 3). [ὦ ζυρέ (a) does not suit the context here (1504 n.). Probably it has been repeated from 1504 by mistake.]

1515 Philokleon takes over Xanthias's 'crab' pun. Salt water was regularly used for boiling fish; cf. Ar. fr. 416, Antiphanes 222.   κύκα: 'mix', by adding salt to fresh water; or possibly, since the verb is sometimes used of turbulent water, it may here mean 'boil'.   ἤν: 'in case'.

1516-37 *The play ends with dancing by Philokleon and the sons of Karkinos, joined presently by Karkinos himself.*

We cannot hope to appreciate this part of the play fully, since the main feature of it was the dancing. The words and music were mere accompaniment, to which the audience will have paid little or no attention. Ar. occupies the time with some variations on the 'crab' pun made in 1507 and some references to pirouettes and high kicks, but it should not be assumed that these have a close correspondence with the movements which the sons of Karkinos performed. They quite possibly arranged their own dances; and anyway the choreography must have been worked out after, not before, the composition of the words and music. These lines are therefore a very shaky foundation for any conclusion about the style of the dancing of Karkinos's sons, or the ways in which their dancing differed from the older style of dancing which Philokleon tried to demonstrate in 1484-95. But it is noticeable that 'moving in a circle' or 'spinning round' or 'pirouettes', which are not mentioned at all in 1484-95, appear five times in 1516-37 (in 1517, 1523-4, 1528-9 (twice), and 1530-1). Presumably Ar. was sure that the dancing of Karkinos's sons would include such movements, and it seems fair to infer that they were a prominent feature of the new style of tragic dancing and not of the old. High kicks, on the other hand, were evidently common to both styles (compare 1490-2 with 1523-7 and 1530-1).

Some of the dancing may have been accompanied by music without words, and so the passage may have lasted longer than the time it would take to sing the words straight through. Most of the time was no doubt taken up by an expert display given by the sons of Karkinos. Philokleon must have taken some part; perhaps he did some clowning, with much falling over and picking himself up again, in between dances by the sons of Karkinos. But the idea that he is competing against them is not followed up (at least, not as far as we can tell from the words alone); no winner is declared. Probably it is obvious from the first that Philokleon is a hopeless dancer and the sons of Karkinos are experts, so that the audience's interest is not in being told who is the winner but in watching the experts' performance.

1532–4 seems to imply that Karkinos himself only watched; perhaps Ar. knew when he wrote those lines that Karkinos would not dance because he was too old. But he may have led the procession out of the orkhestra at the end.

Metre: 1516–17 are anapaestic tetrameters, before the dance begins. The remaining lines, accompanying the dancing, are in the metre called 'archilochean': $\times - \cup\cup - \cup\cup - \times - \cup - \cup - -$. 1520 and 1525 are cut short after the eighth syllable. For the scansion of 1526–7 ὦζωσιν see note on that line

The archilochean metre is a rare one, and is nowhere else used for so long a passage as this. It would be rash to say, on the evidence of this passage alone, that it is a metre normally used for gay dance music, or that it is specially associated with epic forms and phrases.

1516 ξυγχωρήσωμεν: 'let us make way'. The chorus move perhaps to the back of the orkhestra, to leave all the rest of it clear for Philokleon and the sons of Karkinos.

1517 ἐφ' ἡσυχίας: 'without interference'. ἡσυχία here as often (e.g. *Lys.* 1224) denotes neither silence nor inactivity, but freedom to do as one wishes without obstruction. For ἐπί with a genitive denoting the circumstances in which an act is done cf. Ais. 3. 191 ἐπὶ σχολῆς. ἡμῶν with πρόσθεν: 'in front of us'. **βεμβικίζωσιν**: 'spin'; cf. 1530–1. βεμβικίζω is found only here, the intransitive βεμβικιάω in *Birds* 1465.

1518–19 ἄγ': 381 n. **μεγαλώνυμα**: 'renowned', a very complimentary adjective which Ar. elsewhere applies to gods (*Clouds* 569, *Th.* 315). **θαλασσίοιο**: a nickname of Karkinos, used also in Pl. com. 134: 1501 n. For the epic form of the genitive cf. 1521–2. [The mss.' θαλασσίου will not scan, and since ἀτρυγέτοιο is certified by the metre in 1521–2 it seems better to adopt a similar form here than Bergk's clumsy θαλασσίου θεοῦ.]

1521–2 θῖν' ἀλὸς ἀτρυγέτοιο: a Homeric phrase, e.g. *Iliad* 1. 316. In this sentence Ar. is taking up again the joke of regarding Karkinos's sons as crabs, as in 1507 and 1515. This does not mean, as has sometimes been supposed, that Karkinos's sons were dressed as crabs and performed crab-like movements in their dance. When Ar. wrote these words he probably did not know what movements they would perform; he just wanted to give the chorus some words to sing meanwhile, and these words are as good as any.   καρίδων: V.-H. Debidour *Aristophane*: *Théâtre complet* i 412 suggests that there is a pun on Χαρίτων: dancers may be called brothers of the Graces, crabs brothers of shrimps. But Χαρίς has ᾰ, and it is doubtful whether the two words are sufficiently alike to make the pun clear to an audience.

1523-4 κυκλοσοβεῖτε: 'move in a circle', 'whirl round', not found elsewhere. σοβέω is used only of scaring away birds in Ar. (e.g. 211), but other authors use it of setting other kinds of object in motion. [So Dindorf's conjecture may be accepted. The reading of **a** does not scan, and may result from an attempt to explain the unfamiliar compound.]   τὸ Φρυνίχειον: internal accusative: 'the Phrynikhan kick'. Cf. 1490-2.

1526-7 ὤζωσιν: 'cry "Oooooh!"' ' To reproduce the noise made by impressed spectators Ar. has stretched out the initial ὤ- to equal two long syllables. The word might well be written ὠώζωσιν.

1528-9 The change from plural to singular verbs has no significance. If the chorus address one of the dancers, that does not necessarily mean that the others have stopped dancing. Still less does it mean that Philokleon alone is dancing, as has sometimes been thought; the following sentence (1532-4) implies that the sons of Karkinos have just been dancing.   στρόβει: 'whirl!', intransitive, as in *Knights* 386. παράβαινε: 'go along', 'proceed'; or possibly 'go sideways' (so Merry, and Roos *Die tragische Orchestik* 100), but I know no parallel for this sense.   γάστρισον σεαυτόν: 'slap your belly'. A number of extant vases show dancers slapping their bellies with their hands; cf. Roos *Die tragische Orchestik* 101-5. ('Hit your stomach with your heel', says Rogers. I should like to see such a movement demonstrated.)

1530-1 οὐράνιον: 'as high as heaven'; cf. 1492. [It is not impossible that οὐρανίαν should be restored here too.]   βέμβικες ἐγγενέσθων: 'let pirouettes be included' in the dance; cf. 1517. The literal meaning of βέμβιξ is 'a top', and in *Peace* 864 Karkinos's sons are called τῶν Καρκίνου στροβίλων, 'Karkinos's tops', but in our line 'let there be tops' or 'become tops!' is probably not the right translation; ἐγ- has more point if the noun is taken to refer to the movement rather than the dancers. (περιφοραί, περιαγωγαί is Σ's explanation. Cf. Roos *Die tragische Orchestik* 96 n. 2.) Likewise στρόβιλος, besides meaning 'top', was the name of a dance movement (Pol. 4. 100, Ath. 630 a), to which 1528-9 στρόβει may refer. There is no evidence to show whether στρόβιλος and βέμβιξ were the same movement or different ones.

1532-3 ποντομέδων ἄναξ: 'lord of the sea', a pompous variation for Karkinos's nickname θαλάττιος. In A. *Th.* 131 the same phrase is used of Poseidon; but Ar. does not mean that Karkinos is Poseidon.

1534 τριόρχοις: 'buzzards'; cf. Thompson *Birds* 286–7. Ar. calls Karkinos's sons so merely because the word sounds as if it might be derived
from τρεῖς and ὀρχέομαι, so as to mean 'three dancers'—a feeble pun;
it is just as well that the audience's attention was probably distracted
from it by the dancing.

1535 εἴ τι φιλεῖτ': 'if you wish'.   **θύραζε**: 'out' from the orkhestra.

1537 The relative clause defines τοῦτο: 'No one has ever done this
before, dismiss a comic chorus dancing'. Cf. E. *Andr.* 170–2 εἰς τοῦτο
δ᾽ ἥκεις ἀμαθίας . . . ἢ παιδὶ πατρός . . . τολμᾷς ξυνεύδειν.

After 1537 the chorus begin to dance, and the dancing may well
continue for a minute or two before the characters and chorus
finally depart, still dancing. [If both chorus and characters dance, it
makes little practical difference whether we read ὀρχούμενος (RΓ) or
ὀρχούμενον (VJ). But 1535 ὀρχούμενοι favours the nominative.] The
claim that this was the first comedy to end with a dance is impossible
for us to check (*Akh.* ends with a song, not necessarily accompanied by
a dance; *Knights* as we have it ends with dialogue, though some have
thought that a choral finale has been lost; the surviving version of
Clouds and all other surviving comedies are later than *Wasps*), but
I see no reason to reject it. Σ *Clouds* 542 says that Ar. used the comic
dance called κόρδαξ in *Wasps*, and if that is true this must be the point
at which it was danced (cf. Roos *Die tragische Orchestik* 145–60); but it
is not clear what grounds Σ had for the statement. There is no other
evidence to show what sort of dance concluded the play.

INDEXES

I. ENGLISH

II. GREEK

(*See also the entries in the English Index under* clothes, dance, imagery, invented words, names, puns)